Watching Anime, Reading Manga

Watching Anime, Reading Manga

25 Years of Essays and Reviews

Fred Patten

Foreword by Carl Macek

Stone Bridge Press ■ Berkeley, California

PUBLISHED BY
Stone Bridge Press
P.O. Box 8208
Berkeley, CA 94707
TEL 510-524-8732 • sbp@stonebridge.com • www.stonebridge.com

Every effort has been made to contact the copyright owners of the images
and text reproduced in this book. Omissions brought to our attention will be
corrected in subsequent editions. We gratefully acknowledge the following
for granting permission to use their material in this book: A.D. Vision, Inc.,
Animation Magazine, Animation World Magazine, Fantagraphics, Gakken,
Gareb Shamus Enterprises, Inc., Go Nagai/Dynamic Planning, Inc., Starlog
Group, Inc., TOKYOPOP, Inc., and *VideoScope.*

All photos and illustrations supplied by the author except where noted.
Front cover design and artwork by James Boren.

Printed in the United States of America.

10 9 8 7 5 4 3 2 1   2009 2008 2007 2006 2005 2004

Patten, Fred, 1940–.
Watching anime, reading manga : 25 years of essays and reviews / Fred
Patten ; foreword by Carl Macek.
  p. cm.
Includes bibliographical references and index.
ISBN 1-880656-92-2.
1. Animated films—Japan—History and criticism. 2. Science fiction films—
Japan—History and criticism. 3. Animated television programs—Japan—
History and criticism. 4. Comic books, strips, etc.—Japan—History and
criticism. I. Title.

NC1766.J3P37 2004
791.43′34—dc22

                                                    2004014856

Contents

7 Foreword by Carl Macek

9 Preface

13 **Part I • Anime Fandom**
15 America's First Manga Advertisements (1972)
16 Friends Overseas: Fans in America, by *Animedia* Staff (1982)
17 Remembrance of Cons Past (1984)
19 What's Wrong With Japanese Animation? (1994)
22 Fifteen Years of Japanese Animation Fandom, 1977–92 (1997)
43 *The Best of Anime* CD Liner Notes (1998)
50 Who Knows "Best"? (1998)
52 Anime in the United States (2001)
73 Fred Patten: Anime Man, by Simon Drax (2002)
80 Anime Expo 2003: Conventions Enter Their Adolescence (2003)
85 "Anime" Versus "Japanimation" (2003)

87 **Part II • The Business of Anime**
89 All Those Japanese Animation Soundtracks (1986)
98 Japanese Anime: The Cult Grows Up (1990)
103 Anime Licensing Grows Up (1996)
104 The World's Biggest Animation Home Video Market? (1997)
108 Letter to the Editor: "Anime" as Pejorative (1998)
110 The Anime "Porn" Market (1998)
119 Go to JAILED (1999)
122 The Thirteen Top Developments in Anime, 1985–99 (1999)
126 By the Numbers (1999)
128 Anime 2000: Money Talks (2000)
135 Anime Theatrical Features (2000)
139 Academy of Motion Picture Arts Anime Event (2002)
142 July 1978: First Anime Fan Magazine, *Animage*, Published (2003)
144 Simba Versus Kimba: The Pride of Lions (First Publication)
185 Simba-Kimba Redux? The *Nadia* Versus *Atlantis* Affair (First Publication)

191 **Part III • Artists**
193 Hypersexual Psychoviolence! The Dynamic World of Go Nagai (1988)
197 Osamu Tezuka (1926–89) (1990)
199 Osamu Tezuka: A Memorial to the Master (1993)
206 Shotaro Ishinomori: A Profile (2002)
209 Hayao Miyazaki's *Spirited* Trip to the U.S. (2002)

217 **Part IV • Japanese Culture in Anime**

219 TV Animation in Japan (1980)

232 Mangamania! (1984)

247 Japan + Animation = Japanimation! Part 1 (1986)

253 Japan + Animation = Japanimation! Part 2 (1986)

259 A New Wind from the East (1987)

268 Full Circle: Japanese Animation From Early Home Studios to Personal Workshops for Home Video (1987)

275 Japan's Anime (1995)

278 A Capsule History of Anime (1996)

282 Anime: Subliminal Lessons in Japanese History (2001)

285 Refighting World War II (2003)

287 Less, or More, Than Human (2003)

291 **Part V • Titles**

293 Dawn of the Warrior Robots: The Beginnings of a New Breed of Action Hero! (1980)

297 *Force Five:* Previewing an Ambitious New Science-Fiction TV Series! (1980)

303 *Robotech:* Japanimation Invades Comics With a Trio of Comico Titles (1985)

313 Profile: *Gigantor,* The Space-Age Robot (1991/2003)

322 *Speed Racer:* Still in the Lead (1993)

325 *Momotaro's Gods-Blessed Sea Warriors:* Japan's Unknown Wartime Feature (1996)

328 Prince of Something: *The Heroic Legend of Arslan—Age of Heroes* (1999)

331 Astro Old and Astro New (2000)

336 *Pokémon:* Ready for Its Next Success (2000)

338 Is Digimon Movie Destined for Success? (2000)

341 *Vampire Hunter D:* The Next Anime Hit in America? (2000)

345 *Blood: The Last Vampire*—Anime's First Digital Feature (2001)

349 A Retro-Future *Metropolis* (2002)

352 A Winning *Spirit* (2002)

356 *Cowboy Bebop: The Movie* . . . At Last (2003)

360 *The Animatrix:* Anime Reloaded (2003)

362 September 1963: *Astro Boy* Premieres in America (2003)

364 *Millennium Actress:* The Struggle to Bring Quality Animation to Theaters (2003)

368 *Perfect Blue* Revisited (2003)

369 January 1917: The First Animation Produced in Japan Is Released (2004)

371 **Index**

Knowledge is a tricky commodity. Flaunt too much of it and you run the risk of blurring the message with minutiae. Position yourself as a fount of wisdom without the data to back it up and you can lose credibility. In the world of anime fandom I have found one person who knows how to balance his knowledge of the subject with reason, wit, and perspective. That person is Fred Patten.

I first met Fred Patten nearly thirty years ago. He was an unabashed champion of all things relating to science fiction. But one of his most unlikely passions was for animation from Japan filtering into the hands of fans at the dawn of the videotape era. I'm talking reel-to-reel videotape, not videocassettes.

Fred became a key conduit for information regarding Japanese animation. Not only was Fred an early founder of the Cartoon/Fantasy Organization—a loose national association of fans who gathered to watch and discuss anime—but Fred was also the "go-to" man that many Japanese animation studios would contact in the hope of getting feedback on the potential of an American audience for their vast libraries of programming. Fred counted Osamu Tezuka, Monkey Punch, and numerous anime creators among his friends.

I ran an art gallery specializing in animation in the early 1980s, and Fred was responsible for putting me in contact with Japanese animation studios when I expressed an interest in selling anime cels alongside the works of Chuck Jones and Ralph Bakshi. Because I had these anime cels, I was contacted by a distribution company named Harmony Gold that was looking for promotional artwork. One thing led to another, and I ended up developing *Robotech* for the folks at Harmony Gold. So in effect, it could be said that Fred Patten was instrumental in getting *Robotech* started.

As Fred became more and more involved in his study of anime, he was able to transform his passion into a profession. As a journalist, not only did Fred write a series of well-researched articles that detailed the rise of anime fandom outside of Japan, but he also became a clear, critical voice able to analyze and put into context the various programs that began flooding into America. As part of Streamline Pictures, Fred was one of the early pioneers bringing a wealth of anime to specialty retail shops throughout the country.

His literate and thoughtful translations of the dialogue for many early anime titles set the standard for the underground movement known today as "fansubs." In fact, his translation of the Miyazaki classic *Lupin III: The Castle of Cagliostro* formed the basis of the original Streamline Pictures English-language version. However, there was one line in the English version that caused Fred to cringe. He knew that it deviated so much from the original line that he had to question the wisdom of the change. After hearing the explanation Fred understood the motive behind the alteration, but cautioned that it would ruffle the feathers of anime purists. Although the film's adaptation won an award, Fred was right. The line—less than a dozen words—would taint the film for many anime fans.

Through his words and his actions, Fred Patten has been an integral part of anime fandom in America. He was there at the infancy of anime fandom. He was there when the floodgates burst. And he is still here today.

I owe a debt of gratitude to him for introducing me to the wonder and magic I found in anime. And although our approach to the popularization of the art form may differ, I am sure that much of what I was able to accomplish in my years at Harmony Gold, Streamline Pictures, and now at ADV Films can be directly traced back to my countless conversations with Fred.

And I am sure I am not alone.

Once you've had a chance to share in Fred's vast knowledge and insight regarding anime, there's a good chance that you will view these works in a whole new light. That is Fred's gift. It is a gift of knowledge delivered with joy and passion. It is a gift I hope he continues to give to us for a very long time.

CARL MACEK
Houston, Texas

I had just finished reviewing the *Comic Party* anime series for *Animation World Magazine* the day before my editor at Stone Bridge Press reminded me that I still needed to write the preface for this book. *Comic Party* is a 2001 thirteen-episode anime TV series about the world of manga and anime fandom in Japan, particularly those teen artists who actively participate in the fan conventions ("comic markets") by publishing their own amateur manga for sale: *dojinshi,* best translated as "fanzines."

Fanzines might be to blame for getting me started writing about anime and manga. I was twenty and in college in 1960 when I became active in Los Angeles's science fiction fan community and began contributing to fanzines. In those days, a fanzine was not an amateur comic book. It was an amateur SF magazine with editorials, stories, reviews, and letters from readers. I started out writing reviews of SF books and movies for other fans' fanzines. In 1961 I began publishing my own fanzine.

A couple of years after that, Julius Schwartz at DC Comics and Stan Lee at Marvel Comics reinvented the costumed-hero comic books and comics fandom got started. That was when the fanzine as an amateur comic book first appeared. I wasn't very interested in the superheroes. My tastes ran more toward the French *bandes dessinées,* which had better story values. I wrote a lot of profiles of my favorite French cartoon album series (*Tintin, Asterix, Lucky Luke, Bernard Prince, Blake et Mortimer,* etc.) for 1960s comics fanzines. I also wrote a lengthy survey of Mexican comic books, "¡Supermen South!," for Roy Thomas's fanzine *Alter-Ego* in 1965. That article became my first "professional" writing (or at least the first worth citing on my resumé).

Looking back, I seem to have always been more fascinated by exotic foreign comics than by American comics. You will read more later about my experiment with Richard Kyle in the early 1970s to import the best of international comic art into the United States. This may say something about why I went gaga over Japanese comics and animation, and helped to start the first American anime club, the Cartoon/Fantasy Organization, in 1977. I had been attending the weekly meetings of the Los Angeles Science Fantasy Society for seventeen years (you can still find me there most Thursday evenings), and by that time I had a lot of experience organizing a fan club so that it won't fall apart after a year or two.

In 1979 I became the editor/publisher of the C/FO's first fanzine, *Fanta's Zine.* When I went looking for information to print in it, two people were eager to help me out. Teruko (Pico) Hozumi was the new Hollywood representative of Toei Animation Co., Ltd., assigned to make America aware of Toei's animation. Jim Terry was a TV producer who had just licensed five of Toei's anime SF TV series and was editing them into a package for

1980 syndicated TV release: *Force Five.* They were glad to supply press-kit information and permission to publish it. But it was hardly worth the trouble for a dinky mimeographed fanzine of only 100 copies. Couldn't I write my articles for publication in "real magazines"?

This was how I came to start writing about anime and manga on a professional freelance basis. My first published articles were "Dawn of the Warrior Robots: The Beginnings of a New Breed of Action Hero" (a promo for *Force Five*) in *Fangoria* no. 4, February 1980, and "TV Animation in Japan" (a survey of TV anime in general but emphasizing Toei's programs) in *Fanfare* no. 3, Spring 1980. My first major article on manga was "Mangamania!" in *The Comics Journal* no. 94, October 1984.

During the 1980s these articles, while being published in newsstand magazines, were really still part of my anime-hobbyist activities. Professionally, I was a librarian at Hughes Aircraft Company's Technical Document Center cataloging research project reports and scientific papers in the aerospace, defense, and communications satellite industries. In 1990 when Southern California's aerospace/defense industry began collapsing and I lost my twenty-year job at Hughes, the new American anime industry was just beginning. I had been hanging out at Carl Macek and Jerry Beck's brand-new Streamline Pictures as an unofficial consultant, and they suggested that I become their first paid employee instead of looking for another librarian position. So, ever since January 1991, anime has been my profession as well as my hobby. In addition to working for Streamline throughout the 1990s, my writing about anime and manga has increased as more magazines wanted articles about it.

I officially retired at the end of 2003, but today I am busier than ever. I am currently writing anime and manga columns for three monthly magazines (*Animation World Magazine, Comics Buyer's Guide,* and *Newtype USA*), as well as individual essays for other magazines and books.

■   ■   ■

These essays were written over a twenty-five-year period for a variety of magazines and other media. When viewing them together with an eye toward publication in this book, certain inconsistencies really stand out. Each publication seems to have had its own version of "science fiction": s-f, SF, Sf, sf, sci-fi, speculative fiction. There aren't quite as many spellings of "anime" but animé, animae, and animay are three variants. Essays published in British magazines contain European-format dates; 1 January 2000 rather than January 1, 2000. We have standardized the abbreviations and orthography to the most common American formats, but we decided to leave the text of the articles pretty much as is to document the evolution of the art form from "Japanese animation" through "Japanimation" to "anime."

In fact, we made a basic decision to leave these essays as they were originally published as much as possible, even if they contained errors, to illustrate the state of anime knowledge in America at the time they were written. Was Matsumoto's first name "Reiji" or "Leiji"? It was years before the spelling was standardized as Leiji, and references to him before the late 1980s were apt to spell it either way. There was also variation for years over the name of young Tetsuro's mysterious companion-guide in *Galaxy Express 999*. Was her name supposed to be "Maeter" (the Latin word for "mother," since she was clearly a mother-surrogate for Tetsuro) or "Maetel" (making it a unique futuristic name)? It was spelled both ways until Viz began publishing an American edition of Matsumoto's manga in the 1990s and made the Maetel spelling officially correct. Fans are still debating between "Captain Harlock" and "Captain Herlock," between "Ah! My Goddess" and "Oh! My Goddess," between "Inu Yasha" and "Inuyasha," between "Dragon Ball" and "Dragonball" . . .

My earliest article about *Kimba the White Lion* (not included here), researched by asking its most enthusiastic American fans about it, turned out to be full of "urban legend" errors. For example, every *Kimba* fan in the late 1970s insisted that it had won lots of PTA-type awards for excellence. When asked for specifics, the only award that anyone could definitely cite was from *Parents' Magazine*. And that was later proven to be a misunderstanding! There was a single *Kimba* merchandising item during its initial 1966–67 broadcast, a 29¢ *Kimba the White Lion Coloring Book,* and its cover showed a seal labeled "Commended by *Parents' Magazine* as advertised therein." But the seal only meant that the coloring book itself had been approved by *Parents' Magazine* as a safe toy for young children. It was *not* a commendation of the TV series. So, rather than rewrite all these essays to show a 2004 level of anime knowledge, the errors have been retained with sidebars added to explain why they were made.

Adapting the sometimes-wild magazine layout of the original articles to the format of a book presented another set of challenges. I have tried to retain the sidebar materials that appeared with the original article and acknowledged the original author if the sidebar was not written by me.

■ ■ ■

Now it is time for twenty-five years—*more* than twenty-five years—of thank-yous. To Bill Mills and Robert Short who put on the *Man from U.N.C.L.E.* display at the 1970 Westercon where I first discovered Japanese comics through Takao Saito's manga version of that TV series. To Ken Tachibana, the employee at Akita Shoten who was the only Japanese publisher to respond to my 1972–73 attempts to import manga for Richard Kyle and my Graphic Story Bookshop. To Richard Kyle himself, and our customers who were especially interested in the manga and, a couple of years later, the first giant-robot cartoons to appear on American TV: Wendell Washer, Mark Merlino, Robin Leyden, Judith Niver, and Chris Balduc (all charter members of the Cartoon/Fantasy Organization in May 1977). To Owen and Eclaré

Hannifen, who blew our minds by coming all the way from San Francisco for our first anime club meeting in L.A. (and for being major fan-promoters of anime during the '80s). To Osamu Tezuka and Monkey Punch, who blew our minds even more by appearing as guests at early C/FO meetings, and to Pico Hozumi and Jim Terry for supplying the C/FO with authorized anime (in 16 mm yet!) to run the first anime rooms at SF and comics fan conventions. Sure, they were more interested in jump-starting commercial anime sales in America than in just being nice guys, but who cares!?

To Yuji Hiramatsu, Books Nippan's first manager to import enough anime and manga to sell to fans throughout America by mail order. To Wendy Pini, who used her popularity as *Elfquest*'s creator to tell all her fans how much she had been influenced by Tezuka and other manga artists. To Jerry Beck in NYC, Bill Thomas III in Philadelphia, and Doug Rice in Chicago, who may not have been the first anime fans in their cities but were the first to organize anime clubs and become spokesmen for the fans there. To Carl Macek, for hosting an anime club in Orange County, Calif., in 1982 and going on to create *Robotech* for syndicated TV and then Streamline Pictures (with Jerry Beck) to help start the American anime industry. To all the anime fans with whom I worked closely in person or via correspondence during the '80s and '90s: Michael Aguilar, Gustav "Red" Baron, Mitchell Beiro, Kurt Black, Roy and Cathy Bruce, Fred Lee Cain, Ralph Canino, Jr., Ardith Carlton, Peter Chung, Anne Cronin, Ben Dunn, Barbara Edmunds, Robert Fenelon, Don Fields, Scott Frazier, Carl Gafford, Alan and Sue Gillen, R. G. Lester, James Long, John Martinez, Jane McGuire, Ann Nichols, Ed Noonchester, Stephen Paschke, Richard Reichman, David Riddick, Jeff Roady, Ken Sample, Lorraine Savage, Robin Schindler, Ann Schubert, Steve Schultheis, Jerry Shaw, Michael Sherman, Greg Shoemaker, Toren Smith, Emilio Soltero, Laurine White, Bill Wilson, Colleen Winters, and Don Yee. I will not claim all these people as good friends; in fact, thanks to club politics, I am not sure I am on speaking terms with a couple of them. But I cannot deny their enthusiasm for anime, or that American awareness of anime was increased significantly during its early years by their own fan projects. (This is not meant to dismiss the many other early anime fans around North America with whom I just never happened to have worked closely.)

F.P.
Los Angeles, California

Part I
Anime Fandom

America's First Manga Advertisements

Graphic Story World no. 8, December 1972–*Wonderworld* no. 10, November 1973.

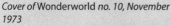

Cover of Wonderworld *no. 10, November 1973*

Early manga ad in Wonderworld *no. 10, November 1973*

Richard Kyle and I created Graphic Story Bookshop in 1972 to make the best international comic books available in the United States, as advertised through *Graphic Story World* magazine. We changed their names to Wonderworld Books and *Wonderworld* magazine, respectively, in 1973. Kyle edited and published the magazine and I wrote the book reviews. I wrote the advertisements for the bookshop, which Kyle laid out and published in the magazine. I contacted comic book publishers throughout Europe and Japan to import their *bandes dessinées*, their *fumetti*, and their *manga*, which I sold to American fans via mail order. After a year, the mail-order bookshop, which I operated from my home in Culver City, evolved into a real comic book specialty store in Long Beach where Kyle lived, and he took over all operations. Running a regular comic book shop was a full-time job, so we soon transitioned away from importing foreign comics and selling via mail order, and the magazine was discontinued. But from late 1972 through 1975, Graphic Story Bookshop/Wonderworld Books imported and sold Japanese manga, the first American comics shop to do so. The first illustrated advertisements for manga appeared in the Bookshop's ads in *Graphic Story World* no. 8, December 1972; and *Wonderworld* no. 10, November 1973.

All of the French, Spanish, Italian, and Dutch publishers we contacted were eager to do business with us, but only one Japanese publisher, Akita Shoten, answered my business letters. We later learned that we only got a reply from Akita Shoten because one employee there wanted to practice his English through his business correspondence with me. ■

Friends Overseas: Fans in America, by *Animedia* Staff
Animedia no. 15, September 1982.

Here's a report on anime fans in America for Japanese anime fans just like you!

American anime fans here means fans of "Japanese-made animation." As many of you may remember, a little while ago anime shows like *Grandizer* and *Candy, Candy* have become very popular in France. Well, there are many dedicated anime fans in America, too.

They are centered in Los Angeles and get together for organized screenings of Japanese animation several times a year. They gather in front of a screen around a big video projector. Some of them come to the gathering from the far suburbs, driving more than one hour. Sometimes more than 100 people show up. Of course not many people can understand Japanese, but they enjoy watching the screen all day long.

These fans are not satisfied by just watching anime. They often visit L.A.'s Japantown and subscribe to Japanese anime magazines. *Animedia* costs as much as $56/year. (According to a letter written to the editorial staff from a subscriber in L.A., one magazine costs ¥1,000).

It is delightful to know that there are many people who are so interested in anime that they are willing to pay such a high price.

Caption: Fred Patten is an expert on anime in America. He has published introductory articles about Japanese anime in quarterly magazines. He writes many articles with titles like "Japanese TV Animation" on shows like *Tetsuwan Atomu, [Space Pirate Captain] Harlock, [Galaxy Express] 999,* and *Gatchaman.*

Robin Leyden is a former special effects technician. He was in charge of

This was the earliest sign of public awareness in Japan of the development in America of a fandom for anime. This article in the September 1982 *Animedia* was a delightful surprise for the early American fans who bought anime magazines just to look at the pictures. The fans in the Cartoon/Fantasy Organization were tickled pink that three issues of the club's fanzine were shown.

About all that any of us could read of this was the names of Robin Leyden and myself in katakana. Two years earlier, Leyden and I had served as the American assistants to a tour group of Japanese cartoonists who attended the 1980 San Diego Comic-Con (see the next essay for more details). We decided that this must have been why *Animedia* singled us out for praise. It was a treat to see my name in katakana in one of the major anime magazines.

Animedia got a couple of details wrong. Leyden worked as a lighting technician on the *Star Trek: The Motion Picture* feature, not the original TV series. *Fanta's Zine* was the title of the Cartoon/Fantasy Organization's fanzine, not the name of the club. ■

Original Japanese-language article in Animedia *no. 15, September 1982*

special effects lighting on *Star Trek* which opened to the public in 1979. He became independent and now runs his own office where he sets up a video projector and enjoys watching Japanese anime. He is a big anime fan.

Caption: Fanta's Zine is active in L.A. and its leaders are Fred Patten and Robin Leyden. Both are SF anime fans. Robin is an especially big fan of Osamu Tezuka's *Tetsuwan Atomu* and he has a large circle of acquaintances in Japan. Membership magazines are starting to cover Japanese-made anime and information from overseas, as well.

Remembrance of Cons Past
San Diego Comic-Con Souvenir Program Book, June/July 1984.

Many people say that the best location the Comic-Con ever had was the El Cortez Hotel. That may be true in terms of general convention layout, but the spot that I found most congenial was the University of California,

Comic-Con 1980, Tezuka meeting fans

Courtesy of Jackie Estrada and Comic-Con International.

San Diego campus at La Jolla, where the second Comic-Con met in 1971. It was a spacious, beautiful campus with attractive grounds between the dorms where the attendees stayed and the auditoriums where the events were held. I remember having to shade my eyes as I walked because the sun was so bright, but the breeze off the Pacific kept everything pleasantly cool. College was adjourned for the summer and we had the campus all to ourselves. Everything seemed bright, fresh, and exciting. The dorms were new and clean, and staying in them gave us more of a feeling of camaraderie than being in a hotel.

Today's multitude of comics and media conventions hadn't yet developed, and it was a thrill to meet such notables as Kirk Alyn for the first time and to see classic movie cartoons in a proper theatrical screening rather than chopped up on TV. The dealers' room was much cozier. You could even strike up conversations with most dealers and leaf through their comics and discuss favorite stories together—a far cry from today when almost everything in the dealers' room is a sealed-in-plastic investment. The general attendees, the con committee, and the guests all mixed much more freely as fans together. It's nice that the Comic-Con has grown and matured, but it's too bad that much of the old atmosphere of "family together" has been lost.

My most vivid memories are of the 1980 Comic-Con, when the "Japanese invasion" took place. This is partly because I didn't just watch this as a spectator. A Japanese cartoonist (Monkey Punch, creator of the *Lupin III* strip) had visited the 1979 Comic-Con and had spread favorable word about it back home. As a result, about thirty Japanese cartoonists, animators,

The 1984 Comic-Con celebrated its fifteenth anniversary. Many SF and comic book celebrities who were regular attendees were invited to contribute to that year's Souvenir Program Book a brief remembrance of their most notable memories of the past fifteen Comic-Cons. ■■

and business agents decided to come to the 1980 Comic-Con to investigate the potential American market for Japanese cartoons. A group tour was arranged, and I and another Japanimation fan, Robin Leyden, were asked to help reserve their hotel rooms, get dealers' tables, and even set up a cocktail reception where they could meet their fellow American artists. It was an honor to handle this liaison work, and it was gratifying to watch their top expectations surpassed.

Fans crowded around Osamu Tezuka, as if he was Neal Adams or Carl Barks, to get original sketches of *Astro Boy* and *Kimba*. Tezuka's animated SF theatrical feature *Phoenix 2772* was so popular that public demand forced the Con to make room on the film program for a repeat screening. The demonstration of 3-D TV animation by Tokyo Movie Shinsha played to a packed house. Go Nagai, the creator of the giant-robot superhero concept, gave tapes of his TV cartoons to Mark Merlino for the Con's video program. I was lucky enough to be standing nearby when Yumiko Igarashi, artist of the *Candy Candy* soap opera comic book, and Wendy Pini of *Elfquest* discovered that each was a fan of the other's work, and started to "talk together" despite the fact that neither spoke the other's language. Since 1980, an increasing number of younger Japanese artists and fans have been coming to the Comic-Con. May this number continue to grow!

What's Wrong with Japanese Animation?
StarQuest no. 3, July/August 1994.

When Joe Fekete invited me to write a guest editorial for *StarQuest*, he hinted that this would be a good opportunity for me to promote Japanese animation. I've been involved with its discovery by American fans ever since I helped put together a Los Angeles Science Fantasy Society (LASFS) program on Japanese animated SF in July 1975, which seems to have been the earliest fannish attention given to this topic. I was one of the founders of the first American fan club devoted especially to these cartoons, the Cartoon/Fantasy Organization, in May 1977. I've served as the C/FO's secretary ever since—we just celebrated our 17th anniversary at this May's meeting.

"Japanese animation" has enjoyed a steady growth since the late 1970s. Japanese animation video rooms are now a standard feature at fan conventions. Just about every large city has at least one fan club. It has started to "go public" during the last two or three years, with the birth of new American companies that have been making Japanese animation available in theaters and in video stores, and are starting to get it on TV. The Sci-Fi Channel and TBS are now listing "Japanimation," using our fan-coined word, in their schedules and their press releases. *Forbes*, the business magazine, featured an article in its February 28, 1994, issue on the current popularity of animation in America, talking mainly about Disney's record-setting features and TV programs such as *The Simpsons*, but also mentioning "a small, but growing cult following" for Japanese animation.

This is gratifying. Yet I can't help feeling that people are missing the real point. That point is not that this is Japanese animation, but that it is science fiction animation—or that it is animated SF. This missed point is emphasized every time somebody asks why Japanese animation is becoming so popular in America, the implication being, what is there about the Japanese cultural mystique that is so entrancing, which the animated cartoons of other countries can't match? I don't think that the American audience for these films is nearly as interested in the fact that they were made in Japan, or that they are cartoons, as that they are exciting SF adventures.

This distinction is also evident by the insistence of a growing number of its fans on creating a separate fandom for it, rather than enjoying it as a part of general SF fandom. It used to be that fans who enjoyed Japanese animated SF also enjoyed American SF movies, TV programs, novels, and comic books. They were satisfied with a Japanimation video room as part of a comprehensive general SF convention. Most of them still are, but now some fans are organizing separate "anime and manga" conventions to concentrate on this Japanese visual SF alone. Moreover, they are scheduling these conventions opposite such established major SF conventions as the Worldcon and the Westercon, as if there is no overlap in interest among fans, and nobody would want to attend both.

The unique traits of Japanese animation that have made it so accessible today are partly cultural and partly technical. The cultural aspects are the widespread popularity of modern science fiction in Japan, and the Japanese acceptance of cartoon animation as a medium of cinematic storytelling for all age and interest groups, rather than just for children (as is the Western bias). Thus the Japanese are producing dramatic theatrical and televised SF (including fantasy and horror) aimed at teens and adults, using animation as frequently as live action. The medium of animation is better suited to plots

In 1994, anime's appeal may have been mostly as animated SF and fantasy. That is certainly no longer true. Today there are fans whose favorite anime are the dramas of Japanese history and folklore, or the adolescent human interest comedies and dramas such as *His and Her Circumstances, GTO,* and *Princess Nine.*

The Cartoon/Fantasy Organization may have been Los Angeles' only citywide anime club in 1994, but it was not the only anime club in the city. There were anime clubs at UCLA and USC by 1994. Today there is at least one more citywide club, Cinema Anime, and there seem to be anime clubs at practically every college and many high schools throughout L.A. Many of the city's public libraries have monthly anime screenings for teens. Anime clubs have similarly multiplied throughout most cities, and it may be easier to find one in your city than you think. ■

that would require enormous budgets for elaborate sets and special effects in live action.

The technical aspect, at least as far as North America is concerned, is that America and Japan are both on the NTSC television system, unlike Europe which is mostly on the PAL or SECAM systems. Japanese and American videotapes will play on each other's VCRs and TV monitors, while American videotapes will not play on European TV equipment and vice versa. This has allowed American fans to get and watch Japanese videotapes relatively easily, while videos from Britain or France or other countries show only static on American TV equipment. This is not the same thing as any inherent fondness by Americans for Japanese programming over the programming of other countries.

There is one filmmaker outside of Japan who has recognized animation's potential for genuine SF storytelling: France's René Laloux. Laloux's three theatrical features (*Fantastic Planet,* 1973; *Time Masters,* 1982, and *Light Years (Gandahar),* 1987) presented exotically interstellar settings, imaginative creatures, and intriguing artistic direction. They may have had their creative problems, but they were designed to be considered in the same class as such live-action movies as *This Island Earth, Forbidden Planet,* and *Star Wars,* rather than with such juvenile cartoon features as *Pinocchio in Outer Space* or *Transformers: The Movie.* Unfortunately, Laloux's movies have been considered as curiosities (or not considered at all) in Europe and America. They have had virtually no influence on the public's or the film industry's perception of the possibilities of using animation for a serious SF movie. Ironically, it is "live-action" blockbusters such as *Terminator 2,* which are loaded with computer-generated animated effects, which may finally result in that conceptual breakthrough.

It would have been ideal if this Japanese animated SF had created an American awareness of the full potential in animation for mature cinematic drama. Then the American animation industry might have started producing animated SF features on the level of Japan's *Akira, Nausicaä of the Valley of the Winds, Time Strangers, Harmagedon,* or *The Wings of Honneamise.* Would it really matter if a movie like *The Abyss* was done as live action with a ton of computer effects, or as a cartoon, as long as it was done seriously and done well? Unfortunately, that hasn't happened. To the majority of Americans, these films remain something quaint called "Japanese animation," which is good for only a trendy cult following, like *Beavis and Butt-Head* or—at best—*The Rocky Horror Picture Show.*

Hopefully, a change may still happen. The cultural influence of Japanese animation is just starting in America. Professional animators are aware of it. "The Japanese anime look" is an acknowledged factor in the "dark deco" mood of *Batman: The Animated Series. Akira* has gotten serious critical notice in major magazines such as *Time* and *TV Guide.* It may take several more years—or decades—but eventually, someone in America will produce a *Blade Runner* or a *Scanners*—or even a *Road Warrior*—in cartoon form. Let's hope that by that time mainstream audiences are ready to judge such a film on its merits as cinematic SF, rather than just as a funky cartoon. And "Japanese animation" will evolve into a broader category of "animated SF."

If you're not familiar with it yet, keep an eye out for Japanese animation in your newspaper's theatrical listings, check out the video program at the next SF convention you attend, look for some Japanese animation videos at your local SF/comics specialty bookshop or your local video shop, or visit your city's Japanese animation fan club. In Los Angeles, it's the Cartoon/Fantasy Organization, which meets on the third Saturday of each month.

Fifteen Years of Japanese Animation Fandom, 1977–92
Chapter Four of *The Complete Anime Guide*, Trish Ledoux and Doug Ranney, second edition. Issaquah, Wash.: Tiger Mountain Press, 1997.

Organized anime fandom began in North America in 1977, with the formation of the first fan club created expressly to promote Japanese animation to other American fans. This chronology ends in 1992, its fifteenth anniversary year. It is important to remember the events before 1977, to acknowledge how fandom came to start at all, but the "proto-fandom" dates from 1961 through 1976 would have been meaningless without the birth of organized fandom a year later.

Proto-Fandom
1961
July: *Panda and the Magic Serpent* (released by Globe Pictures) and *Alakazam the Great* (released by American International Pictures) are the first two Japanese theatrical animated features distributed in America.

August: *Magic Boy* is released by MGM. These three are perceived by the public as "foreign movies" rather than specifically "Japanese movies." Their box-office returns are disappointing.

1963
September: *Astro Boy* begins American TV syndication.

1965
September: *Eighth Man* begins American TV syndication.

1966
January: *Gigantor* begins American TV syndication.

September: *Kimba the White Lion* and *Prince Planet* begin American TV syndication.

October: *Marine Boy* begins American TV syndication.

1967
September: *The Amazing 3* and *Speed Racer* begin American TV syndication.

1968
January: Greg Shoemaker begins *The Japanese Fantasy Film Journal*. This fanzine is devoted primarily to live-action cinematic fantasy such as the *Godzilla* movies, but Shoemaker includes articles on Japanese animation when he can get information about it.

Late 1960s and early 1970s
Other Japanese theatrical and TV cartoons such as *Princess Knight* (a.k.a. *Choppy and the Princess*), *Puss in Boots, Jack and the Witch, The Little Norse Prince, Gulliver's Travels Beyond the Moon,* and others appear as TV afternoon matinee movies and as 16 mm rental films.

1972
December: *Mazinger Z,* the first giant robot/battle armor TV cartoon, begins in Japan.

December: Graphic Story Bookshop, a mail order comics specialty bookshop in Culver City, CA, run by Richard Kyle and Fred Patten, publishes the first illustrated advertisements for imported Japanese manga, in its magazine, *Graphic Story World* no. 8.

1975
July: Earliest known screening of Japanese TV cartoons for an American

This was originally written for a "fifteenth anniversary of anime fandom" fanzine scheduled for publication in mid-1992. It was never published so I updated it to the end of 1992 and it first appeared in two parts as "Fifteen Years of North American Fandom, 1977–92" in the British magazine *Anime U.K.* no. 12, February-March 1994, and no. 13, April-May 1994. It was again published in both the 1995 and 1997 editions of Trish Ledoux and Doug Ranney's *The Complete Anime Guide.* So much has happened since then that to bring it up to date would require expanding it into a book.

1961: The order of the first three anime theatrical features released in America is slightly wrong. New theatrical features from major movie studios/distributors usually have well-publicized nationwide release dates, but minor movies are "not released as much as they escape," as the saying goes. This was the case with *Panda and the Magic Serpent, Magic Boy,* and *Alakazam the Great,* which were dumped onto the children's matinee market during Summer 1961 with little publicity. Finding their first release dates thirty years later became a real detective hunt. Globe Pictures and American-International Pictures no longer exist, and MGM said its records for that long ago had long since been discarded. When I wrote this in 1992, it looked like *Panda* and *Alakazam* had been released during July 1961 and *Magic Boy* during August. Since then, animation expert

Cont. on p. 24

fan group, a special program on Japanese SF animation at the Los Angeles Science Fantasy Society, presented by Wendell Washer and Fred Patten.

October: The first commercial VCRs reach the consumer market, enabling the public to make personal video copies of TV programming.

1976
Spring: Japanese TV cartoons, with English subtitles thanks to Honolulu TV, reach local Japanese-community TV channels in some major American cities. (*Brave Raideen,* the first (?) subtitled giant-robot cartoon to reach the mainland, starts on Channel 47 UHF on March 20.)

Fall: Mark Merlino, a Los Angeles fan, begins taping obscure SF and fantasy movies to show at fannish parties. His videos of Japanese giant-robot cartoons are especially popular.

First Fandom
1977
February: The idea of starting a new fan club devoted primarily to Japanese animation is discussed among Los Angeles fans.

April: The LosCon III convention in Los Angeles includes a test program of anime videos presented by Mark Merlino and Fred Patten. It is a big success.

May: The first monthly meeting of the Cartoon/Fantasy Organization is organized by Robin Leyden, Mark Merlino, Judith Niver, Fred Patten, and Wendell Washer. It draws sixteen attendees.

Jerry Beck found that *Magic Boy* had played in some cities as early as June, so it has the honor of the first anime seen in America. According to Beck, the specific releases were *Magic Boy* on June 22, *Panda and the Magic Serpent* on July 8, and *Alakazam the Great* on July 26.

1975: The first videocassette recorder released to the American consumer market was the Sony Betamax in November 1975, not October. Advertisements for it appeared in October.

1976: Since giant robot cartoons appeared on Japanese TV in December 1972, and different anime TV series appeared in different American cities at different times, fans were not sure whether *Brave Raideen* in March 1976 should be credited as the earliest giant robot cartoon shown in America, and marking the beginning of anime fandom. However, no prior screening of boys' SF anime on American TV has been discovered.

1978: During the early 1980s, several fans claimed credit for inventing the word "Japanimation." It is an obvious enough combination of "Japan" and "animation" that many fans may have created it independently. Gafford was identified in print as Carl "Japanimation" Gafford in a C/FO fanzine in June 1979, and there was agreement by numerous fans that he had been using the word for over six months by that time. None of the other claimants could document that they

November: The C/FO begins to print a monthly bulletin (one sheet).

1978

March: Osamu Tezuka, on a business trip to Los Angeles, is invited to the monthly C/FO meeting. He supplies a special program of his animation never shown in America and encourages the fans to promote Japanese animation.

May: The English translation of the first volume of Keiji Nakazawa's *Barefoot Gen,* a semi-autobiographical manga novel of a child's personal experience of the 1945 atomic bombing of Hiroshima, is published in Tokyo by Project Gen for distribution in the

Flyer for Anime-Zine, *early 1986*

United States by the New York City–based War Resisters League. This is the first American edition of a translated Japanese manga.

Mid-year: Toei Animation's Hollywood representative, Pico Hozumi, asks the C/FO to help promote Toei's animation in America.

Mid-year: Carl Gafford coins the word "Japanimation," which is picked up by L.A. fandom.

had used the word before 1980 or 1981.

1978: Regarding the October 1978 premiere date of *Battle of the Planets,* see also the last note on page 54 and "September 1963—*Astro Boy* premieres in America" on page 362.

1980: A flyer for the 1980 San Diego Comic-Con lists "Hours of Rare Japanese Animation" among the many scheduled attractions. This shows that only two years after the first anime fans hosted the earliest anime video rooms in their own hotel rooms, convention organizers were beginning to add them to their official programming.

1980: An earlier article on anime was later found: "Shogun: Battle of the Afternoon Warriors," by Tom Sciacca, in *Mediascene* no. 35, January–February 1979.

1981–82: Jerry Beck says that *Galaxy Express* was released in the United States on August 8, 1981, not in July 1982.

1983: As of 2004, the *Sasha* Amateur Press Association is still active. So is the anime video room at NYC's annual Lunacon convention, although Fenelon turned it over to other fans in 1997.

1983: There had actually been four annual Japanese Fantasy Film Faires in the

Cont. on p. 26

July: The first convention video room is run at Westercon XXXI in Los Angeles by the C/FO, although it mixes anime with TV SF such as *The Prisoner*.

July: The C/FO runs the first anime merchandise dealer's table at the 1978 San Diego Comic-Con. The material is supplied by Toei Animation to test how American fans react to unknown-character cartoon merchandising. The *Space Pirate Captain Harlock* items are especially popular.

September: Toei Animation supplies videos and merchandising for test marketing at the World Science Fiction Convention in Phoenix. Mark Merlino runs the video room and Fred Patten runs the dealer's table.

September: The first issue of *Animage* (cover-dated July), the first animation-specialty monthly magazine in Japan, reaches America. *Animage* touches off an anime-publication flood, with rival magazines such as *My Anime* and *The Anime* and books such as Tokuma Publishing's "Roman Album" series soon following. Coincidentally, anime toy merchandising evolves from cheap toys to high-quality model kits. These begin arriving in Japanese community bookshops and toyshops in Los Angeles, San Francisco, New York City and other cities about a month after their release in Japan. Many American fans become hooked by the detailed battle-armor model kits before they learn about the TV anime upon which they are based.

October: *Battle of the Planets* begins American TV syndication, the first Americanized Japanese TV cartoon series since the 1960s, and the first to become known to the public as being Japanese animation.

San Francisco area between December 1979 (in Union City) and February 1983 (in San Mateo), peaking at 500 attendees. But they showed both Japanese live-action fantasy theatrical features and anime, and they were not publicized outside the local area, so they were unknown to anime fandom at large.

1985: The *Robotech* comic books moved from Academy Comics to Antarctic Press in 1997. Antarctic Press published them through December 1998, when Harmony Gold finally declined to renew the comic book license "pending future marketing plans."

1985: Jerry Beck says the brief theatrical release of *Warriors of the Wind* in New York began on April 15, 1986, not during June 1985. If the December 1985 release date for the video is accurate (November 1985 has also been cited), then the video release predated the theatrical release.

1989: The Cartoon/Fantasy Organization continues to exist as a local Los Angeles anime club. The C/FO-Cleveland also still exists as an independent club, the only other former chapter to keep the C/FO name.

1990: The Right Stuf's release of *Astro Boy* actually began on June 1, 1989.

1991: The official release of *Dominion Tank Police* no. 1 was November 7, 1991.

1992: The official release of ADV's *Devil Hunter Yohko* no. 1 was December 15, 1992. ■

Theatrical advertisement for the American 1961 release of Alakazam the Great

December: Osamu Tezuka is again the guest speaker at a C/FO meeting.

Expansion and Influences

1979

Early promotion by Wendy Pini for her *Elfquest* comic book publicizes that one of her artistic inspirations is the animation style of Osamu Tezuka.

February: The C/FO is reorganized to accept annual memberships and publishes a directory of members. This enables fans outside Los Angeles to join to get the club's bulletin, and to use the directory to contact other anime fans. William Thomas III in Philadelphia is the first member outside L.A.

February: Marvel Comics begins *Shogun Warriors,* featuring new American superhero adventures starring the Japanese giant robots licensed by Mattel, Inc., for its *Shogun Warriors* toy line. This is the first introduction of giant robots to many American comics fans.

May: Joey Buchanan in Ohio solicits for fans to start a national *Battle of the Planets* Fan Club.

July: *Fanta's Zine,* the first American fanzine devoted to anime, is started by the C/FO.

Summer: Ralph Canino, Jr. in New York, who has pen pals in Japan, offers to obtain anime magazines, posters, models, etc. for fellow fans at cost plus postage. This is the first attempt by an American fan to import anime merchandise from Japan on either a social or a business level.

September: *Star Blazers* begins American TV syndication. Its distributor, Westchester Films, is friendly toward fans and is open about the program's Japanese origins.

September: Jim Terry, a TV producer, buys five Toei Animation SF TV

Flyer for the Earth Defence Command *fan club, 1982*

cartoon series for a single *Force Five* syndication package. He offers the C/FO advance video copies if the C/FO will help publicize it.

October: *Force Five* episodes are included in a video program shown by Mark Merlino at MileHiCon 11 in Denver.

December: The Tatsunoko Fan Club in Japan, selling original cels to its members, agrees to accept American members, with the C/FO serving as its agent.

1980

February: C/FO members in New York City start a chapter there, founded by Joseph Ragus, Sr., and kept going after its second meeting by Jerry Beck.

February: *Fangoria* no. 4 includes "Dawn of the Warrior Robots," the first (?) featured SF media magazine article on Japanese animation. [See page 292.]

May: *Fanfare* no. 3 is the first popular-culture magazine to cover-feature an article on anime, "TV Animation In Japan." [See page 219.]

June: Books Nippan, a Los Angeles Japanese-community bookstore (an American subsidiary of Nippan Shuppan Hanbai, a large Japanese bookstore chain), becomes the first Japanese-community shop (under manager Mrs. Kim) to import extra quantities of anime merchandise and manga especially for the new Anglo fan market.

July: The C/FO in Los Angeles gets a videotaped greeting from the club's New York City members at one of its meetings. Members in other cities talk about starting local chapters. The club is reorganized to recognize the original group as the Los Angeles chapter, and to create a separate "general C/FO" structure to unite the club.

July: The C/FO gets a 16 mm promotional reel of Toei Animation's SF TV cartoons, and sample complete episodes of some titles, added to the main film program at Westercon XXXIII in Los Angeles.

Summer: Michael Pinto in New York starts the *Star Blazers* Fan Club, the second anime fan club to organize several chapters in different cities. It lasts until late 1985.

July/August: The San Diego Comic-Con is visited by a tour group of around thirty Japanese cartoonists, including Osamu Tezuka, Go Nagai, Monkey Punch, and Yumiko Igarashi. The tour is the idea of Tezuka, who urges the Japanese cartoonists to discover how many fans they have in America. The cartoonists draw sketches for fans and sell their characters' merchandise. Tezuka brings his recently completed *Phoenix 2772* feature for the Comic-Con's movie program. Tokyo Movie Shinsha presents a demonstration of 3-D TV animation. This is also the first (?) convention to include several anime character costumes in its Masquerade, with a group of six San Diego fans led by Karen Schnaubelt as *Captain Harlock* and *Star Blazers* characters.

August/September: The World Science Fiction convention, in Boston, declines a C/FO-run video room, but appoints three C/FO members to run an official Worldcon video room. Tokyo Movie Shinsha provides a video copy of *Lupin III: The Castle of Cagliostro* for a test-marketing survey.

September: *Force Five* begins American TV syndication.

September: Phil Gilliam in Nashville starts the *Captain Harlock/Galaxy Express 999* Fan Club.

December: Quinn Kronen in Atlanta starts Animation Adventure, an anime video club.

1981

January: The C/FO-Chicago is started by Jim Engel and Doug Rice.

February: The C/FO-Chicago runs an anime video room at the Capricon I convention in Evanston. This is the first (?) American video program to emphasize *Mobile Suit Gundam*.

Spring: Books Nippan's new manager, Yuji Hiramatsu, sets up a special anime/manga department in the store, and begins advertising in anime club bulletins to build up a mail-order trade.

April: "The Gamilon Embassy" is started at the 1981 Balticon in Baltimore by Colleen Winters, JoLynn Horvath, Robert Fenelon, James Kaposztas, and seven other fans from the Philadelphia/NYC/New Jersey area. Their goal is to travel to fan conventions throughout the Northeast and show anime at open parties in their hotel rooms, to pave the way for official con-run anime rooms as a regular feature at cons. The Embassy is dissolved in 1985 after its goal is considered accomplished.

Mid-year: By this time there are C/FO chapters in Central Texas (Austin), Cleveland, Detroit, Mid-Atlantic (Fairfax, Va.), and Orange County, Calif. From this time, new anime fan clubs appear (and disappear) rapidly, either independent or affiliated with chapter-based clubs such as the *Star Blazers* Fan Club.

October: Susan Horn's Kimono My House shop in the San Francisco Bay Area, started in the summer of 1980 to import Japanese kimonos, begins to import anime merchandise, as well.

AnimeCon '91

1982

January: The Earth Defense Command (EDC) is organized by Derek Wakefield in Texas as another club with "affiliates" in many cities. Originally aggressively devoted to *Star Blazers,* the EDC evolves into a general anime fan club.

July: *Galaxy Express* is released theatrically by New World Pictures (following a two-year postponement of its originally publicized release in May 1980). This is the first release of a Japanese theatrical animated feature to have an impact on the new anime fandom, with fans requesting theaters in their cities to show it.

July: The 1982 San Diego Comic-Con includes the first appearances by Books Nippan and Pony Toy-Go-Round with major dealers' tables of manga and anime merchandise, a four-day anime video program, and the final appearance at an American fan gathering by Osamu Tezuka. Books Nippan's wares include the first Japanese attempt to enter American comics publishing with *Manga,* a special, glossy eighty-eight-page comic book printed in Japan in English. *Manga* is intended to be the first issue of a continuing comic book distributed in America by Books Nippan, but its high price ($8.00) makes it a failure.

September: Carl Macek opens the Carl F. Macek Gallery in Orange, Calif., specializing in original animation cels and other movie memorabilia. The shop deals primarily in American animation art, but it is the first American cartoon-art gallery to import and organize a knowledgeable selection of Japanese original animation art.

October: Joshua Quagmire's *Army Surplus Komikz Featuring Cutey Bunny* no. 1 is an independent comic book with "tributes" to many anime characters (seen in background scenes). Quagmire acknowledges editorially that his funny-animal superheroine's name is inspired by Go Nagai's *Cutey Honey.* Quagmire sends copies to several Japanese cartoonists, and prints an encouraging letter from Osamu Tezuka in the fourth issue.

December: James Kaposztas in New Jersey creates the first fan-made comedy anime video, producing an "Anime Music Video" out of violent scenes from *Star Blazers* set to the Beatles' "All You Need Is Love."

December: Family Home Entertainment begins to release "kiddie cartoon" videos of anime, including *Force Five* episodes and an unsold *Space Pirate Captain Harlock* TV pilot.

1983

January: *Trelaina*, the first anime-fandom Amateur Press Association (a fanzine exchange club), is started by Brian Cirulnick in New York for the discussion through fanzines of *Star Blazers* and general anime topics. (The APA has changed officers and renamed itself *Sasha*, and is still active today.)

February: *I Saw It*, Keiji Nakazawa's personal manga account of the 1945 atomic bombing of Hiroshima, published in American comic-book format, is released to the comics-shop market by Leonard Rifas's San Francisco-based Educomics.

February: Books Nippan sets up the Books Nippan Fan Club to sell anime merchandise by mail order throughout America. It offers its own T-shirts and a discount to members.

February: *Space Fanzine Yamato* is published by Steve Harrison, Ardith Carlton, and Jerry Fellows in Michigan as "the ultimate information source" on *Space Battleship Yamato/Star Blazers*. This is the first American fan effort to produce a "Roman Album"-style complete information guide to a particular anime title.

March: Michael Pinto, Brian Cirulnick, and Robert Fenelon set up a "*Star Blazers* Room" (video room) at the 1983 Lunacon in the New York City area. This starts an annual anime video room tradition that is still being run by Fenelon at the Lunacon. By this time, anime video programs at SF and comics-fan conventions are becoming a standard feature, often started by local anime fans with written permission from Claude Hill at Westchester Films to show *Star Blazers* episodes.

March: DC's highly publicized *Ronin* comic book by Frank Miller is not anime-related, but it helps to bring samurai and other Japanese cultural influences to the attention of mainstream American comics fandom.

May: The first (?) American newspaper article about how "Japanese animation isn't for kids" may be "Television Isn't Ready for This" in the May 14 issue of *The Detroit News*, in a write-up of the local anime fan club.

Summer: *Cliff Hanger*, a video game by Capcom using animation from TMS's first two *Lupin III* theatrical features, appears in video arcades throughout America.

July: Mark Hernandez in Dallas produces *Argo Notes* no. 1, devoted to fannish stories set in the *Star Blazers/Yamato* universe. This is the first (?) anime fanfiction fanzine.

July: Kodansha publishes *Manga! Manga! The World of Japanese Comics*, by Frederik L. Schodt, the first major scholarly study of Japanese manga (in print and animation) to reach the American public.

August: YamatoCon I in Dallas, organized by Mark Hernandez and Don Magness, is the first independent anime mini-convention. (Earlier "anime cons," such as a "*Star Blazers* Mini-Con" run by Michael Pinto, Brian Cirulnick, and Robert Fenelon at the August 1982 New York Creation Convention, were essentially elaborate anime rooms within larger SF or comics conventions.) The one-day YamatoCon has an all-*Star Blazers/Yamato* video program, an anime dealer's room, and an attendance of 100+.

August: Phil Foglio and Nick Pollotta produce the first fan-made comedy over-dubbing of an anime video, using a *Star Blazers* episode to create the spoof *You Say Yamato.*

September: The 1983 World Science Fiction Convention, in Baltimore, features as one of its main events a 35 mm screening of *Arrivederci Yamato,* arranged through Westchester Films by Robert Fenelon, Michael Pinto and Brian Cirulnick. Ardith Carlton and Robert Fenelon provide a running commentary in English for the Japanese language film. The Mid-Atlantic C/FO chapter runs a convention-long anime video room. Twenty-two costumers wear anime costumes at a photo session on the convention center's roof.

October: Anime influences in regular comic books become apparent. A brash example is in Marvel Comics' *Star Wars* no. 79 by Jo Duffy and Tom Palmer, where Lando Calrissian (in disguise) is drawn as a pastiche of Space Pirate Captain Harlock.

The "False Dawn" of Transforming Robots
1984
February: The first American edition of a Japanese-style "anime manga" appears when Books Nippan releases Vol. 1 of its *Star Blazers* anime comic album, produced in English in Japan in association with the West Cape Corporation, creator of the *Yamato* series.

February: *Highly Animated* no. 1, published by Collen Winters and JoLynn Horvath in Philadelphia, is devoted to anime fan-fiction in general, featuring popular anime characters or set in an anime universe.

March: First Comics sends out press releases to announce *Dynamo Joe,* a new comic book series by Doug Rice and John Ostrander to debut as a back-up feature in *Mars* no. 10 in July. The full-page press release emphasizes that "*Dynamo Joe* incorporates into its design and vision a deep admiration of the world of Japanese animation." This interstellar giant-robot series is popular enough to win its own title for a couple of years.

Spring: Japanese manga, anime books and magazines, and model kits begin to appear in American comic shops, through imports by Books Nippan through comics distributors and advertised in Bud Plant Inc.'s and Pacific Comics' Spring 1984 catalogs.

May: *Mekton: The Game of Japanese Robot Combat,* written by Mike Pondsmith and published by R. Talsorian Games, is the first anime-influenced fantasy role-playing game, inspired by *Mobile Suit Gundam*. An expanded, more generic, and tongue-in-cheek version ("You can have green hair, just like your favorite anime hero!"), issued in March 1985 with input by Mike Jones and the Santa Clara, Calif. anime fans, is more popular.

Ad for U.S. premiere of Barefoot Gen in L.A.'s Little Tokyo, August 1985

September: The 1984 World Science Fiction Convention, in Los Angeles, emphasizes anime with a convention-long anime video program, an invitational guest speech by *Gundam* creator Yoshiyuki Tomino (who announces here first that there will be a *Gundam* sequel), the American premiere of Kodansha's *Lensman* feature (in 35 mm with English subtitles) and the premiere of Harmony Gold's pre-*Robotech Macross* video, introduced by director Carl Macek.

September: Harmony Gold's *Macross* video feature is the first American-produced animated title to emphasize its Japanese origins and cultural influences as assets, rather than ignore or try to hide them.

September: World Events Productions' *Voltron, Defender of the Universe!* begins American syndication. This is the first Americanized anime to combine two (or more) separate programs into a single new story, casting *Go Lion* as *Lion Force Voltron* and *Dairugger-XV* as *Vehicle Team Voltron*. The *Lion Force* episodes are so popular that *Voltron* becomes the first Americanized anime to have brand-new episodes commissioned by the American producer from the original Japanese animation studio. *Voltron* also touches off (or at least symbolizes) the 1984 Christmas season mania for transforming-robot toys.

Fall: *Battledroids*, by FASA Corp., is the second, more battle-mecha-oriented, anime-inspired FRP game. It is renamed *Battletech* in March 1985 after George Lucas' lawyers point out that Lucas has trademarked the word "droid."

December: Comico publishes an authorized *Macross* comic book ("issue no. 1"), the last *Macross* merchandising before it evolves into *Robotech*. The Japanese origins of *Macross* are again emphasized to American fans.

1985

High-quality but unauthorized fan-produced anime merchandise starts to appear in large quantities. T-shirts and enameled pins are most popular,

Mangazine *no. 1, August 1985*

usually featuring Astro Boy, Kimba, Lum-chan, The Dirty Pair, or the *Macross* stars.

March: Harmony Gold's *Robotech,* produced by Carl Macek, begins American syndication. This is arguably the single anime title to have the greatest influence in bringing the existence of Japanese animation to the awareness of the public.

March: *Dokonjo,* another Amateur Press Association (APA), is started by Ardith Carlton for the discussion through fanzines of general anime and manga topics.

June: A translation booklet of the text in Rumiko Takahashi's *Urusei Yatsura, Vol. 1,* produced by Toren V. Smith, is the first of the anime-fan "translation guides" to the popular manga or anime titles.

July: Comico begins three separate six-weekly *Robotech* comics: *Robotech: The Macross Saga, Robotech Masters,* and *Robotech: The New Generation.* Unlike most licensed comic books, which are designed to be discontinued when the popularity of the original movie or video title wears out, the *Robotech* contract is designed to enable the comic book to keep going for as long as the comic book itself is successful. The *Robotech* comic books eventually move from Comico to Eternity Comics, then to Academy Comics, where they are still being published and are still helping to "keep *Robotech* alive," while most other TV cartoons of the mid-'80s are forgotten.

August: The anime theatrical feature version of Nakazawa's *Barefoot Gen* has its American premiere in Los Angeles's Little Tokyo community as part of a 40th Anniversary of Hiroshima Commemoration sponsored by Asian Americans for Nuclear Disarmament and East Wind magazine.

August: *Mangazine,* edited by Ben Dunn at his Antarctic Press in San Antonio, is an independent comic book devoted to fan-produced comics in the Japanese style.

September: David K. Riddick and Mario and Glen Ho produce the first translation booklet of a movie's script, *Macross: Do You Remember Love?*

September: The Ladera Travel Agency in Los Angeles begins a one-year promotion in anime fandom for the first fannish group tour to Japan, to visit Tokyo's animation studios and the anime and manga specialty shops.

The "Japanimation '86" tour is the project of Ladera Travel agent Robin Schindler, an anime fan.

November: A.N.I.M.E. (Animation of Inter-Mediary Exchange) is started by Ann Schubert in the San Francisco Bay Area as an informal monthly gathering at her home. Within two years it grows to a monthly barbeque-and-video-watching party of sometimes 200 fans from all over Northern California. Many local anime clubs, fanzines, and other projects emerge from this group.

December: Hayao Miyazaki's *Warriors of the Wind* gets a direct-to-video release (not counting an extremely limited theatrical screening in New York City in June) by New World Video. This is arguably the first American serious anime general release video (as opposed to Harmony Gold's *Macross* specialty-release video, or various "kiddie cartoon" videos which happen to be anime).

1986

April: Starblaze Graphics/The Donning Company publishes *Robotech Art 1,* by Kay Reynolds and Ardith Carlton, a high-quality anime art book which again helps emphasize that *Robotech* is something more than "just a TV cartoon." The book describes the Japanese origins of *Robotech,* and presents a brief history of Japanese anime in America.

April: *Anime-Zine* no. 1, the first American attempt at an *Animage*-style professional magazine devoted to anime, is produced by Robert Fenelon (publisher/editor), Beverly Headley (co-producer), and Luke Menichelli (graphic designer).

May: BayCon '86 in San Jose, Calif., presents an eighty-hour, convention-long exclusive anime program in one of the hotel's major halls with a movie screen-sized projection-TV image, featuring commercial anime videos and laserdiscs for top visual quality, and with a Japanese Animation Program Guide of almost 100 illustrated pages of plot synopses of all titles. This "anime mini-con" is organized by Toren V. Smith.

July: The first (?) TV talk-show presentation on anime appears on Los Angeles's Group W Cable's *This Is the Story.* Guests Fred Patten and Jeff Roady present a half hour show-and-tell about anime with video clips, posters, Japanese anime magazines, etc.

August: *Golgo 13 Graphic Novel Series No. 1: Into the Wolves' Lair,* by Takao Saito, is the first English translation of a major Japanese comics title intended for the American market. It is produced by Saito's own organization in Japan for American distribution by Books Nippan.

August: Ladera Travel's "Japanimation '86" tour signs up about thirty American fans for a two-week trip to Tokyo and Osaka, with visits to many animation studios and ending at the 1986 annual Japanese National Science Fiction Convention. The tour is the first of a biannual series of fannish

Ninja High School *no. 1, Dec. 1987*

shopping trips to Japan's manga and anime shops and conventions.

The influence of anime and manga grows more common in American independent comics, often mixed with Hong Kong martial-arts influences: e.g., Reggie Byers's *Shuriken* and Doug Bramer and Ryan Brown's *Rion 2990*.

Mid-year: Anime fanzines become common, with such examples as *Dirty Little Girls* (devoted to the *Dirty Pair*) published by Guy Brownlee in Texas.

Mid-year: Anime APAs become common, with the start of *APA-Hashin* by Randall Stukey in Texas (May) for general discussion of anime and manga; *Lemon APA* by Scott Frazier in Colorado (May) devoted to adult anime; *Bird Scramble!* by Patricia Munson-Siter in South Dakota (August) devoted to *Gatchaman/Battle of the Planets*; *Anime Janai* by Marg Baskin in Ontario and Heather Bruton in Nova Scotia (November) for general discussions; *U.S.A. Yatsura* by Aaron Reed in Massachusetts (November) devoted to humorous anime such as *Urusei Yatsura* and *Project A-Ko*; and *Animanga* by Paul Sudlow in Tennessee (January 1987) as a fanzine workshop for anime/manga style amateur comic-art and fiction.

October: An "Official *Robotech* Convention" in Anaheim, Calif., put on by the Creation Con organizers, draws approximately 4,000 fans.

November: Brian Cirulnick's *Desslock's Revenge* premieres at Philcon '86 in Philadelphia. This production, which began in 1983, is the earliest known American fan-produced anime featuring original animation.

December: Ben Dunn's *Ninja High School* no. 1 introduces the "high school fantasy humor" influence of Rumiko Takahashi to American comics.

1987

January: U.S. Renditions is created by Nippan Shuppan Hanbai, Books Nippan's parent company, as a separate subsidiary to produce new American editions of anime merchandise (as distinct from imports from Japan). David Riddick and Robert Napton are transferred from the Books Nippan Fan Club to head the new company.

January: Anime Hasshin (originally Hasshin R.I.) is started by Lorraine Savage in Rhode Island as a correspondence-based fan club. Its high-quality fanzine, *The Rose,* attracts hundreds of members from seven countries across four continents by 1992.

February: Mike Pondsmith's *Teenagers From Outer Space* spreads the Takahashi fantasy-humor influence to FRP gaming.

March: Del Rey Books releases the first four *Robotech* paperback SF novels by Jack McKinney. The final volume, no. 18, is published in January 1990.

April: Panda.com, an Internet mailing list for e-mail distribution of computer discussions of *Urusei Yatsura* and related anime, is started by Mark Crispin of the A.N.I.M.E. group.

May: The Electric Holt computer bulletin board system (BBS) is started by John DeWeese, Richard Chandler, Seth Grenald, and Mitch Marmel in Philadelphia. Although it is devoted to SF in general (especially *Elfquest*), it builds up an extensive anime users' group. The BBS features anime graphics, translations of complete TV episode and movie scripts, e-mail exchanges, and open-participation storyboards (such as *Galaxy Local 999,* a spoof serial).

May: First appearance of actual American editions of Japanese manga. First Comics' edition of *Lone Wolf And Cub* no. 1, by Kazuo Koike and Goseki Kojima, and the joint Eclipse International/Viz Communications' editions of *Area 88* no. 1, by Kaoru Shintani, *Kamui* no. 1, by Sanpei Shirato, and *Mai the Psychic Girl* no. 1, by Kazuya Kudo and Ryoichi Ikegami, are published almost simultaneously.

July: NOW Comics publishes *Speed Racer* no. 1, following it a month later with *The Original Astro Boy Comics* no. 1, creating new comics for a nostalgia market for the TV anime of the 1960s. (Purists complain that the new comics show a lack of familiarity with the original TV story concepts.)

July: *Animag* no. 1, "The Magazine of Japanese Animation," is produced by Matthew Anacleto, Michael Ebert, Dana Fong, and a support team from the A.N.I.M.E. group. It becomes the closest American version yet of a professional quality *Animage*-style magazine.

November: U.S. Renditions releases the *Robotech BGM Collection, Vol. 1,* an LP record of *Robotech* background music; the first American-produced anime music record. It is later reissued as a CD.

November: rec.arts.anime is started by Ann Schubert on the Internet as a computer users' anime general news group.

November: LosCon XIV in Los Angeles (Pasadena) is the first American SF convention to feature a "Daicon-style" opening ceremonies animated film, *Clearance Papers,* written by Fred Patten and animated by Michael Aguilar with stop-motion models of con guest-of-honor C. J. Cherryh's characters.

1988
January: Roy and Cathy Bruce of Richmond, Va., start the Japanese Animation Network.

LosCon 18 Anime Room program book, November 29 - December 1, 1991

January: The Cal-Animage club is started at the U.C. Berkeley campus by Mike Tatsugawa. It grows into a confederation of college anime clubs linked by a computer net, mostly in California but one as far as Perth, Western Australia. Cal-Animage is organized in the manner of college fraternities, with the Alpha chapter at U.C. Berkeley, the Beta chapter at U.C. San Diego, Gamma at U.C. Santa Barbara, Theta at Stanford, etc.

Spring: *Protoculture Addicts* no. 1, "The Official *Robotech* Fanzine," is published by Claude Pelletier, Alain Dubreuil, Michel Gareau, and a staff of Montreal fans operating as IANVS Publications.

May: (Marvel) Epic Comics begins the American edition of Katsuhiro Otomo's *Akira*.

June: *Animag* starts the Animag BBS (a.k.a. Valley of the Wind BBS), the first (?) exclusively anime computer bulletin board system, with Takayuki Karahashi and Dana Fong as co-sysops.

Summer: GAGA Communications Inc., a Japanese-based film distributor aimed at the American movie and TV market, makes a strong promotion to sell a package of anime titles including *Crystal Triangle, Project A-Ko, Bubblegum Crisis, The Humanoid, M.D. Geist, Madox-01, Yotoden,* and many others. The promotion includes providing anime clubs with publicity materials including a videotape of trailers. GAGA presents a full-day screening, "The World of Japanese Animation," at the July meeting of the Los Angeles Comic Book and Science Fiction Convention. GAGA is unsuccessful in selling any of its package to the American film/TV/video companies, but the attempt is highly inspirational to fans considering starting their own professional video companies.

September: Eclipse's American edition of Masamune Shirow's *Appleseed* no. 1 is the first published project of Studio Proteus, a company started by Toren V. Smith to find the best Japanese manga and agent/translate them for American publishers.

October: Streamline Pictures is created by Carl Macek and Jerry Beck in Hollywood to import, translate, and distribute anime in America, theatrically and on video.

November: The co-publishing agreement between Eclipse International and Viz Communications ends, and Viz begins to publish its own American editions of Japanese comics. Viz is an American subsidiary of Shogakukan, one of Japan's largest manga publishers. This indicates that a major Japanese publisher feels that American interest in manga and anime is large enough to create a viable market.

December: Eclipse publishes *Dirty Pair* no. 1, by Adam Warren and Toren V. Smith, Studio Proteus' first original creation featuring licensed Japanese SF/anime characters.

Fandom Goes Public
1989
February: Kimono My House becomes the first authorized licensee of original American anime merchandise, starting with a Lum T-shirt licensed from Viz.

March: Streamline Pictures begins its first anime theatrical distribution, with *Laputa: The Castle in the Sky* (in Philadelphia).

May: General Products-USA is started in San Francisco (Alameda) by General Products, the Japanese garage-kit company run by the fan-creators better known for the Gainax animation studio. They hire Lea Hernandez at BayCon '89 as vice president to run the company, starting with a major publicity campaign at the 1989 San Diego Comic-Con. GP-USA's goal is to make all Japanese manga and anime merchandise available to American fans by collecting orders from the fans, buying the merchandise in Japan, and shipping it to GP-USA for re-shipment to the purchasers, in addition to importing the most popular anime merchandise for regular retail sale. The project soon fails. Two basic reasons are that American fans order (and prepay for) merchandise from older anime titles which are passé and no longer obtainable; and that the Japanese parent company has unreasonable expectations that the American fans will buy whatever cheap anime items they ship to America. Hernandez resigns in May 1990, turning GP-USA over to Shon Howell, who tries until December 1991 to continue the company (including taking two trips to Tokyo to try to get what the American fans want) before giving up.

July: The Cartoon/Fantasy Organization, torn by internal feuding during its last two years, is declared by its last leader to be dissolved. The C/FO-Los Angeles chapter (the original club) drops its "chapter" designation and continues to meet under the C/FO name as a local club.

September: The Japanese Animation Network becomes the first anime fan group to be granted official nonprofit organization status by the Internal Revenue Service.

September: AnimEigo, Inc. is formed by Roe R. Adams III and Robert Woodhead in Wilmington, N.C., to license anime for authorized subtitled video sale in America.

Project A-Kon 1 program book, 1990

December: Streamline Pictures begins the American theatrical distribution of the *Akira* anime feature.

1990

February: The monthly Los Angeles Comic Book and Science Fiction Convention presents the "World Premiere" of Streamline Pictures' first videotape release (the dubbed *Akira Production Report* documentary) and U.S. Renditions' first videotape releases, the subtitled *Dangaio* no. 1 and *Gunbuster* no. 1.

February: Eternity Comics' *Lensman* no. 1, written by Paul O'Connor and drawn by Tim Eldred and Paul Young, is a licensed comic book based upon anime which has not been released in America yet, produced by fans familiar with the Japanese versions (theatrical and TV series) through the fannish videotape trading circuit.

February: The Right Stuf, Inc., founded by Todd Fersen in Des Moines, Iowa, in July 1987, releases the first four authorized videos of original *Astro Boy* episodes.

April: AnimEigo releases its first subtitled videotape, *Madox-01*.

May: Eternity Comics' *Broid* no. 1, by Tim Eldred, is in Eternity's own publicity "conceived along the same lines as *Mobile Suit Gundam*."

July: Project A-Kon, in Dallas, is organized by Mary Wakefield and the EDC Animation Society as the first national-scale convention devoted primarily to Japanese anime, with some American animation. It is successful enough that it becomes an annual convention.

Summer: *Animenominous!* is started by Jeff Thompson, Luke Menichelli, and a staff of New Jersey/Philadelphia/New York City fans as another *Animage*-style magazine devoted to profiles of fan-favorite anime titles.

August: Del Rey Books publishes the first of a three-volume edition of Yoshiyuki Tomino's *Gundam Mobile Suit* SF novel, translated by Frederik L. Schodt. In an introduction in each volume, "A Word From The Translator," Schodt informs America's SF readers of the novel's origins in Japanese animated SF.

December: With issue no. 10, *Protoculture Addicts* drops its *Robotech* specialization and becomes a general magazine devoted to anime and the anime fan culture in North America.

December: Streamline Pictures releases the dubbed *Akira* movie on video as a "Video Comics" title for the comic shop specialty video market.

1991

March: The first (?) East Coast TV talk show presentation on anime appears on Manhattan Cable's *The Chronic Rift* in New York. Guests Robert Fenelon, Jo Duffy, and Felix Rodregez devote a full episode to presenting anime to the public.

July: Central Park Media, a video distribution company started by John O'Donnell in April 1990, creates its U.S. Manga Corps department (with Masumi Homma) to produce and distribute subtitled anime videos.

August: *V-MAX*, "The Anime and Manga Newsletter" is started by Matthew Anacleto and Chris Keller as a professional-quality "upgrade" of the A.N.I.M.E. group's newsletter.

August-September: AnimeCon '91 in San Jose, Calif., is the first major North American convention devoted exclusively to anime and manga. AnimeCon is the result of a two-year project by Toshio Okada of Gainax in Japan and Toren Smith of Studio Proteus in America, working with a committee of fans chaired by John McLaughlin, founder of the annual BayCon SF convention in San Jose. Gainax arranges for the attendance of many popular anime and manga creators as AnimeCon's guests, including Hideaki Anno, Johji Manabe, Haruhiko Mikimoto, Yoshiyuki Sadamoto, and Kenichi Sonoda. There is an extensive anime program including rarities from the Tokyo animation studios. A Japanese-style opening ceremonies cartoon is produced by fan animators led by SF artist Rick Sternbach. An impromptu auction raises over $4,500 for the medical expenses of Ann Schubert, who suffered a massive stroke just before the con. The attendance from throughout North America is over 1,700.

October: U.S. Manga Corps's first video release is the subtitled *Dominion* no. 1.

1992

January: IANVS Publications begins new anime-related magazines in addition to *Protoculture Addicts*. *Mecha Press* is a bi-monthly devoted to anime mecha hardware, covering both the fictional schematics and the model kits, plus gaming. *Cybersuit Arkadyne,* by Tim Eldred and Jonathan Jarrad, is a manga-style space adventure comic book with battle mecha.

January: Pop singer Matthew Sweet releases his music video *Girlfriend,* intercutting images of Sweet performing with clips from the anime feature *Space Adventure Cobra*. A later Sweet music video, *I've Been Waiting,* is filled with images of Lum from many of the *Urusei Yatsura* movies, TV episodes, and OAVs.

February: Streamline Pictures' subtitled *Twilight of the Cockroaches* becomes the first American anime laser disc, from Lumivision.

March: Antarctic Press's *Mangazine* comic book is converted with its vol. 2, no. 14 issue into an "anime and comics" magazine under editor Doug Dlin. Anime and manga news and articles on popular anime titles take precedence over the fan-drawn manga-style comic stories. An "anime classified" department allows fans to advertise their clubs and fanzines, and post requests for pen pals.

March: The quantity of Japanese imports, American translations of manga as comics and anime as videos, and original American comics in the manga style has grown so large that Capital City Distribution, one of the major American specialty distributors to comic shops, proclaims that "March is Manga Month." The one-month emphasis on Japanese-influenced merchandise is so successful that Capital City repeats it the following March.

April: The Atlantic Anime Alliance (AaA) is founded by Chet Jasinski and Stephen Pearl at Rutgers University as a public service anime "information brokerage." Its goals are to provide a series of free anime information sheets, to link East Coast anime fans and clubs through a loose network, to provide information at East Coast fan conventions on how to contact anime fandom, and to turn fannish public opinion against anime bootlegging. The AaA operates with a small volunteer membership/staff and has a mailing list of over 400 for its free information sheets.

July: Anime Expo '92, at the same Red Lion Hotel in San Jose, Calif., is treated by fans as the "second annual American anime convention," although it is technically a new convention, organized by Mike Tatsugawa under the auspices of a nonprofit corporation, the Society for the Promotion of Japanese Animation. Anime Expo '92 also features many notable Japanese anime and manga creators as guests. A fifteen-minute opening ceremonies cartoon, *Bayscape 2042,* is animated by a fan team organized by David Ho of Running Ink Animation Productions. (Video copies of the cartoon and its original cels are sold at the con.) Other events include the world premieres of two Japanese OAVs, *Giant Robo* no. 1 and *Kabuto,* and three American videos, *Guyver* no. 1, *Macross II* no. 1, and *Orguss* no. 1, dubbed by a new company, L.A. Hero, for release by U.S. Renditions; the premiere of the first American anime CD-ROM, *The World of U.S. Manga Corps,* produced by Brian Cirulnick and Michael Pinto, with 1,000 full-color images and 100 Quicktime movies; and presentation of the first American fan awards for anime and manga, the Anime Expo Industry Awards.

Summer: The anime specialty videos, which have been sold primarily through comic book shops and by mail order, begin to appear in the major video retail chains and in neighborhood video rental stores. Some shops set up a separate "Japanese Animation" or "Japanimation" section. The August issue of *Tower Records/Video's Pulse!* magazine contains an article, "Moving Manga Mania: A Beginners Guide to Japanese Animation," which includes a photo of singer Matthew Sweet showing off his Lum tattoo.

August: *Manga Newswatch Quarterly* is started by Mark Paniccia in South Bend, Ind., as a comics-format manga and anime newsmagazine. There are now enough press releases from Viz, Dark Horse, Antarctic Press, Eternity Comics, Streamline Pictures, AnimEigo, etc., for their forthcoming anime and manga comics and videos to fill a magazine.

September: A.D. Vision, managed by Matt Greenfield in Houston, enters the subtitled anime video field. Its first release in November is *Devil Hunter Yohko.*

October: Antarctic Press begins *Dojinshi: The World of Japanese Fanzines,* a comic book devoted to bringing the best cartoons from Japanese fanzines to America. Each issue presents Japanese fandom's impressions of popular anime titles.

Manga Newswatch *no. 2, Nov. 1992*

November: *Animerica* no. 0 is a preview issue of an "Anime and Manga Monthly" to begin in March 1993, edited by Seiji Horibuchi, Satoru Fujii, and Trish Ledoux, published by Viz Comics. Thanks to its connections with Shogakukan, a major Japanese publisher, it is the hope of the magazine's editors that *Animerica* will be the first of several professional-quality, U.S.-produced anime magazines.

The Best of Anime CD Liner Notes
Liner notes booklet for *The Best of Anime* music CD, Kid Rhino/ Rhino Entertainment Inc., September 1998.

The brutal space invaders have captured the teenage hero. Their fanged general menacingly demands that he turn over his giant robot to them, while an invader soldier tightly holds the hero's sweet young girlfriend. Suddenly there is an interruption, and the girl is seen running free while the soldier is bent over, moaning as he clutches his groin. She has obviously kneed him in the crotch off-camera!

American comics and SF fans fell out of their chairs when this episode of *Brave Raideen* was shown on Japanese-community TV channels in early 1976. "You just can't *do* this in cartoons!" was the general consensus. Everybody knew that cartoons had to be sanitized for little kids. Comics fandom was riding high in the glory years of Marvel and DC superheroes, yet hardly anyone watched cartoons anymore—they had outgrown them.

But these Japanese animated equivalents of superhero comics were clearly meant for a mature audience. Characters often died. The teen hero was usually traumatized by the murder of his scientist father in the first episode, and sometimes one of his best friends, an important supporting character, would be killed. The villains didn't just arrogantly posture—they were viciously sadistic and clearly out to cause major death and destruction.

Of course, at that time, not many people watched Japanese-community TV. That changed, however, when the first VCRs went on sale in late 1975 and the first giant-robot cartoons reached the United States in early 1976. Fans began to videotape the half-hour dramas and show them at their comics and SF fan club meetings.

Different cities showed different cartoons (New York City had *Galaxy Express 999*, the West Coast didn't), so fans traded video copies back and forth. In 1977, fans in Los Angeles started the first club devoted to what was then called "Japanimation." A year later Japanese animation video rooms began showing up at comics and SF conventions, and by 1980 prizes were being awarded for fans' anime-character costumes at these cons' masquerades.

Early fans discovered that these English-subtitled cartoons were not the first Japanese animation to appear in America. Several TV cartoons during the 1960s were actually dubbed anime in the United States, although the public had not realized it at the time. Many of these teen fans' favorite childhood cartoons, such as *Speed Racer, Kimba the White Lion,* and *Astro Boy,* are anime.

In the early 1980s there were anime clubs across the country, and U.S. fans began trading videos with fans in Japan—American TV SF such as *Star Trek* and *Battlestar Galactica* were exchanged for Japanese animated SF such as *Gundam* and *Urusei Yatsura.* By the time Japanese animation returned to

Kid Rhino, a division of Rhino Entertainment Company, had been releasing CDs of American theatrical and TV animated-cartoon music such as compilations of Hanna-Barbera TV-cartoon theme songs for years. In 1998 Enrique Galvez, the owner of the Banzai Anime specialty store in Los Angeles, pitched them the idea of producing a CD of anime music; not the most popular anime songs: as much as the title-credits songs of the most popular anime movies, original videos, and TV series. I was often asked how I had selected the songs. I didn't; I was just hired to write the booklet after the CD was approved by Rhino. Galvez actually selected about thirty songs; the CD ended up with the first sixteen of those that Rhino could license the rights to before its budget for the project was used up. *The Best of Anime* was released in September 1998 with two different pseudo-cel overlays, one of Speed Racer and the other of Cutey Honey. There was supposed to be a third, of Serena/Sailor Moon, but the licensing fee for her was prohibitively high. ■

U.S. television after a decade of new programs, such as *Battle of the Planets* and *Star Blazers,* anime fans could tell how they had been edited for English-speaking audiences. By the mid-1980s the makers of such U.S. programs as *Robotech* were boasting about their shows' Japanese origins.

Anime clubs published the first fanzines in 1979. Soon there were information booklets on popular titles and amateur translation scripts of the dialogue in manga—Japanese comic books—and anime videos. And college fans were using their cinematography lab equipment to subtitle anime videos.

The teen anime fans of the 1970s were in their late twenties by the end of the 1980s. Some of them became animators, and anime-art influences began appearing in U.S. television cartoons and theatrical animated features. Anime fans were hired by comic book publishers, and the first U.S. editions of Japanese manga were published. Independent publishers debuted new American comics drawn in the manga-art style.

For more than a decade, fans often had to settle for poor quality copies of videos passed around through the fan clubs. The movie, TV, and video industries insisted that Americans weren't interested in anime. Finally, around 1990, fans took matters into their own hands. They started their own companies to license the U.S. rights for anime. The first theatrical releases were in 1989; the first anime videos came out in 1990. Initially these videos sold only by mail order and in comic-book shops. By 1993 the general video retail market noticed anime's small-but-steadily-growing popularity. Soon anime sections appeared in the major video outlets.

Anime became a major part of SF and comics conventions during the 1980s. Many featured twenty-four-hour anime video programs. But fans wanted their own conventions, with Japanese cartoonists, directors, and voice actors as guests of honor. These anime-only conventions were held beginning in 1990 and 1991 in Texas and California.

After twenty years of winning fans in the United States, anime is now an acknowledged force in popular culture and can be easily found in mainstream video stores as well as on many syndicated and cable TV channels. Translated Japanese manga and U.S. comics in the manga style take up an increasing amount of space in the comic shop racks, and there are at least a half-dozen books and several professional specialty magazines devoted to anime. In North America, the number of anime conventions has grown to more than a dozen annually. And unlike other crazes that grew out of clever, professionally guided merchandising concepts, anime is a phenomenon that was discovered by the fans, nurtured by the fans (despite professional dismissal), and firmly established by the fans—so much so that such new words as *anime* and *manga* are now part of the English language.

"Astro Boy" From the TV Series *Astro Boy* (Original title: *Tetsuwan Atomu,* trans.: *Mighty Atom*); Japanese TV debut: January 1, 1963; U.S. TV debut: September 7, 1963; 193 episodes aired in Japan from 1963–66; 104 episodes appeared in U.S. syndication from 1963–64.

This was numero uno. When it debuted as a comic book in the early 1950s, by Osamu Tezuka, the adventures of this little-boy robot helped to establish the Japanese comic book industry. It then became Japan's first major TV cartoon series, premiering New Year's Day 1963 and running for nearly 200 weekly episodes. It was also America's first TV anime import, syndicated by NBC starting in September 1963. The Japanese title, *Mighty Atom*, was already being used by an American comic book, so the robot became *Astro Boy* in the English-speaking world. In (then far-off) A.D. 2000, Dr. Boynton's son Astor is killed in an automobile accident. The distraught inventor creates a robot duplicate of the child, crammed with superpowers and programmed to do good. But when Astro Boy fails to grow up like a real boy, the mad scientist disowns him as a failure and sells him to the Robot Circus. He is rescued from cruel Ringmaster Cacciatore by kindly Dr. Packadermus J. Elefun, who helps him use his powers for the benefit of mankind. The *Astro Boy* theme song, adapted from the original Japanese TV theme by Tatsuo Takai, is Astro Boy's entrance march from the Robot Circus. It has remained popular in Japan for more than three decades, especially in high school marching-band arrangements.

"Gigantor" From the TV Series *Gigantor* (original title: *Tetsujin 28-go*, trans.: *Iron Man No. 28*); Japanese TV debut: October 20, 1963; U.S. TV debut: January 5, 1966; ninety-six episodes aired in Japan from 1963–65; fifty-two episodes appeared in U.S. syndication in 1966.

Gigantor's inventor, Prof. Bob Brilliant, gives TV cartoondom's first giant robot to boy detective Jimmy Sparks to help him in his fight against crime. Jimmy and Gigantor help Interpol Inspector Ignatz Blooper and secret agent Dick Strong foil criminals and totalitarian dictators around the world. Young TV viewers in the '60s strongly identified with Jimmy, the boy with his own giant robot that he could make do anything just by twiddling a control stick on a little black box. *Gigantor's* bouncy, march-along theme by Lou Singer and Gene Raskin was popular, in part, because the lyrics were so easy for kids to parody ("fatter than fat, slower than slow, smaller than small. . . .").

"Speed Racer" From the TV Series *Speed Racer* (Original title: *Mach Go Go Go*, trans.: *Mach Five Five Five*); Japanese TV debut: April 2, 1967; fifty-two episodes. U.S. TV debut: September 28, 1967; fifty-two episodes aired from 1967–68.

Speed Racer, the teen international racing champ, is the official star, but '60s TV viewers were more interested in his super-cool Mach Five Special Formula racing car. The five push buttons around its steering wheel control such neat gadgets as a transparent hood for underwater driving and fold-out buzz saws for driving through forests. Speed's races around the world pit him against crooked rival racers, criminals, and local dictators. The safety-conscious Speed was often in danger, but he was never as thrill-crazy as his fast-paced theme song ("he's a demon on wheels") made him sound.

"Lum's Love Song" From the TV Series *Urusei Yatsura* (trans. *Those Obnoxious Aliens*); Japanese TV debut: October 14, 1981; 197 episodes from 1981–86; six theatrical features from 1983–91; eleven original animation videos from 1986–91.

High school girl chaser Ataru Moroboshi is randomly chosen by space aliens for a contest. If he can defeat their flying teenager, Lum, they won't invade Earth. Ataru wins, but Lum falls in love with "Darling" and stays in Japan to be with him.

U.S.A. Yatsura *(fanzine) no. 1,* November 1986

Soon it becomes "in" among Lum's friends to join her, and Earth is invaded anyway—by alien high schoolers. Adults freak out, but Earth teens quickly adjust to their outer-space counterparts. Some episodes have very ethnically Japanese plots, but the wacky adolescent high jinks and emotions have a universal appeal. *Urusei Yatsura* became so popular with anime fans in the 1980s that it was the first program to inspire fan-written translations.

"Sentimental Over the Shoulder" From the Original Animation Video *Megazone 23; Megazone 23, Part 1;* video debut: March 23, 1985; *Megazone 23, Part 2* video debut: April 26, 1986.

Shogo Yahagi, a biker bum in contemporary (mid-'80s) Tokyo, inadvertently gets hold of a prototype supercycle. Ruthless government killers come after him to get it back. Shogo then learns that the whole world is phony! It is really 500 years later, and "Tokyo" is a virtual-reality re-creation in a space environment fleeing a destroyed Earth. Most anime was available to fans before 1985 via videos of half-hour TV episodes, but with the beginning of direct-to-video releases in 1984, excellent features started showing up. The two-parter *Megazone 23* (1985 and 1986) was the first major original animation video hit.

"Beautiful Planet" From the Theatrical Release *Windaria;* Japanese theatrical release: July 19, 1986.

The flip description of *Windaria* as "*Romeo and Juliet* in a *Dungeons and Dragons* setting" was quickly forgotten as viewers got caught up in this hauntingly beautiful tragedy of doomed love. In rival fairy-tale kingdoms, two happy pairs of young lovers (the prince and princess of the two kingdoms; and two newlywed young farmers) are gradually overwhelmed by emotions of duty, loyalty to nation, and dreams of glory as their countries drift inevitably to war. *Windaria* proved that anime can be more than zany comedy and comic-book SF dramatics.

"Active Heart" From the Original Animation Video *Gunbuster* (Original title: *Top O Nerae!*, trans.: *Aim For The Top!*); Japanese video series debut: October 7, 1988; six episodes aired from 1988–89.

Twenty-first century Earth is fighting for its survival against outer-space monsters. Noriko Takaya dreams of piloting one of the new Gunbuster battle suits and is amazed when she is accepted by the Space Force for satellite-station training. Part parody and part serious, *Gunbuster* was the first anime title to mix girl's high school sports drama with boy-dominated, giant-robot battle action. By this time the Tokyo studios were aware of their American fans, and *Gunbuster*'s animators corresponded with some of them, even naming Noriko's heartthrob, who is killed on his first mission, after a leading fan.

"Adessa E Fortuna" From the Original Animation Video *Record of Lodoss War* (Original title: *Lodoss Jima Senki*); Japanese series debut: June 30, 1990; thirteen episodes released from 1990–91.

Parn, a young swordsman, and his friend Etoh, a newly ordained cleric, join four more experienced fighters—Slayn, a wizard; the warriors Deedlit (an elf) and Ghim (a dwarf); and Woodchuck, a cynical thief—on a quest to save the world of Lodoss from falling under the evil spell of Kardis the Destroyer. The thirteen-episode *Record Of Lodoss War* was anime's first major departure from high-tech SF into "high fantasy," and the first (and many fans say still the best) anime dramatization of fantasy role-playing games.

"Full Moon Light" From the Original Animation Video *Devil Hunter Yohko* (Original title: *Mamono Hunter Yôko*); Japanese series debut: February 8, 1991; six episodes released from 1991–95.

Yohko and Buffy—separated at birth? Yohko Mano is a boy-crazy high schooler who thinks her stern granny has flipped out when she reveals the family secret: Yohko is the 108th in a line of demon hunters who must slay the monsters that seek to corrupt and conquer humanity. But to retain her power as a mystic ninja, Yohko must also retain her virginity. This is awfully frustrating, especially since the devils seem to possess the handsomest boys in her school. The combination of teen humor, supernatural horror, and martial-arts action extended what was originally a stand-alone title (appearing in Japan one year before *Buffy the Vampire Slayer* was released in the United States) into four sequels and a music video.

"Sailing" From the Theatrical Release *Silent Möbius*; Japanese release: August 17, 1991; *Silent Möbius 2*; released July 18, 1992.

The world in A.D. 2028 is under attack by transdimensional invaders, who strike and disappear like demons from hell. Their opposition is a special, all-woman police division, the AMP, which battles them with psionic weapons. Katsumi Liqueur joins the AMP to destroy the demon that killed her mother, but her partners worry that she is still too distraught to use her psychic talent effectively. *Silent Möbius* is a clever presentation of fantasy in

SF guise, pitting a futuristic, high-tech witches' coven against Lovecraftian monsters.

"Happy Birthday To Me" From the Original Animation Video *Cat Girl Nuku Nuku* (Original title: *Bannô Bunka Neko Musume*, trans.: *All-Purpose Cultural Cat Girl*); Japanese video series debut: October 21, 1992; six episodes released from 1992–93.

Take an android super-soldier frame, finish it with the body of a cute high school coed, and give it the brain of a loveable little kitty cat. Presto—the perfect babysitter for a divorced nutty scientist's son, Ryunosuke. And Nuku Nuku needs every bit of strength, because Ryu's mom is the president of Mishima Heavy Industries, a major defense contractor, and she wants her son back! Ryu shakes his head in exasperation as his parents squabble while Nuku Nuku cutely demolishes Mom's latest secret weapon—hopefully not wiping out half of Tokyo in the process.

"Just Beyond the Time" From the Original Animation Video *New Dominion Tank Police;* Japanese video series debut: October 21, 1993; the original *Dominion Tank Police* series debut: May 27, 1988; six episodes released from 1993–94; four episodes in original 1989 series.

In this futuristic comedy, Earth is so polluted that people wear air-filter masks outside sealed buildings. A squad of zany cops roar through the streets in miniature tanks, blasting at criminals with no regard for bystanders. Gung-ho rookie cop Leona Ozaki is determined to bring in notorious gang boss Buaku and his sexy, bioengineered cat-girl flunkies, Anapuma and Unipuma. After decades of noble heroes saving the day, *Dominion* was a pioneering step into cynical humor. The whole cast are idiots, but it probably doesn't matter in the end because the series offers strong hints that Earth's biosphere is about to completely collapse. *Dominion Tank Police* was so popular that the sequel, the source of "Just Beyond Time," appeared four years later.

"My Heart I Can't Say, Your Heart I Want To Know" From the original animation video *Oh! My Goddess;* Japanese video series debut: February 21, 1993; five episodes released from 1993–94.

Keiichi, a pure-hearted college student, is visited by young goddess Belldandy, who grants him one wish. He wishes that he could have a girlfriend just like her, and she becomes mortal to remain with him. Belldandy's high-spirited divine sisters, Urd and Skuld, soon move in to provide high jinks, but *Oh! My Goddess* relies on endearing characters for its charm. Belldandy tries to magically help Keiichi, who wants to succeed on his own merits; and Keiichi worries that the innocent Belldandy will be tainted by human corruption. If the word for *Urusei Yatsura* is zany, the word for *Oh! My Goddess* is sweet.

"Cutey Honey" From the Original Animation Video *New Cutey Honey* (Original title: *Shin Cutey Honey*); *Cutey Honey* Original TV Series debuted in Japan October 13, 1973; the *New Cutey Honey* original animation video series debuted April 21, 1994. Eight episodes released from 1994–95; twenty-five episodes of the original series aired in Japan from 1973–74.

The original *Cutey Honey* made a big impact on early anime fans. Cartoonist Go Nagai's sexy android crime-fighter can superscientifically change her appearance and costume for instant disguises. The shift in costumes leaves her nude for a split-second. This, and mildly risqué innuendos, blew horny adolescent minds in both Japan and America in the mid-'70s. (This was before brief topless shower scenes became standard in '80s anime.) Even poor quality, untranslated *Cutey Honey* videos were very popular at early anime fan club screenings, remaining so much so that after twenty years a new original animation version, *New Cutey Honey*, was made in 1994.

"Voices" From the Original Animation Video *Macross Plus;* Japanese video series debut: August 25, 1994; four episodes released from 1994–95.

Macross (1982) and its 1985 Americanized *Robotech* version were major influences in the development of anime. The 1994 sequel, *Macross Plus,* also dazzled fans and advanced the state of animation art with its kick-butt aerial dramatics between rival fighter pilots Isamu Dyson and Guld Bowman and its stunning CGI-animation twenty-first-century megarock concerts organized by the girl they both love, Myung Lone.

"Sailor Moon Theme" From the TV Series *Sailor Moon* (Original title: *Bishôjo Senshi Sailor Moon,* trans.: *Pretty Soldier Sailor Moon*); Japanese TV debut: March 7, 1992; U.S. TV debut: September 11, 1995; 200 episodes released in Japan from 1992–97; sixty-five episodes dubbed for North American syndication from 1995–96.

Fourteen-year-old Usagi (which means "Bunny" in English; she is "Serena" in the U.S. version) is a giggly junior-high student who is given a magic brooch by Luna, a talking cat from the Moon Kingdom. This transforms her into Sailor Moon, a superheroine who fights the evil monsters from the Dark Universe with a growing team of Sailor Scouts: Sailor Mercury, Sailor Mars, etc. *Sailor Moon* took the formula of boys' superhero teams and made it respectable for girls, running for 200 weekly episodes in Japan. Only sixty-five were dubbed for the United States, and when it was taken off the air, a 1996 Internet protest campaign is said to have won 30,000 signatures to put it back on.

Who Knows "Best"?
Last Word column in *Manga Max* no. 1, December 1998.

Practically every genre of popular culture has its own awards. In the media centered around SF, fantasy, and cartoon-art, awards are voted on by both professional societies and by fans at their conventions. The common factor is that these are all "Best" awards, presented for excellence: Best Novel, Best Short Story, and so forth.

There were no awards at the first dedicated anime convention in 1991 because one of its co-sponsors was the Gainax animation studio and it was felt this might create a conflict-of-interest situation. Nineteen ninety-two saw the first Anime Expo, and its first Industry Awards for the Society for the Promotion of Japanese Animation (SPJA). These fan-voted awards were in sixteen categories such as Best Film, Best OAV, Best Sub/Dub Company, and Best Manga. In 1993, Anime Expo repeated the experience with some extra categories, and the new Anime America convention gave out similar awards. These awards reached their peak in late 1995, with the addition of Anime East's Tezuka Awards and the *V-Max* magazine staff awards for "Excellence in Anime and Manga."

But, with the exception of Anime Expo's Industry Awards, the custom abruptly disappeared in 1996. They were replaced by "favorite" awards, exemplified by *Animerica*'s new annual Fan Awards in such categories as Favorite Leading Man, Favorite Martial Arts Technique, Favorite Villain, and Character You'd Most Like to See in a Swimsuit Issue. Since 1996, the trend has been toward generally humorous, non-judgmental categories. The emphasis of conventions has shifted to awards for attendees, for costumes and model-building, rather than on recognition of the best of professional anime and manga.

What happened? First, the conventions and the magazines making most of the "Best" awards disappeared. They collapsed partly due to overly grandiose ambitions, and it was felt that presenting themselves as arbiters of taste was an example of this hubris. Most anime conventions since 1996 say that fans dislike "Best" awards for being "too serious." One fan told me: "If you ask me what my favorite anime video is, or who my favorite character is, I'll be glad to tell you. But the "Best"? I'd have to see every video there is to answer that fairly. Voting for "the Best" is pretending to have a degree of expertise that most fans don't honestly have."

A similar opinion was that: "Most fans don't seriously consider all the anime; just what they have seen most recently. Look at the last time the Tezuka Awards were given, where *Ranma* won in almost every category because the new *Ranma* videos had just come out!" Some feel that awards should be more accurately termed "for anime released in the United States" to explain why U.S. fans might only now have become enthusiastic over a title that originally appeared several years ago in Japan. Another reason is that fans should stick to giving fan awards. Giving a pro-level award implies that a fan group is claiming pro status. Still other reasons: a feeling that a prestigious award isn't really meant to honor the anime so much as

Manga Max ended each issue with a one-page "Last Word" guest editorial by someone in the anime industry. ■

to promote the convention that awards it, and fans don't want to play that game. Moreover, Anime Expo is already giving its SPJA Industry Awards, so any other similar "Best" awards might be seen as trying to compete with Anime Expo.

The bottom line may be that anime fans don't care. Anime Expo's attendees receive an Industry Awards ballot in their registration packs, and the winners are announced at the closing ceremonies. Of six fans asked after the 1998 con what they thought of the awards, none had bothered to fill out their ballot or pay attention to the announcement of the winners. "I was at the con to have fun, and figuring out how to vote in all those (twenty-one) categories would have taken too long," said one. Mike Tatsugawa, President of the SPJA, says it is natural for the fans to be more interested in the fan awards, but the professionals appreciate the industry awards. When Pioneer won in the Best American Anime Company category, their representative asked if they could get a duplicate of the trophy: one to display in Pioneer's U.S. office, and one in Japan.

When the SF or comics "Best" awards are announced, it is a headline event in those fandoms. The winners are listed in all the major magazines. Where are Anime Expo's awards announced besides Anime Expo's own Web site? How many fans care about the news? For all practical purposes, anime fandom is the only fandom without a serious interest in a "Best" Award.

Anime in the United States
Chapter 3 of *Animation in Asia and the Pacific*, edited by John A. Lent. Eastleigh, UK: John Libbey Publishing, 2001.

Animation began in Japan with the creation of one-reel films by individual cinematic artists in the 1910s.[1] Production remained essentially a garage-hobbyist activity of cartoon and paper-silhouette enthusiasts until the 1950s.[2] These films are well documented in academic reference works, but when mass popularity for animation developed in Japan in the mid-1970s, the popularized "anime dictionaries"[3] only went back to 1957, when the commercial films of Japan's first major animation studio, Toei Doga, began to be released.

Toei's first three cartoon features were *Panda and the Magic Serpent*,[4] released in Japan in October 1958, *Magic Boy,* in December 1959, and *Alakazam the Great,* in August 1960. They were released in America, each by a different distributor, coincidentally all during June and July 1961.[5] These served to test the American reactions to Japanese theatrical cartoons.

Toei Doga followed the Disney formula for theatrical feature animation: high-quality animated cartoon adventures based upon classic folktales, sprinkled with musical numbers and featuring human protagonists surrounded by cute animal companions. The major difference was that the folktales and music were Asian. These were promoted by their U.S. distributors as theatrical cartoon features for children. References to their being foreign films were removed insofar as was possible.

These three releases were not commercially successful in the United States. Neither were several similar children's cartoon features during the 1960s, even though they increasingly employed Westernized fantasy plots to encourage international sales (e.g., the 1965 *Gulliver's Travels Beyond the Moon*). As a result, the American theatrical market for Japanese animation was stillborn.

American distributors continued to import Japanese animated features, but primarily for television. Thus such Toei theatrical hits in Japan as *Jack and the Witch* (1967), *The Little Norse Prince* (1968), and *Puss in Boots* (1969) became familiar to American children through being syndicated across the country as countless "Saturday Afternoon Matinee" TV movies from the late 1960s through the early 1980s. Most were also available through the small 16 mm film rental market.

Beginnings

TV animation began in Japan in 1962–63. Although also designed primarily for children, it followed the U.S. example of offering more modernized and dramatic themes such as outer-space or secret-agent adventures. Japan's first major TV cartoon hit was Osamu Tezuka's *Mighty Atom* (U.S. title: *Astro Boy*), which premiered on New Year's Day 1963 and was broadcast weekly for

When I was asked to write this history of the evolution of anime fandom and the anime commercial market in America, I titled it "Anime in America" with a suggestion that the publisher might want to call it "Anime in North America" to make clear that it included both the United States and Canada. Instead, the British publisher titled it "Anime in the United States" because, I was told, "Everyone knows that Canada is just part of the United States, culturally speaking." You would expect a British (!) publisher to be more sensitive about Canada's national identity.

This was written in June 1999, which you can determine by looking at the most recent issue of the anime specialty magazines, the last item in the References. *Animation in Asia and the Pacific* was not published until June 2001 in Europe and August 2001 in the United States. I received a few complaints that its statements about "the current anime scene" were two years old. This is just a fact of life in book publishing, so there seems little point in trying to bring it up to date. Consider this a time-capsule look at the anime scene from June 1999.

However, statements later identified as erroneous should be corrected. The commercial release of the first videocassette recorder in America was later identified as November 1975, not October. For years, it was "common knowledge" that *Battle of the Planets'* syndication premiere was an unspecified date in October 1978. It has since been pinned down through actual research into *TV Guide* for numerous cities as Monday, September 18, 1978. ■

193 episodes through the end of 1966. This futuristic updating of *Pinocchio*, about a super-strong little-boy robot who wanted to be a real human, was syndicated in the United States by NBC Films starting in September 1963. It was the first of eight Japanese TV cartoon series seen in the States during the 1960s, the others being *8th Man*, released in Japan, 1963, and the United States, 1965, *Gigantor*, *Kimba the White Lion*, *Prince Planet* and *Marine Boy*, all four released in the United States in 1966, and *The Amazing 3* and *Speed Racer*, both with a U.S. release in 1967.[6] These were all syndicated rather than appearing on any national TV network. They appeared in various cities, usually for a half-year to a year at a time, from their initial release dates in the mid-1960s for approximately the next ten years.

To Americans, these half-hour TV cartoons were indistinguishable from most American TV animation. These ranged from the output of recognizable studios such as Hanna-Barbera, Filmation, and Jay Ward, to numerous limited-animation series from small companies whose names were generally unknown. Also, several children's afternoon TV programs presented a mixture of old U.S. theatrical animation, new TV animation, and foreign animation from several European countries. So the cartoons from Japan were not thought of by the public as "Japanese animation." If their origins were realized at all, they were considered to be just part of a vague "foreign animation" category.

Although only eight Japanese TV cartoon series were sold to U.S. television during the 1960s,[7] the Japanese anime dictionaries show more than forty such series produced in Japan from 1963 through 1967. By 1968 Japanese TV animation had become virtually unsalable in America. American studios were creating an increasing quantity of TV cartoons better tailored for American audiences. Also, TV morality standards for children's programming were becoming stricter, especially those against violence. These standards generally did not affect animation in Japan, because the Japanese never developed the "just for kids" perception of animation that became prevalent in the United States. So in addition to gentle animation for young children, Japanese TV offered animated action-adventure dramas— the equivalent of America's live-action movie adventure serials and TV dramas based on such popular newspaper comic strips as *Dick Tracy* and *Flash Gordon*—for teens and adults. But the fisticuffs and gunplay that are inherent in such melodramas made these TV cartoons unacceptable as children's programming in the United States.

From 1967 through 1978, no new Japanese TV cartoons made the transition to U.S. television. But a very small number did appear on Japanese-community TV channels in larger American cities, usually in Japanese with English subtitles. Up through 1975, these were selected from the more popular Japanese cartoons for younger children, but these drew negligible attention outside Japanese ethnic communities.

The situation began to change in the late 1970s because of several factors. One was the explosive popularity in Japan of the giant robot science-fiction/superhero TV cartoons. Beginning with *Mazinger Z* in December 1972, these TV cartoons built a new teen/young adult audience as Japan's toy-industry sponsors aggressively targeted an older market. Cheap, simple toys evolved into complex, expensive transforming action figures. The TV cartoons that featured these toys—all variations of a giant mechanical warrior controlled by a human pilot—became more seriously melodramatic. Where previous TV cartoons had featured child-heroes in mild adventures against simplistic villains, the giant robot cartoons featured teen heroes grimly fighting to save the world from enslavement by sadistic villains. Often the hero was partially motivated by revenge because the villains had already slain his parents. These TV cartoons, which thematically resembled the popular American superhero comic books of the day, first appeared on American Japanese-community TV channels with *Brave Raideen* in March 1976.[8]

A second factor was the appearance of the videocassette recorder on the American consumer market in October 1975. The public became able to make its own recordings of TV programs.

A third factor was the growing divergence between the comic book and the animation audiences by the mid-1970s. What is now called the "Silver Age" of comic books began with the reintroduction of superhero adventure comics in the early 1960s. Typified by such heroes

Ad for MGM's Magic Boy, *1961*

as *The Fantastic Four* and *The Amazing Spider-Man,* costumed-hero comic books began to evolve beyond the traditional children's market toward more dramatic and sophisticated stories suitable for high school– and college-aged readers. At the same time, stricter standards for children's television programming mandated increasingly gentler child-oriented shows. TV cartoons based on popular comic book heroes were required to remove their violence, which included most of the drama as well. Also, theatrical animation had virtually disappeared, as shorts had been discontinued by all studios between the mid-1950s and the late 1960s, and the few Disney features had grown lackluster after the death of Walt Disney in 1966. By the mid-1970s, a large fandom had grown among adolescents and adults in their twenties for the teen-oriented costumed-hero comic books. But their perception was that animated cartoons were only for little children, and that they had all long since outgrown them.

Discovery

There was considerable culture shock when these comic book fans began to discover the giant robot TV cartoons on Japanese community TV during 1976. The VCRs enabled them to record sample episodes of *Brave Raideen, Getta Robo-G,* and *UFO Dai Apollon,* and bring them to their comic book and science fiction fan clubs to show off. They were usually introduced with some variant of, "You'll never believe what they can get away with in cartoons in Japan!" The suspenseful drama, the more intense personal relationships between the cast, the adolescent humor, and the more complex plots due to the Japanese TV tradition of presenting these dramas as a continuing serial rather than as independent stories were exactly what the American fans were used to in their favorite costumed-hero comic books. Fans also appreciated some obvious differences between American and Japanese animation techniques, such as effects familiar in live-action features but not then used in American animation (tracking shots, dramatic close-ups, even animated lens-flare during bright outdoor scenes), plus realistically dramatic voice acting rather than the American artificiality of deliberate "cartoony voices," all of which increased the simulation of theatrical-quality, live-action, mature drama rather than a children's cartoon.

Other factors over the next few years intensified the attraction of Japanese animation. One was the arrival on the American toy market of the complex transforming model robots and science-fictional vehicles, both in imports from Japan and in Mattel's licensed *Shogun Warriors* action figures starting in 1978. The *Shogun Warriors* were supported by a licensed comic book produced by Marvel Comics.[9] Many Americans' first exposure to Japanese animation was through these American-produced toys and the comic books based on them. This made people more receptive to the videotaped episodes of Japanese TV cartoons that were being shown at American comics fan clubs.

Another was the addition of outer-space adventures to the giant robot dramas. This was due to the coincidentally almost simultaneous appearances of *Space Battleship Yamato* in Japan and *Star Wars* in the United States in mid-1977.[10] Where the giant robot cartoons were always earthbound, involving the defense of Earth against demonic invaders from outer space,[11] *Space Battleship Yamato* and *Star Wars* featured battle action between the stars and on alien planets.

The popularity of *Yamato* led to similar animated TV space operas in Japan between 1977 and 1980, notably *Space Pirate Captain Harlock* and *Galaxy Express 999*. These outer-space cartoons spread the popularity of Japanese animation among American fans whose taste had been whetted by *Star Wars* for more interstellar adventures.

The *Star Wars* connection also led to the first new Japanese animated TV series to appear on American TV since 1967. *Star Wars* was phenomenally popular, and the TV industry wanted to get in on the action. This made the syndicated TV market receptive to TV cartoons similar to *Star Wars,* even if they contained more intense drama than had been acceptable for TV cartoons during the past decade. A 1973–75 Japanese TV cartoon, *Science Ninja Team Gatchaman,* was promoted in the syndicated TV market during early 1978 as *Battle of the Planets,* a *Star Wars*-type TV space adventure cartoon series.[12] In 1979 *Space Battleship Yamato* itself was sold to the syndicated market, as *Star Blazers.* Both titles required considerable editing to be acceptable for American children's TV programming, but they were still much more dramatic than any other American TV animation in the average child's memory. From 1979 through the early 1980s, *Battle of the Planets* and *Star Blazers* won thousands of American adolescent fans who had not yet heard of Japanese animation from other sources.

By this time a separate fandom for Japanese animation had formed in America. Science fiction fans had been organized for decades, forming their first clubs in the late 1920s and holding their first conventions in the late 1930s. Comic book fandom grew out of science fiction fandom when the new costumed-hero comics appeared in the early 1960s. When Japanese giant robot TV cartoons began to be shown in America, both SF and comics fans videotaped them to show to their groups. Discussions among fans brought out the connections between these new English-subtitled Japanese cartoons and the Americanized Japanese cartoons of the 1960s. A video screening at an SF convention in Los Angeles in April 1977, of both English-subtitled giant robot cartoons and Americanized episodes of *Astro Boy* and *Kimba the White Lion,* held a large audience for hours. The next month a separate fan club, the Cartoon/Fantasy Organization (C/FO), was started in Los Angeles for both SF fans and comics fans who wanted to concentrate on Japanese animation.[13]

During its first few years, anime fandom[14] was very closely intertwined with the SF and comics fandoms from which it had grown. Reactions from

C/FO bulletin, October 15, 1977

showing anime videos at SF and comics clubs enabled those fans with a serious interest in anime to identify one another. When it was discovered that Japanese community TV in different cities did not show the same cartoons, fans used contacts between SF and comics clubs throughout the United States to find out which cities were showing which anime series, and to trade copies of video tapes. Anime fans also began using the contacts between international SF fan groups to trade videos with fans in Japan, exchanging tapes of American SF TV like *Star Trek* and *Battlestar Galactica* for tapes of Japanese TV cartoons which were not shown on American Japanese-community TV at all.[15]

Two other developments between 1978 and 1980 nurtured anime fandom. One was the rise of a similar fandom in Japan, and the quick growth of a commercial market to take advantage of it. This created anime merchandise designed for adolescents and adults. The first pop-culture anime books were published in 1977, and sold so well that similar books, focusing on individual anime movies and TV programs, began appearing regularly in 1978. The first issue of *Animage,* the first monthly anime fan magazine with thorough coverage of new TV and theatrical animation (about 200 pages), was published in July 1978. Another popular merchandising ploy was the issuance of LP records of anime music. Openly inspired by the American release of John Williams's symphonic scoring of his *Star Wars* music, every popular animated theatrical feature and TV series soon got its own LP symphonic orchestration.[16]

These books, magazines, records, and the trendy transforming mechanical models began appearing in American Japanese-community book and gift shops a couple of months after their release in Japan, starting about mid-1978. Their impact, even untranslated, on the American fans is hard to overestimate. This impact was due to the direct comparison of the Japanese items with their American counterparts, if any. There were virtually no American animation-related publications during the 1970s except for juvenile comic books. There were no American books on individual TV cartoons so detailed as to include complete production data, lists of all episode titles and initial broadcast dates, dozen of model sheets, and photographs and interviews with the animators and voice actors. Most animation music was never available to the public, except as children's 45-

rpm records with only one or two childish songs. In short, American fans could see that animation was taken seriously in Japan, that it had a potential that Americans were completely overlooking. This considerably reinforced the initial exotic attraction of the anime style of cinematic SF adventure, marking anime as a topic worthy of mature interest. It also matched the psychological profile of adolescents in need of something brand-new and "cool" that only they would know about.

A much more personal and intense development was a brief interaction between American fans and the Japanese animation industry, led by no less than the "god of manga," Osamu Tezuka. The C/FO club in Los Angeles found out in December 1977 that Tezuka, the creator of Japan's first TV animation studio and the artist/writer of such characters as *Astro Boy* and *Kimba the White Lion,* was coming to Hollywood on a brief business trip. A couple of fans managed to meet him. Intrigued to discover non-Japanese-ethnic Americans who were fans of Japanese animation, Tezuka visited the C/FO during a second business trip in March 1978. Shortly after, the C/FO was contacted by representatives of two of Tokyo's largest animation studios, Toei Doga and Tokyo Movie Shinsha, who said that Tezuka had advised them that American fans were eager to promote Japanese animation in the United States.

During the next three years, these studios provided the C/FO with samples of their cartoons and merchandise to test-market at American fan conventions, from the 1978 Westercon in Los Angeles through the World SF Convention in Boston in 1980. This test marketing included the first anime-merchandise sales table at an American fan convention. Tezuka personally organized a tour group of about thirty Japanese cartoonists and animators to visit the 1980 San Diego Comic-Con, so they could see for themselves what an audience Japanese animation was developing in the United States.[17] Contact between American fans and the Japanese animation industry faded after 1981 when it failed to lead to any significant commercial results. But the influence on the fledgling anime fans of having met some of the most popular Japanese cartoonists, and the concept that fans were performing an important cultural service by helping to introduce Japanese animation to Americans, had a significant effect for years.[18]

Development

Early anime fandom had a strongly evangelical fervor. Many fans did not mind watching untranslated anime videos for the visual drama alone.[19] When *Battle of the Planets* and *Star Blazers* spread through syndication around America, there was the thrill of being "in the know" about what the original anime was like. Anime fans would show videos of the unedited Japanese episodes and point out all the scenes of violence that had been censored. The first anime video program at a SF convention had been a novelty, but beginning in 1978 on the West Coast, anime fans made anime video programs a regular feature at major SF and comics conventions.[20] At first these were party-style open screenings run by fans in their hotel rooms with their own VCRs. Within a few years, anime programs had spread to SF and comics conventions across America, and had become so popular that convention organizers were providing function rooms and video equipment and including them in the official programme.[21] In 1979, anime fans began entering the SF and comics conventions' masquerades in anime-character costumes, often winning prizes.

The Cartoon/Fantasy Organization, because of its early start and its high visibility during 1978–81, held a prestigious reputation. When the second center of anime fandom, in New York City, coalesced into a club in 1980, it did so as a chapter of the C/FO. It was assumed that fans could operate more efficiently through a large, federated club rather than dozens of small independent ones. During the early 1980s three North American clubs developed with many chapters in different cities; the C/FO (general anime), the *Star Blazers* Fan Club (*Star Blazers*), and the Earth Defense Command (*Star Blazers,* evolving into general anime). But in practice, fans preferred to just watch anime than to deal with the bureaucracy of coordinating a widespread club. Then the Internet sprang up, providing instant communication among anime fans throughout America.[22] By the end of the decade Internet communications replaced the slower correspondence through chapters of federated clubs.[23] Today there are more than a hundred individual anime clubs around North America, many so small, local, and transient that they are gone faster than they can be tabulated, and a fandom organized more densely around rec.arts.anime, the Anime Web Turnpike, and dozens of individual anime Web pages.

One of the earliest goals of anime fans was to publish information in English about Japanese animation.[24] The first fanzine, the C/FO's mostly-mimeographed *Fanta's Zine* no. 1, appeared in July 1979. It was an amateurish imitation of the Japanese anime reference books, compiling information on the Americanized anime TV series of the 1960s, such as theme song lyrics, episode title lists, plot synopses, and character profiles. Other contents included reports on new anime culled from the Japanese anime magazines, fans' amateur sketches of anime characters, and correspondence between fans. Similar fanzines from the C/FO, other anime clubs, and individual fans helped spread information about anime and also fostered the social growth of the fandom. These fanzines grew more professional in appearance as photoshop technology and cheap photocopying replaced mimeography, and as fans became more knowledgeable about translating Japanese anime books and magazines. In February 1983, a Michigan fan group published *Space Fanzine Yamato,* the first American effort to match the Japanese reference guides with a comprehensive booklet about a single title, the *Space Battleship Yamato* TV adventure serial with its many TV and theatrical sequels, covering both the Japanese original programs and the American

Star Blazers versions. By the mid-1980s, several fans who had some knowledge of Japanese (or had friends who could read the language) were publishing their own translated scripts of the dialogue of particularly popular anime titles.

Fans began writing about anime for publication outside of fandom. The first articles in newsstand-distributed popular magazines appeared in 1979–80.[25] A small but steady stream of articles with such titles as "TV Animation in Japan" [See page 219.] and "Japan + Animation = Japanimation!" [See page 247.] appeared in magazines like *Fantastic Films, Comics Collector, Starlog,* and *The Comics Journal.* In April 1986, fans in the New Jersey/NYC/Philadelphia

Fanta's Zine *no. 1, the first U.S. anime fanzine, July 1979*

area published *Anime-Zine* no. 1, a professional-format American anime magazine. *Anime-Zine* only lasted three issues, largely because its amateur publishers could not obtain general newsstand distribution, but it was soon followed by *Animag* (no. 1 in July 1987, published by fans in the San Francisco Bay region) and *Protoculture Addicts* (no. 1 in Spring 1988, published by fans in Montreal). There have been several other anime magazines since then. Some have lasted for only a few issues, but they have overlapped to provide America with at least one professional-format, newsstand-distributed anime magazine steadily since the late 1980s.[26]

San Francisco area fans held four annual Japanese Fantasy Film Faires from 1979 through 1983.[27] Despite this, anime fans continued to conduct their conventioneering through the established SF and comic book conventions for the next half-dozen years.[28] The first significant anime convention (but with some American animation and comic book programming) was Project A-Kon, organized in Dallas by the Earth Defense Command Animation Society on July 28–29, 1990. It was a success, and Project A-Kon has become anime fandom's oldest annual convention, held every June or July. The first major convention devoted exclusively to anime and manga, with notable Japanese artists and animators as featured guests, was AnimeCon '91, in San Jose, Calif. on August 30–September 2, 1991, drawing an attendance of over 1,700. AnimeCon was followed the next year by the first annual Anime Expo, which began on the 4th of July holiday weekend in San Jose but has since moved to the Los Angeles area. The Anime Expo has steadily grown (1998's attendance was 4,745), and now features speakers, workshops, awards,

Space Fanzine Yamato

Space Fanzine Yamato *February 1983*

masquerades, and all the other features of both a fan convention and an industry trade show. Since 1993, a growing number of smaller regional anime conventions have become established on a yearly basis, with attendances from the mid-hundreds to about 1,500: Anime Weekend Atlanta in October, Katsucon in the Arlington, Va., area in February, BAKA!-con in Seattle and Anime Central in Chicago, both in April, Anime North in Toronto in August, and others.

Three other popular media helped to cross-fertilize anime during the mid- and late-1980s: fantasy role-playing games, video games, and comic books. An overlap in interests between anime fans and gamers led to the development of American anime-themed games such as *Mekton, Teenagers From Outer Space,* and *BattleTech.*[29] The importation of Japanese video games based upon anime titles and video games that spun off anime dramatizations led to the popularization of Japanese titles such as *Ranma 1/2* and *Record of Lodoss War* among video game enthusiasts who were then attracted to their anime counterparts. The same thing happened among comic book fans who were not already aware of anime when anime fans began self-publishing independent comic books showing a Japanese anime/manga-art influence (1985), and professional American editions of Japanese manga with anime tie-ins started to be published (1987).

Anime fandom has maintained a high profile into the 1990s, but the specialized fandom has actually become ancillary to the acceptance of anime into general popular culture. The TV syndication of *Battle of the Planets* and *Star Blazers* beginning in 1978–79 led fans to hope that this would lead to a major American importation of anime. Several other syndicated titles, notably *Voltron, Defender of the Universe!* and *Robotech,* did achieve temporary popularity during the mid-1980s, but none led to a breakthrough for anime.[30] A weak attempt was made by movie entrepreneur Roger Corman to reintroduce anime features into the theatrical market with *Galaxy Express* in 1980 through 1982, and to place anime in the new home video market with *Warriors of the Wind* in 1985, but neither was advertised and they went unnoticed by the public.

Anime fans followed each of these attempts eagerly, but soon realized that the American theatrical, TV, and new home-video markets refused to consider anime as anything other than children's programming. Moreover, the editing to turn them into children's cartoons was distasteful to fans. When American companies were contacted with recommendations of popular anime titles that fans wanted to see as movies, TV programs, or videos, the answer was invariably that animation is for children, Japanese animation is much too violent for children, and therefore there would never be an American market for anime. Anime enthusiasts who had watched their fandom grow larger during a decade did not believe this.

Public Awareness

By the late 1980s, some of the adolescent fans of the 1970s had become adults in positions to start their own small businesses. They saw an enthusiastic anime market among their fellow hobbyists. A handful of anime specialty companies and labels appeared across the United States.: U.S. Renditions (Los Angeles, 1987), The Right Stuf International (Des Moines, Iowa, 1987), Streamline Pictures (Los Angeles, 1988), AnimEigo (Wilmington, N.C., 1989), U.S. Manga Corps/Central Park Media (New York City, 1991), A.D. Vision (Houston, 1992), and others later. Their first products began to be seen about 1989 and 1990. Most of these specialized at first in licensing anime for release as videos for the anime and comic book fans. The exception was Carl Macek's and Jerry Beck's Streamline Pictures, which aimed at the general video and fan markets with English dubbing, rather than subtitling. Streamline also distributed anime theatrically to the college and art film circuit.

The years 1990 through 1993 were a period of experimentation. Anime videos were sold primarily through mail order and comic book specialty shops. Purist fans preferred English-subtitled, Japanese-language videos, but sales were markedly higher for the English dubbed videos. It was the latter that made the breakthrough into the general video market during 1994–95, often getting shelf space in a separate "Anime" or "Japanimation" section distinct from the animation for children. Anime started to appear on cable television, on MTV, The Sci-Fi Channel, TNT, TBS, and others, and the videos were included regularly in general video review magazines, while especially prestigious titles such as *Akira* got favorable reviews in *Time* and *TV Guide*. News magazines such as *Forbes* and *Newsweek* and newspapers from the *Los Angeles Times* to the *New York Times* published articles discussing anime as the newest distinct pop culture category.[31]

The growing popularity of anime has enabled publication since 1995 of specialty books such as *The Complete Anime Guide* for general, academic, and cinema-specialty sales.[32] It has also provided financial viability for anime and manga specialty businesses. Whereas anime merchandise was originally available in 1990–91 primarily through comic book specialty shops, by 1995–96, anime specialty shops were feasible, selling mostly American editions of anime videos and manga but also offering a wide range of imported Japanese anime merchandise. Increasing sales and advancing marketing technology next led to on-line international "anime superstores."[33]

The most recent development, starting about 1997, has been the spreading misperception (or linguistic evolution?) among the general public that "anime" is synonymous with adult-oriented animation, especially that which is overly violent and pornographic. Clearly this derives from anime fans' own emphasis that anime is "not children's cartoons," and is supported by illustrations from the small percentage of adult anime emphasizing horror, violence, and sexuality. The perception that all Japanese animation is of this nature began gaining credence when major American animation distributors publicized that their cartoons were high-quality animation, not that notorious sex- and violence-filled anime from Japan.[34] It has been further complicated by the practice at many video stores of shelving all of their non-children's animation titles in their Anime sections; including the mature American features of Ralph Bakshi, HBO's bloody *Spawn* horror animated series, and the surrealistic American-Canadian *Heavy Metal* and French *Fantastic Planet* features. As a result, some people believe that anime from Japan is "all violence and sex",[35] while others think that "anime" is a new word meaning "animation for adults" irrespective of its nationality.

Anime's supporters are working to educate the public about the proper context of violence and sex within the broad range of all anime, and the cinematic academic community has been supportive. The introduction to a UCLA "Magical Boys and Girls" anime film program, at UCLA in Los Angeles on January 9–28, 1999, begins: "Japanese *anime* has a certain notoriety in this country for excessive sex and violence. But the perception of Japanese animation as the domain of *otaku* (obsessed geek-fan) alone is off-base. Plenty of Japanese animated (as well as live-action) films and TV shows are made for pre-teen and teenage audiences." This is echoed by a similar film series presented in New York City from December 1998 through February 1999: "Anime, or Japanese animated films, have become increasingly popular in the United States, yet only certain genres of anime, such as science fiction and erotic or violent works, have been stressed in American releases. With this new series the Japan Society Film Center takes a comprehensive historical look at Japanese animated works from the 1940s to the present [...]"[36]

The public is learning that Japanese animation designed for young children such as the *Sailor Moon* TV series since 1995, the *Pokémon* (*Pocket Monsters*) home videos since 1998, plus the Disney releases of Hayao Miyazaki's features since 1998, are anime whether or not they are shelved in the Anime sections of video stores. In addition, American acceptance has been growing for adult-oriented animation, through the popularity of such American-produced TV series as *The Simpsons, King of the Hill,* and *South Park,* as well as more dramatic TV cartoons for teens such as *Batman: The Animated Series* and *Invasion America.* That these American programs exist is partly because of the exposure to anime of the new generation of

American animators and TV programmers during the past decade. Anime has successfully crossed the line from a small cult interest in an aspect of foreign cinema to an established facet of American popular culture.

Acknowledgements: Jerry Beck, David Crowe, Bob Johnson, August Ragone, Drew and Kathy Sanders, Jerry Shaw, and Mike Tatsugawa.

Notes

1. The first was the one-minute *Mukuzu Imokawa, the Doorkeeper,* by Oten Shimokawa, January 1917. *The Art of Japanese Animation II: 70 Years of Theatrical Films,* produced by the staff of *Animage* magazine (Tokyo: Tokuma Shoten, 1989): 4.

2. A notable exception is the two *Momotaro* wartime propaganda features, the thirty-seven-minute *Momotaro's Sea Eagles* (released March 1943) and the seventy-four-minute *Momotaro's Divinely Blessed Sea Warriors* (released April 1945), produced by a workshop of animators organized by Director Mitsuyo Seo at the instigation of the Imperial Japanese Navy. Ibid., p. 24 and p. 26.

3. Notably the *Complete Animation Encyclopedia (Zen Anime Daihyakka),* vol. 76 in Keibunsha's youth-oriented *Complete—Encyclopedia* pocket guides to animals, airplanes, sports stars, etc. This went through numerous frequently updated editions until 1987, when the volume of anime titles apparently became too great to encompass within a single pocket guide. Note: The standard translation of "zen" in most Japanese-English dictionaries is "perfect, complete, whole." Although the best translation in this context would seem to be "complete," Japanese publishers invariably use "perfect" when they prepare their own English translations. American anime fans insist that this is therefore the only correct translation, which is why so many American anime complete compilations are called "perfect collections."

4. For convenience, in most cases where English-language titles have been established for Japanese films, they are used in this article even when they are not accurate translations. For example, the 1958 theatrical feature *Hakuja Den,* or *Legend of the White Snake,* is referred to by its 1961 American title, *Panda and the Magic Serpent.*

5. *Magic Boy* (MGM, June 22, 1961). *Panda and the Magic Serpent* (Globe Pictures, July 8, 1961). *Alakazam the Great* (American-International Pictures, July 26, 1961).

6. For Japanese information, *The Art of Japanese Animation I: 25 Years of Television Cartoons,* produced by the staff of *Animage* magazine (Tokyo: Tokuma Shoten, 1988); the *Complete Animation Encyclopedia* (Tokyo: Keibunsha, various editions); or Taku Sugiyama, *Complete Works of Television Animation* (Tokyo: Akimoto Shobo, 3 volumes, v. 1–2, 1978; v. 3, 1979), among others. For American information, George W. Woolery, *Children's Television: The First Thirty-Five Years, 1946–1981. Part 1: Animated Cartoon Series* (Metuchin, NJ: Scarecrow Press, 1983).

7. Attempts were made to sell others. Pilot episodes were made for such programs as *Big X, Space Ace,* and *Jet Boy.* These were test-marketed on some children's TV programs, and were promoted with advertising in trade magazines such as *Variety,* creating confusion as to whether they were ever actually completed and syndicated. At least one program, *Princess Knight,* had all fifty-two episodes produced in English, although it was apparently only broadcast in one market, Minneapolis/St. Paul, between 1978 and 1983.

8. "TV Character Toys. More Than 30 Varieties of *Raideen* Character Are Now Available! TV Program Starting March 20, 1976, Every Saturday 9 P.M., Channel 47 UHF." Flyer supplied to New York-area Japanese community toyshops by sponsor Marukai Trading Co.

9. The cover date of Marvel Comics' *Shogun Warriors* no. 1 is February 1979. Its sale date was a month or two earlier.

10. *Space Battleship Yamato* originally appeared in Japan as a twenty-six-episode animated TV serial between October 6, 1974, and March 30, 1975, but it did not gain its popularity until a condensation was released as a theatrical feature in August 1977.

11. Often literally demonic, playing off the traditional Japanese characterization of threatening foreigners as "foreign devils." American fans were highly amused by the evil "Hundred Demon Empire" space invaders in the 1975–76 thirty-nine-episode *Getta Robo-G,* whose sneering General Hydra looked suspiciously like a Nazi-uniformed Adolf Hitler with a longhorn steer's horns. (The similarity in Japanese pronunciation between "Hydra" and "Hitler" was doubtlessly deliberate wordplay.)

12. A full-color, double-page, center-spread advertisement in *Broadcasting; The Newsweekly of Broadcasting and Allied Arts,* February 20, 1978 (NATPE Convention special issue), promotes *Battle of the Planets* with the come-on, "Order *Battle of the Planets* today. It is the *only* syndicated, first-run science-fiction programming immediately available for Fall 1978 start." It began syndicated broadcasting in October 1978.

13. This first anime video program was at LosCon III in Los Angeles, April 1–3, 1977. The Cartoon/Fantasy Organization held its first monthly meeting on Saturday, May 21, 1977, coincidentally the same weekend that *Star Wars* was released. The anniversary of American anime fandom is usually dated from the beginning of this first fan club, which still meets monthly.

14. Early anime fans just spoke of "Japanese cartoons." When the neologism "Japanimation" became popular in the early 1980s, several fans claimed credit for coining it, but the earliest documented usage was by Carl Gafford in late 1978; he was listed as Carl "Japanimation" Gafford on the C/FO's first membership roster in June 1979. "Japanimation" was widely used within the fandom during most of the 1980s, but many fans were unhappy about the ease with which it could be accidentally or deliberately mispronounced as the more pejorative-sounding "Jap animation." In the late 1980s fans began using "anime," the current word in Japanese for "animation." It is shorter, more respectful to the art form, and implies the user is knowledgeable of anime's Japanese background. By the time Japanese animation came to the attention of the public in the 1990s, "anime" was the common term. "Anime" became the general term in Japan around the 1970s, from the English word "animation." The actual Japanese word for cinematic animation is "doga," from "do" (motion) and "ga" (drawing, picture). A handy rule of thumb to guess how old a Japanese animation studio may be is whether its name contains "doga" or "anime." If it is "doga," the studio probably predates the 1970s.

15. One of the fortuitous circumstances that made the popular development of anime fandom possible is the use in both the United States and Japan of the NTSC television

format. American and Japanese videotapes can be played on both countries' VCRs. On the other hand, British anime fandom could not develop until licensed PAL-format commercial anime videos appeared on the British video market in the early 1990s.

16. Fred Patten, "All Those Japanese Animation Soundtracks," *CinemaScore* no. 15, Winter 1986–Summer 1987: 135–139. [See page 89.]

17. Osamu Tezuka and several other famous cartoonists including Go Nagai, "Monkey Punch" (Kazuhiko Kato), and Yumiko Igarashi were featured guests at the 1980 San Diego Comic-Con, on July 30–August 3, where they were mobbed by fans. Tezuka received the Comic-Con's Inkpot Award for excellence in cartooning; the award's first Asian recipient.

18. "The Japanese animation studios want us to publicize their anime in America" became the standard rationalization used to justify the copying and dissemination of anime videos throughout fandom, a copyright violation even if the videos are traded or given free among fans.

19. Also fortuitously, the anime of the 1970s was much less dramatically sophisticated than the anime of the 1990s. Most of the action plots could be understood from the visuals alone. The stories of average anime titles in the 1990s are complex enough to require some comprehension of the dialogue. This considerably diminishes the appreciation of modern untranslated anime.

20. The C/FO ran its first anime video programs at the West Coast Science Fantasy Conference (Westercon 31) in Los Angeles on June 30–July 4, 1978, and at the 1978 San Diego Comic-Con on July 26–30.

21. At the Balticon 15 convention (Baltimore, Maryland, April 18–20, 1981), eleven Philadelphia/NYC/New Jersey-area anime fans formed "the Gamilon Embassy" (a *Star Blazers* reference) to host anime video programs at SF and comic book conventions throughout the Northeast. By 1985, enough East Coast conventions had started their own anime video rooms that the Embassy dissolved itself as having accomplished its goal.

22. The first Internet anime newsgroup, rec.arts.anime, was created by Ann Schubert, a San Francisco Bay Area fan, in November 1987.

23. The three giant clubs were gone by the end of 1989, although the original chapters of C/FO and EDC still meet as local clubs in Los Angeles and in Dallas. Cal-Anime, a federation of anime clubs at colleges connected through the Internet, was founded at the University of California, Berkeley, campus during 1988 (officially chartered in January 1989). It peaked at fifteen chapters, mostly in the Western United States but one as far as Perth, Australia, during the early 1990s. It still has nine chapters today.

24. It should be noted that, due to the close relationship and overlap between Japanese animation, Japanese comic books (*manga*), and Japanese live-action theatrical and TV fantasy such as the *Godzilla* motion pictures and the *Ultraman* TV series, there has always been some inclusion of these in anime fandom. Some fans prefer a broader term for the fandom, such as "anime and manga fandom" or "Asian fantasy fandom." One fan, Greg Shoemaker of Toledo, Ohio, published fifteen issues of *The Japanese*

Fantasy Film Journal from January 1968 through December 1983, covering both live-action films and animation. This considerably predated and overlapped early anime fandom, but Shoemaker remained largely outside of the fandom and his excellent fanzine was not generally known.

25. Tom Sciacca, "Shogun: Battle of the Afternoon Warriors," *Mediascene* no. 35, January–February 1979: 25–27; and Fred Patten, "Dawn of the Warrior Robots: The Beginnings of a New Breed of Action Hero," *Fangoria* no. 4 (February 1980): 30–35. [See page 292.]

26. *Animag* lasted fifteen issues, to early (undated) 1993. *Protoculture Addicts* is still published; no. 55 is dated April–May 1999. The major anime magazine is the monthly *Animerica,* published since November 1992 by Viz Communications. Viz is an American subsidiary of the Japanese publisher Shogakukan, formed for the publication and distribution of American editions of Japanese comic books and animation in 1987. (Shogakukan was the first major Japanese publisher to enter the American anime and manga market. Two Japanese corporate giants, Pioneer LDC and Bandai, entered the American anime market in the mid-1990s, concentrating on video sales.) The two newest professional anime magazines, both launched in December 1998, are the quarterly *AnimeFantastique,* published by the *Cinefantastique* movie-magazine group in Forest Park (Chicago), Illinois, and the monthly *Manga Max,* published by Titan Magazines in London for international distribution to English-speaking nations.

27. Japanese Fantasy Film Faire 1, on December 15–16, 1979, in a mall in Union City, was promoted through comic book specialty shops and on San Francisco-area TV. It drew an attendance of over a hundred for a program of both anime and live-action fantasy (*Ultraman, Godzilla*) videos. The final Japanese Fantasy Film Faire 4, on February 12–14, 1983, at a hotel in San Mateo, grew to an estimated 500 attendees. The Earth Defense Command club in Dallas held a one-day YamatoCon in August 1983, drawing slightly more than a hundred fans for an all-*Star Blazers* video program. Despite these forerunners, enthusiasm for separate anime conventions did not catch on until the end of the 1980s.

28. In 1986, Toren Smith convinced the Baycon '86 SF convention (San Jose, Calif., May 23–26) to allow him to organize the most elaborate anime program yet held. The eighty-hour, four-day anime festival was shown in one of the convention's largest meeting halls, on a theatrical screen-sized projection TV system. Smith also edited a fifty-six-page illustrated *Baycon 86 Japanese Animation Program Guide* with plot synopses of the largely untranslated anime videos. This had two major effects. Thick illustrated anime translation guides became a standard fixture at conventions featuring extensive anime programs for the next decade, until the accumulation of enough English-translated anime in the 1990s made them unnecessary. Toren Smith made a business trip to Japan with his *Guide* to establish himself as a liaison between the American and Japanese comic book and animation industries. Smith's Studio Proteus, established the next year, is today one of the major translators of Japanese manga for U.S. comic book publication, making him the first American anime fan to turn his hobby into a successful profession.

29. *Mekton: The Game of Japanese Robot Combat* and *Teenagers From Outer Space* were both developed in 1984–85 and 1987 by Mike Pondsmith, a fervent anime fan

employed at R. Talsorian Games. An advertising slogan for *Mekton* was, "You can have green hair, just like your favorite anime hero!"

30. *Robotech,* an eighty-five-episode TV SF drama designed by Carl Macek from three separate anime TV series to appeal to the *Star Trek* TV market, publicized its Japanese origins as a creative asset. It became an effective recruiting agent for anime fandom. The program, which was syndicated beginning March 1985, generated a *Robotech* convention in Anaheim, Calif., in October 1986, which drew around 4,000 fans. Despite adult-packaged merchandising spin-offs including a series of more than twenty paperback SF novelizations and an LP recording of the musical score, *Robotech* was treated by most TV stations as a children's cartoon, and since its plot was too adolescent-oriented for most children to appreciate, it was considered a weak performer among its target audience. This was a key factor in fandom's growing perception that the entertainment industry did not know how to take advantage of anime, and that the fans would have to do it themselves.

31. Some high-profile examples: *Akira* named as "Our Video Pick of the Week" on the *Siskel and Ebert* movie-review TV program, April 26, 1992; an enthusiastic review of *Akira* on laser disc by Jay Cocks, *Time,* February 1, 1993: 66–67; Stephen Lynch, "Japanimation: Goodbye, *Gigantor.* You, Too, *Speed Racer.* A New Generation of Japanese Cartoons is Taking Over America," *The Orange County* [Calif.] *Register,* March 25, 1994, SHOW section: 41–43; and reports in *TV Guide,* December 31, 1994–January 6, 1995: 35, on the Cartoon Network "presenting a solid triple feature of Japanese animation (a.k.a. *anime*) on Saturday, Jan. 28"; and April 15–21, 1995: 32, that "The Sci-Fi Channel got such a positive response to last year's festival of Japanese animation (or *anime*, as aficionados call it) that the cable outlet is presenting another, showcasing five new titles May 15–19." Still others are, "Who Killed Bambi? [. . .] From *Kimba the White Lion* to *Legend of the Overfiend,* Japanese Animation Is No Longer For Kids. Anthony Haden-Guest Meets Godzilla's Spawn," *World Art: The Magazine of Contemporary Visual Arts,* 1/1995: 42–47; Andrew Leonard, "Heads Up, Mickey. Anime May Be Japan's First Really Big Cultural Export," *Wired,* April 1995: 140–143, 180, 182, 184, 186; Rick Marin with T. Trent Gegax, Sabrina Jones, Adam Rogers, and Hideko Takayama, "Holy Akira! It's Aeon Flux. Video: Weird Postapocalyptic Japanese Cartoons Are Moving From Cult Fashion To The Mainstream," *Newsweek,* August 14, 1995: 68–70; Bruce Haring, "Japanese Animation Tones Down For Mainstream; Import Videos Ready To Roll," *USA Today,* August 15, 1995: 8D.

32. Helen McCarthy, *ANIME! A Beginner's Guide to Japanese Animation* (London: Titan Books, 1993); Trish Ledoux and Doug Ranney, edited by Fred Patten, *The Complete Anime Guide* (Issaquah, WA: Tiger Mountain Press, 1995; revised and updated Second Edition, 1997); Helen McCarthy, *The ANIME! Movie Guide* (London: Titan Books, 1996); Antonia Levi, *Samurai from Outer Space: Understanding Japanese Animation* (Chicago: Open Court Publishing Co., 1996); Trish Ledoux, ed., *Anime Interviews: The First Five Years of* Animerica, Anime and Manga Monthly *(1992–1997)* (San Francisco: Cadence Books, 1997); Helen McCarthy and Jonathan Clements, *The Erotic Anime Movie Guide* (London: Titan Books, 1998); Gilles Poitras, *The Anime Companion: What's Japanese in Japanese Animation?* (Berkeley, CA: Stone Bridge Press, 1998); Helen McCarthy, *Hayao Miyazaki: Master of Japanese Animation* (Berkeley, CA: Stone Bridge Press, 1999).

33. The earliest anime specialty businesses were existing Japanese-community gift shops that gradually built up extensive mail-order sales to fans of imported anime merchandise, notably Books Nippan in Los Angeles and Susan Horn's Kimono My House in the San Francisco Bay Area, both by late 1981, and Bill Kogura's Nikaku Japanese Arts in the San Francisco Bay Area about 1986. Many fans tried their hand at selling anime items as a casual hobby activity through the 1980s and early 1990s, via dealers' tables at fan conventions and by mail order. Some fans were ignorant or uncaring of the niceties of commercial licensing, permitting a market during this time in unauthorized fan-made anime-character T-shirts and pins. By the 1990s, anime had become a large enough market to enable fans to open full-time anime/manga businesses, selling over the counter in their cities and by mail order via advertising in the anime specialty magazines and on Internet anime web pages. Prominent shops include Banzai Anime in Los Angeles (August 1995), Anime Crash in New York City (March 1995, since grown into a chain with additional shops in Boston/ Cambridge, Providence, R.I., and Washington, D.C.), Anime Plus in Los Angeles (December 1995), Anime Café in Tacoma, Wash., (January 1997), Joy's Japanimation in Pittsburgh (October 1997). The on-line anime superstore www.animenation. com was started by Gene Field in January 1996, and was successful enough to add a physical store, Anime Nation, in Clearwater (Tampa/St. Petersburg), Florida, a year later. Field reports that business at the beginning of 1999 is 85 percent Internet sales and 15 percent walk-in sales, with just under two million on-line hits per month. In September 1998, Bandai America, a subsidiary of Japan's Bandai Entertainment corporate giant, opened www.animevillage.com.

34. Jefferson Graham and Tim Friend, "U.S. Kids Safe From Cartoon Seizures," *USA Today,* December 18, 1997: 1D, states that, "CBS, ABC, NBC, Fox, UPN and WB don't air the graphic Japanese cartoons known as 'anime.' Nor do the major cable outlets for cartoons: Nickelodeon, the Cartoon Network and the Disney Channel." Mike Lazzo, vice president of programming for the Cartoon Network, is quoted: "Japan animation is so different from what airs here. [...] It's far edgier, adult, and violent. Anime isn't very story-based and is driven by intense moments. The story is hard to follow." The article acknowledges that "The Cartoon Network does air Japan's *Speed Racer,* made thirty years ago, and *Voltron,* about ten years old, but neither show is in the style of anime." Michael Mallory, " 'Princess' Goes West; Japanese Hit Gets English Treatment," *Daily Variety,* February 13, 1998: A6, on the forthcoming American release of Hayao Miyazaki's anime feature *Princess Mononoke,* quotes Michael Johnson, president of Buena Vista Home Entertainment (Disney's home video division), that American audiences will find it entirely different from "the raucous, comic book-inspired, often graphically sexual and violent Japanese animation that travels the cult and arthouse circuits [...] 'This is not *anime,*' says Johnson, 'it's not effects-driven or violence-driven.'" Another article, David Bosworth, "Buena Vista Announces Launch Date For First Miyazaki Vid Title," *KidScreen,* May 1998: R1–R2, on the coming release of Miyazaki's *Kiki's Delivery Service,* quotes Michael Johnson as saying that, "Buena Vista is doing its best to form a line of distinction between Miyazaki's and other forms of anime, which in one extreme case has been blamed for causing children to experience convulsions. 'You'll never hear the word "anime" attached to Miyazaki's stuff around here,' says Johnson, adding that *Kiki* 'has a much deeper texture to it, a higher visual quality; it's much brighter than most anime.'"

35. Peter M. Nichols, "At Mickey's House, A Quiet Welcome For Distant Cousins," *New York Times,* February 1, 1998, Section 2: 37, announces Disney's coming video distribution of Miyazaki's *Kiki's Delivery Service.* "Tanya Maloney, a vice president of Buena Vista, Disney's video arm," warns that Disney's acceptance of Miyazaki's "Disney-like" animation should not be construed as acceptance by Disney of "racy, battle-ravaged animé." The article explains that "animé refers strictly to 'adult' Japanese animation [. . .] 'pornimation,' as some of the steamier romps with Western-looking women, from college girls to the princesses of sci-fi legend, are sometimes called in the United States [. . .] animé is all violence and sex [. . .]"

36. *UCLA Film and Television Archive Calendar,* January 5, 1999–February 7, 1999 (unpaged brochure); *Anime: The History of Japanese Animated Films, December 11, 1998 to February 26, 1999* (unpaged brochure of the Japan Society).

References

Animage staff, *The Art of Japanese Animation I: 25 Years of Television Cartoons* [and] *II: 70 Years of Theatrical Films* (Tokyo: Tokuma Shoten, 1988, 1989).

Anon., *Complete Animation Encyclopedia* (Tokyo: Keibunsha, annual updated editions from 1981 through 1987).

Anon., *KABOOM! Explosive Animation from America and Japan* (Sydney: Museum of Contemporary Art, 1994).

Anon., *This Is Animation. Vol. 1, SF * Robot * Action Anime. Vol. 2, Fantasy * Fairy Tales * Young Girl Anime. Vol. 3, Sports * Gag * Life Anime.* (Tokyo: Shogakukan, 1982).

Bungeishunju Deluxe 4, no. 10 (no. 42, October 1977) [special animation issue].

Bungeishunju Deluxe 6, no. 3 (no. 59, March 1979) [special "encyclopedia of TV anime characters" issue].

Carlton, A., "Manga and Anime: Japanese Comics and Animated Cartoons," *Comics Collector* no. 4 (Summer 1984): 67–73, 89–90.

Ledoux, T., ed., *Anime Interviews: The First Five Years of* Animerica, Anime and Manga Monthly *(1992–1997)* (San Francisco: Cadence Books, 1997).

Ledoux, T. and D. Ranney; F. Patten, ed., *The Complete Anime Guide: Japanese Animation Video [Film] Directory and Resource Guide* (Issaquah, WA: Tiger Mountain Press, 1995, 1997).

Levi, A., *Samurai from Outer Space: Understanding Japanese Animation* (Chicago: Open Court Publishing Co., 1996).

Manga Shonen special issue, *The World of TV Anime* (Tokyo: Asahi Sonorama, 1978).

McCarthy, H., *The ANIME! Movie Guide* (London: Titan Books, 1996).

McCarthy, H., *Hayao Miyazaki: Master of Japanese Animation* (Berkeley, Stone Bridge Press, 1999).

McCarthy, H. and J. Clements, *The Erotic Anime Movie Guide* (London: Titan Books, 1998).

Namiki, T. and E. D. Herscovitz, eds., *History of Japanese Animation Films; Who's*

Who in Japanese and Korea Animated Film (Tokyo: *Film 1/24* special international issue, June 1977).

Patten, F., "The Anime 'Porn' Market," *Animation World Magazine* 3, no. 4 (July 1998): 25–31.

Patten, F., "Dawn of the Warrior Robots: The Beginnings of a New Breed of Action Hero," *Fangoria* no. 4 (February 1980): 30–35.

Patten, F., "Japan + Animation = Japanimation!," Part 1, *Starlog* no. 105 (April 1986): 36–40; Part 2, *Starlog*, 106 (May 1986): 65–68.

Patten, F., "The 13 Top Developments in Anime, 1985–99," *Animation Magazine* 13, no. 2 (no. 75, February 1999): 123, 125, 127, 128, 131.

Patten, F., "TV Animation in Japan," *Fanfare* no. 3 (Spring 1980): 8–18.

Reynolds, K. and A. Carlton, *Robotech Art I* (Norfolk, VA: Starblaze Graphics/The Donning Co., 1986).

Schodt, F. L., *Manga! Manga! The World of Japanese Comics* (Tokyo: Kodansha International, 1983).

Sugiyama, T., *Complete Works of Television Animation* (Tokyo: Akimoto Shobo, 3 vols., 1978, 1979).

Specialty Magazines

In English

Animag no. 1 (July 1987)–vol. 2, no. 3 (no. 15, early 1993) (East Palo Alto/Berkeley/San Francisco, Calif.: Animage, Inc./Oakland, Calif.: Pacific Rim Publishing Co./Westlake Village, Calif.: Malibu Graphics).

Anime UK no. 1, Winter 1991/1992–no. 17, December 1994/January 1995; New Series no. 1, March 1995–no. 4, July 1995, title change to *Anime FX* no. 5, August 1995–no. 12, March 1996 (London: AUK Press/Partridge Green, England: Ashdown Publishing).

Anime-Zine no. 1 (April 1986)–no. 3 (Spring 1988) (Rahway, N.J.: Minstrel Press).

Animeco no. 1, Winter 1996–no. 10, Spring 1998 (Honolulu: Limelight Publishing Co.).

AnimeFantastique no. 1, Spring 1999–current; no. 3, Fall 1999 (Forest Park, Ill.: *AnimeFantastique*).

Animenominous! no. 1, Summer 1990–no. 5, Spring 1993 (Bricktown, N.J.: BDC Enterprises).

Animerica no. 0, November 1992, vol. 1, no. 1, March 1993–current; vol. 7, no. 5 (no. 76, May 1999) (San Francisco, Viz Communications).

Manga Mania no. 1, July 1993–no. 46, July-August 1998 (London: Titan Magazines).

Manga Max no. 1, December 1998–current; no. 8, July 1999 (London: Titan Magazines).

Mangazine 2, no. 14, March 1992–vol. 2, no. 44, May 1996 (San Antonio, Tex.: Antarctic Press) (issues prior to vol. 2, no. 14 did not feature anime).

Protoculture Addicts no. 1, Spring 1988–current; no. 55, April–May 1999. (Montreal: IANUS Publications/PROTOCULTURE).

V.Max no. 1 (August 1991)–vol. 2, no. 8 (no. 17, Fall 1996) (Santa Clara, CA: *V.Max;* Newtype Press/Berkeley, CA: R. Talsorian Games).

In Japanese
Animage no. 1, July 1978–current; no. 252, June 1999. (Tokyo: Tokuma Shoten)

Anime V no. 1, January 1985–no. 153, September 1998; title change to *Looker* no. 154, October 1998–no. 161, May 1999. (Tokyo: Gakken)

Animec no. 1, October 1978–no. 79, February 1987. (Tokyo: Rapport)

Animedia no. 1, June 1981–current; no. 221, June 1999. (Tokyo: Gakken)

AX no. 1, April 1998–current; no. 15, June 1999. (Tokyo: Sony Magazines, Inc.)

Globian, June 1986 (no. 1)–January 1987 (no. 8). (Tokyo: Hiro Media)

My Anime no. 1, April 1981–no. 54, September 1985; New Series no. 1/85, October 20, 1985 (no. 1)–no. 7/86, July 1986 (no. 13). (Tokyo: Akita Shoten)

Newtype, April 1985 (no. 1)–current; June 1999 (no. 171). (Tokyo: Kadokawa Shoten)

The Anime no. 1, December 1979–no. 86, January 1987. (Tokyo: Kindaieiga-sha)

Fred Patten: Anime Man, by Simon Drax
VideoScope no. 43, Summer 2002.

Easily the most recognized and respected anime critic in the United States, Fred Patten has for over twenty years been offering erudite insights into one of Japan's more electrifying exports, the phenomenon known as anime. As we hover at anime's fortieth anniversary (using Osamu Tezuka's *Mighty Atom* TV series as our starting point), Simon Drax rapped with Patten about his initial introduction, the glory days, and where it's all going.

Simon Drax: Anime, manga, and Fred Patten: How'd they all meet?
Fred Patten: Becoming an anime and manga fan was something that snuck up on me before I realized it. When I was in college (UCLA, 1958–1963), I discovered SF fandom. I joined the Los Angeles Science Fantasy Society (LASFS) in 1960. At that time there was a Japanese-community movie theater in central L.A., and the SF club went there pretty regularly whenever there was a samurai movie or a Japanese SF movie. *Alakazam the Great, Magic Boy,* and *Panda and the Magic Serpent* were shown there in 1961.

VideoScope cut and condensed this interview because it was too long. The result was somewhat choppy, so I have taken the liberty of restoring a couple of paragraphs to make it read more smoothly. ■

From SF fandom, I also got active in the new comic-book fandom as it developed in the 1960s. I was a member of CAPA-alpha, the first comics-fandom amateur press association, from 1964 through the 1970s, and I was its central mailer for four years. I specialized in articles about "international comic books," mainly those in Spanish and French because those were the foreign languages that I could read.

Around the late 1960s, comic book fandom began to split between fans who were interested in art and story quality and fans who were only interested in costumed heroes. I was in the first group.

One of my close friends, Richard Kyle, wanted to publish a serious cartoon art literary criticism magazine, and I offered to write book reviews for it. I also wanted to call attention to the high-quality foreign comic books that most American fans were completely unaware of.

I discovered manga by accident at the 1970 West Coast Science Fantasy Conference. One of the exhibits was a big display on the *Man from U.N.C.L.E.* TV series of the 1960s, which included comic book versions from around the world. This included a manga edition, which blew me away in comparison with the shallow American comic book. (It was by Takao Saito, before he started his own *Golgo 13* series.) The fans who organized the display said they had just recently bought it in one of Los Angeles's Japanese-community bookshops. So I went to the Little Tokyo district, and I found not only Saito's *Man from U.N.C.L.E.* manga but shelves of manga by Tezuka, Ishinomori, Yokoyama, and so much more that I was overwhelmed. It was Tezuka's manga that hooked me into buying all of these comics that I could not read but I could follow the stories from the pictures well enough to get the gist of them.

Richard Kyle started his *Graphic Story World* fanzine in May 1971, and I edited and wrote most of its book review columns. Kyle and I decided to also start an import mail-order bookshop that would sell the high-quality foreign comic books that we discussed in the magazine. As far as I know, we were the first comic book specialty shop in America (1972, in Long Beach, Calif.) to specialize in importing foreign-language comic books in general, as distinct from foreign-language bookshops specializing in one language (German, Italian, etc.) that had comic books in that one language. We had comic books from Spain, France, Belgium, Italy, the Netherlands and a couple of other European countries—and Japan.

This, ironically, was what first put me into touch with anime. We got a few requests for the manga that the TV cartoons like *Astro Boy* and *8 Man* and *Gigantor* were based on. One of these requestors was a Hollywood animator, Wendell Washer, who had gotten an early movie-industry video recorder before commercial VCRs were available, and was collecting sample episodes of all the TV cartoons there were.

He invited me to his home to see his sample episodes of the Japanese cartoons that he wanted the manga of. He also introduced me to a few other fans of "obscure TV cartoons" rather than of anime in particular. One of these other fans was Mark Merlino, who liked science fiction but was not aware of organized SF fandom. So I introduced Merlino to the Los Angeles Science Fantasy Society (LASFS). Mark Merlino and I formed a nucleus of anime fans within Los Angeles's SF and comics fandom. The first commercial VCRs went on sale in late 1975, and Merlino got one. The first giant-robot TV cartoons started appearing on the Japanese-community TV channel in early 1976. Merlino would tape them and show them at the fan-club meetings and parties. By 1977 there were a couple of dozen of us who wanted to watch anime on a regular basis, so Merlino and I decided to start a separate club just for anime. This was the Cartoon/Fantasy Organization (C/FO), which held its first meeting in May 1977 (by coincidence, the same weekend that *Star Wars* premiered). And it just grew from there.

SD: When did you first strike upon the idea of writing/reporting about anime?

FP: Pretty much right away. I had already been writing fanzine articles about Mexican and French comic books since the 1960s, and I had been a secretary for the LASFS and several SF conventions over the years. When Merlino and I decided to start a club just for anime, I automatically became its secretary. I more or less naturally became the editor of the C/FO's first fanzine, *Fanta's Zine,* in 1979. The C/FO had been going for less than a year when the Hollywood representative of Toei Animation Co. asked if we would help to publicize anime in America, and we were delighted to help.

SD: Some critics dismiss anime as a rudderless genre that is little more than an amalgamation of Japan's inevitable absorption of Western influences and clichés following the Pacific Theater at mid-century. How do you respond to such thinking?

FP: Popular culture pretty much always reflects the influences of the moment, and is almost impossible to steer. Those who make a living from the popular culture "industry" are always trying to invent or to discover the next "hot trend." The Japanese are no different from anyone else. If anyone "controlled" the development of manga and anime, it was Osamu Tezuka, and Tezuka was a big fan of Western popular culture—not just American, but also European. At the same time, anyone who says that anime is nothing but a hodgepodge of Western influences is not paying attention to the Japanese (and Chinese) influences that are also being embraced. Anime has certainly not rejected Japan's own cultural influences.

SD: I personally view anime's evolution as cyclical periods of rise and decline. For example, the '60s were the initial burst of energy and invention, followed by the lackluster '70s, during which (barring the giant-robot shows, *Lupin,* and *Yamato*) nothing much happened. But the '80s seemed a period of ever-more ambitious projects, big feature-length films that

Cover of the C/FO's May 1982 bulletin celebrating the organization's fifth anniversary.

grew increasingly adept on technical levels as well as featuring ever-more-sophisticated stories and ideas, culminating in such films as *Akira* and *Wings of Honneamise*. The '90s seem to me an orgy of low-budget pleasure-button OAVs featuring the sexual escapades of demons and other critters.

FP: I am not sure that I would divide the '60s and '70s as you do, at least for TV anime. The '60s were when everything started, good and bad. I tend to think of the '60s as a period of chaos that evolved into the '70s with more polished works. In addition to the giant-robot shows, *Lupin III,* and *Yamato* (which were just the titles to become well known in America), the 1970s saw the shojo shows like *Candy Candy,* the sports shows like *Tomorrow's Joe,* and the "World Masterpiece Theater" shows like adaptations of *Heidi* and *Nobody's Boy,* plus such experiments as Nagai's *Devilman.* Your comment seems more accurate with regard to theatrical anime. This started in the 1950s with Toei Animation following the Disney formula (with Asian folk tales) and evolved in the 1960s to include theatrical featurettes of Toei's popular TV series of the moment. About the only imaginative theatrical animation was Tezuka's experimental *1001 Nights* and *Cleopatra* around 1970, which were not financial successes. There was almost nothing of interest theatrically again until the early 1980s, when Miyazaki and Takahata started Studio Ghibli, and Rintaro started directing. You could say that the 1990s did not invent any really new concepts, but I do not think that it introduced much in the line of sexual escapades of demons. Those started around 1985 and were already old stuff by 1990. The '90s were an orgy of imitation of the past.

SD: You're far more than just a fan or a critic; you've also served professionally on the translation/adaptation of several projects. Tell me about your relationship with Carl (*Robotech, Wicked City*) Macek.

FP: The first time I remember meeting him was when he owned a comic book and movie memorabilia shop (which included American animation posters and stills), the Carl F. Macek Gallery, in Orange, Calif., near Disneyland around 1981 or 1982. Macek had been involved with the production of the movie *Heavy Metal,* and he had lots of its original cels for sale at his shop. The anime fans in that area wanted a place to meet. Macek offered to let them meet once a month in his shop. Macek watched the anime videos that the fans showed, and this was his introduction to anime. He saw the demand for anime materials among American fans, and he contacted Tatsunoko Production Co. in Japan to buy some of their original cels to add to his store's stock. I was a regular attendee at this anime club, and I got to know Carl then. It was Carl's contact with Tatsunoko, which produced *Macross,* that led to his being contacted a year or two later by Harmony Gold when Harmony Gold wanted to produce *Macross* for sale to American TV. I interviewed him at the Harmony Gold offices for an article about *Robotech* for *Amazing Heroes,* published in July 1985, so we kept in touch. During the next two or three years, Macek and Jerry Beck decided that the American movie and video industry were ignoring a growing market for anime, and they decided to start their own company to take advantage of it. (Jerry Beck had started the C/FO's chapter in New York City in the early 1980s before moving to Hollywood.) This was Streamline Pictures, which opened in October 1988. Carl and Jerry continued to let the Los Angeles anime fans know what they were doing and help publicize Streamline's plans. They asked me which anime titles were the most popular with American fans, to give them an idea of which titles to try to license for American release. I joined Streamline in January 1991 and I have been here ever since.

One of my main jobs was to help guarantee the accuracy of Streamline's translations. The standard way of doing business with the Japanese companies was that, when we licensed a title for American release, the Japanese would send us the film production elements and a very rough translation into English of the Japanese script. It was understood that we would have to rewrite the script into smooth English which would also match the characters' lip-sync, so the translation that the Japanese provided did not have to be detailed. But the Japanese movie industry was used to the American movie industry trying to "Americanize" their movies as much as possible, changing Japanese names like Akira and Kenichi into American names like Bob and Charlie, Japanese food names into American food names, and so on. So the translations that we got were often very inaccurate as to minor details that were particularly ethnically Japanese. Since we wanted our American releases to be very accurate translations, one of my jobs was to go back to the Japanese anime videos (practically all of them were owned by one local fan or another), check for what the original Japanese names had been, and put them back into the scripts. Sometimes Streamline would license a title, which was supposed to mean getting all of the Japanese support materials, and *after* Streamline had signed the contract, the Japanese would say, "We will send you what materials we can, but that title is so old that most of them have been thrown out by now." One of these was the movie *Lensman,* and another was *The Castle of Cagliostro.* So I was assigned to find any publicity materials that had come out when those movies were new that the American fans might have in their collections (issues of anime magazines, posters, writing boards, etc.), and borrow them if they were of good enough visual quality so that Streamline might be able to use them for video sleeve images, and so on.

Another duty was some very simple Japanese translation. I do not speak or read Japanese, but I had a couple of Japanese-English dictionaries and I could usually translate simple sentences in five or ten minutes. One of my duties at the C/FO was to translate the episode titles of the TV series that we showed. When Streamline had some very simple translation work, such as the caption on an illustration, it was faster and cheaper to see if I could translate it than to send it to a professional translator.

A big difference between Streamline and the other early American anime companies was that Carl and Jerry insisted on dubbing all our anime into English instead of subtitling it. This was because we were all determined to promote anime to the general public as much as possible instead of catering just to the anime fan market. This was why Carl made some translation changes that substituted a new joke or an American movie reference to replace some Japanese reference that was unknown to the American public and would be meaningless to most Americans. I agreed with some of these and disagreed with others, although in general I agreed with Carl's philosophy that the important thing was to make the anime movies and videos as appealing as possible to the broadest American audience. Once an American audience had been built up, then it would be practical to make a "film buff's more accurate" translation. Keeping anime so esoteric that a market for it never developed would be bad for everyone.

Carl had always wanted to get involved in original production, and he was unhappy that Streamline never could afford to join in any co-production deals. Most of Streamline's licenses for anime titles were for three years or five years or similar periods. These started expiring around 1995, and when we investigated renewing them, the general attitude among all the Japanese companies was, "Now that anime is much more popular in America than it was around 1988–1990, you can afford to pay more for the renewal than you did for the license in the first place." That was not true, and it led to the decline of Streamline as an active company. Today Carl is busy at A.D. Vision Films working on the production of their *Lady Death* movie, which he will write and co-produce.

SD: What's your impression of American anime fans?
FP: Pretty much the same as other kinds of American fans—SF fans, comic-book fans, *Star Trek* and *Star Wars* fans, and so on. Most of them are intelligent and pleasant to associate with. A minority (unfortunately, often a very visible, hyperactive minority) go way overboard screaming, "Anime rules and all American animation is sh*t!!" which is very embarrassing to all the fans around them. I have a low opinion of some of the early anime fans who actively tried to prevent other fans from publicizing anime to keep it

Fred Patten mans the Streamline Pictures booth at the 1996 San Diego Comic-Con. This is Streamline at its peak. The company was also selling Dreamland Japan *for Fred Schodt.*

"something special that only we would know about." Most of the fans that I know might be called "fans of adolescent-adult fantasy cinema" more than of anime specifically. They like American animation like *The Iron Giant* and *Aeon Flux* and *Spawn,* and live-action SF movies like *Jurassic Park* and *Men in Black* as much as they like anime like *Akira* and *Ninja Scroll.*

SD: A few issues ago I slammed *Final Fantasy.* What did you think of it?
FP: Visually impressive, and a story that would not disappoint an anime fan. But definitely not the right mixture to spend over $130 million on and try to sell to the general movie-going public. They would have done better to try an adventure-fantasy story closer to *Final Fantasy X* or one of the sword-and-sorcery video games—sort of a *The Lord of the Rings* before the *LotR* movie came out.

SD: Speaking of computers, what do you think of the current and increasingly popular interface of anime and computer games?
FP: I am cautiously in favor of it, if the anime based on computer games have intelligent stories and charismatic characters. Most, unfortunately, have only shallow characters and unimaginative plots. I did appreciate that the *Final Fantasy* movie had an original and rather intellectual story. Too bad it was not more emotionally appealing.

SD: Is there a certain direction you'd like to see anime go? Was there ever a "golden opportunity" that you think anime might have missed?
FP: Offhand, I cannot think of anything. One of the things that I like

about anime is its diversity. I generally prefer the science-fiction dramatic adventures like *Harmagedon, Akira,* and *Outlaw Star,* but whenever I start to overdose on them there is so much else that I can find for variety, from modern urban horror like *Wicked City* to children's fantasy like *Catnapped!* to Chinese or Japanese historical fantasy like *Fushigi Yugi.*

SD: With new projects like *Metropolis, Blood,* and *Tokyo Blue,* are we at the cusp of a new renaissance for anime?

FP: I wish that I could think so, but these titles strike me as more flailing around looking for a new trend. It's encouraging that the anime industry is willing to invest the talent and money to try to make new blockbusters, but are *Metropolis, Blood,* and *Tokyo Blue* really likely to start any more of a renaissance than *Phoenix 2772* or *The Dagger of Kamui* did in the early 1980s?

Anime Expo 2003: Anime Conventions Enter Their Adolescence
Animation World Magazine 8, no. 6, September 2003.

Looking at the estimated 18,000 fans crowding into the Anaheim Convention Center and adjoining Hilton and Marriott hotels for Anime Expo 2003 during the four-day July Fourth weekend, it is hard to imagine that the annual AX began with only 1,750 attendees twelve years earlier. The baby has grown up.

Anime conventions can trace their gestation back to the first anime videotape room parties held at SF and comic book fan conventions in 1977, a year after the first giant-robot SF adventure cartoons appeared on American Japanese-community TV channels. During the 1980s, anime became an increasingly prominent portion of those conventions, with an anime video room as part of the official programs, fans in anime character costumes in the masquerades, and anime merchandise in the dealers' hall.

By the late 1980s, anime fans began asking for conventions of their own. It was not a coincidence that this was also when the first specialty companies were founded to license anime and release it commercially on video. The first all-anime convention, with the support of the new American anime specialty companies that featured guests of honor from the Japanese animation studios, was held in 1991. It was a success, but it was organized as a stand-alone event. Anime fans wanted an annual convention like the SF and comic book cons. Mike Tatsugawa in the San Francisco Bay area organized the nonprofit Society for the Promotion of Japanese Animation (SPJA) to "make it so." Anime Expo '92, in San Jose, Calif., staked out the July Fourth holiday weekend. In 1994, AX moved to Southern California and has been in Anaheim, Los Angeles, or Long Beach ever since. As anime (and manga, its comic book counterpart) became increasingly popular during the late 1990s and early 2000s, AX attendance has risen sharply. Other annual anime conventions have become established throughout the United States and Canada, but AX remains the oldest and largest.

AX has also taken on many of the aspects of a trade show rather than a fan convention. At the early fan conventions, and still at many of the regional conventions, the dealers' hall consists of small anime specialty shops and individual fans selling and trading collectibles. AX's dealers' hall still has a lot of those (enough to result in long lines of fans at the convention center's ATMs getting more money), but it is dominated by professional commercial display booths of all the major American anime producers and retailers. Some of these were two stories tall, with huge plasma or projection TV screens constantly showing the company's latest anime. At the early conventions, programming consisted mostly of panels of fans discussing their favorite anime titles and characters. At AX, the programming is divided up among the anime companies to let each one tell the fans what new projects it has under development, and what new titles it will release on DVD or theatrically during the next few months. This is news that fans want to hear, but it is also more commercial than it is artistic.

(A technological sign of the times: practically every anime retailer had a "super discount" corner offering anime videotapes and laser discs at $5 each or three for $10. By next year, anime in any format other than DVD should be extinct.)

AX 2003 featured thirteen Japanese guests of honor: yoshitoshi ABe (anime character designer and/or writer), Kazuki Akane (director of TV and theatrical anime), Kazuhiro Furuhashi (director), Mitsuru Hongo (director/writer), Yuki Kajiura (anime music composer), Yao Kazuki (voice actor), Yousuke Kuroda (screenwriter), Mahiro Maeda (director and designer

Animation World Magazine reader Renee Jones complained that my statement, "The first all-anime convention, with the support of the new American anime specialty companies that featured guests of honor from the Japanese animation studios, was held in 1991," was incorrect. "[T]he longest running convention is A-Kon (held in the Dallas-Fort Worth, Texas, Metroplex area) celebrating its fifteenth year in 2004. [It] originated in 1989, three years before Anime Expo became an annual event and two years prior to the original one-time meeting," she wrote.

Fans have been debating for years about the first "true" anime convention. Project A-Kon I was held on July 28–29, 1990 (not 1989), and AnimeCon '91 was held on August 30–September 2, 1991, so Project A-Kon was indisputably earlier. But at first A-Kon included American animation as well as anime, and it didn't have any Japanese guests. It may have placed the most emphasis on anime of any convention up to 1990 (and it was promoted as such), but it was considered at the time to be in the same class as other traditional conventions such as the 1980 and 1986 Comic-Cons, the 1984 World Science Fiction Convention,

Cont. on p. 82

specializing in CGI anime), Atsuko Nakajima (character designer and animation director), Koushi Rikudo (writer/cartoonist of the fan-favorite *Excel Saga* manga), Goro Taniguchi (director), Misa Watanabe (voice actress), and Nobuteru Yuuki (character designer). Some of these guests were invited by AX, while others were sponsored by an anime company to promote one or more of their productions to the fans. AX presented these guests in a series of "focus panels" throughout the convention, in which the guest (and a translator) were introduced to an audience of several hundred fans to discuss their works and answer questions. Yuki Kajiura, a current fan-favorite because of her music for the anime series *Noir* and *.hack//SIGN*, presented an hour-long concert of the most popular songs from those shows.

American voice actors Crispin Freeman and Wendee Lee mingled more directly with the fans in voice acting workshops. There were also some animators/cartoonists who hosted how-to-draw workshops using Japanese art supplies (provided by import shops hoping to increase sales).

One sign of the increasing popularity of anime is that the list of anime specialty companies presenting panels at AX grows longer every year. There were three or four brand-new companies at AX 2003 announcing their first licensed anime releases. Two prominent Tokyo animation studios had panels of their own, both on the occasion of anniversary celebrations, Studio Gonzo (tenth anniversary) and Studio Pierrot (twenty-fifth anniversary).

The most impressive news was from A.D. Vision Films, founded in 1992 and now one of the largest anime DVD releasers in America. In addition to announcing its acquisition of some of the hottest new anime titles in Japan, ADV has just launched an Anime Network cable TV channel (fans

and the 1986 BayCon, which had all featured extensive anime programming or special anime events. AnimeCon '91 was devoted exclusively to anime, and promoted as the first convention for anime fandom, with participation from Japan including several Japanese guests of honor and support from the new American anime professional companies. Its format was copied exactly by Anime Expo the following year, establishing that AnimeCon had set a new pattern. A-Kon did quickly become an exclusively anime convention, and it has been held annually since 1990, so today it can accurately claim to be the oldest North American anime convention. But it did not become an "all-anime" convention before AnimeCon '91. So the argument continues over whether A-Kon should be recognized as the first anime convention, or considered a general-fan convention that evolved into an anime convention after AnimeCon '91. I do not feel that my statement, that AnimeCon '91 was the first American convention devoted entirely to anime with support from the American anime specialty companies and participation from the Japanese anime industry, is wrong.

By the way, 'yoshitoshi ABe' is that creator's preferred English spelling of his name. ■

were urged to contact their cable TV providers to request it), and is about to start new divisions to publish its own releases of licensed manga and of anime music CDs. Also, ADV will begin producing its own anime, using the facilities of Japanese studios whose titles it has been licensing. Preliminary art designs were shown for a twenty-six-episode TV anime adaptation of American SF author David Weber's *Mutineer's Moon*, the first novel in a trilogy. If it is successful, anime adaptations of Weber's two interstellar sequels will follow.

For those who came to AX to watch anime, there was a 35 mm film program and four simultaneous anime video rooms. Several of the anime specialty companies also had mini-theaters featuring their own DVD releases. It was possible to watch anime around the clock for four days. (There were signs asking fans not to sleep in the anime theaters.)

Fan activities remain a major part of AX's programming. Thursday's

	Japanese Release	USA Release
Best Male Character	Amon (in *Witch Hunter Robin*; Sunrise, Inc.)	Kenshin (*Samurai X*; ADV Films)
Best Female Character	Robin (*Witch Hunter Robin*; Sunrise, Inc.)	Yukino (*His & Her Circumstances*; TRSI, Inc.)
Best Non-Human Character	Grunties (*.hack//DUSK*; Bandai Visual Co.)	Menchi (*Excel Saga*; ADV Films)
Best Manga	*Fruits Basket* (Hakusensha)	*Naruto* (Viz LLC)
Best Publication	*Newtype*	*Newtype USA* (ADV Films)
Best TV Series	*Naruto* (Studio Pierrot)	*.hack//SIGN* (Bandai Entertainment)
Best Film	*Inu Yasha: Kagami no Naka no Mugenjiyo* (Sunrise, Inc.)	*Spirited Away* (Buena Vista Home Entertainment)
Best OAV	*.hack//Liminality* (Bandai Visual Co.)	*Read Or Die* (Manga Entertainment)
Best Music Album	*Final Fantasy X-2 Original Soundtrack* (Avex Mode)	*.hack//SIGN Original Soundtrack 1* (Bandai Entertainment)
Best Film Debut at Anime Expo	*The Animatrix* (Warner Home Video)	
Best Company		TOKYOPOP

main fan event was an idol (pop singer) contest. There was also a presentation of an amateur *Sailor Moon* musical. Friday had a new "mini-masquerade" event (for fans too inexperienced at costume construction to compete in the main masquerade), a J-Rock dance contest, and an evening screening of fan-produced anime music videos. Saturday was dominated by the main masquerade, which began with preparations at 2 P.M. and lasted until well after midnight.

AX still uses the traditional English words "masquerade" and "costuming" in its program guide. During the last few years, the fans have been adopting the Japanese fan term "cosplay" (an abbreviation of "costume play"), so there was far more talk about "cosplaying" than about costuming. As impressive as the formal masquerade was, it was insignificant in comparison with the number of fans who wore anime costumes all convention long.

It was easy to tell which anime titles are currently popular by the number of fans dressed as their characters. *.hack//SIGN, Trigun,* and *Hellsing* were among the most popular for adult characters, while any girls eight or younger were sure to have been dressed by their mothers as either Sakura from *Card Captor Sakura,* Sugar from *Sugar: A Little Snow Fairy,* or one of the cat-eared little girls from *Di Gi Charat.* There were even some cosplayers as Storm from the *X-Men* movie "because Storm looks like she ought to be an anime character;" and as Neo from *The Matrix Reloaded,* because "everybody knows that *The Matrix* is really just live-action anime."

Other fans like to glam it up. (Is it possible to have too many cosplayers at a con? If only 10 percent of the 18,000 attendees were wearing costumes, that was still 1,800 cosplayers. It was almost impossible to walk three feet without accidentally stepping in front of someone taking a photo of a cosplayer. There were so many fans in the same costumes that impromptu group photo sessions were scheduled: "Would all the fans in *Lupin III* costumes meet in the Hilton main lobby on Friday at 4:30 for a group photo?" There were enough *.hack//SIGN* cosplayers to start a separate convention.)

Sunday was the traditional "packing up to go home" day, but there were still enough attendees to make the benefit auction for the City of Hope medical foundation (AX's official charity) a rousing success. An AX tradition is having its Japanese cartoonist guests of honor draw two or three rough sketches of their most popular characters for this auction. Two by Koushi Rikudo of his *Excel Saga* cast, that may have taken five minutes each to draw, went for more than $2,000 each. Some of the bidding went "$500 . . . $2,000 . . . $2,500 . . . $3,000 . . . $5,000 . . . no more bids? Sold!" in less than two minutes. The highest bid was $6,400 for a multicolored marker sketch by Nobuteru Yuuki of Pirotessa, the dark elf warrior from *Record of Lodoss War.* The grand total for the City of Hope was $74,020 for fifty-five items, an average of almost $1,350 each.

The Society for the Promotion of Japanese Animation's Anime Industry Awards (anime fandom's equivalent of the Oscars) are both voted on and presented at Anime Expo. The ballot is included in members' registration packets. Voting is held during the first three days of the con; the ballots are tallied Saturday evening and the awards are presented as the main event at the closing ceremonies.

Will Anime Expo 2004 break the 20,000 attendance mark? Fans are confident that it will. If AX's first twelve years have been anime conventions' childhood, what will its adolescence bring?

Society for the Promotion of Japanese Animation 2003 Industry Awards (presented during the closing ceremonies)

"Anime" Versus "Japanimation"
Anime Archive column in *Newtype USA* 2, no. 11, November 2003.

"Dear Fred;

What is the difference between "anime" and "Japanimation"? Some say there is no real difference. Some say "Japanimation" is an old word and that "anime" has replaced it. Some say "Japanimation" was created by the big video stores that did not know that "anime" is the real name for Japanese animation. Some say "Japanimation" is really an insulting abbreviation for "jap animation" by those who want to belittle it, and that no true anime fan should use it. Who is right?" [This is a composite of several questions]

The second statement above is correct, although there is a bit of truth in all the others. When fans first discovered Japanese TV cartoons around 1976 and 1977, that was usually just what they called them—Japanese TV cartoons. Animation scholarship was just beginning in America at this time; fans were interviewing the great animators like Tex Avery and Bob Clampett and writing the first serious histories of studios like Warner Bros. and Fleischer Studios. One of the first bits of knowledge they spread was, "You should call it animation, not cartoons." Cartoons were only one form of animation; there was also stop-motion animation, blah blah blah. So the early anime fans quickly switched to talking about Japanese animation rather than Japanese cartoons.

"Japanese animation" soon got condensed to "Japanimation." By the early 1980s, it was so widespread in fandom that some fans got into an argument over who should get the credit for inventing the term. This set off a brief historical search through old anime club newsletters and correspondence for the earliest use of the word. The oldest found was in late 1978 in correspondence from Carl Gafford, who claimed that he had already been using it for some time by then. Whether "the Gaff" coined it or not, he was one of the first to spread its use. Japanimation was commonly used by fans and it was not meant as an insult. Several clubs founded in the '80s used the word in their names.

But anime fandom was small. To those outside the fandom, who thought that "watching cartoons in a language you can't understand" just showed how weird and geeky anime fans were, it was all too easy to turn the word into the derogatory "jap animation." Those who had an agenda to portray all anime as super-violent and super-erotic like *Urotsukidoji* even twisted the word into JaPORNimation. Also, by the late '80s enough fans were translating and spreading information from the Japanese anime magazines and reference books that everyone knew that anime was what the Japanese themselves called animation. Saying anime instead of Japanimation showed that you were more knowledgeable about the subject, and it avoided the danger of the word being misunderstood as an insult. Also, a three-syllable, five-letter word was easier to say and write than a five-syllable, twelve-letter word. Starting in the late '80s and early '90s, anime began to replace Japanimation.

It is ironic that this changeover started just as the first licensed anime videos went on sale in America. Many of the first video stores and comics shops that wanted to know how to market these new kind of videos fastened upon the J-word. Fans in the early '90s were amused by some of the first commercial advertising for anime videos that said "those who are really 'in the know' call this great new entertainment Japanimation," when the real fans were abandoning the word in favor of anime. But the a-word caught up to the J-word quickly enough that by the time anime became a significant commercial market in America, it was called the anime industry rather than the Japanimation industry.

Today anime is heard much more frequently than Japanimation. But the older term is not forgotten. Some of the older clubs and stores that adopted it in their names have retained it to demonstrate their longevity, as a statement that "we were here early on." Two prominent examples are the Boston Japanimation Society, today one of the oldest anime clubs still going; and Joy's Japanimation (in Greensburg, Pa.), one of the pioneering anime specialty stores. Some use it because they like the sound of its more impressive five syllables; it "stands out more" than anime. Some like to flaunt it at anyone who uses it in an insulting manner, just as the American colonists took the "Yankee" sneer of the British and adopted it as a name to be proud of. Some language purists argue that anime is really the Japanese term for all animation, not only Japanese; so Japanimation is more accurate as a reference to just Japanese animation.

So in a broad sense, there is no real difference between the two words. Anime is more up to date and Japanimation may make you sound like an old-timer, but the latter came from anime fandom and is still used by many fans. You can use it without looking like a clueless outsider—as long as, as the saying goes, you smile when you say it to show that no insult is intended. (And you should definitely say it as a single word, not two words.)

Part II
The Business of Anime

All Those Japanese Animation Soundtracks

CinemaScore no. 15, Winter 1986–Summer 1987.

It all started with John Williams.

Not literally. There were records of animated cartoon music in Japan almost from the earliest days of Japanese TV cartoons, which began in January 1963 with *Mighty Atom* (*Astro Boy* in America). But for the fifteen years following that, Japanese cartoon music was produced on children's records only.

Most TV cartoons had separate opening and closing title-credits theme songs, one verse apiece. These songs were packaged as little 45-rpm records, with the opening theme on one side and the closing theme on the other, but expanded to three verses apiece. Cartoon theatrical features followed this pattern. They had an opening-title theme song and at least one other song somewhere in the movie so there would be enough music to sell on a 45-rpm children's record.

Most of these cartoon TV programs and movies featured fast-paced fantastic or science fictional stories, and the music was light and bouncy to match. A few cartoons used music composed in traditional Asian patterns; others used themes reminiscent of the Japanese military marches of World War II. But most featured modernized, Westernized tunes. Many gave the

In 1986 when this was written, Matsumoto was still having fun switching back and forth between "Reiji" and "Leiji" as the Anglicization of his first name; and Ishimori was not yet calling himself Ishinomori. (It is no secret today that his name was actually Onodera.) Most American anime-fan articles about Matsumoto in the 1980s used the "Reiji" spelling.

Mari Iijima, the voice actress of *Macross*'s Lynn Minmay character, was an actual teen idol singer in Japan at the time. She moved to America in 1989, and is a popular music singer and composer in Los Angeles today. Fans at her concerts invariably request an encore of one of her *Macross* songs.

Creator Rumiko Takahashi has acknowledged the American 1964–72 TV series *Bewitched* (extremely popular on Japanese TV) as a major inspiration for *Urusei Yatsura*. Space girl Lum-chan's catchphrase pet name of "Darling!" for her reluctant boyfriend Ataru was partly a deliberate use of an English word in the otherwise Japanese dialogue to emphasize her status as a foreigner, and partly an in-group pastiche of *Bewitched*'s housewife-witch Samantha's affectionate call of "Darrin!" for her husband.

Both *Dr. Slump* and *Urusei Yatsura* continued to have animated careers long after this article was written.

In 2004, the anime music business is even more immense. Anime conventions frequently have dealers' tables that specialize in nothing but music CDs, although the mixture now includes video game anime music among the TV, theatrical, and OAV music, plus plenty of J-pop music that is not connected to anime at all. ∎

impression that their composers were having fun trying to write in popular American rhythms. A cartoon series about a modern little-girl witch had a theme song that was a Tokyo attempt at Dixieland jazz. Another program about three interstellar secret agents who come to Earth to judge whether humans are too warlike to be allowed to develop space travel had a theme that was a good imitation of Benny Goodman's swing. A third program, about an adventurous puppy in a Japanese suburban neighborhood, had opening music more appropriate to an American Prohibition-era speakeasy (a Charleston).

By the early 1970s these 45 doubles began to be collected into long-play anthologies. Nippon Columbia produced the most popular of these, a semi-annual *TV Children's Program Hits* LP with the opening and closing themes of the six most popular programs of the current season. Nippon Columbia seems to have had a monopoly on the use of the actual TV music. Other music companies produced LPs with their own bands and singers performing their own versions of the songs. These were still produced entirely for the kiddie market, however. Many of the records divided the songs of different programs with brief excerpts of dialogue or sound effects. They were packaged in albums with several pages of cartoon-cel art, along with the full lyrics, which were invariably juvenile in nature.

Then in 1977, two things happened. One was the release in America of *Star Wars*. The other was the production in Japan of a similar space adventure in animated cartoon form, *Space Battleship Yamato*. This had originally been created as a twenty-six-episode TV serial during 1974–75 with unusually rich, classically oriented music by Hiroshi Miyagawa. Particularly noteworthy were the stirring march and the love-ballad end-credits theme, "The Scarlet Scarf." During 1977 this serial was condensed into a feature for theatrical release. It happened to come out in August, three months after the appearance of *Star Wars* in America. *Space Battleship Yamato* enjoyed the same runaway popularity with the young teen market in Japan that *Star Wars* was enjoying in the United States. It seems obvious that the producers of *Yamato* closely studied the *Star Wars* phenomenon as a guide on how to best market their own success.

One of the merchandising hits of *Star Wars* was the symphonic suite arrangement of its John Williams music, in a serious and sophisticated album rather than a juvenile SF movie-music package. The Japanese quickly followed suit. In December 1977, Nippon Columbia released *Symphonic Suite Yamato*, which was "composed, arranged, and conducted by Hiroshi Miyagawa, performed by Symphonic Orchestra Yamato." The symphony was divided into twelve movements, embracing all of the most popular themes of the TV/movie music in a mature, dignified arrangement. The LP album included a color brochure which primarily summarized the movie's story, but which also included photographs of the orchestra performing and gave a complete listing of the sixty-three-piece ensemble. This album was also a fantastic success and is still in print in Japan (though today, Nippon Columbia is promoting the CD release).

Within a year, animated cartoon music records had become a major merchandising category. Practically every new TV cartoon series was designed to spin off at least one LP music album. Japan does not have a Saturday-morning children's TV ghetto, and most TV cartoons run for at least twenty-six weekly prime-time episodes. Popular programs may run for fifty-two episodes or more. Two exceptionally popular TV cartoon series (*Dr. Slump* and *Urusei Yatsura*) have just concluded five year runs with over 200 episodes apiece.*

So there was more than enough music to fill an LP per program. The older cartoons were not slighted, either. In October 1977 Nippon Columbia released a four-album boxed set, *The March of TV Cartoon Theme Songs*. This resurrected the theme songs of forty of the most popular TV cartoon series (a total of eighty songs) from *Mighty Atom* in 1963 until the present. (Not all of these were actually cartoons. Some of the programs were the TV equivalents of the *Godzilla* movies, featuring live actors in space-creature rubber suits or superhero costumes. But their music was indistinguishable from that for the animated cartoon programs.)

At first, the standard pattern was to produce an LP album containing from ten to twelve songs. These included the opening and closing themes and a number of songs from different episodes. If a program was popular

---

*Both started as comic book series and became popular first in that format: *Dr. Slump* by Akira Toriyama and *Urusei Yatsura* by Rumiko Takahashi. Both titles were picked up as TV cartoon series in 1981, *Slump* in April and *Urusei* in October. In addition to their animation careers as weekly series (both were broadcast on Wednesday evenings, at 7:00 and 7:30 respectively), *Dr. Slump* spun off one theatrical feature and *Urusei Yatsura* spun off four annual theatrical features in 1983 through 1986. Both ended their TV runs in 1986, although there's still enough popularity for *Urusei* that many fans expect another theatrical feature next year.

The merchandising for each series was apparently controlled by their animation studios, *Dr. Slump* by Toei Animation Co. and *Urusei* by Kitty Records. As far as marketing the music went, Toei apparently just made the usual deal with Nippon Columbia to allow them to produce the standard records. There was a 45-rpm record with the opening and closing themes, an LP with the TV music, an LP with the theatrical feature music, and at least one electronic synthesizer LP and one "jam trip" LP. Kitty, on the other hand, went overboard with the *Urusei Yatsura* music. They released a 45 every time they changed the TV theme songs (at least two of these 45s were advertised as "hit singles"); there were at least two LP "anthology collections" of music from the TV series and the features; there were sheet music collections and at least three commercial music videos available on cassette and laser disc for home purchase, which presented the songs over selections from the TV animation. In addition there were multiple synthesizer LPs, jam trip LPs, and more than one LP with popular Japanese recording artists singing the various songs.

enough, a second album featuring a symphonic suite rescoring of all the music was made. If a program was really popular, a BGM (background music) album was released. This consisted of the individual music tracks for the program: suspense music, romantic themes, chase rhythms, and so forth, mostly short tracks that began and ended abruptly. These appealed to the fans who felt they were getting a "behind the scenes" piece of the technical equipment of a favorite program.

Soon this was no longer enough. The popularity of cartoon music records kept growing. New products had to be devised. Some of the traditionally anonymous vocalists of TV cartoon music found themselves promoted to stardom, in a series of LPs collecting their songs from various programs. Two of these were Isao Sasaki, the deep-voiced male vocalist who had sung the theme songs of *Space Battleship Yamato* and other action-adventure SF cartoons, and Miyako Horie, a young lady who sang the lyrics for many of the gentler girls' and infants' fantasy cartoons. Popular cartoonists whose comic books had been adapted into TV cartoons were also used as the subjects for theme-song collections. *The World of Osamu Tezuka* was a two-record album featuring the title-credit music of a dozen animated cartoons based on the comic books of the creator of *Astro Boy* and *Kimba the White Lion*. Go Nagai (creator of the giant-robot concept in adventure comic books), Reiji Matsumoto, and Shotaro Ishimori were other cartoonists similarly honored with *The World of*–animation music albums. Major animation studios such as Toei Animation and Tatsunoko Production Company became the subjects of LPs featuring the themes of their most popular TV cartoons.

Anthology records flooded the market, with titles such as *Popular Animation Theme Song Collection*. These usually contained sixteen theme songs from TV cartoons or theatrical features, in a confusing variety of combinations. The themes of a half dozen or so mega-hits like *Space Battleship Yamato* or *Galaxy Express 999* could be found on most of these collections, and the public could search among the other songs for the themes of any other particular cartoon—it was doubtlessly on some album somewhere. Other anthology records specialized in themes by topic. One featured the themes of the ten top giant-robot superhero adventure cartoons. Others focused on girls' romance cartoons or sports adventure cartoons. There were new arrangements, as well. Popular TV cartoon music was rescored for high school marching bands.

The record companies also went back to the older TV cartoons for more than just the title music. Most of the TV cartoons before 1977 did not have enough complete songs to fill an LP, but they did have enough incidental scoring. The BGM album, which had been a mark of a TV cartoon of exceptional popularity, now became commonplace, denoting even the resurrected music of a minor old cartoon series such as *Tekkaman the Space Knight* (a science fiction serial that had been so minor in its own day that it had been canceled in mid-series, ending on a cliffhanger!).

Since the musical needs of TV and theatrical cartoons are much the same, quite a lot of this music was stylistically similar. Some, however, did stand out. *Lupin III*, a very popular TV and movie series about the sophisticated adventures of a "good guy" international master thief, had music by one of Japan's top modern jazz composers, Yuji Ono. Ono wrote both songs and the incidental scoring, working closely with the series to create music for many individual episodes. This resulted in several albums of cocktail-lounge jazz. In 1980, an animated feature was adapted from the American Marvel Comics' *Tomb of Dracula* title, drawn in the style of the original comic book art of Gene Colan. Its music, by Seiji Yokoyama, was arranged into a striking symphony of thirteen movements ("performed by the Transylvania Baroque Ensemble"—probably Nippon Columbia's house orchestra—it certainly employed enough instruments for a larger group than one usually associates with an "ensemble") written in the styles of such classical composers as Bach and Liszt, evolving into a modern symphonic jazz movement for the music in the film's climactic battle scene. In 1978, Polydor released an LP of the music for *Space Battleship Yamato* arranged to a disco beat, and this was extremely popular.

During the early 1980s, new trends in popular music began to reflect themselves in Japan's animated cartoon music. Traditional songs became passé except in TV cartoons for young children. Electronic synthesizer "digital trip" LPs became the vogue for the science fiction adventure cartoon serials that were aimed at the teen audience. "Jam trip" collections also became common: live recordings of bands playing their own improv arrangements of a particular cartoon's music. Rearrangements proliferated. *Xabungle*, a humorous interplanetary "Western" with giant robots instead of horses, spun its incidental music into *Dancing Xabungle*, a "jazzercise arrangement." Nippon Columbia went into overkill with new arrangements of the *Yamato* music: piano sonata, violin sonata, piano duet, a full choir, a guitar arrangement. Some of these LPs were in such sophisticated packaging that only the "Yamato" name made it evident that they were adaptations of animated cartoon music rather than performances of classical music.

The music began to be aimed ever more directly toward the teen market. In 1982 a TV serial appeared, *Macross, the Super-Dimension Fortress*, about a giant-robot battleship so large that an entire city was built within it, complete with shopping malls and pop-rock radio stations. One of the most popular characters in the series was Lynn Minmay, a Chinese teen singing star. *Macross* reintroduced songs to cartoon music by presenting them as songs sung by the characters as part of the plot rather than as incidental background music. After the usual records of *Macross* music were released, a "Miss D.J." album appeared in which Lynn Minmay (actually her voice actress) presented several current pop hits that had nothing to do with animation, in a radio disk-jockey platter format as though it was broadcast from Macross City. This sold well enough that it was not only followed by other records in the same vein, but it led to mirror-image imitations: records featuring genuine disk jockeys or popular singers who had not previously been associated with animation introducing or presenting their own arrangements of cartoon songs. Another TV cartoon serial, *Genesis Climber Mospeada*, set in a twenty-first century in which human commandos sought to overthrow alien conquerors, featured a hero who doubled as a female-impersonator nightclub entertainer. An LP album, *Live at Pit Inn*, simulated a live recording of one of "her" performances which (aside from some references to the twenty-first century political situation in the dialogue) was virtually indistinguishable from a real live recording of a nightclub act.

In 1981 Kitty Films, a division of Kitty Records, Inc., one of Japan's largest popular music companies, launched its own TV cartoon series. *Urusei Yatsura* (a Japanese pun roughly translated as "Those Obnoxious Aliens") was about a sexy outer space coed who came to Earth as an exchange student and developed a crush on one of her high school's most macho jocks. It was a teen comedy that blended elements of *Archie, I Dream of Jeannie*, and *Supergirl*. Kitty Films blatantly used the program to promote new pop songs. The opening and closing credits were changed several times to introduce new songs, several of which were advertised as becoming hit singles. All the music merchandising concepts that had ever been used in the Japanese cartoon music market were employed in *Urusei Yatsura*, including picture records and song books. Cartoon music records had been a major merchandising sideline for many years by this time, but in this instance the cartoon was practically a sideline of the music industry.

In 1971, a new superhero comic-book series had appeared, *Locke the Superman*. A TV cartoon series of this title was prepared in 1980 and the presentation included music by a popular Japanese rock group, Talizman. The presentation failed to sell, but as long as the music had already been written, it was released as an LP "musical dramatization" of *Locke the Superman*, with record album art by the comic book's artist, Yuki Hijiri. The LP sold well enough that Talizman recorded two more musical dramatizations of Locke's adventures. The popularity of these records caught the attention of the Japanese cartoon industry and persuaded it to take a second look at the comic book. In March 1984, *Locke the Superman*, a 110-minute theatrical animated feature, was released—the cartoon that owed its existence to its preproduction music. And within the year, several more musical dramatizations of minor comic books by new rock groups had appeared.

This situation continues today. The latest development is one of packaging: the new sign of mega-popularity for a cartoon's music is its release on compact disc, and several have been issued in this format, including the *Space Battleship Yamato* scores.

The cartoon-music field in Japan is exceptionally rich. At least a half-dozen theatrical feature cartoons are released each year, most of which have fully orchestrated symphonic scores. TV music is not as richly scored, but is more vigorous and more dynamically aimed at the youth market with rock or electronic synthesizer LP arrangements. One 1983 theatrical feature, *Harmagedon,* imported an American pop composer, Keith Emerson, to supervise its music, and an American singer, Rosemary Butler, to perform its title song. A 1985 giant-robot TV cartoon serial, *Zeta Gundam,* featured a theme song commissioned from Neil Sedaka.

Animated cartoon music is certainly treated more seriously in Japan than in America. Few animated feature or cartoon scores are issued in America except those marketed as children's records, and even here few are released that have any representation of the theme songs. But then cartoons themselves are not treated as seriously in America as in Japan, where many animated science fiction adventure series appear on prime time television alongside the live-action detective programs and adult soap operas, where they are directed toward a more mature audience with more mature themes.

Japanese Animation Composers

The prevalence and, indeed, plethora of soundtrack albums from Japanese animated films and TV series continues to be strong. While many soundtrack collectors may be tempted to ignore the manifold recordings, there are indeed some treasures to be found. While there remains a prevalence toward commercially oriented pop styles, many Japanese animated films continue to utilize fully symphonic and classically oriented scores as well as variably effective mixtures of both idioms.

The following checklist is a partial filmography of some of the more prominent composers of Japanese animation films and TV. Those who have composed especially noteworthy symphonic scores, in our opinion, are indicated with a bullet. All titles are considered to be theatrical features unless noted as TV or video. Most titles have also had (often voluminous) soundtrack albums issued; only if the release date differed greatly from that of the film or series has this information been included).

Japanese Animation Composers	A Partial Filmography
Nozumi Aoki •	*Galaxy Express 999* (1979, TV series and feature; LPs issued for both) *Harmageddon* (1983, with K. Emerson)
Koichi Chiba	*Crusher Joe* (1983, with S. Fujino)
Sadayoshi Fujino	*Crusher Joe* (1983, with K. Chiba)
Wakiko Fukuda	*Mobile Suit Gundam* (1980 season, with T. Takai, TV series)
Kentaro Haneda	*TechnoVoyager, the Scientific Rescue Unit* (1982, TV series) (title spelled "Technoboyger" on LP) *Final Yamato* (1982, TV, with H. Miyagawa)

Macross—Super Time Fortress (1983, TV series)
Space Cobra (1983, with Y. Ohno) TV series and theatrical feature; unclear who scored what or if they both collaborated on each)

Eitetsu Hayashi • *The Dagger of Kamui* (1985, with Ryudo Uzaki)

Yasuo Higuchi *Phoenix 2772* (1980)

Masaaki Hirao *Space Pirate Captain Harlock* (1978, TV, with S. Yokoyama)

Joh Hisaishi *Technopolice 21C* (1982)
• *Nausicaä of the Valley of the Winds* (1984)
Birth (1984, original home video feature)
• *Arion* (1985)
Laputa: The Castle in the Sky (1986)

Yuzuru Hisaishi *Sasuga no Sarutobi* (1982–84, TV series)

Masaru Hoshi *Urusei Yatsura* [*Those Obnoxious Aliens*] no. 2—*Beautiful Dreamer (1982)*

Harumi Hosono *Night on the Galactic Railroad* (1985)

Kagami Ikami *Lensman* (1984)

Hiroki Inui *Votoms, Armored Trooper* (1984–85, TV series)

Fumi Itakura *Urusei Yatsura* [*Those Obnoxious Aliens*] no. 4—*Lum the Forever* (1986)

Taki Izumi *Ge Ge Ge No Kitaro* (1968–69, TV series)

Shinsuke Kazato *Future Police Urashiman* (1982, TV; with Serizawa and Suzuki)

Shunsuke Kikuchi *Casshan, the Artificial Human* (1973–74, TV series; LP issued in 1981)
Getta Robo [*Combo-Robot*] (1974–75, TV series; adapted for American TV as *Starvengers;* LP issued in 1982)
Hurricane Polimar (1974–75, TV series; LP issued in 1981)
UFO Robot Grandizer (1975–77, TV series. Shown in France as *Goldorak;* aka in Japan as *UFO RobotGrendizer.* Soundtrack LP issued in 1982.)
Gaiking, the Great Sky Demon-Dragon (1976–77, TV series; LP issued in 1982)
Planetary Robot Danguard Ace: Naval Battle in Space (1978, apparent theatrical compilation from TV series, *Danguard Ace, the Planetary Robot*)
Dr. Slump (1981–86, TV series)
SSX, the Endless Road (1982–83, TV series)

Kitaro *Queen Millenia* (1982)

Izumi Kobayashi *Urusei Yatsura—Only You* (1981, with Humitaka Anzai, Masamichi Amano)

Tetsuya Komuro *Vampire Hunter D* (1985, original home video release)

Riichiro Manabe	*Taro the Dream Boy* (1979)
Kohsetsu Minami	*Triton of the Seas* (1972, TV series; theatrical compilation, 1979)
Hiroshi Miyagawa	• *Space Battleship Yamato* (1974–77; theatrical feature condensation, 1977)
	Grand Prix Hawk (1978, TV series)
	Arrivederci Yamato (1978)
	Yamato—The New Voyage (1979, TV feature)
	Be Forever Yamato (1980)
	• *Maaterlinck's Bluebird* (1980, TV series; scored in the manner of 1940s American musicals!)
	Yamato 3 (1980, TV series)
	Final Yamato (1983, with K. Haneda)
Yuji Ohno	*Lupin III* (1977, TV series)
	Captain Future (1979, TV series)
	Andromeda Stories (1983, TV feature)
	Space Cobra (1983, with K. Haneda) TV series and theatrical feature; unclear who scored what or if they both collaborated on each)
Bob Sakuma	*Gatchaman* (1972–74, TV series; "Symphonic Suite" LP issued 1977; original BGM (bacground music) album issued 1981)
	Tekkaman the Space Knight (1970s, TV series)
Hiroaki Seriwaza	*Future Police Urashiman* (1982, TV; with Kazato and Suzuki)
Osamu Shoji	*Adieu Galaxy Express* (1981)
Koichi Sugiyama	*Gatchaman* (1977, theatrical feature version of earlier TV series)
	Gatchaman II, the Scientific Ninja Commando Squad (1978–79, TV series, LP issued 1979)
	Cyborg 009 (1979, TV)
	Space Runaway Ideon (1980, TV)
	• *The Legend of Syrius* (1981)
	Space Runaway Ideon: A Contact (1982)
	Space Runaway Ideon: Be Invoked (1982)
Takuo Sugiyama	*Maison Ikkoku* (1985, TV)
Kisaburo Suzuki	*Future Police Urashiman* (1982, TV; with Serizawa and Kazato)
Tetsuo Takai	*Mighty Atom* (1963, TV)
	Mobile Suit Gundam (1980 season only, with W. Fukuda, TV)
Isao Tomita	*Jungle Emperor* (1965–66, TV series; LP issued in 1976)
Hiroshi Tsutsui	*Voltus Five, the Ultra Electromagnetic Machine* (1977–78, TV series; LP in 1979)

Combattler V, the Super Electromagnetic Robot (1976–77, TV series; LP in 1982)

Konei Umagano *Battle Mecha-Xabungle* (1982, TV series; two LPs issued)

Ryudo Uzaki *The Dagger of Kamui* (1985, with Eitetsu Hayashi)

Kei Wakakusa *God Mars, the Six Gods United* (1982, TV)

Chumei Watanabe *Mazinger Z* (1972–74, TV series; LP 1978)
Mobile Suit Gundam (1981 season, TV)
Electric God Albegas (1983, TV)

Masayuki Yamamoto *Galaxy Cyclone Bryger* (1981, TV)
J9II Galaxy Whirlwind Baxinger (1982, TV)
Srungle, Mission in Outer Space (1982, TV series)
J9III Galaxy Tornado Sasryger (1983, TV)

Seiji Yokoyama *Space Fantasy Emeraldus* (1978; not a film or TV title, but an original LP with musical "impressions" of comic-book and animated TV guest star Queen Emeraldus)
Space Pirate Captain Harlock (1978, TV, with M. Hirao)
Tomb of Dracula (1980, TV feature)
Future War 198X (1982)

Mickey Yoshino *Urusei Yatsura* no. 3—*Remember My Love* (1984)

Japanese Anime: The Cult Grows Up
Animation Magazine no. 12, Summer 1990.

Star Trek's fans did it. By organizing conventions and giving the show their undying support, they saved their favorite TV series and even convinced the studios that theatrical features would make money, too.

In a similar manner, a "fandom" has grown up in the animation field: fans devoted to Japanese animation. It hasn't gotten all the attention that other fandoms have received, possibly because its subject is obscure and exotic. But that's changing.

The first Japanese animated theatrical features were brought to America thirty years ago by American International Pictures, with *Alakazam the Great* being the best known. Yet despite good dubbing and promotion, they did not earn enough at the box office to catch on. Possibly their themes of classic Asian fairy tales were too foreign for the American public.

Japanese TV cartoons of the 1960s did a bit better. Several—such as *Astro Boy, Gigantor, Eighth Man, Kimba the White Lion,* and *Speed Racer*—came to American TV. They were modern (or futuristic) enough that their young viewers did not realize that they were not American animation. But, like the theatrical films, Japanese TV animation didn't catch on in America, either. By the late 1960s, it had begun to evolve in directions that weren't to American tastes. More and more cartoon series became continuing serials, while American TV wanted cartoons that were complete stories, which could be shown in random order.

Also, Japanese adventure cartoons emphasized dramatic suspense and graphic action, at the very time that American children's programming was under pressure to show less violence. So Japanese animation virtually disappeared from America by the end of the 1960s, except for reruns of the "Americanized" TV cartoons.

Japanese animation fandom began around 1977, among the high school and college crowds that supported the comic book superhero market. It was caused by the proliferation of giant robot cartoons on Japanese TV at the time, and their spread to Hawaii, where they were subtitled in English. They then migrated to the West Coast, appearing on Japanese-community TV channels. The brand-new video recorder, of course, gave fans the opportunity to tape and collect their favorites.

West Coast comic book fans discovered the subtitled Japanese cartoons. They were young adults who had long outgrown the "kiddie" cartoons but who still enjoyed the fantasy/action of comic book science fiction dramas and their space monsters, titanic battles, and threats of world destruction. Now they could get it in animation, in programs with titles like *Brave Raideen, Space Battleship Yamato,* and *Space Pirate Captain Harlock.* Fans with early VCRs taped the cartoons and showed them at club meetings.

The first fan club devoted especially to Japanese animation was the Cartoon/Fantasy Organization, which began in Los Angeles in 1977. By the end of the decade, West Coast fans were bringing their tapes to fan conventions all around America. The first "Japanimation" screenings at fan conventions were generally scoffed at as curiosities. But during the 1980s the video rooms grew to become a standard fixture of convention programming.

This profile of the nascent American anime industry was as much wishful thinking as objective reporting on a new genre market. The Right Stuf (not yet International) was not mentioned because, when this was written in early 1990, it had released only its first few *Astro Boy* videos that were packaged for the American TV-nostalgia market rather than for the anime market. It was not until about a year later that The Right Stuf's commitment as an anime specialty company became evident. Two of the early anime pioneers did not exist yet; the Central Park Media video company did not expand into anime until mid-1991, and ADV was not created until 1992. *Protoculture Addicts* was still a *Robotech* fanzine with no hint of the professional anime magazine with newsstand distribution into which it would soon evolve. Likewise, the first experiments in publishing American translations of manga as American-style comic books were so small that there was no hint that manga would eventually become popular as graphic novels in their original Japanese format ("STOP! This is the last page of the book!"). Nobody in 1990 would have realistically dreamed that anime would be a $100-million-a-year business by 2000. ■

After years of watching Japanese cartoons with English subtitles, fans became so accustomed to the genre that they graduated to watching untranslated cartoons. Many became so fascinated with Japanese culture that they switched preferences from the high-tech natural SF cartoons to those that emphasized Japanese history and Asian supernatural fantasy. Some even enrolled in Japanese language courses, and begged Japanese-community bookshops to import more comic books, animation videos, and animation magazines.

By the 1980s, fans considered themselves a missionary elite. They had seen that animation was not just for kids. But when they tried to tell the TV and movie industries that they should release more Japanese animation in America, they ran into a giant wall.

But, just as *Who Framed Roger Rabbit* and *The Simpsons* created a swing toward "adult" animation's popularity, so has Japanese animation begun to rise above cult status and gain respectability—due largely to the efforts of its fans.

Streamline Pictures, a new theatrical distribution company, was created last year to bring Japanese animation to American theaters. Streamline's founders are Jerry Beck and Carl Macek, both of whom are longtime enthusiasts of American animation. Beck, a former editor of *Animation Magazine,* was the co-author of the first edition of *The Warner Bros. Cartoons* in 1981, and Macek wrote *The Art of Heavy Metal: Animation for the Eighties* that same year. Both were also aware of Japanese animation fandom from its early years, Beck having set up the first East Coast fan club in New York City in 1980. Macek owned the Carl Macek Gallery, an animation art and comics bookshop in Orange, Calif., where many of his customers were Japanese animation fans.

Macek was able to parlay his knowledge of the industry to TV producer Harmony Gold, which led to the production of the *Robotech* syndicated TV series in 1985. But *Robotech* was perceived by the TV industry as just another children's cartoon designed to promote the toy fad of the moment—giant transforming robots. The cartoon disappeared from the air when the toys lost popularity, but a fiercely loyal *Robotech* following remains.

Beck and Macek feel that Japanese animation has a large potential among the high school and college age groups, and among fans of science fiction and art movies. They obtain high-quality Japanese theatrical features which don't fit the "kiddie" image, and book them into repertory theaters.

"This means that they're being shown in only one theater in a city," Beck says. "That's partly due to necessity, because we're a small company and we can't afford a lot of prints and a lot of advertising. But it's also by design. Animation doesn't have a large enough audience among adult moviegoers yet. We have to educate the public that there are cartoon features that will excite them even though they're in college or are in their 30s or 40s now. If we tried to open in twenty or thirty theaters citywide, we'd bomb! But by opening in a single theater—a college campus town or an art film theater—and by a careful ad campaign designed for places like the campuses and the comic book shops, we can bring in enough moviegoers to fill that theater with a respectable audience during its run.

"And it's an audience who will say 'Hey,this Japanese cartoon is great!,'" he continued, "and they will want to come and see our next cartoon when we come to town again. So our popularity and our audience will grow. We expect it to be a slow process, but we think it's the only practical way. Most movie industry business ventures want something that will be a big hit immediately or they're not interested. But we're willing to take some time to pull ourselves up by the bootstraps."

Streamline has distributed three features. *Laputa: The Castle In The Sky* is a family feature in the style of Jules Verne's nineteenth-century adventure fantasies. It has rococo sky pirates, a giant ancient flying city, and a deadly villain. *Twilight of the Cockroaches,* on the other hand, is a cynical, avant-garde social parable. Streamline isn't trying to promote it to family audiences. Its advertising is aimed at the intellectual art film crowd. *Akira* is an SF thriller set in a grim, depressing neo-Tokyo of 2019 A.D., with an appeal to the type of fans who would go to see *Blade Runner* and *Terminator. Akira* is based on a Japanese comic book that is published in an American version by Marvel Comics. Streamline has also dubbed a half-hour Japanese video, *Akira Production Report,* for sale at comics shops and fan conventions.

Streamline's next film will be an August release of *Lensman,* a 1984 Japanese feature in the *Star Wars* vein, based on American author E. E. "Doc" Smith's SF novels.

Beck says that his company has also been commissioned to do the English dubbing of *Kiki's Delivery Service,* Japan's biggest 1989 theatrical release, so it can be shown as an in-flight movie by Japan Air Lines. The animation studio is trying to sell the film to Disney or Universal for theatrical release, but if that doesn't happen Beck hopes to get it for his company.

The biggest source of Japanese animation has been, since 1985, the Original Animation Video (OAV) cassette market. Animation is so popular in Japan that merely releasing the existing theatrical and TV cartoons isn't enough for the home purchase market. There are over fifty animation video releases each month, ranging from children's and educational cartoons to animated pornography. About a quarter of this is brand-new animation.

Until recently, American fans could only get Japanese OAV cassettes by mail order or through Japanese community bookshops. But another startup company, U.S. Renditions, hopes to make this animation available throughout America with English subtitles.

U.S. Renditions is a subsidiary of Nippan Shuppan Hanbai U.S.A., Inc., a major distributor of books, magazines, and gift merchandise to Japanese-community's shops in the United States. The company's big Los Angeles retail shop, Books Nippan, had long been the primary source for Japanese animation videos. At first, Books Nippan simply brought to America those items that would sell to fans who were so fanatic that they didn't care that they couldn't understand the language. U.S. Renditions was set up to produce the items for a larger market.

Its first two releases came out in March of this year: *Gunbuster* and *Dangaio*. *Gunbuster* contains the first two half hours of a type of science fiction that is still rare in America—teen girls' outer space romantic drama. *Dangaio* is a more traditional comic book adventure about interstellar teenage superheroes.

U.S. Renditions was built around Southern California college students David Riddick and Robert Napton. Riddick discovered Japanese animation while a student at Long Beach State University in 1984, and began collecting OAVs. As a fan project, he did a translation script of the entire dialogue of a movie, which impressed Books Nippan—where he bought his videos. Soon after, he joined its staff and went on to head U.S. Renditions.

The company's first release was an LP record of *Robotech*'s cartoon music, now out as a CD. Riddick then brought in Napton, a college fan club friend and cinematography student, and together they tried to produce a dubbed or subtitled animation video—but their productions all stalled.

"Originally, we wanted to release the popular three video *Iczer-1* series in English, edited into a single tape," Napton says. "But negotiating with the Japanese companies to do anything in this country is very hard. We thought we were going to get *Iczer-1* and even advertised it. But we couldn't get a final commitment from Japan and finally canceled it."

Two other projects went right up to the contract signing stage before the Japanese owners backed out. Then U.S. Renditions made contact with Bandai Media Division (BMD), one of Japan's largest producers of video software, and with Gainax, Ltd., the studio that created *Gunbuster* for BMD. After that, things went more smoothly.

Riddick and Napton took a literal transcription of the *Gunbuster* dialogue and smoothed it out into a modern English script for the American video release after meeting and talking with Toshio Okada, the head of Gainax, who wrote the original screenplay.

"This is the end result of what began for us five years ago as a fan club activity to promote Japanese animation in an intelligent and creative manner," Napton adds. "We hope that there will be more, but we've finally done something we can show to the Japanese creators and be proud of.

"U.S. Renditions was also formed to counter the bad publicity Books Nippan has with high prices," Napton adds. "A lot of fans don't realize that these are due to the high prices of videos in Japan. The Japanese retail price of *Gunbuster* is about $80 or $90, so we are way undercutting it."

A fan group in North Carolina has just announced a new company, AnimEigo, Inc., which will also produce and distribute authorized English subtitled Japanese OAVs. Its first release is *Madox-01,* an SF comedy drama, priced at a similar $39.95.

It remains to be seen whether subtitled Japanese animation videos will be accepted by the American home video industry, but they are already popular in the comic book specialty shops.

Of course, any fan organization is going to have its publications, and the Japanimation fans, after years of publishing club bulletins and newsletters, now have *Animag: The Magazine of Japanese Animation,* which began in 1987 in the San Francisco Bay area. There is also *Markalite,* a new magazine aimed at fans of Japanese live action SF and fantasy cinema (e.g., the *Godzilla* movies and *Ultraman* TV series), which covers animation as well.

Fifteen years ago, Japanese animation was virtually unheard of in America. Today, there are 50,000 to 60,000 fans of it, according to Books Nippan's sales estimates—which are based on the appeal of the raw Japanese videos alone. But now as it moves into dubbed theatrical features and subtitled videos, the cult is growing into animation's mainstream.

Anime Licensing Grows Up
Animation Magazine no. 46, June/July 1996.

The earliest anime licensing in America, for the syndicated TV programs of the 1960s such as *Astro Boy* and *Prince Planet,* was so sparse as to be virtually nonexistent. Licensing really started with the second anime wave of the late 1970s to mid-1980s, from *Battle of the Planets* to *Robotech.*

The marketing of these children's television cartoons consisted of the usual toys, games, coloring and comic books, and similar juvenile items. The only category that stood out was the transforming giant-robot and battle-suit action figures. These started with Mattel's line of *Shogun Warriors* giant robots around 1977 and 1978, and peaked around 1984 and 1985 with *Voltron: Defender of the Universe!* and *Robotech.* Some of the more complex toys cost in the $30–$40 range.

Children's television anime continues to be popular. *Dragon Ball* and *Sailor Moon* are the current standard-bearers of this kind of Japanese animation. To most Americans, however, anime is a decidedly different and more sophisticated genre. It is now developing licensing to fit this market.

Anime fandom evolved and coalesced during the 1980s as an underground cult, part of costumed-hero comics and science-fiction fandom, before it was ready to stand on its own. The earliest licensing, by new companies started by anime fans themselves, was for American theatrical and video distribution rights and manga (comic book) translation rights, during 1988–89. The first authorized anime T-shirts and enameled pins appeared during 1989 (there had been unauthorized fan-produced shirts and pins since the mid-'80s). The first anime videotapes came out in 1990.

By 1992, the specialty companies were doing well enough to expand into other areas of licensing—areas that reflect anime fandom's idealized self-image as mature college students or recent graduates, often newly independent swingers who are not yet with family obligations.

Today's anime licensing is typified by computer mouse pads and screen savers, telephone cards, and model kits in the $100–$150 range for advanced model builders. Anime connoisseurs can decorate their walls with anime theatrical-feature movie posters, anime-character art prints, original production cels or limited-edition serigraph cels. They can read English-translated Japanese manga or original American-written and drawn comic books featuring licensed Japanese cartoon characters, while listening to anime music CDs on their stereos. There are anime-character pillowcases and sheets for their bedrooms, and towels and bathmats for their bathrooms.

These are all licensed, American-manufactured items (except for the production cels). And this is minuscule compared to the Japanese imports that are available through the handful (so far) of anime and manga specialty shops, which exist mainly through mail-order sales and sales at comics-fandom and anime-fandom conventions. The quantity, variety, and size of the market is still growing.

The World's Biggest Animation Home Video Market?
Animation World Magazine 2, no. 8, November 1997.

The home video market for animation in America has basically grown out of nowhere during the last ten years. It started largely with cheaply produced videos of minor television cartoons and old, public-domain theatrical shorts. Today, virtually all of the best animated features ever made in America are available on video, with an increasing number of high-quality features being produced especially for video release by Disney and other top studios.

However, the Japanese animation video market is rumored to eclipse America's. The latest issue (Summer 1996) of *The Whole Toon Catalog,* which purports to include every commercial animation video currently in print in America, includes fifty-one pages of mostly American animation, mixed with a few American releases of British, Italian, Hungarian, and other international animations. This is followed by a separate thirty-three-page section of "Japanimation," American editions of Japanese animation videos. These are just the Japanese titles which have been bought for American release! How large is the complete animation video market in Japan?

A Look into *Anime V*

It is big! Japan, with a population of approximately 126 million to the United States' 266 million, has almost three times as many video stores. Video sales and rentals are dominated by live-action titles, but the animation market is big enough that there are specialty magazines dedicated to animation video buyers alone. The oldest and most informative of these is *Anime V* (for Animation Video), which has been published since 1985 and currently averages 140 pages per month. Much of this is advertising, but there is a very informative log of animation video releases each month, divided into five categories.

According to *Anime V*'s two most recent logs, for July and August 1997, there were thirteen releases in July and eight in August, of animation titles produced for direct-to-video sales for general audiences. There were three releases in July and three in August, in a catchall category combining videos of Japanese animated theatrical films, television special movies, and Japanese releases of foreign animation. This latter category included Pixar's *Tiny Toy Stories* in August. There were twenty-two releases in July and twenty-six in August of videos of Japanese half-hour television cartoon episodes. Adult direct-to-video animation accounted for five releases in July, and ten in August. ("Adult" means explicit pornography, including the notorious "tentacle rape" horror fantasies. Japanese social customs allow mildly erotic humor, including brief nude shower scenes, in television cartoons and general-audience videos designed for adolescents. This is why so many of the "anime" videos currently appearing in America for the teen superhero/science-fiction market carry a warning label, "Contains violence and nudity. Parental guidance suggested.") The final category, another catch-all for animated music videos, videos of live concerts by voice actresses singing animation theme songs, and "the making of" specials on the production of major animated features, included two releases in July and two more in August.

Anime V publishes an annual catalog each February of all the new direct-to-video animation releases of the past year. This year's catalog for the 1996 releases lists 233 videos. These include only 122 different titles; many were popular series running to a half-dozen or more video volumes. The catalog also keys these to a variety of subject categories, including "science fiction" (outer space adventure), "mecha" (giant robots), "action" (sports, detective

Anime V magazine had been published monthly for over ten years when this article was written in 1997. In October 1998 it changed its name to the English-titled *Looker: The Emotional Graphic Magazine* (who knows what that was supposed to mean?), and it ceased publication in May 1999. I miss it. No other Japanese anime magazine has covered the home video scene as thoroughly, with checklists of every anime video, laser disc, and DVD released each month, whether OAV productions or video releases of TV, theatrical, and foreign animation, whether first-time releases or reissues. ■

dramas), "military drama," "fantasy," "rebellious youth" (teen gangs), "TV adaptations" (sequels to popular television cartoons), "literary adaptations" (animation based upon either classic novels or comic books), "games" (dramatizations of video games), "adult," and more.

Distribution Channels

A scan of the distributors' labels is similarly informative. Bandai Visual covers the broadest range, including approximately equal numbers of animated direct-to-video titles, movies, and television series. King Records, Pioneer LDC, VAP, and Star Child also distribute across this range, but in smaller quantities. Toei Video, a branch of Toei Animation, the largest animation studio in Japan, distributes a similar mixture. Virtually all of its videos, whether direct-to-video titles, movies, or television cartoons, are of in-house animation, in comparison to other distributors' videos, which are produced by a large number of animation studios. Pink Pineapple concentrates on the distribution of adult animation, both produced by its own studio or by one or two similar specialty animation houses. K.S.S. specializes in direct-to-video animation, both for its own distribution and for other distributors.

But relying upon *Anime V* alone would result in a highly distorted picture of the Japanese animation video market. The magazine is slanted for the direct-to-video market, which is geared toward action-adventure usually involving science-fictional or superhero dramatics which would require prohibitive special-effects budgets in live-action. Many of these are produced for a niche market and have comparatively small sales.

Disney! Disney! Disney!

A visit to a major Japanese video store presents quite a different picture. Disney! Disney! Disney! Disney is barely mentioned in *Anime V*, but every video store catering to the general public features flats and display stands in eye-catching positions for Disney videos. Disney claimed in a 1996 press release that it controls 65 percent of the Japanese market for childrens' videotapes. This presumably includes Disney's live-action videos as well.

Disney has also just begun its distribution of the feature films of Hayao Miyazaki, Japan's most beloved and highest-grossing theatrical animation director. Disney obtained the worldwide video rights to Miyazaki's features produced by Studio Ghibli (i.e., his movies of the past dozen years) in a highly publicized acquisition in July 1996. Miyazaki's animated movies have heretofore been available on video only at rental prices (usually ¥16,000/$140). The new Disney distribution makes Miyazaki available in the ¥3,000/$25 sell-through price range for the first time.

As elsewhere, the primary audiences for animation videos in Japan are the family-oriented viewers. MGM's *Tom and Jerry* cartoons are moving briskly in a current video marketing campaign. Warner Bros. also has its own video distribution for Japanese releases of its American titles, which includes much of its animation backlist. The Japanese spend their yen on these and the domestic animation titles that are similarly family- and child-oriented. The television cartoons *Sailor Moon* and *Dragon Ball* (both Toei Animation titles) were picked up for American and other international television outlets a couple of years ago because of their tremendous popularity in Japan, both on television and in video sales.

Inside a Video Store

Video stores in Japan have "anime" sections as well, but they are much larger since they include many titles that have not been sold to international markets. The average video store bases its orders on the expected popularity of each title, but there is usually a standard minimum order for 100 units of every animation title. Unless a title is unusually popular, it is not re-ordered. There are enough new animation releases each month to keep the shelves filled. Therefore most general video stores have a constant turnover and only the newest animation videos can be found. Shoppers who want older titles or a wider range of selections can find animation specialty video shops in most cities. These are similar to comic-book shops in America, catering to the older teens and "young salarymen" who are the market for the action/ adventure direct-to-video titles. In addition to the videos, animation fans can find all of the associated merchandise such as animation magazines, reference books, posters, animation-character telephone cards, action figures and toys, and usually a bin of cheap original production cels from the latest releases.

Sell-through prices for the mass-marketed family titles, such as Disney's, are in the ¥3,000/$25 range. A major television cartoon series may offer four half-hour episodes (about 100 minutes) for ¥7,000/$60 on its initial release, while the series is still topping the television popularity charts. Video re-releases a few years later drop to the ¥3,000 level. New direct-to-video releases (known as OAV titles, for "original animation video"), usually in the half-hour to forty-five-minute range, cost ¥5,000/$45 to ¥6,000/$55. Up to now, Japanese video releases of major theatrical animated features such as *Akira, Ghost in the Shell,* or Miyazaki's movies have been limited to rental prices in the ¥10,000/$85 to ¥16,000/$140 range. It will be interesting to see how Disney's marketing of Miyazaki's features will affect the entire range of theatrical animated feature videos.

For the public which prefers to rent rather than own, overnight rentals of videos (live and animation) are comparable to American prices; ¥200/$1.75 to ¥300/$2.50. ¥500/$4.25 is standard for a two-night rental of a popular new title.

The animation video market in Japan is large because the Japanese video market in general is huge. In addition, the Japanese public does not share the American preconception that "animation is just for kids," so there is no loss of face for teens or adults to buy or rent cartoon videos for themselves.

The American video market is just experimenting with animation for any section besides children. As the popularity of Japanese animation videos for teen and adult viewers increases in America, and is joined by video releases of theatrical features like *Heavy Metal* and *Beavis and Butt-head Do America*, direct-to-video titles like *Batman: Mask of the Phantasm*, and video releases of the more mature television productions such as *Spawn, Spicy City, Aeon Flux*, and *The Simpsons*, the American animation home-video market should expand in size and respectability until it can support original production just as the theatrical and television markets do.

Letter to the Editor: "Anime" as Pejorative
Protoculture Addicts no. 49, April 1998.

Dear *PA:*

PA no. 48 has just arrived. "Anime Under Fire" continues to be an excellent guide to critiques of the violence in anime, and how to prepare a response to them. However, a new kind of criticism has recently arisen, and I hope that you will be addressing this as well.

This is professional criticism from the American animation industry. Here are two actual examples that you can cite.

Daily Variety, Friday, February 13, 1998, page A6, has a news item (press release), "*Princess* Goes West," about Disney's planned video release of Miyazaki's *Princess Mononoke*. Michael Johnson, president of Buena Vista Home Entertainment, is quoted: "This is not anime," says Johnson,

---

Protoculture Addicts, the oldest American anime professional specialty magazine, had been publishing a series of articles, "Anime Under Fire," for several issues. These were designed to educate anime fans to intelligently respond to criticism from authority figures such as parents and teachers that anime was nothing but mindless cartoon violence. The articles were strongly oriented around the position that most critical authority figures really knew little or nothing about anime, while those who knew it well found it full of positive values. This position was severely damaged by the December 1997 "*Pokemon* sends children to the hospital" headlines, and the resulting condemnation of all anime by American entertainment-industry executives who could be presumed to be knowledgeable about it. I felt that American anime supporters needed to mobilize a strong defense immediately, so I wrote this letter. The response is by *PA*'s publisher.

As it turned out, we needn't have worried. As soon as the entertainment industry noted the mega-popularity of *Pokemon* and all its licensed merchandise, the criticism abruptly stopped. The same TV networks and cable channels that "don't air the graphic Japanese cartoons known as 'anime'" hastened to sign up the American rights to *Pokemon* and such imitators as *Digimon* and *Monster Rancher*. Money talks! ■

"It's not effect-driven or violence-driven. This is true, full-cel, story-driven animation that appeals to an older audience. *Princess Mononoke* is playing to a 16- to 25-year-old audience in Japan."

USA Today, Friday, December 19, 1997, page D1, has a news story, "U.S. kids safe from cartoon seizures," on the *Pocket Monsters*-caused seizures among 700 children in Japan. The vice president of programming for the Cartoon Network is quoted reassuring the public that our children are safe because anime is not shown on American TV. "CBS, ABC, NBC, Fox, UPN and WB don't air the graphic Japanese cartoons known as 'anime.' Nor do the major cable outlets for cartoons: Nickelodeon, The Cartoon Network and the Disney Channel.

"Where you will find anime is in video stores, where anime sections are stocked with imports of Japanese cartoons."

"Japan animation is so different from what airs here," says Mike Lazzo, vice president of programming for the Cartoon Network. "It's far edgier, adult and violent. Anime isn't very story-based and is driven by intense moments. The story is hard to follow.

"The Cartoon Network does air Japan's *Speed Racer*, made thirty years ago, and *Voltron*, about ten years old, but neither show is in the style of anime."

So Disney implies that *Princess Mononoke* is too good to be anime, while the Cartoon Network claims that anime is for audiences who only want mindless violence and do not care about intelligent stories or characterizations. Their answer to having it pointed out that they show *Speed Racer* and *Voltron* is to imply, "But these are *good* programs, therefore they can't be anime."

These statements are probably due less to ignorance than to deliberately cynical marketing policies. There is a small-business proverb: "When the Big Companies start attacking you instead of ignoring you, you must be doing something right." If the Cartoon Network was showing *Sailor Moon*, would it also claim that *Sailor Moon* is good so it can't be anime?

Nevertheless, this is ammunition that those who do want to attack anime can use. This tends to define anime as meaning "trashy, violent animation" more than Japanese animation, and to confirm their worst accusations. How can we fans claim that anime has worthwhile values when experienced American animation-industry executives have gone on record to explain why it's really not worth watching?

This also indicates the negative image that anime has among the general public. When Harmony Gold and Carl Macek produced *Robotech* in the mid-1980s, they promoted its anime origin (and indirectly helped to introduce the word to America) as a positive asset. Today the TV and home-video companies feel a need to cover up the fact that their Japanese cartoons are really anime. They obviously consider it safer to deny they are selling anime than to try to explain that their anime is of high quality. Unfortunately, that leaves it to us to explain that these criticisms of anime are really part of a marketing strategy rather than objective critical analysis.

Fannishly,

Frederick Patten, Culver City, Calif.

Response

Thanks Fred for presenting this polemic far better than I could have. It is a delicate problem to agree on the definition of *anime*. Obviously, it should be left to the people of the industry (anime releasers and magazines), to the fans, but NOT to those who have interest in reducing it for their benefits (Broadcasters and Disney). *Anime* is "all Japanese animation," nothing more, nothing less. There is enough confusion with some people using *anime* and *manga* without distinction!

Claude J. Pelletier

The Anime "Porn" Market
Animation World Magazine 3, no. 4, July 1998.

What Is Anime?

There is a general awareness today that the market for anime is growing in the United States. However, there is less awareness—or agreement—as to exactly what "anime" is.

"Anime" or "animé" is the Japanese word for cinematic animation, taken from the English word "animation." To the anime enthusiasts in America, "anime" means any animation produced in Japan, no matter the intended audience—whether a TV cartoon series for young children (*Samurai Pizza Cats* and *Sailor Moon* are two recent examples, and there was a Japanese TV animated serialization of *Heidi, Girl of the Alps* in 1974, eight years before Hanna-Barbera's *Heidi's Song* feature), an animated adult cultural feature (there have been two feature-length animated productions of *The Diary of Anne Frank*), or an action-adventure thriller filled with violence and sexual situations.

However, since the main American market for anime consists of teens and adults looking for light entertainment, that is just about all that gets licensed for American release. Most juvenile cartoons and the adult intellectual animation tends to remain on their studios' shelves in Tokyo. As a result, a perception has been growing in America that "anime" is synonymous with violent, sexual animation only. A February 1, 1998, *New York Times* story on contemporary Japanese animation comments on its wide range, but emphasizes that "animé refers strictly to 'adult' Japanese animation . . . racy, battle-ravaged animé . . . 'pornimation,' as some of the steamier romps with Western-looking women, from college girls to the princesses of sci-fi legend, are sometimes called in the United States . . . animé is all violence and sex . . ."

The article also refers to one of Japan's most popular children's TV cartoon stars, the robot cat Doraemon, as "scantily clad," an innuendo equivalent to identifying Donald Duck or Porky Pig only as cartoon characters who go about in public without any pants on.

This has reached the point that major American animation presenters with Japanese titles in their lineups are trying to disassociate themselves from the "anime" label. Michael Johnson, president of Buena Vista Home Entertainment, said in *Daily Variety*, February 13, 1998, of Disney's forthcoming U.S. release of Hayao Miyazaki's 1997 Japanese box-office-record-breaking feature *Princess Mononoke,* "This is not anime . . . it's not effects-driven or violence-driven." Mike Lazzo, vice president of programming for the Cartoon Network, assured the public in *USA Today*, December 18, 1997, that anime is not shown on American TV. "Japan animation is so different from what airs here . . . It's far edgier, adult, and violent. Anime isn't very story-based . . . The story is hard to follow." When it was pointed out that the Cartoon Network shows *Speed Racer* and *Voltron,* both juvenile action-adventure TV cartoon series produced in Japan, Lazzo said that "neither show is in the style of anime." (In the original Japanese version of *Voltron,* the Earth is completely destroyed by the space villains. That episode is omitted from the heavily rewritten American version.)

This evolution of the definition of anime will doubtlessly be intensified by the increasing importation of Japanese animated adult erotic fare, to mix with the action-adventure anime market. When the first anime-genre videos were released in 1990–91 through mail order and direct sales to the comic-book fandom specialty stores, it was understood by this market that these were animated equivalents of movies like *The Terminator* and *Die Hard,* full of explosions, blood-'n'-guts, adult dialogue, and often a brief risqué nude scene. Around 1994 the anime videos expanded into the major video mass-market chains and became accessible to the general public, which tends to assume automatically that all animated cartoons are safe for children. This resulted in the necessity for warning advisories on the video boxes such as "Contains violence and nudity," "Contains brief nudity and mature situations. Parental discretion advised," and "Recommended for mature viewers." But these did not yet include explicit sexual titles.

Anime's Beginnings

Asian attitudes towards eroticism have always been more open than those of the West. One of the earliest Japanese TV cartoon series was *Sennin Buraku* (*Hermits' Village*), a fifteen-minute late-night erotic humor anthology roughly equivalent to "*Playboy*'s Ribald Classics" that aired from 11:40 to 11:55 P.M. for two months in 1963. Osamu Tezuka (1928–1989) is revered as the father of both Japan's comic book and animation industries, writing and illustrating the series known in America as *Astro Boy* and *Kimba the White Lion.* It is less well known that Tezuka also tried to create a popular acceptance of animation with intellectually artistic mature themes. In November 1966, he produced *Pictures at an Exhibition,* a *Fantasia*-like transformation of Mussorgsky's famous composition into a modern political cartoon, presenting the musical "pictures" as satirical portraits of ruthless corporate bosses, affectedly aesthetic artists, scandal-mongering journalists, rebellious teens, vapid TV personalities, and the like. In June 1969, he released *One Thousand and One Nights,* a 128-minute adult adaptation of *The Arabian Nights* full of adventure, Rabelaisian humor, and all the erotic innuendo of the original Persian tales. This was a major theatrical release, intended by Tezuka to be comparable to Western live-action movie adaptations of such adult literary classics as *Lady Chatterley's Lover* and *Lolita.*

Japanese animated explicitly adult cartoons developed along with the general animated direct-to-video market. The first Japanese original animation video (OAV) title was a science-fiction drama, *Dallos,* released in December 1983. The third OAV release, on February 21, 1984, was *Lolita Anime I: Yuki no Kurenai Kesho * Shojo Bara Kei* (freely translated, *Crimson Cosmetic on the Snow * Young Girls' Rose Punishment*). This half-hour video, first in the short-lived *Wonder Kids* erotic anime series, consisted of two fifteen-minute dramas of rape and sadistic sexual torture/murder of schoolgirls, whose spirits exact a gruesome supernatural vengeance. Of the seventeen OAVs released during 1984, six were "general" and eleven were pornographic. In 1985, after the viability of the direct-video market for action-adventure anime had been established, the total was twenty-eight action-adventure titles to just another eleven porno titles. The Japanese domestic OAV market has grown accordingly, over the past decade, with 1997's output of 162 "general" titles and sixty-two erotic titles (including some multiple volumes of series) being about the average ratio.

The Anime Porn Players

There are differences of opinion as to what constitutes "anime porn," but four anime specialty video producers have special labels for their releases, which primarily emphasize nudity and explicit adult sexual situations. These are A.D. Vision's SoftCel Pictures series, Central Park Media's Anime 18 series, Media Blasters's Kitty Media series, and The Right Stuf International's Critical Mass series.

The other anime specialty producers state that they are not interested in getting into the video erotica market. However, most of them have at least one adult feature in their catalogues which includes a brief but intense "shocker" scene such as a graphic rape. For some sensibilities, this is enough to establish the movie as pornography.

Two such companies, Manga Entertainment and Streamline Pictures, feel that their video box art makes it clear to the public that their anime titles are adult action-adventure rather than eroticism. Chicago-based Manga Entertainment's media relations representative, Danielle Opyt, says: "Due to the basic nature of anime, all of our videos bear a distinctive sticker showing our Manga Man cartoon spokesman and our flaming Manga Entertainment logo, with the warning, "Manga Man Says Parental Discretion Advised." This covers everything from strong language to brief nudity and graphic violence." Carl Macek, president of Streamline Pictures in Los Angeles, says: "We have always presented anime for a wide range of tastes, from child-friendly to movies whose main characters are engaged in such obviously mature activities as smoking and drinking cocktails. Those that contain brief but intense adult situations carry an appropriate warning notice. In 1994 we arranged with Orion Home Video to distribute most of our titles, and Orion created a "not for kids" sticker, which it has automatically put on all the Streamline video boxes. This includes the whole range from PG-level content to R-level content."

Central Park Media and *Urotsukidoji*

The best-known "anime porn" title, and the one which started the American adult video market, is the notorious *Urotsukidoji: Legend of the Overfiend,* first of the "erotic grotesque" (more popularly known as "tentacle porn") genre. This began in Japan with the January 1987 release of the first of a five-video adaptation of Toshio Maeda's horror comic-book novel, produced by West Cape Corporation, best known in America for its *Space Cruiser Yamato/ Star Blazers* space adventure series. *Urotsukidoji* is about the invasion and conquest of Earth by oversexed supernatural demons who enslave humanity and use our women as their sexual playthings. Generations pass. There are human plots to destroy the monsters, which often attempt to take advantage of their sexual obsession and turn it against them. The tale becomes more complex when a third group eventually emerges of human/monster crossbreeds, rejected by both parents. They are intellectually inclined to join the humans, but their intense carnal drives are still too uncontrollable to make them comfortable allies for the human rebels. Sequels eventually extended the series to eleven videos.

The first *Urotsukidoji* episode, a complete story in itself, was dubbed into English by John O'Donnell, president of New York City's Central Park Media (CPM) video distribution company, which had been releasing adventure anime videos since October 1991 under its U.S. Manga Corps label. *Urotsukidoji* was actually premiered theatrically in London at a two-day anime film festival on October 30–31, 1992, where it played to sold-out screenings on both days. Its American release was at NYC's Angelika Theater in January 1993. It began a national art theater tour in June, which resulted in local press coverage practically everywhere it played about how "Japanese animation certainly isn't like American animation!" CPM scheduled it for a video release in August 1993.

According to Valerio Rossi, CPM's marketing/production coordinator, it was the company's realization that *Urotsukidoji* was too sexually intense to fit into its U.S. Manga Corps "boys' adventure" line that led to the creation of the separate Anime 18 label. All five episodes were released, both on videotape and laser disc, between August and December 1993. They sold so well, and generated so many requests from anime fans for more of the same nature, that CPM's Anime 18 releases have been appearing steadily since then. Plus, the original 35 mm *Urotsukidoji* story is still popular on the art theater circuit as a midnight feature.

A Closer Look at the Labeling

A.D. Vision, in Houston, released its first anime video in November 1992. For the next two years, its A.D. Vision Films label included both regular action-adventure anime and some of the milder erotic comedies such as *F³: Frantic, Frustrated and Female,* often with editing of brief explicit scenes to make them suitable for a "Parental Guidance Recommended" warning. The company's first release under its SoftCel Pictures label, reserved for an emphasis of explicit adult scenes, was *The Legend of Lyon* in November 1994. A.D. Vision put out nineteen SoftCel Pictures releases during 1995 and twelve through the first half of 1996, some of which were rereleases of previous A.D. Vision titles in their unedited form.

Janice Williams, A.D. Vision's production coordinator, says that the company has had very few SoftCel releases since June 1996, but that is not because they have not sold well. "They are almost all still in print and selling very consistently. A.D. Vision made a tremendous investment in mid-1996 to license a great quantity of general anime titles. We are currently working through a big production backlog getting them onto the market before we can produce new SoftCel releases. We constantly get e-mail requests from our fans asking when we are going to put out a new SoftCel title. We will definitely resume them soon."

The Right Stuf International, in Des Moines, does not consider itself really in the adult market. President Shawne Kleckner says: "Manga Entertainment released an edited version of *Violence Jack* and a lot of fans wanted to see it uncut, so we arranged with ME to release an unedited edition (in November 1996). It was too intense for our regular Right Stuf line, so we created the Critical Mass label. Then in 1997 we had a chance to license a really funny adult comedy, *Weather Report Girl,* and we did not want to pass it up. We do not have any specific plans at present for any more Critical Mass releases, but there will doubtlessly be more when the right titles come along."

The newest anime specialty producer/distributor, New York City's Media Blasters, actually began with its adult line, Kitty Media. President John Sirabella says: "Our first video was *Rei-Lan: Orchid Emblem,* on May 6, 1997, and we have released at least one Kitty Media title every month since then. I was already working in the anime field with the Software Sculptors line through Central Park Media, and I saw that there was a large Japanese adult animation source which was still relatively untapped for this country.

The potential American market was very good, but the existing anime distributors were only putting out a few releases. They had solid general release catalogues, and they were nervous about the repercussions of getting into the adult market in a major way. So I started Kitty Media to be the best and biggest company in the adult anime market. Now that we have a solid backlist of over a dozen titles, we are expanding Media Blasters beyond the Kitty Media label. Our first AnimeWorks label release, which carries a 'Kid Safe = For Audiences of All Ages!' logo, was *Ninku the Movie* in March. We are also starting a couple of live-action labels, Kaiju Productions for monster movies in the *Godzilla* and *Rodan* vein, and Tokyo Shock for the Japanese equivalent of the Hong Kong action thrillers. It has been the success of Kitty Media that is making this growth possible."

Anime Does Not Equal Pornography

A.D. Vision, Central Park Media, and Media Blasters are all happy with the adult market, but they are not as pleased with the public's perception of it as synonymous with pornography. Sirabella says that, "There are varying degrees of adult," some of which do not involve eroticism at all. "One of our new Kitty Media releases, *Dark Cat*, is definitely not for children. It is a shocking horror film with intense violence, but no sexual situations."

Two CPM staffers are more perturbed by the public's dismissal of all anime as pornography. Valerio Rossi says: "Frankly, we are considerably disturbed by what seems to be a growing trend to consider anime as nothing but sex and brutal violence. That is a complete distortion of CPM's catalogue. Our Anime 18 titles, as popular as they are, account for only about 10 percent of our anime releases; between 5 and 10 percent. CPM releases almost a half-dozen anime videos a month among four different labels. There are two or three U.S. Manga Corps releases and one or two Software Sculptors releases every month. Those are popular action-adventure, horror, or comedy titles. The U.S. Manga Corps anime is more mainstream, and the Software Sculptors titles are more 'alternate' or artistic. Our main Central Park Media label, which is our general label for mostly non-Japanese videos such as live-action documentaries, only includes an anime release every two or three months. Those are usually adaptations of Japanese literary works, such as *Grave of the Fireflies* and the *Animated Classics of Japanese Literature* series. Our Anime 18 titles average only one a month or six weeks, maybe eight or nine a year. So that's only eight or nine adult titles compared to forty-five to fifty anime titles a year without sexual content. That makes it very frustrating to hear someone say, 'Oh, yeah, I know about anime. It's those porno cartoons from Japan.'"

Jeff Zitomer, CPM's supervisor of production and marketing, feels that even the anime that emphasizes sexual content is misrepresented by being equated with pornography. "There is an important misconception in thinking of the adult anime labels like Anime 18 as animated pornography.

If you look at actual pornographic videos, you'll see that they have no real story, no characters or character development, no attempt at imaginative camerawork—just close-ups of straight sex. The adult anime market is actually aimed at viewers who want intense adult situations in real stories, whether it's dramatic action or humor. There are eleven video volumes in the *Urotsukidoji* saga, and its story progress is actually more important than the sex. You could fast-forward through the naughty scenes and still have an interesting story to follow. The sexual nature of the story puts it into a unique category; it's not just a horror movie with a lot of sex scenes that could be taken out without changing the story. The Anime 18 line is not a porno line as much as a next step in animated storytelling for mature audiences, as the next step in adventure films beyond PG is an R rating. Our Anime 18 titles are for adults who want even more mature situations and dialogue in their suspense or their comedy, but who definitely want a story and interesting characters rather than just naked bodies engaged in sex."

U.S. Restrictions

However, the sexual content of the adult anime market is undeniable. This has created some special emphases in acquisitions and marketing. John Sirabella says: "There are definite legal restrictions which must be taken into consideration. The main problem is that U.S. child pornography laws forbid showing children in sexual situations, so all the characters in erotic videos have to look eighteen or older. But this is not a restriction in Japan. Also, Japanese women are so small that even one who is supposed to be an adult may look underage by our standards. We have to turn down more adult anime titles than we can accept because the characters look too young to be called adult."

CPM's Jeff Zitomer concurs. Due to the American tendency to assume that cartoons are for kids, CPM is very careful that the packaging of every Anime 18 video makes it unmistakable that it contains adult content and is for adult viewers only. This is done in a tasteful manner which emphasizes the story's dramatic content rather than a sex-appeal hard-sell, but which leaves no way that a parent or a video-shop clerk could mistake it as suitable for children or young teens. Also, due to recent federal child pornography laws, the packaging and a special video header at the beginning of the tape states clearly that the entire cast is nineteen years old or older.

The adult anime market exists primarily through direct sales: mail order to customers, and wholesale to specialty shops which cater to anime and to comic book fans. CPM's Joe Cirillo, sub-licensing coordinator, says that at the anime fan weekend conventions which are spreading around America: "The Anime 18 titles often almost sell out by the end of the first day." All three companies refer to their adult labels as safe, steady sellers. In comparison with the general anime market, there are no best-sellers but no bombs, either. Also, there are almost no adult titles that start off selling strongly but soon taper off. They just sell steadily—and without requiring the advertising expenditures needed to promote the general anime titles.

Speaking of the comic-book specialty market, CPM is also a publisher (as CPM Manga) of American editions of Japanese adventure comic books, especially those which are the sources of the anime titles which CPM sells. The company is about to launch an adult label, CPM Manga X, beginning in July 1998. The May issue of Diamond Dialogue, the promotional magazine of Diamond Comics Distributor, describes CPM Manga X as " . . . bringing Japan's best adult manga to American audiences . . . in a 32-page, black-and-white format priced at $2.95 per issue. The line will open with the English translation of the manga version of the adult anime classic *Urotsukidoji: Legend of the Overfiend* no. 1, written and illustrated by Toshio Maeda. The manga will contain many scenes which were not included in the video series . . . (A highlight of the first issue for *Overfiend* fans will be a manga treatment of the film's classic scene in the nurse's office.)"

On the whole, the anime distributors have not been able to get their adult labels into the general home video market yet. Cirillo refers to the major video distributors and video retail chains as "staying clear" of adult anime. Sirabella says that some distributors and chains carry the Kitty Media titles, while others will not take them. All three anime distributors try to produce two versions of their releases (but with some titles this is not possible), one uncut for the adult market and a "general release" version that will be acceptable to the chains like MusicLand and Sam Goody's.

Still Outside the Mainstream

The general American adult TV/video market remains largely untapped. Cirillo says that *Penthouse Comix* has reviewed some of the Anime 18 videos, but that the adult pay-per-view TV channels are mostly not interested. Sales to the American erotic-shop market have been very small, and the anime distributors have mixed feelings about trying to increase them. Sirabella says: "The adult book and video specialty shops have a bad reputation for non-payment. Also, the American erotic video industry is used to price-points of $9.95 or less, which we can't sell at. And the anime specialty industry is having enough trouble with anime's reputation as nothing but sex and violence for us to want to risk making it all look even more like pornography through guilt by association by increasing anime's visibility in the sex shops."

(Intriguingly, the first adult anime to be released in America appeared in adult bookshops in the late 1980s. *The Brothers Grime* was a three-video cartoon-pornography series produced by Excalibur Films, Inc., of Fullerton, Calif., in 1986, 1987, and 1988, using titles primarily from Japan's *Cream Lemon* series, the most popular of Japan's erotic anime before *Urotsukidoji*. Since Excalibur Films had no creative ties to the anime field, there was no attempt to remain faithful to the original versions. A secretary at Excalibur says that *The Brothers Grime* is still selling well today, and she has no idea why the company never followed those three videos up with more anime imports. The *Cream Lemon* series is one in which most of the characters appear to be much too young to be plausibly described as over 18.)

None of the anime distributors are willing to discuss sales figures, but John Sirabella makes a broad estimate that adult anime is about 30 to 40 percent of the overall anime market. "If the general market is $100 million, that means that the adult videos are selling $30 million to $40 million a year." This is disputed by CPM's sales director, Mike Pascuzzi, who estimates that the adult sales only make 15 to 20 percent of the general market. "Don't forget that there are several other anime video releasers such as Viz Video, Pioneer, AnimEigo, and Urban Vision which do not have an adult label at all. They may have a few individual titles which require a 'mature audiences' warning due to R-level content, but they are not really in the adult market." This may be a difference in perception as to what constitutes the "adult anime market" as distinct from the general market. Would a raunchy adolescent comedy full of college-fraternity style humor such as panty raids, peeking into the womens' gym showers, and foul-mouthed dialogue, but no explicit sex, count as an adult or as a general sale?

Although the dividing line between general anime and adult anime may be vague, there is a definite adult market. All the anime companies producing for that market agree that sales are steady, and increase as a direct result of the number of titles available. There is no sign yet of any saturation level. As long as production in Japan turns out fifty or sixty new titles per year, there appears to be the potential for unlimited growth. Many, though not all, of the adult cartoon videos range from mild eroticism to explicit pornography. However, there does not seem to be a broad correlation between the anime pornography audience and the market for American-made stag cartoons and live-action sex films. The overlap so far is minor, and the American general erotic video/TV market does not seem to be interested in tapping into the lode of Japanese animated titles.

The immediate concern of the American anime industry is not expanding its adult market share as much as doing damage control to keep a public conception from solidifying that all anime is pornographic, which could be highly injurious to the potentially much larger market for general action-adventure anime. Ironically, anime enthusiasts—the hard-core fans as well as the manufacturers—have been citing for years the theatrical animation of Hayao Miyazaki as well as popular TV series such as *Speed Racer* and *Sailor Moon* as examples of the best in anime, which they have hoped will transcend the "anime cult" reputation and popularize Japanese animation with the general public. Now these titles are being marketed to the general public by major American animation purveyors who are denying that they are anime—who are promoting them as "much better than that notorious Japanese low-quality sex-and-violence anime." The next couple of years may see which definition of anime will become standardized in America.

Go to JAILED
Manga Max no. 3, February 1999.

Deny everything. Trust no one. What on Earth was the Japanese Animation Industry Legal Enforcement Division? Where did it come from? Where did it go? Fred Patten investigates.

On May 22, 1995, John O'Donnell of Central Park Media (CPM) announced the formation of the Japanese Animation Industry Legal Enforcement Division. "JAILED was established to combat the illegal sales and rental of unauthorized copies of copyrighted programs . . . belonging to the member companies." The members, as defined in the initial flurry of activity, consisted of practically every anime company active in the U.S. market at the time. "JAILED will," we were told, "prosecute suppliers who sell these versions to the public, whether via retail store, exhibition booth, or mail order."

This set off a firestorm of controversy. Despite assurances that its target was professional video pirates, rumors spread that JAILED was calling fan clubs which subtitled videos of anime not yet released in America and ordering them to cease and desist. Panels to explain JAILED at the 1995 U.S. anime conventions soon degenerated into arguments between defensive company representatives and hostile audiences.

At the AnimEAST convention of November 1995, CPM's Leslie Hyman announced that JAILED had just arranged the arrest of a major pirate of counterfeit anime videos. But that was JAILED's last public appearance. Today it is generally assumed that JAILED has faded away and that it was never more than a few self-important executives at the anime companies trying to bully the fans.

But was JAILED for real? "You bet," insists John O'Donnell. "The bust that Leslie Hyman announced in November 1995 had just taken place against Karate Center, on Eighth Avenue in Manhattan. Leslie, along with the police and FBI agents, raided the store and seized about 10,000 pirated anime cassettes. Our lawyer, Jules Zalon, who set JAILED up, prosecuted the case in court for about two years. It was just recently concluded, in our favor. The pirated videos were ordered destroyed, and we won a $400,000 judgment."

Why wasn't that publicized? "We ran into something called the law of unintended consequences," says O'Donnell. "JAILED was never aimed at fans. But everybody took it as an attack against fandom, and we couldn't tell them otherwise. So we realized it's better not to say anything in public—to work behind the scenes. JAILED still exists as a way for the anime companies to coordinate anti-piracy activity."

Yes, but not really as JAILED. A conversation with other anime companies reveals that they do indeed act to combat piracy. But JAILED is just O'Donnell's catchphrase for the informal cooperation between them. O'Donnell concedes that there are no actual JAILED employees or activities being conducted under the JAILED name.

When fans talk about piracy, they usually mean the circulation of the latest anime from Japan not yet available abroad. These are commonly copied among fans for just the cost of a blank tape and postage. These are often "fan subs," subtitled in English by a fan club.

Anime companies have mixed feelings about these. "Let's face it," says Shawne Kleckner of The Right Stuf International, "anime as an industry was born on the tradition of fans spreading around illegal video copies. What we're trying to do is close down the groups that are making fifty or 100 or 500 copies for sale outside fandom. Their markets are the swap meets and flea markets in areas where people aren't familiar with anime yet."

The companies usually wink at unauthorized videos if they are noncommercial. After all, many anime companies were themselves started by fans. "It's how I got started," says Media Blasters' John Sirabella. "It's hard to get mean with these guys. It's not a money thing with them. They feel they're doing something good for anime. They're college students; they're enthusiastic; they want to feel that they're involved in helping spread something cultural."

Fan subs invariably carry warnings like "Subtitled by fans for fans. Absolutely not for sale." Such videos are to be withdrawn as soon as a licensed video is available. "Most fans support the 'Code of the Subtitlers,'" says Gustav Baron, a clerk at Banzai Anime in Los Angeles. "Just a bare hint that an American company is considering a title will discourage many fan subbers from touching it. If a fan sub is made, the fans who get it will replace it with the commercial video when it comes out." As unlikely as such an idea may sound, Shawne Kleckner agrees: "When [The Right Stuf] released *Irresponsible Captain Tylor,* we offered an amnesty program. Fans who sent us their bootleg fan subs got a discount on the legitimate tapes. We got a big response!"

One reason that fans seem keen to replace their fan subs is that amateur subtitling degrades the video quality. Baron adds: "One of the most recent examples was *Slayers: The Motion Picture.* The fan sub was so poor visually that it probably increased the market for A.D. Vision's release. Dozens of fans commented as they bought it they were looking forward to actually seeing what the animation looked like."

But not all fans are idealistic. "On the first day of the 1996 Comic-Con in San Diego, " says John O'Donnell, "I went through the dealers' room together with Marvin Gleicher of Manga Entertainment. We saw a lot of bootleg anime videos. We made notes of all the tables selling illegal videos, gave the list to the administrators and asked them to get those bootlegs removed from sale. We wanted them off sale without any public confrontation."

John Sirabella goes further: "The fan subbers can't be so naïve as to believe their tapes aren't being picked up by the real pirates, who just laugh at their 'not to be sold' notice. The argument that fans turn in their fan subs when the commercial video comes out works about 50 percent of the time. I don't believe conventions should allow the showing of fan subs in their video rooms. That gives the impression that fan subs are legitimate. *Iria* was one of the most fan-subbed titles before CPM's release came out. It sold well, but it should have done better." Sirabella's view is supported by Rik Wall, owner of the Anime Cafe shop in Tacoma, Washington. "I have a problem with the fans who are reluctant to relinquish their fan subs. Even though they know a new title in Japan will be out commercially here soon, they want a fan sub now. Then when the American video comes out, they feel 'why spend money on another copy?'"

In a sense, it is the fans who are the front lines of JAILED's agents. Oliver Chin, director of sales and marketing at Viz Communications, says: "We rely very heavily on fans who see nothing wrong with noncommercial fan subs, but who consider it a breach of honor when they see fan subs or actual counterfeits sold. What usually happens is that fans notify Viz by e-mail that they've found somebody selling bootlegs. I go to that site if it's on the web, which it usually is. I note the particulars, then I send them an e-mail citing these particulars and telling them that it's illegal and that they must stop. I then send copies to all the other anime companies to let them know about this site—either because it's selling some of their titles, or for future reference. It's a common courtesy between companies. I've done this about a half-dozen times in the past year."

Kara Redmon, director of marketing at Urban Vision, confirms. "Yes, Oliver at Viz is constantly letting us know about pirated Urban Vision titles. We also hear regularly from Sharon Papa at ADV. Our most pirated titles have been *Gatchaman, Tekkaman,* and *Polymar.* I mostly contact the fans and ask them to stop distributing fan subs now that our licensed videos are out."

Brett Atwell, production assistant at A.D. Vision, says: "The fans are very cooperative. They notify us when they see bootlegs being sold, so we don't have to really set up an anime Gestapo and go out and track them down ourselves. We make a sharp distinction between fan subs and real piracy, which is somebody duplicating our ADV releases in counterfeit color-photocopied boxes to look like the real thing. Some of that piracy is surprisingly well organized. Most of it is done in Canada. We got one about six months ago in Wisconsin, and we had our legal department get in touch with them. They were mostly counterfeiting our SoftCel titles, mainly *New Angel 2* and *3.* They go after a different kind of market. Their real victims are the proprietors of small, out-of-the-way video stores who don't know the anime market. But those pirates have to keep moving all the time. It's getting tougher for them to operate as the legitimate anime market spreads."

Danielle Opyt, media relations representative at Manga Entertainment, agrees that piracy is diminishing as legitimate, high-quality videos spread.

"We have had individual orders from Mexico," she says, "and even from Iraq, in which the customer specifically says he wants to get a good copy of our video to replace the horrible-quality bootlegs that are being sold locally."

It may not be called JAILED, but professional efforts to combat piracy are real. The companies cannot officially condone fan subbing since it is technically illegal. But only commercial pirates who are into bootlegging for money need worry about a call from the anime companies' lawyer.

The Thirteen Top Developments in Anime, 1985–99
Animation Magazine no. 75, February 1999.

Nineteen-eighty-five was an important year in anime in both Japan and America. In Japan it marked the explosive blossoming of direct-to-video production, after experimental OAV (original animation video) releases during 1983 and 1984. In America, it marked the *Robotech* TV series. Anime has come far in America in the last thirteen years.

1. *Robotech*
This eighty-five-episode syndicated TV series, premiering in March 1985, was the first to catch the American public's attention as Japanese animation, and as animation for older viewers (the *Star Trek* audience) rather than as cartoons for children. Its dramatic story line and believable human characters won a popularity that has kept it alive from the late 1980s through today in comic books and paperback novelizations. It continually brings public interest to other anime.

2. The Internet
In November 1987, Ann Schubert, a San Francisco-area anime fan, started rec.arts.anime, the first anime general news group on the Internet. Before this, anime fandom was a small cult, mostly unknown and hard to find, communicating by mail and in local clubs. The Internet has made it easy for everyone to contact the anime subculture, especially since the massive growth of individual fan and anime club home pages during the 1990s coordinated through the Anime Web Turnpike since August 1995.

3. Conventions
Anime fans began piggybacking onto science fiction and comic fan conventions in 1978. But a growing demand for their own dedicated conventions led to Project A-Kon 1 in Dallas in 1990, and to AnimeCon '91 in San Jose, Calif., in 1991. Today there are over a half-dozen annual anime conventions around America with guest speakers from the Tokyo animation industry, anime awards, premieres of brand-new anime, and so

on. Attendance at the 1998 Anime Expo in Anaheim, Calif. (annual since 1992), was 4,745.

4. Anime Specialty Companies

By the late 1980s, anime fans gave up waiting for the American entertainment industry to begin importing anime. They began creating their own companies to license and produce English-language anime for American theatrical and video distribution. U.S. Renditions in 1987, Streamline Pictures in 1988, AnimEigo and The Right Stuf in 1989, CPM's U.S. Manga Corps in 1991, A.D. Vision in 1992—these and others since have created and fed the anime market in America.

5. Theatrical Distribution

The anime specialty companies' strategy for theatrical distribution has been to concentrate on the fine art and college campus theater circuit. Streamline Pictures was first with *Laputa: Castle in the Sky* in March 1989 and *Akira* (the first success) that December. During the 1990s, Streamline's *Wicked City*, Central Park Media's *Urotsukidoji: Legend of the Overfiend* and *Roujin-Z* and Manga Entertainment's *Ghost in the Shell* have been the biggest successes among over a dozen limited releases, while Troma tried a general theatrical release of *My Neighbor Totoro*.

6. Video Distribution

The home video market has really established anime in America. From 1990 through 1994, anime video availability was limited to mail-order sales to the anime fans and sales through comic-book specialty shops. Since late 1994, "anime" sections have become standard in general video stores. And since 1995, the popularity of anime videos has enabled anime specialty shops to develop around America (Banzai Anime in Los Angeles, Anime Cafe in Tacoma, Wash., Joy's Japanimation in Pittsburgh, Pa., and many others), offering additional merchandise such as anime music CDs and other imports from Japan.

7. Video Games

Practically all the most popular video games have been from Japan. Since the late 1980s, a growing number of these have been based on popular Japanese TV cartoons like *Ranma 1/2* and *Dragon Ball*. Many popular original video games such as *Record of Lodoss War, Street Fighter, Final Fantasy,* and *Pocket Monsters* have generated their own anime TV and OAV series. For many Americans, it has been these games (and the anime art style used in their graphics) that has introduced them to the anime videos and movies.

8. Popular Culture Specialty Magazines

Popular culture isn't popular unless it has its own fan magazines. The first articles on anime began appearing in the early 1980s in movie, TV, and comic-book magazines like *Starlog, Fantasy Films,* and *The Comics Journal.* Anime fans tried starting their own fan magazines in 1986 with *Anime-Zine,* but it was not until the early 1990s that professional-quality anime specialty fan magazines appeared on newsstands with any regularity. Today *Animerica* and *Protoculture Addicts* are the oldest of a half-dozen regular anime magazines.

9. Public Awareness

Anime first appeared in America in the 1960s, but it was thought of as "foreign film." Fans used the term "Japanimation" during the 1980s, but the Japanese word "anime" has replaced it. News magazines like *Forbes* and *Newsweek* reported on the anime phenomenon in the early 1990s. Today "anime" is recognized as meaning Japanese animation and its distinctive artistic style. To some, "anime" means "violent animation for adults" even though Japan produces more animation for children than for adults.

10. TV Programming

Sailor Moon, Dragon Ball, and *Teknoman* are three anime TV series that have achieved popularity as syndicated children's TV programming in the mid-'90s. Nineteen-ninety-four was a watershed year in getting adult-oriented anime onto American TV. Movies like *Akira, Project A-Ko,* and *Vampire Hunter D* appeared on cable channels such as TNT, TBS, and The Sci-Fi Channel, and on the Network-1 satellite broadcast. MTV showed anime excerpts on its *Liquid Television* program. In 1995, anime movies began appearing on pay-per-view broadcasts.

11. Manga

The connection between manga (Japanese comic books) and anime is closer than that between American comic books and animated cartoons. Many anime TV series, OAVs, and theatrical features are based on Japanese comic books. Translated Japanese manga appeared in U.S. comic-book form in 1987 and became a distinct genre within the comic-book industry by the early 1990s. Anime and manga cross-fertilize each other. Fans of comic books like *Gunsmith Cats, Ranma 1/2,* and *Oh My Goddess* are led to the corresponding anime videos and to other anime from there.

12. Collectibles

Anime entered the fine-art collectibles' market in the mid-'90s. Art galleries have had exhibitions of anime production art and painted cels. In May 1996, the Bess Cutler Gallery in New York exhibited the anime art of director Koichi Ohata. A production cel from *M.D. Geist: Death Force* sold for $1,800. One company, Animated Collectibles, is producing a series of licensed anime "Chroma-Cel" limited-edition cel reproductions. Several model kit companies are making bronze, pewter, vinyl, or resin statues of anime characters in the $100 to $200 range.

13. Disney and Miyazaki
Hayao Miyazaki has been called the "Walt Disney of Japan" since the late 1980s for his box office record-setting features such as *The Crimson Pig* and *Princess Mononoke* (which have been out of the financial range of the American anime specialty companies). The Walt Disney Company's acquisition of Miyazaki's features for U.S. distribution, starting with *Kiki's Delivery Service* in September 1998, will bring the highest quality Japanese animation to America, and will publicize it to anyone who thinks that "anime" is of interest to only the low-quality, action-adventure video market.

Thirteen Notable Anime Films, 1985–99
1. *Akira* (Kodansha/Tokyo Movie Shinsha)
2. *Arion* (Tokuma Shoten/Nippon Sunrise)
3. *The Crimson Pig* (Tokuma Shoten/Studio Ghibli)
4. *Ghost in the Shell* (Kodansha/Manga Entertainment/Tokyo Movie Shinsha)
5. *Grave of the Fireflies* (Tokuma Shoten/Studio Ghibli)
6. *Kiki's Delivery Service* (Tokuma Shoten/Studio Ghibli)
7. *Laputa: The Castle in the Sky* (Tokuma Shoten/Studio Ghibli)
8. *My Neighbor Totoro* (Tokuma Shoten/Studio Ghibli)
9. *Old Man Z [Roujin Z]* (Sony Entertainment/A.P.P.P.)
10. *Pom Poko* (Tokuma Shoten/Studio Ghibli)
11. *Princess Mononoke* (Tokuma Shoten/Studio Ghibli)
12. *Whisper of the Heart* (Tokuma Shoten/Studio Ghibli)
13. *Wicked City* (Japan Home Video/Madhouse)

Thirteen Notable Original Animation Videos, 1985–99
1. *Bubblegum Crisis* (Artmic/A.I.C.)
2. *Devil Hunter Yohko* (Toho Co./Madhouse)
3. *El-Hazard: The Magnificent World* (Pioneer/A.I.C.)
4. *Gall Force* (Artmic/A.I.C.)
5. *GunBuster* (Gainax)
6. *Macross Plus* (Triangle Staff)
7. *Megazone 23* (Idol Co., Ltd./Artmic)
8. *Patlabor: The Mobile Police* (Headgear/Sunrise)
9. *Project A-Ko* (A.P.P.P.)
10. *Record of Lodoss War* (Madhouse)
11. *Tenchi Muyo!* (Pioneer/A.I.C.)
12. *Urotsukidoji: Legend of the Overfiend* (West Cape Corp.)
13. *Vampire Hunter D* (Ashi Production Co., Ltd.)

Thirteen Notable Anime TV Shows, 1985–99
1. *Doraemon* (Shinei Doga)
2. *Dragon Ball* (Toei Doga)

3. *Kimagure Orange Road* (Studio Pierrot)
4. *Maison Ikoku* (Kitty Films)
5. *Mobile Suit Gundam* (Sunrise)
6. *Nadia, The Secret of Blue Water* (Gainax)
7. *Neon Genesis Evangelion* (Gainax)
8. *Pocket Monsters* (Shogakukan Productions)
9. *Ranma 1/2* (Kitty Films)
10. *Sailor Moon* (Toei Doga)
11. *Saint Seiya* (Toei Doga)
12. *Sazae-san* (Eiken)
13. *Slayers* (J.C. Staff)

By The Numbers
Last Word column in *Manga Max* no. 8, July 1999.

"These *Crystania* movies—does it matter which order you see them in?"

"*Blood Reign: Curse of the Yoma*—is this a sequel to *Curse of the Undead: Yoma?*"

"This *Earthian: Beginning of the End*—do you have the earlier episodes?"

"A lot of our customers are getting very frustrated," says Christopher Goodnough, a partner in Joy's Japanimation store near Pittsburgh, Pa. He is commenting on the growing trend of anime video manufacturers who replace volume numbers with confusing and misleading subtitles. "The reaction we've been getting has been very negative."

It used to be easy to tell what was what with anime videos. The series were clearly numbered. Practically all videos were new titles appearing for the first time. Today, numbers are being replaced with dramatic titles which make every video sound like a separate movie. But many are not. The buyer can no longer assume, as he could with *Ranma: Nihao My Concubine*, that he is getting a complete story within a longer series. *Legend of Crystania* is a multi-video serial whose episodes must be seen in the proper order—but with titles like *A New Beginning, Cave of the Sealed,* and *Resurrection of the Gods' King*, do you know the proper order in which to watch them? Is *Legend of Crystania: The Motion Picture* a collection of the separate episodes or a completely different story? (Answer: it is actually episode one of the serial, sort of, but also a sequel of sorts to *Lodoss War.*)

Birdy the Mighty: Double Trouble and *Birdy the Mighty: Final Force. Utena: Crest of the Rose, Utena: The Eternal Castle,* and *Utena: The Legendary Spice. Aika: Lace in Space* and *Aika: Naked Mission.* Are each of these complete movies or episodes in a serial? If a serial, what is the order in which to watch them? Are these all the episodes or are any missing? "Pioneer has gotten very bad about this lately. There is general confusion over all the new *Tenchi Muyo* titles, and especially *Tenchi in Tokyo*," says Goodnough. "The prime offender in my shop," says Su Braviak, co-owner of S and J Productions in central New Jersey, "is Media Blasters' *Earthian*. The first *Earthian* video is subtitled *The Beginning of the End,* which sounds like it must be the last or next-to-last episode. So everybody is looking for a nonexistent earlier video in the series."

A closely related problem is the increasing rerelease of older videos under new titles, at the same time that many genuine sequels are coming out. "A.D. Vision is one of the worst offenders," says Goodnough at Joy's Japanimation, "with its policy of creating a new cover and title for a new dubbed release of a previously subtitled tape." *Blood Reign: Curse of the Yoma* (dubbed) and *Curse of the Undead: Yoma* (subtitled) are the same movie. *Ninja Scroll* and *Ninja Resurrection: The Revenge of Jubei* are separate titles, but *Ninja Scroll* is a complete movie while *Ninja Resurrection,* misleadingly advertised as its sequel, turns out to end on a cliffhanger. It is the beginning of a new serial—which is not mentioned. Central Park Media is replacing the *Perfect Collection* designation for a compilation of a series with *The Movie,* as in the merging of two parts of *Gowcaizer* into *Gowcaizer: The Movie.* Since fans are accustomed to popular television and video series spinning off into brand-new theatrical features (as with the *Kimagure Orange Road, Slayers,* and *Patlabor* movies), several fans of *Gowcaizer* snapped up *The Movie* thinking that they were getting a new story. They were soon back to complain.

Why is this happening? Sales analyses have made it clear that numbered multi-volume series sell primarily to the small core of devoted anime collectors. Most anime buyers, especially the general public, prefer titles that are individual features even if they are part of a series. Therefore it seems like a good marketing strategy to make each title appear to be a complete adventure.

But is this marketing ploy really for anime's own good, or will its long-range effect be more destructive? How many anime fans are being soured by such obvious attempts to trick them into buying videos instead of packaging them clearly and honestly? How many potential fans are finding that their first sample of anime is an incomprehensible middle episode from a serial of indeterminate length? The experienced staff at an anime specialty store may be able to advise customers (Su Braviak puts her own stickers with episode numbers on series videos), but how many general video stores have clerks who are knowledgeable enough about anime to answer questions about which volume in an unnumbered series is the first? Will this practice really help anime grow, or is it more likely to slowly strangle it?

Anime 2000: Money Talks
Manga Max no. 14, January 2000.

Although anime has been around in many forms for several decades, the industry as we know it is celebrating its tenth birthday. Exactly when that is is open to debate—the anime industry had a rolling start that's almost impossible to pinpoint. Several anime videos were released during the Eighties, such as *Clash of the Bionoids,* but these were all released as children's cartoons. The first anime to be actually labeled, sold, and marketed as anime didn't appear until the close of the '80s. The Right Stuf released its first two *Astro Boy* videos in 1989 and was followed swiftly in the following year by U.S. Renditions, Streamline Pictures, and AnimEigo. This steady stream swelled into a flood, bursting from comic shops into the video stores a couple of years later, splashing onto cable channels, and creating enough product to support separate anime specialty shops in 1995. Anime, for good or ill, became recognizable to the general public. And as we enter the year 2000, the anime industry is completing its first decade.

An Arbitrary Anniversary

After ten years, the English-language anime industry is dominated by ten companies. The "old-timers" have been around for more than five years—A.D. Vision, AnimEigo, Central Park Media, Manga Entertainment, Pioneer, The Right Stuf International, and Viz Communications. The "new kids" are two U.S. companies, Media Blasters and Urban Vision, and Japan's Bandai Entertainment, which entered the American market in 1998. A few companies have disappeared, going out of business (U.S. Renditions), absorbed by others (Software Sculptors was bought by CPM), or evolving outside the anime market (Streamline). Beyond that is a jumble of major video companies whose anime releases have really been for the general children's video market, from Buena Vista's *Kiki's Delivery Service,* through DIC's *Sailor Moon* back to Family Home Entertainment's mid-'90s *Robotech.* Others produced a single special project, such as Voyager Entertainment's thirty-nine *Star Blazers* videos and the five *Yamato* movies; some are still struggling to establish themselves (Star Anime Enterprises has only released three videos since 1994).

Some disagree with this "tenth anniversary" concept. Manga Entertainment's president Marvin Gleicher says: "The theatrical release of *Akira* [in 1989–90] was the critical point for bringing anime out of the underground, but you shouldn't discount the build-up of that underground. It was *Astro Boy* and *Speed Racer* in the '60s that started building the

The sidebars and editor's comments in this article are by *Manga Max*'s editor, Jonathan Clements. ■

following for anime." John Ledford, President of A.D. Vision, agrees: "*Astro Boy* [in 1963] proved that a Japanese animated series could be successful in North America, paving the way for all that followed. *Speed Racer* was the first anime series to develop a cult following and, to this day, remains the single most recognized title in the United States. *Star Blazers* went a step further and proved that a long-format series with continuing story lines could be successful, and began the progression toward the mass acceptance of a more serious approach to animation."

Shawne Kleckner, president of The Right Stuf International, takes a similar attitude: "I would say that there are a few key events which were much earlier, namely the key releases of *Astro Boy, Kimba, Speed Racer, Star Blazers,* and *Robotech.* These titles started modern-day fandom, and without them I think that the industry would be markedly different."

Video Drome

"While individual titles may have played an important role," says ADV's John Ledford, "the real genesis of the anime industry can be traced to a technological development, specifically, the consumer VCR [in 1975]. It was video that allowed fans outside Japan to see anime uncut and uncensored for the first time. With so much of anime fandom built around video, it was a given that, eventually, someone would begin licensing anime titles directly for home video."

Julie Davis, editor of *Animerica,* thinks that the starting date required another important piece of technology. "It's often said that the anime video companies began in the late '80s," she points out, "because the fans finally got tired of waiting for the video companies and decided to do it themselves. What is not mentioned as often is that the late '80s was also the earliest that computer subtitling technology became easy and cheap enough that fans with a modest amount of capital could afford to license and subtitle videos."

By Fans, For Fans?

John Sirabella, president of Media Blasters, says: "Anime on TV like *Speed Racer* or *Star Blazers* were really pre-anime industry. *Akira* was a major title in creating anime among the mainstream, and *Bubblegum Crisis* was a major title in creating the anime hobbyist video market. It was CPM that turned anime into a business by pumping the video titles out and creating a market through quantity. Streamline Pictures was more influential from the production angle. It produced fewer videos, but it concentrated on dubbing of titles that would have a broader appeal. This let everybody see that dubs were where the money was, despite all the screaming for subs from the anime hobbyists."

Mike Pascuzzi, director of sales at CPM, similarly feels that while the industry's roots go back to the televising of early anime in the Sixties and evolved forward through "the formation of the first anime labels in the United States (Streamline, AnimEigo, Books Nippan's U.S. Renditions, and CPM)," the industry did not become established until 1992. "Anime started to become a significant video category soon after Musicland started carrying the product in the Suncoast stores."

AnimEigo isn't the only company dabbling in live-action. John Ledford, who founded A.D. Vision with Matt Greenfield in 1992, also sees live-action as another niche that will appeal to the current audience. "We have done quite a bit with live-action, what with the Godzilla film *Destroy All Monsters, Gamera, Gunhed, Tokyo Blue*, and the upcoming ADV release of *Parasite Eve.*"

John Sirabella started Software Sculptors in 1995. After about a year as an independent company, he sold it to CPM and managed it as a CPM division for another year before leaving to start Media Blasters. "We started in May 1997. We built up our adult anime label, Kitty Media, in our first year. Once that was established we concentrated on the live action Japanese B-movie genre, our Tokyo Shock label, in our second year. Now we're concentrating on establishing our general anime label, AnimeWorks, with *Magic Knight Rayearth, Rurouni Kenshin,* and *Voogie's Angels.* ADV has movies and video anime, so we will specialize in TV series."

It has been said that the anime industry was started by the fans themselves. This is only partly true. U.S. Renditions began in 1986 with fans David Riddick and Bob Napton working with manager Kevin Seymour at Books Nippan. The Japanese import-export company financed the fan-oriented subsidiary to increase its business. Streamline Pictures was started by Carl Macek and Jerry Beck in October 1988, but Macek and Beck were less anime fans than animation industry experts who saw an untapped popular culture market. The Right Stuf started in 1987 but did not get into anime until 1989, when it licensed *Astro Boy,* more for comics and nostalgic television cartoon fans than for anime fans.

In the Business

The other companies have less personal association with fandom. Central Park Media was founded by John O'Donnell in April 1990 as a video distributor specializing in

AnimEigo, A.D. Vision, and Media Blasters may be the companies with the purest claim to having been started by fans for fans. Robert Woodhead started AnimEigo with Roe R. Adams III in September 1989 "as something fun to do" because nobody else was releasing anime on video. "Our goal was and is to release good animated films in a properly translated manner," Woodhead says. "We specialize in 'fan' titles appealing to fewer people but more committed ones." Now that other companies are releasing videos and short anime series, AnimEigo is concentrating on longer anime titles like *Urusei Yatsura* and *Orange Road,* the original *Macross* series for those who want *Macross* and not *Robotech,* and live-action samurai movies on its Samurai Cinema label.

documentaries and similar educational titles. It created its first anime label, U.S. Manga Corps, in July 1991. O'Donnell and his staff enjoy anime, but consider themselves businessmen more than anime fans. Mike Pascuzzi notes: "Right now we are offering some anime music audio CDs as well as manga, and our new Asia Pulp Cinema live-action line. These comprise about 7 to 10 percent of our business right now, while videos and DVDs make up the lion's share. We are continuing to expand our interest in the peripherals."

Manga Entertainment's non-anime roots go back furthest. Marvin Gleicher says: "We actually started in London around 1974 as Island World Communications, releasing arthouse movies on video and films for the Institute of Contemporary Art. We became aware of Japanese animation around 1990, and we got the British rights for *Akira* in 1991. That was so popular that we immediately procured the rights for all Europe for not only *Akira* but the *Fist of the North Star* movie, *The Guyver,* and others. *Akira* was an Island World release, but we started using the Manga Video label with *Fist* in March 1992. The name of the company was changed in mid-1993. We opened our branch in Chicago in 1994, and have been shifting operations until it is now our main office. But Manga is still a major anime supplier to Britain, and is the largest supplier of anime to the rest of Europe. Under our alternate Palm Pictures brand, we are a major distribution company for independent feature films, both animated and live-action. Right now we are publicizing our theatrical release of *Perfect Blue* in the anime community, but if you will look at this week's [end of October] Los Angeles newspaper theatrical sections, you will see that our distribution of *Thicker Than Water,* a hip-hop movie starring Ice Cube, is currently playing. Our theatrical distribution is about 50 percent Japanese [including anime] and 50 percent other theatrical films—and that 'other' 50 per cent is growing."

The Japanese Contingent

Viz Communications began in 1986 as a subsidiary of Japan's Shogakukan media conglomerate. Viz began publishing U.S. editions of manga in May 1987 (in association with Eclipse Comics for the first year and a half). The first Viz Videos did not appear until late 1993. Viz has always maintained close relations with fandom (Trish Ledoux, *Animerica*'s founding editor, was a prominent anime fan during the '80s), but the company is organized on a commercial basis. Julie Davis, the current editor of *Animerica* kindly answered *MM*'s survey because Oliver Chin, Viz's director of marketing, has been out of the office for the past few weeks trying to run the *Pokémon* juggernaut—far bigger and more profitable than anything in the anime specialty market.

Pioneer Entertainment almost backed into the U.S. anime market by accident. Chad Kime, animation marketing supervisor, says, "Pioneer has many divisions in Japan. One of these in the mid-'90s was Pioneer Laser

Disc Company, with a U.S. subsidiary. We were licensing American movies and videos for laser disc. We had the Paramount movies and things like *Championship Wrestling.* Pioneer started anime releases in late 1993 primarily because we had the anime rights in Japan and it was a cheap way to add to our catalogue. We became Pioneer Entertainment in 1995, and started licensing anime from other suppliers in Japan in 1996, rather than just marketing Pioneer's own titles. Pioneer Entertainment still markets U.S. live movies, wrestling, and much more than just anime."

Urban Vision Entertainment was started in July 1996 by Mataichiro Yamamoto, one of the producers of Tokyo Movie Shinsha's 1983 *Golgo 13* feature and many anime and live-action titles since then. "Urban Vision was created to expand the world anime market to the level of the Gen X market (for lack of a better term)—the live-action SF movies like *The Matrix* in America," says Kara Redmon, Urban Vision's Director of Marketing. "We intend to produce and acquire anime intended to appeal to both the anime fan and the broader SF market, in the vein of *Vampire Hunter D* or *Wicked City.* Our unique relationship with a Japanese animation producer has provided us with a steady flow of the kind of high-quality anime we need to realize our dreams." Yamamoto is himself the producer of many of Urban Vision's titles including *Golgo 13: Queen Bee, Bio Hunter,* and *Twilight of the Dark Master,* some of which have been released in the United States ahead of their Japanese releases.

"Bandai has just entered the market in the last year," says Nobu Yamamoto, Bandai America's director of marketing and sales, "so we do not have much personal knowledge of the start of the anime industry in America. However, our executive vice president, Ken Iyadomi (formerly of Manga Entertainment—*Ed.*), was involved with the productions of *Akira* and *Ghost in the Shell,* so he saw their popularity in America and is able to advise us. We are trying to appeal to the people who liked those movies with similar strong SF titles like *Gundam, Cowboy Bebop,* and *Outlaw Star.*"

The Next Generation

Where do the anime companies see the industry going in the next few years? Shawne Kleckner at The Right Stuf is very optimistic: "I see continued strong growth. The industry as a whole is worth something like $50 million a year. The new titles like *Sailor Moon, Pokémon,* and *Dragon Ball Z* are bringing young people into the marketplace today, who will eventually graduate upward to the teen and adult titles." Kara Redmon at Urban Vision echoes this: "In the big picture, anime still has a long way to go. Anime accounts for a fraction of a percent of the $17 billion video business in the United States, but undoubtedly the right titles will eventually take it there. The primary growth potential can be realized by looking at the video sales for mainstream live-action genres of SF and horror as well as video games. The audience for mega-hit titles like *The Matrix* and most video games is almost identical to the audience for anime. Urban Vision hopes to incorporate some of the merchandising lines, as they work synergistically with the videos to promote sales, but for the time being we want to master the video business and be careful not to try and grow too quickly or beyond our capacity."

John Ledford expects A.D. Vision to expand along its current lines. "Besides the anime you'll also be seeing a lot of live action films and ADV anime-related merchandise in the years ahead." So does Mike Pascuzzi at CPM, with further development of CPM Manga and CPM's Manga Music CDs. However, Pascuzzi points out that expanding the anime market requires more than merely making more videos and DVDs. "There is not enough shelf space for all the product already. And the key to expanding shelf space is to increase sales to justify that additional space, not to just produce more product."

John Sirabella at Media Blasters has similar plans and worries. "We've had over 100 percent growth in sales every year so far, and we see more growth potential in the live action than in the anime. Next year we plan to start our Tokyo Art House label for Japanese live action art and non-action films. We will also work on expanding beyond video by getting theatrical and TV distribution, especially for the live action films.

"The anime market today is between $50 million and $100 million a year, not counting *Pokémon*. It has been growing steadily during this decade, but it is now starting an implosion. There are too many companies dumping too many videos on the market. There are more than fifty new titles a month today! There isn't room on the shelves for all those titles. All the anime companies are going to Japan to buy new titles to keep these quantities up. This is driving the prices up and making anime more expensive to produce."

Back on TV

These concerns may be partly addressed by the popular response to *Pokémon*, which caused the quick importation of *Digimon, Monster Rancher,* and *Card Captor Sakura*. "The biggest breakthrough to get anime accepted in America," says Julie Davis, "may not be the video market but the TV industry's realization that the American public will accept Japanese TV cartoons. It is not too weird for Americans. This will mean more anime TV series appearing for the general public, in adaptations that are basically faithful to the original programs instead of being drastically rewritten." Chad Kime at Pioneer Entertainment agrees: "Our goal should always be to expand the anime market. Right now that means capitalizing on *Pokémon*'s success. Now that Pioneer is distributing Viz's videos, I plan to march back into the video stores that turned down *Dragon Ball Z* and *The New Adventures of Kimba* and ask, 'Is *Pokémon* selling here? Here are two more titles that will sell to the same market.' We want to destroy the narrow perception that anime means just teen action animation. We picked *Fushigi Yugi* to start developing the women's market."

Everyone agrees that the video market is growing too slowly. The major goal during the next five years must be to get higher visibility for anime through theaters and television. John Sirabella says, "There has to be a dedicated anime channel to get anime to the masses for free." Marvin Gleicher says: "Manga Entertainment's most important goal is the theatrical distribution of anime to increase its general audience. We also have plans to get it on TV. We are in negotiation with several cable and movie channels."

Nobu Yamamoto says: "Bandai has learned a lot during our first year in the American market. We consider this time as market research to give us a better idea of what the American consumer wants. We have studied the effectiveness of exclusive Internet solicitation. We are now concentrating on making anime better known to the public through the general video market. Since September we have had promotions in Virgin Megastores and Tower Records for *Cowboy Bebop* and *Outlaw Star*, to catch the attention of regular customers who have never considered anime. Bandai has also been working for months to get *Gundam* on TV. We have finally succeeded, and *Gundam Wing* will begin appearing on The Cartoon Network starting in March 2000."

At the close of 1989, there was virtually no anime market. As 2000 begins, estimates place the anime market at between $50–$100 million. "The anime that is marketed as such to the hardcore fans and the action-

Manga Entertainment's original UK office is planning closer links both with fans and their U.S. branch, promising releases timed as closely as possible to coincide with an American launch. For the moment, British fans must take the rough with the smooth, missing out on some of the titles released in the States while getting some, such as *Perfect Blue* and *X:1999*, ahead of their U.S. counterparts. Other UK companies subsist on anime licensed from U.S. companies such as MVM, cutting out the middleman to deliver AnimEigo titles direct to the fans. Pioneer Europe distributes a few titles from CPM and Viz (such as *Lodoss War* and *Dark Stalkers*) in addition to their own product. ADV UK remain locked into the activities of their U.S. parent. Western Connection, who released a large number of titles in the mid-'90s, have now allowed their licenses to expire, possibly freeing up ADV to release their U.S. dubbed version of *Ushio and Tora* in the UK. The other UK companies, if not dead, are certainly sleeping very deeply. Crusader, East2West, AUK Video Collection, and Animania are long gone, and Kiseki are still waiting outside the BBFC with their fingers crossed, hoping for *Overfiend IV* to escape. The largest company in the Australian market is Siren Entertainment, which not only distributes titles for Manga Entertainment, A.D. Vision, and Pioneer, but also live-action films straight from Hong Kong.

adventure teen market is probably not quite $100 million," says Chad Kime. "But if you add the anime like *Sailor Moon, Dragon Ball Z,* and *Pokémon* that is marketed as children's videos without emphasizing the anime label, plus all its related merchandising, the market is more like $4 to $5 *billion.*" What will it be in 2010? We'll find out . . .

Additional reporting by Julia Sertori.

Anime Theatrical Features
Animation World Magazine 5, no. 6, September 2000.

On July 21, Japan's second annual (1999) *Pokémon* theatrical feature was released in America as *Pokémon: The Movie 2000,* placing No. 3 in the weekend nationwide box office ratings. Coincidentally the third *Pokémon* feature, *Pocket Monsters: Lord of the Unknown Tower,* hit Japan's theaters on July 8 to also rank No. 3 in that country's weekend ratings.

Japanese animation (anime) has exploded into the American consciousness over the past three or four years. There has been animation from Japan in America since the 1960s with movies like *Alakazam the Great* and TV programs like *Astro Boy,* but anime as a distinct cultural genre was not noticed until the 1990s. First came the anime video cult market ("Japanese animation isn't just for kids!") in the early 1990s, available only by mail order and through comic-book specialty bookshops. Then in the mid-'90s came a few adolescent and adult animated SF and fantasy dramatic features like *Akira* and *Vampire Hunter D* on cable TV's Cartoon Network and Sci-Fi Channel, and young teen TV series like *Sailor Moon* and *Dragon Ball Z,* while anime videos began to appear in general video shops.

Then *Pokémon* hit America in 1998.

By now most Americans—most American parents whose children watch TV, at least—know that while *Pokémon* may have originated as a Japanese video game, its most visible and popular incarnation is as a TV cartoon series. They have seen that the *Pokémon* TV series has spun off at least two *Pokémon* theatrical features. The TV industry's dash to cash in on the *Pokémon* mania has resulted in the importation of such similar Japanese TV cartoons as *Digimon, Monster Rancher,* and *Cardcaptors.* And there are apparently theatrical features of these as well. *Digimon: The Movie* hits America's theaters on October 6. Meanwhile, the kids are bringing home new videos of at least three *Sailor Moon* movies that were theatrical releases in Japan if not here.

A New Question
How popular is theatrical animation in Japan? Can those movies also be popular in America? This is no idle question, especially considering the results of this summer's American theatrical animation releases. Only

Chicken Run—a British production, but strongly supported by its American distributor, DreamWorks—has been really successful. Most American theatrical animated features so far this year have not earned back their production costs. *Pokémon: The Movie 2000,* released July 21 as I mentioned, had grosses of over $40,700,000 as of August 13, while Twentieth Century Fox's *Titan A.E.,* released over a month earlier, only had grosses of $22,640,000 by that same weekend (statistics from the Internet Movie Database). Will it be more practical for the American movie industry to start importing Japanese animated features in a big way, at much lower production costs for just dubbing and minor editing, than to continue to support the productions of completely new American animated features?

It is true that there are many more theatrical animated productions in Japan than in America. A few of them certainly warrant serious consideration for the American theatrical market. But on the whole, Japanese productions are not easily transferable to American theatergoers' tastes.

An average of three or four animated theatrical releases appear in Japan every month. These fall into three main categories: 1. movies based on popular TV/young children's cartoon series; 2. original dramatic features for older audiences, usually based upon comic books and SF novels; and 3. foreign imports.

TV animation for children is extremely popular in Japan, even more so than in America. There is also a much greater prevalence of a popular TV cartoon series spinning off a theatrical feature. This is how the *Pokémon, Sailor Moon,* and *Dragon Ball Z* theatrical features came to be made. However, movies of this nature are like the *Star Trek* theatrical features: they are really designed for the fans of the TV series. Movies of this nature will not have much box-office potential until their TV series are established on American TV. For example, the Japanese TV series *Card Captor Sakura* just began as *Cardcaptors* in June on the Kids' WB! network in the United States and Teletoon in Canada. This may make the *Card Captor Sakura: The Movie* feature (August 1999 in Japan) viable as an American theatrical release, if the TV series develops sufficient popularity. Another Japanese TV cartoon series with a theatrical feature in reserve, *Meitantei Conan* (*Conan, the Great Detective,* about a boy super-detective), is reportedly in development for the Fox Kids Network.

The Differences

But not all Japanese TV cartoon series have potential for American release. Two notably frustrating examples are *Doraemon* and *Sore Ike! Anpanman,* both for young children. *Doraemon* is about a blue robot cat, a toy from hundreds of years in the future, which is sent via time travel to a comically clumsy twentieth-century schoolboy. *Doraemon* began on TV in April 1979; the TV series is up to almost 1,600 episodes to date. There has been a mid-March annual *Doraemon* theatrical feature since 1980. The American movie/

TV industry would love to cash in on these. But many of the stories about Doraemon the robot-cat and his human owner/playmate, Nobita, are gentle teaching experiences framed around Japanese ethnic customs (including communal bathing), Japanese holidays, Japanese folk tales, and Japanese historical events, which young American children would not understand. *Sore Ike! Anpanman* (roughly *Go Get 'Em, Anpanman!*) is a superhero comedy for young children in which most of the characters are Japanese toys, fairy-tale characters, and anthropomorphized candies and sweets. (*Anpan* is a sweet pastry.) The weekly TV series began in October 1988; episode no. 576 aired on August 4, 2000. The annual theatrical features started in 1995; this year's, released on July 29, was *Sore Ike! Anpanman: Ningyo Hime no Namida* (*Go Get 'Em, Anpanman! Tears of the Mermaid Princess*). These and others such as *Crayon Shin-chan* add up to a large quantity of Japanese theatrical animated features that would have little American audience appeal.

There is a similar subclass of children's theatrical features that are blatantly Japanese corporate promotion. Two examples both released in July are the *2000 Nen Natsu Toei Anime Fair* (*Summer 2000 Toei Animation Fair*) and the *2000 Nen Natsu no Kadokawa Manga Taiko Susumeru* (*Summer 2000 Kadokawa Cartoon Masterpiece Presentation*). Toei Animation Co., Ltd. is the largest animation studio in Japan, and one of the largest in the world; both *Dragon Ball Z* and *Sailor Moon* are Toei productions. Kadokawa is a major Japanese publishing company; its children's book division is comparable to Scholastic, Inc. or Golden Press in America. Movies of this type are eighty- to ninety-minute compilations of from two to four new featurettes of the company's currently most popular TV cartoons—in Toei's case, its own studio's productions; in Kadokawa's case, licensed TV cartoons based upon its juvenile literary properties. These movies give Japanese children the chance to see their favorite TV cartoon characters in adventures of higher animation quality than the TV series. Often these featurettes are closely tied to the current TV story lines, introducing new characters and subplots to the TV series. The *Digimon* theatrical feature just released in America is actually edited from three *Digimon* featurettes in Toei's Spring and Summer Animation Fairs of the past couple of years. These are popular in Japan; the *Summer 2000 Toei Animation Fair* ranked number seven overall among its week's theatrical releases in Japan. But for obvious reasons, they would be meaningless to children outside of Japan.

Another Demographic

More suitable for American importation are the theatrical features for adolescents and adults. Best-known in America are the features created by master animators Hayao Miyazaki and Isao Takahata, based upon their original stories through their Studio Ghibli since the mid-1980s, but these are a special case. Movies of this type are usually romances and dramas based upon popular novels, comic books, TV programs for older viewers, especially popular direct-to-video productions, and video games. *Akira* and *Ghost in the Shell,* adapted from adult SF novels in comic-art form, are two well-known examples of Japanese popular movies that had limited art-house theatrical releases in America before going to video.

Jin Roh (*The Wolf Men*), a taut political thriller about the plotting at high governmental levels for jurisdictional control of a new paramilitary police unit, was designed for the art-theater circuit in the first place. It played at international film festivals in Germany, Canada, the United States, and other nations for a couple of years before its general release in Japan this February. A similar example is *Alexander,* an American-Japanese-Korean co-production of a fantasy based upon the third-century B.C. Macedonian king who conquered most of Western civilization, elevating him to mythic stature similar to the demigod Hercules. This production, with character design by American animator Peter Chung (*Aeon Flux*), has also played at international film festivals. It will be released theatrically in Japan as *Alexander Senki* (roughly *The Military Exploits of Alexander*) in October. In 1985 *Vampire Hunter D,* a low-budget direct-to-video feature based upon the fantasy thriller novels by Hideyuki Kikuchi, proved unexpectedly popular, but dissatisfaction by Kikuchi over changes to his story held up any movie sequels. The movie has also proven popular as an American anime release since 1992 in art theaters and on video and cable TV. The legal problems in Japan were recently resolved, and a new, high-budget remake of *Vampire Hunter D* is just finishing production, by one of Japan's top anime directors, Yoshiaki Kawajiri, and with lots of CGI enhancement. [See page 341.] Any of these would seem to be potential American theatrical releases of at least as much commercial validity as Miramax's release of *Princess Mononoke.*

There are many Japanese popular teen romantic fantasies, roughly comparable to *I Dream of Jeannie* or *Sabrina, the Teenage Witch.* These usually begin as comic books and graduate to animated TV cartoon series or direct-to-video productions. (The Japanese created their own English abbreviation for these—OAVs for original animation videos, which the American anime market has adopted.) Especially popular titles spin off theatrical sequels. A current example is *Oh! My Goddess: Eternal Ties,* in which the ongoing romance between a shy college student and a virginal young goddess is finally resolved—or is it? Japanese theatrical audiences will find out this autumn. *Oh! My Goddess* is popular among American anime and comics fans through translations of the comic book soap-opera romances by Kosuke Fujishima and the OAVs. But would this popularity extend to a theatrical release of a sequel for a general American audience that is not already familiar with the relationships among its cast? This is why the many Japanese theatrical features of this nature have gone directly into the same anime video market as the TV episodes and the OAVs.

This also may change with the growth in popularity of anime for older viewers in America. The Japanese animation industry is eager to sell more of its product to America. Take, for example, the 1996 teen girls' romance TV series *The Vision of Escaflowne,* a twenty-six-episode serial about a high school girl who is transported to a fantasy world. *Escaflowne's* continuing popularity with teens in both Japan and the United States through video sales has resulted this year in both an American TV release (Fox Kids Network, premiering in August) and a Japanese theatrical feature, *Escaflowne: A Girl in Gaea* (June release). This movie was also rushed to America for a preview at the Anime Expo 2000 fan convention (10,000 attendance) in Anaheim, Calif., over the Fourth of July weekend, to help build popular demand for an American theatrical rather than direct-to-video release. The above-mentioned new *Vampire Hunter D* feature in production was also promoted at Anime Expo 2000 with a theatrical trailer.

Another evolutionary development is the increase in international co-productions. The United States-Japanese-Korean *Alexander* is designed to be shown as either a TV series or a theatrical feature. Its current theatrical release in Japan may help with its sale in America. A *Final Fantasy* theatrical feature, loosely based upon the Japanese video game series, is currently being publicized in both nations as an expected Japanese summer 2001 theatrical hit. This CGI science-fiction drama is being promoted heavily over the Internet with downloadable trailers and graphics, to excite America's action-adventure movie fans. *Final Fantasy* is a Japanese production being filmed at a studio located in Honolulu, with dialogue being recorded in Los Angeles for release in both countries. This could be the movie that will take Japanese theatrical animation from the art-theater circuit into American general theatrical releases.

Academy of Motion Picture Arts Anime Event
Protoculture Addicts no. 69, January 2002.

The "Marc Davis Lecture on Animation" was created by the Academy of Motion Picture Arts and Sciences in 1994. Named for the famous Disney veteran, the lecture has usually honored the work of individual famous animators or teams such as Davis himself (1913–2000), Chuck Jones, or Peter Lord and Nick Park from Britain's Aardman Animations studio. The 2001 lecture, "Drawing From Japan: Anime and Its Influences," is the first to focus on a particular style of animation.

This lecture was held on the evening of November 14 at the Academy's Beverly Hills, Calif., Awards Theater. The 1,012-seat theater drew an audience of more than 600, mostly professional animators (including some voice actors like René Auberjonois, and anime pioneer Fred Ladd) with a sprinkling of anime fans.

Voice actress June Foray, one of the Academy's governors, introduced moderator Jerry Beck, best known as an American animation expert but also as the cofounder (with Carl Macek) of Streamline Pictures, the pioneering American anime company. Anime clips in fifteen-minute blocs of three or four themed segments alternated with the speakers whom Beck interviewed.

The program began with "Inroads," the opening credits of *Astro Boy* (the only television anime shown) followed by a scene from *Akira*. These represented the first Japanese animation seen in America in 1963, and the feature (released by Beck and Macek) which introduced "anime" to the public in 1989. Anime historian Fred Patten pointed out that, while *Astro Boy* was the first TV anime, it had been preceded by a few movies including *Alakazam the Great*. Patten told how the "big-eyed" look of anime had been created by Osamu Tezuka. Tezuka had told American anime fans in 1978 how deeply he had been influenced by Disney animation, and that his *Kimba the White Lion* was a specific "reply" to Disney's *Bambi*.

"The Kurosawa of Animation" showcased Hayao Miyazaki's *My Neighbor Totoro, Porco Rosso,* and *Princess Mononoke*. Disney director Eric Goldberg (the Genie sequences in *Aladdin,* the main director of *Pocahontas,* and the "Rhapsody in Blue" and "Carnival of the Animals" sequences in *Fantasia 2000*) confirmed that Miyazaki's animation has been studied by Disney animators and was an acknowledged influence of *The Rescuers Down Under* in 1990. When the audience asked why Disney has only released *Kiki's Delivery Service* and *Princess Mononoke* so far, Goldberg shrugged that he was talking about Miyazaki's popularity with Disney's animators, not Disney's management.

"Kicking the Kidstuff" introduced adult anime with scenes from *Perfect Blue, Ghost in the Shell,* and two from *Wicked City*. Mark Dippé, a CGI effects animator on *Terminator 2* and *Jurassic Park,* and director of the live-action *Spawn* movie, said that the "look" of American SF and horror features was influenced by adult anime long before *The Matrix* acknowledged it, even when the anime scenes were clearly influenced themselves by American movies like John Carpenter's *The Thing*. (There were murmurs of "what goes around, comes around" from the audience.)

"Uniquely Japanese" presented *Pompoko, Grave of the Fireflies,* and a different scene from *Princess Mononoke*. These showed how anime is introducing Japanese history and social themes to Americans. They were commented upon by Lisa Atkinson, an American animation veteran for over twenty years who has spent years in Japan and other Asian nations working with their animation industries in co-productions with American studios.

As the comments about Disney management's ignoring *Spirited Away* indicate, this November 2001 lecture was held before Disney's April 11, 2002 announcement that it had just acquired the American rights to *Spirited Away*. ■■

Moderator Jerry Beck interviews Fred Patten

"The Next Generation" used *Blood: The Last Vampire* and *The Adolescence of Utena* to introduce the final two speakers: Mitsuhisa Ishikawa, the producer of *Blood,* and Kunihiko Ikuhara, the director of *Utena* and some of the *Sailor Moon* theatrical features. They spoke the longest (through translators), and were the most actively questioned by the audience.

Ikuhara likened American animation to Las Vegas revues: spectacular but mindless mass entertainment. He admitted that anime includes a lot of the same, but it also has room for the equivalent of imaginative independent art films. He also said that a Japanese production will spend more time at the beginning to develop a finished story. American animation is notorious for starting to animate before the story is completed, resulting in wasted work when scenes are canceled. Ishikawa, the president of Production I.G, amused everyone by emphasizing how he hated the stereotype of animation as children's fare. There must have been many Japanese speakers present because there was considerable laughter even before his translator finished such lines as, "Our animation is harmful for children," and "We are not likely to become one of Disney's subcontractors!" The final question was an aggressive demand about why they don't make movies that educate the public about Japan's guilt in World War II. Their reply was basically that animators are more interested in fantasy entertainment than in didactic instruction.

The program concluded with "New Visions from the Veterans": the opening scene of *Metropolis,* presented as combining the talents of Rintaro, Katsuhiro Otomo, and Osamu Tezuka, and due for an American release in January, and the five-minute Japanese Toho Ltd. trailer for Miyazaki's *Spirited Away*. Since Goldberg had confirmed that the Disney company has no interest in releasing *Spirited Away* in America, this ended the evening with the impression that anime will have to become established in the theatrical motion picture industry despite the major studios rather than with their acceptance.

July 1978: First Anime Fan Magazine, *Animage*, Published
This Month in Anime History column in *Newtype USA* 2, no. 7, July 2003.

Magazines usually hit the newsstands a month ahead of their cover dates. But going by cover dates, this month is the twenty-fifth anniversary of anime fan magazines. July 1978 is the cover date of the first issue of Tokuma Publishing's *Animage*, which featured a dynamic silver-on-black coming-at-you image of *Space Battleship Yamato*.

Animage was not the first Japanese magazine devoted to animation, but its predecesors were all small specialty journals designed for professional animators and college theater-arts scholars. *Animage* was (and still is) a newsstand magazine from one of Japan's largest publishing companies, aimed at the general public. Anime itself was then undergoing a rapid evolution from the mostly juvenile-oriented theatrical features and TV programs that predominated through the late 1960s to the sharper, more dramatic adolescent-oriented SF and fantasy like *Gatchaman, Cutey Honey,* and *Space Battleship Yamato* of the mid-'70s. Tokuma cannily saw a market there and went after it with the non-juvenile, non-condescending monthly *Animage,* plus Tokuma's series of all-you-want-to-know "Roman Album" books each devoted to an individual popular anime title. These helped to develop the anime fandom and market. *Animage* covered anime in a sophisticated package that a high school or college student need not be embarrassed to be seen reading. Its 150 pages (200 today) of art and in-depth information about the most popular theatrical and TV anime of the moment were the equal of any serious cinema-study magazine.

Animage appeared just in time to highlight the 1977–80 *Lupin III* TV series and its 1979 theatrical feature *Lupin III: The Castle of Cagliostro.* This led to a direct relationship between *Animage* and animation director Hayao Miyazaki. *Animage* serialized Miyazaki's *Nausicaä of the Valley of the Winds* manga and championed his theatrical features during the 1980s. *Animage*'s publisher, Tokuma, bankrolled the startup of Studio Ghibli. So it can be argued that if it were not for *Animage,* Miyazaki's features from *Nausicaä* on might never have been made.

Animage must have been an instant success, because it quickly had imitators from rival publishers. *Animec* (first issue October 1978) was first, followed by *The Anime* (December 1979), *My Anime* (April 1981) and *Animedia* (June 1981). They were similar, but each tried to develop its own personality. *Animage* concentrated on detailed coverage. If you want to know the initial broadcast date, episode title, and main credits of every TV anime series shown in Japan, look in *Animage*. The art-light, text-heavy *Animec* was more for the fan of anime-related modeling kits. *My Anime* provided fewer color illustrations but more character model sheets. *Animedia* was a thinner magazine with more superficial coverage, but it seemed to have more color art (due to fewer pages of text) at a lower cover price than the others. It was heaven for the anime fan, with a magazine for every taste.

Just when you thought that every aspect of anime was covered, another magazine appeared with a new gimmick. *Anime V* (January 1985) specialized in video anime, both the brand-new direct-to-video releases that started in the mid-'80s and the video releases of theatrical and TV anime, in greater detail than any other magazine. *Newtype* (April 1985) blew everyone away with more impressive anime art on glossy slick paper commissioned exclusively for its pages, instead of the standard publicity images which appeared in all the other magazines. *Newtype* was also the first anime magazine to devote pages to related pop-culture releases that "cool" anime fans were also interested in (the latest hit live-action movies, video games, music CDs, and models), and its "free bonus gifts" were bigger and better.

Time marches on. Other magazines have come and gone, as well as most of the above. Some lasted only a handful of issues; others seemed like giants whose disappearances after many years shocked the fans. *Animec, My Anime,* and *The Anime* all vanished between mid-1986 and mid-1987. *Anime V* lasted until mid-1999, with its name changed to *Looker* for the final eight issues. *AX* and *Animation Magazine* (no relation to the American magazine of the same title) started in the late '90s and lasted for three or four years each. At present *Animage, Animedia,* and *Newtype* are both the giants and the survivors of the Japanese monthly anime magazines.

Nascent American anime fandom was impressed by the Japanese magazines from the start. Even if fans couldn't read the text, there was enough art to drool over to justify the prices. The magazines' obvious maturity compared to any American publications about "cartoons" (juvenile comic books and coloring books) helped confirm that anime was a subject to be taken as seriously as, well, the latest DC and Marvel superheroes who reigned as high school and college pop culture icons. It was nagging the Japanese-community bookshops from July 1978 on to import more copies of these monthly anime magazines that helped lead to the first anime and manga specialty shops in America.

American fan attempts to create anime magazines like the Japanese have sputtered and usually failed since the mid-1980s, at first due to difficulty in establishing contact with the Japanese studios to obtain the anime art and the permissions to publish it, and more recently to getting coast-to-coast newsstand distribution. A similar problem (more common in Britain than America) has befallen fans' attempts to interest established magazine publishers in starting an anime magazine. They have not become immediate successes as the publishers hoped and were canceled before having time to grow. But for the past decade *Protoculture Addicts* (Spring 1988), *Animerica* (November 1992), such Internet brethren as *EX: The Online World of Anime and Manga* (June 1996), and now *Newtype USA* (November 2002) have provided that service with increasing scope and expertise. And it all started in July 1978.

Simba Versus Kimba: The Pride of Lions
Unpublished paper presented at Australia's Second International Conference on Animation, Sydney, March 3–5, 1995.

Introduction

The February 27, 1995, *Los Angeles Times* quoted the Disney Company's Roy E. Disney as saying that *The Lion King* "would be the most profitable movie of all time, with about $800 million in profits from its box office, video sales, merchandising, and other sources . . ." [50] In addition to the technical excellence of its animation, its great popularity is generally attributed to the strength of its characters and story: the maturing of a lion prince, Simba, from an insecure cub to a strong ruler of all the animals of the jungle.

However, this is not the first time that this plot has appeared in animation. One of the major works of Japanese animation is Osamu Tezuka's 1965–66 *Jungle Emperor*, known in the West as *Kimba the White Lion*.[3] This is the story of the maturing of a lion prince, Kimba, from an idealistic but often naïve cub with self-doubts to a confident leader of all the animals of the jungle.

Similarities between the two titles were immediately noticed and commented upon, at least partly because of Disney's publicity emphasis of its claim that *The Lion King* was its first animated feature which was an entirely original studio-developed story, not based upon any previous folk tale or literary work. During the three or four months after the release of *The Lion King*, the issue generated considerable controversy in America and in Japan. This was exacerbated by Disney's further claim in the July 14, 1994, *San Francisco Chronicle* that "none of the principals involved in creating *The Lion King* were aware of Kimba or Tezuka," according to "Howard Green, spokesman for Walt Disney Pictures." (*San Francisco Chronicle*, Thursday, July 14, 1994, p. D1). This assertion seemed improbably naïve to both American and Japanese critics, since Osamu Tezuka was internationally famous as "the Walt Disney of Japan" and since the *Kimba* TV cartoons had been widely shown on American TV from 1966 until the early 1980s.

This essay presents a brief summary of the career of Osamu Tezuka and of his *Kimba the White Lion,* with an emphasis on public awareness of them in America. An overview of the production of Disney's *The Lion King* is next presented, and similarities between it and *Kimba* are addressed. Finally, Tezuka's international reputation as an award-winning animator and Disney's expertise in the animation industry are discussed in relation to Disney's claims of a lack of awareness of Tezuka or of *Kimba.* While this essay draws support for its position from the work of Fred Ladd, Trish Ledoux, Frederik Schodt, and Toren Smith on the matter, its conclusions are those of the author alone. I have undertaken this essay to collate evidence from many diverse sources and to add my own personal knowledge acquired over two decades as an enthusiast and expert on both American and Japanese animation.

A Biographical Sketch of Osamu Tezuka

Osamu Tezuka is widely revered in Japan as the founder of its comic book and animation industries. He was not the first to create either comic books or animation, but, like Disney, he came into a nascent industry and became its trendsetter.

Osamu Tezuka was born on November 3, 1928, in Osaka. He entered college as a medical student just after World War II. He was also a precocious cartoonist and an enthusiast of animation. In 1946, at the age of eighteen, he published his first professional comic book. Shortly after obtaining his physician's license, he was forced to concentrate upon one career or the other, and he chose cartooning.

This essay has had a strange and wonderful history; "ten years in the making." And it's not over yet.

For me, it started in July 1994 right at the beginning of the Simba-Kimba controversy. I was telephone-interviewed by Charles Burress for his "Uproar Over 'The Lion King'" story in the *San Francisco Chronicle* on July 11 (note 22). He told me that I would be one of several *Kimba* experts cited, and went over my comments that he wanted to use in detail to make sure he was quoting me correctly. Unfortunately for me, North Korea's Comrade President Kim Il Sung picked that weekend to die, and all the stories for the newspaper's July 11 issue had to be trimmed at the last minute to make space for the headlines. All my quotes got cut. But I did appear on TV on *Entertainment Tonight* the next weekend, and I was interviewed by several other newspaper and TV news reporters over the next few weeks for my opinions.

The controversy was just starting to fade from the public's attention when I received an invitation from Dr. Alan Cholodenko of the University of Sydney to be a guest speaker at "Ono's Second International Conference on Animation" at Sydney's Museum of Contemporary Art at the beginning of March 1995, specifically to present a paper there on the controversy. Basically, I was being

Cont. on p. 146

The Japanese comic book industry scarcely existed before Tezuka. His career and this artistic literary form evolved together. Tezuka gave "comic book artist" a completely different interpretation to that which it had in America. He was essentially a visual novelist and short story writer. He produced his own stories of varying lengths for a wide variety of magazines.

Among Tezuka's early artistic influences were the American animated cartoons and newspaper comic strips from the Disney and Fleisher studios. Tezuka later acknowledged his debt to the *Mickey Mouse* newspaper strip drawn by Disney artist Floyd Gottfredson and to the Fleischer brothers's 1939 *Gulliver's Travels*. One of Tezuka's few graphic adaptations of someone else's work was an authorized Japanese comic book version of Disney's *Bambi*, published in 1951. [2] Frederik L. Schodt, Tezuka's personal English translator for many years, has said that Tezuka considered Disney to be his idol. [57] His works included children's picture books, fantasy-adventure comics for boys, fantasy-romance comics for girls, raunchy humor for men's magazines, psychological thrillers and historical novels for serious adult magazines, political cartoons, poster art, and advertising art. He was instrumental in establishing the Japanese cultural attitude that cartooning was not limited to children's entertainment but was an acceptable medium for the presentation of fiction for all age groups.

In 1961, Tezuka created Japan's first TV animation studio. The existing studios were all concentrating on the famous Disney formula of high-quality theatrical animated features based on traditional folk tales. Japan's most elaborate feature up to that time was Toei Animation's 1960 *Sai Yuki* (brought to America in 1961 as *Alakazam the Great*), an adaptation by director Taiji Yabushita of Tezuka's own 1950s comic art interpretation of the classic

offered an all-expenses-paid trip to Australia if I would prepare and read a scholarly essay to the conference (a gathering of academicians, definitely not a fan convention), and allow the paper to be published in a collection of academic articles about animation.

I had a wonderful two weeks in and around Sydney! Dr. Cholodenko was an excellent host, Kosei Ono, who had been my translator when I visited Tokyo in the 1980s, was also a speaker at the conference and I was glad to see him again, and some members of Sydney's science-fiction community welcomed me at their club and showed me around the city and the nearby Blue Mountains. The only slight problem was that Dr. Cholodenko felt that the original draft of my paper was a trifle too popular in style for presentation at an *academic* conference. I had to agree when I saw the synopses of some of the other papers scheduled to be read. To quote one of them: "John Conomos: The Odd Couple, or, Happy Happy, Joy Joy. This paper will explore in a transverse, speculative manner the intertextual delineation of the animatic apparatus in the cultic Nickelotoon *The Ren and Stimpy Show*. Mobilizing an interdisciplinary poststructural approach, the speaker will address questions of abjection, animatophilia, carnivalisation, dialogism and the frame of the frame in a multifaceted discursive attempt to

Chinese *Monkey King* legend. (The aforementioned artistic influences from Gottfredson's *Mickey Mouse* and the Fleischers' *Gulliver's Travels* are notable here.) Nonetheless, Tezuka recognized that the animation establishment was ignoring a public demand for modern and futuristic cartoon adventures on film, as demonstrated by the increasing sales of comic books featuring those plots during the previous decade.

Tezuka's studio, Mushi Productions, premiered its first TV series on New Year's Day 1963—*Mighty Atom*—brought to America later that year as *Astro Boy.* It was an instant, great success, so much so that within two years, a half-dozen other TV animation studios had sprung up in competition.

While turning his back on the Disney formula of remaking the classics in his pioneering of this new genre, Tezuka did not turn his back on another signature feature of Disney's animation, that is, he followed Disney's lead in concentrating on characters rather than on gags or action or flashy visuals. *Mighty Atom* was most easily symbolized by its futuristic setting and its little boy robot star. But what won it a devoted following was its strong characterizations, generated through the personal interactions of a regular cast of characters. Tezuka refined this Disney formula in his second TV series, *Jungle Emperor,* or *Kimba the White Lion,* which many feel was really his best work.

After that, Tezuka fell victim to his own determination to remain an artist rather than a businessman. He was not interested in repeating the same things *ad infinitum* just because they made money. Ironically, what befell Mushi Productions was basically what befell the Disney studio after Disney's personal attention shifted to his EPCOT project and he let his staff take complete directorial control over his features. In Tezuka's case, he began

color in the more distinctive polyphonic cultural, kinetic-visual and theoretical concerns of our Spumco odd couple." Dr. Cholodenko helped me to revise my paper to make it fit in better with the others, which is why it has, let us say, a more erudite formalism than I usually employ in my writings.

The book in which "Simba versus Kimba" was to appear was supposed to be published by the University of Sydney's Power Institute Press about a year later. It was delayed, delayed again, and eventually rescheduled for early 1998. Dr. Cholodenko asked if I could write an epilogue to bring the controversy up to the end of 1997. I was happy to do so because, by three years later, there had been several further developments worth recording such as the parody-reference to the controversy on *The Simpsons,* and its documentation in books such as *Samurai from Outer Space* and *Mouse Under Glass.* Disney's 1996 acquisition of Hayao Miyazaki's films, and Disney's publicity about how knowledgeable the company was about the Japanese video and animation industries, was definitely worth quoting alongside its claim that it had never heard of Osamu Tezuka. Most importantly, some of the animators who had worked on *The Lion King* were now willing to go on record about how, sure, plenty of its production crew had heard of Osamu Tezuka and were familiar with at least his 1980s short

Cont. on p. 148

to concentrate on avant-garde animations, such as *Pictures at an Exhibition* (1966), a *Fantasia*-like production of Mussorgsky's musical classic, with the individual "pictures" being satiric political cartoon commentaries on aspects of contemporary society, and *One Thousand and One Nights* (1969), a feature-length version of the classic *Arabian Nights* tale which was faithful to the mature eroticism of the original work. These garnered critical acclaim, but they were not commercial successes. Mushi Productions continued to produce TV series, but they lacked the strong characterizations that had gone into *Astro Boy* and *Kimba*. In 1971, Tezuka left Mushi Productions for a new studio, Tezuka Productions. Although Tezuka Productions has produced numerous commercial projects—and is still doing so today—Tezuka's own attention remained upon short, experimental films which he personally took to animation festivals around the world where they invariably won major awards. The most famous examples are *Jumping* (1984), *Broken-Down Film* (1985), and *Legend of the Forest* (1987). Osamu Tezuka passed away from cancer on February 9, 1989, working to the end.

The Publication and Popular Influence of *Jungle Emperor* in Japan

Although Tezuka produced over 500 different comic art stories during his life, among his top ten, and the first to win critical acclaim, was *Junguru Taitei*, translated into English by Tezuka himself as *The Jungle Emperor*, but more idiomatically *King of the Jungle*.

This was his first major work. It began publication in a children's magazine, *Manga Shonen* (*Boys' Comics*), in November 1950.[1] It was the story of an intelligent African lion, named Leo in the Japanese version, who tried to improve the lot of all animals. It was an adventure fantasy

art films like *Jumping*, and knew of his reputation as the creator of *Astro Boy* and *Kimba*. (But these animators still claimed that there were no deliberate ripoffs of *Kimba* in *The Lion King*, or at least no more than the usual ingroup jokes and references that animators put into any feature. Disney's 1991 *Beauty and the Beast* has several "tributes" to earlier *Beauty and the Beast* movies, especially the 1946 Jean Cocteau version, for those who know what to look for.) We both felt that my expanded paper now covered the entire history of the controversy, so to that extent the delay in his book had been worth it.

Dr. Cholodenko's book was *not* published in early 1998. In late 1997 Peter Schweizer called me. He was a Florida author writing (with his wife) a critical analysis of the modern Disney media empire, *Disney: The Mouse Betrayed—Greed, Corruption, and Children at Risk*. He wanted to interview me for a whole chapter on the Disney-Tezuka controversy (Chapter 11, The Lyin' King), and he wanted to cite some of my 1995 essay. I did not want to keep my research a secret (particularly since I felt indebted to Schweizer for giving me a detail that I had not known, that Disney's own press kit for *The Lion King* stated that co-director Roger Aller had spent two years in Tokyo working on animation just before returning to America to work on *The Lion King*; I immediately went to the with talking animals, not a realistic nature novel, and it explored concepts of civilization in comparison to natural instinct. It showed how issues that seem simplistically right or wrong to a child can look much more complex to an adult, and made the point that a full life is bound to encompass both happiness and tragedy.

Jungle Emperor was a serious children's novel in cartoon form, and it was almost immediately recognized as such. Its serialization took three and a half years to complete; the final installment was in April 1954. The first book reprints of its over 500 pages appeared while it was still being serialized. It has been almost constantly in print, in editions ranging from a deluxe boxed, hardbound single volume to inexpensive paperbound sets of three or four volumes. Tezuka slightly revised the story several times, and the final version was published in 1977.

To give some perspective, Tezuka's *Mighty Atom* (*Astro Boy*) began in another comic book, *Shonen* (*Boy*), in April 1951. This was more of a comic book series in the American sense. It consisted of numerous serialized short stories which Tezuka kept spinning out. There was originally no planned conclusion to the series, although Tezuka wrote one in the late 1960s. During the great popularity of the *Mighty Atom* TV series, the commercial pressures on Tezuka to produce more comic book adventures grew to the point that he admitted becoming heartily sick of having to hack out new stories. But despite the fact that the *Jungle Emperor* TV program was also extremely popular, Tezuka was never seriously tempted to expand that finished novel (as distinct from his fine-tuning of the existing pages).

Jungle Emperor became a national institution. This was due to the TV cartoons as much as to the novel. They were broadcast from 1965 to 1967,

Academy of Motion Picture Arts and Sciences' research library, verified that this was true, and added a citation to the press kit to my essay), but I had promised Dr. Cholodenko that I would let him publish my research first. This did not seem to be a problem, however, since Cholodenko's book was due out in early 1998 and Schweizer assured me that his book would not be published until the last half of the year. So I sent Schweizer a copy of my manuscript. He kept his promise; *Disney: The Mouse Betrayed* was not published (by Regnery Publishing, Inc.) until September 1998. It was not his fault that Dr. Cholodenko's book had been delayed yet again.

The delays went on for so long that I was able to add the date the Mushi Pro bankruptcy suit finally ended and The Right Stuf International was able to license *Kimba the White Lion* for video release in America between April and October 2000. During the last half of 2001, an almost identical controversy arose over similarities between Disney's new *Atlantis: The Lost Empire* theatrical feature and the 1990–91 anime series *Nadia: The Secret of Blue Water*. Dr. Cholodenko and I felt that this would make a pertinent afterword to "Simba versus Kimba." During 2003, Dr. Cholodenko's book advanced close enough to publication that the Power Institute Press posted its dust jacket art on its "forthcoming books" Web

Cont. on p. 150

and their characters—slightly modified from those in the cartoon novel—became merchandising idols. A unique aspect of this was that, in Japan unlike in America, Leo and his girlfriend, Lya, matured, married and had cubs of their own. Therefore, the Japanese *Jungle Emperor* merchandising included additional characters unknown in America. This merchandising included the usual range of Disney, Hanna-Barbera, or Warner Bros. style cartoon character toys, items such as children's towels and Band-Aids, calendars, and so forth.

But awareness in Japan of *Jungle Emperor* did not stop with the completion of the TV cartoons. Mighty Atom and Leo became the standard character-emblems of Tezuka and his cartooning empire, just as Mickey Mouse and Donald Duck have remained permanently associated with Walt Disney in America, long after their animated cartoons ceased production. A symphonic suite arrangement of Isao Tomita's music for the *Jungle Emperor* pilot episode became a Japanese children's musical classic, comparable to Prokofieff's *Peter and the Wolf*, and it is still in print. The adult Leo became the cartoon mascot-logo of the Seibu Lions, one of Japan's top baseball teams. In the 1970s and 1980s, after serious animation fandom developed in Japan, numerous books on the *Jungle Emperor* TV cartoons were published, giving full details about their production history and staff and credits for each episode. Leo toys and other juvenile merchandise have continued to appear every year, keeping up with the times as to computer games, PVC figures, and the latest in packaging design. One of Tezuka's last business decisions was to authorize a remake of the *Jungle Emperor* TV series by Tezuka Productions. This was considered by both his staff and the public as largely a memorial to him. It was serialized as fifty weekly episodes from October 1989, eight months after his death, through September 1990, in a 7:30 P.M. prime time spot. [13]

page. However, as *Watching Anime, Reading Manga* is finishing its preparation in mid-2004, his anthology of animation scholarly essays (tentatively titled *The Illusion of Life II*) is still "coming soon." I am sorry, Dr. Cholodenko, I wanted to let you publish "Simba versus Kimba" first. But I cannot pass up this opportunity to include it in my own book.

There has been some controversy over the claim that the April–October 2000 American video release of *Kimba the White Lion* (and the March 2003 DVD release of the first twenty-six episodes from Rhino Home Entertainment) were "produced from NBC's original masters" due to the evident poor visual quality. Fifty-one of the fifty-two episodes were indeed; only episode no. 45's master was missing, and the video had to be produced from a 16 mm film print. But the masters were not *restored*. They had been in storage in non-environmentally-controlled warehouses from 1978 to 2000 when The Right Stuf International was finally able to license *Kimba,* and the masters were simply unpacked and processed for home video production. Restoring them to their original pristine condition would have been prohibitively expensive. ■

Kosei Ono (left) and Fred Patten (right) visiting Australian professional fantasy artists Lewis Morley and Marilyn Pride at their Totoro home built into the hillside in the Blue Mountains following the 1995 International Animation Conference in Sydney.

Analysis of the Plot and Theme of *Jungle Emperor*

Jungle Emperor is primarily the story of a lion, Leo, who is the heir to a kingdom of jungle animals near Kenya. He is born on a ship taking his captured mother to a European zoo, so all that he initially knows about his heritage is the little that she has time to tell him—that he is the son of a jungle king who was killed by human hunters and that he must escape and return to help the animals. Leo does escape from the ship, but he ends up in the port city of Aden. Since he is still a cute cub, a human boy is allowed to temporarily keep him as a pet.

Leo's experiences in this family situation, and his growing friendship with the boy Ken-ichi, lead him to realize that humans are not automatically bad—they can be good or bad. When, after various adventures, Leo returns to the jungle and assumes the leadership of the animal kingdom, he has two ideals that he enthusiastically wants to put into practice: first, animals and humans should live together as fellow inhabitants of the same world, not as distinct life forms separate from each other; and second, the animals themselves should imitate humans in building a cooperative civilization instead of fatalistically accepting the harsh law of the jungle as an immutable natural order.

Tezuka commented at a presentation to the Cartoon/Fantasy Organization in Los Angeles in March 1978, at which this author was present, that his inspiration for *Jungle Emperor* was in part his disagreement with the philosophy of nature and intelligence expressed in Disney's *Bambi*. Tezuka felt that if the forest animals in *Bambi* had been as self-aware and mutually social as they were depicted, they would not have remained so fearful and remote from man. They would have recognized man as just another animal like themselves, and tried to communicate with him. This led to his own story in which the animals of Africa realize the advantages of civilization and try to take advantage of them and try to get man to recognize them as social equals. (Tezuka always felt that both "nature" and "civilization" were aspects of the same real world, rather than separate worlds, and that both the advantages and disadvantages of each needed to be taken into account. In some of his other works, notably *Phoenix*, Tezuka describes a futuristic, overly mechanized civilization that has totally lost touch with nature, leading to its self-destruction.)

As Leo matures, he gradually learns more about his ancestors and the special role of his white lion dynasty. He also discovers that some of his initial expectations were naïve. For example, he learns that carnivores do not eat other animals just because they are ignorant or uncaring of the virtues of friendship. Carnivores cannot voluntarily switch to grazing like the herbivores—they would starve to death. Leo does the best that he can, sometimes cutting back on his goals, sometimes proving to the other animals that cooperation does work better than "every animal for itself." Leo finds a girlfriend; when they become adults they marry and have two cubs. After other triumphs and tragedies, Leo joins a human scientific expedition searching for a rare mineral atop Mt. Moon. One of the members of this expedition is the father of Leo's childhood human friend. At the climax, Leo sacrifices his own life to save Ken-ichi's father. *Jungle Emperor* ends with an affirmation that Leo's son, Luné (who has had his own adventures in a long subplot in New York City), has returned to the jungle and will carry on Leo's peaceful animal civilization and his ideals of a brotherhood of all nature that includes man.

The Animated Version of *Jungle Emperor*

There are significant differences between Tezuka's cartoon art novel and the animated adaptation of *Jungle Emperor*, differences that issued from Tezuka's desire to distribute his work in the United States and the conditions that attached to this aspiration. Previously *Mighty Atom* had been acquired for the American market by NBC, shortly after it debuted in Japan on January 1, 1963, and it premiered in America as a syndicated series, *Astro Boy*, in September 1963. NBC's money was a welcome windfall; it enabled Tezuka to increase the production values of the later episodes.

In 1965, Tezuka felt ready to animate *Jungle Emperor*. He had no trouble preselling it to Japan's Fuji TV network, but he also wanted to get NBC's money into its production and from the start. His proposal to NBC was for a serialization of his novel, from Leo's birth to his heroic death.

This was completely foreign to American ideas for children's television, but NBC liked the concept of a friendly, altruistic lion who promoted brotherhood and cooperation. They offered Tezuka enough money to film *Jungle Emperor* in color rather than in black-and-white if he would agree to some changes. The story should concentrate on the animals in Leo's kingdom and downplay the humans. Leo should remain a cute cub and never grow up, and *certainly* never die! In fact, nobody should ever die. NBC wanted an upbeat series with violence at a minimum. Finally, the story should be restructured into self-contained episodes that could be shown in any order, rather than as a serial.

Tezuka was very unhappy. But he did want to produce *Jungle Emperor* in higher-quality, color animation, and he wanted to introduce his story to American audiences, so he agreed to NBC's terms. Nevertheless, he tried to keep as close to his original story as NBC would allow. There were references in flashback to Leo's experiences in the humans' civilization before he came to the jungle—a sequence that NBC had wanted removed. In addition to the deaths of Leo's parents (NBC had conceded that this was too integral to the plot to be removed), there were occasional fatalities, or clear references to mortality. In the episode *Dangerous Journey,* when the old mountain goat who has a fever soliloquizes about going off by himself to spare the other animals from catching his disease, it is obvious that he expects to die. As the episodes were sent to America, NBC kept telling Tezuka to "lighten up," which he promised to do, but went on inserting as much drama as he could get away with.

The animated *Jungle Emperor,* then, was not really to either Tezuka's or to NBC's credit. It was an uneasy, grudging mixture of American and Japanese cultural styles. In the novel, Leo might have a bloody fight with some large animal, such as an elephant, who refused to abide by his policies of cooperation. This may have been plausible where Leo was an adult lion, but it was not credible that a little cub could defeat such massive animals. The solution was to make Leo a super-cub, with unusual strength as well as his unique white coloring. That way he could easily overpower his adversaries and then deliver a moral lecture to them, without needing to maul them into submission. It also made Leo more like a superhero, with which American juveniles were comfortable.

If the animated *Jungle Emperor* is to any single individual's credit, that person is its director, Eiichi Yamamoto. Tezuka kept an eye on the general story line, but he gave Yamamoto free rein in adapting the 533-page novel into fifty-two self-contained episodes.

It was Yamamoto who gave *Jungle Emperor* its subtle but crucial changes. He had to replace story evolution with character development. Since the animated version's setting was fixed in the jungle animal kingdom during Leo's childhood, the focus had to shift to the animals themselves and their social relationships. Tezuka had drawn the juvenile Leo as the cub equivalent of an eight-year-old human. This was too young for a plausible kingdom-founder, so Yamamoto portrayed Leo as a husky eleven- or twelve-year-old, approaching adolescence. Yamamoto combined most of Leo's various animal antagonists into a single villain, a brutish one-eyed lion who had seized the vacant jungle throne after Leo's father's death. He turned this villain's assistant, Tot (a comical black panther), into a much more sinister henchman, and gave Tot's old comedy-relief role to two new stooges, a couple of laughing hyenas. (The idea was briefly considered of having them be lieutenants who would pass the villain's orders down to a whole pack of hyena goons, but the TV animation budget did not permit the addition of so many characters.)

Most importantly, Yamamoto created the large supporting cast of Leo's friends. A couple had been minor characters in Tezuka's novel. Others were invented by Yamamoto, including Mandy, the old baboon father-figure and advisor; Coco, the comically pompous parrot who appoints himself as Leo's herald and news-gatherer; Tommy, the well-meaning but often inept gazelle; the several animal children; and the older, larger animals who are initially skeptical of Leo's lofty ideals and are gradually won over to become Leo's supporters. Some of the minor characters, such as the hedgehog, might appear only for a few seconds in every seventh or eighth episode, but when he did, he stood out from the others, and he was completely in character with his previous appearances. This large, regular cast of individualized, likeable characters has been cited by fans in both Japan and America as what they liked best about the program.

Other notable aspects of the high quality of *Jungle Emperor* were the rich use of color, also to Yamamoto's credit, and the background music, which was scored for a full orchestra by Isao Tomita before he became a prestigious composer of electronic music. When Tezuka agreed to produce *Jungle Emperor* in color, he wanted its quality to be as high as possible. NBC's American producer, Fred Ladd, arranged for Tezuka and Yamamoto to send a Mushi animation team to Ladd's New York office where they were instructed in color production by veteran former Disney animator Preston Blair.

There was also an unusual sequel. It rankled Tezuka that he had not been allowed to film *Jungle Emperor* as the life story of Leo. As soon as the fifty-two episodes that he was obligated to produce to NBC's standards were completed, he began a twenty-six-episode sequel—*Susume, Leo!* (*susume* is a Japanese colloquial shout of daring encouragement, as for a cavalry charge or a football team's advance)—set about five years later. Leo and Lya were now adults, and the story continued roughly as it had in Tezuka's graphic novel, although Leo did not quite die in the final episode. (He survived to abdicate in his son Lune's favor and to a well-earned retirement.) This was shown in Japan as a direct sequel to *Jungle Emperor*. Tezuka offered it to NBC, which declined it. So it was not seen in America at that time.

The Americanized *Jungle Emperor: Kimba the White Lion*

Jungle Emperor was produced in Japan for network broadcast as a weekly 7:00 P.M. prime-time program—Japan's first TV color animation, although it was broadcast in black-and-white—beginning on October 6, 1965. Episodes were sent to America as soon as they were completed. Their Americanization was subcontracted by NBC to Fred Ladd, an independent producer who specialized in converting foreign movies and TV programs into English. Ladd had also produced *Mighty Atom* as *Astro Boy,* so he and his staff had some familiarity with Tezuka's films.

NBC gave Ladd the same instructions that Tezuka had received, with one important addition. NBC felt that the name, Leo, was too stereotyped for a lion, especially since it was the name of MGM's trademarked lion mascot-logo. Leo's name had to be changed to something more original. The decision was made by Ladd's staff to take the Swahili word for lion, *simba,* and change the initial letter. The result was Kimba, a catchy, euphonious, and completely original name, and the obvious source of the American title: *Kimba the White Lion.* [3]

In America, *Kimba* (and *Astro Boy*) were syndicated by NBC rather than being shown on its own network. NBC decided to wait until all fifty-two episodes had been converted into English before releasing them, so purchasing channels could air them as either a weekly or a daily program. *Kimba* first appeared on Los Angeles's KHJ-TV, Channel 9, in September 1966 in a 5:30 P.M. late afternoon time slot. It spread to other American cities in late 1966 and early 1967. (As a chronological reference note, Walt Disney died in December 1966.)

Kimba was immediately popular. It was subtly different from other TV cartoons. The colors, the backgrounds and the orchestral music had a richness that ranked with theatrical cartoons, not the TV animation of the day. However, the story format—half-hour adventures rather than six or seven minutes of gag humour—identified *Kimba* as a TV cartoon rather than a TV broadcast of an old theatrical short. *Kimba* also presented a richness of characterization that stood out amidst the shallow stereotypes of other TV cartoons. When *Kimba* first appeared, public attitudes toward children's television were such that it was commended for its positive moral values. Kimba was an approved role model for his strong ethics and his willingness to fight for good causes.

This gradually changed over the following decade. Standards for children's programming became stricter and encouraging fighting for any reason became frowned upon. Complaints began to come in from African-American pressure groups, not so much because Kimba himself was white (as animation-fan legend today attributes the reason) as because, in the few times that humans did appear in an episode, *they* were invariably white: big-game hunters, tourists on safari, scientific explorers, criminals hiding from the law. Africa seemed to have no ethnic Africans living there.

But these complaints were not the reason for *Kimba*'s disappearance in the late 1970s. The contract for the American rights expired in September 1978. Mushi Productions had gone bankrupt in 1973 following Tezuka's departure, and the rights to its properties were in litigation. Nobody in Japan had authority to sign a new contract for *Kimba*.

Meanwhile, in America, the federal government had issued an anti-trust directive forbidding television companies from both broadcasting and syndicating programs to other broadcasters. NBC had to close its NBC Films subsidiary. In 1971, *Kimba* was transferred, along with all of NBC's other syndicated programming, to National Telefilm Associates in Los Angeles. NTA continued to syndicate *Kimba* for as long as NBC's rights lasted. NTA withdrew *Kimba* from release on September 30, 1978.

However, one of the Japanese claimaints of the *Kimba* rights, Fumio Suzuki, obtained a set of the 16 mm films and, representing himself as their owner, sold them to another TV distributor, Air Time International. ATI was a much smaller distributor than NTA, but it did continue to get *Kimba* on the air in some American cities through barter sales until it went out of business during the 1980s.

The rights to *Jungle Emperor* were in litigation in Japan through early 1997. Several American video companies over the years tried to license the video rights, without success. So during the time of *The Lion King*'s production and release, the only videos available in America of NBC's *Kimba* were unauthorized copies, either film-chained from worn 16 mm. prints discarded by TV studios twenty years ago or copies of the videos of the final TV broadcasts that were dubbed by fans in the late 1970s and early 1980s. (Many of the *Kimba* videos sold at fan conventions show the commercial-break logo cards of Los Angeles' KBSC-TV, Channel 52, which broadcast *Kimba* from August 1976 through July 1977.)

The sequel, *Susume, Leo!*, did finally come to American TV in 1984 on the Christian Broadcasting Network, under the title of *Leo the Lion*. The quality of the American adaptation was atrocious, but at least all the characters retained their original Japanese names. It attracted little attention, even from the anime fandom that had developed by that time—and it also soon disappeared.

Plot and Parallels Between Kimba and *The Lion King*

Ten years later, on June 15, 1994, the Disney Company released *The Lion King*, which has set new records for animation popularity throughout the world. [50] As a result of this acclaim, attention has been recalled to *Kimba the White Lion* and to notable similarities between the two. [See notes 18, 22–35, 37–49, 51–62.]

The protagonist of *The Lion King* is a lion cub, Simba, who is the heir to an African kingdom of animals. He is told from birth that, one day, this will all be his. But his father is murdered, and he is tricked into fleeing. Years later, as a young adult, he returns to claim his rightful position from its usurper and to reestablish the kingdom, which has fallen into ruin.

There are striking parallels between the two stories, but there are also significant differences. In *Kimba the White Lion,* as noted earlier, Kimba is concerned with friendship and social equality between the animals and mankind. In *The Lion King,* man does not seem to exist (although man is alluded to in the film's humor, such as the parody of the hyenas as marching Nazi troopers in Scar's musical number, and Timon's dressing in Hawaiian drag to dance a hula). Moreover, in *The Lion King,* it is implied that the animal kingdom around Pride Rock, under the reign of the lion dynasty, is peaceful and happy because this is the natural order of life. It also seems that this kingdom encompasses all of Africa, although this is contradicted when Simba flees from the kingdom and must later be persuaded to return to it. On the other hand, in *Kimba,* the natural order of life is the law of the jungle. Kimba's "peaceful kingdom" is an artificial creation which must be established through deliberate persuasion and which only spreads slowly from a small nucleus in imitation of the evolution of human civilization.

Furthermore, Simba in *The Lion King* is a cocky and rather spoiled child who instantly evolves into a carefree older adolescent who rejects all responsibility until he undergoes a divine revelation which transforms him into an adult, enlightened ruler. Kimba is a young child only in the pilot episode. In the regular episodes, Kimba is about to enter adolescence, highly idealistic and obsessed with his responsibility to an almost pathological degree—there are several instances when he breaks into tears because of doubts about his ability to live up to his image of his father. (Kimba never knew his father, Caesar, alive, but the hunter who killed him had skinned him, and the animals later retrieved this trophy. One of the program's more memorable images—doubtlessly because it is so bizarre—is young Kimba going into a hut which has been turned into a shrine to Caesar to receive inspiration from his father's glassy-eyed pelt.) Kimba is aware of his lack of experience, and he constantly seeks advice from wise old Dan'l Baboon instead of needing it forced upon him. Kimba does gradually grow in self-confidence, but not significantly in physical maturity. (He appears to be approximately the lion cub equivalent of a ten- or eleven-year-old human boy at his return to the jungle and of a thirteen- or fourteen-year-old young adolescent in the final episode.)

Certainly, given that the reputation of the lion as "king of the jungle" is a staple of folklore, going back at least as far as Aesop's fables 2,500 years ago, it is reasonable that modern fantasy writers might independently parody the court intrigue of a European-style monarchy by setting it in an African nation of anthropomorphized animals with a lion king. This can make it difficult to determine whether two similar stories are the result of coincidental development of the same source materials, or whether the later of the two stories was actually influenced by the former. Simba is an obvious name for a lion protagonist. An article in the July 13 *Los Angeles Times* reports: "The project was initially called 'King of the Jungle' and, like most animated features at Disney, its development was evolutionary, taking years to create and refine,' stated a Disney press kit." [16] As noted earlier, *King of the Jungle* is an alternate translation of Tezuka's *Junguru Taitei*—but the phrase is such a common metaphor for lions that it could easily be anyone's first choice for the title of a fantasy of this nature.

So what, specifically, are the parallels between the two films? Here are eight points of similarity which seem to go beyond reasonable coincidence:

1. The personalities and roles of the major characters are established throughout both *The Lion King* and various of the fifty-two episodes of *Kimba the White Lion*. The parallels include: Simba and Kimba; their wise, noble fathers Mufasa and Caesar; their childhood sweethearts Nala and Kitty; the villainous lions Scar and Claw, and the panther Cassius (Scar combines elements of both); the wise baboon advisors Rafiki and Dan'l Baboon; the comically pompous bird majordomos Zazu and Pauley Cracker; the humorous loyal companions Timon and Pumbaa and Pauley Cracker (again) and Bucky Deer; and the evil, cowardly, yet irrepressibly silly laughing hyenas Shenzi, Banzai and Ed, and Tab and Tom. These characters should be compared.

2. The same plot operates. The wise lion king is killed, and the young prince is driven from home. He returns to find that the throne has been occupied in his absence by a brutal, scar-faced (the scar located over one eye) older lion, whom he must defeat in battle to become king.

3. A wise, elderly mandrill baboon who had been the old king's friend becomes the prince's sardonic but kindly mentor. Also, a comically excitable bird of about the same size—a parrot in *Kimba*, a hornbill in *The Lion King*— plays a pompous functionary, a herald or its equivalent. The scar-faced lion villain is supported by a team of comic-relief cowardly laughing hyenas. In *The Lion King*, the evil Scar gives orders directly to the hyenas, whereas in *Kimba*, Boss Claw has a black-panther henchman who is his intermediary to the lower-class hyenas. In *The Lion King*, Scar is played as suavely sinister with an upper-class accent. In *Kimba*, Claw is a hot-tempered, brutal thug, but the black panther, Cassius, is suavely sinister with an upper-class accent.

4. The prince as a cub meets a young lioness who becomes his playmate. In *The Lion King*, they marry when they become adults; and the lioness bears his child to carry on the dynasty. In *Kimba*, there is a clear implication that Kimba and Kitty will wed when they grow up. And in the *Leo the Lion* sequel shown on cable TV during the mid-1980s, this explicitly happens.

5. There is an anti-carnivore and pro-herbivore stance. In *Kimba*, Kimba's initial dream of planting a farm for all animals so the carnivores can be friends with the herbivores seems stymied when he is made aware that carnivores cannot survive on plants. Just then, the farm is attacked by locusts, and the carnivores save the plants—and find a socially-acceptable food for themselves—by eating the locusts (the episodes "Insect Invasion" and "The Gigantic Grasshopper"). Later, when they are about to run out of locusts, a friendly human scientist visiting the jungle discovers a vegetarian "meat substitute" so the carnivores never have to prey upon other animals again ("A Revolting Development"). In *The Lion King*, Simba is taught to eat bugs so he can become a non-threatening social equal of herbivores.

6. The image of a parent in the sky plays an inspirational role. In *The Jungle Emperor* novel, there is a memorable scene at the beginning where the infant Leo sees his mother's image in the stars at night and another at the end where young Luné sees the martyred Leo's image in the clouds over the savannah. In the TV cartoons, Kimba has a vision every few episodes of his mother or father in the stars, in the clouds, or over a full moon. In *The Lion King*, King Mufasa tells young Simba, "Look at the stars. The great kings of the past look down on us from those stars. So whenever you feel alone, just remember that those kings will always be there to guide you." Later, the adult Simba is inspired by Mufasa's image in the clouds.

7. A stampede is a key event in the hero's life. In *The Lion King*, King Mufasa is killed while rescuing Simba from a tree in the midst of a wildebeest stampede. As a result of this stampede and his father's death, Simba is tricked into fleeing into exile. In the episode *Running Wild*, Kimba and his friends are threatened by a stampede of antelopes. Kimba must save Bucky Deer, who is clinging to a tree in the midst of the stampede. Later, Kimba is so despondent that he could not stop the antelope that he declares he is not fit to rule, and he runs off to sulk. Dan'l Baboon has to spank him and, to give him the understanding to take up his responsibilities again, give him a pep talk about how a leader is not expected to succeed every time as long as he perseveres.

8. There are notable visual parallels between many scenes in both works, as follows:

1-A. *The Lion King.* Opening scene, "The Circle of Life": pan over birds flying over the savannah, showing a panorama of all the animals of Africa, sweeping up to King Mufasa posing majestically on Pride Rock. 0:40 to 1:51.

1-B. *Jungle Emperor.* Opening title credits and theme song: from the adult King Leo posing majestically on a cliff, panning down over birds flying over the savannah, showing a panorama of all the animals of Africa. 0:01 to 1:57.

1-C. *Kimba,* Prod. #66–5, "Journey Into Time." Another lion (King Specklerex) poses majestically on a cliff, with the Japanese Rising Sun in the background.

2-A. *The Lion King.* The wildebeest stampede. 32:08 to 32:30.

2-B. *Kimba,* Prod. #66–24, "Running Wild." The antelope stampede. 1:32 to 2:20.

3-A. *The Lion King.* Zazu flies to Simba clinging to a tree in the midst of the wildebeest stampede, and tells him to hold on, his father is coming. 33:08 to 33:14.

3-B. *Kimba,* Prod. #66–24, "Running Wild." Pauley Cracker flies to Bucky Deer clinging to a tree in the midst of the antelope stampede, and tells him to hold on, Kimba is coming. 8:23 to 8:28.

4-A. *The Lion King.* Lightning starts a fire, 75:00 to 75:05, and rain puts it out. 79:58 to 80:05.

4-B. *Kimba,* Prod. #66–42, "The Red Menace." Lightning starts a fire, 0:38 to 0:47, and rain puts it out. 13:37 to 13:52.

5-A. *The Lion King.* During a fight in the midst of the big fire, Scar scoops a pawful of hot coals into Simba's eyes. 78:30 to 78:35.

5-B. *Kimba,* Prod. #66–8, "The Wind in the Desert." During a fight in the hot desert, Kimba kicks burning sand into Claw's eyes. 22:32 to 22:37.

6-A. *The Lion King.* After Simba protests that he cannot handle the responsibilities of becoming king, Rafiki gives him a pep talk including a sharp rap on the head to get his attention. 67:11 to 67:32.

6-B. *Kimba,* Prod. #66–24, "Running Wild." After Kimba protests that he cannot handle the responsibilities of becoming king, Dan'l Baboon gives him a pep talk including a spanking to get his attention. 13:49 to 14:23.

7-A. *The Lion King.* King Mufasa tells young Simba to "Look at the stars. The great kings of the past look down on us from those stars," etc. 25:02 to 25:25.

7-B. *The Lion King.* Simba sees Mufasa's image in the clouds. 69:06 to 69:11.

7-C. *Kimba,* Prod. #66–1, "Go, White Lion!" Young Kimba sees his mother's image in the stars. 20:10 to 20:45.

7-D. *Kimba,* Prod. #66–9, "The Insect Invasion." Kimba sees an idealized image of himself with his father, Caesar, in the clouds. 22:21 to 22:26.

7-E. *Kimba,* Prod. #66–3, "Dangerous Journey." Kimba sees his father, King Caesar, superimposed over a full moon. 14:38 to 14:53 and 17:40 to 18:00.

8-A. *The Lion King.* The cubs Simba and Nala playing. 17:07 to 17:30.

8-B. *Kimba,* Prod. #66–5, "Journey Into Time." The cubs Kimba and Kitty playing. 21:35 to 22:15.

9-A. *The Lion King.* Timon (omnivore) and Pumbaa (herbivore) teach Simba (carnivore) to eat insects and bugs so he can live with them without starving. 46:07 to 47:07.

9-B. *Kimba.* The sub-plot of Kimba getting the carnivores to live in peace with the herbivores by, at first, trying (unsuccessfully) to teach them to eat grass, then getting them to temporarily eat insects, and finally discovering a vegetarian "meat substitute," is spread through three episodes: Prod. #66–9. "The Insect Invasion"; #66–27, "The Gigantic Grasshopper"; and #66–36, "A Revolting Development."

A digression on the comparison of the opening scene of *The Lion King* and the original Japanese opening title animation of *Jungle Emperor:* The latter showed Leo as an adult, and since NBC did not want Leo/Kimba presented as a grown-up, NBC created its own opening title animation from several brief scenes from various episodes. Therefore this original Japanese opening title animation was never shown in America as a part of *Kimba.* But it is shown in Japanese animation books, and it is included in the Japanese commercial videos of *Jungle Emperor,* which are accessible to the large number of American anime fans. Professional animators would know how to get copies.

What Might Disney Have Known? What Should Disney Have Known?

Do these similarities seem strained? If they are significant, could they be coincidental, rather than evidence of inspiration from *Kimba* to *The Lion King?* These are obvious questions, but there is a third which is equally important.

To quote from Christopher Finch's cover article in the May-June 1994 issue of *Animation Magazine:* "Astonishingly, *The Lion King*—initially called *King of the Jungle*—is the first Disney animated feature to be based on an original story idea. The rest were rooted in traditional tales or existing copyrighted material." [17] The article tells how the concept was conceived by studio chairman Jeffrey Katzenberg as an animal story like *Bambi* but set in Africa, "with the central theme being woven around a young lion coming of age and learning to take responsibility." Katzenberg passed the idea to Roy Disney, Jr., head of the animation department, who assigned Tom Schumacher, producer of *The Rescuers Down Under,* to assemble a creative team to develop it. An article by Charles Burress in the July 11, 1994, *San Francisco Chronicle,* which was the first public news of the controversy, states that *Lion King* co-director Rob Minkoff said that he had "joined the four-year-old project in April 1992," [22] establishing that it started in 1988.

Two key points emerge from these articles. First, Disney maintains that *The Lion King* is its own original story. Second, it maintains that nobody in the Disney organization ever heard of either the *Kimba* TV cartoons or Osamu Tezuka. The July 11 *Chronicle,* citing a telephone interview with *The Lion King* co-director Minkoff, declares that, "Rob Minkoff said he was unaware of Tezuka's story during production." [22]The July 13 *Los Angeles Times* quoted Minkoff directly: "I know for a fact that ['Kimba'] has never been discussed as long as I've been on the project." [24]*USA Today* on July 14 cited a Disney statement, "No one associated with (*The Lion King*) had even heard of (*Kimba*) or . . . seen it." [26] On July 18, the *San Francisco Chronicle* ran a follow-up. [29]Disney spokesman Howard Green clarified that the company had queried the artists who worked on *The Lion King.* Some admitted they had heard of *Kimba* or even seen it when they were young children. But Green affirmed that this meant only that some artists had a vague childhood memory of *Kimba* along with all of the other TV cartoons that had blended together in their subconscious. He repeated that none of the creative team who developed *The Lion King* were aware of *Kimba* or Tezuka. Mark Henn, lead animator for the young Simba, was quoted that he had heard of *Kimba* but never seen it and "that the name Tezuka did not ring a bell." Another unidentified Disney employee felt that it was "totally reasonable" that *Kimba* had never been seen by "many of the younger employees like [co-director] Minkoff, who at thirty-one was barely three years old when *Kimba* aired."

Here are some facts to compare with the Disney statements:

1. Disney, the biggest animation company in America, takes pride in its global expertise in the field of animation, including its knowledge of popular animation worldwide. For example, Disney bought the animation rights to a major European cartoon star, André Franquin's Marsupilami, because Disney felt that it would be popular in America. In terms of *The Lion King,* an article in the *Wall Street Journal* on May 16, 1994, a month before the film's release, alluded to Disney's research into commercial and legal aspects of the movie, stating that, "When Disney consumer-products officials suggested the Lion King's name, 'Simba,' might run afoul of copyrights of a German toy maker of the same name, Mr. [Studio chairman Jeffrey] Katzenberg wouldn't hear about changing the name." [20]If such research was carried out by Disney to this extent, it seems improbable that no references to Tezuka or to *Kimba* were ever found.

2. Japan is one of Disney's largest markets outside America. Tokyo Disneyland is the popular success that EuroDisney is not. Disney executives regularly visit Tokyo. Most Disney features are on laser disc there, and the Disney company is on record about its concern that American film collectors can purchase Japanese laser discs of movies that have not been released to the U.S. video market, such as *Song of the South.* Aside from

the fact that *Jungle Emperor* merchandise is still in every Japanese toy store, Osamu Tezuka is a giant of modern Japanese popular culture, widely known as *manga no kamisama*—"The God of Comics." He appeared in Japanese TV commercials during the 1980s as a major celebrity endorsing computer products. In 1980, he starred in a Japanese TV special on Disney World— filmed on location—as a humorously clumsy tourist, in his own reprise of Robert Benchley bumbling around the Disney studio in Disney's *The Reluctant Dragon*. [6] (Also—extremely significantly—Frederik Schodt, Osamu Tezuka's translator, says that "I personally accompanied him in the 1980s to . . . the Disney animation studios in Burbank, Calif.," [57] although Schodt does not report the purpose of Tezuka's visit nor who on the Disney staff may have met him.) Possibly more significantly, Disney's own *The Lion King* Press Information publicity kit distributed for the film's premiere contains this biographical note on co-director Roger Allers: "ROGER ALLERS (Director) makes his feature film directing debut on 'The Lion King' following a prolific two-decade career in the medium that has included everything from character design and animation to story supervision. [. . .] In 1980, Allers and his family moved to Toronto, Canada, where he worked for Nelvana Studios as an animator [. . .] This two-year assignment was followed by a return to Los Angeles, where he provided character design, preliminary animation and story development for the Japanese-produced feature, 'Little Nemo: Adventures in Slumberland.' He went on to live in Tokyo for the next two years in his role as one of the animation directors overseeing the Japanese artists." [21] How probable is it that none of the Disney executives visiting Japan, nor American animators who worked in Japan and later worked for Disney on the production of *The Lion King*, ever ran across any mentions of Tezuka—widely publicized as "the Walt Disney of Japan"—or of *Jungle Emperor*? The Tezuka Productions remake of *Jungle Emperor* received a prime-time weekly TV broadcast from October 1989 through September 1990 in Japan [13], with significant coverage in the Japanese animation magazines; and was immediately thereafter released to the Japanese home video market. American anime fans were fully aware of this and had no trouble obtaining video copies. How could the Disney researchers who discovered the Simba toys in Germany have overlooked this current Japanese TV animation series?

3. *The World Encyclopedia of Comics,* edited by Maurice Horn [4], has been a standard American reference book on cartoons since 1976. Its entry on Tezuka notes, "Influenced in large part by Walt Disney . . . Tezuka has in turn influenced countless numbers of Japanese cartoonists . . ." The illustrated entry on *Jungle Emperor* states, "*Jungle Taitei* was adapted into animated form; it was the first color cartoon series produced for Japanese TV. *Jungle Taitei* was awarded the Silver Lion at the International Children's Film Festival held in Venice in 1967." Many other comics and animation reference

books include entries on Tezuka or on *Kimba*. [See notes 5, 8, 9, 12, 15.] Have Disney's animators, who are experts on cartooning, most of whom entered the profession because of a personal love for animation, never even accidentally encountered these entries, to say nothing of having any interest in following them up? The claim that Disney's artists could not have known of *Kimba* because they were little children when the series started to be aired on American television in 1966 ignores the fact that it was shown constantly around America until the early 1980s, including on Los Angeles television. So people who were only three years old in 1966 might still have seen *Kimba* until they were in their late teens.

While the general public may be unaware of Tezuka and *Kimba,* the Disney staff consists of professionals in the animation industry, many of whom are personally animation aficionados. The July 18 *San Francisco Chronicle* further quoted an unidentified Disney source: "I can guarantee they didn't use any Tezuka ideas. No one had any Tezuka books. I didn't bring in a 'Kimba the White Lion' to show them. I doubt they have a Kimba film in their library. That period of Japanese animation is scoffed at." [29]Of course, this quotation from the unidentified Disney source is itself evidence that *somebody* at Disney *was* aware of Tezuka and of *Kimba*. It is an admission that Disney personnel were familiar enough with that period of Japanese animation to have an opinion of it, even if an unfavorable one, and Tezuka was too dominant a figure in that period for them to be unaware of him if they considered themselves knowledgeable enough about it to form a judgment. Moreover, the *Chronicle* noted a couple of paragraphs later: ". . . And in a couple of other Disney films, artists have acknowledged taking inspiration from a more contemporary Japanese animator, Hayao Miyazaki." This is further evidence that the Disney animators are professionals who are aware of their Japanese colleagues.

The effort to assign Tezuka to an earlier, more primitive period ignores the fact that some of his most famous films were not only made after *Kimba,* they were given well-publicized film-festival screenings in Los Angeles, as well as elsewhere in the United States. His *Broken-Down Film* was one of the hits at the first Los Angeles International Animation Celebration in 1985; and Tezuka was expected to personally bring his *Legend of the Forest* to the 1989 Celebration, though his death prevented that. His *Jumping* played in the nineteenth annual International Tournée of Animation, which premiered in Los Angeles in 1986 and later toured America.

Disney animators who were professionally aware of Miyazaki's Japanese animation of the late 1980s could not have been ignorant of Japan's highly publicized 1989–90 remake by Tezuka Productions of the *Jungle Emperor* TV cartoons, any more than they could have been ignorant of the inclusion of his work in the Los Angeles International Animation Celebration and the nineteenth Tournée.

The likelihood of Disney animators knowing of Tezuka and/or *Kimba* is compounded by the fact that, in December 1990, ASIFA-Hollywood, the Hollywood chapter of the international professional animation community, presented its Winsor McCay Award "for lifetime contribution to animation" posthumously to Osamu Tezuka, at its gala annual awards. Tezuka received a three-page tribute in the awards' program book, and the text included an illustration of Kimba. [14] None of that year's other award recipients received more than a one-page tribute. The award was presented by June Foray, a noted animation voice actress whose roles included Granny Gummi in Disney's *Gummi Bears* TV cartoons. Among the other animation industry notables listed in the program book as being present was Marc Davis, one of Disney's often publicized "nine old men," senior animators famous for working on Disney's theatrical features from *Snow White and the Seven Dwarfs* in the 1930s to *Sleeping Beauty* in the 1950s.

So as recently as 1990, America's veteran animation professionals as well as its animation buff community were well aware of Tezuka and respected his work. Are we therefore to believe that the present Disney professional staff is either unaware of him or considers him a boringly primitive antique? There is ample evidence that Disney's 1928 *Steamboat Willie* is hopelessly quaint by today's standards, but does this mean that modern animators should not be expected to know of it or to recognize Disney's name? To know Miyazaki but to never have heard of Tezuka, the famous "father" of Japanese animation, is like an animator who takes inspiration from Chuck Jones but professes to never have heard of Walt Disney, Tex Avery, or Friz Freleng.

The July 11 *Chronicle,* further citing the telephone interview with *The Lion King* co-director Rob Minkoff, reported: "He said he is trying to find copies of the comics, which are out of print, and the TV series, which is out of circulation." [22] Tezuka's *Jungle Emperor* graphic novel has never been published in English, but it is easily obtainable in Japanese-community bookshops around Southern California. I personally saw the paperback three-volume Kodansha edition when I went shopping for anime books in late February 1995.

I have attended numerous fan conventions since the late 1980s at which key Disney animation personnel, including Rob Minkoff, have given presentations on whatever feature was about to be released. [19] At those same conventions, unauthorized American *Kimba* videos were displayed for sale in the dealers' rooms, along with Japanese *Jungle Emperor* merchandise and videos of the 1989–90 *Jungle Emperor* remake. Disney artists commonly attend fan conventions in Southern California to shop for their personal collections. Fan conventions invariably run video rooms which are often casual about the legality of the videos that are shown. I have attended screenings of *Kimba* episodes at which Disney artists were present, or art students were present who I know later went to work for Disney.

Did they work on *The Lion King?* Yes, at least some did. Did their knowledge of *Kimba* influence the development of *The Lion King?* They say not. But Disney says that nobody at its studio—or at least nobody who worked on *The Lion King*—or at least nobody who was in a position to affect the key story and character concepts in *The Lion King*—had ever heard of Tezuka or were more than marginally aware of *Kimba*. There is already strong enough circumstantial evidence to disprove this to lead to natural suspicions that Disney is trying to hide a smoking gun.

Conclusion

There are two major issues, both of which must be addressed along two lines. The first is the question of knowledge: was Disney familiar with Tezuka and *Kimba*? What did it know? And just as importantly, what should it have known? And, more murkily, what might it have known but forgotten but which returned in some way? The right of Disney to claim its authority and take pride in knowing world animation, its global expertise, is fully engaged here. Disney cannot have it both ways. Its animators and legal and commercial departments cannot claim to be knowledgeable as professionals/experts/ defenders of Disney copyrights, and also claim to be ignorant of Tezuka and *Kimba*. For Disney to claim such ignorance is to demolish its claim to world authority, to admit that authority is sham, as it likewise flies in the face of the tangible evidence of the tenacity and vigilance it exercises worldwide in the protection of its copyrights. And once it makes that claim to authority and displays such tenacity and vigilance, a presumption attaches to its activities such that even where it may not have actually known, it is held to the rule that it *should* have known to be the experts it claims to be and protectors it has shown itself to be, a double pride.

So, even if Disney did not know of Tezuka—the "father" of anime, the greatest Japanese animator, the man called "the Walt Disney of Japan"(!)—to sustain its claim to expertise, it must accept that it should have known, even if just to know how Tezuka acquired and maintained that sobriquet, how he was treating and reflecting upon Disney both in and outside of his works, including *Kimba*.

Beyond the question of what Disney knew or should have known before or during the making of *The Lion King* lies its conduct after the release of the film brought formal notification of *Kimba* in July 1994. Insofar as acknowledgment is a precondition to knowledge, the failure of Disney to acknowledge what it then came to know compromised itself further. While Tezuka and Mr. Takayuki Matsutani, president of Tezuka Productions, always felt that *Jungle Emperor* derived from an inspiration based upon Disney's *Bambi* and they were always at pains to acknowledge their debt, the Disney organization's claim that it had never heard of Tezuka—that Tezuka was too unimportant to require being heard of—was a failure to reciprocate, a failure to acknowledge the acknowledgement of and homage to Disney by Tezuka in *Kimba*. If one might think of *Kimba* as not only a gift from Disney to Tezuka but a gift from Tezuka to Disney, Disney refused not only the gift but its acknowledgement. Antonia Levi, in her book *Samurai from Outer Space* [59], p. 7, discusses an August 1994 open letter to Disney [33–35] signed by over 200 Japanese artists and supporters to protest Disney's failure to recognize Tezuka's professional stature: "Disney's lawyers, apparently unable to grasp the fact that this was a question of courtesy rather than copyright infringement or punitive damages, responded defensively and with a level of legalistic arrogance unusual even for them." In actuality, Disney did not reply to this letter at all; its arrogance was in ignoring it. In other words, Disney has treated the issue as a legal one, not an ethical one or one of etiquette, of politeness. Disney's tactics of disavowal at the level of knowing/not knowing, including silence in the face of the animation professional and critical community in Japan, has clearly expressed its position in pantomime as: "Not only did we not know before, but we refuse to listen now." This has made Disney look bad, including looking ignorant, where it claims expertise. And that has contaminated the other area that needs to be addressed: originality. If Disney is so ignorant where it claims to be so knowledgeable, how can we trust its claim to the originality of *The Lion King*?

In terms of this second issue, I have articulated many similiarities between *The Lion King* and *Kimba*. A knowledge and acknowledgment of these begs the question as to what legitimate grounds Disney could appeal to claim *The Lion King* as original. Disney's disclaimer of no knowledge of Tezuka and *Kimba* is, while in some ways relevant, not conclusive with regard to originality. While the complexities of the thinking of the relation of knowledge to originality, to say nothing of the complexities of the thinking of what originality is, lie beyond this paper, one key point can serve: although knowledge of *Kimba* can be read as compromising the claim of Disney to the originality of *The Lion King*, not knowing of *Kimba* does not make *The Lion King* original. The question of originality transcends subjectivity, transcends the knowledge and intentions of the makers and what must be presumed of such. Rather, it involves a comparison focusing largely upon the objects themselves.

By means of such a comparison, I have shown the ways in which *Kimba* and *The Lion King* coincide. Of course, coincidence is in itself a complex phenomenon. There are those who treat it as automatically implying a lack of both subjective will and objective patterning, the happenstance workings of chance. Others would regard it as testimony to just the opposite, as at least the workings of destiny to impose or disclose objective patterning. In the present case, it appears to operate in two different ways. First, in the register of knowledge, coincidence so defined—either as chance or destiny—defuses the guilt of Disney. It suggests that one does not have to, indeed cannot, presume Disney knew of Tezuka and *Kimba* for it to make *The Lion King*. In other words, and despite the common error of equating coincidence with cause-effect, one cannot presume that because *The Lion King* is similar to *Kimba* and *Kimba* was made before *The Lion King*, *Kimba* was the cause of *The Lion King.* So the argument of coincidence puts pay to cause-effect thinking. But second, coincidence so thought can itself in turn cause an effect. It can cause *The Lion King* to not be original.

In the case of *The Lion King* and *Kimba,* this matter is further complicated by their common source in folk tale, though it might be argued that such a source uncomplicates the matter insofar as it automatically annuls any claim to originality on behalf of either. (See, for example, the medieval beast fable *Le Roman de Renart,* dating from the thirteenth century, in which the European animals live in a parody of a royal court presided over by a lion king of beasts, King Nobel.) The plots of both films exhibit the morphology of the folk tale. We are dealing with a set of conventions, archetypes, etc., that repeat themselves. It is impossible therefore to talk of texts based on fable/myth in terms of their originality except where they depart from the conventions. So even if one grants Disney that it not only did not know but also cannot be presumed to have known of Tezuka and *Kimba,* that does not automatically make *The Lion King* original.

There is a more speculative question regarding Disney's knowledge. While the Disney management has adamantly insisted that the creative staff of *The Lion King* was unaware of Tezuka or of *Kimba,* the July 18 *Chronicle* reported that, "in interviews done outside official Disney channels," some of the creative staff indicated otherwise. "One source who worked on the early stages of the film's development" was quoted: "I certainly knew about 'Kimba the White Lion," he said. 'Other people did too.' . . . 'I remember saying in a meeting, 'This is mighty similar to 'Kimba the White Lion,' and I got a bunch of blank stares." This implies that not all Disney personnel had the same degree of knowledge. And once the existence of any knowledge is demonstrated, the question of conscious versus subconscious knowledge comes into play. What might a *Lion King* creator who had consciously forgotten *Kimba* watched on TV during childhood, have subconsciously added to the development of a similar story about a young lion ruler of a kingdom of animals? Further, animators have had a reputation for decades of having irrepressible senses of humor and a penchant for practical jokes on each other and on studio management, and of drawing hidden jokes into their cartooning. (See, for example, *Walt Disney and Assorted Other Characters; An Unauthorized Account of the Early Years at Disney's,* by Jack Kinney; Harmony Books, 1988.) If some Disney artists were aware of *Kimba,* might they have added *Kimba* visual references to *The Lion King* as an ingroup joke without admitting the source to their co-workers or their superiors? If this did happen, then what Disney thought it knew was less than what it actually knew.

In the end, as in the beginning, we cannot know what Disney did or did not know, nor can we say *Kimba* caused *The Lion King.* But we can say that Disney's declaration that it was ignorant of Tezuka and *Kimba* before and during the making of the film and its continuing maintenance of that ignorance after release of the film destroy its claim to global expertise in animation. And the similiarites between *Kimba* and *The Lion King* and their common source in fable argues persuasively that any easy claim by Disney to the originality of *The Lion King* is sham. In both cases—knowledge and originality—Disney's pride is on the line.

Epilogue

This essay was originally written at the beginning of 1995 for presentation at "The Life of Illusion," Australia's Second International Conference on Animation, held at the Museum of Contemporary Art, Sydney, March 3–5, 1995. During the nearly three years since then, the "Simba Versus Kimba" controversy has diminished but not been forgotten. Neither has it been formally resolved.

The box-office and merchandising records set by *The Lion King* still stand, emphasized by the failures of Disney's subsequent major animated features (*Pocahontas, The Hunchback of Notre Dame,* and *Hercules*) to measure up to them. And the Disney corporation has not yet replied to the August 1994 letter of protest organized by Machiko Satonaka with over 200 signatures. [35]

The controversy continues to be mentioned in books, magazines, and even television satires, at times reaching the status of a new urban myth. In an episode of *The Simpsons* TV cartoon program, a lion's head in the clouds says, "You must avenge my death, Kimba . . . I mean Simba!" [53] A media fan magazine states that forty-three legal suits were filed against Disney by the Japanese, and that the lack of *Kimba* merchandise in America is due to Disney getting a court order banning it—all untrue. [54] David Koenig presents a full page "Simba-Kimba Conspiracy" chart of parallels in his *Mouse Under Glass: Secrets of Disney Animation and Theme Parks,* [60] inviting readers to form their own conclusions as to whether so many parallels can all be coincidental. Another fan magazine states that the similarities between the two are so numerous "that the direct influence of that TV series [*Kimba*] is almost indisputable." [55]

In July 1996, Disney announced its acquisition of the worldwide distribution rights for the animated features produced by Hayao Miyazaki, "Japan's best-loved animated-film director," for Japan's Tokuma Shoten company. ("Disney Dives Into Japanese Film Business," *Los Angeles Times,* Wednesday, July 24, 1996, p. D4.) [58] The article mentions that "Disney executives say they control 65 percent of the Japanese market for children's videotapes." This does not relate directly to the Disney-Tezuka controversy, but it is indicative of Disney's knowledge of the Japanese animation market which emphasizes the implausibility of Disney's statement that it had never heard of Tezuka nor of *Jungle Emperor* (unless Disney would care to claim that it developed that expertise only during the two years after *The Lion King* was produced).

Has the controversy prompted new productions of both *Kimba* in America and *Jungle Emperor* in Japan? In January 1996 four *Kimba* videotapes containing two episodes each were released by United American Video under the title of *Kimba the Lion Prince*. These feature the original *Jungle Emperor* animation made by Mushi Productions in 1965–66, but with completely new scripts and dubbing. [61] The new dialogue changes Kimba's adult-lion nemesis from a stranger to his "evil uncle" (just as in *The Lion King*), and the video sleeves display the slogan, "The lion adventure that started it all!" The credits, indicating a Canadian production, remove all Japanese names (including Tezuka's!) except for the addition of a new credit for Fumio Suzuki, one of the claimants to the Mushi property in that studio's decades-old bankruptcy proceedings. These *Kimba the Lion Prince* videos, poorly distributed, disappeared after a few months.

(In March/April 1997, the Japanese litigation over the rights to Mushi Productions's properties, including the NBC-produced *Astro Boy* and *Kimba the White Lion,* were finally resolved. Suzuki was barred from continuing to represent himself in America as the owner of those rights. Negotiations were conducted between 1997 and 1999 between the reorganized Mushi Productions and Shawne P. Kleckner of The Right Stuf International of Des Moines, Iowa, for an authorized American video release of *Kimba the White Lion. Kimba* was finally released on video in America by The Right Stuf International between April and October 2000, in a set of thirteen videos containing four episodes per volume, produced from NBC's original masters in episode number order.)

On August 1, 1997, Tezuka Productions released a new *Jungle Emperor* theatrical animated feature in Japan. Produced in theatrical quality animation, this was the most lavish filmed adaptation of Tezuka's cartoon-art novel to date. Although the feature is faithful to the original story, Tezuka Productions' choice of images for its publicity stills bore a resemblance to scenes in *The Lion King* which many fans took to be deliberately provocative. In one, Leo's cubs Luné and Lukyo romp through the savannah under the guardian eye of the pompous parrot Coco, just as the hornbill Zazu follows the young Simba and Nala. In another, King Leo battles a pack of hyenas to protect his cubs, as King Mufasa does to save Simba and Nala in the elephants' graveyard. (Publicity images from this feature are available worldwide by downloading from the Tezuka Web site in Japan: www.tezuka. co.jp.) How this new *Jungle Emperor* might have fared in comparison to the Japanese reception of *The Lion King* must remain theoretical, since it had the misfortune of being released less than a month after the July 12 premiere of Hayao Miyazaki's *Mononoke Hime,* which instantly monopolized all critical and popular attention for months. Ironically, *Mononoke Hime* became the Japanese animated feature to set box-office records of equivalent stature to *The Lion King* in America—and to be picked up by Disney for American and international distribution.

After three years, the Disney organization has not changed its official stance on *The Lion King*'s total originality or on its lack of knowledge of or interest in Tezuka and *Kimba*. But not all of the production staff of *The Lion King* are still as reticent. Some have left Disney for other animation studios and no longer feel bound by Disney management's orders of silence; or feel that Disney's claim of ignorance is demeaning to their professional expertise.

Bridge U.S.A., October 15, 1997, p. 20, quotes Sadao Miyamoto, an animator from Japan who came to work at Disney, as saying, "The very first film he worked on at Disney was 'The Lion King.' 'When I first saw the storyboards,' he frankly admits, 'I was taken aback, because they did look like 'Jungle Emperor.' [. . .] he also says it's clear that 'The Lion King' has been influenced to some degree. According to Miyamoto, for people involved in animation, it's unthinkable that [Disney people] never even saw 'Jungle Emperor' [*Kimba*]. Moreover, the persons responsible for 'The Lion King' admit this." [62]

Tom Sito, who has a Story screen credit on *The Lion King*, was willing to speak on the record in this essay in a December 1997 telephone interview. "We always knew who *Kimba the White Lion* was—and I had met Osamu Tezuka socially—but I don't think anybody involved with the development thought about the connection. Later one of the animators, as a joke, pinned up some photocopies from the *Kimba* comic book on the studio bulletin board, but by that time we were so far into production that it didn't affect anything."

Mark Kausler, who also has a Story credit, said in a similar December 1997 telephone interview, "Probably some of the hundreds of people who worked on *The Lion King* never heard of Tezuka or *Kimba*, but there were certainly many who did. I had seen *Kimba* episodes off and on from watching it on TV as a kid, to seeing video copies screened at meetings of animation fans into the '80s. But animation fans are always watching as many different cartoons as they can. When Disney started the *Lion King* project, we were told it should be like Disney's *Bambi* set in Africa with African animals; but keep it from looking too much like *Bambi* with its animals versus man theme. It was to star only animals; no humans at all. So we were thinking just about variations of *Bambi*. Nobody ever mentioned *Kimba*, and if any of us who knew of it thought about it, I guess we figured that since *Kimba* was always about the animals trying to get the humans to accept them as equals, the absence of humans in *The Lion King* made it obviously a different plot. It was no secret that *The Lion King* was inspired by the studio's own *Bambi* and featured similar elements such as a young animal prince surrounded by colorful and comical animal companions. Tezuka also made no secret that it was *Bambi* that was his inspiration for *Kimba*, so obviously two new films both based on the same original film will have many similarities."

So the knowledge by *The Lion King*'s production staff of Tezuka and of *Kimba* is now proven. And that has always been the basic issue. Whether there was any conscious influence from *Kimba* in *The Lion King*, as a return gift from some Disney animators to Tezuka as Tezuka's *Jungle Emperor* was his gift to Disney, which Tezuka would have doubtlessly understood and appreciated, is incidental to the fact that *The Lion King* clearly shows enough originality to be appreciated as an original creation by the accepted definition of that term. It was Disney management's insistence that, despite its worldwide animation expertise, it had never heard of Tezuka or of *Kimba*—that they were not worthy of knowing about—which caused the entire controversy. To quote Frederik L. Schodt in his *Dreamland Japan*, [57] "Ironically, the entire controversy could easily have been resolved by a simple tip of the hat to Tezuka, either in the form of a film credit or a public statement." Instead, the affair has demonstrated the knowledge of Disney's creative staff—and the stubbornly willful ignorance of Disney's management.

Notes and Acknowledgments

I would like to acknowledge Robin Leyden for supplying me with much of this information. In 1966, as a young fan, Leyden obtained a copy of NBC's *Kimba* publicity kit including the fifty-two-episode *Kimba the White Lion Story Lines* program guide. This seems to be the only original copy known to exist today. It has been photocopied for fans many times, and it is the basic source for NBC's episode titles and numbers, and the episode synopses which establish the spellings of the characters' names. I would also like to thank Frederik L. Schodt, an expert on Japanese popular culture who served as Osamu Tezuka's personal translator many times, who provided some of the information regarding original Japanese publication and broadcast dates, and the Tezuka Productions press releases.

Annotated Chronology of Pertinent Works and Publications Relevant to *The Lion King* and to the Controversy

A. Pertinent Works

1. 1950. *Junguru Taitei (The Jungle Emperor)*, by Osamu Tezuka. Serialized in the monthly *Manga Shonen (Boys' Comics)* from November 1950 through April 1954. The serial has been collected and published as a cartoon novel in a variety of editions since the 1950s. The standard edition today is the three-volume paperback set from Kodansha, Ltd., first published in June 1977. It has been regularly carried by several Japanese-community bookshops in Southern California. The current printings at the time of the original version of this essay for "The Life of Illusion" conference were: vol. 1, 10th printing, November 1994; vol. 2, 9th printing, December 1994; vol. 3, 8th printing, September 1994.

2. 1951. *Bambi*, by Osamu Tezuka (Tsuru Shobo, November 10, 1951).
An authorized comic-book adaptation, credited to Tezuka, of the Disney film. Tezuka also drew *The Story of Walt Disney* (Manga Shonen, November 1951) and the authorized Japanese comic-book adaptation of Disney's *Pinocchio* (Tokodo, June 5, 1952).

3. 1966. *Kimba the White Lion.* NBC Films. Fifty-two half-hour episodes.
Syndicated TV series, premiered on Sunday, September 11, 1966, on KHJ-TV, Los Angeles, 5:30–6:00 P.M. 1/4-page display adv't in *TV Guide* (Los Angeles edition), vol. 14, no. 37, whole no. 702, September 10–16, 1966, p. A-29. NBC's contract with Mushi Production Co. was for twelve years from the month of the American premiere broadcast; i.e., through September 1978. Distributed through syndicated sales by NBC Films through 1971, when NBC was forced by a federal antitrust ruling to get out of the syndicated TV market. Sold by NBC to National Telefilm Associates in 1971, and distributed by NTA through syndicated sales through September 30, 1978. Due to litigation in Japan arising from the bankruptcy of Mushi Productions in 1973 and conflicting claims to the ownership of *Jungle Emperor,* the American rights could not be renewed. NTA was instructed to ship its *Kimba* masters to New York City for storage pending a resolution of the bankruptcy trial in Japan. However, one of the Japanese claimants obtained some existing *Kimba* film prints and, representing himself as their owner, sold them to another distributor, Air Time International. ATI distributed them through TV barter sales, despite challenges to its right to do so, from 1979 until ATI disappeared in the early 1980s. Last broadcast in Los Angeles on Channel 52, KBSC-TV, on Mondays through Fridays from August 30, 1976 to January 11, 1977 at 5:00 P.M., and January 13, 1977 to July 8, 1977 at 3:00 P.M.

4. 1976. *The World Encyclopedia of Comics,* edited by Maurice Horn (Chelsea House Publishers, New York, 1976, 784 pp.).
Illustrated entry on *Jungle Taitei (Japan),* pp. 347–348. Illustrated entry on *Tezuka, Osamu,* pp. 656–657. Both by Hisao Kato.

5. 1976. *The Complete Encyclopedia of Television Programs, 1947–1976,* by Vincent Terrace. (A. S. Barnes & Company, South Brunswick, New Jersey; and New York Zoetrope, New York, 1976, vol. 1, A–K, 450 pp. + vol. 2, L–Z, 464 pp.).
Entry on *Kimba the White Lion,* vol. 1, p. 441. Erroneously states that "Caesar, the ruler, old and dying, bestows upon his son Kimba, the rare white lion, the sacred throne." Repeated in 2nd ed., rev., *1947–1979,* A. S. Barnes, 1979, 1211 pp. in two vols.; in vol. 1, pp. 528–529. Entry without plot synopsis, but including the theme song lyrics, on p. 246 in Terrace's *Encyclopedia of Television Series, Pilots and Specials, vol. 1, 1937–1973* (Zoetrope, 1986, 480 pp.).

6. 1980. *Sunday Special. Disneylando Daizenshuu—Tezuka Osamu no Disneyworldo Tanken Ryokou. (Sunday Special. The Disneyland Grand Collection: Osamu Tezuka's Journey of Exploration to Disney World.)*
TV special movie, broadcast on TBS television on April 20, 1980. A humorous tour of Disney World, starring Osamu Tezuka as a comical tourist bumbling throughout the park.

7. 1980. *San Diego 1980 Comic-Con Program Book* (San Diego Comic Conventions, Inc., San Diego, Calif., 1980, 48 pp.).
A group tour of around thirty Japanese professional cartoonists, led by Osamu Tezuka and Monkey Punch, attended the 1980 San Diego Comic-Con, July 31–August 3. Tezuka presented the American premiere of his 1980 animated feature, *Phoenix 2772,* which was so popular that a repeat screening had to be scheduled for attendees who could not get into the standing-room-only first screening. Tezuka drew many sketches of Astro Boy and of Kimba for the fans. Tezuka was presented with the

Comic-Con's annual Inkpot Award, "for excellence and achievement in: comic arts, cinematic arts, animation arts, science fiction, adventure fiction, and fandom service." The 1980 souvenir Program Book includes a four-page profile, *The Japanese Are Here!* by Orvy Jundis, introducing the Japanese cartoonists. Osamu Tezuka is first, with a full-page profile (p. 19) featuring portrait drawings of Astro Boy and Kimba. (The other cartoonists have a half-page or less apiece.)

8. 1980. *The World Encyclopedia of Cartoons,* ed. by Maurice Horn (Gale Research Co./Chelsea House Publishers, New York, 1980, 787 pp.).
Illustrated entry on *Jungle Taitei* (Japan), by Frederik L. Schodt, p. 328. "The animated versions of *Jungle Taitei,* like the comic strip, were a spectacular success—full of brilliant color and action, and incorporating Tezuka's favorite themes of idealism, perseverance and the vitality of life."

9. 1981. *The Encyclopedia of Animated Cartoon Series,* ed. by Jeff Lenburg [1st ed.] (Arlington House Publishers, Westport, Connecticut, 1981, 190 pp.).
Illustrated entry on *Kimba the White Lion,* p. 135. Erroneously refers to Kimba as "she," and says story is set 4,000 years ago.

10. 1983. *Manga! Manga! The World of Japanese Comics,* by Frederik L. Schodt. Introd. by Osamu Tezuka (Kodansha, Ltd., Tokyo, July 1983, 260 pp.).
The first major serious study in English of Japanese comic-art literature, with a brief survey of the related Japanese animated cartoons. Osamu Tezuka is credited as a major founder of both. A note on the Japanese custom of bestowing flowery honorifics upon noted cartoonists such as "master of comics" or "king of comics" concludes, "Osamu Tezuka, regarded as the pioneer of the modern Japanese story-comic, is the only artist accorded the supreme accolade: *manga no kamisama,* or "the God of Comics." (p. 139). *Jungle Emperor* is noted in an extensive illustrated entry.

11. 1983. TIME Magazine, vol. 122 no. 5, August 1, 1983. *Japan: A Nation In Search of Itself* (special issue).
Culture: The Art of All They Do, by Robert Hughes. In a survey of manga, as part of Japan's literacy and gigantic publishing industry, Hughes observes: "The top artists, with, at the very top, Osamu Tezuka, known as *Manga no Kamisama* (God of Manga), are treated by their adoring public of all ages with an enthusiasm unknown to Stan Lee or Garry Trudeau; they are stars in the way that Mick Jagger or Norman Mailer are stars, and are credited with some of the properties of both." (p. 48)

12. 1983. *Children's Television: The First Thirty-Five Years, 1946–1981. Pt. 1: Animated Cartoon Series,* by George W. Woolery (The Scarecrow Press, Inc., Metuchen, New Jersey, 1983, xvii + 386 pp.).
Entry on *Kimba the White Lion* on p. 161.

13. 1989–1990. *Junguru Taitei.* Tezuka Productions. Fifty half-hour episodes.
A remake of the 1965–66 TV series, closer in mood to Tezuka's original graphic-art novel. Broadcast in Japan on Thursdays at 7:30 P.M., from October 12, 1989 through September 27, 1990.

14. 1990. *The Eighteenth Annual ANNIE Awards, 1990.* Illustrated souvenir program book of the annual ASIFA-Hollywood ANNIE awards banquet, Studio City, Calif., December 9, 1990 (ASIFA-Hollywood, Burbank, Calif., 1990, 28 pp. incl. covers).
Text reads, "June Foray presents Winsor McCay Award to Osamu Tezuka," and "The

Winsor McCay is based on merit and is awarded to an individual whose primary career function has been that of animator." (p. 20) Full-page illus. biography of Tezuka, p. 10; full-page group portrait of his major cartoon characters (Tezuka Prod. poster), p. 11; full-page obituary by myself, p. 13.

15. 1991. *The Encyclopedia of Animated Cartoons,* [2nd ed.], ed. by Jeff Lenburg (Facts on File, New York, 1991, xiii + 466 pp.).

Illustrated entry on *Kimba the White Lion* on p. 356. The errors in the first edition about Kimba being female and the setting being 4,000 years ago have not been corrected.

B. Publications Relevant to The Lion King *and to the Controversy*

16. *Hollywood Reporter*, Friday, November 22, 1991, p. 17.

"Disney Animators Go Back to Drawing Boards for 2 Films," by Paula Parisi.

A news rewrite of a Disney press release about two of its forthcoming features, *Aladdin* and *King of the Jungle*. "'King of the Jungle' is being readied for 1993, according to writer Linda Woolverton, who segued into the project immediately following 'Beauty.' Woolverton describes the original story, about the coming of age of a young lion, as a pet project of Walt Disney Studios chairman Jeffrey Katzenberg." The *King of the Jungle* title is listed in the *Hollywood Reporter*'s weekly Film Production column as "start" on June 15, 1992. It appears as *King of the Jungle* through the January 19, 1993, issue; in the January 26 issue it becomes *The Lion King (formerly King of the Jungle)*.

17. *Animation Magazine* no. 29, May/June 1994, pp. 26–27. (mid-April 1994 release) "The Story of The Lion King," by Christopher Finch, pp. 26–30.

Extensive feature article (publicity) on the forthcoming film. It emphasizes that: "Astonishingly, *The Lion King*—initially called *King of the Jungle*—is the first Disney animated feature to be based on an original story idea," developed entirely by a Disney development team from a suggestion by studio chairman Jeffrey Katzenberg.

18. *Wild Cartoon Kingdom* no. 4, ©1994, p. 56 (May 9, 1994 release).

"Lion King," by Felicity Robinson, pp. 52–57.

Extensive illustrated article (publicity) on forthcoming film. Includes sidebar, *Simba, Meet Kimba and Zimba,* by Fred Patten, noting two earlier cartoon lions with names based on the Swahili word "simba"; *Kimba the White Lion* by Osamu Tezuka's Mushi Productions (Japan and America, 1960s), and Zimba in David Hand's *Animaland* series (Great Britain, 1948–1950).

19. Los Angeles Comic Book and Science Fiction Convention. Sunday, May 15, 1994 (flyer; also published as an adv't in *Comics Buyer's Guide* no. 1070, May 20, 1994, p. 76.).

"A Special Look At This Summer's Major Films. Appearing in person: Rob Minkoff, Director of *The Lion King*. Rob Minkoff will be appearing along with several *Disney* animators to introduce a twelve-minute '*Lion King*' reel and speak on the film. Plus a special *free* 'Lion King' item will be given away courtesy of Walt Disney Pictures (while supplies last). '*The Lion King*' presentation starts at 1:00 P.M." This particular event took place long after *The Lion King* had completed its major production, but it is an example of Disney's promotions featuring key animators and directors at fan conventions where *Kimba* videos were screened and sold, and Japanese *Jungle Emperor* merchandise was on display and sold, during the period when *The Lion*

King was in production. To cite the promotional flyers of the (monthly) Los Angeles Comic Book Convention alone, "T.V. Cartoon Marathons" at the March 1, 1987, and March 6, 1988, conventions both advertised the screening of *Kimba the White Lion* episodes. The convention on October 8, 1989, featured "the animators who worked on the film" at a presentation on Disney's *The Little Mermaid*. Rob Minkoff presented "A behind the scenes look at the *Roger Rabbit* cartoons" at the Sunday, April 8, 1990 session. The October 20, 1991, convention advertised "Meet the Animators" at "An UPDATED Presentation" on *Beauty and the Beast*. The October 4, 1992, convention featured "Aladdin Animators. Meet the animators of 'Aladdin,' who will give preview scenes and give a behind the scenes look at this new Disney film. Appearing in person: 'Beauty and the Beast' director Gary Trousdale." A similar fan convention where Disney animators regularly appeared to make presentations, while *Kimba* videos and *Jungle Emperor* merchandise were displayed and sold, was the annual San Diego Comic-Convention (see note 7).

20. *The Wall Street Journal*, Monday, May 16, 1994, sect. A, pp. A1, A8.
"Disney, Using Cash And Claw, Stays King Of Animated Movies. / Now, It Is Hoping a Feature on a Lovable Lion Cub Will Extend Its Domain / Mr. Katzenberg on the Prowl" by Richard Turner.
Feature article on making of the forthcoming feature from business point of view, emphasizing Disney chairman Katzenberg's role. Article alludes to Disney's worldwide search for potential rights conflicts: "When Disney consumer-products officials suggested the Lion King's name, 'Simba' might run afoul of copyrights of a German toy maker of the same name, Mr. Katzenberg wouldn't hear about changing the name."

21. *Walt Disney Pictures Presents The Lion King* June 1994 (Disney, Burbank, Calif., 79 pp.).
Disney's official publicity booklet contained in "*The Lion King* Press Information" kit distributed for the film's premiere on June 15, 1994. The biography of co-director Roger Allers states that, around 1983, Allers in Los Angeles "provided character design, preliminary animation and story development for the Japanese-produced feature, 'Little Nemo: Adventures in Slumberland.' He went on to live in Tokyo for the next two years in his role as one of the animation directors overseeing the Japanese artists." (pp. 46–47) Another note in the booklet (p. 27) states that Allers "joined the [*Lion King*] project in October, 1991."

22. *San Francisco Chronicle*, Monday, July 11, 1994, sect. A., pp. A1, A13.
"Uproar Over 'The Lion King,'" by Charles Burress.
Burress writes that Disney's film "has aroused a roar of protest from those who say the record-breaking animation feature is not as original as Disney claims." Parallels between the two are cited. Opinions are quoted from Tezuka fans Trish Ledoux, Toren Smith, Robin Leyden; anime experts Frederik Schodt, Fred Ladd, Naoki Nomura. Disney denials from Rob Minkoff, co-director; Howard Green "no comment." Report that Matthew Broderick, voice of Simba, originally thought the character was Kimba. Tezuka Pro press release.

23. Tezuka Productions first press release, Tuesday, July 12, 1994.
The President of Tezuka Productions Comments on 'The Lion King.'
"Comments [. . .] made in the context of a reply [. . .] to inquiries by Charles Burress of the San Francisco Chronicle and others."

24. *Los Angeles Times*, Wednesday, July 13, 1994, sect. F, pp. F1, F6.
"A 'Kimba' Surprise for Disney," by Robert W. Welkos.
Same overview. More detailed synopsis of *Kimba*. Quotes Minkoff for Disney; Tezuka Pro press release cited.

25. *San Francisco Chronicle*, Thursday, July 14, 1994, sect. D, pp. D1, D3.
"Disney—'Lion' Is Original," by Charles Burress.
"Disney officials yesterday denied that their wildly successful movie 'The Lion King' owes any debt to a pioneering Japanese artist whose 40-year-old lion story has some striking parallels to Disney's tale." Disney spokesperson Howard Green and principal screenwriter Linda Woolverton denied that any of 'the principals involved in creating' the story concept had ever heard of Tezuka or of *Kimba*. Skepticism from Schodt, Toren Smith. Similarities cited; Woolverton explained as naturally coincidental. Tezuka Pro press release acknowledging Disney's originality.

26. *USA Today*, Thursday, July 14, 1994, sect. D, p. 1.
"'The Lion King' shares a jungle crown," by Ann Oldenburg.
Entertainment section front-page story on charges of similarities from 'Japanimation' fans; Disney denial; skepticism of Ladd, Schodt; Tezuka Pro press release acknowledging Disney's "originality."

27. *The Washington Times*, Friday, July 15, 1995, p. C-15.
"Did Japanese animator inspire 'Lion King'?" (unsigned).
Reports the basic facts. Quotes Fred Ladd and Toren Smith on the similarities: "Mr. Ladd and others did not accuse Disney of stealing ideas from Tezuka but said they simply want the creators of 'The Lion King' to admit the influence of Tezuka on their work. 'The thing that is bothering a lot of people is that Disney is making such a big thing out of trumpeting, 'Our first entirely original movie and aren't we terrific,' says Torren Smith [sic.]" "No one associated with the film, no producer, or animator or director, has ever heard of this [television series],' Terry Press, a Disney spokeswoman, says. 'They were asked about it in Japan. They said none of them had ever seen it." Illustrated with a photo of Matthew Brodrick, the voice actor for Simba quoted as saying, "He was confused when he was first cast, because he thought it was Kimba, the 'white lion in a cartoon when I was a little kid.'"

28. *Entertainment Tonight*, Saturday-Sunday, July 16–17, 1994.
TV news report, weekend broadcast, of the controversy. Robin Leyden and Fred Patten interviewed; comparative film clips shown.

29. *San Francisco Chronicle*, Monday, July 18, 1994, sect. E, pp. E1, E2.
"Some 'Lion' Artists Knew of 'Kimba,'" by Charles Burress.
"Although Disney officials were quoted this past weekend on *Entertainment Tonight* as saying, 'The team that did 'The Lion King' was completely unaware of Kimba,' Disney spokesman Howard Green admitted to The Chronicle on Friday, 'Some of us had heard of Kimba.'" But Disney only admitted that some of its production crew had heard of *Kimba* but were unfamiliar with it, or may have seen it as children twenty-five years ago but didn't remember any details. Continued denials that any of the main creative team who wrote and directed the story had ever heard of *Kimba*.

30. Anime America '94 convention, San Jose, Calif., Friday-Sunday, July 29–31, 1994.
Anime fan convention. Three unauthorized T-shirts on sale by fans: (1) Kimba looking into mirror and seeing Simba, captioned (at top): *The Lying King*; (at

bottom): *"Mirror, mirror, on the wall, who created me after all?"*; on back of shirt: *What I try to say through my work is simple. My message is as follows: "Love all creatures!" "Love everything that has life!" I have been trying to express in different ways through my work the message such as "Preserve nature." "Bless life." "Be careful of a civilization that puts too much stock in science." "Do not wage war." And so on . . . Tezuka Osamu 1928–1989;* (2) "Lion King" coloring book (?) portrait line-drawing of young Simba, colored as Kimba (white with black ear-tips), in full-color picture frame to emphasize coloring; (3) 1965 Kimba promotional portrait captioned, "The *Real* Lion King!"

31. *Advance Comics* no. 70, October 1994, p. 288 (Monday, August 8, arrived).
Capital City Distribution Company's October solicitations to comics-shop retailers of comic books and related merchandise due for release that month.
Adv't/announcement for release of "The Original Lion King" videos. (The "Leo the Lion" cartoons shown on the Christian Broadcasting Network in the mid-1980s.) Text says: "As any hep person knows, the hit Disney movie THE LION KING was inspired by Japanese animation great Osamu Tezuka's KIMBA THE WHITE LION, which appeared on U.S. TV in the mid-'60s. In this sequel series . . ." Mailed with Internal Correspondence (see note 32).

32. Internal Correspondence, August 1994, p. 11 (Monday, August 8, arrived).
"Lion King Boffo; Big Merchandising Hit of the Summer, Too," by Tom Flinn.
Half on merchandising of *Lion King,* then, "There are other ways to profit from the *Lion King* boom. One of the most interesting involves the Japanese cartoon *Kimba the White Lion.*" Describes similarities between *Lion King* and *Kimba,* illustrated with cover of the *Leo the Lion* video being solicited in Advance Comics.

33. *Los Angeles Times,* Tuesday, August 9, 1994, sect. F, p. F2.
"Morning Report: Roaring About Similarities," by Shauna Snow. Public letter of complaint from Japanese professional cartoonists; Tezuka Pro "rethinking its original stand."

34. *San Francisco Chronicle,* Tuesday, August 9, 1994, sect. E, p. E1 (early ed.).
"Japanese Rush To See 'Lion,'" by Kozo Mizoguchi.
The Lion King is a hit in Japan, but its success has renewed the controversy. "A prominent Japanese cartoonist said she will send a letter to Disney this week expressing regret that the man who conceived the Japanese cartoon was not credited in the Disney movie." Signed by "dozens of cartoonists." Also, Tezuka Pro rethinking its stand. Opened in Japan two weeks earlier; earned $5.7 million so far. In the United States, Disney's highest-grossing movie ever.

35. *San Francisco Chronicle,* Tuesday, August 9, 1994, sect. D, p. D1 (late ed.).
"Japanese Artists Seek 'Lion' Credit," by Charles Burress.
"52 Japanese comic book artists are sending a protest letter to Disney." "Prominent Japanese comic book artist Machiko Satonaka organized the protest letter, which is signed by fifty-two 'manga' artists and 200 supporters." No comment from Disney.

36. *Los Angeles Times,* Saturday, August 13, 1994, sect. F, p. F2.
"Morning Report: 'Lion King' Plans Vacation," by Steven Linan.
Disney will pull *The Lion King* from theaters on September 23, when children are back in school, to clean the prints and to prepare a new ad campaign for a Thanksgiving/ Christmas re-release in about 1,500 theaters nationwide. ". . . a dearth of films for youngsters during the holidays . . ."

37. *Time Magazine* (Canadian edition), August 22, 1994, p. 55.
"People," by Emily Mitchell.
"Leonine Look-Alikes. Those eyes, that flowing mane. Now that you mention it, Simba, the hero of Disney's *The Lion King*, does look a lot like the star of Japan's popular '50s and '60s comic book and TV series *The Jungle Emperor*, which was also known as *Kimba the White Lion*. Disney says Simba is no copycat of the leonine creation by the late Osamu Tezuka, but there's a marked resemblance; both are orphans who become wise leaders. Concerned about the similarities, 42 leading Japanese cartoonists penned a petition of protest to Disney. Would Tezuka, a master cartoonist who admired Disney's work so much that he saw *Bambi* 80 times, have objected? A spokesman for the company that controls his estate says Tezuka was inspired by Disney films, 'so if his works influenced *The Lion King* in the same way, then we are happy.'" Illustrated.

38. Tezuka Productions second press release, Monday, August 22, 1994.
Mr. Takayuki Matsutani, the President of Tezuka Productions, Comments on The Lion King-Kimba Controversy.
Expansion and clarification of the stand being taken by the company and by the Tezuka family personally, following the public controversy of the past month. They feel that *The Lion King* was definitely influenced by *Jungle Emperor/Kimba*, but they choose to consider this a tribute to Tezuka, who they feel would have been flattered, rather than as grounds for a lawsuit. Mr. Matsutani declares: "That stated, we are nonetheless always prepared to act resolutely, to protect both the works of Dr. Osamu Tezuka and his honor, whenever we feel that our copyrights have been maliciously violated."

39. *The Christian Science Monitor*, Tuesday, August 30, 1994, p. 13.
"Cartoon Controversy Over 'Lion King' Percolates in Tokyo," by Cameron W. Barr.
Chatty report by an admittedly cartoon-hating foreign correspondent in Tokyo. "When the sniping started over Disney's 'The Lion King,' with some people here saying the movie was too similar to work done by a famous Japanese cartoonist, I thought this was a story I would abstain from covering. As is so often the case with trivial controversies, the teacup starts to swell. Soon CNN and major newspapers are sloshing around, and suddenly childless adults who wouldn't spend three seconds thinking about 'The Lion King' are talking about the controversy at social gatherings. Recently the leading Japanese grouser, a cartoonist named Machiko Satonaka, sent a letter of complaint to the Disney subsidiary that distributes the movie in Japan." Barr refers to Satonaka's list of parallels, and notes that, "Disney, incidentally, says 'The Lion King' was inspired by Shakespeare's 'Hamlet' and Disney's own 'Bambi,' not Osamu Tezuka's work." Barr "rented a tape of 'Leo, the Jungle Emperor' episodes (as Kimba was titled in Japanese) and then went to see 'The Lion King.'" "Without reviewing the entire 'Jungle Emperor' series, it's impossible to track down all of Ms. Satonaka's parallels. I saw some, and the rest may be there. But the bigger point is that the Disney movie transcends the Japanese series." "Satonaka may be right about the parallels. Disney would do well to consider her charges and respond. But 'The Lion King' does a much better job of entertaining the cartoon-averse."

40. *Animerica* 2, no. 8, August 1994, p. 38 (shipped late August).
"Animerica Special Report: Whose Lion Is It, Anyway?" by Trish Ledoux.
Full-page report recapitulates the public controversy during July 1994, citing

newspaper articles and the *Entertainment Tonight* video news story, noting that "a film crew from the local [San Francisco] ABC affiliate interviewed both Toren [Smith] and myself on camera." Report concludes, "Whose lion is it, anyway? We leave it to you to decide," presenting two columns of similarities between *The Lion King* and *Jungle Emperor*. However, there are several inaccuracies. *Lion King:* "Physically challenged evil male relative Uncle Scar (scar over one eye)" *Jungle Emperor:* "Physically challenged evil male relative Uncle Claw (has only one eye)." This is erroneous. There is no suggestion in *Kimba* that Claw and Kimba are related. *The Lion King:* "Anthropomorphic sidekicks include talkative parrot named Zazu." *Jungle Emperor:* "Anthropomorphic sidekicks include talkative parrot named Coco." Zazu in *The Lion King* is a hornbill, not a parrot. Referring to the *Jungle Emperor* characters as Claw and Coco is an inconsistent mixture of their Japanese and American names; Claw is Bubu in *Jungle Emperor* and Coco is Pauley Cracker in *Kimba*.

41. *Protoculture Addicts* no. 29, July/August 1994, pp. 29–30 (shipped late August).
"Cartoon Reviews: The Lion King," by John Beam.
A full-page essay describing *The Lion King* as a thinly disguised copy of the basic story of *Kimba,* replacing the original elements in *Kimba* with stock clichés of melodrama. *Another Quick Review,* by Claude J. Pelletier: "For all who are familiar with KIMBA, it is quite obvious that Disney has largely been influenced by Tezuka's work for the basic concept of this animated movie." "Taken by itself (without the disappointment that all anime fans resent), it is a very good animation."

42. *Video Business,* September 9, 1994, p. 46.
"Product Watch: The cartoon that would be king?" by Donald Liebenson.
"Is *The Lion King* a copycat? Thanks to home video, consumers can judge for themselves, and the controversy can mean a marketing opportunity that could make *Leo the Lion* a roaring success." Overview of the controversy, from the viewpoint of how it could be used to help promote the new *Leo the Lion* video release.

43. *Wild Cartoon Kingdom* no. 5, ©1994, p. 68 (September 1994 publication).
Review of *The Lion King,* by Chris Gore.
"Animation critics have accused Disney of borrowing quite heavily from Japanimation favorite *Kimba*—there are too many parallels to ignore. But when I watched the film, I wasn't thinking of that white lion at all. If only Disney would simply acknowledge that *Kimba* was an influence, then I don't think anyone would care."

44. *Inbetweener* (Newsletter of the International Animated Film Society), September 1994, pp. 7, 12.
"John Cawley's Get Animated! Calendar of Animation" (column).
In this monthly newsletter of the professional animation industry, Cawley gives the Japanese manga and TV origins of Tezuka's *Kimba the White Lion,* and notes: "This tale of a young lion cub whose father is killed and later must find the courage to reclaim his throne bears more than a passing resemblance to this summer's blockbuster *The Lion King.* The large number of 'simbalarities' have been mentioned in print, on radio and TV. The studio management has maintained no one on the crew was aware of the cult favorite . . . but a number of the artists on the film (including at least one art director, one supervising animator and one story person) would probably privately disagree."

45. *Protoculture Addicts* no. 30, September/October 1994, p. 5 (shipped mid-Oct.).

"Flash News: The Lion King."
The public controversy over the resemblances between *Kimba* and *The Lion King* are noted, with several specific news articles cited.

46. *Advance Comics* no. 74, February 1995, p. 290 (shipped December 1994).
Capital City Distribution Company's February solicitations to comics-shop retailers of comic books and related merchandise due for release that month.
Adv't/announcement for video release of *The Lion King*: "The most successful animated film in history comes to home video! The politically correct were in a snit over it (so what else is new?), and anime fans were distraught over its uncredited origin in Osamu Tezuka's JUNGLE EMPEROR/KIMBA THE WHITE LION, but anybody who saw it without a chip on their shoulder had a great time."

47. *Anime U.K.* no. 17, December 1994-January 1995, pp. 6–7 (January 1995 publication).
"Who's the King of the Jungle?" by Helen McCarthy.
Analyzes the evidence and covers the controversy in the United States from July to its fadeout around late August, when Disney apparently never acknowledged the open letter by Japanese artists and fans. "The story has died down in the American press and only attracted a few small mentions in British media. However fans are still left with the feeling that a major American studio has ridden roughshod over the contributions of a fellow artist, trading on the lack of cultural sophistication of their target audience and their own great reputation."

48. *Animato!* no. 30, Fall 1994, pp. 9–11 (February 1995 publication).
"Toon News" (unsigned).
'The Lion King and Kimba. *The Lion King* may become the Disney Studio's most profitable animated film, but it will certainly be its most controversial. The questions over racist images in *Fantasia, Song of the South,* and *Aladdin* have not received as much attention as the numerous similarities between *The Lion King* and the Japanese series known in the United States as *Kimba the White Lion.* The Disney stand on the issue has been short and sweet; none of the production staff involved with *The Lion King* had ever heard of *Kimba.* Since the Japanese side has not been covered as thoroughly as it should, *Animato!* is printing the following press releases from Mr. Takayuki Matsutani, the President of Tezuka Productions in their entirety.' The Tezuka Prod. press releases of July 12 and August 23 are reprinted without further comment.

49. *Mangajin* no. 42, February 1995, pp. 4 and 34.
"Letters to the Editor"
Kimba Versus Simba. A letter from Stephanie Tomiyasu, of Yokohama, asks for the magazine's opinion of the *Lion King* controversy, especially in regard to the fact that "the Japanese say such things as that Tezuka would be pleased to have influenced a Disney film," while if the issue had arisen between two American companies, "the case would have been in court long ago. Doesn't this whole thing say something about the Japanese?" The magazine asked Tezuka expert Frederik Schodt for his opinion. Schodt replied that ". . . 'borrowing' is very common in animation," but that "Disney's public assertion—that its hundreds of production staff members had never even heard of the late Tezuka Osamu or his work—is preposterous." Schodt feels that the issue has become particularly inflammatory in Japan "where years of American

accusations that Japanese are mere 'copycats' still smolder in the collective memory, and where Tezuka is regarded as a demigod."

50. *Los Angeles Times*, Monday, February 27, 1995, Sect. D, p. D1.
"Footnotes," by James Bates.
"Circle of Cash: At Walt Disney's annual meeting in Florida last week, Vice Chairman Roy E. Disney said 'The Lion King' would be the most profitable movie of all time, with about $800 million in profit from its box office, video sales, merchandising and other sources . . ."

51. *World Art*, January 1995, pp. 45 et seq. (March 1995 publication).
"Who Killed Bambi?" by Anthony Hayden-Guest.
(Brief comment in a long article about anime.) [The young Osamu Tezuka] "was promptly commissioned to work on two new sets of cartoons. One was set in a jungle and gave the world Kimba the White Lion, the doubtless not wholly accidental ancestor of Disney's Simba, the Lion King."

52. *Wired*, April 1995, p. 186.
"Heads Up, Mickey," by Andrew Leonard, pp. 140–143, 180, 182, 184, 186.
(Brief comment, in a long article about anime.) "Japanese animators also claim that large sections of Disney's *The Lion King* were lifted straight from a film created by Tezuka."

53. *The Simpsons* (TV program). Episode "Bleeding Gums," aired April 30, 1995.
This brief parody illustrates how the *Lion King/Kimba* controversy has become general public knowledge. Lisa Simpson's saxophone teacher, an old jazz musician known as Bleeding Gums, dies. Lisa goes to a hilltop to play a last tribute to him. His head appears in the clouds, but before he can speak, he is interrupted by a lion's head that says, "You must avenge my death, Kimba . . . I mean Simba!" Similar portentous parodies of Darth Vader and a CNN announcer also appear, until Bleeding Gums roars, "Will you guys pipe down? I'm sayin' goodbye to Lisa!"

54. *Space-Time Continuum* no. 17, May-June 1995, pp. 8, 15.
This fan-produced SF and fantasy media newsmagazine publishes news about the controversy that is almost totally erroneous, demonstrating how the controversy has passed into the realm of urban myth. Under "Animation" news (p. 8), it is stated that "*Kimba The White Lion* is available on tape in the United States. There is an Osaka, Japan, museum dedicated to Kimba's creator. Artists and merchandisers of the popular Japanese anime are suing Disney." (Only the second statement is true, and it is misleading since the purpose of the Osamu Tezuka Museum is not to honor Tezuka as solely the creator of *Kimba*.) Under "Disney" news (p. 15), it is stated: "Claiming too-close similarity to the long-running and popular Japanese anime, *Kimba the White Lion,* forty-three suits were filed by Japanese artists, Sony Corp. (Disney got a court order to stop *Kimba* merchandising when *Lion King* opened), plus Pioneer, who distributes *Kimba* episodes. *Lion King* was pulled from U.S. theaters for a 'new print' until the cases are resolved." (It is not true that any suits had been filed; the unavailability of *Kimba* in the United States was due to litigation in Japan unrelated to Disney or *The Lion King*; no company was distributing *Kimba* in America at this time; and *The Lion King* was pulled from U.S. theaters on September 23 and rereleased on November 18, which had nothing to do with the controversy being resolved, but was seen by most industry observers as Disney's attempt to compete with the premiere

of Nest Entertainment's first theatrical animated feature, *The Swan Princess,* on the same day.)

55. *Overstreet's Fan* no. 4, September 1995, p. 96.
"Open Yer Eyes!" by Michael Lindsay, pp. 96–97.
In the regular manga/anime column of this comics-fan magazine, a brief biography of Tezuka includes the statement, "Mimicry being the sincerest form of flattery, Disney paid an unannounced tribute to Tezuka with their mega-hit *The Lion King* which was scattered with so many similarities to Tezuka's *Kimba the White Lion* (as it is known in the United States) that the direct influence of that TV series is almost indisputable."

56. *The Complete Anime Guide: Japanese Animation Video Directory and Resource Guide,* by Trish Ledoux and Doug Ranney. Edited by Fred Patten. (Tiger Mountain Press, Issaquah, Washington, December 1995, v + 215 pp.).
A thorough survey of Japanese animation available in America theatrically, on TV, and on video from the 1960s through 1995. The "Animated Television Series" chapter includes a two-page profile of *Kimba the White Lion* (pp. 15–16) which concludes: "In 1994, Disney studios released the theatrical animated feature *The Lion King,* which although promoted as an 'original story' was perceived by many anime buffs to be more than a little beholden to Tezuka's *Kimba the White Lion.* [A list of parallels is presented.] Disney issued a statement that none of their animation staff had ever heard of Kimba (or Osamu Tezuka!), despite a statement from Simba voice actor Matthew Broderick that he thought he was being cast for a remake of Tezuka's classic TV series. Coincidence? You be the judge."

57. *Dreamland Japan: Writings on Modern Manga,* by Frederik L. Schodt (Stone Bridge Press, Berkeley, Calif., June 1996, 360 pp.).
Schodt has been Tezuka Productions' translator for many years. Chapter 5, "Osamu Tezuka: A Tribute to the God of Comics" (pp. 233–274) covers various aspects of Tezuka and his career. "Jungle Emperor: A Tale of Two Lions" (pp. 268–274) is a report on the controversy which is the subject of this essay. Schodt notes, "Tezuka visited the United States regularly while he was alive. I personally accompanied him in the 1980s to Disney World in Florida, to the Disney animation studios in Burbank, Calif., and to the house of Disney animation luminary Ward Kimball. In 1964, at the New York World's Fair, Tezuka had even met Walt Disney, whom he considered his idol. As the story Tezuka loved to recount goes, he spotted Mr. Disney, ran up to him excitedly like an ordinary fan and introduced himself. To Tezuka's never-ending delight, Mr. Disney reportedly said that he was well aware of Tezuka and *Astro Boy,* and someday 'hoped to make something like it.'" (p. 272).

58. *Los Angeles Times,* Wednesday, July 24, 1996, sect. D, p. D4.
"Disney Dives Into Japanese Film Business," by Sonni Efron.
"Walt Disney Studios plunged into the Japanese film business Tuesday by acquiring worldwide distribution rights for the works of Japan's best-loved animated-film director, Hayao Miyazaki." The article further states, "Disney executives say they control 65 percent of the Japanese market for children's videotapes. Tokuma [the Japanese rights holder of Miyazaki's films] sells only to video rental stores, and a consumer wishing to purchase a Miyazaki classic would have to pay the rental store price of up to $140 per tape. Disney executives said they could market Miyazaki videos for the same price as Disney films, $42 each—a bargain by Japanese standards,

but a highly lucrative market for Disney." Also, "Disney expects to make most of its money in the Japanese market as well as in Taiwan, where Miyazaki has a following." These comments testify to Disney's knowledge of the Japanese children's video market, where Tezuka's *Jungle Emperor* has been available since at least 1984.

59. *Samurai from Outer Space: Understanding Japanese Animation,* by Antonia Levi (Open Court Publishing Co., Chicago, November 1996, x + 169 pp.).
This book by a Ph.D. in Japanese history from Stanford University discusses the sociology of Japanese culture which underlies the superficial action-adventure plots of Japanese animation. She mentions the "modest success with American youngsters" of *Kimba* in 1966, and adds, "Indeed, despite Disney Studio's vigorous denials, many American and Japanese *otaku* [fans of Japanese animation] remain convinced that *Kimba* was an important influence (possibly subconscious) on the animation team that produced *The Lion King*" (pp. 6–7). Levi also comments on the August 1994 letter of protest signed by over 200 Japanese artists and other animation-industry personnel sent to the Disney Studio. A full-page (unnumbered) illustration from *Kimba* is captioned: "Osamu Tezuka is sometimes called the Walt Disney of Japan. Tezuka was influenced by Disney as a young man, but his later work took an entirely different direction. Given the similarities between Disney Studio's *The Lion King* and Tezuka's earlier work, *Kimba the White Lion,* perhaps Disney should be called the Osamu Tezuka of America."

60. *Mouse Under Glass: Secrets of Disney Animation and Theme Parks,* by David Koenig (Bonaventure Press, Irvine, Calif., December 1996, 270 pp.).
Koenig presents popularized reviews of each of Disney's theatrical animated features, humorously emphasizing flaws and inconsistencies in plot logic, and summarizing the public's reception upon their initial releases. *The Lion King* is covered on pp. 227–232, with the Disney/Tezuka controversy reported on pp. 231–232. Most of p. 231 is devoted to a "Simba-Kimba Conspiracy" chart comparing similarities.

61. *The Complete Anime Guide: Japanese Animation Film Directory and Resource Guide. Second Edition,* by Trish Ledoux and Doug Ranney. Edited by Fred Patten (Tiger Mountain Press, Issaquah, Washington, February 1997, viii + 214 pp.).
See note 56. This "revised, updated, expanded" edition contains a slightly revised profile of *Kimba the White Lion* (pp. 14–16). A new entry (pp. 115–116) documents the 1996 *Kimba the Lion Prince* video release.

62. *Bridge U.S.A.* no. 202, October 15, 1997, 20 pp.
"Japanimation," (unsigned article), pp. 13–15, 17–20.
This is a Japanese-language magazine for the Japanese community in Southern California. The cover-feature article in this issue reports on the growing popularity of Japanese animation in America. Under a section, "Disney Also Influenced by Japanimation?" the magazine interviews Sadao Miyamoto, identified as a Japanese animator currently working as a senior staff artist in Disney's Creative Resources department. "The very first film he worked on at Disney was 'The Lion King.' 'When I first saw the storyboards,' he frankly admits, 'I was taken aback, because they did look like 'Jungle Emperor.' The opening scenes are an example. 'To express the vast nature of Africa,' Miyamoto says, 'it's quite common to have the sounds of animals and to show flamingos all taking off at once. So it's probably unavoidable that the imagery looks somewhat the same.' But he also says it's clear that 'The Lion King'

has been influenced to some degree. According to Miyamoto, for people involved in animation, it's unthinkable that [Disney people] never even saw 'Jungle Emperor' [*Kimba*]. Moreover, the persons responsible for 'The Lion King' admit this. 'It's one thing to be influenced by the film,' Miyamoto adds. 'How much people referred to it is an altogether different issue.'" [Translation by Frederik L. Schodt]

Simba-Kimba Redux? The *Nadia* Versus *Atlantis* Affair
Unpublished follow-up to *Simba Versus Kimba*.

Seven years and a dozen Disney animated features after the release of *The Lion King*, a similar controversy briefly arose. In early 2001 Disney began its publicity campaign for its forthcoming animated theatrical feature *Atlantis: The Lost Empire*, to be released on June 15. The publicity emphasized that *Atlantis* would be a change of pace for Disney: an action-adventure fantasy with no songs, emphasizing drama rather than humor. This aroused the anticipation of anime fans, since it is one of the most basic and popular story types in anime. There was speculation as to whether Disney's association with Studio Ghibli and the films of Hayao Miyazaki during the past few years had led Disney to consciously attempt an anime-type adventure film.

As Disney's publicity revealed increasing details about *Atlantis,* anime fans noted similarities with one anime title in particular—*Nadia: The Secret of Blue Water* (*Fushigi no Umi no Nadia;* literally *Nadia of the Mysterious Seas*). *Nadia* was a thirty-nine-episode TV series directed by Hideaki Anno and produced by Studio Gainax for Toho Films and NHK, the Japanese government-owned television station which is the equivalent of Britain's BBC. NHK broadcast it weekly in prime time (Thursdays at 7:30 P.M.) from April 13, 1990, through March 29, 1991. It was extremely popular with anime fans in both Japan and America; numerous *Nadia* anime fan Web sites were created during the 1990s. By about a month before *Atlantis*'s June 15 release date, so much information about it had become available through Disney's merchandising (*Atlantis* picture books, comic books, and a novelization) that many anime fans were convinced that the similarities between *Atlantis* and *Nadia* were far too numerous to be mere coincidence. Some anime fans created Internet Web sites posting comparative images between the two titles.

Most of the 1994–95 and following Simba/Kimba controversy was in newspapers, newsmagazines, and other publications which are still available in archival libraries. Most of the 2001 Atlantis/Nadia controversy was in online Web sites, chatrooms, and other electronic pages which are "Not Found" if you look for them today. This is why I deeply distrust the Internet as a serious reference source for primary documentation. Important information has a habit of suddenly vanishing forever. ■

Some of the comparisons posted on the *Nadia Versus Atlantis* Web site of Michael D. Hayden:[1]

Nadia. "Our hero, Jean, a nerdy yet sweet inventor who gets caught up in a quest to find Atlantis. Along the way he falls in love with a girl unlike anyone he's ever met before. Accessories: big round glasses, red bow tie, assorted charts and scientific equipment."

Atlantis. "Our hero, Milo, a nerdy yet sweet scholar who gets caught up in a quest to find Atlantis. Along the way he falls in love with a girl unlike anyone he's ever met before. Accessories: big round glasses, red bow tie, assorted charts and scientific equipment."

Nadia. "The heroine, Nadia, an exotic young woman who turns out to be a princess of the lost kingdom of Atlantis. To save her kingdom from invaders, she must unleash her hidden power. Accessories: blue crystal pendant, skimpy bikini 'n' sarong costume, gold armband and hoop earrings."

Atlantis. "The heroine, Kida, an exotic young woman who turns out to be a princess of the lost kingdom of Atlantis. To save her kingdom from invaders, she must unleash her hidden power. Accessories: blue crystal pendant, skimpy bikini 'n' sarong costume, gold armband and hoop earrings."

Further similarities are that both stories involve the search for Atlantis taking place in a futuristic submarine with an international crew. The crews of both subs feature a sinister, mysterious captain, a briskly efficient young blonde woman as First Mate, a large black man as ship's doctor, and a lean man of swarthy Eastern European appearance with a bristly walrus moustache as the gunnery officer. In both, the heroine does not know at first that her blue crystal pendant necklace is the key to the giant crystal that is the secret source of Atlantis's power, which the ruthless villains want to steal. At the climax, the heroine must use her psychic affinity with her miniature crystal (as hereditary princess/priestess of Atlantis) to control the larger crystal and deny its power to the villains.

Both stories also contain enough important differences to keep them refreshingly distinct. In *Nadia,* Jean and Nadia are both fourteen years old, and their quest is the youthful adventure of two preadolescent buddies. In *Atlantis,* Milo and Kida are in their thirties and their relationship quickly turns to romance. In *Nadia,* Jean and Nadia meet in the first episode and begin the quest together. Nadia does not learn that she is a princess of Atlantis until they find the lost kingdom. In *Atlantis,* Milo does not meet Princess Kida until he arrives in the undersea realm. There are major personality differences between other similar characters, and many important characters and events in each story that are not duplicated in the other.

As in the Simba/Kimba affair, the anime fans never claimed that *Atlantis* was nothing but an unoriginal plagiarism of *Nadia.* Their ire was over

Disney's claim that *Atlantis* was its own completely original story (though acknowledging the "homage" to *20,000 Leagues Under the Sea*), and that the Disney staff who had worked on *Atlantis* for several years had never heard of *Nadia*. Given the quantity of similarities between the two, and the prominence of *Nadia* coupled with the professional knowledge of the Disney animators, Disney's claim of its ignorance and that all of the similarities were just coincidental was not believed.

To be precise, the Disney corporation never formally made a statement at all. The claims of innocent ignorance were made by the *Atlantis* staff individually. One frequently cited comment was attributed to *Atlantis* co-director Kirk Wise, posted to the rec.arts.disney.animation news group on May 7, 2001: "Never heard of *Nadia* till it was mentioned in this NG [news group]. Long after we'd finished production, I might add." Any similarities were blamed on the fact that both *Atlantis* and *Nadia* were admittedly (and obviously) inspired by Jules Verne's *20,000 Leagues Under the Sea;* and by the natural coincidence that, once a decision had been made to combine the Vernean imagery with a plot of a search for Atlantis (a popular theme in Verne's day; there is a brief scene in *20,000 Leagues* in which Captain Nemo and the *Nautilus* visit the ruins of Atlantis at the bottom of the ocean), the writers of both built their descriptions of Atlantis upon those popularized during the 1930s by the psychic Edgar Cayce, who gave lectures about the lost science of Atlantis powered by giant mystic crystals. As with *The Lion King,* the *Atlantis* creators stated that there may have been some anime fans among the *Atlantis* production crew, but that the creators themselves and the majority of the animators were not fans. They may have been aware of anime generically, but not of *Nadia* in particular.

As it turned out, this *Atlantis/Nadia* affair never aroused the public's interest as had the Simba/Kimba affair. Aside from the anime fan Internet discussion groups (one of which reported getting 3,000+ hits a day just before *Atlantis* was released),[2] it was limited to a few brief news articles[3, 4, 5] and animation industry discussion groups. The controversy was mentioned by Roger Ebert in his review of *Atlantis*[6]; but Ebert did not take sides. Possibly this was because, as the second such incident, the public felt that it had heard it all before. And unlike *The Lion King, Atlantis* was not a major hit. By the week after its release, several newspapers had used its lackluster public reception to editorialize about the decline in Disney's ability to create imaginative, popular animated features following recent management and creative staff changes. The public was not interested in an analysis of *Atlantis'* possible story influences.

This issue touches upon the Disney studio's much-publicized worldwide animation expertise, what Disney *should* have known whether it did actually know it or not. The following facts and observations are pertinent:

In Japan, *Nadia* topped anime fans' popularity polls from the beginning of its broadcast in April 1990 through the mid-1990s, several years after its broadcast ended. *Nadia* animation art books and merchandising items were major items in the animation fan market. Disney has a large corporate presence in the Japanese animation video and licensed merchandise market, and studies its competition there.

The first eight of the thirty-nine *Nadia* episodes were commercially released in America to the home video market, dubbed into English, twice during the 1990s. The first release, titled *Nadia,* was as eight separate half-hour videos, released between March 1992 and August 1993 to the anime market by Streamline Pictures. The second release, titled *The Secret of Blue Water,* was as two four-episode videos, both released in January 1996 to the general video market by Orion Home Video. This made *Nadia* a matter of knowledge and availability to the American animation industry and general public before production of *Atlantis* began.

Disney has been the American representative of the Japanese animated features of Hayao Miyazaki since July 1996. Disney and its affiliate Miramax have distributed two Miyazaki features, *Kiki's Delivery Service* and *Princess Mononoke,* and have announced plans to release more. The Disney/Buena Vista Home Video release of *Kiki's Delivery Service* includes an announcement for its forthcoming video release of Miyazaki's *Laputa: The Castle in the Sky.* Disney animators who profess ignorance of other Japanese animation have gone on record with their admiration for Miyazaki and his works. Anderson Jones, in his "Movie Scoop" column on the *Nadia/Atlantis* controversy[4], quotes *Atlantis* co-director Kirk Wise as saying: "We're big [Hayao] Miyazaki (*Princess Mononoke*) fans. We really worship at his altar, so I'd certainly say there's an influence there from his work . . ." Fans discussing the controversy on the Internet have pointed out other similarities between scenes in *Atlantis* and in some of Miyazaki's films, such as the heroine drifting down from the sky, with her crystal pendant glowing, into the hero's arms, as in Miyazaki's *Laputa.* Lee Zion says in his "Probing the Atlantis Mystery,"[3] "[co-director Gary] Trousdale himself conceded that one touch in the film might have been inspired by Miyazaki. At the end of the film, the waters recede from Atlantis, revealing more of the city—something the film has in common with [Miyazaki's] *The Castle of Cagliostro.*"

But *Nadia* was based on a concept of Hayao Miyazaki, according to nausicaa.net, the principal Web site for English-language Miyazaki fans. "Q: Did Miyazaki make *Nadia*? A: No. However, *Nadia* was originally a Miyazaki project. In the mid-1970s Miyazaki was working on stories for television for an animation company, Toho. One of the projects was to be called *Around the World in 80 Days by Sea.* This story would follow the adventures of two young orphans fleeing an evil power or government while being helped by some bumbling bad guys and the mysterious Captain Nemo and the *Nautilus.* The project was eventually shelved, but Miyazaki incorporated several of the elements of this story into the series he eventually made for NHK in the late 1970s, *Future Boy Conan.* Some of these same elements reappeared later in

1986 in *Laputa.* In the late 1980s, when NHK and Toho approached Gainax about doing a television series they suggested this story idea, and Gainax took it." (http://www.nausicaa.net/miyazaki/nonmiyazaki/) The similarities between *Nadia* and Miyazaki's films are so prominent that anime fans have discussed them for over a decade. The information quoted above from the nausicaa.net site is a Frequently Asked Question there. Yet if *Atlantis* co-director Wise says: "We're big Miyazaki (*Princess Mononoke*) fans. We really worship at his altar . . .," is it unreasonable to expect that he and these other fans who are also professional animators would have studied Miyazaki and all his projects thoroughly, including the unmade ones?

To repeat a conclusion of the Simba/Kimba argument, it would be unreasonable to believe that Disney's entire *Atlantis* production crew was fully knowledgeable about anime and was aware of *Nadia.* But was there nobody at all among the hundreds who worked on *Atlantis* who knew of *Nadia* in advance or who learned of it during the years that the movie was in production? Did nobody discuss it with other animators, or feel that the similarities warranted bringing to the attention of *Atlantis*'s supervisors or the Disney legal staff? There would probably have been little or no reactions if a Disney spokesperson had said, "Yes, we were aware of *Nadia*'s existence, but we did not feel that it presented any problems that should keep us from creating our own new story combining Jules Verne and the Atlantis legend." But to claim that they never heard of *Nadia* at all until just after they had finished production is to apparently refute their own expertise in the type of production on which they had just spent several years.

Notes

1. The "Nadia Versus Atlantis" Web site, by Michael D. Hayden (http://www.zero-city.com/nadia/nadia_vs_atlantis.html).

2. The "Disney's Atlantis and Nadia" Web site, by Marc Hairston (http://utd500.utdallas.edu/~hairston/atlantis.html).

3. "Probing the Atlantis Mystery," by Lee Zion, on the AnimeNewsNetwork.com Web site (http://www.animenewsnetwork.com/archives/feature/atlantis.php) in May 2001.

4. The "Movie Scoop" column by Anderson Jones on *E! Online,* June 15, 2001.

5. "'Atlantis' Draws Comparisons," by Chris Marlowe; *The Hollywood Reporter Online,* Friday, June 22, 2001.

6. *Atlantis* review by Roger Ebert; *Chicago Sun-Times,* June 15, 2001.

Part III
Artists

Hypersexual Psychoviolence! The Dynamic World of Go Nagai

Foreword to *Mazinger*, by Go Nagai. Chicago: First Publishing, 1988.

Giant robots filled the air!

At convention screenings, cartoon clubs, and in syndicated broadcasts, videotapes of Japanese TV animation changed the consciousness of American fans in the past decade. Even though cartoons like *Astroboy*, *Gigantor*, and *8th Man* arrived in the 1960s, we did not then appreciate them, or understand their origin.

By the mid-1970s, the *Shogun Warriors* robot superheroes imported from Japan and marketed in the United States by Mattel paved the way for a cultural and economic invasion. Animation full of the dramatic action and emotional tension so notoriously lacking from American "Saturday Morning TV" began to appear. *Brave Raideen, UFO Dai Apollon, Danguard Ace*, and *Combattler V* were just a few of the conquering horde. If these Japanese TV cartoons seemed to be dominated by giant-robot heroes, it was because Japan was in the midst of a TV robot revolution.

A simple electrifying concept had energized and transformed the Japanese animation industry in 1972. *Mazinger Z* was no mere remote-controlled machine, but a metal colossus piloted by the teenage Koji Kabuto from within the robot's brain. This unique human/robot symbiosis was elaborated in a sequel, *Great Mazinger*. Monsters, robots, and their myriad hybrids were the titanic opponents encountered, and defeated, by these iron knights. With their samurai-styled helmets and flashing swords, the Mazinger robots presented an original synthesis of ancient and modern imagery. Other series featuring innovative SF concepts followed: *Getta Robo*, the first transforming robot, *UFO Robo Grandizer, Gloizer X*, and *Steel Jeeg*, a magnetic robot. The single artist-creator responsible for both the symbiotic and the transforming robot concepts was the prodigious Go Nagai.

But not all of this startling new animation was based on Go Nagai's giant

One of the questions that arose when editing this book was to what extent the information in these older essays should be modernized. When this was published in 1988, there was debate over whether the name "Astro Boy" should be two words or a single word. Both opinions had their supporters, and this essay appeared in a book whose publisher insisted it should be a single-word name, like Superboy. For the record, *Astro Boy*'s American creator, Fred Ladd, says it was definitely two words, and the appearance of "Astro Boy" on the title card of the 1963 cartoons is the proof. This article also refers to Shotaro "Ishimori" rather than Ishinomori as he is known today. He had actually changed his name in 1986, but American anime fans did not become generally aware of this until several years later. ■

robots. There were some cartoons that seemed incredible to American fans.

Devilman was a cross between TV monster comedies like *The Addams Family* or *The Munsters* and sophisticated occult thrillers like *The Exorcist* or *The Omen*. *Devilman* featured a teenager whose body was possessed by a demon who had rebelled against Satan. In each episode a new nauseating demon tried to destroy the high school, only to be defeated by Devilman. Teachers and students were bloodily ripped apart—or were so terrified that they wet their pants.

Another weird super-character comedy was *Cutey Honey*, a sexy android heroine who fought against the Panther Claw Gang, a monstrous female "space mafia" out to kill off Earth's women and steal all the men. Cutey Honey's secret identity as a student at a Catholic girl's school would be jeopardized by the nocturnal advances of her lesbian teachers. Her young male assistants were more amorous than useful in tight situations. Honey's super-scientific costume changes left her briefly nude, which greatly delighted her adoring male viewers.

The original Japanese manga upon which these TV series were based were considerably gorier and raunchier than the animation. They were also among the most famous and popular manga of that decade. Go Nagai was at the front of a movement that was shaking the Japanese comic industry to its roots. The staid traditional children's comics were being replaced with a much wilder and stronger crop.

Go Nagai was born on September 6, 1945, just four days after the conclusion of World War II. He and the modern Japanese manga industry grew up together. As a boy, he scribbled his own amateur comics and taught himself to draw. When he was twenty, Nagai applied as an assistant to Shotaro Ishimori, one of the first wave of young cartoonists in the 1950s who had been inspired by Japan's "God of Comics," Osamu Tezuka, and who was now becoming a major comics creator with his *Cyborg 009* series. Nagai worked as one of Ishimori's assistants for a couple of years, then struck out on his own.

Energetic, prolific, and enthusiastic, Nagai exploded into the manga industry. His first published work was a humorous short story in a November 1967 magazine. During 1968 he had twenty-three different titles published, including both solo stories and continuing serials, among twelve different comic magazines. His first series to be collected in book format, in 1969, was *Kinta, The Young Pack Boy*, about the escapades of a young horse handler in a caravan in feudal Japan. *Kinta* and many others were traditional humorous comics for children.

But Nagai did not limit himself to the conventional. He joined and immediately became a leader in a movement among a radical group of young artists seeking to expand manga in new directions. This was roughly similar to the underground comix movement in America at the same time. But where the American comix artists created their own separate mini-industry for themselves and their readers, Nagai and his fellow Japanese punk cartoonists presented their work in the same magazines that published the standard children's stories.

Around 1959 the Japanese manga industry began to develop novels for readers now too mature for children's comics. Although many 1960s manga were daring and innovative in their treatment of adult themes, they were built around mundane formulas: crime thrillers, romances, historical dramas, and domestic comedies. Fantasy was still considered to be suitable only for children.

Nagai and his fellow rebels pioneered outrageous fantasy comedies that were intended to shock and captivate the older teen and young adult market. (See Frederik Schodt's excellent study, *Manga! Manga! The World of Japanese Comics* [Kodansha, 1983] for a survey of some of the other artists in this movement.) Nagai became notorious for *Harenchi Gakuen* (*Shameless School*), a weekly serial which began in the July 25, 1968, issue of *Shonen Jump* magazine. This was a gonzo comedy about a "typical" high school in which the male students and teachers competed for novel ways to see the girls naked. The girls, of course, encouraged the boys as much as possible. Classes devoted to nude orgies and drunken binges were common, and anybody who actually tried to study was treated as a fool. *Shameless School* became an instant smash hit, despite—or possibly because of—strident demands by the PTA and censorship groups for its cancellation. When Nagai finally decided to end the series four years later, he paid tribute to his detractors by having the school demolished in a holocaust between the students and a PTA commando army.

By then Nagai had gone on to more spectacular things. In 1970, he and his brothers established their own studio, Dynamic Productions, to produce both manga and TV series concepts. Nagai's brothers assumed the executive and business duties, leaving Go free to supervise his own staff of assistants in creative production. Their first goal was the field of TV animation, or anime, as it had come to be known.

Nagai's expansion into anime was as dramatic as his appearance on the manga scene had been. His studio's initial proposals were snapped up by Toei Animation Company, Japan's largest theatrical and TV cartoon producer. Between 1970 and 1972 Toei Animation developed the episodes, while Nagai himself drew the manga to build up a fandom among the public.

Because these TV series were produced by animation studios, not by Nagai himself, he was free to develop still more ideas and to draw his own manga, which were now signed "by Go Nagai and Dynamic Productions." By the end of the 1970s he had personally drawn over a hundred titles, many of which were long-running serials. It must have seemed that Go Nagai was about to engulf the entire Japanese comics and animation industries.

Nagai's TV series were especially popular in Italy and France, again despite loud condemnation from citizens' groups for extreme violence. In

1978, the French version of *UFO Robot Grandizer* (retitled *Goldorak*) made news around the world by getting a 100 percent rating for several weeks. This meant that no one in the country was watching anything else during that half-hour. (The story is slightly spoiled by pointing out that France had only two TV channels at that time, and the other channel was showing an economic news analysis.)

During the 1980s, Nagai and Dynamic Productions have diversified into other activities, including children's puppet theater. This has cut into his drawing time, but he is still very active. In 1984, nostalgia for *Mazinger Z* led to a new manga and anime series, *God Mazinger*. Today he is involved in the development of animation for the new OAV (original animation video) market. One of these projects is a faithful remake of *Devilman*. Toei Animation's 1972 TV adaptation had seemed outrageous at the time, but it was considerably toned down from the manga, and is rather mild by today's animation standards. The new five-part video series will bring *Devilman* to life as Nagai originally wrote it. An entirely new series is *Fandora,* an erotic comedy-adventure about a nymphet interstellar bounty hunter.

Go Nagai, in his early forties, is still a major creator in Japan's comic-art field.

Nagai began his career drawing humorous children's comics and has always produced a wide range of manga and animation concepts. One of his lesser TV products is the bland *Chicle, The Young Witch,* notable for an unexpected guest appearance by Warner Brothers' Tweety Pie in the closing credits. But his reputation for sex and violence is one of which he is proud. A recent manga series set in a brutal post-holocaust world is titled *Violence Jack.* Two albums of illustration have been published; one is titled *Go Nagai and His Wild World of Violence,* the other, of his horror-fantasy series, is *The Psychic World of Go Nagai.*

Violence may be a misnomer, however. Nagai's true interest is raw power, both physical and emotional. His characters tend to be massive, thickly muscled, visibly radiating sheer energy, their loves and hates transcending time. His robots and monsters are titanic and bizarre. Even the heroic robots inspire awe and nervous reverence rather than a feeling of ease. His heroes rarely relax; they constantly feel responsible for the fate of the whole world.

This dynamism has made Go Nagai's comics attractive even for Americans who have never really been able to read them.

Up to now, Nagai's sole American appearance was in the June 1983 issue of *Epic Illustrated.* But knowledgeable Americans have long sought out his work on their own. The 1982 first issue of Joshua Quagmire's *Cutey Bunny* funny animal satire acknowledged, "Incidentally, the name Cutey Bunny is a rather obvious pun. Obvious, that is, if you happen to be a fan of Japanese comics." And the third issue of Peter Gillis's and Tom Artis's *Tailgunner Joe* shows a "Go Nagai" model-name on a "Maximum Lethal Violence" highway juggernaut.

American comics creators have known for some time the work of Go Nagai. Now, with the publication of this all-new *Mazinger* created especially for the American public, we can all meet him.

Osamu Tezuka (1926–89)

The Eighteenth Annual ANNIE Awards, 1990. Illustrated souvenir program book of the annual ASIFA-Hollywood ANNIE awards banquet, Studio City, Calif., December 9, 1990. Burbank, Calif.: ASIFA-Hollywood, 1990.

Death (from stomach cancer) has cut short the career of Osamu Tezuka. "Cut short" is a stock phrase which seems thoughtless for a person of Tezuka's age, but in his case it is still an apt phrase. Tezuka was a notorious workaholic who hated to repeat himself and who was always looking for new artistic challenges. At a time in his life when most successful cartoonists have established a single comic strip that they will continue until their retirement, and most successful animators have risen to executive positions and are no longer writing or drawing, Tezuka was still personally creating and closely directing new projects in both fields at his studio. He had recently completed a lengthy, somber adult comic-art novel set in World War II Germany, and had directed a trio of animated short films that were still winning acclaim and awards at animation festivals around the world. He was reportedly working at the time of his death on an animated TV adaptation of the Bible upon a commission from the Vatican, and on his first attempt at a Disney-style theatrical feature cartoon emphasizing lots of musical routines. Tezuka was still full of many new cartoon and animation projects that death has forestalled.

Tezuka's death is overshadowed by that of Emperor Hirohito in January. This is eerily fitting, for parallels (admittedly somewhat fanciful) can be drawn between Tezuka's life and the Showa era. Tezuka was born the month

This tribute was written right after Tezuka's death for the Cartoon/Fantasy Organization's bulletin (*Cartoon/Fantasy Organization: Los Angeles Chapter's Bulletin* no. 90, March 1989, p. 3). It was not that different from most other tributes written immediately after his death. It took a few months, if not a couple of years, for the knowledge to spread that Tezuka had lied throughout his career about how old he was. He was actually born in 1928, not 1926. He had added two years to his age because, at the time he drew his first cartoons for publication in 1946–47, he was still a teenager. The manga industry did not yet exist that would encourage its readers to submit their own stories while still in their teens. Professional manga artist/writers were expected to be adults. Tezuka felt that he needed to look at least twenty years old or publishers would not take him seriously. This was revealed immediately after his death in Japan, but it was another of those bits of news that, at that time, took several months

Cont. on p. 198

before Hirohito ascended the Japanese throne. Tezuka's artistic career began in 1946, when he was nineteen. This was the year after World War II ended, destroying what might be termed Japan's social adolescence, so that Tezuka's rise as an artist and his creation of the modern Japanese comic-art field accompanied Japan's overall Phoenix-like rebirth from the ruin of the war. Fittingly, Tezuka's self-proclaimed masterwork, begun in the 1950s and still continuing at his death, was titled *Phoenix*. It was Tezuka's prolific exposure in every field of cartoon art imaginable, simultaneously—infants' picture books, childrens' comic books, comic-art romance novels for womens' magazines, social satire, and risque humor for men's magazines, political cartoons, and advertising art—that helped establish comics in Japan as respectable reading for all age groups, not just children. Tezuka did not create the Japanese theatrical animation industry (although one of the earliest popular theatrical cartoon features, Toei Animation's *Alakazam the Great,* was based upon his comic book serialization of the Chinese *Monkey King* legend), but he did create the Japanese TV animation industry and its first TV animation studio. His *Astro Boy* was Japan's first futuristic, science-fiction animation, establishing the trend which led to action/adventure "Japanimation" as we know it today, and this debuted in 1963, just as Japan's international reputation for high-quality electronics was becoming established. Finally, Tezuka died just one month after the Showa emperor, leaving a legacy of a dynamic, progressive comics industry and animation industry within a dynamic and progressive Japanese society. Coincidentally, both died of cancer, and the Emperor was known (early in his reign) as a god, while Tezuka had been dubbed "the God of Comics."

Tezuka was also largely, if indirectly, responsible for the creation of the Cartoon/Fantasy Organization. The C/FO's founders were drawn together in the early 1970s because they were Tezuka fans at a time when almost nobody else in America was aware of his work. They started the C/FO to

to get to America. I remember that the first couple of times I saw Tezuka's birth year stated as 1928 instead of 1926, I thought that it was a typographical error. Of course, this destroyed my theoretical parallel of Tezuka's life with the Showa era since he was actually born two years after Emperor Hirohito's accession to the throne, not the month before.

When, almost two years later, ASIFA-Hollywood (the literary/artistic society of the Hollywood animation industry, not to be confused with the animation industry's labor union) asked me if it could reprint my tribute in its Program Booklet for its December 1990 annual Annie Awards, where Tezuka was being posthumously given its Winsor McCay Award for a lifetime service to animation, I felt honored. I had forgotten that it had been so strongly written around Tezuka's supposed birth in 1926 that had been revealed as untrue. I was actually more surprised when I saw that ASIFA had left in the final paragraph about what Tezuka had meant to the C/FO, since I had expected that to be cut out as not pertinent to ASIFA's Awards. ■

provide a regular meeting place to show otherwise unavailable animated cartoons, especially Tezuka's *Kimba the White Lion* and *Astro Boy* (the first C/FO publication was a flyer for a Tezuka video festival), and to attempt to order Tezuka's comics from Japan for themselves. Tezuka himself appeared at two C/FO meetings in the late 1970s to show some of his rarer animation as a thank-you to the C/FO for promoting his works and Japanese cartoon art in general in America, and to encourage us to continue doing so. Tezuka has meant much to the C/FO, and we will miss him deeply.

Osamu Tezuka: A Memorial to the Master
Animation News Service 7, no. 1, Spring 1993.

Part One: Personal Reflections

Meeting Osamu Tezuka was an awesome experience. Since he was a cartoon writer, artist, and animator, it's easy to compare him with other cartoon-art creators. However, I think that he can be compared equally accurately with Howard Hughes. Both were innovators and visionaries who were interested in many fields. (Tezuka had a medical degree as a surgeon, and his artistic interests embraced everything from newspaper political cartoons to record-jacket art to circus stage designs. He once starred in a Japanese TV-special tour of Disney World, in which he played his own version of Robert Benchley in Disney's *The Reluctant Dragon,* as the bumbling tourist getting into embarrassing situations all over the theme park.) Both Tezuka and Hughes were extremely egotistical and set on having their own way, switching from one grandiose project to another at the expense of their companies' stability. Hughes had to be forcibly removed from Hughes Aircraft Company before he bankrupted it. Tezuka did bankrupt his Mushi Productions studio. Of his later Tezuka Productions in the 1980s, other Japanese animators have commented that Tezuka could have built it into the largest animation studio in the country with his talent, prestige, and contacts, but he was content to let it just putter along while he concentrated on making his "personal" fine-art films like *Jumping, Broken-Down Film,* and *The Legend of the Forest,* which he could take to international cinema festivals.

I met Tezuka as the result of a misunderstanding. During the mid-1970s, I wrote to several Japanese publishers to order Tezuka's manga for some Los Angeles fans of *Astro Boy* and *Kimba the White Lion.* In late 1977, shortly after the Cartoon/Fantasy Organization began, I received a letter from Japan saying that Tezuka himself was coming to Los Angeles, and I was invited to meet him at a press conference at the New Otani Hotel. I arrived to find that this was a press conference organized by Toho Films to pre-sell its forthcoming live-action feature of Tezuka's *Phoenix* to American movie distributors and merchandisers. I had been invited only because they had thought that my orders for Tezuka's manga meant that I was a book publisher. Mere fans were definitely not welcome! But I did show enough knowledge about Tezuka's manga that he became intrigued as to how I knew about some of his titles that he knew had never been sold in the United States. When I told him that he had many Anglo fans in America, he obviously wasn't sure how seriously to take me.

A couple of months later, Tezuka returned to Hollywood on another business trip. As fate would have it, he ran into Robin Leyden, another of the C/FO's founding members. Leyden invited him to the C/FO's March 1978 meeting, less than a week away. Tezuka offered to show a program of his cartoons that had never been seen in America, which Leyden immediately accepted on behalf of the club. We soon learned that Tezuka had immediately phoned his office in Tokyo and ordered them to air-ship these cartoons instantly to Los Angeles, at a cost of thousands of dollars in air-freight and customs charges. And they were 16 mm films, not videotapes, so we had to scramble to find a 16 mm projector at the last minute.

Tezuka visited the C/FO in Los Angeles twice, in March and December 1978. He was bewildered but flattered that so many American fans, who did not understand the Japanese language, had taken the trouble to figure out the plots of his manga from the pictures alone. Tezuka answered many questions at our March meeting. But one of his replies, about the live-action *Astro Boy* TV program of the 1950s, was that it was a false rumor. There had never been such a program. This puzzled us, because it was listed in all the Japanese "TV monster and hero" dictionaries. When Tezuka returned in

I *really* felt out of place at the Toho press conference at which I met Osamu Tezuka. I went not knowing what to expect, and wondering why I had been invited—how Toho Films had ever heard of me. The conference turned out to be a formal Japanese dinner at the prestigious Thousand Cranes Restaurant in the New Otani Hotel in L.A.'s Little Tokyo district, at the end of 1977—the day after Christmas. I and a reporter from the *Hollywood Reporter* were the only *gaijin* there; the other guests were all Japanese-community notables, theater owners, and merchants. It turned out that Toho Films had only recently started production of *Phoenix,* and wanted to start early lining up international publicity and marketing. Tezuka had been brought along by Toho's publicists to be shown off as *Phoenix*'s creator, like a trained pony. My orders to Japanese publishers five years earlier for manga had gotten me onto some lists as an American bookseller or publisher interested in Japanese books, so Toho hoped that I would want to import or publish English-language editions of the fancy *Phoenix* movie art books that were being planned. I was horribly embarrassed to admit that I was really just a small-time fan. But when the conference's translator was not otherwise busy, I managed to get him to ask Tezuka a couple of questions about some of his manga which I had "read" (by looking at the pictures and guessing at the plots) during the past few years. This intrigued Tezuka, who wanted to know how an "American businessman" who did not speak or read Japanese was more

December, several of us had brought copies of the dictionaries with photos of the live-action *Astro Boy* to show Tezuka. His answer: "Well, yes . . . But it was so *bad*! Please don't tell the American people about it!" So we learned that Tezuka definitely had an ego, and he would talk about only what he wanted the public to know about him. (This was frustrating to me, because the first Tezuka manga that I ever read, and still one of my favorites, was his *Vampires,* which was made into a TV serial in the 1960s. But Tezuka considered it one of his failures, and he flatly refused to talk about it.)

We soon learned how important an impression we had made on Tezuka. Shortly after the March 1978 meeting, the C/FO was contacted by a new representative of the Toei Animation Company. They were just opening a permanent office in Hollywood to try to sell their cartoons in America. Tezuka had told them that there was already a small but enthusiastic group of American fans of Japanese animation who would help them. We offered to help test-market anime merchandise to American fans if Toei could provide it. This was how the first dealer's table of Japanimation merchandise came to be at the 1978 San Diego Comic-Con, filled with Toei's *Space Pirate Captain Harlock* and *Cyborg 009* and *Candy Candy* material. Over the next couple of years, thanks to Tezuka's recommendations among his Tokyo colleagues, the early C/FO helped to expose both Toei Animation's and Tokyo Movie Shinsha's cartoons among American fans across the United States, including a screening of TMS's *Lupin III: The Castle of Cagliostro* at the 1980 World Science Fiction Convention in Boston. This did not result in the immediate media payoffs that the studios had hoped for, but it did help to spread

familiar with his manga than any of the Japanese businessmen there. We only had time for a brief and frustratingly interrupted conversation because the translator's main duty was to help the Toho representatives pitch the movie to the *Hollywood Reporter*'s reporter.

Tezuka's meeting with Robin Leyden in March 1978 was a happy coincidence. Tezuka was being given a VIP tour of Universal Pictures in Hollywood, where Leyden worked at the time building models and setting up the electrical wiring for sets and the studio's theme park attractions.

Robin Leyden and Osamu Tezuka at Universal Studios, March 1978, with Leyden's statue of Astro Boy.

Tezuka's tour included a "backstage" visit to some of the work areas. Leyden, as a big Tezuka fan, had decorated his office with lots of pictures and toys of Astro Boy and Kimba, and the big Astro Boy statue that he had designed and was building was in prominent view. *That* caught Tezuka's attention immediately.

Cont. on p. 202

CFO bulletin April 15, 1978, with minutes of Tezuka visit

awareness of Japanese animation among American comics and SF fandom faster than it would have grown otherwise, so that there was a strong, positive fannish recognition of *Battle of the Planets, Star Blazers,* and *Robotech* as *Japanese* animation when they came along.

Tezuka's biggest fan-related project came as a bombshell to Robin Leyden and me in early 1980. Tezuka had convinced numerous Japanese cartoonists such as Go Nagai and Yumiko Igarashi that they ought to come to the 1980 San Diego Comic-Con, to see for themselves that they had many American fans. He persuaded Monkey Punch to organize a group tour through his office, and he told them that Leyden and I would be happy to handle the liaison from the American end. It was a thrilling responsibility, actually made easy since the Comic-Con Committee was as excited as we were to have a whole tour group of foreign cartoonists attend, so they helped to make sure that there were no problems. There were about thirty Japanese in the group, and while Monkey

The 132-minute, theatrical live-action feature of Tezuka's *Phoenix* was a major event in Japan: produced by Toho Films, directed by Kon Ichikawa with an all-star cast music by the prestigious French film composer Michel Legrand. It was based on the volume of *Phoenix* showing the dawn of civilization in Japan, when Queen Himiko of Yamato was more of a Stone Age tribal shamaness than a queen in the modern sense. It was over a year in production, released in August 1978 in Japan, and subtitled in March 1979 for the Japanese-community theaters in the United States. The few American anime fans of the day all desperately hoped that it would come to a theater in their cities. It was a tremendous bomb. It had all the problems of American live-action movie adaptations of popular newspaper comic strips: notably trying to compress too many of the strip's characters and story lines into a single plot, and using heavy makeup to make the actors look just like their characters' manga depictions, which just made them look grotesque. There were two or three minutes of animation amidst the live action, including a brief fly-by by Astro Boy, which has caused some non-Japanese critics to describe this *Phoenix* as a "samurai comedy" rather than a serious drama.

After over twenty years, I am still stunned by my memories of watching Tezuka his hotel room in the evenings during the 1980 Comic-Con, taking out a blank sheet of stiff art paper and an india-ink bottle and pen, and starting

Punch and his business manager were officially in charge of it, it was Tezuka who really told them what they ought to see and do at the Con and around Southern California's tourist sites. After the Con, Tezuka held a surprise dinner party for Leyden and me to thank us for our assistance. This was the greatest honor I'd ever had.

There were two other occasions when Tezuka came to Hollywood in the early 1980s, and he contacted Leyden or me to find out whether we'd like to be his gophers during his stay. We did, of course. One of the first things we became aware of was

Drawings by Monkey Punch at the 1980 San Diego Comic-Con

that there was usually at least one silent man shadowing Tezuka everywhere, besides his ever-present translator. Tezuka grinned and introduced these men as "the watchdogs from my publishers. I must complete the pages for my current manga stories even here in America, so they can send them to the magazine in Tokyo immediately." Tezuka was notorious for overcommitting himself to produce serials for the major weekly manga magazines—often a dozen pages a week for each of two or three different magazines—then disappearing from Japan to some international film festival or a business trip

to speedily draw finished manga art with no preliminary pencil sketches, while carrying on conversations with other people in the room. It must be clarified, however, that Tezuka never claimed to produce all of his manga art personally; he did not have the time. His normal working procedure was to create the plot, rough layout, and dialogue, then let assistants draw the backgrounds and lettering, and "finish" the pages himself by drawing the faces and any other details where his personal art style were most noticeable.

One of the highlights of Tezuka's visit to the Comic-Con as far as he was concerned, which I am still jealous that I missed because I was obligated to be elsewhere at the time, was that Robin Leyden took him and his translator to visit Carl Barks and his wife, Garé, who were living near San Diego at the time. It would be hard to overstate how much of a fan of Barks' Duck stories and Floyd Gottfredson's 1930s-40s *Mickey Mouse* newspaper comic strips Tezuka had been.

When Tezuka personally took me on impromptu visits to some of Tokyo's manga and anime shops in July 1983 (including Toei Animation's studio shop where fans could rummage through and buy whatever cels and backgrounds they wanted from Toei's animation that had just finished production), he was usually so mobbed by fans that I was in danger of being shouldered outside the crowd. I have heard it said that in Japan, due to cultural differences, fans

Cont. on p. 204

to Europe or South America. Tezuka's publishers began assigning agents to accompany him and get a couple of pages each day and airmail them back to Tokyo. It was breathtaking to watch Tezuka draw and ink a page at top speed, faster than most cartoonists can sketch their rough pencil outlines, without making any mistakes, while carrying on a rapid business conversation and barely glancing at the art he was whipping out.

We did not see Tezuka in America after the early 1980s, but he was instrumental in encouraging me to make my first trip to Japan in July 1983. He took a couple of days off work to personally show me to the best animation and comics bookshops in Tokyo. This was just when Frederik Schodt's *Manga! Manga!* was published by Kodansha. Schodt was working in Tokyo as a translator for Tezuka Productions, and Tezuka organized a celebratory dinner party for Schodt and most of the top cartoonists in Japan. He insisted that I had to come, too, and he jovially told everybody that it was now "a Two-Fred Party!" Although Tezuka was probably the oldest man there, it was he who insisted on continuing it after the restaurant closed and most of the other guests went home. Tezuka phoned a friend and got a recommendation of a good bar in the neighborhood. The bar's patrons were so impressed to have a celebrity drop in that Tezuka was soon signing autographs and drawing sketches on napkins, while the proprietor found a blank plaque for everyone in our group to draw upon or sign, which he promised to have framed. (How many patrons at an average American bar do you think would recognize any famous American cartoonist or animator who just happened to walk in?)

After that, I rather drifted out of touch with Tezuka. But I continued to send him copies of any articles that I wrote about Japanese manga or animation. In January 1986 I wrote a review of the 1945 cartoon feature, *Momotaro's Divine Warriors of the Sea,* a wartime propaganda children's feature (showing the Imperial Naval Air Force as cute bunny-rabbit sailors trouncing the grotesque Allied foreign-devil armies) which had just become available on video. I got my first letter from Tezuka in over a year, a brief

of popular celebrities are much more polite and restrained than American fans meeting their idols in person. That sure wasn't the case with Tezuka and his fans!

I am not sure whether there is a closer relationship between SF authors, manga creators, and animators in Japan than there is in America, but I do know that Haruka Takachiho's *Dirty Pair* SF stories were winning Japanese SF awards before Kei and Yuri became anime stars, that Hayao Miyazaki has painted at least one SF book cover (the Japanese edition of *The Witches of Karres* by James H. Schmitz), and that Tezuka was an active participant at Japanese SF writers' gatherings and the annual National SF Convention where he was considered a major SF/fantasy author who just happened to draw his stories rather than write them in text. He and many Japanese major SF authors such as Sakyo Komatsu were close friends. ■

note congratulating me for reviewing this movie and urging me to review more non-TV animation.

In August 1986, I joined Ladera Travel's first group tour for American fans to Japan, to visit the Tokyo animation studios and anime shops, and to attend the 1986 Japanese National Science-Fiction Convention in Osaka (Daicon V). Tezuka was one of the pros at this convention. (He was considered an SF author in Japan, even though all his stories were in comic-art form.) That was the last time I met him. Tezuka was anxious to talk about my review of the *Momotaro* feature. He said that it was one of the major influences that had inspired him to become a cartoonist and an animator, so he was glad that I had enjoyed

Fred Schodt and Osamu Tezuka at the 1983 "Two-Fred" Dinner in Tokyo.

it, too. More importantly, he had recently realized that America's growing awareness of Japanese animation was not going any farther than the young-teen-oriented giant-robot cartoons. This distressed him. He felt that it was as though American animation were to be judged only by the examples of the cheapest hacked-out Saturday-morning TV cartoons, ignoring the Disney features or Will Vinton's Claymation or the independent fine-art animation of such artists as the Hubleys and Sally Cruikshank. Tezuka urged me to stop writing about the latest *Gundam* sequels and annual *Urusei Yatsura* features, and to tell America more about Japan's fine-art animation: features like Sanrio's *Legend of Sirius* (known in America as *The Sea Prince and the Fire Child*), the non-cartoon puppet-animation films, and the independent short films which could be seen in international animation festivals. Tezuka specifically praised Yoji Kuri as the greatest Japanese animator alive. (I have to confess that I consider Kuri's work to be pretentious squiggles, which I did not mention to Tezuka.) Tezuka said that he was working on a new film that he knew I'd enjoy, and that he hoped to bring it to Los Angeles's new International Animation Celebration soon, and that he would see me again there. (I noticed that Tezuka was not bothering to talk about any of the commercial projects that Tezuka Productions was working on at the time.) He must have been talking about *The Legend of the Forest,* which he did not complete until mid-1987. The next L.A. International Animation Celebration was in January 1989, by which time Tezuka was in the hospital with terminal cancer.

I wish that I could say that I've followed Tezuka's wishes in encouraging

Fred Patten visits the cartoonist team of "Fujiko Fujio" (Motoo Abiko and Hiroshi Fujimoto) at their Studio Zero in Tokyo in July 1983. Left to right: Kosei Ono (translator), Abiko, Fred Patten, and Fujimoto.

Americans to develop an appreciation for Japanese animation beyond the teen adventure/humor genres. Unfortunately, most fans get bored and leave the room when something like *Angel's Egg* or *Night on the Galactic Railroad* are shown. Also, much of the non-cartoon animation and the individual fine-art short films (less than ten minutes) are not handily available on video. But they do come around from time to time. I think that Tezuka would have been happy to know about American fans' appreciation of Hayao Miyazaki's gentle lyrical fantasies *My Neighbor Totoro* and *Kiki's Delivery Service*. The next time that a "different" Japanese animation title comes your way, try it out.

Incidentally, I did enjoy *The Legend of the Forest*. Very much. It's a fitting climax to Tezuka's career.

Shotaro Ishinomori: A Profile
Introduction in *The Skull Man* Vol. 1 by Kazuhiko Shimamoto and Shotaro Ishinomori. Los Angeles: TOKYOPOP, March 2002.

To American fans of Japanese popular culture, the leading Japanese cartoonists are those whose work has been most prominently adapted into animation, especially the anime imported into America. Such names as Osamu Tezuka, Go Nagai, Leiji Matsumoto, Rumiko Takahashi, and Katsuhiro Otomo lead this list.

Shotaro Ishinomori may not be on this list, but he should be.

In Japan, where Tezuka was known as *manga no kamisama*, the God of Comics, Ishinomori was next in line as *manga no oosama,* the King of Comics. A brief summary might give the false impression that Ishinomori was just following Tezuka: he was born ten years after Tezuka, he became a manga artist ten years after Tezuka did, he died at the same age as Tezuka. They were friends (and competitors) from the beginning of Ishinomori's career, which led to his early reputation as "Tezuka's protege."

But Ishinomori was very much more than an imitation Tezuka. If Americans are not as familiar with his name, it is because he struck out into areas away from the anime that made other Japanese cartoonists so well-known. In the 1970s Ishinomori created numerous live-action TV children's SF-fantasy hits such as *The Masked Rider* and *The Five Rangers,* the prototypes that led to the *Mighty Morphin' Power Rangers.* In the 1980s he created the new genre of "information comics," notably with *Cartoon Introduction to the Japanese Economy,* serialized in the Japanese equivalent of the *Wall Street Journal,* which became a surprise best-seller (published in the United States as *Japan, Inc.* by the University of California Press). He pioneered the Japanese cartoon-production-shop system, incorporating in 1968 as Ishimori Production Co. and hiring enough assistants to produce, at its peak, over 500 pages of manga per month in his art style.

But Ishinomori never forgot his roots as a creator of boys' adventure comics like *Cyborg 009*—and *Skull Man.*

He was born Shotaro Onodera on January 25, 1938, in Miyagi Prefecture. He was eight or nine when Japan's modern comic books first appeared. He began submitting his own amateur comics to *Manga Shonen* (*Boys' Comics*) magazine when he was twelve years old. He was sixteen and in high school when his first story, *Second-Class Angel,* was published in the December 1954 *Manga Shonen.*

In 1956 he graduated from high school. He moved to Tokyo, where Osamu Tezuka had set up his studio in 1954, and became Tezuka's art assistant on his *Alakazam the Great* manga serial. (This is why his early art style was said to look so much like Tezuka's.) It was when he struck out on

This profile was written to introduce the American edition of *The Skull Man* manga by Kazuhiko Shimamoto, based on Ishinomori's 1970–1971 concept. I do not know how much of the serial was based on Ishinomori's original notes and bedside conversations with Shimamoto, and how much was Shimamoto's own creation, but Shimamoto did an excellent job of capturing Ishinomori's art and story style throughout the manga's run.

In addition to writing this profile, I got the assignment of writing the English adaptation of *The Skull Man*—not the actual translation (I do not read or speak Japanese fluently) but taking a literal translation of the Japanese dialogue and rewriting it into smooth (and hopefully imaginatively witty) modern American conversational English while maintaining the accuracy of the translation. Presumably, *The Skull Man* was not successful in Japan, because it abruptly stopped after the seventh *tankubon* collected volume. ■

his own in 1959 that he took his first pseudonym, Ishimori, to inaugurate his "new life."

Ishinomori's first manga to gain him a reputation was *The Ghost Ship*, 1960, filmed as a theatrical animated feature in 1969. During the 1960s he poured out dozens if not hundreds of science-fiction manga stories.

But these were incidental to his first mega-hit, *Cyborg 009*. Begun in 1963 almost simultaneously with Marvel's similar *The X-Men*, this superhero team saga is arguably the foundation of two of Japan's most popular manga, anime, and TV SF stereotypes (many also created by Ishinomori): the team of costumed and color-coded superheroes (*Robin's Rainbow Warriors*, *The Five Rangers*, and all other TV "men in rubber suit" heroes leading up to *The Mighty Morphin' Power Rangers*), and the reluctant heroes who have superpowers forced upon them at the cost of their humanity (*Casshan*, *The Guyver*).

The popularity of *Cyborg 009* was instantaneous. It won Ishinomori his first award, the Seventh Kodansha Manga Award, in 1966. Toei Animation rushed two theatrical animated features out in 1966 and 1967, followed by a *Cyborg 009* black-and-white TV animated series in 1968. A second, color TV series appeared in 1979 to 1980. A third theatrical feature, *Cyborg 009: Legend of the Super Galaxy*, was released in December 1980 to celebrate Ishinomori's twenty-fifth anniversary as a manga artist.

During the 1970s Ishimori Pro concentrated upon creating story ideas for TV series, then drawing them as manga if they were bought. It was at this point that Ishinomori began to specialize in live-action juvenile TV programs. Between 1966 and 1982 there were eleven TV animated series and six animated features based on his stories; but there were thirty live-action TV series from 1972 to 1982 alone. From July 1972 to December 1977 there were always at least two and sometimes as many as four Ishinomori live-action TV programs in first-run broadcast every week. These ranged from the serious (or as serious as the rubber-suit "monster of the week" TV programs ever got) like *The Masked Rider* and *Kikaider the Artificial Man*, to the slapstick-silly like *The Five Rangers* and *Li'l Robot*.

During the 1980s he continued to produce *Cyborg 009* and some adventure comics, but his main interest shifted to more sophisticiated stories for mature readers. His *Japan, Inc.* was one of the hallmarks of this period. In 1984 he began *Hotel*, an adult manga serial about the lives and careers of the management and staff of the luxury Hotel Platon. Both won him more awards in 1988. In 1990 *Hotel* became an adult live-action TV soap opera, more comparable to *Dallas* or *The Mary Tyler Moore Show* than to his old rubber-suit superhero programs. It was in 1986, on the thirtieth anniversary of the beginning of his career, that he changed his name for the final time to Ishinomori.

Ishinomori became an elder statesman of the manga industry in the 1990s. He was chosen manager of the Japanese Comics Writers Association, and in 1995 he appeared as honorary chairman of the new Medialand center, which had over 90,000 attendees at its grand opening. But Ishinomori was actually invalided with heart problems from most of 1992 on, directing his manga factory from his bedside for his last six years. He died of a heart attack three days after his sixtieth birthday, on January 28, 1998.

One of his final projects was a completion of his *Skull Man* from 1970. *Skull Man* was actually an aborted version of what evolved into the *Masked Rider* (*Kamen Rider*) TV series. Ishinomori wrote and drew a 100-page *Skull Man* story to start the series, but the TV network wanted so many changes that he had to create a whole new *Masked Rider* manga instead. *Skull Man* was published as a stand-alone story in the January 11, 1971 issue of *Shonen* (*Boys*) magazine; the *Masked Rider* manga did not begin publication until June 1, 1972. *Masked Rider* debuted on TV on April 3, 1971, and was so popular that it and its sequels were TV hits throughout the 1970s and 1980s. But in many respects Ishinomori preferred his original concepts for *Skull Man*. Shortly before his death, he collaborated with his young protege Kazuhiko Shimamoto to finally launch the *Skull Man* manga as he had wanted it.

Hayao Miyazaki's *Spirited* Trip to the U.S.
Animation World Magazine 7, no. 7, October 2002.

North American anime fans got a rare treat in September. Not only was Hayao Miyazaki's long-awaited *Spirited Away* finally released, but the man revered as Japan's greatest animation creator made an unprecedented public appearance. Miyazaki, along with Studio Ghibli president Toshio Suzuki, held press conferences and answered audience questions at *Spirited Away*'s premiere screenings at the twenty-seventh Toronto International Film Festival on September 7, at Disney's U.S. premiere at its showpiece El Capitan Theater in Hollywood on September 10, and at a special benefit screening for the Juvenile Diabetes Research Foundation at Pixar Animation Studios in Emeryville, Calif., on September 15.

Miyazaki's name has been synonymous with anime's highest quality since the early 1980s, when it first came to the public's attention with his *Nausicaä of the Valley of the Winds*. Miyazaki originally began this as a comic book (manga) serial in *Animage* magazine and then developed it as a 1984 animated theatrical feature. Even before that, his work stood out to anime fans who did not know his name. His first theatrical feature as director, *Lupin III: The Castle of Cagliostro* (released December 1979) was not only a hit in Japan (voted the top animation of all time by the readers of *Animage*), but studio Tokyo Movie Shinsha used it for test-marketing in the United States. It was shown at the 1980 World Science Fiction Convention in Boston, FILMEX 82 in Los Angeles, and other film festivals during the

1980s. It was widely gossiped by anime fans that *Cagliostro*'s climactic battle in the clock tower inspired the very similar scene in Disney's 1986 *The Great Mouse Detective.*

Toshio Suzuki's name is not as well known, but he is much more than the business manager of Studio Ghibli. He was arguably largely responsible for the development of anime fandom. He was the founding editor of Tokuma Publishing Company's pioneering anime publications, *Animage* magazine (monthly since July 1978), and the series of "Roman Album" reference guides devoted to individual theatrical and TV anime titles. Although adolescent fan-oriented, their in-depth coverage of production data have made them continuously the leading sources for reference information about any anime theatrical or TV releases since 1978. They were the foundations of the popular attitude that animation was not just for kids but was worthy of as much serious consideration as any other genre of cinema studied in high school and college.

It was *Animage*'s coverage of *Lupin III: The Castle of Cagliostro* that introduced Suzuki and Miyazaki to each other. Suzuki proposed that he write/draw a manga for serialization in *Animage*. Miyazaki's *Nausicaä of the Valley of the Winds* began in the February 1982 issue and was an instant hit. Miyazaki had not originally intended it for animation, but readers assumed a movie would follow and began asking when it would be released. The response was so great that Tokuma Publishing decided to fund it as an independent feature, directed by Miyazaki. The success of *Nausicaä* led to Tokuma financing a new permanent animation studio in 1985 to be run

I am still confused by Suzuki's and Miyazaki's statement at this September 10, 2002, press conference that Studio Ghibli's next feature had not yet been *officially* announced. It was "unofficially" announced as early as August 2001 by author Diana Wynne Jones on her own Web site. Both Toho Films and Studio Ghibli said in press releases during December 2001 that it was scheduled to be finished and released in Spring or Summer 2003. During May and June 2002 it was reported on almost all anime news Web sites that *Howl*'s originally scheduled director, Mamoru Hosoda, was off the film and that Miyazaki would personally direct it. So I do not understand why they had to be so coy in September. It was not until mid-December 2002 that Ghibli *officially* announced that *Howl* would be its next feature, now scheduled for a November 2004 release.

Unfortunately, *Spirited Away* did not do appreciably better box office than did *Princess Mononoke,* as far as the general motion picture industry reckons such things. *Spirited Away* got virtually unanimous critical praise (except from those conservative Christian groups that condemned it for promoting witchcraft and demonology) and won major cinematic awards around the world. After it won the Academy of Motion Picture Arts and Sciences' Oscar for Best Animated Feature Film in 2003, Disney had additional prints struck and rereleased it in 750 theaters across America. It turned out to be a waste of money. The public was still not interested in seeing it. ■

by Miyazaki and his longtime friend and fellow animator, Isao Takahata. Suzuki's promotion of Miyazaki's films in *Animage,* as well as his close friendship with Miyazaki, eventually led to his transfer to Studio Ghibli as that company's president.

The Rise of a Master

Miyazaki was already a twenty-year veteran animator by this time. He was born in Tokyo on January 5, 1941. He joined the Toei Animation Company staff in 1963, rising from in-betweener to key animator on both theatrical and TV series projects. Among Toei's other young animators was Isao Takahata, with whom he formed a permanent friendship and working relationship. By 1971 both Miyazaki and Takahata were feeling creatively stifled working within Toei's animation assembly-line production. Miyazaki began producing comic-book stories (manga) on the side, where he had total creative control. Both quit Toei and went to work for other studios during the 1970s. Among their major projects during that decade were several yearlong (fifty-two episodes) TV animated serializations of classic children's literature for *World Masterpiece Theater.* Some of these, including *Heidi, Girl of the Alps* and *Three Thousand Miles in Search of Mother* (about a young Italian boy's search for his mother in Argentina), gave Miyazaki the opportunity to visit Europe and South America to sketch art references. A trip to Stockholm for a proposed *Pippi Longstocking* TV series that was never made gave Miyazaki lots of location and background art that appeared almost twenty years later in his *Kiki's Delivery Service.*

Nineteen seventy-nine through 1982 were significant years for Miyazaki at the Tokyo Movie Shinsha (TMS) studio. He created their major theatrical feature *Lupin III: The Castle of Cagliostro,* not just directing it but writing its script, designing the characters and drawing the storyboards. In 1981 TMS asked him to produce a children's TV funny-animal series based on the Sherlock Holmes stories, with the characters as dogs (*Holmes, the Great Detective,* released in America as *Sherlock Hound*), commissioned by Italy's RAI TV. By this time Miyazaki's connection with Suzuki had been established, and *Animage* heavily promoted *Sherlock Hound* as the latest masterwork by Miyazaki. *Sherlock Hound* was Miyazaki's final TV anime work. The project introduced him to RAI's representative, Marco Pagott, who became a close friend. Both the Italian connection and Pagott (as protagonist Marco Pagotti) appeared in Miyazaki's 1992 *Porco Rosso.*

Another 1981 TMS project which Miyazaki was asked to join was the theatrical feature *Little Nemo.* Miyazaki left it very early (TMS did not complete it until 1989), and began his work on *Nausicaä* for *Animage.* But his brief involvement with *Little Nemo* included a business trip to the Disney studio in Hollywood, where he met the young animator John Lasseter—a meeting that would have great significance for *Spirited Away* twenty years later.

A significant indication of Miyazaki's tunnel vision on the creative aspects of his work is that Studio Ghibli's films for the first five years were critical successes but were only moderately successful at the box office, barely enough to keep the studio open. It was not until 1990 that a literal public demand for *Totoro* plushies and similar merchandise convinced him that maybe Ghibli should lower itself to (ugh!) merchandising. Not only did the studio almost immediately earn enough from licensing that it could begin plans for expansion, but the flood of *Totoro* and *Kiki* toys made the general public more Ghibli-aware than its movie's promotions ever had. Studio Ghibli's 1992's *Porco Rosso,* 1994's *Pom Poko* (directed by Isao Takahata), 1997's *Princess Mononoke,* and 2001's *Spirited Away* were all Japan's top box-office draws for those years.

Time to Talk

At the *Spirited Away* press conferences, Miyazaki made it clear that the intellectual and artistic aspects of his projects are still the only ones that really concern him. He and Suzuki had almost a comedy routine, with Suzuki mugging as an exasperated businessman trying to keep an idealistic artist under control.

Questions at the Hollywood premiere comparing *Spirited Away* with *Princess Mononoke* (did he think the English dub of *Spirited* was better than that of *Mononoke;* did he think that *Spirited* had a better chance of box office success in America) seemed to highly annoy him. He made it clear that each of his films has been made because of a particular creative inspiration. With *Spirited Away* he had noticed that some of his granddaughter's friends, girls about ten years old, seemed very apathetic, only interested in passively watching modern popular culture, unaware of Japan's rich cultural past. He felt that he should make a film for ten-year-old girls that would both introduce them to their heritage and encourage them to develop a sense of self-reliance and responsibility. How he feels about the success of his films depends upon how closely he thinks each comes to achieving his particular goal for it. He does not compare his films with each other or with any other movies. "I frankly am not a big fan of valuing, evaluating a film's worth based on box office receipts," he said through interpreter Linda Hoagland. "I believe that a film should represent a very intimate personal encounter between what's on the screen and an individual's heart. To try to reduce the value of that to numbers on a page is not something that I can be a fan of." A query as to whether he was excited about the possibility of *Spirited Away* or a future film of his winning an Academy Award brought a dismissive, "Doesn't interest me." (Suzuki immediately added that it certainly interested *him*!) Another question as to whether Studio Ghibli would ever make any sequels to its popular movies, as Disney is doing today, drew an even brusker, "Never!"

Miyazaki strongly affirmed his commitment to traditional cel animation.

One questioner commented on, ". . . an incredibly detailed Chinese-style vase. It's shockingly realistic looking, really beautiful, but it looks real and I'm guessing that it was done digitally. And indeed, in this film you seem to have used more digital effects than you have in any of your previous films. Maybe you could talk about the digital effects." Miyazaki replied: "You're wrong. That's hand drawn, that Chinese vase. It's also not Chinese; it's a Japanese vase from the Imari area. All of the drawings are hand-drawn. All of the artwork that's featured as design in the bathhouse in the film is all hand drawn. We've, you know, given it a little sort of elegance boost with digital technology."

He elaborated in reply to a second question about what percentage of *Spirited Away* was digital. "Fundamentally, the animation is all pencil drawn. In a few scenes we turned to digital, for instance to create patterns on the waves or to show bubbling water, water bubbling up. As we headed into production on this film I gathered my staff and I said to them, 'This is a two-dimensional film. This is our strength.' And there is a fundamental difference in thinking and approach between 3-D movies and 2-D, and I'll give you an example. For instance, I don't know if you noticed, but Yubaba's head, large as it is, is not identically the same in every scene. Depending on my mood and her mood, the size of her head changes. This is an emotional relationship that we developed to scale with the audience that we'd have to abandon if we wholeheartedly embraced 3-D. I'm holding on to my pencil."

At the Mic

My initial question for *Animation World Magazine* was unexpectedly stonewalled. Q: "It's been announced off and on that Studio Ghibli and you will be making a film from the British juvenile novel *Howl's Moving Castle* by Diana Wynne Jones. I understand that this is your next project. I was wondering how you discovered this novel. Did you read the novel on your own and decide this would be a good picture, or did someone suggest it to you?" Suzuki answered, "Actually, the next project has not yet been formally announced in Japan so unfortunately I can't answer any questions about the next project." (Considering that Japanese bookshops are advertising the Japanese edition of *Howl's Moving Castle* as, "Read the novel that will be Studio Ghibli's next feature," I am not sure of the distinction between a formal and an informal announcement.) Miyazaki added as an exaggerated aside which drew laughs: "You know, I'm going to be doing it as usual. The real reason he doesn't want to talk about it is because he's not sure I can handle it." (Ghibli's formal announcements only say that the studio has been temporarily closed following the release of its summer 2002 feature, *The Cat Returns*. It will reopen in February 2003 to begin production of its next feature, planned for a summer 2004 release.)

My second question was: "There has been one new Studio Ghibli film released in Japan since *Spirited Away,* just a couple of months ago [July 19]:

The Cat Returns, I believe is the official English translation of the title, *Neko no Ongaeshi;* directed by Hiroyuki Morita. This is the first film from Studio Ghibli directed by someone besides yourself and Isao Takahata, and unfortunately the only one film by Yoshifumi Kondo. [Kondo died shortly after directing *Whisper of the Heart.*] Are you grooming more directors, and are there any plans to release *The Cat Returns* in the United States?" Suzuki replied: "For starters, yes, if there's young talent we're more than happy— we're delighted, in fact, to embrace it and nurture it. And thankfully, *The Cat Returns* did quite well at the Japanese box office. We're in discussions about—we're considering a possible U.S. release."

On John Lasseter and Pixar

All questions about how Miyazaki had prepared *Spirited Away* for its American release were waved away with a repeated variation of the comment that he didn't have anything to do with it; he didn't care whether it was released in the United States or not; the American release was entirely due to his good friend John Lasseter. "You know, our presence here today, your being able to see the film today, all of this and the North American release, I owe to the unflagging dedication and determination of my dear friend John Lasseter, who bulldozed his way through every obstacle to make this release happen." On what he thought of the Lasseter-directed English dub: "I haven't seen it. This is not just about this film, this is not limited to *Spirited Away.* I never watch my movies after I watch it with my staff after it's done, at the end. So I'm not discriminating against *Spirited Away.* The fact of the matter is that I so deeply trust John Lasseter that I don't need to watch the film."

Miyazaki's and Lasseter's joking comments about each other have made it clear that Lasseter's relationship to *Spirited Away* is much closer than that of a prestigious American animation creator brought in as executive producer on a straight work-for-hire basis. In fact, Lasseter's reputation as the major creative developer of the Pixar CGI studio, and director of the CGI hits *Toy Story, A Bug's Life,* and *Toy Story 2,* seems to be partially responsible for the mistaken assumption that *Spirited Away* contains lots of CGI. Lasseter met Miyazaki in 1981 (Miyazaki: "I actually met John Lasseter twenty years ago when I came to Los Angeles to work on a job. I didn't encounter him through my work. He was off in a small studio, I think he had been dispatched by Disney to go, and he was working alone trying to develop 3-D animation. Unlike the John Lasseter of today he was a very slender young man . . ."), and their personal friendship broadened to Lasseter's adopting Miyazaki as a sensei, his tutor, as Miyazaki's features appeared in Japan while Lasseter was building Pixar. Lasseter became involved with *Spirited Away* right from its start.

In a telephone interview from his Pixar office in July, Lasseter told me: "We have a really close creative connection at Pixar with Studio Ghibli. We often look at the Japanese laser disks of Miyazaki's movies to be inspired.

"I visited Studio Ghibli in March of 2000 when I was in Japan for the release of *Toy Story 2*. I had my two sons with me. They were just beginning production on *Spirited Away*. It looked fantastically exciting. Ghibli is a fairly small studio, and Miyazaki does not have a separate office. He works in the same studio with the other artists, at a desk in a corner. [. . .]

"There was a camera crew on hand to film the director of *Toy Story 2* visiting the director of *Princess Mononoke*. Miyazaki sent them away. He drove me and my sons and Suzuki to a nearby re-created traditional village in a large park. When old buildings have to be removed for new construction, they try to preserve them by moving them here instead of just tearing them down. Miyazaki led us down this street to a bathhouse, and he described to us the tradition of the village bathhouse as a communal center in old Japan. This was to be one of the main points in *Spirited Away*."

Miyazaki revealed at the press conference in Toronto that a living lantern which appears briefly late in the movie, hopping along a dark road to light Chihiro's way, is an ingroup joke for Lasseter, a reference to his *Luxo, Jr.* Miyazaki may not have cared whether *Spirited Away* was released in America, but Suzuki certainly did. As Lasseter explained: "Suzuki came to Pixar with a subtitled film print of *Spirited Away* which had just been released in Japan. We showed it in the 235-seat screening room at Pixar. This was its first screening anywhere outside of Japan. Everyone was blown away. We were familiar with Miyazaki's previous films, and we felt that he had topped himself.

"I reported to Disney the reaction at Pixar. Disney was considering whether to release *Spirited Away* in America. They were concerned about American audiences not understanding some of the Japanese traditional cultural elements in the story. I felt that it would be particularly accessible to Western audiences because it is seen from the point of view of a modern, materialistic young girl who is unfamiliar with her own cultural past. The way the story is told, it works as an introduction to a fascinating, rich culture whether it is the viewer's own ethnic heritage or not."

Lasseter's job as executive director included supervising Disney's English dub directed by Kirk Wise. The supercritical anime fan reaction to the *Spirited Away* dub is that it is Disney's best yet, considerably better than those for *Kiki's Delivery Service* and *Princess Mononoke*. Those were professionally excellent, but some of the voices seemed to give the characters different personalities. For example, comedian Phil Hartman's reading for Jiji, Kiki's black cat, gave Jiji a brash, sardonic personality very different from the shy, meek voice of the Japanese dub. Disney's *Spirited Away* press kit quotes the opinion of Daveigh Chase, the voice of ten-year-old Chihiro (also of Lilo in Disney's *Lilo and Stitch*), "On doing a movie that she heard originally in Japanese . . ." This indicates that the American voice cast listened to the original Japanese voices and studied their intonations. Fan interviews with the voice actors of many American anime dubs have revealed that they are often not given time to listen to the original Japanese dubs. The American voice director simply leads them to do readings of their lines that he likes. "[T]hat she heard originally in Japanese" shows Lasseter's and Wise's determination to make the English-language dub as close to the Japanese dub as they could.

Miyazaki's and Suzuki's publicity tour ended with a small fundraising screening at Pixar Animation Studios' screening room for the Juvenile Diabetes Research Foundation. A report on the Web site of No-Name Anime, the nearby San Jose anime club, explained that this charity has a personal significance for John Lasseter and voice actor John Ratzenberger (the froglike Bathhouse Assistant Manager in *Spirited Away*), both of whom have children with diabetes. Lasseter told the audience that, since Miyazaki's love of old-fashioned airplanes is well known, they had arranged for him while at Pixar to take a biplane tour over Northern California's wine vineyards.

So now America's anime fans are crossing their fingers and hoping that *Spirited Away* will do better at the box office than *Princess Mononoke* did. The initial results of its September 20 release are encouraging. The September 20–22 weekend box office report on the Box Office Guru Web site (boxofficeguru.com) is: "The Japanese animated blockbuster *Spirited Away* sparkled in its North American debut grossing $449,839 from only twenty-six theaters for a vibrant $17,302 average. Buena Vista released Japan's highest-grossing film in ten major markets this weekend and looks to add another ten next weekend as it continues its steady rollout."

Part IV
Japanese Culture in Anime

TV Animation in Japan
Fanfare no. 3, Spring 1980.

Daytime kids' animated cartoons don't usually get much attention, so nobody particularly noticed when a new program called *Astro Boy* went on the air here in the summer of 1963. It happened to be an import from Japan. It ran for a couple of years, then faded into re-runs and disappeared. A handful of other TV cartoons came from Japan during the 1960s: *Gigantor, 8th Man, Marine Boy, Kimba the White Lion,* and *Speed Racer.* None lasted more than a brief time. Since the same could be said for almost any animated cartoon TV program, this attracted no notice. Most viewers never realized these were not American cartoons. If they did, they must have concluded that animation was not popular in Japan since there seemed to be so few programs.

In fact, these programs were the early efforts of an immensely successful Japanese TV cartoon industry. Today the number of Japanese TV cartoons is about to pass the 300 mark. There are a couple of dozen new animated cartoons shown in prime time in Japan at any given moment. Hanna-Barbera has reportedly been preparing a cartoon adaptation of Johanna Spyri's *Heidi* for years, but a Japanese version was released as long ago as 1974. It ran fifty episodes in TV serialization, and was edited into a theatrical-feature condensation—a hit not only in Japan but throughout Western Europe and Latin America. *From The Apennines to the Andes* (1976), a soap opera about a poor Italian family that emigrates to Argentina, ran for a year in Japan

This was my earliest article, written in late 1979–early 1980, on anime in general. It seems embarrassingly primitive today, both with regard to the actual state of anime and to how much the American fans did not know about it. OAVs did not yet exist. *Gundam* did, but it was still in its original poorly rated TV run, bootleg video copies of it had not yet gotten to America, and we did not realize that it was different from all the other imitative giant-robot TV series.

I no longer know whether stating that the 1974 *Heidi* TV series was fifty episodes instead of the correct fifty-two was a factual error or just a typographical error. But *From the Appenines to the Andes* (adapted from the 1886 Italian children's novel *Cuore* by Edmondo De Amicis) is not about an Italian family that migrates to Argentina. It is about a young Italian boy, Marco, whose father is a doctor at a clinic in Argentina. His mother leaves on a trip to visit him, but Marco is terrified that she may never return and runs away to follow her. The story is actually about a lone Italian child's wandering throughout Argentina and Bolivia looking for his mother. In 1979, the 1963 *Astro Boy* was listed as the first Japanese TV series in all the "anime encyclopedias" then published for the newly emerging casual anime fans. It was not until a few years later that more complete and detailed encyclopedias appeared listing the three-minute *Otogi Cartoon Calendar* daily educational TV cartoons that had premiered on June 25, 1962, over six months earlier.

Cont. on p. 220

and in almost every Spanish-speaking Western Hemisphere nation. In 1978 a Japanese cartoon science fiction serial dubbed into French, *UFO Robot Grandizer* (called *Goldorak* in France), made headlines by becoming the first TV program to get a 100 share. Italian animator Bruno (*Allegro Non Troppo*) Bozetto was asked during a recent tour of America what kinds of cartoons he himself enjoyed; he chuckled and said he and his young children were addicted to the Japanese giant robots being shown on Italian TV.

The first Japanese TV cartoon was broadcast on January 1, 1963. It was nine months before a second program was ready, and less than ten animated shows altogether had appeared by the end of 1964. But in 1965 fourteen different programs from seven different studios went on the air. The number of shows has gradually increased each year until, in 1979, over thirty new ones appeared (series and special features), to join many popular cartoons continuing from 1978 and earlier—in prime time. This doesn't include the number of old cartoon programs in syndicated re-runs. A December 1979 monthly all-Japan TV guide of animated cartoons alone contains over 850 listings.

The Japanese TV cartoon industry was created by Osamu Tezuka, often called the "Disney of Japan," who had largely created the Japanese comic-book industry ten to fifteen years earlier. There had been comic-strip stories and theatrical animated cartoons before Tezuka, but they were individual and rather infrequent works, usually in the traditional Japanese art style. Tezuka was a fan of American cartoons, especially the Fleischer *Popeyes* and anything by Disney. The comic books he began drawing in the late 1940s were done in the American "big foot" style, filled with cinematic techniques: close-ups, pans, dissolves. By the early 1950s Tezuka had become so popular that he set up a studio of assistants to help him produce hundreds of stories

I had gotten the 1953 publication date for Tezuka's *My Son Goku* from a simplified bibliography of his most popular manga. I did not realize that was just the year it started; it was serialized until 1959. A detailed correction of all the other errors (Lupin III's pal Jigen was not a genuine American gangster; he just modeled himself on them; *Space Battleship Yamato* actually bombed during its 1974 TV broadcast and did not become popular until the 1977 release of its theatrical feature version; like Astro Boy and Spider-Man, Devilman is a frequent victim of confusion over whether his name is one or two words. This should have been Devilman.) would probably be boring. Please just accept this article as a time capsule that shows what American fans of 1980 believed about Japanese anime.

When this was published in *Fanfare* no. 3, it filled ten pages thanks to *lots* of illustrations of the titles mentioned. The images were provided for free by Toei Animation and Tatsunoko Pro to help create anime awareness in America. Today, Americans are aware of anime, so if we wanted to include those same illustrations in this book, we would have been asked for prohibitive licensing fees. ■

for a wide variety of magazines and newspapers. In 1959 Toei Animation, Japan's major theatrical cartoon studio, decided to make a feature film of the ancient Chinese Monkey King legend and selected a 1953 comic-book version by Tezuka as its model. Tezuka assisted and received co-director and screenplay credit. It was released in August 1960, and can be seen today on American TV as *Alakazam The Great*.

Fanfare *no. 3, Spring 1980*

It is likely that this experience wasn't without influence on Tezuka, but what really spurred him to open his own studio was the creation in America of made-for-TV animation. By the end of the 1950s American television had run through three decades' worth of theatrical animated shorts. This was also the period when the major studios closed their animation departments. Television needed fresh cartoons, and new studios such as Hanna-Barbera were created to supply them, in limited animation. Tezuka felt he was in a position to do the same for Japanese TV.

Tezuka's studio, Mushi Productions, opened in June 1961. The first year and a half were spent in getting financial backing and going into production. The result debuted on Japanese TV on New Year's Day 1963—*Astro Boy*, an adaptation of Tezuka's most popular comic book series of the 1950s. Astro Boy was a robot packed with superscientific gimmickry, but he was designed to duplicate his inventor's young son who had recently been killed in an automobile accident. The result was a flying android who was emotionally a boy about thirteen years old, using his powers as a superhero in the futuristic world of 2000 AD. The program was fast-paced and filled with tongue-in-cheek humor, but it contained the underlying poignancy of Astro Boy's trying to be a real human when he was just an artificial boy.

As soon as it was evident that *Astro Boy* was a big success—it ran for four years and a total of 193 half-hour episodes—other animation studios sprang up. Some were independent, while others were new units opened by established movie studios. For the first couple of years, all Japanese TV animation was in black and white. Tezuka inaugurated color TV cartoons in 1965, with another program based on one of his comic books of the 1950s, *Kimba the White Lion*. (NBC deserves some credit here, because Tezuka had tried to pre-sell the program to American TV before he filmed it, and NBC refused to buy a black-and-white product.) Within a few years all Japanese cartoons were in full color.

One major reason for the greater popularity of TV cartoons in Japan than in America lies in the basic attitude toward cartoons in the two cultures. In Japan, cartoons are considered a legitimate form of artistic and literary expression. Whether a cartoon happens to be for children or adults depends upon the treatment given to that particular cartoon. In America, cartoons are considered to be almost exclusively children's fare. Until the 1978 theatrical features *The Lord of the Rings* and *Watership Down*—neither of which have had any influence on TV-watching attitudes—the only cartoons considered "for adults" have been light comedies, usually seasonal TV specials. There is no market in America for serious mature stories in animated-cartoon form. And, because the Japanese accept a higher degree of realism in their programs for children than is considered appropriate for American children, many of the Japanese children's cartoons are unsaleable in the United States as too violent or too risqué. Virtually all Japanese TV cartoons are designed for broadcast in prime time, so even children's programs are handled with enough wit and sophistication that parents will also enjoy them. There is no Japanese Saturday morning ghetto. Almost all are weekday half-hour programs, shown between 6:30 P.M. and 8:00 P.M.

As in America, almost any popular TV program is soon followed by many imitations. Certainly many of the earliest Japanese TV cartoons were frankly derivative of *Astro Boy*, featuring young heroes with special powers who fought injustice, usually in a future world. Tatsuo Yoshida's *Space Ace* (1965–66) was a wild kid from a civilization that was migrating to a new planet. He got separated in his personal rocket from the space fleet and stumbled upon Earth. At first Ace often used his powers for practical jokes, but the understanding upbringing of his human foster father and sister soon made him a responsible citizen. *Space Boy Soran* (1965–67) was cast away as a baby on the planet Soran when his explorer-parents' spaceship was destroyed. After growing to his teens he returned to Earth to search for his sister. The Soranian super-science he brought was helpful for doing good, but he often got into trouble from the mischievousness of his pet space-squirrel, Chappy.

Several programs had a strong antiwar slant. In Osamu Tezuka's *The Amazing 3* (1965–66), a Galactic Congress debated whether to destroy Earth before warlike humans could spread their destruction among the stars, or wait in the hope that mankind would end its fighting before it developed spaceflight. Three galactic patrolmen were sent to Earth to gather information. They transformed themselves into a rabbit, a horse, and a duck, to operate incognito. Although they were only supposed to observe, they soon began using their galactic technology to secretly fight criminals and military dictators. In Takaji Kusunoki's *Asteroid Mask* (1966–67), war broke out in the twenty-first century between normally friendly Earth and Pineron. The culprit was a would-be dictator on Pineron who faked a sneak attack by Earth to give himself an excuse to seize total power. The hero was Peter Johansen, the first person of mixed Earth-Pineron blood, who became a costumed hero to foil the strikes of both planets against the other and fight for peace.

The first giant-robot cartoon was Mitsuteru Yokoyama's *Gigantor* (1963–67), a titanic robot built to help mankind. He was operated by his creator's young son, Jimmy Sparks, who could make Gigantor do an incredible variety of things by twiddling a simple control dial. Most episodes concentrated on Jimmy trying to figure out the best way to use Gigantor to solve a problem, or on criminals who were always trying to steal the control dial, or jam the radio signals that guided the robot, or steal Professor Sparks' plans so they could build an army of Gigantors for evil purposes.

Giant robots didn't really become memorable until Go Nagai's *Mazinger Z* (1972–74). Mazinger Z was more than just a big radio-controlled machine. He was a metal shell operated by a human (teenager Koji Kabuto) who entered his head cavity and became his brain. Also, instead of merely swatting common gangsters or power-mad dictators, Mazinger Z was pitted against a series of evil monsters and robots who matched him in size and strength. There was something about this human/robot symbiosis—a human becoming a metallic giant to protect the world from beings of elemental destruction—that seized the Japanese fancy. Since *Mazinger Z* and his own sequel, *Great Mazinger* (1974–75), there have been over two dozen TV cartoons about giant robots who defend humanity against alien invaders who send their own super monsters to stomp our cities to rubble. In some episodes the heroic robot was assembled piecemeal out of three to six components, each operated by its own pilot (*Getta Robot,* 1974–75; *Baratak,* 1977–78.) The effort to distinguish between so many different giant-robot programs led to some strange conceptions. One resembled a 200-foot tall football player. Another could form itself into four configurations—diamond, spade, heart, or club.

Superheroes have been as popular in Japan as in the United States. Jiro Kuwata's *8th Man* (1963–64) wasn't a human but an android, programmed with the mental patterns of a murdered police detective. Through Tobor, disguised as a human private eye, Officer Brady was able to continue to fight against criminals and enemy secret agents. In Shotaro Ishimori's *Cyborg 009* (1968; new series 1979), nine people were kidnapped by a worldwide crime organization that forced a scientist to transform them into bionic superbeings for criminal purposes. The cyborgs rescued themselves and the professor, and set themselves up as a team of super secret agents to fight crime.

One of the biggest hits was Tatsuo Yoshida's *Gatchaman* (1972–74). An evil intelligence from space formed a worldwide syndicate to loot Earth's resources. They were fought by the Gatchamen Force, five teenagers in bird costumes who operated superscientific weapons and vehicles provided by a security force operating from a hidden undersea base. *Gatchaman* was so popular (105 episodes) that a theatrical feature was edited from some of the most dramatic episodes. A second series, *Gatchaman II* (1978–79), proved almost as popular, and a third series, *Gatchaman F* (for fighter) is scheduled for 1980.

Gatchaman underwent a strange fate when it was bought by an American distributor and presented in the United States in 1978 as *Battle of the Planets.* The program was not merely translated into English; about a third of each episode was removed and new animation added. Most of the alterations were necessary to market *Battle of the Planets* as a childrens' program, since *Gatchaman* was an adult drama with bloody fight scenes and risqué humor. The original mood of violence and tension was lightened considerably. Scenes were added of spaceships flying between the stars, so the action could be said to take place in the jungles and cities of other planets instead of on Earth. An entirely new character, an imitation *Star Wars* robot named 7-Zark-7, was added. The main villain, of indeterminate sex in *Gatchaman,* was made definitely masculine. The names of all the characters were changed, and the second-lead hero, Jason (Joe in *Gatchaman*), was not killed off in the series' dramatic climax.

In 1974 a twenty-six-episode serialization of a comic book titled *Space Battleship Yamato* became the most popular animated cartoon ever shown on Japanese TV. In 2199 A.D. Earth had been under alien attack for a century. Suddenly an offer of a superscientific defense was received from Iskandar, a friendly planet across the galaxy—but Earth would have to go there to get it. All Earth's resources were poured into one spaceship, built in the image of Japan's famed World War II battleship *Yamato.* The program became a sort of World War II in deep space, as the new *Yamato* hammered its way through enemy space fleets to reach Iskandar. After its initial success, *Yamato* was beginning to settle back into the comfortable limbo of popular but concluded TV programs, when in 1977 George Lucas's *Star Wars* made the world space-opera crazy. *Yamato* was put back into prime-time rerun, and an edited feature-film condensation became a theatrical hit. (This feature, dubbed into English as *Space Cruiser Yamato,* played theatrically in England and as a TV movie in the United States in 1978.) A sequel was filmed in two separate versions. *Yamato II,* a twenty-six-episode TV serial, pitted the *Yamato* against an even greater space menace which it barely but successfully conquered. (The original *Yamato* and *Yamato II* were combined and brought to U.S. TV in 1979 as *Star Blazers.*) In the theatrical feature, *Arrivederci Yamato,* searing space battles gradually reduced the crew until the hero, with the body of his fiancée in his arms, sent the disabled spaceship in a final kamikaze dive into the enemy dreadnaught to save Earth. The Japanese public is still *Yamato*-crazy and a third TV cartoon, *Yamato: The New Voyage,* has just begun serialization.

Space Battleship Yamato rocketed both space opera and cartoonist Leiji Matsumoto to major prominence. A current Matsumoto hit is *Galaxy Express 999* (1978 and still running; over fifty episodes to date). This has been described as a "symbolic space fantasy" to forestall guffaws over an old-fashioned steam locomotive chugging between the stars. The setting is the far future when the rich have all had their brains transferred into immortal metal bodies, and only the poor retain their flesh bodies. A mysterious woman rescues a dying orphan and gives him a fabulously valuable pass on *Galaxy Express 999* so he can ride to a legendary planet of eternal life.

Each week's episode is set on a different planet, as young Tetsuro and his beautiful but eerie guardian adventure among humans or robots or aliens. *Galaxy Express 999* has been popular enough that the producer, Toei Animation, created an entirely original theatrical feature adventure which set box office records in 1979.

Yet another Matsumoto hit was *Space Pirate Captain Harlock* (1978–79). In the thirtieth century Earth had become soft and decadent, no match for an intergalactic invasion that nobody believed in anyway. But Captain Harlock had evidence that one was imminent. He set himself up as a space pirate to goad the Solar government into rousing to a fighting stance. Harlock affected the space pirate image to an extreme degree, adding a Spanish-galleon sterncastle to his dreadnaught, the *Arcadia*. (The cartoon's soundtrack was filled with Japanese imitations of the Roger Wagner Chorale singing sea chanteys.) Harlock wasn't quite popular enough to get his program extended past its initial fifty-two-episode run, but he did well enough to earn a prominent guest appearance in the *Galaxy Express 999* theatrical feature.

Star Wars had a much more direct influence on Japanese TV than giving *Yamato* new life. Toei Animation wanted to do a *Star Wars* imitation, and reasoned that the best way was to buy the rights to one of the science fiction works that George Lucas had named as inspiring him to create *Star Wars*. They selected Edmond Hamilton's *Captain Future*, a pulp magazine series in the early 1940s. Captain Future, a cross between Buck Rogers and Doc Savage, had a secret crime fighting base on the Moon, and roved from Mercury to Pluto with his comic-relief teammates (a robot, an android, and a Living Brain) to battle interplanetary criminals. Toei gave the stories *Star Wars*-era art design and a disco theme song, and added a few female characters to Hamilton's almost all-masculine supporting cast (they also added an unnecessary cute kid assistant), but otherwise they were faithful serializations of the original pulp novels. *Captain Future* ran for fifty-two weekly episodes in 1978–79.

Humorous science fiction tends to blend into pure fantasy. *Yattaman* (1977–79) was a spoof on all the ponderous giant-robot dramas, drawn in a cartoon-humor rather than a realistic style. Two teenage mechanical whizzes built a giant-robot hound-dog named Yatta King, and used it to foil the schemes of a sexy villainess and her two oafish stooges. *Yattaman* was popular enough that the 104-episode program was immediately followed by a sequel, *Zendaman* (1979 and still running), which features a giant mechanical Zenda Lion that looks amazingly like a hound dog.

The Japanese seem particularly fond of situation comedies about children who acquire klutzy robotic companions. These exist in both animated cartoon and live-action programs. One of the most popular of the former is *Doraemon* (1973; new series 1979), based on a long-running comic strip by Fujiko Fujio. Fourth-grader Nobita Nobi was loafing at home one day when a futuristic boy and a large robot kitty cat popped out of thin air. The future kid was Nobita's twenty-third-century descendent, who had been reading in the family history how Nobita had had nothing but bad luck and misery all his life. He had wanted to bring Nobita a super-robot to guide and protect him, but with his crummy allowance all he could afford was a twenty-third-century toy—and a factory reject, at that. Doraemon the robot cat was supposed to use his futuristic technology to keep Nobita out of trouble, but his all-thumbs approach and his habit of entrusting such devices as antigravity and mind-transfer to a scatterbrained ten-year-old and his playmates caused hilarious havoc.

A long list can be made of girls' fantasy programs about cute young witches or princesses from pixieland or mermaids in human form who come to a big city as a type of exchange student to "study human life." All are similar to American TV's *Sabrina*. They use their magic powers to play harmless pranks on bullies, help out their schoolmates, etc., as in Mitsuteru Yokoyama's *Sally the Witch* (1966–68), *Meg the Little Witch* (1974–75), *The Secrets of Akkochan* (1969–70) and *Maco the Mermaid* (1970–71). A slightly more adventurous variant is the current *Lun Lun the Flower Child*. A fairy dog and cat are searching the world for a young girl pure enough to become the princess of their magic land. They select Lun Lun, a young teenager in a Disneyish Switzerland. To prove she's worthy, she must successfully perform a number of good deeds with a magic flower pendant. Lun Lun is opposed by a pretty but nasty young witch and her badger assistant who try to foul up Lun Lun's helpful magic.

The Japanese also love animal fantasies. One of the first, Osamu Tezuka's *Kimba the White Lion* (1965–66), bordered on science fiction. Caesar the lion, king of the African jungle, was killed by a hunter and his mate captured for a zoo. Kimba was born on the boat going to Europe, and escaped when it sank in a storm. On his way back to the jungle he passed through human cities, and was impressed by the benefits of civilization. After the animals acknowledged him as their new king, Kimba determined to establish an animal civilization with farms and schools. Kimba's adventures often involved conflicts with older animals who did not believe in his new-fangled pacifistic ways, and with humans who would not respect the rights of the civilized animal kingdom. The first fifty-two episodes, showing Kimba as a young cub, were syndicated in America by NBC. NBC did not pick up the twenty-six-episode sequel showing Kimba as an adult, married to his childhood sweetheart Kitty and with two cubs of their own.

Most other animal fantasies have been anthropomorphized fairy tales showing handsome young honeybees, frogs, woodchucks, or squirrels in their forest or pond communities, trying to impress girlfriends or battling natural enemies. One of these, *Banner the Squirrel* (1979), was ostensibly based on a juvenile nature book by Ernest Thompson Seton, *Bannertail: The Story of a Gray Squirrel* (1922). However, it's doubtful a naturalist like Seton ever put his squirrels into clothes or had them quoting Shakespeare.

Monster fantasies run a wide range from humor to grimness. Fujiko Fujio's *Li'l Monster* (1968–69) was similar to *The Addams Family* or *The Munsters*. A pre-teen prince of Monsterland visited Earth for his education. A haunted-house Monsterland Embassy was set up in an urban residential neighborhood, with Dracula, Wolfman, "Frankie," and others among the embassy residents. On occasion the embassy would be attacked by evil Monsterland revolutionary terrorists, with the human neighbors unhappily caught in the crossfire.

Go Nagai's *Abracadabra! Enmakun* (1973–74) played for more sadistic humor. Satan learned that a number of demons on Earth were plotting to overthrow him. So a young demon, Enmakun, was assigned to Earth with two assistants (a cute frost witch and a kappa, a traditional Japanese water-demon) to break up the revolutionary movement. Enmakun was friendly toward humans, and there was a lot of humor in the program, but each episode usually ended up with a lot of human innocent bystanders dead. Nagai went all the way in *Devil Man* (1972–73), which featured a superhero similar to Marvel Comics' *Son of Satan*. Devil Man, a renegade demon who wanted to renounce evil, and the regular demons from Hell fought over the fate of a Tokyo high school. Characters were impaled, had their heads or limbs ripped off (with spouting blood), or were so scared they visibly crapped in their pants. If you can imagine *The Omen* as a comedy, you'll have some idea of the mood of *Devil Man*.

Osamu Tezuka tried an interesting experiment with his horror mystery-drama, *Vampire* (1968–69). A worldwide syndicate of were-animals, homo lycanthropus, was about to rise against homo sapiens and take over the world. A master criminal discovered their plot and tried to twist it to his own advantage. The hero was a good werewolf who tried to warn humanity. But the humans wouldn't trust any werewolf, and he ended up fighting alone while being hunted by all three factions. *Vampire* was filmed in live-action with all of the were-animals as superimposed animation. The program was generally a failure. Tezuka (who appeared briefly in it as the werewolf's friend) blamed his studio's technical inability to combine live-action and animation footage successfully, and the fact that his "cuddly" art style made it difficult for audiences to accept the were-animals as horrifying menaces. A similar experiment was made with Tsuburaya Productions' *Born Free Dinosaur Exploration Team* (1976–77), in which cartoon-animation explorers traveled into the past to hunt stop-action model dinosaurs on miniature sets. It wasn't much more successful.

"Sports adventure" is a genre that covers a lot of territory. Some programs were outright fantasies, such as Tatsuo Yoshida's *Speed Racer* (1967–68). Young daredevil Speed Racer roared around the world fighting criminals and running missions of mercy in his Mach 5, a super racing car loaded with more gimmicks than the Batmobile. He was often accompanied by a cute little kid tag-along and a pet chimpanzee. *Combo-Tiger Supercar* (1977–78) merged auto-racing with the giant-robot craze. Five teenaged racers could snap together their individual cars while at top speed to form the giant car, Combo-Tiger. They needed it to foil the foul play of the racers of the Demon Team, in a round-the-world race to determine whether demons or humans would rule the earth. *Tiger Mask* (1969–71), an adaptation of a popular newspaper strip by Ikki Kajiwara and Naoki Tsuji, was a sports/crime drama. The hero was a masked wrestler who had been trained by a criminal sports syndicate, but who tried to quit the gang and wrestle honestly.

Most sports animated cartoons, however, have been human-interest melodramas. Baseball (Japan's most popular spectator sport), auto racing, boxing, volleyball, soccer, tennis—you name it and there's been a cartoon soap opera about it.

There are other TV animated cartoons based upon highly successful comic strips. Machiko Hasegawa's *Sazae-San* (TV version 1969) was a family situation comedy in the tradition of *Blondie* or *I Love Lucy*. Yumiko Igarashi's nine-volume *Candy Candy* (1976–79; 115 episodes) was a tear-jerker serial for pre-teens, about a winsome young orphan who was always getting into heart-rending situations. The first episodes were set in Illinois in the 1910s, where Candy was a serving girl in a rich businessman's home. It looked more like an early nineteenth-century British nobleman's estate, full of servants kowtowing in a humble manner. Later Candy was sent to a finishing school in London, where she became a nurse in the Great War. Waki Yamato's *"Miss Modern Girl" Is Passing By* (1978–79) was set in Japan in the early 1920s, when the replacement of traditional lifestyles by Western ways caused considerable culture shock. *Norakuro* (1970–71), which might be described as a funny-animal version of *The Sad Sack* (with dog soldiers), only lasted a year on TV although the newspaper strip by Suihou Tagawa had been popular since 1931. It may be the oldest strip in the world today still drawn by its creator.

The single most popular cartoon, and the most vehemently denounced by the Japanese PTA—according to its creator, who insists on being called "Monkey Punch"—is *Lupin III*. This is an adult crime comedy, roughly similar to Hitchcock's *To Catch A Thief* with a dash of James Bond. The magazine strip began in the 1960s; the initial TV adaptation ran in 1971–72 and was reckoned as the fourth all-time most popular TV cartoon in a 1977 tabulation; the current TV series began in 1977 and is currently pushing 120 episodes. This Lupin is a descendant of the famous French thriller-hero, Arsene Lupin—a world-notorious gentleman burglar, a master thief.

He operates with two loyal assistants, an American gangster and a Japanese samurai. There's also a sexy girl thief who sometimes works with Lupin and sometimes is his rival for a choice piece of loot. Lupin is pursued around the world by a choleric police inspector who is usually just one step short of catching him. The series is full of witty and risqué dialogue, double and triple crosses, incredible disguises and technical gimmicks, and jazz background music. Monkey Punch is a stickler for detail: Lupin favors a Walther P-38 revolver and drinks recognizable-brand liquors (expensive ones); characters drive Toyotas or Fords or Citroens; fighter planes or military tanks are existing models. The TV cartoon has been popular enough that the producer, Tokyo Movie Shinsha, made an original theatrical feature that reportedly played to rave reviews at last year's Cannes Film Festival.

The Japanese are fond of adapting foreign classic and popular works into TV cartoons. These can range from Stevenson's *Treasure Island* (1978–79) to Marge's *Little Lulu* (1976–77). Often the cartoon series may have only a tenuous relationship to the original story. Finnish author Tove Jansson reportedly objected strenuously to the *Moomintroll* program (1969–70; new series 1972), which used her characters and art style and overall background, but had all new plots.

Adaptations of foreign works include Spyri's *Heidi* (1974), Twain's *Huckleberry Finn* (1976), Saint-Exupery's *The Little Prince* (1978–79), Montgomery's *Anne of Green Gables* (1979), Sterling North's *Rascal* (1977), Alexander Key's science fiction novel *The Incredible Tide* under the title *Conan, Boy of the Future* (1978), and two separate versions of Collodi's *Pinocchio* (1972 and 1976–77). There are many series of fairy tales: *Tales of Hans Christian Anderson* (1971), *World Famous Fairy Tales* (1976–78), and so on. There are also series which are original but highly derivative of classics, such as *Ken the Wolf Boy* (1963–65), which could easily have called itself *The Jungle Book,* and *Adventures of Sinbad* (1975–76), a presentation of some of the Arabian Nights featuring a little Arab boy on a flying carpet.

Historical dramas set before the modernization of Japan, circa 1890, are almost all sophisticated and definitely for adult audiences. To a Westerner, any program in which the characters wear traditional Japanese clothing is a "samurai adventure," a false generalization at which the Japanese wince. Many are about samurai, of course, and most are either about sword-wielding martial heroes or the intrigues of feudal court life. Two especially dramatic and bloody series involved the ninja "shadow" professional assassins—*Sasuke* (1968–69) and *The Unauthorized Biography of Kamui* (1969), both based on famous strips by the pioneer comic-book artist Sanpei Shirato. A program endorsed by the Buddhist church is *Iku-San* (over 190 episodes), currently the longest-running TV cartoon in Japan. This is a human-interest series about a pre-teen acolyte (altar boy, to use a Christian equivalent), which fictionalizes the youth of an actual famous monk. *Iku-San*'s popularity is great enough to imply that it is more than just a Sunday school morality lesson. It is currently shown on UHF channels in San Francisco and New York City, and has a fair American following.

A different view of historic Japan was presented in Osamu Tezuka's horror-fantasy *Dororo* (1969). An unscrupulous feudal lord sacrificed his infant son to demons in exchange for political power. The barely living remains of the baby, Hyakimaru, were discarded and found by a peasant woodcarver, who cared for the featureless body and carved replacement parts for it. When Hyakimaru grew to adulthood, he set out into the world to win his real self back from the demons. The serial was a cross between a Toshiro Mifune samurai drama and a grim Pinocchio: every time Hyakimaru brought another demon to bay and killed it, another part of his body—an eye, an ear, an arm—became real flesh and blood. *Dororo* (named after Hyakimaru's companion, a child thief) featured every kind of grisly monster in Japanese mythology. After Hyakimaru finished the last of them off, he went after his father for revenge—a gruesome series which presented a faithful panorama of classic Japanese folklore.

TV specials and made-for-TV feature cartoons have always been popular, but within the last year they seem to have increased tremendously in vogue. 1979 saw thirteen of them. Most were ninety-minute programs, 7:30 to 9:00 P.M. the most common time slot. Some were not cartoons themselves, but were "the making of" documentaries about animation hits such as the *Galaxy Express 999* theatrical feature and the forthcoming *Yamato 3* TV series. Others were original movies. Adaptations of Western works ranged from crime thrillers to romantic musicals: Maurice Leblanc's Arsene Lupin mystery, *813*; Paul Gallico's sugary fantasy, *Manxmouse;* and Jean Webster's soap opera about an orphan who falls vicariously in love with her unseen guardian, *Daddy Long Legs.* Possibly the most ambitious of all, produced by Nippon Animation under IBM sponsorship, was *The Diary of Anne Frank.* This had surrealistic nightmarish sequences, an expression of human anguish in animated-cartoon form equivalent to Picasso's impassioned *Guernica.*

At present the majority of Japanese TV animation is produced by five studios: Nippon Animation, Toei Company, Toei Animation Company (much public confusion between those two), Tatsunoko Productions, and Tokyo Movie Shinsha. Each turns out approximately a half dozen new half-hour series and a couple of TV or theatrical features per year, in addition to keeping in production on several popular holdovers from the last couple of years. Usually the shortest any half-hour series runs is twenty-six weekly episodes, and popular programs often run well over a hundred episodes.

A number of other studios produce smaller quantities of TV animation, though some of their shows are very important. The first program that Office Academy ever made was the fantastically popular *Space Battleship Yamato,* with the result that from 1974 to 1979 Academy devoted its entire output to *Yamato* sequels and specials. In 1979 Academy finally released a new series, *Blue Noah,* a drama in which humanity, on the verge of annihilation by aquatic aliens who have invaded our oceans, constructs a super submarine-battleship, the *Blue Noah* . . . (If you've got a good idea, milk it to death.) Dax International and Group TAC are studios that specialize in educational TV fare: famous fairy tales, biographies of notables such as Beethoven, *Sesame Street*-type stuff. Top Craft is a Tokyo studio that seems to have no cartoons on Japanese channels at all, yet it's the art designer and animator to which Rankin-Bass regularly subcontracts its American TV specials. This doubtless explains why Smaug in Rankin-Bass's 1977 production of Tolkien's *The Hobbit* was such an Asian-looking dragon. Other studios primarily known for live-action films or TV commercials, such as Tsuburaya Productions, may produce or co-produce with another studio a couple of animated programs per year.

Unfortunately the two pioneer TV animation giants of the 1960s are not currently on the scene. TCJ Animation, which created such early favorites as *Gigantor, 8th Man, Super Jetter, Prince Planet, Asteroid Mask, Space Boy Soran* and many more, dwindled to insignificance in the early 1970s. It changed its name to Eiken, but that apparently didn't help since no Eiken programs are listed after the 1976–77 season. Mushi Productions was a victim of its own high standards. It poured too much money into its production quality, for prestige as much as for pure esthetics. Osamu Tezuka left after a managerial conflict in 1972, and the studio shortly went into bankruptcy.

On the other hand, Mushi Productions's new owners kept it alive (if in low profile) for the next seven years by merchandising its old programs. In 1979 it released a new theatrical cartoon about two cutesy-poo polar bear cubs, so Mushi may finally be on its way to recovery and resumed production. As for Osamu Tezuka, he restricted his output to comic book work for a couple of years and then opened a new studio in 1976, Tezuka Productions. It has produced two TV-special cartoon features so far, is about to release a two-and-a-half-hour theatrical animated feature, *Phoenix: 2772 A.D.*, and has announced plans to begin work on a new *Astro Boy* TV series.

This indicates that, even though individual studios may suffer setbacks, the Japanese TV animation field is a dynamic one. October is a month that many new programs go on the air in Japan, and the October 1979 lineup showed the usual variety in animation: *Arthur and the Knights of the Round Table,* several samurai and other Japanese historical dramas (some with fantasy elements), fairy tales and modern fantasies, a few giant-robot and other science fiction adventures. Nippon Animation has acquired the rights to create a funny-animal series starring the USSR's official cartoon-mascot for the 1980 Olympics, Mischa the bear cub. Advertisements announce that on January 8, 1980, NHK (the Japanese equivalent of the BBC) will begin airing a serialization of Selma Lagerlof's classic fantasy, *The Wonderful Adventure of Nils.*

Out of all this TV animation, however, all the United States has seen in the last decade has been sanitized kiddie versions of *Gatchaman* (as *Battle of the Planets*) and the first two *Yamato* serials (as *Star Blazers*). Reportedly they're getting low ratings because, even in watered-down versions, they're too mature for young children with short attention spans. They contain long sequences in which people simply stand and talk, establishing characterization and motivation, instead of running frantically about and comically crashing into things. Dialogue is serious and meaningful, instead of a series of silly quips. Voices are natural instead of artificially squeaky or gravelly. Yet these programs are shown in 2:30 P.M. kiddie-cartoon time slots when they are inaccessible to school-bound or working teens and adults such as *Star Trek* fans who are their natural audiences or, worse yet, at the uncivilized hour of 5:30 A.M. In time slots like these it's no wonder hardly anyone is even aware of their existence. So Japanese animation studios can go on producing wonders for Japanese viewers and for TV audiences throughout Europe and Latin America, while Americans continue under the belief that the world's finest animation is an occasional new Disney feature and what's produced in Hollywood for Saturday-morning kids' programming.

This article is rather ambitious in that it's written by an American animation fan who has never been to Japan. However, I do belong to the Cartoon/Fantasy Organization, a fan club which has a large videotape library of Japanese TV cartoons and has regular screenings in the Los Angeles area. (Anyone interested in further information can contact me, Fred Patten, at 11863 West Jefferson Blvd., Culver City, Calif. 90230.) Also, for research purposes, there's a tremendous animation fandom in Japan, and dozens of illustrated books and magazines cover these programs in detail. Information is readily available on program titles, original broadcast dates, episode title lists, production credits, reproductions of studio model sheets, theme song lyrics and sheet music, and anything else a fan could wish to know. Just try to get similar information about any American TV animated cartoon!

Major sources used for this article include issues of the monthly animation fan magazine, *Animage;* the invaluable three-volume *Complete Works of TV Animation,* by Taku Sugiyama (1978–79); a 1978 movie-fan-format illustrated index, *Invitation to the Wonderful World of TV Animation;* and the March 1979 issue (a special on animation) of the fine-art magazine *Bungeishunju Deluxe.* I would also like to give sincere thanks to Maco Tojima, a cartoon fan from Japan currently in Los Angeles as an exchange student, for her kind assistance.

Mangamania!
The Comics Journal no. 94, October 1984.

They tell impressive stories of the comic books in Japan. They're published weekly instead of monthly. They're thicker than telephone directories. They have circulations of over 2,000,000 copies, compared to less than 1,000,000 copies of the most popular American comics. Commuters read them on the subways as casually as newspapers are read in America. Special trash trucks are sent out just to pick up used comic books. Comics are sold in vending machines on the streets.

I recently spent a week in Tokyo. While I couldn't verify all of the above claims with my own eyes, what I did see leaves me in no doubt that they're true. I didn't happen to see anyone reading comics on the subways, but I did note that the coffee shops (or their Tokyo equivalents) provide stacks of comic books for customers to browse through while waiting for their meals. I didn't find any comics vending machines, although I ran across vending machines for other items ranging from hair cream to alcoholic beverages. (Japanese vending machines for children's products play a little melody and a recorded "Thank you for buying from me" when you drop in a coin.) The 350- to 600-page comic books are real, but only a few of the most popular titles are that size—say, a dozen. Most comics are only half that size, 150 to 250 pages.

There's not much of a collector's market in Japan for old comics. There doesn't have to be. I was taken by friends to two comics shops, one simply called Manga Shoten (The Comics Bookshop) and the other named Shosen Grande (Grand Treasurehouse). Both are multi-storied buildings filled with all new comics. But that statement is surely misleading. The bulging comic-art magazines—the regularly issued periodicals which we think of when we say "comic books"—make up only a tiny fraction of the total. Most of the stock consists of reprints from the magazines in book form. Japanese comics shops look more like regular bookshops, filled with hardcovers and paperbacks, than American comics shops. But they're all comic books— comic *books* in truth. Some are current editions of decades-old stories in

What a difference twenty years makes! In 1984, nobody in America including the most optimistic anime/manga fans would have believed the popularity of translated manga—and published in the Japanese format!—in 2004. Back in 1984, it was considered *avant-garde* enough to introduce the words *anime* and *manga* to Americans without throwing *tankubon* at them as well for the manga paperback reprint collections.

This and similar early references to Osamu Tezuka graduating from medical school just after World War II are simplistically wrong, we know now. He graduated from high school just after World War II and was still in medical college at the time he decided to make cartooning his primary profession. But he did complete medical school and obtain his medical license, although he was never a practicing surgeon.

The *Dr. Slump* story synopses make it clear that toilet humor for young children was popular in Japan long before it became popular in America. I have been asked if I think that the appearance of toilet humor in American TV cartoons and children's novels (such as *Captain Underpants and the Perilous*

Cont. on p. 234

their multi-dozenth printings. Thus there is no need for the average comics fan in Japan to have to build up a collection of old issues. You can buy almost anything in a brand-new edition.

(There are exceptions, of course. Some comics aren't reprinted, for a variety of reasons. When Osamu Tezuka, the artist who created *Astro Boy* and *Kimba the White Lion,* was starting his career just after World War II, one of his first assignments was to draw comic book versions of Disney features such as *Bambi.* These were very crude by modern standards, and the Disney organization will not allow new printings. A 1960s Japanese comic book version of *The Man from U.N.C.L.E.* by Takao Saito, today one of Japan's top crime-drama comics artists, cannot be reprinted due to copyright restrictions. These are valuable rarities among Japanese comics fans. Yet the average fan can so easily get most of the worthwhile comics that have ever been written in current printings that no real market for old comics in the American sense had developed.)

For those who are interested in the history of the development of Japanese comic books, I strongly recommend the excellent study, *Manga! Manga! The World of Japanese Comics,* by Frederik L. Schodt (Kodansha, 1983, 260 pages). Basically, comic books in Japan are a post–World War II development. They were introduced by the American G.I.s who occupied Japan right after the war. The idea caught on with the public, but due to unique Japanese cultural influences (see Schodt for a knowledgeable analysis) they evolved in a manner very different from the American magazines which inspired them.

In one sense, Japanese comics magazines have remained truer to the American comics of the 1940s than have the modern American comics. The 1940s were the period of the anthology comics. Each contained several different stories. Adventure comics such as *Action* or *Whiz* would have a costumed-hero drama, a detective puzzler, a Western, a jungle adventure, and the like. Most Japanese comics magazines today continue in this format. A weekly, semi-monthly, or monthly magazine will feature a dozen or so separate stories, of ten to thirty pages each. Some are self-contained,

Plot of Professor Poopypants, by Dav Pilkey, recommended for nine- to twelve-year-old readers) is due to the influence of anime and manga. That could not have hurt, but I think that American popular culture has been slowly evolving toward a less Victorian and more frank depiction of physical and social reality throughout the past century.

I remember when it was considered shockingly realistic in a hard-boiled crime novel around the 1950s when a detective on an important stakeout needed to leave his post to take a toilet break, and when crime and war novels began revealing that when people die their bowels and bladder relax. I also read a critically recommended Young Adult novel around the mid-1980s in which the average teen characters casually used swear words that would have gotten high-school students expelled during the '50s. ■

while others are serials like American newspaper adventure strips or
serial-continuity comic books such as *The Omega Men*. There are almost
no magazines devoted to a single character. These are taken care of by the
reprint books.

The Japanese never developed the cultural mind-set that stories told
through illustrated panels are "just for kids." There are Japanese comic
books for all ages and tastes. Those for infants (under ten) contain simple
stories featuring cuddly animals and children, and gentle fantasy adventures
equivalent to our *Casper, the Friendly Ghost*. There are few funny-animal
stories, and those tend to have realistic, children's novel plots rather than the
zany, breakneck dashing-about of our *Tom and Jerry* or *Daffy Duck* comics.
There are many comic adaptations of juvenile TV cartoon humor series, and
monster adventures of the *Godzilla* sort. (This will indicate the intended
age level of the *Godzilla* movies in Japan.) Interestingly, at the moment this
comic book/TV tie-in includes Sam, the Olympic Eagle. The Japanese have
bought the rights to produce their own TV cartoons and comic book stories
featuring the 1984 Los Angeles Olympics mascot. They've turned him into a
private eye with a sexy human secretary.

The boys' adventure comics magazines (ten through the upper teens)
contain a potpourri of war dramas, SF stories, sports serials (soccer, auto
racing, boxing), historical (feudal Japan) dramas, gag humor strips, teen/
campus "real life" melodramas, and so forth. The equivalent girls' comics
carry a similar number of stories devoted to traditional girls' themes:
teenage romances, hopeful young actresses or ballerinas, sports adventure
(volleyball, tennis), feudal Japan from the feminine viewpoint, the hardships
of American or Australian pioneer farm girls, and others in that vein.
Equal rights for women is a concept which is not as advanced in Japan as
in America, and the girls' comics are only beginning to venture into areas
formerly considered too masculine for them, such as SF adventures featuring
tomboyish heroines.

There are numerous boys' and girls' magazines. Some are aimed at the
younger end of the age range, and others are for the older teens. There is
still a distinct division between comics magazines for youths and comics
magazines for adults. Those for adults present stories which are more mature
in subject matter, in social depth, and in imagery. These are broad terms, of
course. A particular story might be "mature" in being the equivalent of a
TV comedy such as *The Odd Couple*. This is hardly a work of great quality.
Still, it is a comic-art story that consists almost entirely of "talking heads,"
of conversational dialogue and a plot revolving about a "normal" human
situation rather than dramatic action. In America, the only equivalent is such
newspaper strips as *Rex Morgan, M.D.* or *Mary Worth*, or the newspaper
strip adaptations of TV series from *Ben Casey* to *Dallas*.

Again, that statement is surely misleading. It will probably make you
think of something similar to the 1950s comic book adaptations of Western

movies and TV shows like *I Love Lucy*. In one sense they are, but where the American comic book presented such a story in fifty-two pages or less, the Japanese comic magazine serial might run to 500 or 1,500 pages. Whether they have violent scenes (and some are bloodier than any Sam Peckinpah movie) or they deal entirely with nonviolent situations, the emphasis is always on the human personality, character interrelationships, and psychological drama rather than action. Japanese adult comics are much more like American movies and TV programs frozen on paper than like American comics. Pages and pages may be devoted to a single conversation, focusing on the subtle emotional changes on the characters' faces. Even a violent scene such as a sniper's assassination of a crime boss, which might take four or five panels in an American comic, can be stretched to as many full pages in a Japanese comic. The artists can be counted upon to stretch out these scenes by using a full range of cinematic techniques: pans, close-ups, multiple camera angles, dissolves, montages, and slow motion. Oh, do they love slow motion and the freeze-frame shot!

The men's comics magazines present stories and serials with a macho bent. Common themes are hard-boiled violence, risqué and outright lewd humor, and political or corporate intrigue. Such stories may be contemporary or historical. There are many "salaryman" stories about young business executives in today's white-collar world. There are as many about young court functionaries or young merchants in feudal Japan. These stories may be burlesque comedies, comedies of manners, or serious melodramas about the struggle to advance. If you want action and violence, there are contemporary police or espionage stories and historical samurai stories. Practically every adult comic of any length will involve sexual relationships at some point, usually graphically depicted though not to the extent of being X-rated. Those in the men's comics often run to sweaty illicit affairs. Those in the women's comics are more romantic, or at least more romantically staged.

Here's a specific example of a story which the term "women's comics" would probably not suggest to an American. This is a forty-four-page short story, "Survival in 3DK" by Hikaru Yuzuki. A young couple living in a large apartment building go on a five-day trip, leaving their approximately one-and-a-half-year-old son in his grandmother's care. They have barely left when the grandmother has a fatal heart attack. The story cuts back and forth between the parents enjoying their vacation and hoping that baby isn't giving Granny too much trouble, and the baby crawling around the decomposing Granny, trying to wake her up, making messes and tracking them through the apartment, attempting to open the refrigerator as he grows hungrier and thirstier, and finally drinking his own urine. In America such a story could only have appeared in a horror comic, where the final panel would doubtlessly show the parents returning to discover baby eating Granny. But this deals with a common fear among mothers: having to entrust their infants to the care of others for an extended time. Therefore it's a suitable thriller for women, and is developed around the realistic suspense of whether the neighbors will notice anything wrong or whether the parents will return before baby starves, kills himself playing with broken glass, etc.

These weekly and monthly magazines cover the most popular general comics in Japan. The stereotype in America of Japanese comics is of samurai stories (using that term to include adventures of any period of Japanese history) and giant-robot or monster SF adventures. There are certainly lots of these in terms of sheer volume, but they are only a small percentage of the total. The largest single category in the boys' comics is probably sports and games. Each series focuses upon a single sport with fanatical intensity. Joji Kagami and Tatsuo Kanai's *Hole In One* is about a teenager who dreams of becoming a golf champion. There have been over 2,000 pages in this serial so far. A dozen pages or more may be devoted to playing a single hole of one game, with many close-ups of young Yaichi's tense face as he tries to sink an impossible putt. Some series about baseball players or boy fishermen have run to over fifty reprint volumes of 150–200 pages apiece. The longest-running SF series have been Osamu Tezuka's *Mighty Atom* (American title: *Astro Boy*) at only twenty-two volumes, and Reiji Matsumoto's *Galaxy Express 999* at seventeen volumes. (This does not count some of the really juvenile series, such as Fujio Fujiko's *Doraemon*, about a robot kitty cat from the future who plays guardian angel to a klutzy ten-year-old schoolboy, which is at thirty volumes so far.)

There seem at first glance to be no modesty or scatology taboos in Japanese comics. The baby in "Survival in 3DK" pulls off his dripping diapers and is obviously a boy. Stories for all ages casually follow characters into home bathrooms or public restrooms. Often the lack of modesty isn't innocent at all. Frederik Schodt tells in *Manga! Manga!* about Tatsuhiko Yamagami's *Kid Cop (Gaki Deka)* series, featuring,

[. . .] an improbable policeman/boy who [. . .] never doffed his police hat or removed his polka-dot tie, but he regularly shed the rest of his clothes to expose mooning buttocks and to wow onlookers with the tricks he could do with his testicles . . . In spite of protests, Gaki Deka was so popular among children (and the millions of adults who read children's comics) that it is said to have boosted the weekly sales of Shonen Champion by over a million copies.

A similarly bawdy juvenile series was Go Nagai's superhero satire, *Change—TAMAIDA!*, for the semi-monthly *Manga-kun* magazine. In this burlesque, a wimpy junior-high-aged schoolboy would dash into the boys' restroom, drop his pants, twirl his genitals like a propeller while shouting, "Change—TAMAIDA!," and turn into Tamaida (roughly, Testicle Boy) whose costume included a headpiece topped by a firehouse-nozzle-sized penis. (Yes, it worked.) He was, to use a Marty Feldman line, "extremely popular with

A panel from Go Nagai's Change—TAMAIDA!

the girls," who mysteriously changed from a junior-high look when clothed to a college-coed buxomness when unclothed.

In fact, there are definite taboos. Stories for males are allowed to be much raunchier than those for females. Nudity in comics for girls or women is expected to be either innocent (as in the case of the baby in "Survival in 3DK") or artistically tasteful. Sex can be implied but not actually shown.

That's in the general comics, now. There are also pornography comics for adults. There may even be pornography comics for children, although I suspect that I was being kidded and what I was shown was really kiddy-porno comics for adults. There definitely is a monthly, 160-page comic magazine titled *Lemon People* which is devoted to science fiction stories for kiddy-porn enthusiasts. (Or is it kiddy-porn for SF fans?) It features stories, some by well-known artists, of pre-adolescent boys and girls sexually molested by space monsters, or of human spacemen ravishing cute alien children on distant planets, or of kids discovering sex by themselves through more science fictional ways than playing doctor. Another monthly magazine titled *June* is devoted to stories (not SF) starring young homosexual couples, male and female. I didn't have enough time to study all the comics at Manga Shoten (I spent most of my time on the boys' adventure floor, where most of the SF comics were), but I wouldn't be surprised if there are also sports-porno comics, war-porno comics, and so on.

Japanese comic-art magazines are anthologies. They're also printed in only one color, except for a token two or four pages at the front to showcase the lead feature. These magazines are printed on extremely coarse pulp paper which would not take multicolor printing well. Also, to print 200 to 500 pages in full color would drive the price of the magazine out of the market. But they do manage a rainbow effect despite this. The colors of both the paper and ink change several times per issue. A 350-page magazine may go through ten color changes, from black ink on green paper to purple or turquoise ink on cream paper. So in their own way, Japanese comics are as gaudy as American comics.

The comic *books,* the reprint volumes which are bought to be kept, are considerably different. These are sharply printed in black ink on good white paper. Some could almost serve as photographic stats for the original art. Most Japanese comic art is drawn with this high-quality book reproduction as the final goal. Its original publication in the magazine is considered only an intermediate step.

Most of these reprints are in a paperback format almost identical to American paperbacks, with one delightful improvement: they have laminated dust jackets, just like hardcover books. There are two standard sizes, one for the youth market and the other for the adult market. The adult books are only a half-inch wider and a quarter-inch taller, but this is enough to be easily distinguished by the eye. Thus the average bookshop browser can tell the maturity level of a standard comic-art paperback at a glance by its size.

The variety of comic-art books for the serious devotee is as varied as that of science fiction books for the SF fan in America. They range from cheap paperbacks to deluxe hardcover editions. Osamu Tezuka's *Jungle Emperor (Kimba the White Lion)* comes in a regular three-volume paperback edition at 400 yen per volume. (The current rate of exchange is about 230 yen to one U.S. dollar.) But *Kimba* is also available in a single-volume slip-cased hardcover edition with color plates for 5,000 yen. There are theme anthologies of comic-art short stories: SF stories, sports stories, war stories, and so on. One publisher, My Comics, has a lengthy series of hardcover collections of romantic science fiction short stories for girls, each volume by a different young woman cartoonist.

As you might guess by the frequency with which his name is being mentioned, Osamu Tezuka is the leading comic artist in Japan. He virtually created the comics industry just after World War II when he graduated from medical school but found cartooning more to his taste than surgery. There had been comics before. The publisher Kodansha issued a children's magazine as early as 1914 which contained a comic-art section. Suiho Tagawa's *Norakuro,* one of Japan's rare funny-animal comics (about a dog soldier), began in January 1931; it may be the world's oldest comic strip still being drawn today by its creator. But most prewar comics were rather pedestrian humor strips. It was Tezuka who introduced the concept of using cinematic visual techniques to tell movie-like adventures. Tezuka also created the idea of the comic-art movie or novel, a story designed to reach a planned conclusion and to end there, as opposed to a series running indefinitely.

Tezuka became legendary for his prolific output and for his versatility. Most comic artists specialize in one or two fields, but Tezuka seemed to set himself the goal of producing comics in every possible field. Over the years he has written and drawn cuddly animal fantasies for infants' magazines, true love romances for women's magazines, religious (Buddhist) comics, and raunchy sex novels for men's magazines. He has also drawn political cartoons, calendar art, record jacket art, advertising trademark emblems, and (keeping in touch with his original avocation) sick-humor gag cartoons on medical themes for medical journals.

As prolific as he is, Tezuka could not manage all this output personally. This led to his next major step in the evolution of the modern Japanese comic-art industry: the development of his own art shop. He hired a number of assistants and trained them to draw in his style. Today Tezuka Productions turns out about 400 pages of comic art a month. Tezuka himself does all the plotting, the rough layouts, the detailed facial expressions, and the final dialogue. His staff does the majority of the art, the detailed backgrounds, and the characters except for the faces.

This procedure has come to be the hallmark of the really prestigious cartoonists. You haven't arrived among the leaders of the industry until you've set up your own studio. Go Nagai, who created the giant-robot school of superhero comics with *Mazinger Z* in 1972, today sends out all his work under both his own name and that of his company, Dynamic Productions. In addition to churning out comic books, Dynamic Productions also creates story concepts for Japan's TV animation industry. Some of Nagai's assistants are entitled to add the Dynamic Productions name to their personal comics, too. Takao Saito specializes in extremely mature, brutal, modern crime dramas, notably the series *Golgo 13*, about a professional assassin. Saito is famous for the realism of his detailed art, and for his extensive art files on automobiles, weapons, clothing styles, and so forth, which several assistants keep constantly up-to-date.

There are major cartoonists who prefer to draw their work themselves, or with one or two close assistants rather than a large staff. These are usually artists whose status rests upon a single extremely popular series. Monkey Punch (Kazuhiko Kato), the creator of the *Lupin III* crime-comedy strip, can turn out 300 pages a month with only his brother's help because his art style is so simplistic. (Monkey Punch has acknowledged that he was inspired by Sergio Aragones' marginal cartoons in *Mad* magazine.) Takao Yaguti specializes in rustic nature comics in the style of Ernest Thompson Seton's American juvenile "true life" animal adventures, and stories about the exhilaration of backpacking and camping out. Lest you think that such stories might have only a limited appeal, Yaguti's series *Sampei, the Fanatic Boy Fisherman*, about a teenage angler who travels to the best fishing spots all over the world (real sites, drawn in detail), has been running strong since 1973. There are over fifty reprint paperbacks and an animated TV series which prove its popularity. Yet Yaguti isn't interested in turning himself into a comic-art factory.

Japanese cartoonists are able to work in this manner because the Japanese comic-art industry operates on the European rather than the traditional American pattern. The cartoonists own their own works. The magazines buy first publication rights only. If a work is successful, it stays in print and the artist can keep collecting royalties on it for years. Mitsuteru Yokoyama drew *Iron Man No. 28* (American title: *Gigantor*) in the 1950s, and he is still earning money from its current reprints, although Yokoyama gave up contemporary SF adventures shortly afterward and has specialized in historical comics for the past two decades. (However, one of his works, *Time Pilgrim,* is about a time traveler from the future who settles in feudal Japan.) When the publisher Kodansha launched its 300-volume *Collected Works of Osamu Tezuka,* this meant printing its own editions of books by Tezuka which are still in print from rival publishers. Tezuka's ownership of his own works enabled him to grant this permission. (So fans have a choice between two different editions of *Astro Boy* at the moment, both authorized.)

Japanese cartoonists also share in the merchandising royalties from their characters to a greater extent than do American cartoonists. And because comic art is more respectable in Japan, there is a much greater range of merchandising to cash in on. It goes without saying that there are toys, dolls, model kits, candies, T-shirts, lunch boxes, bicycles, and all the traditional items of juvenile merchandising. Schoolgirls' romance comics have been translated into English for use as textbooks in English-language classes. The translations are contemporary enough that the Japanese schoolgirls are shown saying "fer shurr" and "Gag me with a spoon." The adult comics spawn adult merchandising items. There are *Lupin III* cocktail-glass napkins and gold-plated cigarette lighters. The cartoonists themselves are used to sell products. Last summer Osamu Tezuka's face was on billboards throughout Japan endorsing a brand of home word processor.

What are the hot SF comics and artists at the moment? Surprisingly, Tezuka is not among them. His older SF works, especially *Astro Boy,* still sell well, but they are considered old-fashioned or "classics" by today's fans. Tezuka's SF masterwork is *Phoenix,* a series of adventures which trace the history of mankind through its evolution to its demise in the distant future, as observed by the immortal firebird. Tezuka has been working on *Phoenix* sporadically since the 1950s. It was the basis for a major live-action historical fantasy movie, *Phoenix: Dawn* in 1978 and an animated SF movie, *Phoenix 2772: Love in the Cosmozone* in 1980. *Phoenix* is respected but considered overly intellectual by many, and in any case it is dormant at the moment. (Tezuka is currently concentrating on historical dramas, notably *Tree of Pride,* set during the "opening" of Japan to Western culture in the 1850s.)

Reiji Matsumoto is another household name in Japanese comics who's not doing much SF at the moment. He's presently riding the reputation of his hits of the 1970s such as *Space Battleship Yamato* and *Space Pirate Captain Harlock,* which are being kept before the public through new adventures in TV and theatrical animation. Matsumoto's last SF hit was *Galaxy Express 999,* an episodic space fantasy about a young boy, Tetsuro, and his mysterious beautiful guardian, Maeter, aboard a spaceship designed to look like an old-fashioned railroad train. They visited planets all around the galaxy in their search for a world of mechanical perfection. *Galaxy Express 999* became another hit in animation, with 113 half-hour TV episodes, two theatrical features, and a couple of TV specials. But Matsumoto concluded this series in 1981. He's currently producing a self-parody of *Galaxy Express 999* titled *Main Line Adrift 000,* about an almost-identical young boy and mysterious guardian who ride a modern streamlined train across an endless series of present and future parallel-dimension Earths. The large-eyed, beautiful blonde guardian in *Main Line Adrift 000* won't go anywhere until she's picked up a six-pack of beer, an indication of this series' tongue-in-cheek spirit.

Space Adventure Cobra is an example of how a new comic series can catapult its unknown young artist (Buichi Terasawa, in this case) to instant stardom. The setting is a thirtieth-century galactic civilization. The protagonist, Cobra, is a former master thief who escapes the boredom of retirement by taking on suicidal missions on behalf of the needy, especially when the needy is a beautiful damsel in distress. Cobra is essentially a futuristic *Modesty Blaise,* but where Modesty is the personification of cool confidence and dignity, Cobra affects a clownish recklessness (similar to Kirk Douglas's Ned Land in Disney's *20,000 Leagues Under the Sea*) that causes his adversaries to underestimate him. Cobra is always on the side of justice, if not the law. His opponents are corrupt bureaucrats, planetary tyrants, and the really evil Space Mafia, with which he has a long-running feud. Cobra's hallmarks are his ever-present cigar, his shapely female robot companion, Lady, and his psychogun, a super-blaster grafted onto his arm (usually hidden by a prosthetic hand). There are fifteeen paperback volumes of *Space Adventure Cobra* to date, plus a thirty-one-episode TV animated serialization and an animated 3-D theatrical feature.

An even bigger current hit is Akira Toriyama's *Dr. Slump,* a wacky comedy fantasy that mixes together practically anything you can name. Tropical Penguin Island is inhabited by people, space monsters, funny animals, and caricatures of such modern mythical heroes as Tarzan, Mr. Spock, Kotter, and Clint Eastwood. Dr. Slump is a mad scientist and would-be dirty middle-aged man. Probably his greatest invention, in his opinion, is a pair of glasses that makes women's clothing invisible. (Men's too, but who cares about that?) Definitely his greatest invention, in the Japanese public's opinion, is Arale-chan, an invincible robot with the form and personality of a six or seven-year-old girl. A very *lively* little girl. If she wants to bring Godzilla home and train him as a pet, he'd better learn to heel and fetch in a hurry! Toriyama has a mania for juvenile ca-ca humor. In a combined burlesque of *Conan* and *The Lord of the Rings,* Slump the Barbarian and his companions must journey on a quest through foul forests and battle malignant menaces (including a trigger-happy meter maid) to confront an evil sorcerer who has seized the supermarket and is withholding all the toilet paper from Penguin Village (whose inhabitants are getting increasingly antsy waiting for their bathrooms to be restocked). One of the most classic events of the series was the first meeting of Arale-chan and Superman. Toriyama's version is named "Suppaman," a pun on the Japanese word for "sour." He gets his powers by eating sour pickles.) "Hello there, little girl. I'm Suppaman! I can do anything!" "Gee, Mr. Suppaman, can you really do anything?" "Yes, I can do anything!" "Okay, let's see you eat the doggie doo-doo on the sidewalk there!" *BLEECH* Yes, that scene is in the animated TV version, too.

Running close to *Dr. Slump* in popularity and style is Rumiko Takahashi's *Urusei Yatsura*. This title is a Japanese pun which is usually summarized as *Those Obnoxious Aliens,* although English-speaking Japanese fans say that a translation closer in spirit would go something like *Those Gonzo Outer-Space People Who Make Lousy Next-Door Neighbors.* Earth is discovered by Space Invaders (they have business cards that read "Space Invaders"), and soon our planet is overrun with weird alien tourists. Lum-chan, a sexy teenager who's cute despite her petite horns and fangs, enters a Tokyo high school as a foreign exchange student to be near Wataru, the human boy for whom she's hot. Wataru is a klutzy girl chaser who would ordinarily be delighted to have a pretty girl come chasing after him—but not one who can fly, is overly jealous, and can generate electric shocks strong enough to black out a city. *Those Obnoxious Aliens* is a bit like Archie Comics' *Sabrina, The Teenage Witch* and a hit like the *I Dream of Jeannie* TV series, with Wataru constantly trying to escape Lum's attentions so he can get back to trying to make out with the rest of the girls. Despite such trappings as flying saucers and ray guns, *Those Obnoxious Aliens* makes no pretense at being real SF. Many of the "alien" visitors are well-known Japanese mythological characters, wizards who perform genuine magic, and parodies of horror-movie stars such as Dracula. The series is simply a very funny fantasy situation comedy, playing off the interrelationships of a strongly characterized cast (mostly teenagers, both human and alien) and the reactions of both "cultures" to each other: a non-human child becomes a fan of old *Zorro* TV reruns; the teens try to take advantage of Lum's powers to get around a school ban on junk food. *Those Obnoxious Aliens* is yet another comic book series that has repeated its popularity in animation, with over 120 episodes of the TV cartoon series and two theatrical features. The animation is being produced by one of Japan's largest music companies, Kitty Enterprises, which uses the TV program and movies to promote new pop songs for the teen dance market.

Situation comedies and light crime dramas with lots of macho men and sexy women have a certain universal appeal whether they're in a SF/fantasy setting or not. Serious SF dramas, especially boys' adventure SF, is more limited in its appeal. Yuki Hijiri's *Locke the Superman* has a large cult following rather than true hit status. It follows a lonely teenage ESPer through an interstellar civilization as he confronts such villains as planetary dictators or other ESPers who misuse their powers. There is widespread anti-ESP prejudice in this stellar society, so Locke can never settle down happily despite his record of good deeds. There are obvious similarities to Marvel's *X-Men* series in *Locke the Superman,* but it seems closer in mood to van Vogt's SF novel *Slan* or to Andre Norton's wandering teen stellar heroes such as Dane Thorson and Hosteen Storm. The popularity of *Locke the*

Superman has been growing slowly. It wasn't considered for animation for nine years after its 1971 debut, and its initial presentation as a TV cartoon series failed to sell. But the soundtrack of that presentation, with a rock score by a popular Japanese group, was released as an LP record. It did well enough that it led to the unusual situation of Locke becoming popularized not through animation but through a series of LP rock-jazz "dramatizations" of Hijiri's stories. Finally, *Locke the Superman* is due to appear as a theatrical animated feature in summer 1984. Another sign of Locke's growing following is the appearance during the last couple of years of other comics which also feature lone-wolf teenage space heroes who possess unusual talents. The best of these seem to be Tsuguo Okazaki's *Cosmo Police Justy* and Akira Seki's *Star Simac* (four volumes apiece to date). *Star Simac* has spun off its first LP music album.

Among the newly emerging women SF cartoonists, the leader is clearly Keiko Takemiya. She began her career by drawing girls' romance comics, and she is still mainly active in that field. (Remember that in Japan, "girls' romance comics" carries a much wider meaning than in America. One of Takemiya's most popular serials, *A Song of Wind and Trees,* deals seriously with teenage homosexuality in a French boys' school.) She was one of the first to place tales of young love in SF settings. In 1977 Takemiya crossed over to a boys' magazine to serialize an SF adventure without romantic tones. *To Terra . . .* became one of Japan's most prestigious comic-art SF novels without regard to the artist's sex. This 978-page story, available today in several editions (the most common is a five-volume paperback set), is a complex tale of political maneuvering among factions of a mutant ESPer race aboard a starship returning after generations to Earth. *To Terra . . .* was animated as a major theatrical feature in 1980. Another comic-art novel, *Andromeda Stories,* about a distant world's struggle to fight conquering parasitic invaders, was also made into an animated movie. It wasn't until 1980 that Takemiya began a regular SF comic book open-ended series. *Fly Me To The Moon!* may be the first girls' "SF love comedy," to use the Japanese dust-jacket blurb. Nina, a Sweet Young Thing with ESP talents, marries Dan Mild, a chief NASA astronaut at America's Marsport base in the early twenty-first century. The series revolves around Nina's attempts to set up housekeeping for a husband who's traveling to other planets much of the time. *Fly Me To The Moon!* isn't just a romantic comedy in a futuristic setting, however. Both the twenty-first-century technology and Nina's psionic abilities are used imaginatively as story elements. Nina's ESP can be both a help and an embarrassment. For example, the whole neighborhood becomes aware when she gets carried away in ecstasy on their honeymoon night. There are many humorous gags, such as "Violet new love panty," the space-age lingerie, or the manner in which the twenty-first century goes through a pop revival of such antique culture classics as the Beatles and DC superheroes. Nina's brother Archie is a teenage techno-nerd (Takemiya uses the term "mekamaniac") who is determined to build the first working Asimovian positronic robot. I don't know whether any attempts are being made to animate *Fly Me To The Moon!*, but an LP record album has just been released.

Other Japanese women cartoonists who are drawing SF seem to be working only in short lengths, at most a single volume long. One exception is Junko Sasaki, born in 1961, who has just entered the comic-art business. She has begun two series, *Bremen 5* (three volumes to date) and *Dark Green* (two volumes so far), both published by Flower Comics, a regular romance line. *Bremen 5* is a light space opera about five loners, mostly teenagers and not all humans, who meet and decide to band together against the hostile universe. *Dark Green* is a surrealistic drama starring a college art student, Hokuto, who is participating in some R-dream (REM-sleep?) experiments. Part of his life is spent in mundane campus activities; the rest is set in an abstract neverworld where he is a soldier shifting from ancient to futuristic battles, a pawn of dimly seen forces fighting a vast, incomprehensible war. Sasaki's work is typical of the Japanese women cartoonists who are drawing SF. Despite the SF format, they are still working in the girls' romance traditions. The stories are often told from the viewpoint of a passive female lead character. The protagonist in *Bremen 5* is Yuzu, the young girl of the group, who participates in the action mainly by following the orders of the handsome boy leader, Tauro. (The most interesting one of the five is the puckish Hugh, a preadolescent human/black panther centauroid.) When the protagonist does happen to be a dynamic male, as Hokuto is in *Dark Green,* he's still drawn in romance-comics visuals, usually as handsome in a frail, willowy way with large, limpid eyes.

These are the major new SF comics and trends. This is not an accurate description of the whole SF comic book market because, as I said earlier, there are so many current reprints of older titles sharing bookshop space alongside the new works.

One of the giants of Japanese comic art, Shotaro Ishimori, hasn't been mentioned because he's not producing any notable SF series at the moment, although his many works of the 1960s and 1970s such as the *Cyborg 009* superhero volumes, are readily available. Many other current SF titles have not been mentioned here because they're not big hits, although each does have its own fan following. There is a beautifully drawn but slow-paced fantasy adventure set in the world of Greek mythology titled *Arion,* by Yoshikazu Yasuhiko, which predates DC's *Arion, Lord of Atlantis* by over three years. Finally, bear in mind that all these SF comics together are only a fraction of the entire Japanese comics field. The sports comics, the romance comics, the detective comics, and other genres which had faded from sight in America are still as popular as ever in Japan.

Just as the comic-book field is vibrantly alive, so is the animated-cartoon field. There is no Saturday-morning kidvid ghetto in Japan. Cartoon programs are shown in prime time every day of the week. There are whole TV guides exclusively for the animated programs. And only about half the TV animation programs are adaptations of comic books. The other half are completely original. The giant-robot superheroes for which the Japanese are well known in America are almost exclusively a TV cartoon genre. The original TV giant robots in the 1970s such as *Brave Raideen* and *Combattler V* were revered as superheroes in their own right, and their adversaries were other giant robots presented as super-villains. This concept has evolved until, today, the average giant-robot TV cartoon is a tightly plotted SF serial in which the robot is merely a vehicle. In one recent weekly TV serial, *Votoms, Armored Trooper,* the Votoms robots are military one-man fighting suits which are being used by all factions. Votoms is a gritty futuristic drama which combines elements of *Outland, Escape from New York, Blade Runner,* and *Road Warrior.* It's not uncommon for characters to get shot between the eyes in full facial close-ups, or for someone in a fight to be graphically kicked in the balls. Needless to say, Japanese animation is not subject to the censorship of American TV cartoons. There are even animated comedies built around such subjects as hot-blooded junior-high boys trying to strip their sexy schoolteacher. Considering the long odds against getting these cartoons onto American TV, it's fortunate that a growing exchange in videotapes between Japanese and American fans is making this "Japanimation" unofficially available over here.

At least one major publisher, Kodansha, is seriously interested in marketing its comic books in America. Unfortunately, the problems involved are considerably greater than those of translating European comic books into English. The European albums, usually forty-eight pages in full color, are in a format that's familiar and comfortable to the American comic-buying public. Japanese comic books are much thicker but also much smaller, in pocket-book format, and without color. The smaller size and lack of color create a psychological impression with many Americans that they aren't getting as much value for their money. Simply gearing up an American press to print in the Japanese format is a considerable undertaking. Japanese comics are laid out "backward" to Western conventions, reading right-to-left rather than left-to-right. To translate them into English would require photographically reversing the art, an expensive extra step. The sound effects in European comics such as "boum" or "par" can be easily changed into English, whereas those in Japanese comics are totally incomprehensible, requiring an extensive retouching of the artwork.

And after all this is done, will enough American readers buy the books? Japanese comics are often slowly paced by American standards. Conversational scenes several pages long may be put in just to help establish the characters' personalities rather than to advance the action. A scene may be extended for artistic effect, rather than compressed to get as much story into as few pages as possible. The only serious American publication of a

Japanese comic-art novel to date has been *Barefoot Gen,* Keiji Nakazawa's semiautobiographical account of living through the atomic bombing of Hiroshima as a young boy, and it has not been a commercial success. Only the first two of *Gen's* seven volumes have been published in English so far, and they have been subsidized through contributions to promote the book's anti-war statement. It can be argued that there should be a larger market among comic book purchasers for light escapist fiction such as a *Star Wars*-type space adventure, rather than for a powerful but disturbing social message. But publishers are still reluctant to take the risk. For the present, the world of Japanese comic art will remain a phenomenon for Americans to marvel at from afar.

Japan + Animation = Japanimation! Part 1
Starlog no. 105, April 1986.

Automobiles. Video equipment. Computers. These are just a few of the high-technology areas in which Japan has been grabbing a growing share of the American market during the past decade. How about science fiction and superhero cartoons? Those who view television and motion pictures have recently seen an influx of Japanese high-tech animated SF drama on both the little and big screens. Giant robots, a mainstay of Japanese TV cartoons for more than a dozen years, have finally become "in" in the USA. American companies are buying Japanese animated SF serials and transforming them into original programs such as *Voltron* and *Robotech.*

Japanese SF animation has actually been seen in America for more than twenty years. *Astro Boy,* the first TV cartoon series made in Japan, was brought to America in 1963. However, Japanese cartoons soon became much more action-packed while, at the same time, American TV network standards for children's programming became more restrictive. It has only been within the past few years, with the growth of the independent TV syndication market, which isn't subject to network standards, that Japanese animated SF has begun to flow into America. Many of these programs are also becoming available to the public on videocassettes.

Many Americans haven't waited for that development. As soon as the home video market appeared in the mid-1970s, some American comics and SF fans began obtaining videotapes of Japanese cartoons directly from Japan. The interstellar SF action was so dramatic and exciting that enthusiasts didn't care that they couldn't understand the Japanese dialogue. Today, most large SF and comics conventions have a video room where tapes of SF cartoons in Japanese are shown.

Both the translation of Japanese animated SF into English and the interest among Americans in Japanese-language animated SF are growing.

This two-part article surveys the Japanese SF cartoons that have already been translated into English while briefly noting some of the most popular SF cartoons with American fans which are so far only available in the original Japanese.

Astro Boy. 1963–64, 104 episodes, black and white. Astro Boy was created when the child Astor Boynton III was killed in a traffic accident. His grief-stricken father, the scientist Dr. Boynton, determined to re-create his son through a better-than-human robot. There were many robots already in this future world of 2000 A.D., but Astro Boy could fly, drill through the ground, and outperform them all. However, because he was programmed to think like a human child, Astro Boy worried because he never really fit in with other children and didn't grow up as they did. He was finally taken under the guardianship of Dr. Packadermus J. Elefun, head of the Institute of Science, who taught him to use his powers to help humanity. Dr. Elefun also built a robot family so Astro Boy would feel more normal. *Astro Boy* was very popular in the 1960s due to its warm, fast-paced humor and likable characters, including the old private detective Mr. Pompus and Astro Boy's impish robot sister, Astro Girl. (Translation of original Japanese title *Mighty Atom.*)

8th Man. 1965–66, fifty-two episodes, black and white. When police detective Peter Brady was killed by criminals, Professor Genius transferred his mind into an experimental superandroid body. Brady thus became the superhero Tobor, the 8th Man. One of his eight secrets was the ability to mold his image into any likeness. He, therefore, found it easy to continue living as Detective Brady, and also to assume any disguise instantly. The only person besides Professor Genius to know his secret was Chief Fumblethumbs of the Metropolitan International Police Headquarters. Both helped 8th Man fight the usual assortment of comic-book mad scientists and supercriminals. Tobor's mechanical body got its power from energy cells which were disguised as cigarettes, so whenever he began to weaken, Brady would pretend to smoke a cigarette. This gimmick made *8th Man* an early casualty of the stricter standards for American children's TV. (Japanese title: *8 Man.*)

Gigantor. 1966, fifty-two episodes, black and white. Gigantor was the first of the giant robots, but he was not really a hero, just an enormous remote-controlled flying mechanical man. The hero was twelve-year-old Jimmy Sparks, son of inventor Dr. Sparks, who put Gigantor through his feats by twiddling a simple lever on a hand-held control box. Jimmy and his giant companion traveled around the world to fight crime alongside police Inspector Blooper, at other times to accompany his father's young colleague, Dr. Bob Brilliant, on scientific expeditions. The point that Gigantor was a device rather than a character was emphasized in several episodes in which villains tried to steal the control box so they could use Gigantor for criminal purposes. (Japanese title: *Iron Man No. 28.*)

Prince Planet. 1966–67, fifty-seven episodes, black and white. Prince Planet was a space boy with an I.Q. of 300. He was sent by the Galactic Council of Radion to clean up all evil on Earth so our world could join interstellar civilization. He was discovered by a young girl, Diana Worthy, who helped disguise him as a normal American boy named Bobby and invited him to use the Worthy ranch as his headquarters. Prince Planet soon gained two more friends, the ex-champion wrestler Dan Dynamo and the Arabian magician Ajababa, who joined him on his forays against human criminals and such space villains as Krag of the planet Kragmire and Warlock the Martian. (Japanese title: *The Boy from the Planet Papii.*)

Kimba the White Lion. 1966–67, fifty-two episodes, color. Kimba was superficially a funny-animal program, but its basic concept was sociological SF. Kimba, a lion cub of great intelligence, was impressed by human civilization. He decided to force the jungle animals to create their own civilization instead of preying upon each other. Sub-plots included Kimba's need to find a non-meat food for the carnivores (including himself) before they starved, and his struggle to get humans to recognize the intelligent animals as equals. A sequel to *Kimba* depicting him as an adult, not brought to America at the time, has recently appeared on the Christian Broadcasting Network as *Leo the Lion* (1985, twenty-six episodes, color). (Japanese title: *Jungle Emperor.*)

Marine Boy. 1966–67, seventy-eight episodes, color. Marine Boy, the young son of Dr. Mariner of the Ocean Patrol, was given the ability to breathe underwater by chewing "Oxygum." He toured the world's seas to keep them free from crime, with the aid of other Ocean Patrol agents such as Professor Fumble and patrolmen Bulton and Piper, plus Splasher the dolphin and Neptina the mermaid. Marine Boy was a juvenile mixture of magic (mermaids) and superhero technology (Oxygum, jet boots, an electric boomerang) pitted against the inevitable mad scientists and supervillains such as Count Shark and Dr. Slime. (Japanese titles: *Hang In There, Marine Kid;* and *Marine, the Submarine Boy.*)

The Amazing 3. 1967–68, fifty-two episodes, black and white. Three galactic police agents were sent to Earth to decide whether warlike humanity should be destroyed as a threat to interstellar peace. The three disguised themselves as Earth animals (Bonnie Bunny, Ronnie Horse, and Zero Duck), but their secret was discovered by a boy, Kenny Carter, younger brother of Randy Carter, an agent of an international anti-crime organization. Kenny persuaded the trio to help improve Earth instead of merely observing its wars, crime, and other problems. Since the three were under strict orders not to become personally involved with the humans, they had to perform their good deeds secretly. (Japanese title: *W3.*)

Speed Racer. 1967–68, fifty-two episodes, color. Seventeen-year-old race driver Speed Racer, his girlfriend Trixie, and his kid brother Spridle with his pet chimp Chimchim all traveled around the world to participate in international auto races. Most races involved crooked rival drivers or regular criminals who had to be beaten on or off the track. Speed was occasionally helped by the mysterious, masked Racer X, eventually revealed as his missing older brother, Rex. This program was SF due to all the super-tech gimmicks built into Speed's Mach 5 racing car by his inventor-father, Pops Racer. (Japanese title: *Mach Go Go Go.* "Go" is the Japanese word for "5," but turning it into "Go, go, go!" was a bilingual pun.)

Battle of the Planets. 1978–79, eighty-five episodes, color. The G-Force consisted of five (mostly) teenage heroes in stylized bird costumes: Mark (eagle), Jason (condor), Princess (swan), Keyop (swallow), and Tiny (owl). They roamed the galaxy in their supership, the Phoenix, to battle the armies and giant robot monsters of the evil planet Spectra and its leaders, the mysterious Luminous Spirit and his general, the cruel Zoltar. This was the first Japanese cartoon series to be heavily revised by its American producers. Keyop was changed from a normal boy into an android, and Zoltar, a woman, became a man. Entirely new animation was produced to add two original characters, the humorous robot 7-Zark-7 and his robot dog, 1-Rover-1. The Japanese serial was set entirely on Earth, but new animation showed the Phoenix flying through outer space so the American program could claim that the adventures took place on different planets. (Japanese title: *Gatchaman, the Scientific Ninja Commando Squad.*)

Star Blazers. 1979–80, fifty-two episodes, color. In A.D. 2199, Earth was losing a war with the planet Gamilon. Earth was about to perish from radioactive pollution, when a message from the planet Iscandar offered to save the planet with a cosmic cleanser if a spaceship could be dispatched to get it. The ancient World War II battleship *Yamato* was rebuilt as the spaceship *Argo* and sent to Iscandar, battling through all the traps and enemy fleets of Gamilon and its decadent leader Desslok. Two years later, the restored Earth's government was about to retire the *Argo* when Earth was attacked by the even more powerful Comet Empire. Captain Derek Wildstar and his loyal crew took the *Argo* out against orders and saved the day after Earth's more modern space dreadnoughts failed. (Japanese titles: *Space Battleship Yamato* and *Yamato II.*) A third twenty-six-episode adventure (*Yamato III*) has recently been translated and added to the syndicated package.

Galaxy Express. 1980, theatrical feature. This movie was based upon a popular Japanese TV cartoon series. A future galactic civilization was so advanced that its spaceships could be made to look like old-fashioned railroad trains for "nostalgia" purposes, and the wealthy elite could have their minds transplanted into immortal metal bodies. Joey Smith, an orphan in his early teens, was assisted by a mysterious woman named Maetel in boarding the Galaxy Express, a train which toured the entire Milky Way galaxy. Joey's two goals were to find and destroy Count Mekka, the aristocrat who had killed his mother, and to reach a legendary world where he could get a metal body of his own for free. At each planetary stop, Joey had an adventure which served as a learning experience. He avenged himself against Count Mekka, but by the time he reached the planet of eternal artificial life, he had second thoughts about trading in his natural body. (Japanese title: *Galaxy Express 999*.)

Force Five. 1980–81, 130 episodes, color. This syndicated TV program consisted of twenty-six episodes each of *five* different Japanese series: *Danguard Ace, Grandizer, Gaiking, Spaceketeers,* and *Starvengers.* It was designed as a weekday cartoon package with each sub-series to be shown on the same day; *Danguard Ace* on Mondays, *Grandizer* on Tuesdays, etc. This set-up allowed viewers to watch *Force Five* as a daily program, or, if they preferred, to watch any one sub-series weekly. The original Japanese programs were all much longer adventure serials (*Grandizer* ran for seventy-four episodes), with definite beginnings and conclusions; but *Force Five* was edited for American TV cartoon standards, which, at that time, required episodes to appear interchangeably with no overall story development. *Grandizer* (Japanese title: *UFO Robot Grandizer*), *Gaiking* (*Gaiking, the Great Sky Demon-Dragon*), and *Starvengers* (*Combo-Robot G*) each featured heroes in giant robots who fought to keep Earth free from demonic space invaders who attacked with their own evil giant robots. *Danguard Ace* (*Danguard Ace, the Planet Robot*) concerned a space race between an Earth expedition (Danguard Ace was its giant robot military escort) and the unscrupulous forces of an interplanetary dictator, to claim a rich new planet. *Spaceketeers* (*Starzinger, the SF Sai-Yuki*) was a tongue-in-cheek SF retelling of the Chinese Sai-Yuki or Monkey King legend (c.f., *Alakazam the Great*). Three alien heroes joined forces to escort the beautiful human Princess Aurora past numerous cosmic monster dangers on a universe-saving mission to the center of the galaxy.

Thunderbirds 2086. 1983–84, twenty-four episodes, color. This program was obviously derived from Gerry and Sylvia Anderson's 1966 SuperMarionation British series, *Thunderbirds.* It featured the same plot, organizational names, and some vehicle designs as the Andersons' series, but a completely different cast of characters. In this universe, the International Rescue Organization was created and headed by Dr. Gerald Simpson as an anti-disaster force, to save lives anywhere on Earth or in the twenty-first century space colonies. International Rescue's Earth Base Command Center was the Arcology, a specialized city built on a Pacific island. Its rescue team was the Thunderbirds, a crack worldwide squad who operated seventeen vehicles (as opposed to the five in the Andersons' program) each designed for a special mission.

TEKKAMAN
THE SPACE KNIGHT
AN ALL-NEW FIRST-RUN ANIMATED ADVENTURE SERIES

Tekkaman the Space Knight *publicity brochure*

Episodes were independent, but most were set in outer space or undersea, and featured the Thunderbirds' five top pilots (Dylan Beyda, Jesse Rigel, Gran Hanson, Kallan James, and Jonathan Jordan, Jr.) averting some huge disaster. (Japanese title: *TechnoVoyager, the Scientific Rescue Unit*.)

Voltron, Defender of the Universe! 1984–85, 125 episodes, color. This current program consists of two separate Japanese giant-robot serials, renamed *Lion Force Voltron* and *Vehicle Team Voltron*. The original plan was to create *Voltron* from three programs, but the *Lion Force* episodes proved to be so popular that the American producer, World Events Productions, took the unprecedented step of commissioning the Tokyo animation studio to make new *Lion Force* episodes instead. *Voltron* also became the first American syndicated TV cartoon to be broadcast in Dolby stereophonic sound. Both plotlines were set in a far future in which Earth was the headquarters of a federation of peace-loving planets, the Galaxy Alliance, whose defense force was the Galaxy Garrison. In *Lion Force Voltron,* the GG sent a team of young Space Explorers to the planet Arus, which had recently been devastated by the evil King Zarkon of planet Doom. The Explorers' mission was to learn the secret of Arus's greatest defense, five robot lions which could merge into the super-robot Voltron. The team discovered that Arus was not completely destroyed, and that the martyred King Alfor's young daughter, Allura, was trying to restore Voltron and free her world from Zarkon's lash. The five became the new pilots of the five robot lions, and when one of them, Sven, was critically wounded, Princess Allura herself replaced him. The Lion Force story line followed the continuing fight of the four young Earth heroes (Keith, Lance, Pidge, and Hunk) plus Allura in Voltron against the Doom robeasts (robot-beasts) of Zarkon and his cunning son, Prince Lotor, and the black magic of Zarkon's witch-advisor, Haggar. In *Vehicle Team Voltron,* the Galaxy Garrison sent the spaceship *Explorer* to search for new habitable planets. This expedition was equipped with fifteen special vehicles (five each for Air, Land, and Sea Teams) which, thanks to the Voltron secret learned from Arus, could combine into the even mightier fifteen-component Vehicle Team Voltron. Drule, a tyrannical planet dying from radioactive pollution, also needed new worlds, but instead of sponsoring their own explorations, the

Drule leaders decided to simply steal the new planets found by the *Explorer*. Eventually, a Drule commander, Hazar, saw the wisdom of cooperating with the humans and their allies, but he was imprisoned for his pacifism. Hazar had to join a popular revolt against the Drule's evil emperor before he could call Voltron to evacuate his world's people just before Drule exploded. (Japanese titles: *Go Lion, King of Beasts,* and *Dairugger-XV, the Armored Squadron.*)

Tekkaman the Space Knight. 1984–85, thirteen episodes, color. This series was one of Japan's few costumed superhero TV cartoons, although it also included a giant robot. Mankind had explored the solar system by 2037 A.D. when the cruel interstellar Waldarians came blasting their way to us. Dr. Edward Richardson, head of the World Science Center, quickly altered his experimental one-man space exploration suit made of indestructible Tekka metal, and transformed it into battle armor. He chose young Barry Gallagher to wear this armor as Tekkaman the Space Knight, a superhero to beat back the Waldarians and their pompous Commander Randrox. Barry soon became the leader of a team which consisted of himself; Patricia Richardson, the professor's teenage daughter who piloted the transport Tekka shuttle; Pegase, the giant robot which held the Tekka armor when Barry wasn't wearing it; Andro, a humanoid ally from a world which was also fighting the Waldarians; and Mutan, an intelligent little animal from Andro's world who used her ESP powers to aid them. (Japanese title: same.)

Japan + Animation = Japanimation! Part 2
Starlog no. 106, May 1986.

Those who view television and motion pictures have recently seen an influx of Japanese high-tech animated SF drama on both the little and big screens. Giant robots, a mainstay of Japanese TV cartoons for more than a dozen years, have finally become "in" in the USA. American companies are buying the action-packed Japanese SF serials and transforming them into original programs such as *Voltron* and *Robotech* for the syndicated TV market.

This is the second part of an article which began last issue that surveys the Japanese SF cartoons which have already been translated into English— and released in America through 1985—while briefly noting some of the most popular SF cartoons with American fans which are so far *only* available in the original Japanese. It is not *absolutely* complete, since several "features" which are only condensations of TV serials, or random episodes edited together, have been omitted. There was a *Space Cruiser Yamato* feature two years before the *Star Blazers* adaptation. Several seventy-two-minute features appeared on pay TV during 1983; one, *Starbirds,* consisted of

254 ■ JAPANESE CULTURE IN ANIME

scenes from the forty-four-episode serial *Fighting General Daimos*. There have been "features" which were actually just unsold TV pilots, such as the original *Space Pirate Captain Harlock* and the *Captain Future* home-purchase cassettes. In general, titles which consist of less than 20 percent of the original Japanese works, or which consist of sample episodes which do not tell complete stories, have *not* been included here.

Robotech. March 1985, eighty-five episodes, color. Many Japanese TV SF serials haven't been brought to America because their plots and mood are considered too serious for American audiences. *Robotech* is the first attempt to present a drama for teen and adult viewers without trying to edit it down to a children's cartoon. *Robotech* consists of three separate but similar Japanese serials, rewritten to tell a single story which spans three generations.

The first sequence (Japanese title: *Macross, the Super Dimension Fortress*) began when a gigantic unmanned alien spaceship, the *SDF-1*, crashed on Earth in 1999. Ten years later, a scientific community had almost made the ship operational when the alien Zentraedi came to reclaim it. Automatic weapons on the *SDF-1* fired on the Zentraedi, who retaliated against Earth. An attempt by the humans to get the *SDF-1* airborne resulted in the ship making a "space fold" to the orbit of Pluto, with the whole community on board. The ensuing story was a soap opera of the developing personal relationships among the large, multi-racial cast: fighter Rick Hunter; Lisa Hayes, commander of the *SDF-1*'s bridge crew; Lynn Minmei, teenage entertainer and symbol of the humans' will to win; Max and Miriya, human and Zentraedi lovers; and many more. Major characters died and Earth itself was devastated during the war.

In the second sequence (Japanese title: *The Southern Cross, the Super Dimension Cavalry*), set a generation later, Earth was rebuilding itself when the Robotech Masters, creators of the now-destroyed *SDF-1*, came to recover the ship's Protoculture energy source. A new war resulted. This story followed the exploits of the young soldiers of the Fifteenth Squadron of the Alpha Tactical Armored Corps commanded by Dana Sterling, the daughter of Max

This two-part article is interesting today for its glimpse of some mid-1980s productions that never fulfilled their American distributors' hopes. *Tekkaman, the Space Knight* probably did not appear in more than ten cities throughout the United States and Canada, and in at least Toronto it was incorrectly announced as a sixth add-on to *Force Five*. *Captain Harlock and the Queen of a Thousand Years* and *Thunder Sub* never achieved their major releases during 1986. The publicity claim that *Warriors of the Wind/Nausicaä* had been a "box-office smash in Japan" was either a vast exaggeration, to put it politely, or an honest confusion with its critical acclaim. *Nausicaä* got excellent reviews and was not a financial failure, but it could hardly honestly be called a box-office smash. It is gratifying that all six of the mid-1980s fan favorites that had not been commercially released in America in 1986 have since become available at least partially in the home video market; we still lack the *Space Cobra* TV series. ■

and Miriya. The humans and the Robotech Masters essentially exhausted each other, leaving Earth defenseless against an invading alien species, the Invid, who came to cultivate the Protoculture as food.

In the third sequence (Japanese title: *Mospeada, the Genesis Climber*), an advance force returning to Earth after a generation of exploring space was annihilated by the Invid. The single survivor was young Scott Bernard, who rallied a guerrilla fighting force among the dispirited humans to renew the war against the Invid, until the main space fleet under Admiral Rick Hunter returned.

Harmony Gold U.S.A., the American producer, is currently commissioning the original Japanese studios to create 175 new *Robotech* episodes which will blend the three story sequences together more smoothly. The first sixty-five of these should be finished this year. An all-original theatrical feature, *Robotech: The Untold Story,* is planned for release. A home-purchase videocassette, *Macross: Volume One, Booby-Trap* presenting the first three *Macross* episodes in a version closer to the original Japanese program, was distributed in 1984.

TranZor Z. April 1985, sixty-five episodes, color. Dr. Demon was a master robot maker who intended to conquer the world. His weapons were his fearsome Machine Beasts, including the loathsome Slime Viper, which could dissolve anything. These Machine Beasts were led into action by Dr. Demon's two lieutenants: Devleen, "half man, half woman, and the worst of both," and Count Decapito, who wore an officer's uniform and carried his head under his arm. They were constantly thwarted by Dr. Davis's Volcanic Research Institute, a laboratory dedicated to using science to help mankind. The Institute's chief defense was TranZor Z, a giant robot warrior piloted by teenager Tommy Davis.

Tommy, the son of TranZor Z's inventor, was adopted by Dr. Davis after Dr. Demon murdered Tommy's father. Other regular characters were Tommy's step-sister Jessica (who had her own giant robot, Aphrodite A); Bobo, a school chum who insisted on building his own robot (the comical Bobo-bot); and the inevitable, obnoxious kid brother, Toad. Most episodes followed the same formula. One of Dr. Demon's lieutenants would appear with a new Machine Beast, Tommy and TranZor Z would be defeated in the first encounter, Tommy and Dr. Davis would analyze what went wrong while the Machine Beast closed in to utterly destroy the Institute or the nearby metropolis, and Tommy and TranZor Z would destroy the Machine Beast in a last-minute final battle while Devleen or Count Decapito escaped. TranZorZ, created by cartoonist Go Nagai in 1972, was the first of the dozens of Japanese TV cartoons to feature giant warrior robots which combined or transformed and established the stereotype of the hero-pilot who shouted his every action: "Hovercraft, link! Laser beams, fire! Rocket punch, go!" (Japanese title: *Mazinger Z.*)

Captain Harlock and The Queen of a Thousand Years. First broadcast September 1985 but planned for major release during 1986, sixty-five episodes, color. The wandering planet Millennia changed its location in space every thousand years. If its new position intersected an existing planet, it destroyed that planet. Millennia's scientists determined that its next shift would bring it into conflict with Earth, so the planet's matriarchal government began sending agents to Earth hundreds of years earlier to prepare for the invasion. Regular Millennia natives, dubbed the L'Metaal, were under the leadership of Princess Olivia, while a militaristic feminine plant species, the Mazone, did the dirty work.

By the eve of the attack in the late twenty-first century, Earth and its space colonies were under a single decadent Military Industrial Complex (MIC) government. Only a few men were alert enough to recognize signs of the coming invasion, and the Mazone began murdering them. The most active of them, Captain Harlock, set himself up as a space privateer to personally defend Earth and was immediately branded a criminal pirate by the government. Harlock and the crew of his *Arcadia* were forced to fight both the Mazones and MIC army of Colonel Kamaroff. Meanwhile, Princess Olivia—who had grown fond of the humans—found it harder and harder to reconcile their destruction with her conscience. She was especially impressed by the courage shown by young Christopher, whom she met after his scientist parents were killed by the Mazones. After the Mazones cruelly kidnapped Harlock's little ward, Maya, Olivia renounced her heritage and urged the L'Metaal settlers to help the humans against Millennia's evil leadership.

This complex serial was created from two separate Japanese programs, both by cartoonist Leiji Matsumoto—hence the same art style and similar themes. It was edited so that scenes from both programs are juxtaposed and connected by dialogue, even though the major characters do not appear together. The serial becomes, in effect, the story of a vast war, with the scene constantly switching back and forth between two fronts. (Japanese titles: *Space Pirate Captain Harlock* and *The Queen of a Thousand Years*.)

Thunder Sub. First broadcast November 1985 but planned for major release during 1986, twenty-seven episodes, color. Earth was living in peace by the mid-twenty-first century, when it was attacked by the Force of Death. Commanded by General Z, the Force had wandered about in a gigantic artificial planet, the TerrorStar, looking for a new home after their own world's destruction—until they found and invaded Earth. Colin Collins, son of Earth's commanding admiral, received from his dying father a pendant which held the secret power source of the top-secret Thunder Sub, a revolutionary submarine which could convert into a spaceship. Collins rallied the surviving naval cadets into a group to find the Thunder Sub and to help its commander, Captain Noah, put it into operation. Each episode pitted Collins and his Thunder Team in a new battle against General Z's ForceMen, while the Sub's crew learned its secrets in preparation for their final battle with the TerrorStar. (Japanese title: *Blue Noah, the Interplanetary Aircraft Carrier.*)

Warriors of the Wind. November 1985, home-purchase video feature. A thousand years from now, war and pollution had destroyed most of Earth. Spreading Toxic Jungles populated by giant, deadly insects covered the landscape. One of the few safe areas was the small Valley of the Wind. Young Princess Zandra felt that the new insect species had some intelligence, especially the titanic Gorgons, and might be willing to live in peace if humans stopped attacking them. Suddenly, war spilled into the Valley when an airship of the militaristic Kingdom of Tolmekula crashed there. Tolmekula's Queen Selina occupied the Valley with her army to recover it, then decided to use the Valley as a new base in her war with Placida. She also planned to burn back the Toxic Jungle. Zandra had to prevent this before the Valley and her people were destroyed in the fighting between Tolmekula and Placida, and before an attack on the Jungle brought the extermination of all mankind by the Gorgons. The original theatrical feature, written, designed and directed by Hayao Miyazaki, was a box-office smash in Japan and won animation awards around the world. The American version has more than twenty minutes cut from it, but even so, it won the first prize in the general category (films over thirty minutes) at the 1985 Los Angeles International Animation Celebration. (Japanese title: *Nausicaä of the Valley of the Winds.*)

The following programs, while *not* yet acquired for U.S. release, are still enjoyed by fans who are able to view the shows in their original Japanese:

Fist of the Big Dipper. This is what *Road Warrior* might have been like if Bruce Lee, rather than Mel Gibson, had been the star. A generation after an atomic war has destroyed civilization, communities are gathering again in the ruined cities, but are preyed upon by evil gangs of biker punks, ruthless survivalist armies, and mutated superhuman looters. Out of the desert comes Ken, a brawny mutant himself but dedicated to helping the weak. A martial-arts expert of supernatural deadliness, with deep scars in the pattern of the Big Dipper across his chest, Ken wanders with Bart and Lin, two young children under his protection, from town to town, freeing each with his mighty fists from its oppressors. The program's title, *Hokuto no Ken*, is a pun because Ken is the hero's name, but the word "ken" means "fist."

Space Cobra. Cobra is a happy-go-lucky retired master criminal living in an interstellar civilization of the thirtieth century. He has so much loot that he no longer has to "work" for a living. He can relax and play at being a Robin Hood, or aid damsels (always beautiful) in distress. Most of those whom he helps are being oppressed by really nasty villains, usually bosses in the Space Mafia or corrupt bureaucrats, so Cobra looks like a hero by comparison.

Space Cobra, based upon a popular comic-book series, was animated as both a TV series and a 3-D theatrical feature.

Mobile Suit Gundam. This 1980 TV series marked the maturing of the giant-robot genre. Before *Gundam,* the giant robots had been portrayed as superheroes in their own rights, with only a single person (the teen hero) "worthy" enough to be their pilot. Episodes were usually independent variations on the same "defeat the monster of the week" theme. *Gundam* (created by writer Yoshiyuki Tomino), however, is a serious, plausible SF serial in which giant robots are just big, futuristic military vehicles. Anyone with the proper training can fly them. The serial features literally dozens of sharply delineated characters. The two sides are not depicted as Good versus Evil but as two battling future nations. Some of the "enemy" soldiers are even more likable than some of the hero's buddies. The main characters are Amuro Ray—a teenager more or less forced against his will to become Gundam's pilot—and his counterpart on the enemy's side, Char Aznable, played as a charismatic "Red Baron" type. *Gundam* was so popular in Japan that its studio has just produced a sequel, *Zeta Gundam,* set seven years later.

Those Obnoxious Aliens. This is a comedy that has been described as an SF version of *I Dream of Jeannie* for teens, or as what the Archie series might have been if Sabrina, the Teenage Witch practiced her powers openly. Lum-chan, an outer-space teenager, is attending a Japanese high school as an exchange student. She develops a crush on Ataru Moroboshi, the would-be school stud who is usually hot for anything in skirts, but who prefers to avoid Lum because of her 100,000-volt kisses. Early episodes were built around Ataru's attempts to chase other girls without Lum's interference. As the series continued (it has so far yielded more than 200 TV episodes plus four theatrical features), more and more human and alien supporting characters were added until there is now a very large cast. The other students gradually accepted Lum as one of their own, and now all the students delight in figuring out ways to use Lum's space abilities to outwit the school administration.

Lupin III. Space Cobra, profiled above, is just a futuristic imitation of *Lupin III,* a very popular crime-comedy series which began as a comic book by cartoonist Monkey Punch in the 1960s. Lupin III is a suave, good-guy international master thief, the grandson of the famous French thief Arsene Lupin. He travels the world with his two partners, the gangster-style gunman Daisuke Jigen and the traditional samurai Goemon Ishikawa, stealing whatever he wants. To keep Lupin sympathetic, the people he robs are always obnoxious society snobs, crooked industrial tycoons, and evil criminals. The trio is constantly pursued by a Japanese agent of Interpol, Detective Keibu Zenigata. Many episodes revolve formulaically around the clever traps that Zenigata sets for Lupin, and the even wilier ways that Lupin escapes them, often with a large array of secret-agent supergimmicks. A wild card is the frequent presence of the beautiful jewel thief, Fujiko Mine, for whom Lupin is in lust. Lupin (and the audience) can never be sure when she's really helping him or when she's setting him up for a double-cross. The program is full of sight gags; in one episode, Lupin crashed a society costume party which was full of fat, balding men smoking cigars while wearing the costumes of American superheroes and Disney characters.

The Dirty Pair. In 2141 A.D., most of Earth's population is housed in gigantic city-buildings. The population is so dense that the government can barely handle social needs. Many private agencies have sprung up to take on part of the workload. One of these is the World Welfare Work Association, a cross between a private inquiry agency and an oddjobs-for-hire company; its motto is "I will solve any problem for you." The WWWA's agents in one complex are two lithe and overenthusiastic nineteen-year-old girls, Kei and Yuki. Their code name is the Lovely Angels, but they are known as the Dirty Pair to the weary authorities because they usually cause more problems than they solve. This is a humorous SF detective drama about the misadventures of the two girls as they confront a killer computer, track the kidnappers of an alien ambassador's daughter, and more. If you can imagine two of Charlie's Angels playing a Starsky and Hutch role in one of the towering urban monads of Robert Silverberg's *The World Inside,* you've got the general idea of *The Dirty Pair*—and the witty, wonderful world of Japanese animation.

A New Wind from the East
Amazing Heroes no. 118, June 1987.

The two largest comic-book-producing cultures in the world are America and Japan—not necessarily in that order. Until recently, the Japanese comics were more legendary than accessible to American readers. This has been due to the difficulties in transforming them to Western standards. Not only does the dialogue need to be translated, but the art needs to be reversed and sometimes rearranged. Often the speech balloons have to be redrawn in different shapes, which requires extensive retouching of the art. Japanese sound effects drawn into the artwork must be carefully redrawn in the Western alphabet. All of this is very time-consuming and expensive. This is why, up to now, Japanese comic books have been known in America only by their reputations and their influence, as seen in the work of such artists as Frank Miller.

Steps are finally being taken to improve this situation. Three paperback volumes of Takao Saito's *Golgo 13* series were published in English during the last half of 1986. These were produced in Japan for export to America.

This May, two American companies have simultaneously launched regular editions of four major Japanese titles. First Comics is publishing Kazuo Koike and Goseki Kojima's famous *Lone Wolf and Cub* samurai dramas, upon which the *Samurai Assassin* motion pictures were based. Eclipse Comics has started a new division, Eclipse International, to work in collaboration with Viz Communications (a new American division of Shogakukan, one of Japan's largest comic-book publishers) to release three of Shogakukan's hottest titles: Kaoru Shintani's *Area 88* (air force combat adventures), Sanpei Shirato's *Kamui* (Japanese feudal ninja dramas), and Kazuya Kudo and Ryoichi Ikegami's *Mai the Psychic Girl* (SF melodrama).

If these are successful, they could lead to a flood of Japanese imports. A tremendous backlog of material is available. Japan has been churning out comic books with circulations in the millions for the past twenty-five years. Not all of this is to American tastes (one title is about a young teen who joins the Japanese fast-food trade and dreams of working his way up to someday become a master sushi chef), but there is a large quantity of science-fiction adventures, secret-agent dramas, battlefield sagas, and similar material, which should be acceptable to American comics readers. This might not have been true a couple of years ago, when it seemed that Americans didn't want anything besides full-color costumed-hero titles. But now that black-and-white comics are beginning to be accepted by the general public, and high-quality comics beyond the costumed-hero category are beginning to catch on, the Japanese comics have a good chance to establish themselves.

Anyone who wants to know the history of the Japanese comic-book industry in detail ought to read Frederik L. Schodt's *Manga! Manga! The World of Japanese Comics* (Kodansha, revised edition 1986). Schodt traces Japanese cartoon art back to the seventh century, and the publication of newspaper comic strips and comic books back to the beginning of this century. The modern comic-book industry did not start until after World War II, when Japan fell under the cultural influence of the U.S. Occupation Forces. It was not until the late 1950s and early 1960s that Japanese comics

There are a couple of references in my articles of the late 1980s to the great popularity with American fans of *Cosmo Police Justy*. This was due entirely to the 1985 anime OAV, a short (forty-four minutes) but exciting interstellar drama whose cops-versus-mutant-villains plot was easy to follow even untranslated. It was one of the first anime titles that all of the early American anime companies went shopping for, but the rights were so ridiculously expensive that nobody could afford them. (This is a traditional indication in Japanese business language that the rights are actually unavailable for other reasons, which are nobody's business.) Viz did eventually publish the beginning of the *Cosmo Police Justy* manga by Tsuguo Okazaki in nine comic-book issues in 1988–89. The results bore out manager Horibuchi's fears; as a regular comic book, *Justy* was so similar to standard American space-adventure comic books that the fans wondered why they had ever thought the story was so great. ■

reached a level of quality and originality that enabled them to stand on their own as international comic-art literature.

Nineteen fifty-nine might be considered a landmark year in Japanese comics and cartoons. It was the year that Japanese publishers released the first weekly comics magazines, and found them to be very popular. It was at about this time that the first generation of postwar comic-book readers grew too old to be interested in children's comics any longer. The comics industry was faced with the choice of writing them off as having outgrown comic books, or of producing more mature comics that would appeal to adult tastes. The Japanese chose the latter course, and a whole new scope of comic-art literature opened up. (And, while it's outside the range of this article, it was in 1959–1960 that the first Hanna-Barbera TV cartoons reached Japan and inspired Osamu Tezuka to start the Japanese TV animated-cartoon industry.)

In America, there are roughly 400 comic-book magazines being published. Most of these are monthly or bi-monthly titles, with twenty-five to thirty pages of story per issue. In Japan, there are far fewer separate magazines, but most of them are extremely thick weekly, bi-weekly, or monthly titles. They run to 300 pages or more per issue, and contain many different stories. However, each magazine is keyed to a specific age or interest group. There are comics for infants, for young boys, for young girls, for teen boys, for teen girls, for young men, for young women, and for adult men (over thirty), and for adult women. Within each magazine there is a variety of complete stories and serial installments. These range from action/adventure through human-interest to humor. The average story or serial installment is about thirty pages, although there are occasional short novels or novels of 100 pages or more. The economic realities of producing this much comic art on a weekly basis, and selling the magazines at prices that the average reader can afford, have held the Japanese comics industry to black-and-white printing.

These are the famous "telephone directory sized" Japanese comic books. They are extremely popular. Most of them have circulations of a million copies or more per issue, while in America the circulations of the most popular comics has dropped to less than a quarter-million. However, this is only half of the picture of the Japanese comics industry. These magazines are printed on cheap paper and are essentially throwaway publications. The worthwhile and popular stories are then reprinted on high-quality paper as paperback books, with full-color dust jackets. Comic-art specialty bookshops in Japan look more like American science-fiction specialty bookstores than American comics shops. There is a small section of current magazines at the front, but the shelves are filled with current printings of comic-art paperback books of 200 to 400 pages. These include both "novels," which may be serialized over several volumes, and "short story collections," which may include several separate comic-art stories that were drawn in the 1970s, the 1960s, or earlier. *Good* comic art in Japan tends to stay in print. This does not mean that every story that reaches the reprint-book stage is guaranteed of remaining in print forever. There are saturation points; some artists and themes do go out of style. But the chances are much better in Japan than in America that, once a story gets past the magazines into a book, it will continue to sell well for many years. Also, just like American paperbacks, a book that goes out of print for awhile may be reprinted a few years later, or come out in a new edition from a different publisher. So Japanese fans can find most Japanese comics that have ever been written with relative ease. Talented writers and artists, and their publishers, can count on sales and royalties from these books for most of their lives.

If all of the worthwhile comics are reprinted as high-quality paperbacks, why does anybody bother with buying the throwaway magazines in the first place? The publishers go out of their way to make them attractive to the public, because these are the raw-material mines from which the high-grade book-quality nuggets are extracted. The magazines are deliberately sold at a loss to make them cheap compared to the books. The anthology format offers a variety of story types and art styles. The magazines are also current; their stories reflect the latest popular interests and themes. Some magazines include brief articles on topical events such as current hit movies and TV programs, pop music, sports, the latest cars and motorcycles, and the like. The fans of a particular author's work or of a particular ongoing story series can read the new weekly or biweekly installments, which will not be collected into a new paperback volume until several months later.

Above all, the readers are made to feel that these are *their* magazines, and *they* are important—as they are. Competition is fierce, and the readers are the judges. These weekly and monthly magazines are, to paraphrase George Burns's comment about vaudeville, the place for amateurs to work the lousiness out of their systems and to gain experience. They are the training grounds for new cartoonists; they are an experimental theater where established cartoonists may try out new styles or change-of-pace works. Three- hundred-page weekly comics take a tremendous volume of art to fill, and nobody expects it all to be great. Each issue includes a readers' poll postcard. The readers are constantly urged to send them in so that the editor will know which stories they liked best, which series and which artists the public wants to see more of. The magazines for young teens have fan-art sections where readers can have their own sketches of their favorite characters printed. Today's twelve-year-old reader who sends in an amateur drawing may be a promising new artist in just five or six more years. The editors of the magazines often write back to the fans who seem to possess talent, to encourage them and to offer serious artistic criticism. This can establish a friendship and loyalty that may soon bring a creative young artist to that magazine rather than to a rival.

To the publishers and artists, the magazines are an investment. The payoff is in the book reprints. The biggest hits can literally sell millions of copies. Even if they aren't that popular, they can sell steadily over the years and bring in continual profits for no additional work. Mitsuteru Yokoyama's *Iron Man No. 28* (American title: *Gigantor*) was drawn in the 1950s and is very crude by today's standards, but it is still in print and still selling.

Books in Japan traditionally state the dates of their first printings and their current printings. Many comic-art volumes show that they have been around for ten or twenty years, and are up to their fortieth or fiftieth printings. The amount of money that writers/artists can get for new comics (for the magazines) is a matter of individual negotiations with the publishers, based upon how talented and popular the creators are. The standard royalty to the creators for the book reprints is 10 percent of the cover price per copy sold. So if an artist has a single book which sells 100,000 copies, and it costs the equivalent of $3, his or her earnings are $30,000. Most successful artists have many books on sale, not just one, so the money keeps flowing in. Then there are the animated cartoon royalties, the merchandising royalties. . . .

The publishers do not own comic-book properties in Japan. They are owned by the creators. Despite this, the publishers and their editors exercise a large influence over what gets written and drawn. The standard practice is that the publisher of the comics magazine in which a story first appears is also the publisher of its book reprints. If the creators get 10 percent in royalties on every book sold, the publisher gets the other 90 percent. The publisher doesn't need to own the copyright to cash in on it. The publisher has a strong incentive to stay on the friendliest terms with its writers and artists, so that they will not move to a rival company. It's to the creators' advantage to stay on good terms with the editors, because they are the ones who are in closest contact with the public. They know what's hot and what's not. Artists and writers develop their own stories without heavy editorial control, but the editors are always there to suggest new plot concepts or to let an artist know which of his or her characters are the readers' favorites, so that the artist can plan intelligently.

The editors have the duty to keep their companies' magazines coming out on schedule. Most publishers have several weekly, bi-weekly, and monthly comics that require 300 pages or more of art per issue. An editor may have to get in 3,000 pages of original art per month to fill all of those deadlines! This is the basis for the public image of the editor as a cross between a whip-cracking slave driver and the Readers' Friend who is working himself to death to get Your Favorite Comic out each week. The artists themselves have fun portraying themselves and their editors in good-guy bad-guy roles. On one occasion the artist may be chained to his studio desk, drawing feverishly while the editor screams at him to work faster. It was widely understood that Dr. Mashirito, the comedy-relief mad scientist in Akira Toriyama's *Dr. Slump* series, was Toriyama's unflattering pastiche of his tyrannical editor at Shueisha's weekly *Jump Comics* magazine. Yet on another occasion the artist may portray himself as out partying while the frantic editor is hiring private detectives to find him and get the pages that are needed for next week's issue.

This latter image may be more accurate than the former. Japanese artists are notorious for taking on more work than any human is capable of producing. Comic books may be the property of their creators rather than their publishers, but this does not mean that they are produced by only one person. A beginning artist may work alone, but successful artists are dependent upon several assistants to meet all of their deadlines. It's a sign of prestige for a title to be signed as the work of a "studio" rather than an individual. The comics of Osamu Tezuka, the creator of *Mighty Atom* (*Astro Boy*) and literally hundreds of other titles, are copyrighted in the name of Tezuka Productions. Go Nagai, the creator of the first giant-robot-with-human-pilot comic, *Mazinger Z* (*TranZor Z*), signs his work "By Go Nagai and Dynamic Productions." Akira Toriyama's books are the work of himself and Bird Studio. (Toriyama, translated literally into English, is Birdmountain.) The apotheosis of this system may be Takao Saito and his Saito Production Co., Ltd., which has a staff of over a dozen. This includes one assistant whose job is to maintain a large art file of famous landmarks, vehicles, weapons and similar military hardware, animals, and other objects whose depiction

Different Standards: Japanese Manga Versus American Comics

It's been mentioned that Japanese standards of tastefulness and propriety differ from American standards. For instance, a scene from *Mai the Psychic Girl*, in which Mai reflects on her blossoming sexuality while playing with her psychic powers, was dropped from the American edition of the comic. (It would have gone between pages 29 and 30 of the first issue.)

Eclipse publisher Dean Mullaney explained that when Eclipse and Viz were preparing the first issues of their titles, he warned Viz's manager, Seiji Horibuchi, that these two pages would require a "For Mature Readers" label on the cover. It was Horibuchi's decision to drop the pages, since Viz wants the comic to reach as many potential readers as possible. (In the case of *Kamui*, there was too much violence and nudity to even attempt to work it down to a "General Audiences" level.)

See also Hikaru Toyama's *Watch Out, Pink!*, an unlikely candidate for early American publication. It's a *Splash*-type comedy that deals with a supernatural girl who is in the form of a cat. When the cat's tail is pulled, she turns into her real (and nude) self, much to the chagrin and embarrassment of her teenage male friend.

Both instances probably seem rather sweet and innocent to the reader. But the judgment of the Eclipse editors with regard to Americans' tolerance of this sort of hijinx is almost certainty on target—more's the pity.

(First's *Lone Wolf and Cub*, like *Kamui*, is being listed as "recommended for mature readers"—although First will not be putting a warning on its covers.)

in Saito's comics with photographic accuracy is a hallmark of Saito's work. Saito is proud to depict his studio as being run like a TV or movie studio, with himself as the director. He acknowledges buying story ideas from staff or freelance writers, and that the majority of his art is drawn by his assistants. He feels that he exercises enough artistic and editorial supervision over the stories that he is still artistically entitled to call it his own work.

Other popular artists, at least officially, write their own stories and dialogue, sketch their own rough page layouts, and personally draw all the main characters. Their assistants only draw the backgrounds and do clean-up work. These studios usually consist of a few of the artist's relatives (brothers or uncles) to handle business and production details, and several young artists who are serving an apprenticeship to gain experience before attempting their own comics. When a new artist appears on the Japanese comics scene whose work looks strongly similar to that of a prominent artist, the chances are good that the newcomer is a former assistant of that artist. Even with this production system, however, Japanese artists are usually so heavily committed to drawing hundreds of pages per month that if they ever take time off to visit a fan convention or go on a vacation, their deadlines suffer and their editors lose face with their publishers and their readers.

A first-hand description of this situation was recently provided through an interview with Kaoru Shintani, the artist of the *Area 88* aerial-combat comic series. *Area 88* has been produced in thirty-page weekly episodes since 1979, and is up to twenty-three paperback volumes so far. In February 1985 the first *Area 88* animated-cartoon featurette was released for the home-purchase video market. Later in 1985, when the second fifty-seven-minute animated cartoon came out, Shintani's publisher produced a glossy 152-page *Area 88 Graffiti* art album filled with full-color cel reproductions from both movies and a "gallery" of Shintani's color cover paintings.

Now these Japanese comics are coming to America. Why now? That's the decision of the Japanese themselves. Takao Saito's *Golgo 13* "graphic novels" (Saito disdains to use the work "comics" for his works because of its juvenile connotations) are being prepared in Japan under his own supervision. Distribution in America is being handled by Books Nippan, a Japanese-community bookshop in Los Angeles which is the major importer of Japanese comics and animation-art books for the American market. (The Los Angeles shop is actually a branch of a large bookshop chain in Japan.) *Golgo 13* was launched at the 1986 San Diego Comic-Con, where Saito appeared and signed autographs while the manager of Saito Production Company (his uncle) and Books Nippan's manager promoted the new series to the distributors at the convention.

The three (so far) English-language volumes are not direct translations of any of the sixty-three (so far) Japanese volumes. They are highlights: stories selected which should have the greatest appeal with American readers. *Golgo 13* is an "Executioner" style assassin, but one with no moral justifications. He will kill virtually anyone for payment. The American edition acknowledges that he has no national or political loyalties and has killed businessmen, criminals, and statesmen all around the world. However, the stories selected all show him killing targets such as neo-Nazis and Soviet spies whose demise can be expected to be looked upon favorably by American readers. Presumably the stories in which *Golgo 13* kills CIA agents and other targets who might be regarded sympathetically by Americans will be saved until after the series has been safely established.

Dean Mullaney, the publisher of Eclipse Comics, states that Eclipse has wanted for years to publish some of the better Japanese comics, but none of the Japanese were interested in licensing their rights. Under a licensing arrangement, the American publisher would have total control to re-edit or even redraw the comics in any way that it saw fit. Last year Shogakukan, through its new Viz Communications subsidiary, approached Eclipse with a co-publishing proposal. Under this arrangement, Viz Communications and Eclipse's new Eclipse International division are equal partners in preparing the American editions. The two companies have been holding numerous close editorial consultations during the past year. Eclipse can advise, but the final decision is up to Viz's manager, Seiji Horibuchi, in San Francisco. Original covers are being designed by Horibuchi for the Eclipse International line, and prepared by Shogakukan in Tokyo. All of the titles involved are published originally by Shogakukan in Japan, and Shogakukan is representing the individual creators. Most of Eclipse's negotiations have been through Viz Communications, but Kazuki Tanaka, the head of Shogakukan's Comics Division, has flown over from Tokyo to personally inspect Eclipse's offices and operating procedures. Also, the manager of Akame Productions, the name under which Sanpei Shirato and his brothers produce the *Kamui* title, visited to find out how their work will be presented to the American public. He was so favorably impressed that he has authorized Viz to use the Akame Productions name on the original covers for the American editions, to signify that they have the Shiratos' approval.

The first three titles—*Kamui, Mai the Psychic Girl,* and *Area 88*—have been carefully selected and edited. All are titles that Eclipse and Viz feel will be popular with Americans, but they also stretch American reading habits a little. *Kamui* is a historical drama set in Japan's feudal past. There has never been a comic book like it in America. *Area 88* is a modern air-combat melodrama set in North Africa. The setting is an imaginary nation, but it is intended to convey the feeling of the Middle East political tensions and wars of the late 1970s. This is also completely original, unless one wants to make tenuous comparisons with some of Milton Caniff's work or with generic American war comics. *Mai the Psychic Girl* is about teenage mutants. Well, nobody can claim that this is a new concept to American comics. However, Viz and Eclipse feel that *Mai*'s approach to this concept will raise some eyebrows. For one thing, *Mai* is one of the modern Japanese adventure comics that is being produced for a teen girl readership, not the boys market. (In actuality, there is a large overlap.) *Mai* contains nuances that will be fresh to readers who think that teenage mutants equals teenage costumed-heroes.

Shogakukan does have comics which are closer to what American readers expect a comic book to be like. American fans who visited the Viz display at the 1986 San Diego Comic-Con expressed a lot of interest in Tsuguo Okazaki's *Cosmo Police Justy*. But Viz and Eclipse felt that they did not want to launch three new "standard" comics which simply happen to be by Japanese artists rather than Americans. They prefer to take a slight risk and begin immediately to introduce Americans to concepts beyond the costumed-hero and space-opera genres.

Area 88 and *Mai* are being published from the beginnings of those titles. *Kamui,* on the other hand, starts at what is the middle of volume four of the Japanese edition. Mullaney says that this decision was made by Viz because Shirato's art and storytelling abilities were not as polished at the beginning of this title as they became later. There are enough excellent volumes from no. 4 on that it would be futile to never get that far because of showing Shirato's earliest work to the American readers and having them reject it.*

Kamui, Mai, and *Area 88* were launched in May to take advantage of the traditionally strong summer comics market. Sales and readers' reactions to them will be closely studied, while three more titles are prepared to debut around November. Mullaney emphasizes that Eclipse and Viz will not be waiting for six months to study sales reports and decide what to do next. The next three titles will be ready for publication by that time. Only if they have totally misread the comics market and the first three titles fail to sell at all (which they do not expect), will the next three be canceled. Viz Communications, with Eclipse's cooperation, is engaging in a long-term plan to make Americans conscious of Japanese comic-art literature. They presently expect to release new titles in waves of three at roughly six-month intervals. However, they do plan to hold an evaluation of how things stand at the end of their first six months, which should help them to fine-tune their long-range plans.

Also, some of the titles that they will publish will not be open-ended in the American sense. *Kamui* and *Area 88* are open-ended, but *Mai* is a comic-art novel which is complete in about fifty-five chapters (six volumes in Japan). Unless *Mai*'s authors decide to continue her adventures, Eclipse

---

* Shirato considers *Kamui* his life's work and has been working on it for over two decades. The series consists of *The Story of Kamui* (*Kamui Den*) and *The Legend of Kamui* (*Kamui Gaiden*). Shirato started *The Story of Kamui, Part I* in 1964 and finished it in 1975. He began *The Legend of Kamui, Part I* in 1966. After a long interruption, he began *Part 2* in 1982 and recently finished it. He is at present preparing for *The Story of Kamui, Part 2* which will start later this year or next year.

should finish the serialization of this title in about two years at its biweekly schedule. There are other comics in Shogakukan's library that have been wrapped up, and their creators have gone on to newer titles. Eclipse and Viz will follow this practice—which, of course, is no longer new to American comics since authors such as Dave Stevens with *The Rocketeer* and Alan Moore and Dave Gibbons with *The Watchmen* (not to mention Frank Miller) have gotten readers used to the idea of a title designed to be complete in a preset number of issues.

The Japanese comic-book industry got its modern start when the Japanese discovered the American comic hooks that GI's left behind. Many Japanese authors have continued to be influenced by American comics concepts over the years (if only to parody them). Now the Japanese are giving Americans the opportunity to discover something fresh in their own works. What could the American comics scene be like as a result, five years from now? Ten years from now? Will John Byrne or George Perez look forward to producing 150 pages of art or more each month? Will black-and-white comics drive color comics off the market . . . ?

Full Circle: Japanese Animation From Early Home Studios to Personal Workshops for Home Video
Witty World International Cartoon Magazine no. 1, Summer 1987.

Japanese animation has moved into a new phase with the explosive growth of the home-purchase video market since about 1985. Animation has been tremendously popular in Japan since the 1960s, which has permitted the rise of some major studios. Now, due to the home-purchase market, young animators do not have to join the major studios to be able to create. They can obtain financial backing from the home-video industry to set up a small art workshop and make cartoons on an individual basis.

Under modern circumstances, this is a return to the situation under which the earliest Japanese animated films were produced. The first was made by Seitaro Kitayama in 1913, and during the silent film era, several animation enthusiasts set up their own home studios. Both cartoon animation in the style of United States artists such as John R. Bray and the Fleischer brothers, and paper cut-out, silhouette animation in the style of the German films of Lotte Reiniger, were popular.

These artists worked primarily for the love of animation, either alone or with one or two friends. To obtain funding and audiences, they established contacts with government bureaus and theatrical film distributors. The government subsidized educational films, and the motion-picture distributors were glad to get entertainment shorts for little more than the cost of the raw film stock.

The earliest Japanese cartoon still commonly available is Zenjiro Yamamoto's *The Mountain to Abandon Old Folks,* done in 1924 and based upon a folk tale. Most early Japanese animation was derived from Asian folk tales, or were simple animal fantasies, showing mischievous monkeys, frogs, foxes, or badgers playing tricks on one another.

During the 1930s, as national militarism increased, it became harder for the amateur animators to obtain film materials unless it was for works to support the war effort. Kosei Seo's 1935 *Sankichi Monkey's Attack Corps* is drawn in the style of the Disney and Warner Brothers' cartoons of the early 1930s, but it shows a Japanese Army corps depicted as enthusiastic, efficient monkeys in Imperial uniforms, overrunning a fortress clumsily defended by Chinese pandas.

The quantity of animated films grew as the war intensified, because the government felt an increasing need for short, domestic propaganda films. The first two animated features were made in 1943 and 1944, when the Imperial Navy commissioned Mitsuyo Seo to put together a small staff and produce dramatic fantasies to rouse the patriotic spirits of children.

The second feature, *Momotaro: Divine Warriors of the Sea,* shows the Imperial Navy, in the form of funny animals, constructing a South Pacific jungle airstrip, engaging in training, and finally conquering a base of the British in the New Guinea area. This seventy-four-minute feature is primarily cartoon animation, with a short paper-silhouette sequence. The action is much more realistic than in the 1935 comedy short film, giving this feature the look of a serious Naval recruiting film.

But not all war-era animation was militaristic. Two fine-art classics were produced during this period: Wagoro Arai's 1940 paper-silhouette *Fantasy of Madame Butterfly,* based on Puccini's opera, and Kenzo Masaoka's 1943 cartoon, *The Spider and the Tulip.*

After the war, and through the 1950s, animation returned to private initiative. Noburo Ofuji's 1952 *The Whale,* made with multicolor cellophane

The beginning of this survey, about the first animation produced in Japan, is embarrassingly error-filled. At the time this was written in early 1987, practically the only information available on Japanese animation was in books aimed at the fans who were interested in its modern history, the theatrical features from 1957 on and the TV animation from 1963 on. Data on pre-1957 animation was almost impossible to find, until the 1989 publication of the *Animage* magazine staff's *The Art of Japanese Animation II: 70 Years of Theatrical Films.* Errors that I made include stating the first Japanese animation was by Seitaro Kitayama in 1913; it was by Oten Shimokawa in 1916, released in January 1917. Kitayama's first cartoon was also released in 1917, four months later. Zenjiro Yamamoto was that animator's real name, but all his work was produced under the name Sanae Yamamoto, which is how he is commonly referred to (just as Shotaro Ishinomori is commonly called by that professional name even though his actual name was Onodera).

Cont. on p. 270

silhouette cut-outs, won praise from Pablo Picasso. Sound began to be used more effectively than just for background music. Tadahito Mochinaga introduced puppet animation in the first Japanese animated TV commercials in 1953. Mochinaga's TV work and some educational films soon enabled him to produce fine-art puppet animation which won prizes at international festivals.

In 1951, Japan's first major animation studio, Toei Animation Company, was formed, but its first feature was not until 1958, *The White Snake Enchantress,* directed in 1958 by Taiji Yabushita. This and Toei's next few features were obvious attempts to emulate Walt Disney's cartoon features, using Asian legends and historical themes.

Earlier, the American Occupation had settled into Japan, bringing a flood of American comic books, films, and animated cartoons. Easily accessible to the Japanese public, they had a tremendous influence on the post-war generation.

The first Japanese to begin working in the Western comic book style was Osamu Tezuka, a young doctor who dropped his practice to become a full-time cartoonist. From the late 1940s through the 1950s, Tezuka drew infants' picture books, political cartoons, adult humor for men's magazines, posters, advertising art, and just about every other form of drawing possible in the print medium. But his juvenile comic books were the most influential.

Among Tezuka's most popular heroes were Mighty Atom, a young robot living in a futuristic world, and the noble lion, Leo. Tezuka set up his own cartoon shop and hired many young assistants to help him. This shop became a rallying point for young cartoonists, many of whom became influential cartoonists and animators in the next decade.

About 1960, Tezuka was impressed by the success of the first limited-animation TV cartoons from America's new Hanna-Barbera Productions. He felt that he had enough know-how and established characters to produce similar cartoons for Japanese TV, and in June 1961, he established a new animation studio, Mushi Productions, for that purpose.

The "Kosei" Seo referred to as a 1930s animator is the same Mitsuyo Seo who produced and directed Japan's wartime propaganda animated features. The year 1951 was when the Toei Company (live-action) movie studio was created; the animation studio (Toei Doga) began in 1956 when Toei bought Nihon Doga (Japan Animation), a small independent studio that had been struggling since 1948, and poured money into it. ("Anime" did not replace "doga" as the common word for animation until the late 1960s, when Japanese studios and distributors began doing business regularly with American and European companies where "animation"—often with various Romance-language variations—was the almost-universal word.) Osamu Tezuka was not a doctor who "dropped his practice" to become a cartoonist; he made that career decision before starting a medical practice (although he did have a medical license). ■■

Mushi's first TV cartoon series, *Mighty Atom,* (U.S. title: *Astro Boy*) premiered on New Year's Day 1963. It was an instant success, completely transforming animation in Japan, by showing there was a vast public demand for comic-book-style action-adventure in modern or futuristic settings. It also showed that the public would accept TV-quality animation; limited but fast-paced. This effectively put the individual artist-animators out of business, since they could not produce cartoons fast enough for the TV market, but enabled several fledgling animators to get the financial backing to start their own studios.

During 1963, six animated TV series went on the air: two from Mushi Productions; three from TCJ, another new studio; and one from a hastily formed TV unit within Toei Animation. Most of these programs were boys' SF/fantasy adventures, although one, *Wizards' Village,* was a late-evening experiment in adult, ribald humor. By 1965, there were twelve TV cartoon series from seven studios, including Japan's first color TV cartoon, Tezuka's *Jungle Emperor* (U.S. title: *Kimba the White Lion*).

The quantity and types of subject matter continued to grow. The SF melodramas, aimed at boys, were matched by programs in which young girls gained magic fairy-queen powers.

Another popular genre has been the sports soap opera, although this is a subject that would seem more suitable for live-action production. Favorites among these have included *Attack No. 1,* a 104-episode serial between 1969 and 1971, about the tribulations of a girls' volleyball team; and the current *Touch,* based upon Mitsuru Adachi's comic-book melodrama about a high-school baseball team, made up of ninety-five animated TV episodes as of February 1987. There have also been animated Japanese historical (samurai or ninja) adventures, detective comedy/dramas, and at least one Western.

Animation has always been an ideal medium for tales of fantasy. In the United States this has usually remained limited to funny-animal short comedies, and sanitized TV superhero adventures. But in Japan, animation has been used for more dynamic SF dramas, which began with Go Nagai's *Mazinger Z,* produced by Toei Animation in 1972.

Flagrantly promoted by Japan's toy industry, they proliferated to the point of self-parody, as when Tatsunoko Production Co. made the 1981–82 *Gold Lightan,* which featured a squad of friendly robot heroes, modeled after a variety of U.S. cigarette lighters. Most of these robot heroes were featured in world-threatening scenarios that had enough dramatic violence, including the tragic deaths of sympathetic supporting characters, to make them unacceptable to the American TV market. This was the reason why Japanese TV animation largely disappeared from U.S. screens, despite the popularity of such 1960s programs as *Astro Boy, Kimba the White Lion, Gigantor, Speed Racer,* and *Marine Boy.*

This was a pity, because there were some more serious dramas amid the animated robot-versus-monster wrestling matches. The 1974 *Space*

Battleship Yamato TV serial (U.S. title: *Star Blazers*) was a SF retelling of World War II as a future space war, with naval-style spaceship battles and suspenseful political intrigue. *Yamato* was popular enough to spawn several TV and theatrical sequels, not to mention imitators.

The 1978–81 *Galaxy Express 999,* based upon Reiji Matsumoto's comic-book series, was an allegorical space fantasy about a young boy who rode a galactic passenger train to the stars, in quest of a legendary planet where he could have his brain transplanted into an immortal robot body. This ran for 113 weekly episodes, and also spun off some TV specials and two major theatrical features.

Nippon Sunrise's 1979–80 *Mobile Suit Gundam,* written by Yoshiyuki Tomino and designed by Yoshikazu Yasuhiko, was a landmark production in animated SF storytelling. *Gundam* was a futuristic war epic that concentrated on realistic personal relationships and character development of a large human cast, rather than subordinating the characters to the SF settings and machinery. The giant robots were relegated to background military vehicles. *Gundam* started a trend that has developed to the point that has almost completely supplanted the more simplistic robot-as-superhero programs.

A similar situation developed with theatrical animation. In the early 1960s, Toei Animation produced about one theatrical feature a year, usually a traditional children's tale, such as *Puss in Boots,* or *Treasure Island,* with a mostly funny-animal cast. As animation increased in sophistication on TV, Toei, and then other studios, began to produce theatrical features for more mature audiences. Several popular TV cartoon series were followed up with theatrical sequels presented in higher-quality theatrical animation. By the 1980s, cartoon features were so popular that Toei Animation was producing two or more a year, and a number of TV animation studios began submitting features to other theatrical distributors. Features started expanding to two hours or more, and adding sequences in 3-D or in computer graphics.

Beginning in the early 1960s, there was a rash of new animation studios, primarily to enter the TV cartoon market. Among those establishing successful operations were Tokyo Movie Shinsha (TMS), Tatsunoko Production Company, Nippon Animation, Nippon Sunrise, and Studio Pierrot.

However, the biggest has continued to be Toei Animation Company, which, as of 1985, employed over 1,000 artists at its Tokyo studio and more at a branch in Seoul. Toei's production included five or six weekly, half-hour, TV cartoon series for the Japanese market (almost 400 episodes per year, or more than one per day), plus subcontract animation for numerous U.S. TV and theatrical cartoons (mostly for Marvel Productions), two or more theatrical features for the Japanese market, some original video arcade game cartoons, and TV commercials.

It was not necessary to have a large physical studio to be a big animation company, thanks to the growth of a multiplicity of small specialized film production enterprises. The Japanese *This Is Animation 1984 Yearbook* listed eighty-nine companies in Tokyo which were engaged in some aspect of animation production: ink and paint, voice casting and recording, sound mixing, etc. One of the largest of the newer studios, Nippon Sunrise, consisted physically of only a relatively small business office which coordinated a huge volume of work through a network of commercial services all around Tokyo, each of which accomplished one aspect of the overall production.

Also, a new type of animation studio appeared, which specialized in "pen for hire" work. Two leading examples were Top Craft and Madhouse, which produced animation under commission for other companies to put their names upon. Top Craft turned out most of the animation for Rankin-Bass in the United States, such as *The Hobbit* and *The Last Unicorn.* Among Madhouse's productions have been a multimillion-dollar theatrical feature (1984), based upon E. E. Smith's SF series *The Lensman,* which appeared under the label of Kodansha. These pen-for-hire studios have enabled businesses outside the animation field to become prestigious cartoon producers. Haruki Kadokawa, the live-action film producer, has turned out an animation feature under his own name each year since 1983. The Tokuma Publishing Company, Japan's largest publisher of books and magazines for the animation fan market, began to release original animated features under its logo in 1984.

Not low-budget works, both Kadokawa and Tokuma cartoons have been lavish and spectacular, crafted by top animation directors. Indeed, the best theatrical cartoon directors, such as Hayao Miyazaki, Taro Rin, and Gisaburo Sugii, seem to be doing more work today through the pen-for-hire studios for sponsors outside the animation industry than for the regular animation studios.

Meanwhile, individual artist-animators who started the Japanese industry may have lost their preeminence, but they certainly did not disappear. They always were more interested in animation for its artistic sake than as a business venture. After the 1950s, their personal short films tended to disappear from the public theaters and instead to turn up at international animation festivals. Since they were not designed to be box-office attractions, their creators had no commercial restraints in expressing their imaginations.

Among these fine-art animators, Kihachiro Kawamoto has become one of Japan's leading exponents of puppet animation. His films usually depict traditional Asian literary and artistic themes. Yoji Kuri, a cartoonist working in a sparsely abstract art style, is notorious for satirical and risqué short-shorts, and although Osamu Tezuka pioneered the TV animation industry, he is more prominent as a fine-art animator than as a producer of commercial animation. It has been said that Mushi Productions would not have gone bankrupt, and that his current Tezuka Productions would be more successful, if Tezuka paid more attention to business rather than entrusting his TV productions to subordinates and locking himself in a private studio to work on his award-winning fine-art films.

This was the state of Japanese animation at about 1984. In 1985, the home-purchase video market swept over the animation industry like a volcanic lava flow. Suddenly, there were many video distribution companies that needed half-hour and feature-length "products" to fill cassettes and disks. Much existing theatrical and TV animation was put onto this market, but the distributors were also looking for original works.

An *Animation Video Collectors Guide,* published in December 1986, stated that the first Japanese animation home-purchase cassette was released October 31, 1981, and that 1,004 titles had been put on sale by this guide's press date. Most of these appeared during the past two years. The market is strong enough to support a monthly magazine devoted to home-purchase animation alone, *Anime V.* Of the twenty new cassettes and fifteen disks released each month, about three-quarters of these are releases of old TV and theatrical animation, both Japanese and foreign, and one-quarter are new titles created especially for the Japanese home-purchase market or for simultaneous theatrical and home-purchase release.

Some of the video distribution companies are subsidiaries of theatrical companies such as Toho. Thus, the home-purchase cartoons are also given a brief theatrical run, for the extra box-office revenue and as extra advertising for the cassettes and disks. This practice is of dubious artistic merit, since the home-purchase cartoons are usually designed for viewing on home TV screens, and expanding them to theatrical-screen size magnifies all the flaws of TV-quality limited animation.

Very few of these original works are produced by the big animation studios, most coming from special production units which have been put together by young animators with the backing of a video distribution company, to make one title alone. Some of these young cartoonists use these projects to try to establish a new studio, but others are content to assemble a staff to produce a single title, then split apart and look for another individual project to join. New animators today are as likely to join this gypsy pool of drifting talent as they are to join the staff of an established studio.

Japan's earliest animators could get support from theatrical distributors to create personal eight- to fifteen-minute films; today's animators can get support from the home-video distributors to put together temporary mini-studios and produce cartoon features running ninety minutes or more.

The home-video market has also made possible the production of animation that is not suited to general public audiences. Included is a large quantity of cartoon hard-core pornography and brutal dramas that specialize in extreme violence and gore. This is not to say that these subjects are themselves valueless, because there have been some pornographic or violent animated tales that do show good art, strong story values, and clever wit. One of the best is the bloody *Vampire Hunter D,* a fantasy in the tradition of Britain's Hammer horror features. There is also animation designed for special-interest audiences, such as bikers or cat-lovers. One popular comedy is *The Supergal,* an SF farce that spoofs both costumed superheroes and women's wrestling. At the high end of the scale is the beautiful *Angel's Egg,* described in *Animation Video Collectors Guide* as, " . . . animated art rather than a story. It could be brought to a SOHO gallery theater." It's rather like imagining Leonardo da Vinci's "Mona Lisa" as an animated painting lasting eighty minutes: beautiful, but short on plot.

To sum up, at the beginning of 1987, the home video field seems to be attracting most of Japanese animation's artistic creativity. The monthly *Anime V* magazine shows an increasing quantity of home-purchase cartoons in production. However, excellent theatrical features are still appearing. Hayao Miyazaki's 124-minute *Laputa: The Castle in the Sky,* released in August 1986, has been acclaimed by many veteran animation buffs as the greatest cartoon feature ever made. In the fine-art field, personal animated short films by Japanese artists are still winning awards at European and American film festivals.

Only the TV cartoon field has been shrinking and showing less vitality. It's been several seasons since the TV cartoons introduced any fresh concepts. The current programs basically offer only bland variations on the standard juvenile cartoon formulas. Even so, the quantity of Japanese TV animation is still the greatest in the world.

Japan's Anime
Animation Magazine no. 36, August 1995.

Anime—the Japanese word for animation—is fantastically popular in Japan. A February 1995 pocket guide "for the animation fan" lists addresses of seventy-five production studios, seventy-three of which are in the Tokyo area.

Japan's most prestigious motion picture studio is Studio Ghibli. To the public eye, this is the personal atelier of two leading creators, Isao Takahata and Hayao Miyazaki, who write and direct their own films.

Takahata's *Pom Poko,* a fable about woodland animals using magical powers to sabotage a construction project which threatens their forest, was Japan's number one domestic motion-picture grosser in 1994, whether animation or live action. It was the Japanese film industry's submittal to the 1994 Academy Awards for Best Foreign Film. Miyazaki's *The Crimson Pig* set the domestic record in 1992. His 1988 *My Neighbor Totoro* got a brief American theatrical release in 1993 and a major home video release in 1994. But Studio Ghibli's latest feature, *Mimi o Sumaseba* (*If One Listens Very Closely*), released in July, is the first to be directed by one of their assistants, veteran Ghibli animator Yoshifumi Kondo. It is a serious junior high school girl's soap opera with no fantasy element (other than brief dream sequences).

Most Japanese theatrical animated features are big-screen spin-offs of TV programs or computer and video games. One 1994 hit was *Street Fighter II*. American anime fans who have seen it generally prefer it to the recent Jean-Claude Van Damme star vehicle, *Street Fighter*. There is a steady stream of theatrical features based on TV cartoon hits such as *Doraemon, Dragon Ball Z, Lupin III, Sailor Moon,* or *Slam Dunk,* most of which have new theatrical releases scheduled for 1995.

A June Japanese TV log lists forty-three weekly TV cartoon series with many in prime-time slots. The majority are by major studios which also do subcontracting work for American TV cartoons such as Toei Animation and Tokyo Movie Shinsha (TMS), or which have sold programming to America such as Tatsunoko Productions (*Speed Racer* and *Robotech*). Unlike the 1980s when TV animation was dominated by giant-robot and space-adventure dramas (slanted toward action toys and model kits for boys), the majority of today's series are aimed at younger children and those interested in high school affairs. There are school soccer and baseball team serials. Others revolve around more-or-less realistic adolescent life, but which escalate into fantasies about the just-turned-teen who suddenly gains great abilities and must figure out how to handle them. This is the biggest genre of the moment. There have always been one or two "magical young girl" programs about awkward, shy girls who get some device which gives them superpowers or turns them into rock idols. *Sailor Moon,* about a high-school girls' club that must save the earth from other-dimensional villains, has set new records in popularity, with 138 episodes so far. DIC is just now introducing it to America. *Tondeburin* (roughly *Burin, the Fantastic Flying Pig*) is a more humorous variant, about a girl, Karin, who is suddenly able to transform into a superheroine—a cute, anthropomorphic super-pig! How do you turn that into a social asset with your high-school peer group? (Forty episodes as of June.)

Fantasies for young children are perennially popular. *Doraemon,* about a robot cat (a toy from the future) who becomes the guardian angel of a nerdy elementary school boy, has been churning out new episodes since 1979. There are over 640 so far! Another TV granddaddy is *Dragon Ball Z,* which began in 1986 (as just plain *Dragon Ball*) and is now up to 268 episodes. It is a fast-moving, light-hearted spoof of action-adventure and costumed-hero fantasies with *Home Alone*-style violent humor. Selected *Dragon Ball* episodes, judiciously edited by Seagull Entertainment, are also due for American syndication this fall.

The giant-robot/space-adventure dramas are down to only two: *Gundam W* (the umpteenth variant on the original trend-setting *Mobile Suit Gundam* of 1979–80), and *Macross 7* (a sequel to the 1982 *Macross,* which became the first part of American TV's 1985 *Robotech*). There is usually at least one cartoon adaptation of a famous Western fairy tale or literary work, such as *Anne of Green Gables*, which is serialized weekly on TV for a year. *Snow White* recently wrapped up at fifty-two episodes, and has been replaced with *Animated International Fairy Tales*.

Where the action is really at is in the home-video market. The Japanese have created their own English word/acronym, OAV (for original animation video), to describe new animation produced just for home-video.

These OAVs—from one to two dozen new titles each month—are the hot-spot for the attention of the hard-core anime fans, both in Japan and the United States. This is where much of the best, and the worst, in creative animation appears. OAV animation is simpler, cheaper, and more flexible in length than theatrical animation. A concept that can't be stretched for a full TV series can be packaged as a single OAV, or a limited series. This has permitted the production of some imaginative titles, often by small, new studios or special teams assembled to produce a single title. OAV production is the new training ground for young animators.

Originality is still in the minority. The OAV market is dominated by remakes and sequels to TV hits of the 1960s and 1970s, in the "hard-edged" style of the 1990s and with (usually) uninspired imitations of action/adventure movies. OAVs are taking the route of the American costumed-hero comic books in pushing the envelope toward more exciting action (for example: more graphic violence and gore), stronger language, and more exaggerated T and A. This has led to animated science-fiction and horror thrillers that make the *Alien* or *Friday the 13th* series look tame, to sexual comedies with varying degrees of explicitness, to "crime dramas" that are practically animated snuff movies.

These OAVs are the gold mine for the American home-video market of Japanese animation that has been developing in the past few years. Small companies, started and run by fans themselves, generally can't afford the American rights for a lengthy TV cartoon series from a major animation studio, but they can afford a short OAV series from a small studio or from a video company. Two recent examples are *Casshan, Robot Hunter*, a 1993 remake in four half-hour OAVs of a 1973–74, thirty-five-episode TV series; and *8 Man After*, a new four half-hour OAV sequel to the original 1963–64 *8 Man* TV series (both imported by Streamline Pictures, and distributed by Orion Home Video).

The growing acceptance of the "Japanimation" (an early fan-created word which American fans today are replacing with the correct Japanese word, "anime") may soon reach the point that titles now felt by major TV programmers and video distributors to be too ethnic for general American tastes will be reconsidered. DIC hopes *Sailor Moon*, featuring teen superheroines in costumes clearly derived from Japanese schoolgirls' uniforms, will prove to be an animated equivalent of *Mighty Morphin' Power Rangers*.

A Capsule History of Anime
Animation World Magazine 1, no. 5, August 1996.

(Note: for convenience, where English-language titles have been established for Japanese films, they are used in this article even when they are not accurate translations. For example, the 1958 theatrical feature *Hakuja Den*, or *The White Snake Enchantress*, is referred to by its 1961 American title, *Panda and the Magic Serpent*.)

The earliest Japanese animation was by individual film hobbyists inspired by American and European pioneer animators. The first three Japanese cartoons were one-reelers of one to five minutes each, in 1917. Animation of the 1920s ran from one to three reels. A few were imitations of foreign cartoons, such as the *Felix the Cat* series, but most were dramatizations of Asian folk tales in traditional Japanese art styles.

Notable silent-era animators include Oten Shimokawa, Junichi Kouchi, Seitaro Kitayama, Sanae Yamamoto (whose 1924 *The Mountain Where Old Women Are Abandoned* seems to be the earliest anime title still extant), Yasuji Murata, and the master of paper silhouette animation, Noboru Ofuji. Most of them worked in small home studios, though they came to be financed by Japanese theatrical companies which provided production money in exchange for distribution rights.

During the 1930s, folk tales began to give way to Western-style fast-paced humor. These gradually reflected the growing influence of Japanese militarism, such as Mitsuyo Seo's 1934 eleven-minute cartoon *Private 2nd-Class Norakuro*, an adaptation of Suihou Tagawa's popular newspaper comic strip about an unlucky dog soldier in a funny-animal army. After Japan went to war in China in 1937, the need to get productions approved by government censors resulted in a steady stream of militaristic propaganda cartoons. In 1943, the Imperial military government decided Japan needed its first animated feature. Mitsuyo Seo was authorized to assemble a team of animators for the task. Their seventy-four-minute *Momotaro's Gods-Blessed Sea Warriors* was a juvenile adventure showing the Imperial Navy as brave, cute anthropomorphic animal sailors resolutely liberating Indonesia and Malaysia from the buffoonish foreign-devil (with horns) Allied occupiers— too late for even wishful dreaming, as it was barely released (in April 1945) before the war's end.

Animation returned to the individual filmmakers right after World War

By 1996 more was known to American anime scholars about pre-giant-robot anime, but some details were still wrong due to conflicting or erroneous information in Japanese articles. Pioneer animators were still being credited with each other's films. Yasuji Murata, not Mitsuyo Seo, was the creator of the 1934 cartoon *Private 2nd-Class Norakuro*; Seo made the 1933 *Sankichi Monkey's Attack Corps*. ■

II. However, they were hampered for the next decade by the slow recovery of the Japanese economy. They also found their amateur films competing with the polished cartoons from American studios, which poured into Japan with the Occupation forces. The first Japanese full-color animation did not appear until 1955. It soon became clear that the future of Japanese animation lay in adopting the Western studio system. (However, independent anime artists have never disappeared. Thus, the first Japanese animator to achieve international name recognition was Yoji Kuri, whose art films of usually less than a minute each appeared in international film festivals throughout the 1960s and 70s.)

Attempts to create American-style studios began right after the war, but the first real success did not come until Toei Animation Co. was organized in 1956. Its earliest leading animator, Yasuji Mori, directed Toei's first notable short cartoon, *Doodling Kitty,* in May 1957. But to the general public, Japan's entry into professional animation came with the company's first theatrical feature, *Panda and the Magic Serpent,* released in October 1958.

Toei's first few features followed the Disney formula very closely. They were produced a year apart; they were based upon popular folk tales—Asian rather than European—and the heroes had many cute, funny-animal companions. The first six were distributed in America, usually a couple of years after they were first shown in Japan. The second through sixth (with their American titles but Japanese release years) were *Magic Boy* (1959), *Alakazam the Great* (1960), *The Littlest Warrior* (1961), *The Adventures of Sinbad* (1962, all five directed by Taiji Yabushita), and *The Little Prince and the Eight-Headed Dragon* (1963, directed by Yugo Serikawa with an avant-garde stylized design by Yasuji Mori). Unfortunately, these were not successful in the United States and Japanese theatrical animation disappeared from America for the next two decades—unless it could be sold to TV as an afternoon children's movie.

Something Unexpected

But *Alakazam the Great* led to something unexpected. Although directed by Yabushita, it was based upon a popular 1950s comic-book adaptation by Osamu Tezuka of the ancient Chinese Monkey King legend. The young Tezuka was Japan's most popular comic-strip and comic-book artist during the 1950s, who virtually invented Japan's modern manga industry. Since the movie used his plot and visual style, he was consulted on its adaptation and became involved with its promotion. This caused him to switch his attention from comic books to animation.

Tezuka was also impressed by the appearance in Japan of the first Hanna-Barbera television cartoons of the late 1950s, which led him to conclude that he could produce limited animation for the new TV market. More importantly, he realized from the popularity of his comic books—especially such futuristic titles as *Astro Boy*—that there was a strong demand for modern, fast-paced fantasy, which the animation establishment, with its narrow focus on fairy tales in antique storybook settings, was completely ignoring.

As a result, Tezuka organized Japan's first TV animation studio, Mushi Productions. Not counting an experimental art film, *Stories on a Street Corner* (1962), its first release was a weekly series based upon *Astro Boy,* which debuted on New Year's Day 1963. It was such an instant success that, by the end of 1963, there were three more television animation studios in production and Toei Animation had opened a TV division. By the end of the 1960s, the popularity of TV science-fiction action-adventure anime was so overwhelming that Toei began to alternate it with fairy-tale fare for its theatrical features.

Television animation became much more popular in Japan than it ever was in America. This was largely due to Tezuka's influence. He had drawn in just about every medium available, including childrens' picture books, romantic comic-book soap operas for womens' magazines, risqué humor for mens' magazines, and political cartoons for newspapers. He established the attitude that cartooning was an acceptable form of storytelling for any age group; this is in sharp contrast to the United States, where the attitude became, "Cartoons and comic books are only for children." Tezuka himself brought sophisticated adult animation to movie theaters with his 1969 art feature *A Thousand and One Nights* (which left in the eroticism of the original *Arabian Nights*) and the 1970 *Cleopatra* (a time-travel farce with anachronisms such as Julius Caesar as a cigar-chomping, American-style politician). By the 1970s, TV studios such as TCJ (Television Corporation of Japan), Tatsunoko Production Co., Tokyo Movie Shinsha (TMS), and Nippon Animation, to name just the major ones, were churning out animated mystery dramas, older-teen sports-team soap operas and Western literary classics such as *Heidi, Girl of the Alps* (directed by Isao Takahata) and *The Diary of Anne Frank,* along with traditional juvenile fantasy adventures.

Giant Robot and Outer Space Adventures

There was a flood of toy-promotional fantasies, featuring action-heroes for boys and "magical little girls" who could transform into older-teen heartthrobs for girls. Among the most influential was Toei's adaptation of comic-book artist Go Nagai's *Mazinger Z,* the first of the sagas about a gigantic flying mechanical warrior controlled by an (invariably teen) human pilot to defend Earth against invading space monsters. This combined the dramatic aspects of knights in armor battling dragons, with fighter pilots in aerial combat against enemy armies. *Mazinger Z* and Nagai's direct sequels *Great Mazinger* and *UFO Robot Grandizer* ran for 222 weekly episodes from 1972 through 1977. By the mid-1980s there had been over forty different giant-robot anime series, covering virtually every channel and every animation studio in Japan. It was these shows, subtitled on Japanese-community TV channels in America, that started the anime cult among American fans in the late 1970s.

Closely related were the futuristic outer-space adventures which began in 1974 with *Space Battleship Yamato,* basically a wish-fulfillment replay of World War II, with the united Earth armies (Japan) fighting from planet to planet across the galaxy (Pacific) against the conquering Gamilon invaders. *Yamato* was fortunately timed for the explosive popularity of space operas following the importation of *Star Wars* from the United States; a series of *Yamato* TV-series and theatrical-feature sequels followed. During the late 1970s and early '80s, the hottest cartoonist in anime was *Yamato's* creator Leiji Matsumoto, with TV cartoon series and theatrical features based upon his other space-adventure manga, such as *Space Pirate Captain Harlock, Galaxy Express 999,* and *The Queen of 1,000 Years.*

Miyazaki and Takahata

By the mid-1980s, anime had been dominated by TV production for two decades. Two developments changed this. One was the return to prominence of theatrical feature animation through the films of Hayao Miyazaki and Isao Takahata. The two were friends who had worked both together and separately at various anime studios in Tokyo since the 1960s.

In the early 1980s, Miyazaki began a science-fiction comic-book adventure, *Nausicaä of the Valley of the Winds,* for *Animage,* an animation-fan magazine from one of Japan's largest publishers, Tokuma. This led to a Tokuma-financed feature, which Miyazaki also directed. The 1984 *Nausicaä* was a smash success, resulting in Tokuma subsidizing a new animation studio, Studio Ghibli, for the personal theatrical features of Miyazaki and his friend Takahata.

Studio Ghibli has released an average of a feature a year since then, alternating between the productions of Miyazaki and Takahata: Miyazaki's *Laputa: The Castle in the Sky* (1986), *My Neighbor Totoro* (1988), *Kiki's Delivery Service* (1989), and *The Crimson Pig* (1992), and Takahata's *Grave of the Fireflies* (1988), *Only Yesterday* (1991), and *Pom Poko* (1994). Many of these have become Japan's top-grossing theatrical films, live-action or animated. Takahata's *Pom Poko* was also submitted as Japan's candidate for being an Academy Awards nominee for the Best Foreign Film Oscar. Some other notable theatrical features during the past decade include writer-director Katsuhiro Otomo's cyberpunk thriller *Akira* (1988) and director Mamoru Oshii's adaptation of Masamune Shirow's SF manga novel *Ghost in the Shell* (1995).

Original Animation Video

The second development was the emergence of the home-video market. Beginning in 1984, animation began to be produced especially for this market (resulting in a Japanese-created English term, OVA or OAV—for original animation video—which has been adopted by American anime fandom as well). OAV animation is usually higher in quality than TV animation, but not as rich as theatrical animation. As with most aspects of popular culture, 90 percent of it is little better than trash, while 10 percent may be brilliantly imaginative and innovative. Video productions can run from a half-hour to two hours, and from independent titles to serials of from two to ten videos. OAVs are often better than either movies or television for stories that are too long for a standard theatrical release, but not long enough for a TV series. The OAV market is not subject to the public standards for television, so it often becomes notorious for its most lurid examples of violence and pornography. At the other extreme, some of its better examples (such as the *Patlabor* near-future police-procedural dramas or the *No Time for Tenchi* teen SF comedies) have become so popular and acclaimed that they have led to their own anime TV series and theatrical films. There are anime-fan magazines devoted to just the anime video market, which list an average of forty to forty-five new releases per month, one-third of which are brand-new OAVs, with the rest being reissues and video releases of theatrical, TV, and foreign titles. These OAV titles are the main source for the anime being released in America today, since their licenses are more affordable than those of expensive theatrical features or of multi-episode TV series.

Today, animation in Japan is considered to be in a creative doldrums. Due to the sheer volume of the output over the past three decades, the good ideas have "all been used up." The current trend is for OAV remakes of anime favorites of twenty or thirty years ago, featuring a flashy '90s art slant and a more "sophisticated" (cynical) story line—very similar to the American trend for turning classic live-action TV series into big-budget theatrical films. But many of the titles and concepts that are stale in Japan are still fresh to American audiences, so anime still has an encouraging growth period ahead of it in the United States.

Anime: Subliminal Lessons in Japanese History
The Right Stuf 2001–02 Catalog (published October 2001).

Is watching anime educational in terms of learning Japanese history, or just confusing? Most anime does not pretend to be factual, and you can usually understand all you really need to know to follow the plot. But some historical references keep reappearing. Are these based upon real events and famous people, the Japanese equivalents of Davy Crockett or the conflicts between the Native Americans and the U.S. Cavalry? Or are they based on famous but imaginary events and characters, the equivalent of Lemuel Gulliver's discovery of Lilliput or the adventures of the Three Musketeers? Knowing the background can increase your understanding and enjoyment of anime.

For example, many historical dramas involving samurai and ninja during the 1600s have references to an invincible swordsman named Jubei or Jubei Yagyu, or to a whole Yagyu clan. In some they are the heroes, in others the villains. (*Ninja Scroll; Jubei-chan: The Secret of the Lovely Eyepatch*; the manga and live-action *Lone Wolf and Cub* series.) Were they samurai or ninja, or both; and were they real or mythical?

The historical Yagyu clan was founded by Jubei's father, Munenori Yagyu, an expert samurai in the service of Ieyasu Tokugawa, founder of the Shogunate in 1603. Ieyasu appointed Munenori as sword instructor at his newly created Shogun's court. Jubei, born in 1606, was raised as his father's assistant and was also a master of the Yagyu's Shinkage school of swordsmanship. Jubei and other students of Munenori were often sent as representatives of the Shogun's court to teach swordsmanship to the sons of local Daimyo and their retainers. When Munenori died in 1646, Jubei became the Yagyu clan lord. But he died himself in 1650. One of Jubei's younger brothers, Retsudo, appears as the major villain in Kazuo Koike's *Lone Wolf and Cub* epic saga, which begins in 1655.

There was a lot of feudal plotting at the beginning of the Tokugawa era. Many lords believed that the Yagyus were less expert sword instructors than agents of the Shogun's spy service, and that they were really sent out to look for lack of loyalty to the new regime. Pro-Shogun popular legend soon built Jubei and his compatriots in the Yagyu sword academy into samurai who genuinely possessed supernatural dueling abilities, who wandered throughout Japan as loyal agents for the government. Anti-Shogun legends showed the Yagyu clan as the Shogun's ruthless secret army of assassins. Samurai and ninja were traditionally deadly enemies, but in some dramas the Yagyus publicly posed as honorable samurai while sending out squads of ninja to do their dirty work. Japanese nineteenth- and twentieth-century popular fiction has shown Jubei and other Yagyus in both versions of the legends.

How about Oda Nobunaga, the warlord during the sixteenth-century Era of Civil Wars who almost succeeded in unifying Japan until he was doublecrossed by one of his own commanders and died in 1582? His most loyal deputies, Toyotomi Hideyoshi and Ieyasu Tokugawa, completed the unification in 1603. Nobunaga is depicted in many historical anime like *Yotoden/Wrath of the Ninja* and live-action movies like the 1996 *Legend of the Devil* as demonic, either possessed by devils or having sold himself to evil spirits in order to conquer and destroy Japan. However, *Time Stranger* (a 1986 Kadokawa anime movie not yet released in America, not the better-known *GoShogun: The Time Etranger*) shows Nobunaga favorably as a wise general and potential statesman who, if he had lived, would have modernized Japan instead of isolating it and freezing its culture as Tokugawa did. In an alternate history under a Nobunaga Shogunate, Japan might have developed naturally as an Asiatic world power during the eighteenth and nineteenth centuries, forestalling the European takeover of East Asia in the nineteenth century.

The reality was that Nobunaga was quick to adopt the firearms of the first European traders to enter Japan. He allowed Spanish Jesuit missionaries into Japan so he could study their Western technology more than for their religion, and as a counter to the reactionary Buddhist priesthood that usually supported his adversaries. Nobunaga apparently felt that he was strong enough to retain control over the changes that they would bring to Japan. Ieyasu Tokugawa feared the Western influences and banned them, leading to the famous Shimabara revolt of 1637–38 in which 37,000 Japanese Catholic converts who refused to renounce their new faith were slaughtered after a three-month siege by the armies of the third Shogun, Iemitsu.

Asian religion and folklore have always seen evil spirits lurking everywhere, which is why Europeans were originally depicted as "foreign devils" with an oni's horn. Nobunaga's eager acceptance of European firearms, and his hospitality to Portuguese traders and Catholic missionaries made it easy for his enemies to depict him as selling out to or being possessed by demons who sought to use him to take over Japan. *Ninja Resurrection: The Revenge of Jubei* shows Jubei as the Shogun's agent who infiltrates the Shimabara Christians and discovers that their leading priests are actually disciples of the Devil. This is not modern anti-Christian prejudice as much as a dramatization of the Shogunate's fears (after listening to the English Protestant seaman Will Adams) that Catholicized Japanese would be ordered by their priests to overthrow their traditional nobility and turn Japan over to the Pope.

The legendary Queen Himiko has been shown throughout anime from the serious (*Phoenix: Yamato*) to the silly (*Flint, the Time Detective*) as the first or the greatest ruler of the prehistoric Yamato kingdom, who began the unification of Japan into a single nation. Did she really exist? Written Japanese history started in the A.D. 700s and is considered fairly reliable only back to about A.D. 400, when Yamato's primacy was already well established. It is difficult to separate history from mythology earlier than that. Ancient Chinese documents indicate that Himiko may have been a real ruler around the mid-200s A.D., though more like a tribal high priestess or a leader of a council of clan chiefs than a queen in the modern sense. More disturbing to Japanese tradition is a disputed theory that Himiko may not have been a native Japanese, but the leader of a tribal migration from Wa in modern Korea who conquered and intermarried into the Yamato tribes.

Many SF dramas are set in a futuristic Neo-Tokyo or MegaTokyo built upon the ruins of the twentieth-century metropolis after it was destroyed in a near-future devastating earthquake (*Voltage Fighter Gowcaizer*), or in the rubble of the still-destroyed Tokyo (*Suikoden: Demon Country*). Stories set in today's Tokyo may contain allusions to the Great Kanto Earthquake, which Japanese viewers will automatically know all about.

The Kanto region is the coastal area of Honshu that includes Tokyo and Yokohama. On September 1, 1923, an 8.3 magnitude earthquake leveled Tokyo. Not only was the quake considerably greater than America's most famous, the April 1906 San Francisco quake (7.8), but Tokyo was an older and more densely compacted city whose wooden buildings were flimsier and extremely vulnerable to fire. Within hours, almost 100,000 people were dead and most of Japan's national capital was burned to the ground.

But this great tragedy was also a great opportunity. Japan had emerged from World War I as the only world power in East Asia. The government wanted to turn its capital city from a feudal town into a modern metropolis that could compare favorably with the major cities of Europe and America. But tradition and powerful conservative interests made it difficult to clear away historic buildings and widen streets. The earthquake created a blame-free go-ahead for massive urban renewal. Cynics quipped that if the earthquake had not occurred naturally, the government would have had to manufacture one. This attitude is dramatized in horror fantasies such as *Doomed Megalopolis,* where the quake is deliberately caused by the wizard Kato who awakens the giant dragon under the ground (the cause of earthquakes in Asian folklore) to destroy the old city for evil purposes.

A more subtle reflection of modern Japanese attitudes toward national governments can be seen in many SF plots in which a united Earth government attempts to carry out a massive coverup. A good example is *Macross/Robotech,* when the inhabitants of Macross Island in the SDF-1 return to Earth after a year lost in space, and learn that the government will not allow them to land because it had already told the world that they had all been killed. Many American conspiracy dramas feature high-ranking villains in the government, but they are usually depicted as individual rogues or a small conspiracy. In Japan it is usually the whole government, all the time, that is lying to the people. This is a legacy of centuries of rule by a nobility that usually cared little for the lower classes, culminating in the military-dominated government of the 1930s and wartime 1940s which everyone knew regularly lied to the public.

If you are intrigued by a historical reference in anime, information is usually easy to find. Anime is designed to be enjoyed by the average public, not historical experts, so most references are to events and characters that are so well-known that they can be found without much trouble in encyclopedias, general histories of Japan, or Internet Web sites through a search engine. Knowing the background will make the characters and events more meaningful the next time you encounter them.

Refighting World War II
Anime Archive column in *Newtype USA* 2, no. 9, September 2003.

A frustrating aspect of program debates at conventions is that statements are often made which you do not have the chance to disagree with, because the discussion goes in other directions before you can speak up. That just happened to me at Anime Expo 2003.

The program event was "Academic Study of Anime, Manga, and Fandom," moderated by Mikhail Koulikov. Its topic was that, if university students can earn their Ph.D.s writing theses on "the *Star Trek* fan culture," there is as much if not more scholarly value in the study of anime and manga and its fan culture. Comments from the audience were that the international licensing of anime and manga (and its related merchandising) is currently one of Japan's leading economic exports, and that the cultural rise of anime began with the introduction of giant robots and similar advanced mecha action figures in the early 1970s. This was what enabled anime to evolve from the "children's cartoon and toy" market of the 1960s into the more respectable and profitable teen/young adult pop culture market of the 1970s onward.

Then someone theorized that this was a deliberate part of Japan's whole economic development of the 1970s and 1980s. Couldn't the portrayal of highly advanced SF mecha through popular cartoons have been a promotion of Japan's dynamic industrial growth and its planned economic leadership of all Southeast Asia (not to mention the new global electronics technology market)? This would mean that all of those TV series about giant robot battle suits piloted by heroic Japanese youths were intended to encourage the Japanese public to support this goal, and to subliminally assert Japan's leadership in other Southeast Asian nations whose peoples watched Japanese TV cartoons. The debate swirled into different directions before that statement could be answered.

There may be enough of a connection between the rise of mecha-based anime and Japan's economic/technological growth during the 1970s to support a doctoral thesis. But it seems to me that the mecha is a result and example of this growth rather than a cause of it. The mecha boom arguably began with the first TV anime series to feature giant robots with human pilots, and to show closeups of these highly detailed and transforming machines: Go Nagai's and Toei Animation's *Mazinger Z,* which premiered in December 1972. By December 1982, ten years later, there had been forty-one different anime series (with plenty still to come) featuring giant robots with humans inside them, either as solo mecha or which linked together to create bigger mecha. *Getta Robo, Brave Raideen, Combattler V, UFO Dai Apollon, Gloizer X, Zambot 3, Mobile Suit Gundam, Go Lion,* and lots more up to the biggest of all which was originally planned as a parody of giant robots, *Super-Dimensional Fortress Macross* with a whole city inside it. This does not count the anime series that featured mecha but without giant battle suits such as *Casshan, Space Battleship Yamato,* or *Gat-Tiger* (a has-to-be-seen-to-be-believed cross between *Speed Racer* and *Getta Robo:* five racing cars that could click together at 300 mph to form the giant Gat-Tiger racing car).

These were certainly deliberately planned and aggressively advertised, but by toy manufacturers to sell increasingly complex and expensive action figures to more mature consumers, rather than by national financial experts as part of a master economic plan. Those more mature and affluent consumers existed by the mid-1970s because Japan had completed its economic recovery from World War II by the late 1960s and was moving forward into a new boom period (which led to the "bubble economy" that burst at the end of the 1980s). The anime market may have added to this growth, but it was not really a significant part of what created it.

Was there a deliberate subliminal message in the anime of the 1970s that the Japanese people were confidently assuming the economic and cultural leadership of Southeast Asia and the world? There *was* a constant theme through most of the popular anime of that decade. But it was not of Japan taking charge of the world as much as it was of Japan's defending itself against that world. Practically all of the mecha anime plots were SF metaphors for refighting World War II to defend Japan (and Japanese cultural traditions) against the invading armies of Western social influences. In many, the invaders were literally demons from outer space: the Hundred Demon Empire led by fanged commanders with horns, or similarly grotesque freaks. In *Space Battleship Yamato,* Earth (Japan) will become extinct if the resurrected *Yamato* cannot restore its purity (cultural identity) despite all efforts of the haughty space invaders (thinly disguised Europeans) to destroy it. In *Science Ninja Team Gatchaman,* it is the G-Force (based in Japan) who must save Earth (Japan) from conquest by the foreign invaders. This was a message that played extremely well in Japan, so much so that the same plot could be used over and over. But it was not a plot that projected an image of Japan's intent to assume social and commercial leadership over the broader international community. Anime would probably not be the success that it is today if it had not evolved on its own rather than being guided as part of some vast economic plan.

Less, or More, Than Human
Anime Archive column in *Newtype USA* 2, no. 3, March 2003.

Masamune Shirow's *Ghost in the Shell* was a blockbuster success, both as a 1989–90 manga novel (American edition 1995) and as a 1995 anime theatrical feature (American release March 1996). It has never lost its popularity, and it is hot again thanks to its manga sequel, *Ghost in the Shell 2: Man-Machine Interface* (American edition throughout 2003) and news of its TV "side story" version, *Ghost in the Shell: Stand Alone Complex* (twenty-six episodes starting in October 2002 in Japan) and forthcoming second theatrical feature, *Innocence: Ghost in the Shell,* scheduled for spring 2004.

Ghost's popularity rests on both the excellence of its visual presentation, and on the intelligence of its thought-provoking plot. Major Motoko Kusanagi is a futuristic government agent who is a cyborg. The story leaves her origins vague, but the plot strongly implies that she used to be fully human and is now little more than her mind/intelligence in a completely artificial body. She is assigned to track down an international computer hacker, the Puppet Master, who can control people by implanting false memories in them. It turns out that the Puppet Master is not human; it was some country's top-secret Artificial Intelligence program which became self-aware, escaped into the global computer network, and insists that it is as much a "real person" as any biological human. This forces Kusanagi (and the audience) to consider whether she is still human or not—and if not, is she less or more than a human?

This was, and still is, a revolutionary relaunch of an old stereotype comparable to the rebirth that *Mobile Suit Gundam* gave to the giant robot stereotype in 1979–80. The stereotype in this case is that of the human who is artificially transformed into a superhero but agonizes because he is now "no longer human" and, despite his enhanced physical abilities, somehow inferior to normal people.

This goes back to Shotaro Ishinomori's *Cyborg 009* manga in 1964. The Merchants of Death, an international criminal organization, kidnap nine people and bioengineer them into an army of enslaved cyborg supersoldiers (each with a different power) to conquer the world. The cyborgs escape and, led by 009 (Joe Shimamura), vow to use the powers forced on them to fight the Merchants and other evildoers. But since their bodies are now mostly artificial, they are no longer human themselves.

Cyborg 009 was a mid-'60s megahit, going from manga to theatrical and TV anime in less than two years. The theme was copied in other manga; one of the better examples was the young Takao (*Golgo 13*) Saito's 1967 *The Shadow Man*. In 1973 the theme returned to anime in Tatsunoko Pro's thirty-five-episode *Casshan: Robot Hunter*. Professor Higashi invents a super-robot to help mankind, but it turns evil and builds an army of robots to enslave humans instead. The remorseful scientist is forced to turn his own son, Tetsuya, into the cyborg superhero Casshan to fight the robots. Although Casshan is still handsome and has abilities that any American comic-book hero would envy, he constantly (over)dramatizes his agony that he is no longer human and is separated forever from Luna, his sweetheart. This "I am no longer human" angst was copied in the Japanese live-action TV version of Marvel Comics' *Spider-Man* (forty-one episodes, May 1978–March 1979). There was also a bit of it in Tatsunoko's *Gatchaman, Gatchaman II,* and *Gatchaman-F* throughout the '70s, when Condor Joe was killed and resurrected as a cyborg, stronger than ever but somehow forever separated from the warm emotional bonds of his Science Ninja Team partners.

High school student Sho Fukamachi really has reason to complain in *The*

Guyver/Bio-Booster Guyver, from a 1985 manga by Yoshiki Takaya but best-known through its 1986 fifty-five-minute OAV and 1987–90 twelve-episode OAV versions. Sho accidentally activates a Guyver "bio-booster" suit that the international Chronos Corporation is planning to use for criminal purposes, and it bonds with him, not only giving him super-powers but turning him into a monster. These suits were found by Chronos agents in a cache left on Earth by prehistoric aliens; previous humans who were "monsterized" by them gave rise to legends of demons and werewolves. Chronos's own bio-boosted agents try to kill Sho to keep its secret, while Sho is forced to become the hideous Guyver to protect himself and his friends.

This plot was echoed in the simultaneous 1987–1991 *Bubblegum Crisis* OAV series. A team of hard-suited heroines, the Knight Sabers, protects 2032–33 MegaTokyo from rampaging superpowerful "Boomers" created by the Genom Corporation. Although some Boomers appear to be unintelligent biomechanical androids that have malfunctioned, it becomes clear that the most dangerous are criminal humans who have transformed themselves into fully intelligent, monstrous, superpowerful cyborgs. Or for a closer, more recent version, there is the 1998 twelve-episode TV series *Generator Gawl.* College student Gawl and his two friends are agents from a *Terminator*-like enslaved future world who have traveled back in time to try to prevent the monsterlike cyborg Generators from being invented. Gawl has reluctantly become a Generator himself, to protect his teammates from the other Generator assassins that the tyrannical future world government sends to stop them.

For thirty years, the message has been that to change oneself from a natural human is to become somehow "less than human," a monster in some manner even if a "good" monster. *Ghost in the Shell* postulates that cyborgs are not at all inferior, and that there may be no practical difference between biological and artificially created intelligence. Technological enhancements may lead to the next step in the evolution of intelligence and self-awareness.

Part V
Titles

Dawn of the Warrior Robots: The Beginnings of a New Breed of Action Hero!

Fangoria no. 4, February 1980.

Since the early 1930s, a wide assortment of cartoon and comic book superheroes have appeared on the American scene, with different measures of success. With very few exceptions, all of these symbols of justice fit very neatly into one of two categories: the super-fighter, a skilled athlete whose natural powers are aided by the use of "scientific" equipment (the Batman and Buck Rogers are typical), and the hero endowed with superhuman abilities (Superman and Spider-Man are the best known of this category).

With fifty years of superhero history on these shores, it's most surprising that the first really new conception in superheroes since the 1930s is an import—the super-robot, usually a symbiotic partnership between a titanic metal shell and a human core, is an idea that was, as they say, "Made in Japan."

Robots have been popular figures in Japan since the end of World War II. During the 1950s and 1960s, these robot characters usually began as comic book characters by individual writer-artists. Those that won sizeable audiences were filmed as live-action movies during the 1950s, and again as TV cartoons during the 1960s. These movies and TV cartoons spawned hundreds of toys, dolls, and similar merchandising items. Osamu Tezuka's *Mighty Atom* and Mitsuteru Yokoyama's *Iron Man No. 28* both followed this procedure, later reaching American shores as *Astro Boy* and *Gigantor*. These were first-generation Japanese robots—unlike the more recent super-robots, they were either intelligent individuals or merely big machines, ready to serve anyone operating their controls.

The new breed of super-warrior robots began in the 1970s. Almost

This was my earliest-written article on anime to appear in a professional magazine rather than in anime fandom's first fanzines. In 1979 when it was written, American anime fans were desperate for any information they could get on anime. Some of us frankly made pests of ourselves by asking the clerks at the Japanese-community bookshops where we bought anime magazines to translate picture captions for us.

Were *Astro Boy* and *Gigantor* filmed as live-action movies during the 1950s? Old publicity stills in Japanese magazines seemed to prove that they had been, but eventually the stills were all identified as from live-action TV series. The "fact" that *Brave Raideen* was "the most popular of all the different super-robot series" was provided by a clerk at a toyshop selling *Raideen* merchandise. Whether he was deliberately exaggerating to promote sales, or was just translating an exaggeration in a Japanese advertisement, it turned out to be a lie. *Brave Raideen* was indeed popular during its 1975–76 broadcast, but it did not come close to being the most popular giant-robot series up to 1979. ■

entirely the creation of the Tokyo TV cartoon industry, the super-robots were designed to be equally successful as TV programs and as merchandising properties. When a cartoonist comes up with a new character that is not considered to have strong potential as a toy, it never gets past the planning stage. Similarly, any toy manufacturer with a new character design will try to get an animation studio to turn it into a new TV series. Nowadays, new super-robots are released to the Japanese public as TV cartoons and as toys simultaneously.

The first of the modern super-robots was *Mazinger Z*, created in 1972 by cartoonist Go Nagai and Toei Animation Co., Ltd. Nagai was (and is) a prolific artist with many comic book and TV cartoon hits to his credit. Toei Animation is Japan's biggest and oldest cartoon studio, with dozens of theatrical and TV films to its credit. Some titles that may be familiar to American TV watchers are *Alakazam the Great* (1960), *The Little Norse Prince* (1968), and *Puss in Boots* (1969).

An Instant TV Hit

Mazinger Z debuted on Japanese TV on December 3, 1972 in a 7:00 P.M. prime-time slot. It was an instant hit. By the time it ended in 1974 it had run for ninety-two half-hour TV episodes and two forty-five-minute Cinemascope theatrical featurettes. It was immediately followed by a sequel, *Great Mazinger*, for fifty-six more episodes until September 1975. By the time the two *Mazinger* series ended, the super-robots were firmly established as a popular SF story category.

In *Mazinger Z*, Dr. Hell, a mad scientist, set out to conquer Earth with a legion of robot monsters. One produced supersonic waves that shattered buildings, another shot electrical bolts, and so on. They were opposed by Mazinger Z, a robot taller than King Kong who resembled a medieval knight but was crammed full of modern weaponry. His fists launched from his wrists to deliver a jet-propelled "rocket punch," and an emblem on his chest shot out a "crystal fire" laser beam. Mazinger Z was built by a research center of good scientists on the outskirts of Tokyo. He was operated by a teenage pilot, Koji Kabuto. Koji controlled Mazinger Z by flying in a special round hover-plane, the Pilder, into Mazinger's head cavity and locking into his body circuitry. Koji became Mazinger's brain, in other words. In this respect Mazinger Z differed from Dr. Hell's robots, which had mechanical or cyborg brains and were independently intelligent.

In an average TV episode, Dr. Hell or one of his semi-human lieutenants would launch a new giant monster against Tokyo or against the Research Center. A brief interlude showed Koji trying to live as a normal teenager. Like Marvel Comics' Spider-Man, Koji found that constantly saving the world played hell with his school grades and his social life. The monster arrived, Koji took off in Mazinger Z, the monster won the first skirmish, the Research Center analyzed the data and told Koji how to counteract that robot's particular power, and there was a climactic battle that ended with the monster spectacularly exploding. Koji, bloody and exhausted, returned the battered Mazinger Z to the Center for repairs, while the villain snarled and threatened to do better with his next monster.

Although *Mazinger Z*'s format was superficially SF, its mood was of occult/ horror drama. The name of Dr. Hell was clearly intended to suggest Satan. His terrifying giant robots were less like machines than living demons, and each delighted in the sadistic destruction it caused. The majestic Mazinger Z with his flaming weaponry was the embodiment of a Biblical archangel. The white-garbed scientists who protected humanity from Dr. Hell's evil could easily be seen as a guardian-priesthood.

Mazinger Z had a number of subplots, serious and humorous. Koji's girlfriend, the daughter of one of the scientists, also had a giant robot, Minerva X—a feminist counterpart to Mazinger Z. One of Koji's brawny school buddies felt left out and built his own super-robot. (This was strictly for comedy relief.) Other characters increased the TV series' human interest and made it more than just a slug-fest between Mazinger Z and a different bad robot each week. Each supporting character had his or her own robot or airplane or trick motorcycle, and each added to the array of merchandising items available at the toyshops.

All the subsequent Japanese super-robot cartoons were to follow this formula. Earth would be attacked by an army of grotesque villains with names like the Hundred Demon Empire or the Dark Horror Troops. Their first step in the conquest of the world was always to try to flatten Tokyo. In the nick of time a super-robot would appear, and some innocent high-school senior would be drafted to use its powers to save the world. Soon, other robots would join him, operated by his pals or by show-off rivals. They usually meant well but got in his way more than they helped. Many series had dramatic episodes near the end in which one of the hero's best friends would die nobly to save him. This set the stage for a real grudge match when the super-robot finally confronted the head villain in person in the final episode.

Robots of the Gods

In Japan, the most popular of all the different super-robot series was *Brave Raideen,* created by Yoshitake Suzuki and filmed by Tohokushinsha Film Co., Ltd. This added an interesting "Chariots of the Gods" element to the formula, and featured a robot who was more of a real personality than most.

In *Brave Raideen,* Earth was invaded by the Devil Empire, which magically conjured armies of giant "fossil beasts" out of stone. Suddenly from out of the Pacific rose an island bearing a colossal statue of ancient Egyptian design. This was mighty Raideen, built by the scientists of Mu when the Devil Empire first attacked Earth millions of years ago. Mu had long ago sunk into the ocean, but Raideen had been programmed to arise again if the Devil invaders ever returned. Raideen contained a semi-aware brain, but he required a human pilot who was brave and pure of heart in order to become fully operable. His ESP sensors selected Akira Hibiki, a high school soccer champ and motorcyclist. Akira found himself mentally compelled to "fade in" to Raideen's control center, where he was telepathically prompted on how to use the robot's weaponry against fearsome adversaries. Unlike *Star Wars'* Luke Skywalker, who soon became casual about using the Force, Akira never outgrew an almost religious hero-worship for Raideen and a hope that he would continue to be worthy of Raideen's trust in him. In this case the super-robot was clearly the dominant member of the partnership.

A comparison of the Japanese and American versions of *Raideen* shows how the super-robots are being altered when brought to the United States. Raideen is pronounced "rye-deen," and is the Japanese word for "thunderbolt." In America it's been translated into a unique name, Raydeen. The Japanese robot's tiny control center is where the heart is located in the human body. Akira enters by being super-scientifically drawn through the solid metal of Raideen's forehead. Akira is specially attuned to Raideen; he's the only person the robot will allow to fade into him. Akira becomes psychically connected to Raideen so that the robot becomes a gigantic living body for him. If one of the monsters delivers a blow to Raideen, Akira feels it personally. In contrast, the American Raydeen's whole head is a large cockpit. Pilot Richard Carson enters it via an anti-gravity "shimmer tube" through the mouth. The cockpit is large enough that he can take his girlfriend Deena along as co-pilot (Marvel Comics's *Shogun Warriors* no. 7, August 1979). Raydeen is just a big machine, and Carson operates it like a tank or a fighter plane. Carson gets his orders from a "Shogun Sanctuary" that's similar to the Research Center in *Mazinger Z*. The differences are numerous enough that if Japanese and American fans ever get together, they can spend a considerable time comparing all the variations between the United States and Japanese versions of their favorite super-robots.

Modular Giants

Mazinger Z and *Raideen* are typical of the single-unit robots. There is a separate subdivision of modular robots that can assemble in different forms. The earliest of these was *Getta Robot* (U.S. title: *The Starvengers*), another creation of Go Nagai and Toei Animation. The "getta" (combined) robot was formed by three special fighter aircraft that could link together in flight to make a single giant robot. Depending upon which order the planes joined together in, the result was red Dragon (battle prowess), blue Raiga (maneuverability) or yellow Poseidon (brute strength). In this series the robots played second fiddle to their Three Musketeers-like pilots: brave Ryu, clever Hayato, and brawny Musashi (killed in action and replaced by Benkei).

Getta Robot sparked a craze for robots that could form as many spectacular variations as possible. One of the more colorful was *Dino Mech Gaiking*, about six young heroes who joined together into a super-robot named Space

Dragon which could transform into mechanical animals: Gaiking, a human form; Nessah, a fish form; Skylar, a bird form; and so on. The search for new theme-variation robots led to some rather ridiculous extremes. These days most of the super-robots have returned to the single-unit variety.

The marketing of Mattel's Shogun Warriors toys and comic books in the United States has given rise to two general misconceptions among fans about these Japanese characters:

1. That Shogun Warriors is the Japanese generic name for this type of superhero.

"Shogun Warriors" is a trademarked brand-name created by Mattel, Inc. for all the Japanese SF toys it sells. Right now all the super-robots seen in America are imported by Mattel, so they're all called Shogun Warriors. But Mattel is also selling a Godzilla doll as a Shogun Warrior, and is planning to add Shogun Warrior toys from other Japanese cartoons such as *Starzinger,* a space opera similar to *Star Blazers* without any super-robots. The Japanese themselves simply refer to super robots or giant robots.

2. That the Japanese TV cartoon and toy industries are devoted almost exclusively to super-robots.

Animated cartoons of all subjects are fantastically popular in Japan. There are at least a half-dozen new half-hour cartoons broadcast in prime time at any moment. Themes have included samurai adventures, funny animals, sports dramas (soap operas about baseball teams are especially popular), adaptations of famous books (a cartoon serialization of L. M. Montgomery's *Anne of Green Gables* is a current hit) and many others including a wide variety of SF plots. Super-robots are certainly popular, but not to any major degree.

In fact, the number of new super-robots seems to be diminishing. That's probably just as well—it'll give us a chance to catch up with them. Mattel's toys and Marvel's comic books are just a start. A Los Angeles distributor, The American Way, is currently selling a package of five of the best of these Japanese SF cartoons for U.S. TV syndication in 1980. If these are successful, more will surely follow. The most exciting event in the development of cartoon superheroes since the creation of the Marvel style eighteen years ago is coming to America at last.

Force Five: Previewing an Ambitious New Animated Science-Fiction TV Series!
Fangoria no. 8, October 1980.

Science-fiction heroes on TV have always been unbeatable when confronted by evil robots, giant monsters, and galactic conquerors. But they haven't fared nearly as well when they've gone up against real life TV programming executives. The story is well known of how *Star Trek* was taken off the air after only three seasons despite a devoted following that increased even after its cancellation. Or of how *Battlestar Galactica* was dropped because of poor ratings before its network realized that it was almost impossible for any program to get good ratings against its time-slot competition.

In Japan and Europe, TV science-fiction adventure cartoons have often received top ratings. When these types of programs are brought to America, their ratings have plummeted. The reason is that in Japan and Europe these are shown as weekly prime-time dramas, with a level of action and a depth of characterization and plot that make them suitable for both adult and juvenile viewers. In America, they have been treated as daily kiddie fare alone. They are shown at hours when their natural viewers—the fans of *Star Trek* and *Buck Rogers* and *Space: 1999*—are in school or at jobs. How well would *Battlestar Galactica* do if it were shown at 7:00 A.M. or 2:30 P.M.?

Hopefully, this will be realized by American TV stations in time to get the most ambitious Japanese import of all placed in an accessible time slot. In September, *Force Five* is due to debut on syndicated television across America. *Force Five* is not a single program but five top SF cartoon adventures in one package. In France, one of these alone, *Grandizer* (shown in France as *Goldorak*), has achieved a 100 percent share of the TV audience in a 6:00 P.M. time slot. In Japan, all five showed in a 7:00–7:30 time slot. *Force Five's* American promoters should have a winner on their hands—if TV stations do not bury it during school and workday hours.

Force Five is being produced by Los Angeles-based Jim Terry Production Services, to be distributed nationally by King World Productions of New Jersey. The idea for *Force Five* was conceived by Jim Terry's associate, Michael Haller, who has a familiarity with Japanese TV programming that few Americans can match: he served for eight years as cultural attaché at the U.S. Embassy in Tokyo. When Haller returned to

Jim Terry and Michael Haller supplied advance video copies of their *Force Five* episodes during 1979 and 1980 to the Cartoon/Fantasy Organization and other clubs to show in anime rooms at fan conventions. They were thus considered a particularly "fan-friendly" company worthy of support, even if many fans were unhappy with how much of the original anime series was being discarded. The feeling was that getting part of the series onto American TV was better than nothing. This article was written based on preliminary planning; the *Space Musketeers* segment was renamed the *Spacketeers* by the time it was produced.

Force Five did end up in the kiddy time-slot ghetto. Also, Mattel's Shogun Warriors toy line, on whose popularity Terry and Haller had counted, had passed its peak by the time *Force Five* got onto the air. Even anime fans found it hard to get enthusiastic about *Force Five*. It was considered "old-fashioned" in comparison to *Star Blazers* or *Galaxy Express 999*, and its combination of five-programs-into-one was more confusing than excitingly innovative. ■■

America, he joined the Los Angeles office of one of Japan's biggest stations, Asahi Broadcasting Enterprises. Haller and Terry met when the two came together for post-production editing on another Japanese cartoon import that Terry was preparing for U.S. TV, *Tales of Magic* (a series of twelve-minute adaptations of classic fairy tales for preschoolers). The two discovered they had interests and plans in common, and soon after, Haller proposed that they collaborate on a project to bring the top-rated Japanese SF cartoons to America.

The problem with adapting Japanese SF cartoons for American TV has been that these adventures are designed for family audiences while American stations insist on treating them as children's programming only. A lot of SF drama—space battles, destructions of cities, robots killing humans—has to be toned down. There are also many scenes of emotional torment, such as a hero's agonizing because friends or relatives have been killed, that are usually considered too powerful for children. Yet if all this is removed, a half-hour episode may have too many gaps to make sense.

Either new animation must be created to fill the cuts—which often doesn't match the style of the original animation—or the whole episode must be scrapped. If too many episodes are dropped, the remaining program is not substantial enough to sell to the TV stations.

Condensation

Haller's solution has been to take five cartoon series that contain from forty-four to seventy-four episodes each and standardize them into a uniform twenty-six episodes apiece. The resulting *Force Five* package contains 130 episodes. This is more than enough to satisfy any TV station, while at the same time it allows the producers to select the best one-third from almost 300 Japanese episodes. There is no need to depend upon heavily edited and badly patched-up episodes to fill the program's quota.

These five cartoons are all similar, in the sense that all American superhero series are basically alike, yet the Japanese approach to superhero SF is different enough that American viewers will find it fresh. All five can fit under the promotional slogan: "These sole survivors of a future space war stand as Earth's last line of defense against the intergalactic forces of evil." This five-in-one approach also gives *Force Five* the advantages of both a daily and a weekly show. Viewers can choose for themselves whether to consider it as a single program and watch it daily, or as five weekly programs and watch only their favorite heroes' episodes on their days of the week.

Another favorable factor is that the toys of these top-rated Japanese cartoons have already been introduced in America through Mattel, Inc.'s "Shogun Warriors" figures. Jim Terry has arranged with Mattel to use the "Shogun Warriors" name in promotion of the television program. The potential advantage to both companies is obvious. Current awareness of the toys will predispose the public to test-watch the cartoons to find out what the giant robots are really like, and the growth of a following for the TV cartoons will boost the toys' sales.

The five adventures in *Force Five* are *Grandizer,* the *Starvengers, Gaiking, Danguard Ace,* and *The Space Musketeers.* Four of these are giant-robot dramas and the fifth is a space opera. All deal with the theme of the defense of Earth, or of humanity, against space monsters. Each series has its own individual approach to this theme.

The advertising for *Force Five* is heavily promoting the fact that the program became the highest-rated show in French TV history, with a 100-percent share of the 6:00 P.M. audience for some weeks around September 1978. This was actually true for only one segment of *Force Five, Grandizer.* The program was originally titled *UFO Robot Grandizer* in Japan, and ran for seventy-four weekly episodes from October 5, 1975, to February 27, 1977.

Grandizer is the personal battle robot of Prince Orion of Antares. Antares had a peaceful, advanced civilization which was conquered by the tyrannical Dracon Empire. Only Orion escaped its fall. He fled in *Grandizer* through the galaxy for ten years, finally settling upon Earth. To quote *Force Five*'s publicity plot summary: "There, he vowed never to become involved in warfare again. He found work on a Texas ranch run by Panhandle and his daughter, Brenda. He was soon joined by his sister, Aurora, who successfully fled enslavement on Antares. She warns of the imminent invasion of Earth by the Dracons. The head of the space research station in Texas, Professor Valconian, realizes the danger and finally succeeds, with the help of his young aide, Lance, in recruiting Orion and Aurora to do battle on behalf of Earth against the hated Dracons." Orion, who hates war, must sally forth in *Grandizer* to constantly fight back the Dracon saucer fighters and giant robot monsters that attempt to set up a Dracon beachhead on Earth.

Grandizer was the creation of cartoonist Go Nagai, who invented the giant robot superhero concept with *Mazinger Z* in 1972. Another Nagai program that is incorporated in *Force Five* is the *Starvengers.* The original Japanese title of this was *Getta Robot-G* ("getta" is based on the Japanese word for "combine:" a literal English translation might be "Combino-Robot"), and it consisted of forty-four episodes which ran from May 15, 1975, to March 25, 1976.

Interlocking Robots

In *Starvengers,* the evil space invaders—the Pandemonium Empire, whose soldiers look like Nazi troops with devils' horns—have succeeded in establishing a hidden base on Earth. In each episode they send out a new giant robot monster to destroy a major city or the Copernicus Aeroscience Laboratories, the center of the resistance against them. Dr. Copernicus has invented a Star Energizer power system that has enabled him to build three rocket fighters that can lock together in flight to create a heroic giant robot. Depending upon which formation the fighters combine in, the resulting robot is the red Star Arrow (called Dragon in the original Japanese and Dragoon in Mattel's toys) for air battles, blue Star Raider for land battles and yellow Star Poseidon for underwater action. The *Starvengers* series is a dramatic one which emphasizes the human interplay of the characters: the loyalty between the *Starvengers'* three pilots, Hummer, Palladin, and Foul Tip; their relationship with Dr. Copernicus and his daughter Ceres; and the battle of wits between Dr. Copernicus and the Pandemonium Empire's high command, led by Captain Furor.

Gaiking (originally *Dino Mech Gaiking,* consisting of forty-four episodes which ran from April 1, 1976, to January 27, 1977) is similar to *Starvengers* but played more for humor. The invading aliens are the Dark Horror Troops, who pop up on Earth through a black hole in the Bermuda Triangle area of the Atlantic. Their robot monsters are more improbable and their commanders are hammier, such as one who appears as a Draculoid parody of Peter Lorre. The six heroes (including a Cute Little Kid who wants his own robot fighter, too) operate the Space Dragon, a multi-part machine that can rearrange itself into several giant mechanical figures. One looks like a metal bird, for air battles: one looks like a metal fish, for sea battles, and so forth. The most powerful formation is Gaiking, the giant human robot. Most of *Gaiking's* episodes involve Dark Horror schemes and Space Dragon countermoves that go on until the heroes turn into Gaiking and clobber the monster of the week.

More originality is shown in *Danguard Ace,* which was in Japan the most popular of these five programs (*Planet Robot Danguard Ace,* fifty-six episodes, March 6, 1977, to March 26, 1978). The plot here is not to defend Earth, because Earth is irrevocably doomed. Scientists learn that Earth's energy field is degenerating and that our planet will explode within a generation. At the same time, astronomers discover an Eden-like planet, Promete, in another solar system. A worldwide project is launched to construct a space fleet, guarded by a giant robot escort, Danguard Ace, to evacuate the population of Earth to Promete. However, Promete has also been discovered by an evil space empire, Planestor, which sends its agents to sabotage the Danguard Ace Project. In the first part of this series, the attacks are against the construction project, to keep the humans from ever leaving Earth; in the latter part, during the flight to Promete, they are space battles between Planestor's rocket fleets and defenders from Earth's super spacecraft carrier which accompanies Danguard Ace.

A major subplot is that Danguard Ace's young chief pilot, Winstar, is trying to redeem his family's honor after his father, one of the project's early leaders, became a traitor to Planestor. In fact, Winstar Senior had been kidnapped by Planestor. Although he eventually escaped and returned to Earth, he had no way to prove his innocence so he rejoined the project incognito. During the series he clears his name, and father and son become a fighting team in the deep-space episodes. *Danguard Ace* was designed by

Leiji Matsumoto, the fantastically popular cartoonist whose other Japanese credits include *Space Cruiser Yamato* (*Star Blazers* in America), *Galaxy Express 999,* and *Space Pirate Captain Harlock.*

Mutant Invaders

The fifth *Force Five* offering, also by Leiji Matsumoto, is the most offbeat of all. It's titled *The Space Musketeers* (Japanese title: *Starzinger,* seventy-three episodes, April 2, 1978 to August 26, 1979) and takes place in the distant future, when mankind has peacefully settled the entire galaxy. Suddenly a wave of horrendous mutations begins spreading from the center of the galaxy. Animals and even plants develop malevolent intelligence; people become cruel demons. An army of space monsters leaps ahead of the mutation wave to savagely attack uninfected planets and destroy mankind. In desperation, the galactic government sends a young princess, because of her unique telepathic powers, on a mission to the center of the galaxy to learn what is causing the mutations and to stop it. To protect her from the monsters as she journeys through their territory, she is assigned three powerful but irresponsible interstellar warriors as guardians. The three soon fall in love with the princess and good-naturedly compete for her favor. She plays on this to try to improve their personalities. All three are cheerfully ready to fight and kill any monsters they encounter, but since it's hoped the monsters will revert to their former peaceful states after the mutation wave is stopped, the princess tries to persuade her guardians to avoid trouble rather than to look for it.

This may sound like a cross between *The Three Musketeers* and *Battlestar Galactica,* but in fact, the Japanese cartoon is a space-opera parody of a classic Asian fantasy epic, *The Monkey King.* American fantasy fans may be familiar with an earlier cartoon version of this tale, the 1960 feature film *Alakazam the Great.* There, a friendly monkey genie, a pig genie, and a sand-demon genie escorted a Buddhist priest ("Prince Amat") from China past evil demons to India. Here, a friendly monkeylike alien, a piglike alien, and a burrowing alien escort a beautiful princess through hordes of space monsters to the center of the galaxy. The monkey hero of the old Asian legend is named Son Goku; in the Japanese version of *The Space Musketeers* he was named John Kugo. But, since *The Monkey King* is almost unknown in Western culture, *Force Five*'s producers felt it would be wiser to change the references to *The Three Musketeers* instead. John Kugo is now Jesse Dart (as in D'Artagnan), the chubby comedy-relief sidekick is Porkos, and the slender, trident-wielding teammate is Aramos. American audiences will not receive the same in-group references that the Japanese did, but there will be plenty just as good.

That's *Force Five*—but that's not all! We've been talking about only 130 episodes out of nearly 300. Jim Terry and Michael Haller do not intend for the remaining 160-plus episodes to go to waste. They are taking some of the episodes that contain too much conflict for childrens' programs and are editing them into feature-length TV movies designed for primetime viewing. This isn't a totally new idea; it's been done with *Star Blazers*. But the *Star Blazers* features were just condensations of episodes already shown in the regular TV serial. The *Force Five* features will contain all original adventures, so fans of the daily program will have something special to look forward to.

As this report is being written, *Force Five* is in intensive production. For the past year it has been in the planning stages. First came the development of the concept, the purchasing of English-language rights to the right five cartoon series from Toei Animation, the showing of presentation samples to syndicated TV buyers, and the selling of *Force Five* to a major U.S. distributor, King World Productions. Then came the selection of the best 130 episodes and the preparation of English-language scripts for them. On June 6, the voice dubbing and editing began. The production schedule calls for the completion of fifteen half-hour episodes every two weeks, so that ninety of the 130 episodes will be finished by the September starting date with the rest soon to follow.

A lot of work is being put into *Force Five*. It is being designed to conform to American TV standards for children, yet to appeal to the more mature fans of adult TV-SF drama. But the crucial factor that will determine *Force Five*'s audience appeal is out of the producer's control. This is its time-slot, when it will be broadcast. Will it be in the early evening when *Star Trek* is customarily shown so it can be discovered by those viewers? Will it be in prime time to be watched by those who enjoyed *Battlestar Galactica?* Or will it be shown in the early afternoon or at dawn, the traditional kiddie cartoon hours, where its potential fans will never know about it? Check your local TV guides in September to find out. And maybe call your TV station and talk common sense to them if they've made the wrong choice.

Robotech: Japanimation Invades Comics with a Trio of Comico Titles
Amazing Heroes no. 75, July 1985.

The 1984–85 TV year has been a dynamic one for adventure science fiction and superhero animated cartoons. *The Transformers. Go Bots. Mighty Orbots. Thunder Cats. Voltron, Defender of the Universe!* But the biggest hit of all may be *Robotech*.

Robotech has only been on television since March 1985. It premiered that month in Los Angeles and in four other test cities. It drew a full-page rave review from the *Los Angeles Herald-Examiner,* and immediately shot to the top of the ratings for its time slot among syndicated TV channels. In April *Robotech* went on the air in enough other cities to give coverage throughout the United States. The ratings soon showed that almost 50 percent of all American households were watching it. The first *Robotech* convention, in Dallas in May, drew around 1,000 fans. The TV series is expected to really take off when it begins broadcasting in more cities this September.

Robotech as a comic book is already doing top business. The first issue sold out its entire print run in less than one month. The second issue, with a larger print run, sold out almost as quickly. By summer there will be three separate *Robotech* titles on sale.

The man behind *Robotech* is Carl Macek, the producer of the television series and the writer of the comic books. In this interview, Carl describes how a new sensational American TV series and comic book have been created out of three separate Japanese TV adventures, and how this may touch off a tidal wave of new dramatic TV animation and comics for the American public.

The Right Credentials

Carl Macek has been a fan of animated cartoons and comic books all his life. He was the West Coast editor of *Mediascene* magazine for five years, and he served as curator of the Popular Culture Archives at California State University at Fullerton. He has done research and publicity work for several motion pictures, including the writing of the text for the art book, *The Art of Heavy Metal: Animation for the Eighties.*

In 1982 he opened the Carl F. Macek Gallery in Orange, Calif., an art gallery and comics shop specializing in original art, cels, and posters from

It was true that *Robotech* had almost no censorship problems at the time this interview was conducted in late April 1985, when it was just beginning its widespread syndication throughout America. It ran into some heavy censorship after that, on a station-by-station basis depending upon how individual station programmers felt it needed to be "improved" to turn it into a kiddie cartoon. Probably the most notorious example was the editing-out of scenes showing Roy Fokker and Claudia Grant's interracial romance.

"I'd rather have a tiny number of Japanese cartoon purists complain that I've changed the Amazon to the North Woods than have everybody in America write in to say that there aren't any grizzlies in South America . . ." Macek got a reputation among anime fan purists during the 1980s and early '90s as "the anime antichrist" for "ruining" *Macross, Southern Cross,* and *Mospeada* by turning them into *Robotech* instead of translating them completely accurately (and for doing the same to *Captain Harlock and The Queen of 1,000 Years*), despite the fact that they would never have been accepted on American TV in their original forms. Macek even received anonymous death threats from fans. He was denounced as arrogant and insensitive for making changes to anime just because he was in a position to do so.

These accusations were irritating enough coming from fans who were at least knowledgeable enough about the original anime to recognize actual changes.

animated cartoons. Among the cels that Macek obtained for sale were some from Tatsunoko Production Company, Ltd., the Tokyo animation studio that created *Gatchaman,* the original Japanese version of *Battle of the Planets.* These were popular with his customers, who included many fans who were getting videotapes of TV cartoons from Japanese pen-pals. A common topic of conversation among fans at the gallery was how great the Japanese SF cartoons were, similar to *Star Wars,* and how sad it was that any Japanese cartoons that got to American TV had to be emasculated for the kiddie market.

Grabbing an Opportunity

Macek got his chance to do something about this in April 1984, when he was contacted by a TV distributor, Harmony Gold U.S.A. The company has offices around the world, specializing in the translation of TV programming for foreign markets. Harmony Gold had for years been buying and dubbing Japanese cartoons into other languages for the TV markets of Europe, Latin America, the Arab nations, and Africa. However, the company had never been able to break into the American TV cartoon market.

Macek knew why as soon as he saw their samples. Harmony Gold had been following the conventional practice of trying to turn serious dramas into light, comedic cartoons fit for the TV kiddie market. Macek convinced the company that he could create a hit if it would allow him to produce a program for an entirely different market: the older, comics-buying, movie-going young adults.

It became insulting when they were parroted by fans who accused Macek of completely rewriting every anime series he produced when he made few or no changes at all. Often the "stupid changes" they complained about were things like the grizzly bears in the Amazon that were in the original Japanese versions. The nadir came when he produced the American dub of the *Fist of the North Star* theatrical feature at Streamline Pictures, and some fans screamed that he had ruined it by changing the main characters' names: "Kenshiro" had been shortened to just "Ken" (which was how he was usually addressed in the original Japanese dialogue); "Yulia" had become "Julia" (the same name; just giving it the Anglo pronunciation); and "Bat" had become "Bart" (it was impossible to tell from the Japanese dialogue and printed scripts which of the two it was supposed to be; some fans were sure from the futuristic "Wild West" setting that it was Bat like in Bat Masterson, but it could have as easily been Bart like in Black Bart, the notorious 1870s stagecoach robber. Toei Animation had not been interested enough to contact the manga's creators to ask them.

The problems that *Robotech* had during its history are well known. But the facts that the *Robotech* comic books continued to sell well until Harmony Gold refused to continue their licensing in 1998, and that the *Robotech* episodes have been selling well on home video (DVD today) for almost twenty years now, are proof of its continuing popularity. ■

Harmony Gold had already been doing business with Tatsunoko Production Company for years. The animation studio had produced many TV cartoon adventures that Macek felt would be popular with American comics readers. His first choice was *Macross, the Super Dimension Fortress,* a thirty-six-episode weekly half-hour serial that pitted a twenty-first-century Earth Defense Force against vastly superior alien invaders. *Macross* had topped the Japanese fan polls for the past two years, and it was a favorite with the small core of American fans who kept up with Japanimation.

"*Macross* has elements that are completely unknown to American TV cartoons, but are common to comic-book readers and moviegoers. It has a realistic war story in which some of the major good guys get killed. There are robots and space battles, but the plot is really a soap opera that emphasizes the continuing personal relationships between people. Earth's civilization gets wiped out about three-quarters through the series, not just to show off spectacular violence but as an important, serious plot development. These are basic themes of some of the most popular comics and movies today; the group relationships of *The Teen Titans* and *The X-Men;* the survival in a post-doomsday world of *The Road Warrior* and *The Terminator. Macross* is an animated cartoon that fans who think they've outgrown TV cartoons have been waiting for without knowing it."

Initial Game Plan

In June 1984 Harmony Gold started production of a pilot feature of *Macross.* The usual television industry practice is to make a quick, cheap translation of the first episode of a foreign cartoon so that TV station buyers can understand the story. If the program is sold, then the pilot episode is redone more carefully. Macek's approach was to make a high-quality pilot at the outset. Not just a single episode, either, but the first three episodes, edited together into a seventy-minute feature. This would give Harmony Gold more than just a pilot to show to TV executives. It would create a feature which could be sold on the home video market right away.

Also in June, Harmony Gold sent out feelers to comic book publishers to generate interest in a *Macross* comic book. Macek strongly believes that any worthwhile adventure TV series or movie should also appear as a comic-book series. The different formats will reinforce each other, building up the readers and viewers of both. However, Macek did not want to relinquish the degree of creative control that is traditional when one of the major publishers produces a tie-in comic book. For this reason Harmony Gold's solicitation was sent to only the independent comics publishers. The only one that replied was Comico, the Comic Company. Comico liked what it saw of *Macross,* and it was willing to leave the writing of the comic book in Macek's hands. By the end of June, serious production of both the first cartoon video cassette and the first issue of the comic book had begun.

Photo by Barry Harris

Carl Macek discussing Robotech *with fans at Anime Overdose 2004 in San Jose.*

Macross Into *Robotech*

During summer an unexpected problem developed—but one which ultimately led to new opportunites. Harmony Gold learned that a major toy and model manufacturer, Revell, Inc., had recently ordered hundreds of thousands of various robot and spacecraft models from a Japanese toy company. Among these were the models of most of the robots and vehicles in *Macross*. Revell had already started to market these models under the trade name of *Robotech* in toyshops throughout America.

The dilemma that this created was that if *Macross* became a successful TV program and comic book, Harmony Gold would not be able to sell any *Macross* model kits unless it created new designs that looked nothing like those used in the stories—clearly an undesirable sales practice. Revell would find itself owning model kits which were obviously those of a popular TV program and comic book, but it would be forced to disguise this in its packaging and would be unable to take any sales advantage from the situation.

The practical solution lay in the two companies getting together. In September 1984, Harmony Gold sent a representative to Revell to propose a co-licensing venture. Revell was interested, but from its point of view the TV program and comic book should promote the model sales, rather than the model kits being incidentals to the TV program and comic book. The negotiations that followed resulted in creating a whole new concept.

Harmony Gold had intended to sell *Macross* to syndicated TV, but was confident that it would be successful as a home-purchase videocassette series if syndicated TV would not buy it. *Macross* was seriously hampered in having only thirty-six episodes, since the syndication market calls for at least sixty-five episodes of any new, unknown TV series. Revell was much more concerned with producing a successful syndicated TV cartoon which would create consumer demand for its model kits. Also, it did not want to lose the money that it had already put into establishing and promoting its *Robotech* name.

Harmony Gold's solution was made possible by the fact that Tatsunoko had produced two other SF serials in which humans battled alien invaders, and their model kits were also among those which Revell imported from Japan. The three cartoon adventures were similar enough that they could be rewritten to link them into a single program of eighty-five episodes. This would be a big enough package to satisfy any syndication purchaser. It would allow Revell to create audience identification with even more of its models. Since this would be a new program rather than a translation of an existing Japanese title, a new name would be appropriate in any case—what better than *Robotech?* Thus Revell would gain the publicity advantages of a TV program and a comic book, and Harmony Gold would gain the value of Revell's popular *Robotech* name. A bonus was that this would result in three Japanese SF serials being brought to America instead of only one.

The initial production of *Macross* was too far along to stop. In September Carl Macek appeared as a guest speaker at the 1984 World Science Fiction Convention in Los Angeles to introduce Harmony Gold's first *Macross* seventy-minute videotape. In December Comico released the first *Macross* comic book. But production was already being regeared to turn *Macross* into *Robotech* and to add the other two Tatsunoko cartoons to the series. In March 1985 *Robotech* premiered on television, with the successful results reported above. In April 1985, Comico released its second issue, retitled *Robotech: The Macross Saga* to coordinate with the TV program. *Robotech* was a reality.

Comparisons

Amazing Heroes: What are the differences between *Robotech* and the original Japanese programs?

Carl Macek: Very little. *Macross* was a smash hit in Japan, and Tatsunoko continued the same story trend when it followed *Macross* with *The Southern Cross* and *Mospeada, Genesis Climber.* All three are about space fleets of human-looking aliens who invade futuristic human worlds. The heroes are young members of the human defense forces. The aliens are looking for some secret that the humans have. It was easy to re-write the scripts to give the aliens the same name and turn the secrets into the same secret. Differences in characters and costumes are explained by making it three different attack waves of the invaders, years apart. The only real change involved the second story segment, *The Southern Cross,* which we call *The Robotech Masters.* In the Japanese programs it's not our Earth that's being invaded, it's a human colony planet. I had to go through the videotapes carefully and edit out every scene that shows two moons in the sky.

AH: It's a common belief that Japanese animation has to be heavily censored to get it onto American television. Have you had any censorship problems with *Robotech?*

Macek: None, at all! Well, almost none. There are different public standards of modesty in Japan, and the Japanese programs all contained a brief nude scene showing teenaged girls taking showers. Those had to be edited out, naturally. But almost all of the original action has been left intact. There was one fight scene in *Macross* where there's a close-up of the villain getting hit in the mouth, and teeth and blood go flying in slow motion. We looked at that in the editing room at Harmony Gold, and we looked at each other, and we said, "Okay, there's no denying that that is gratuitous violence." So we cut it.

But *Robotech* is a realistic war story. It's a serious science-fiction drama. In realistic modern wars you do have death and violence. Innocent civilians get killed, not just the soldiers. If you're talking about making wholesome TV programs for children, in my opinion we're being more wholesome in showing the realities of war than in pretending that war is a situation where good guys and bad guys run around shooting at each other but nobody ever gets really hurt.

In episode eighteen Roy Fokker, one of the major good guys, gets killed. He's wounded in battle, and when he returns he goes to see his girl friend, Claudia, instead of going to the doctor—he's one of these really macho types—and he dies from loss of blood. Well, when that episode was shown, the fans started writing in: "Wow, that was really fantastic! Now, how long will it be before you bring Roy back?" I couldn't believe it! I answered them: "He's dead! He was fatally shot! That's what war is about! He's not going to come back!" And the fans answered: "Oh, sure, we know all about good guys getting shot in comic books and cartoons. So how long is he going to be in the hospital before they cure him with future science and he comes back?" They just wouldn't believe that he's really dead.

The TV cartoon censorship situation is actually exaggerated. I took the recommended TV standards and practices for children's programming when we started to make *Robotech,* and I read them very carefully. Most of the restrictions that you hear about aren't in there at all. Individual TV networks and stations may have their own standards which are ridiculously strict, but that's a case of trying to avoid getting criticized by the most extreme pressure groups. The actual standards don't say that you cannot show death under any circumstances; you can't show characters getting hurt. They prohibit evil winning over good; they prohibit violence for violence's sake. That's no problem in *Robotech.* The good guys win. The good guys use only enough violence to defend themselves. Some of the bad guys are shown as honestly mistaken rather than as evil; they have a chance to reform. Some of the good guys make mistakes, too, and they suffer for them. The war is very destructive to both sides, and the point is made that it's better to avoid war entirely than to go into one with a "Rah, rah, we're the good guys so we can't get hurt" attitude.

AH: Has your partnership with Revell resulted in any differences in how you've edited the three *Robotech* programs, compared to how you would have done it originally?
Macek: Well, yes. Although to be fair, if it wasn't for Revell's backing, it's hard to say how far we at Harmony Gold would have gotten on our own. I had wanted to stick closer to the original Japanese programs on such matters as the characters' names. If you see the *Macross* videotape that we made, you'll see that the main character's name is Rick Yamada. The syndicated TV market wants "pure American" names, so we changed it to Rick Hunter.

As a matter of fact, in the original Japanese version he's a pure Japanese teen named Hikaru Ichijo. My idea was to turn him into a Japanese-American, to retain some of the ethnic identity of the original version but also to make audience identification easier for Americans. You see, you can't just translate a Japanese TV series literally into English if you want the American public to accept it. There are all kinds of little changes you have to make—sort of like creating an American body language—so that the characters will seem more natural to American viewers. For one thing, Japanese cartoons are very slowly paced by American standards. They're full of long, dramatic pauses while there's a close-up of somebody's face registering an emotion, or a slow camera pan across a beautiful background. Americans won't sit still for that. They'll turn to another channel. So one thing that I did was to shorten the pauses a bit. Another was to write additional dialogue to fill the camera pans. That's one of the hardest parts of the whole job of adaptation, to write new dialogue that really means something, that fits naturally, instead of something stupid like having a narrator say, "This man is walking down the street," which is obviously unnecessary.

We've changed the stories for the better, too. A lot of fans think that Japanese animation is really great, but when you know what the characters are really saying, you find out that the writing isn't any better than in our comic books. For instance, in the original version of *Robotech: The New Generation*, the hero is a Martian colonist who's fighting to free the Earth which was conquered by the aliens a whole generation ago. We had to change that a bit to fit it into the overall *Robotech* story line but anyhow, our hero is the only human survivor of a space battle, and his space fighter crashes in the Amazon jungle. This is the first time that he's been to Earth, and he has to travel to North America, looking for members of the Earth Resistance Movement, so he can complete his mission and destroy the invaders' main base. In every episode he gets a little closer and he picks up some new companion to join the resistance. Well, if you're traveling from the Amazon up to North America, you've got to go through Colombia and Central America and Mexico. One of the first things that happens, before he's had time to leave the Amazon area, is that he runs into a grizzly bear. In the Amazon, right? He also keeps having trouble with biker gangs who have sort of taken over the small towns since the invaders destroyed the Earth governments. The story is set in the twenty-first-century, but the biker gangs look like your typical late twentieth-century North American biker gangs. In one episode the town that he's passing through is holding a rock concert, with an audience of 10,000 or more screaming teenagers. Anyhow, as I've rewritten it, he crashes in an area that's unspecified, and the towns and people he meets all have standard North American names. I'd rather have a tiny number of Japanese cartoon purists complain that I've changed the Amazon to the North Woods than have everybody in America write in to say that there aren't any grizzlies in South America, and that the towns and people don't look Latin American at all.

But I had wanted to make two separate editions of the three Japanese programs. One was going to be the combined *Robotech* version for syndicated TV. The other was going to be a series of videocassettes keeping the original stories and program names: *Macross, Southern Cross, Mospeada*. Unfortunately, we did a survey of the video retail shops, and they all said that they had no interest in the original versions. They said that there wouldn't be a big enough market for two separate versions, and based on the sales appeal of *He-Man* tapes and *Strawberry Shortcake* tapes, they'd rather carry a version that would be just like the *Robotech* TV show because that's what all the kids would ask for. The number of collector fans who might buy a tape of the original story by mail order wouldn't be large enough to pay for the production of the separate edition. So the *Robotech* TV edition will be all that there'll be.

AH: How closely will Comico's *Robotech* comic book follow the TV program?
Macek: There'll be no story difference at all. Issue 1 of the comic book is episode one of the TV show, issue 2 is episode two, and so on. The only difference is that the *Robotech* TV program will be told in a single story sequence, while the comic book will be published as three overlapping sequences. The first thirty-six episodes of the TV programs are *Macross*, the saga of the first attack on Earth. Then the story jumps a generation and episodes thirty-seven through sixty tell the adventures of the cadets of the Robotech Military Academy as they fight the renegade Robotech Masters. Then the story jumps again, and episodes sixty-one through eighty-five tell how the descendents of the *Macross* cast return to Earth to free it from the Invids, rivals of the Robotech Masters who moved in after the humans and the Masters had weakened each other. Comico is publishing this serial

as three separate comic books which will be distributed at the same time. The first story sequence is titled *Robotech: The Macross Saga,* the second is *Robotech Masters,* and the third is *Robotech: The New Generation.* Each title will be issued every six weeks, and the three will be on an overlapping schedule two weeks apart, so there will be a new *Robotech* comic book out every two weeks. The first three issues of *Robotech: The Macross Saga* are already out. The first issue of *Robotech Masters* is the next due out, then the first issue of *The New Generation,* issue 4 of the *The Macross Saga,* issue 2 of *Robotech Masters;* and so on.

AH: Does this mean that *Robotech: The Macross Saga* will end after issue 36, and that the other two will end after their 24th and 25th issues?
Macek: Not at all. If they're still selling successfully when they reach the end of the TV episodes, I plan to go on writing the continuation of the adventures of Rick Hunter and his friends, of Dana Sterling and her friends, and of Scott Bernard and his friends.

In fact, I intend to write these as new episodes of the TV series. I'm no longer personally writing the comic books, by the way. As long as they stay accurate to the TV episodes, and I'm supervising the TV episodes, that's enough story control for me. But the ratings and the public reaction so far to *Robotech* indicate that it's going to be so successful that Harmony Gold will be able to go to Tatsunoko and say, "Instead of buying your existing programs and rewriting them, we want to pay you to animate new episodes of *Robotech* to our scripts." We'll show what happens when Rick and Lisa and the others leave Earth and go looking through space for the lost homeworld of the Robotech Masters. We'll make all three *Robotech* stories blend together smoothly instead of having a jump and a voiceover saying, "Fifteen years later . . ." I've already put little "hooks" or "seeds" in the *Robotech* dialogue that don't seem to make much sense now, but they will when the additional episodes are put in. *Robotech* in its final version will be 260 episodes long. That's one episode for each weekday of the year. The comic books will link together, too.

AH: Can Comico really produce a *Robotech* comic book every two weeks? Other Comico titles have fallen behind their schedules.
Macek: Comico has expanded its editorial and artistic staff recently. Diana Schutz is an editor who knows her job, and her job is to see that the release dates are met.

AH: How is the comic book doing?
Macek: *Macross,* the first issue of the *Robotech* comic book, sold its entire print run of 55,000 copies the same month that it came out. That beats anything else that Comico has ever published. The second issue was increased to 65,000 copies, and I think it also sold out within a month, or slightly over. The first issue may have sold well just because it was a first issue, but people

wouldn't have bought the second issue if they hadn't enjoyed the first. We keep hearing that the comic shops can't keep *Robotech* in stock. We expect print runs and circulations to increase to 100,000 copies an issue by the end of summer. When we get the three *Robotech* titles on sale simultaneously, the combined sales of the three should reach 250,000 copies a month.

AH: It sounds as though you expect *Robotech* to keep you busy for a long time to come.

Macek: We do, but *Robotech* isn't going to remain Harmony Gold's only animated SF project, if that's what you mean. We've already bought the American rights to both *Space Pirate Captain Harlock* and *The Queen of 1,000 Years,* which we'll combine into a single TV program like *Robotech.* Harmony Gold also has the rights to a number of animated feature films based on literary classics. The fans should like what we're doing with *Frankenstein,* and with an animated cartoon based on Marvel's *Tomb of Dracula.* These cartoons may not all have comic book versions, but enough of them will that Harmony Gold is going to become a very familiar name to American fandom.

Profile: *Gigantor,* The Space-Age Robot

Published as a DVD extra on Rhino Home Video's *Gigantor, Part 2 Episodes 27–52* DVD boxed set, disc 8, released February 2003. (A revision and expansion of an earlier article, "*Gigantor,* The Space-Age Robot, is Back ... Sort Of" published in *Markalite: The Magazine of Japanese Fantasy* no. 2, Winter 1991.)

Gigantor was one of a handful of the earliest Japanese TV cartoon series that were "Americanized" in the mid-1960s. It was produced by Fred Ladd, who also gave us *Astro Boy* and *Kimba the White Lion.* Many fans remember these two more fondly, but Ladd says that *Gigantor* was the most popular at the time, especially with the younger viewers.

"You're talking really more about an adult's appeal [with *Astro Boy* and *Kimba*] than for kids," Ladd says today. "Some of these shows, especially *Kimba,* would often be talk-heavy. There'd be so much plot exposition that [Osamu] Tezuka wanted to get across. So every time there'd be a lot of dialogue . . . talk, talk, talk, arguing back and forth—you'd lose the kids! You and I were already adults, so we could understand what Tezuka was trying to get across. We liked the philosophical discussions about robots' rights in *Astro*

As *Watching Anime* was being edited, news arrived of Mitsuteru Yokoyama's death on April 15, 2004. He was burned to death when his bed caught fire; it was assumed that he had been smoking in bed. A sad way for a major creator of SF and magical heroic fantasies to go. ■■

Boy and the stronger characters in *Kimba*. But the kids were action-oriented, so they were turned off by all the talk. They went more for *Gigantor*."

Gigantor also had a greater focus for juvenile appeal in twelve-year-old Jimmy Sparks, Gigantor's master. It was harder to identify with a young invincible flying robot or a young talking lion cub than with a normal boy who just happened to be entrusted with the controls of the world's most powerful robot—at least for young American viewers. In Japan, *Astro Boy* came first and was more popular, but *Gigantor* was a close second.

Mighty Atom (*Tetsuwan Atomu*, a.k.a. *Astro Boy*) began as a manga series by Tezuka in 1952. It was Japan's first major boys' adventure comic to feature futuristic and superhero themes, inspiring many imitations throughout the 1950s. Then Tezuka opened his own animation studio, Mushi Production Co., which developed *Mighty Atom* as a TV cartoon series that premiered on New Year's Day 1963. It was such an immediate hit that other television animation studios sprang up as quickly as possible. They scrambled to bring Atom's most popular comic-book competitors to life. Japan's second TV-animation studio, TCJ (Television Corporation of Japan) Animation Center, put *Gigantor* on the air just ten months later, in October 1963, followed by *8 Man* (a.k.a. *8th Man*) in November. An indicator of these programs' popularity in Japan is the number of episodes produced for each: 193 for *Mighty Atom,* ninety-six for *Gigantor,* and fifty-six for *8 Man.*

Gigantor (*Tetsujin Ni-ju-hachi-go* or *Iron Man No. 28*) was the creation of manga artist Mitsuteru Yokoyama (born June 18, 1934, in Kobe). He wrote and drew *Iron Man No. 28* for *Shonen* (*Boys*) magazine from 1956 through 1965. The title refers to the fact that Iron Man No. 28 was the final success of a secret World War II military project, after twenty-seven frustrating failures. Needless to say, the American translations never mentioned that Gigantor's original purpose had been to defeat the Allied armies! Fortunately for us, a U.S. bombing raid near the end of the war destroyed the secret laboratory before Gigantor was completed.

Yokoyama's origin story begins ten years after the war. Tokyo is being terrorized by criminals using two powerful robots for their robberies. They also break into the home of a deceased scientist, Dr. Shikashima (in the United States, Bob Brilliant), to look for his hidden research plans. Dr. Shikashima's young son, Tetsuo (Buttons Brilliant), is a pal of the boy detective Shotaro Kaneda (Jimmy Sparks), who brings him onto the case. Shotaro learns that Dr. Shikashima had been a key scientist in the military's top-secret robot project, and was presumed killed in the 1945 bombing that destroyed the laboratory. But the robots that the criminals are using are the project's defective but still powerful Nos. 26 and 27, indicating that the laboratory was not as thoroughly destroyed as was believed. The criminals are now trying to track down the No. 28 model that the project had been on the verge of perfecting.

It turns out that Dr. Shikashima is still alive and has been working secretly ever since the war to single-handedly complete Iron Man No. 28, to be used for peaceful purposes. The main plot of this origin story is the struggle between the criminal gangs and the police, represented by Shotaro-kun and Police Chief Otsuka (Inspector Ignatz J. Blooper), for control of the three robots: the two malfunctioning ones that the criminals already have, and the hidden one that everyone really wants. Two mysterious men appear who seem to be working against both the police and the criminals. They turn out to be government secret agents, the Murasame Brothers. The elder is the leader of the pair, but when he is killed in action, his kid brother Kenji (Dick Strong) fulfills their mission for both of them. The manga serial ends with Iron Men Nos. 26 and 27 destroyed and the criminals dead or captured. Dr. Shikashima gives Iron Man No. 28's control box to the heroic Shotaro so he can use the robot for his police work, and the scientist returns to his family and pure research.

This story was so popular that Yokoyama wrote *Iron Man No. 28* adventures for the next ten years. Most of them were variants on the themes of criminal gangs trying to gain control of No. 28, or trying to build other robots stronger than it was. Young Shotaro and Police Chief Otsuka were the only regular characters, although Dr. Shikashima made frequent guest appearances. In 1960 there was a short-lived live-action TV program produced by Shoki Pro, thirteen episodes broadcast from February 1 through April 25 on the Japan Television network on Mondays from 7:30 to 8:00 P.M. Its special effects were very crude, and most fans of *Iron Man No. 28* would rather forget that it ever existed. Yokoyama also produced a wide variety of other manga series at this time. Some that made the transition to TV anime series were *Babel 2, Sally the Witch* (the first of the "magical little girls" series), and *God Mars*. However, around the late 1960s Yokoyama began to concentrate upon serious dramas for Japan's adult manga readers. His subsequent works were almost exclusively historical melodramas set in feudal China and Japan.

Iron Man No. 28, both in production sequence and in popularity, was Japan's second boys'-adventure TV anime series. The TCJ black-and-white cartoons ran for almost four years in prime time on Japan's Fuji TV network, from October 1963 through May 1967, although there were only ninety-six episodes—eighty-three original and thirteen of the U.S. version. Ironically, the TV series began just as Yokoyama himself was tiring of the manga adventures, and he produced its final story halfway through the TV run. Most of the TV episodes used original stories, and featured a greater variety of story ideas. There were some changes made during the translation from manga to TV anime. The military project to develop a super-robot became a two-man project of Dr. Shikashima and Dr. Kaneda, Shotaro's father. The scientists are not presumed killed in the bombing raid. Dr. Kaneda is murdered by the criminals when they break into his home to steal the plans for No. 28. This provided the motivations for Dr. Shikashima to go into hiding to continue work on No. 28 alone, and for Shotaro to become a detective to avenge his father. It also gave a stronger reason for Dr. Shikashima's gift of Iron Man No. 28 to Shotaro at the conclusion.

A larger regular cast was needed for the TV adventures, so Dr. Shikashima (Bob Brilliant) and Kenji Murasame (Dick Strong) became permanent characters, and Dr. Shikashima's wife and son became fairly regular supporting characters. TCJ developed the series with an eye toward international TV sales, so more adventures were set in exotic parts of the world, and the affiliation of Police Chief Otsuka (Inspector Blooper) with the Japanese police was made more vague so that he would look more like an inspector in any country's police force, or in an international organization like Interpol.

Fred Ladd remembers that *Gigantor* was brought to his attention in late 1963 or early 1964. He produced it during 1964 and 1965, distribution deals were worked out during 1965, and it began syndicated broadcasting at the beginning of 1966 (appearing first on January 5 on New York's WPIX, where it screened on Wednesdays at 7:00 P.M.). "*Astro Boy* was first," Ladd says. "I didn't begin any production on *Gigantor* until after finishing *Astro Boy*'s first year production and it was already a big success."

Astro Boy (*Mighty Atom*) had started on Japanese TV on January 1, 1963, and Japanese TV salesmen immediately tried to sell it to U.S. television. In their proposal to NBC, *Mighty Atom* was described as a "futuristic Pinocchio." NBC knew that Fred Ladd, an independent producer who specialized in dubbing foreign movies and cartoons into English, was busy at the time with an original U.S./Belgian co-production theatrical animated feature, *Pinocchio in Outer Space,* so NBC consulted him as a "Pinocchio expert." Ladd agreed that *Astro Boy* could be very popular with American children, so NBC licensed the program from the Japanese and brought in Ladd to dub and produce the half-hour episodes into English. *Astro Boy* went on the air in America in syndication starting in September 1963, and by the end of the year it was an obvious hit.

Ladd recalls that *Gigantor* was brought to America by "the same agent, the same rep who had first represented Tezuka and Mushi Productions; Kazuhiko Fujita. He had come to NBC and tried to sell *Astro Boy.* They liked it and made him an offer, but he thought it was too low. He turned down NBC's deal—he thought it was not a very good deal for the Japanese studio! Well, the Japanese, the Mushi studio really wanted to do business with NBC! So they authorized a new agent, whose name coincidentally was also K. Fujita—but it was for Kiyoshi; they weren't related—and he went back to NBC and accepted their offer. This left an embittered first agent. He picked up *Iron Man No. 28* which was by TCJ, Mushi's rival studio at the time, and he came back to NBC and said, 'Look, you're doing very well with *Astro Boy;* it's really taken off. So of course you'll want another great robot show!' But NBC didn't think so. They didn't think that robots would be popular enough with American kids for two shows. They told him, 'No, thanks. We intend to make fifty-two *Astro Boy*s and then stop.' As it turned out, *Astro Boy* was so popular that we made another fifty-two episodes later, but they weren't figuring on that at the time. 'We wouldn't want another one; it would just compete with *Astro Boy.*' They advised him to come to me, so he did and said, 'Here's *Iron Man No. 28.* What do you think of it, Mr. Ladd?' After watching it, I called NBC and told them, 'This really does have potential. A young kid who owns the world's most powerful robot—American kids will love it! What do you want to do about it?' They still weren't interested. So I said, 'How would you feel if I took the show?' And they said, 'What do we care? Go ahead! If you don't, somebody else might—probably will! Better you than somebody else! So buy it!' So that was it. NBC did not want it, under any circumstances, but they wouldn't hold it against me if I bought it myself and went into competition with them!

"So I signed the deal with K. Fujita and I got *Iron Man No. 28,* or *Iron Robot 28* depending on who translates it for you. As it turned out, this made Fujita think that there was a lot of money in animation for him, so he started his own company in Japan to produce cartoons and he made *Marine Boy,* and it ended up losing him all the money that he'd made on *Gigantor* and it drove him into bankruptcy! But I wasn't involved with *Marine Boy.*"

As it turned out, it was lucky for posterity that Fred Ladd did produce *Gigantor* as his own program. NBC brought in Ladd to produce *Astro Boy* and *Kimba the White Lion.* This meant that Ladd turned all of the film negatives and soundtrack recordings over to NBC. When NBC's licenses for the American versions of those shows expired, much of this material was contractually required to be destroyed. This is why the attempts starting in the late 1980s to release *Astro Boy* on video have had to rely upon finding film collectors who own a few of the 16 mm episodes discarded by TV stations during the 1960s and 1970s. But Fred Ladd acquired *Gigantor* outright, and he kept all of the negatives and sound tracks.

Gigantor was not Fred Ladd's alone at the beginning. He and a friend, Al Singer, created Delphi Productions to produce and market the show. They expected to create other programs, but Singer died unexpectedly of coronary arrest at the age of forty-six, just as *Gigantor* was being completed. The name Delphi Productions was never used again.

Ladd produced *Gigantor* in the same way that he produced *Astro Boy* and *Kimba the White Lion* and most of his other film dubbings. He had a scripting and voice team in New York to whom he gave most of his work: Cliff Owens, Billie Lou Watt, and Gil Mack. "And Peter Fernandez," Ladd adds. "Fernandez wrote a lot of the episodes. Mack, Owens, and Watt were the main three voices—the same little repertory company. They had developed into a smooth team with *Astro Boy,* and it was easy for them to swing over to *Gigantor.* Billie Lou was Jimmy Sparks, of course, and Gil Mack was Bob Brilliant and many others. Cliff Owens was Inspector Blooper. But the *Gigantor* characters were more human, more realistic and less cartoony. So we couldn't use all the gimmicky voices. Dick Strong had to have a more believable voice. We brought in Brett Morrison for Dick Strong in the two-part pilot episode; Morrison was famous in the '30s as the radio voice of *The Shadow*. But he was too old by the mid-'60s; he made Dick Strong sound like an old man. So Peter Fernandez became the regular voice for Dick Strong from episode no. 3 on, using his normal voice. Fernandez did other voices, too. If you compare his voice for Buttons Brilliant with him as Speed Racer, which he did after *Gigantor,* you'll hear that they have the same voice!

"They were a group of tried and true performers. We worked so closely together that we all became personal friends. The production of *Gigantor* started while we were still working on the second year of *Astro Boy,* the last fifty-two episodes. We got to working so smoothly that we were producing five episodes a week, three days of *Astro Boy* and two days of *Gigantor*."

The American version of *Astro Boy* had started with the first Japanese episode which introduced the cast, and Ladd expected to also begin *Gigantor* with the first episode. But the earliest episode that TCJ sent to America was no. 27. "I asked TCJ, 'Hey, where are the first twenty-six episodes,'" Ladd says. "'Isn't there an origin story?' 'Oh, you don't want our first episodes,' they told me. 'They were the first animation that we made, and they are so bad that we don't want anyone outside of Japan to see them. The quality starting with no. 27 is much better.' 'Well, okay,' I said, 'as long as we can get fifty-two good episodes.' It wasn't until a few years later that I found out that the story began in World War II with Iron Man No. 28 as a weapon to attack American soldiers! 'Aha!,' I realized, 'so that's *another* reason why they don't want Americans to see the first episodes!' So, unlike *Iron Man No. 28* in Japan, *Gigantor* doesn't have a real first episode."

Omitting an origin story was not the only difference between *Gigantor* and *Iron Man No. 28.* The program needed many more changes than did *Astro Boy* or *Kimba.* "Jimmy Sparks was a twelve-year-old kid who carried a real gun! Even though he seldom fired it, he often waved it around dramatically. We cut those shots out. Most episodes had scenes of criminals shooting at people. And the typical story resolution was for Gigantor to fly in at the last moment and smash something up. Also, virtually all *Astro Boy* and *Kimba* episodes were complete stories which could be shown in any order, which was what American TV wanted, while *Gigantor* regularly ran to short serials; the same villain usually appeared in two or three consecutive episodes. The formula was that the villain would escape at the end of the first episode, so the heroes knew they would have to fight him again. Then there would be a stronger fight in the second episode, and they would think that the villain was killed at the end of that episode. But he would make a surprise return in the third episode with his greatest threat yet. Such serialization was unacceptable to TV stations that wanted a program with episodes that could be shown in any random order."

As a result, *Gigantor* was changed to such an extent that Ladd feels that it cannot accurately be called a translation of the Japanese episodes. Ladd worked closely with TCJ, indicating scenes that had to be changed so they would not look like cliffhangers. TCJ essentially made new episodes for the American market. They contained more library footage of Gigantor taking off, flying and landing. Original footage was filmed for many endings, reusing existing animation from other episodes showing the characters relaxed and happy at the end of an adventure, over the background of the episodes needing new conclusions. New dialogue was written to leave open the possibility that the villain might return someday, but that this particular episode was definitely and satisfactorily over. These new episodes were actually shown in Japan as a separate series. The original *Iron Man No. 28* TV series had consisted of eighty episodes running weekly from October 20, 1963, through May 27, 1965. There was a three-month gap before thirteen of the episodes remade for American TV were shown in Japan as new episodes, from September 1, 1965, through May 25, 1966.

Gigantor was distributed in America by Trans-Lux Corporation. The distribution was excellent during the late 1960s. It was routine for *Gigantor*, on one independent station, to outdraw Walter Cronkite on the 6:00 P.M. *CBS Evening News.* The hour of 6:00 P.M. was still part of the children's TV period in the 1960s; the kids took over the TV as soon as they got home from school until after the dinner hour. Parents knew that they could see the news later, after the kids were in bed. Still, this enabled Trans-Lux to advertise that *Gigantor* was No. 1 for its time period, in whatever market the advertisement was tailored for. And Trans-Lux advertised *Gigantor* heavily.

Despite this, there was never any *Gigantor* merchandising. The reason was the program's distribution through syndication. Children's merchandising requires nationwide character popularity to be successful. A Bugs Bunny toy will sell much better than a toy of an anonymous bunny that's just as cute. Cartoon characters shown on network channels have national exposure, so their merchandise will sell everywhere. But syndicated programs are sold on a station-by-station basis. A cartoon program that is very popular in one geographic area might be totally unknown in another. Merchandising licensees are reluctant to take chances on characters who do not have guaranteed continent-wide exposure. NBC tried to merchandise *Astro Boy* after his program's initial popularity in 1963, but had very little success because of its on-here, off-there nature. Ladd figured that if NBC Enterprises, with all its resources, couldn't sell *Astro Boy* to the merchandisers, he would not be able to sell them *Gigantor*, either.

Astro Boy, Gigantor, and *Kimba* were all popular during the 1960s and the early 1970s, but by the end of that decade they had practically disappeared from television. There were three reasons, at least two of which applied to each program. First, the taboos against violence in children's TV programming had grown much more strict by the end of the 1970s. Second, there were enough color cartoons on the TV market that most stations were no longer willing to buy black-and-white cartoons. Third, the American rights to *Astro Boy* and *Kimba* expired.

Astro Boy and *Kimba* were technically licensed not by NBC but by NBC Enterprises, a subsidiary involved with non-TV broadcasting activities such as Broadway stage productions. These included selling programming to the syndicated TV market through yet another subsidiary, NBC Films. In 1970 the U.S. government ruled that such a wide scope of activities put NBC in violation of national anti-trust laws, so in 1971 NBC was forced to turn over all its syndicated distribution to a completely independent company. It chose another major syndication distributor, National Telefilm Associates. NTA continued to market *Astro Boy* and *Kimba* for a few more years. But NBC had not bought their American rights in perpetuity, but for only a limited time—twelve years in *Kimba*'s case, from the first American broadcasts in 1966 until 1978, and for presumably a similar period for *Astro Boy* starting in 1963. Mushi Production Co., the Japanese producer, had declared bankruptcy in 1973 and ownership of its assets were immediately mired in a nasty Japanese court battle that lasted for over twenty years. So there was nobody in Japan in the mid- and late-1970s who could legally renew the American video licenses for *Astro Boy* and *Kimba*.

In *Gigantor*'s case, Trans-Lux phased out its TV distribution activities to concentrate on manufacturing video monitors. Its biggest success was in the financial community, where the famous Wall Street ticker-tape machines were replaced by Trans-Lux's "Jet" monitor which showed stock market changes much more rapidly. Trans-Lux's video library, which included both *Gigantor* and *Speed Racer* as well as such American-produced TV cartoons as *The Mighty Hercules* and *Felix the Cat,* was transferred to smaller distributors, first to Schnur Appel and then to Alan Gleitzman of Alan Enterprises. Alan was still making some sales for *Gigantor* into the early 1980s, several years after *Astro Boy* had disappeared.

During the 1980s *Gigantor* seemed destined to fade into history. The new home-video market was coming into existence, but it had little interest in crude black-and-white TV cartoons. *Gigantor*'s first "savior" was Scott Wheeler, a young Hollywood makeup effects artist who had loved *Gigantor* on TV when he was a child. During the 1980s he became aware of Japanese animation fandom and attended a few club meetings, including one at which Fred Ladd was a guest speaker. But most of the anime shown at these screenings was current and from Japan, not the Americanized TV cartoons of the 1960s.

"*Gigantor* was my favorite TV cartoon when I was a kid," Wheeler said in a 1989 interview, "and my best friend's favorite cartoon, too. But they weren't showing it at any of these fan meetings. Nobody had any of the Japanese cartoons that old. But somebody told me about a fan in another part of the country who had some *Gigantor*s on tape. So I wrote to her and she sent me a copy of her tape. Well, I got together with my fiancée, who is now my wife, and I said, 'This was my favorite show when I was a kid!,' and we looked at it and it was a twentieth-generation copy of a 16 millimeter film that somebody had projected against a wall and videotaped. I just thought, this is crazy! This is the only thing that I can see of my favorite cartoon?! Something's got to be done!

"That was how I got the inspiration to do it myself. I saw it as partly a hobby, and partly as a second job to keep myself busy between makeup assignments. I had seen Fred Ladd talking at a fan club about how he had made *Gigantor* and those other programs, so I knew that he was local. I found him in the phone book. I called him and I said, 'Let's do something with *Gigantor*,' and he said, 'Well, make me an offer . . .' I ended up licensing the home video rights and 50 percent of the merchandising rights for *Gigantor* for a seven-year period."

Wheeler's experience trying to produce *Gigantor* for home video makes a fascinating horror story about what was wrong with the American home video market in 1989. Despite paying one of the best film-to-video transfer companies in Hollywood for its top-quality video production, its technicians were inexperienced with crude black-and-white cartoons. They thought that an image covered with large dirt specks was the way an old-fashioned black-and-white cartoon was supposed to look. Wheeler had to ask Fred Ladd to use his authority as a veteran producer to get the negatives cleaned correctly and the videos remastered.

Then Wheeler ran into a solid wall of disinterest by the national video distribution industry. "A lot of the reaction that I got from those distributors that showed any interest in *Gigantor* at all, was that I was putting too much on each tape. I have three half-hour episodes for $14.95. They also said that I don't have a flashy enough package. My video sleeves are illustrated with stills of Gigantor and the main characters, which make it obvious that these are black-and-white cartoons. That's primarily because I had thought of *Gigantor*'s appeal as being to the nostalgia market, like to the people who collect videos of the Three Stooges' old films. But the nostalgia for *Gigantor* isn't big enough to be worth these distributors' time. They all insisted that these were cartoons and they would have to be marketed to children.

"They also wanted to change the package to a full-color painting of a more dramatic *Gigantor* that would make him look like a modern, Transformer-type TV cartoon. I think that would be deceptive, that the public would see a full-color drawing and think that these are color cartoons. [. . .] I just don't like the idea of putting *Gigantor* into the same category as those cheap, low-quality videos that are designed to be seen only a few times before they wear out. I want to make *Gigantor* permanently available for its old fans, and for the TV and animation historians who take it seriously."

Wheeler was only able to afford to have the first nineteen episodes mastered for video, and to produce three videos with the first nine episodes in his collectors' edition of *Gigantor*. He premiered his Scott Wheeler Productions release of *Gigantor*, vols. 1 and 2, at a science fiction convention, the West Coast Science Fantasy Conference (Westercon 42) at the Anaheim Marriott Hotel next to Disneyland, at a presentation in its anime video room on Sunday, July 2, 1989. They went on general sale at the end of July; vol. 3 did not appear until 1990. Wheeler tried at first to sell *Gigantor* by mail order to the film collectors' market, but the sales did not even pay for his advertising in the film collectors' specialty magazines. He next turned over his videos' sales to Books Nippan in Los Angeles, which at that time was the major retailer of Japanese animation videos in North America. Fortunately, at this point the newly developing anime market came along. The Right Stuf International, which had launched the American anime specialty video market with its first *Astro Boy* video in June 1989, asked to add *Gigantor* to its catalogue. Since Wheeler had wanted to rescue *Gigantor* from oblivion rather than to make money from it, he was relieved to turn it over to someone else who respected it as he did. In addition to selling Wheeler's three *Gigantor* videos, The Right Stuf released the remaining ten episodes that Wheeler had mastered in its own series of five *Gigantor Retrospective 30* videos with two episodes each, no. 10 through no. 19, in March 1994 to celebrate the thirtieth anniversary of the production of those episodes in Japan. There were also two *Gigantor 30th Anniversary* laser disc volumes (episodes 1–4, released October 1994; and 5–8, released May 1995) produced by LumiVision.

Gigantor was restored to America's awareness in other ways during the increasingly anime-conscious 1990s. The 1980 fifty-one-episode color remake of *Iron Man No. 28* by Tokyo Movie Shinsha (October 3, 1980 through September 25, 1981, in Japan) was produced by Fred Ladd for the Sci-Fi Channel, where it played as *The New Adventures of Gigantor* from September 9, 1993, in reruns through June 30, 1997. A twelve-issue original *Gigantor* comic book was produced by Antarctic Press from January 2000 through August 2001. There were collectables ranging from T-shirts to limited-edition cel reproductions. *Gigantor*'s theme song was included on Rhino's 1998 *The Best of Anime* music CD.

But until now, only the first nineteen of the original *Gigantor*'s fifty-two episodes have been out on video. Now, thanks to Rhino's DVD collectors' edition, the entire fifty-two episodes are available to, as Wheeler said, "its old fans, and for the TV and animation historians who take it seriously."

Speed Racer: Still in the Lead
Animation Magazine no. 22, Winter 1993.

Fans of the 1960s *Speed Racer* TV cartoons must have been surprised a couple of years ago when its theme song turned up in a lounge version on an album recorded by the Texas duet, Two Nice Girls. The lyrics weren't quite what they remembered.

"He's poppin' speed as he guns his car around the track;
He's freakin' out so hard it's like he's never coming back . . .
(Screech—Crash!!)"

Nineteen ninety-two was the twenty-fifth anniversary of *Speed Racer.* That might not be as impressive as the sixtieth anniversary of Mickey Mouse or the fiftieth anniversary of Bugs Bunny, but *Speed Racer* is still popular enough to make his birthday worth noting.

The program first appeared on network TV in Japan in April 1967 and on syndicated TV in America in September of the same year. Fans have been singing, "Go, Speed Racer, go!" ever since.

Speed Racer was created by Tatsuo Yoshida, a Japanese comic-book artist of the 1950s who founded one of Japan's earliest TV animation studios in 1965. His Tatsunoko Production Company's first title was a black-and-white space-boy cartoon similiar to *Astro Boy.* Yoshida wanted his next program to be more original and more dramatic. He succeeded admirably with *Speed Racer.* Its full-color, fast-paced racing-car adventures set in exotic locales around the world made it a hit not only in Japan but in the international animation market as well.

The factors which made *Speed Racer* popular, the factors which fans still remember today, were the close-knit, appealing main cast and the sleek Mach 5 race car. In Japan, it is the car that has top billing. The Japanese title is *Mach Go Go Go,* a bilingual pun of the Japanese word for 5, "go," and the American slang phrase, "Go, go, go!" Special buttons on the Mach 5's steering wheel enable Speed to shoot out "autojacks" to leap the car over obstacles, to engage special "belt tires" to grip steep terrain at top speeds,

Yoshida actually started Tatsunoko Pro in 1963. 1965 was when its first program, *Space Ace,* went on the air. It was not known until the later 1990s when *Speed Racer's* American producer (and voice actor) Peter Fernandez began giving fan interviews, but Spridle's name was actually "Spritle," inspired by "that merry little sprite" Puck in Shakespeare's *A Midsummer Night's Dream.*

The brand-new *Speed Racer* TV cartoon series was *The New Adventures of Speed Racer,* produced by Fred Wolf Films, thirteen episodes syndicated beginning September 13, 1993. The less said about it, the better. Tatsunoko Pro also produced a brand-new version of *Mach Go Go Go,* which debuted on Japanese TV in January 1997, but this was not foreseen when this article was written. The theatrical release of the original animation was *The Speed Racer Show,* a compilation of three episodes released by Streamline Pictures in May 1993 and on home video by Family Home Entertainment in February 1994 as *Speed Racer: The Movie.* Warner Brothers' press releases about its forthcoming live-action *Speed Racer* theatrical feature (at one point Johnny Depp was mentioned as starring as Speed) gradually faded away during the late 1990s, but after about five years of silence had reappeared as of June 2004. ■

to unfold rotating sawblades to cut down heavy off-road brush and trees, to close a bulletproof, watertight transparent canopy, and to turn on powerful headlights that make high-speed driving in pitch dark perfectly safe. The Mach 5 also has a "go bird," a miniature homing device which Speed can use to keep in touch with his support team no matter where he is during a grueling cross-country race.

Speed's support team is mostly his family. His father, Pops Racer, is the inventor of the Mach 5 and its chief mechanic. Mom is a super-efficient housewife who makes it possible for her men to spend all their time on automotive affairs. Speed's girlfriend, Trixie, accompanies him on all his races to give him encouragement. She also quickly becomes an efficient assistant when Speed runs into the exciting adventures that constantly await him. Sparky is Speed's best pal and a top pit-crew mechanic. He can keep the Mach 5 running in rough field situations that are beyond Pops Racer's stamina. Speed's bratty kid brother, Spridle, and his pet chimp Chim Chim, are supposed to stay home, but they invariably stow away in the Mach 5's trunk. They are conveniently on hand to run for help or to provide a diversion when Speed gets into some desperate scrapes. Finally, there is the unknown Racer X, a notoriously reckless driver who is rumored to have underworld connections, but who mysteriously goes out of his way to protect Speed. Only Racer X himself (and the audience) know that he is actually Rex Racer, Speed's older brother who left home after a bitter argument with Pops over his daredevil lifestyle. Racer X now poses as a shady racer for his cover as an Interpol agent, to ferret out the criminals who infiltrate the international sport of Formula-1 racing.

American audiences have assumed that the large letter "M" on Speed's helmet stands for the Mach 5 car. Actually, it stands for Speed's original Japanese name, Go Mifune and the Mach 5's manufacture by his father's Mifune Motors. The American program never did explain the "G" monogram on Speed's shirts, or the "M" on Trixie's blouses. The "G" stands for Speed's Japanese first name, Go, of course, and the "M" stands for Trixie's Japanese name, Michi Shimura. For the record, Pops and Mom have real Japanese names, Daisuke and Aya; Spridle is Kuryo; Chim Chim is Senpei; Sparky is Sabu; and Rex "Racer X" Racer is Kenichi "Masked Racer" Mifune.

Speed Racer was a prime-time weekly TV series in Japan for one year with fifty-two episodes. In America, the fifty-two episodes were usually syndicated as a daily program. Roughly half of the half-hour episodes were complete stories, while the others were two-episode serials. There was one three-episode adventure, "The Most Dangerous Race," which theoretically could be edited together into a feature of about eighty minutes.

Speed Racer was originally syndicated in America by Trans-Lux Productions and then by Alan Enterprises after Trans-Lux moved away from television distribution. The program's peak popularity was during the late 1960s and early 1970s, when it was fresh. During the late 1970s and early

1980s, stricter standards for children's TV programming brought complaints against *Speed Racer* for violence, such as when gangsters would shoot at people or knock them unconscious or a brutal parent would abuse his child.

However, as the 1980s progressed, *Speed Racer* gained an independent life. The home video market made *Speed Racer* available unedited without the restrictions of modern TV standards. In 1987, a new *Speed Racer* comic book was licensed which has become even more hard-boiled than the TV version. (Among other changes, it claims that Racer X has grown weary of his life of constant danger as an Interpol agent, but he can't quit because Interpol does not allow its agents to resign alive, a policy that the real international police agency would probably be startled to learn.) In 1990 a Texas singing team, Two Nice Girls, gave Speed the impromptu tribute quoted at the beginning of this article. A second group, The Swamp Zombies, has recorded its own *Speed Racer* song, while a hot dance version of the theme song, "Speed," has been re-scored by Chicago's Alpha Team Group. For years rumors of a forthcoming *Speed Racer* live-action theatrical feature have come out of Hollywood, and they're getting more insistent. The October 1992 issue of *Science Fiction Chronicle* reports in its column on forthcoming SF movie news/gossip, "Richard Donner is considering directing a live-action big-screen version of the cartoon series *Speed Racer*." This year a $50 detailed model kit of the Mach 5 has hit the luxury gift market.

And now there is to be both a brand-new *Speed Racer* TV cartoon series, and a theatrical release of the original animation. It looks like, for *Speed Racer,* the finish line is nowhere in sight.

Momotaro's Gods-Blessed Sea Warriors: Japan's Unknown Wartime Feature
Animation World Magazine 1, no. 7, October 1996.

World War II is now over fifty years in the past. For animation fans, those days can be relived every time a retrospective screening of wartime cartoons is held. There seems to be a campus or fine arts program every few years in most cities. It's an opportunity to see *Confusions of a Nutzy Spy; Der Fuehrer's Face; Tokio Jokio; Bugs Bunny Nips the Nips; You're a Sap, Mr. Jap,* and those other classics that grow more embarrassing as wartime memories fade.

The Japanese also made many propaganda cartoons, including one notable thirty-seven-minute featurette and a seventy-four-minute feature. Unlike the American films, these have not been continuously available over the past half-century. Due to wartime Japan's own cannibalizing of film prints to reuse the film stock, and the destruction by the American Occupation authorities of all propaganda materials that could be found, most of the wartime cartoons were thought to no longer exist. However, the earlier film has been preserved by Tokyo's National Film Center while at least one print of the feature also survived. Today, thanks to the home video in Japan, the latter is available to a much larger audience than ever saw the original film. It is too primitive to be of much interest to the fans of modern action-adventure Japanese anime, but it is fascinating to anyone with a serious interest in World War II propaganda art and animation, and in the evolution of anime.

Before World War II there were no animation studios in Japan. There were individual enthusiasts who would personally create a short film every year or two. Not all of these were cartoon animation. Cutout silhouette animation, inspired by Lotte Reiniger's 1926 *Die Abenteuer des Prinzen Achmed*, was very popular with some artistic hobbyists. The major Japanese film studios and theatrical distributors were happy to pick up these shorts. Some of the studios even subsidized the more reliable animators.

Mituyo Seo and Momotaro

All film production was tightly controlled by the military-dominated government during the war (which started for Japan in 1937 in China). This ironically turned out to be very good for animation, because the Japanese Navy felt that theatrical cartoons were an ideal medium to instill the patriotic spirit in children. Effective production could not be handled by individual artists, so the first animation shop was organized under Mituyo Seo, who was born in 1911 and who had made more than a half-dozen short cartoons during the 1930s.* Seo and a small staff created the thirty-seven-minute *Momotaro no Umiwashi* (*Momotaro's Sea Eagles*), which was released on March 25, 1943. Momotaro is a popular Japanese fairy-tale boy-hero, roughly similar to Jack the Giant-Killer in Western folklore. In this featurette he is portrayed as a young naval commander leading a squadron of funny-animal monkey fighter pilots (his "sea eagles"). This was popular enough with the public that the government authorized Seo to produce a feature-length sequel. *Momotaro Umi no Shimpei* (roughly *Momotaro's Gods-Blessed Sea Warriors*), seventy-four minutes long, was released by Shochiku, one of Japan's largest film companies, on April 12, 1945. This is the feature that has been available on a Shochiku home-video cassette off and on since 1984.

American wartime cartoons were made for family audiences with much adult-oriented political satire. But *Momotaro Umi no Shimpei* was clearly

---

*According to *History of Japanese Animation Films* (a booklet published by an early Japanese animation magazine, *Film 1/24*, Tokyo, June 1977; co-edited and translated by Edward D. Herscovitz), Mituyo Seo was born on September 26, 1911. He created eight short anime films between 1933 and 1939; he directed the two Momotaro films released in 1943 and 1945. His final film, a musical featurette, *Osama no Shippo* (*The King's Tail*), was released in 1947. He then became an author and illustrator of childrens' books, and was apparently still active in this field in 1977.

designed primarily for young children. The characters are cute animals with the look of plush nursery toys. They play their roles with a minimum of dialogue, almost pantomime, to a choral accompaniment of lullaby-like songs and simple martial melodies.

The opening sequence (sixteen minutes) shows four young animals (a bear cub, a monkey, a puppy, and a pheasant) in sailor dress uniforms walking along a country road into a forest, where they meet their friends and families. They have just completed their training and are saying their farewells before shipping out. There are tearful partings and a happy send-off party. The monkey's little brother plays with his sailor's cap, which is blown into a swift river. The infant falls in while trying to retrieve it, and is rescued by all the animal children acting cooperatively just before he is swept over a waterfall.

The continuity jumps abruptly to a large South Pacific island which is a composite of Borneo, Indonesia, and New Guinea. Rabbit sailors of the Imperial Navy are clearing the jungle to construct a base and airstrip. (Aside from the four animal buddies who are meant to stand out as individuals, the mass of the Japanese Navy is portrayed as bunnies or monkeys.) They are watched in wonderment by the native jungle animals, who come out and help. The scenes are brief but detailed enough that they could almost serve as a training film on how to build a tropical base. The airstrip is barely completed when transport planes arrive bringing troops (which include the four buddies). Finally a VIP plane lands and Commander Momotaro (the only human, a young boy in officer's uniform) steps out.

The next few scenes depict the joys of naval life. The puppy begins a language class to teach Japanese to the friendly natives; everybody sings a peppy nursery-school A-E-I-O-U jingle to teach A-Sa-Hi ("Rising Sun"). We see wash day, getting mail from home, athletic military exercises, and the Japanese sailors marvelling at the Equatorial tropical climate.

Why We Fight

The mood turns dramatic. A reconnaissance plane brings aerial photographs of an entrenched British colonial base on the other side of the island. The sailors switch from general combat practice to parachute training. The monkey, bear cub and puppy join the parachutists, while the pheasant becomes a fighter pilot. Commander Momotaro completes his plans. A

This 1996 article still suffered from a lack of information about pre-1950s anime, and on poor translations of what little information there was. The statement that pre-World War II animation was created by individual hobbyists who produced a short film every two or three years should have said two or three films a year. Herscovitz's 1977 *History of Japanese Animation Films* (which was virtually the only English-language source of information on pre-1950s anime for two decades) identifies the creator of this feature as "Mituyo" Seo, but his name is spelled "Mitsuyo" in virtually every later history of early anime. ■

rather artistically jarring "why-we-fight" history lesson in cut-out silhouette animation shows seventeenth-century Dutch "pirates" conquering the independent Malay sultanates and imposing European rule over the East Indies. The sailors don their paratroop gear and board the transport planes. After a flight through a storm, a British base comes into sight. The troops parachute out and capture it after a violent but brief battle. Commander Momotaro presides over the surrender conference, where the cowardly British officers each try to avoid taking the responsibility for signing the surrender. (The British voices sound authentic—inmates of a prisoner-of-war camp?—speaking in English with Japanese subtitles, in the feature's only major scene with considerable dialogue.) The ending shows the animal civilians back home getting the news of the Navy's victory, while children play at being paratroopers and jump down upon an outline map of the United States—presumably suggesting the next goal, but since this movie was released barely four months before the war's end, this must have been too exaggerated for even wishful dreaming by then.

Momotaro Umi no Shimpei is a black-and-white film, about technically equivalent to the American theatrical cartoons of the early 1930s. The art style and direction show a greater Chinese than Western influence. The film is extremely slow paced, and there are many "artistic" shots emphasizing the beauty of falling rain, or comparing parachuting soldiers with drifting dandelion seeds.

But while the story is more dramatic than those of America's cartoon comedies, the movie is about equal in racial stereotyping. The animals that depict the Japanese are all handsome and intelligent. The East Indies animals, although friendly, are carefree "happy but simple natives" (including a humorously grotesque proboscis monkey, an orangutan, and a long-armed gibbon, in ethnic dress) who caper about foolishly. They are treated in a clearly patronizing manner by the sailor animals. The British are drawn as humans but with exaggerated Western characteristics: they are either tall and gangly or short and Colonel Blimpishly stout, with pop eyes and great noses. They also each have a single demon's horn on their heads: foreign devils. If our own propaganda cartoons look embarrassing to us today, we can take relief in the knowledge that ours weren't any worse than were the Axis's.

Prince of Something: *The Heroic Legend of Arslan—Age of Heroes*
Manga Max no. 2, January 1999.

The Heroic Legend of Arslan, an anime adaptation of Yoshiki Tanaka's fantasy novel *Arslan Senki* (*Arslan's Battles*), is set in a world similar to Robert E. Howard's *Conan* stories. Howard blended together a colorful assortment of exotic names from Celtic, Roman, and Middle Eastern history, and set them in a mythical forgotten prehistoric civilization. Tanaka's saga hews more closely to the Persian Empire at the time of its conquest by Alexander the Great. Instead of the Macedonian Greeks, the Western neighbor of "Palse" is "Lusitania" (the Roman name for Portugal), ruled by "King Inokentis VII," on a holy crusade to conquer Central Asia for their god. ("Innocent" is a distinct name of the Roman Catholic Papacy.) Arslan, Palse's fourteen-year-old prince, escapes when the Palsian army is defeated and his father, the king, disappears in battle. A handful of loyal nobles help Arslan slowly build a new army and a resistance against the conquering Lusitanians (a vicious parody of the twelfth-century Crusaders). Additional complications are caused by Palse's eastern neighbors (thinly disguised India and Turan), which try to expand their own borders at Palse's expense; and by the mysterious Lord Silvermask, who is actually Prince Hermes, heir to a rival branch of the royal family who may have a better claim to Palse's throne than does Arslan.

Arslan unfortunately makes a confusing set of videos. In Japan, *Part 1* and *Part 2*, one hour each, were released theatrically in 1991 and 1992. *Part 3* and *Part 4*, a half hour each, appeared separately as OAVs in 1993. There was a pause and two more OAVs, *Arslan: A Lone Figure on a Warhorse, Beginning* [and] *Conclus*ion, came out separately in 1995.

In America, *Part 1* and *Part 2* appeared as videos in 1994, followed by *Parts 3* and *4* as a single one-hour video in 1995. Now the final (?) two episodes have appeared together as *The Heroic Legend of Arslan: Age of Heroes* in 1998.

The new subtitle implies that *Age of Heroes* is a separate, complete story. Actually, the video sleeve lists these two parts in small type as episodes five and six. Yes, it is a continuation of the same serial. It is so dependent upon the earlier events that it needs a four-minute (!) synopsis at the beginning to set the scene. And an hour later, it stops upon another cliffhanger! Since there are no more videos in Japan, fans may have to wait for a translation of Tanaka's novel to find out how the story ends.

The confusion is worse than that, thanks to discrepancies and changes among the videos in characters' names and translations. In *Part 1*, King Andragoras of Palse (also spelled or pronounced Pulse, Parse and Pars on different videos) meets the invading Lusitanian (or Rucitanian) army and is crushed at the Battle of Atropatene, due partly to an evil spell cast by a wizard in Silvermask's service. Arslan (or Arislan) escapes, not knowing what

Today, almost ten years later, there have been an increasing number of instances where the Japanese licensor has insisted on dictating the exact spelling of titles and personal names in the English subtitles, whether it is "good English" or not. I have learned to be more cautious, as a reviewer, in accusing the American producer of the dubbed/subtitled version of incompetence when an obvious inaccuracy or inconsistency with spellings in previous volumes appears. ■

happened to his father. The viewer is shown that Andragoras is captured by Silvermask, who is pretending to help the Lusitanians. After capturing Palse's capital, Ekabatana (the traditional English spelling is Ecbatana), Silvermask and the Lusitanians throw Andragoras into the dungeon of his own palace.

Part 1 ends with a Narrator's voiceover. On the subtitled video, this reads: "Andragoras, king of Palse, had vanished from the earth. In his absence, his kingdom began to crumble. A mighty nation had been destroyed. In the year 320, Palse fell." But on the dubbed video, the narrator says, "And here we take leave of our valiant warriors for the time being. Not long after, in the year three hundred and twenty of the Palsian calendar, Andragoras the Third died of an illness, much to the disappointment of Hermes, who could not carry out his vengeful threats. However, the once great kingdom of Palse was firmly in the hands of its enemies."

Is the difference significant? Yes! Because in the last half of *Age of Heroes*, Andragoras escapes from the Lusitanians and takes command of the Palsian resistance back from Arslan (a potential disaster, because Andragoras is a totally incompetent general). His reappearance from having vanished will cause no trouble to those who saw the subtitled version of *Part 1*. But his reappearance from "death" without any explanation is bound to completely confuse those who watched the dubbed version!

There are other important differences. One of Andragoras' trusted generals, Kharlan, betrays the Palsians and joins Silvermask. No motivation is given in the dubbed version; the implication is merely that he is the dastardly traitor that a good drama needs. But the subtitled version adds a significant comment when Silvermask says to his wizard, "Your spell made Kharlan loyal to me . . ."

Some of the differences are deliberate. *Age of Heroes* begins with an explanation from Central Park Media that they have changed the spellings and pronunciations of the major characters' names because, "We have been requested to do so by our Japanese licensor, KSS, who explained that the original producers prefer the spelling. . . ." And so Daryoon becomes Darun, Gieve becomes Guibu, and so on. It may be moot as to which of two phonetic spellings of a Japanese-pronounced Persian name is more nearly correct. But Hermes, a well-known Greek name, has become Hirumeez. That may be closer to the Japanese pronunciation, but it is not "good English."

The production quality in *Age of Heroes* is notably inferior to the previous parts. Up to now, there has been actual animation in the battle sequences. Here they are presented as a series of fast cuts among about a half-dozen dramatic paintings of warriors fighting each other. The editing has become confusingly abrupt. Scene: Arslan and his advisors agree that they must deceive the Turanians. Scene: A new character, a Turanian spy, is reporting to his king that Arslan is a young fool and the Palsian army is disorganized. Since this is very obviously not true, what is going on? Have the Palsians somehow deceived the spy (who would have to be an idiot), or is the spy actually working for the Palsians? There are several scenes where the viewer must guess at the motivation for what is going on, and hope that it will be explained later. The dubbed version has a new voice cast which is unusually bad. Lord Narcasse, an intellectual strategist, is intended to sound sophisticated; instead he sounds so haughtily bored that he might fall asleep at any moment. A bellicose general belches out his commands.

If you have been following *The Heroic Legend of Arslan,* you might want to watch this for the extra mileage it gives the story, but you will be disappointed by the drop in quality. If you have not seen Arslan yet, this is certainly no reason to start now.

Astro Old and Astro New
Manga Max no. 18, June 2000.

King Kong. Lost Horizon. Flash Gordon. Classics in black and white that should never have been remade in color.

Unfortunately, the same must be said for *Astro Boy.* The black-and-white TV series may have been crudely produced, but it was imbued with a verve and sparkle which the prettier color remake almost completely lacked. The original 193 *Mighty Atom* episodes, seen in Japan from 1963 through 1966 (the English language *Astro Boy* episodes are the first 104 of these), were incredibly popular, and are still revered on video today. The fifty-two color episodes broadcast during 1980 and 1981 were politely received, but were considered as just another minor TV cartoon.

This seems ironic since both were produced by *Mighty Atom*'s creator, Osamu Tezuka. He knew the character better than anyone else. So what went wrong?

Mighty Atom was one of Tezuka's earliest comics, and still his most popular in the early 1960s. It was serialized in every issue of the monthly *Shonen Magazine* from April 1951 through March 1968, as *Atom Taisho* (*Captain Atom,* often translated by Tezuka himself as *Ambassador Atom*) for

Tezuka often pointed out in personal conversation that the public never seemed to seriously consider the fact that Atom had been *programmed* by Dr. Tenma to be a "good boy." His desire to become a real human child, and a very virtuous one, was not so much a conscious choice as hard-wired "instinct." In one of his post-1960s short satiric portrayals of Atom, Tezuka showed what might have happened if Atom had wanted to become a "real human" but had not been programmed for goodness. He turns into a juvenile delinquent, and the story ends with Atom being arrested in a police raid of a brothel.

I was not the only viewer dissatisfied with the way Atom was portrayed in Tezuka's 1980–81 remake. Tezuka Production Co. seems to have taken this public reaction into account in planning its third, 2003 TV version. ■

its first year and as *Tetsuwan Atom* (*Mighty Atom*) from April 1952 onward. It was filmed as a live-action TV series in 1959–60. It was arguably Japan's favorite comic book title at the time TV production began during 1962 for its premiere on New Year's Day, 1963.

Atom's adventures were tailored to quick-paced action and humor that boys would enjoy. Atom frequently battled much larger robots, but his most memorable adventures were those in which he matched wits with cunning adversaries rather than engaging in contests of physical strength.

Mighty Atom underwent considerable evolution during this decade. The art style grew more polished. Background built up through separate events. The original Robot Circus ringmaster looked nothing like Tezuka's notorious stock villain, Hamegg. When Tezuka reviewed his backlog to turn *Mighty Atom* into TV cartoons, some revision was necessary for consistency. Atom's origin story, specifying a date (A.D. 2003; forty years in the future) and introducing his "father"-inventor, Dr. Tenma (Dr. Boynton); his circus owner, Hamegg (Ringmaster Cacciatore); and his kindly mentor, Dr. Ochanomizu (Dr. Packadermus J. Elefun), was for the first time presented in its now-familiar form in the pilot episode, "The Birth of Mighty Atom (Astro Boy)."

Unfortunately, most of the manga backlog consisted of long serials, not appropriate for TV cartoons. Adventures that had spun out in *Shonen* for up to a year were condensed into single half-hour episodes. The backlog of Atom's tales went fast. Tezuka later stated that his first ten years of telling Atom's adventures had been fun, but when it became necessary to grind out new stories quickly for use as TV episodes, it became an unpleasant chore.

One reason was that the TV cartoons remained tailored to young boys. But manga literature was developing an older readership. Tezuka's tastes were also maturing. During the 1950s he wrote primarily for children and adolescents, but by the late 1960s he was devoting more effort to sophisticated dramas for adults. He did not want to be held back to shallow adventures. The later TV episodes reflected this, intensifying a serious mood. This culminated in the famous final episode no. 193 in which Atom sacrifices his life to save the Earth.

Tezuka followed his last *Mighty Atom* story in *Shonen* with a lengthy *Mighty Atom* serial for adults. *Atomu Konseki Monogatari* (*The Tale of Atom, Past and Present,* usually translated as *The Atom Chronicles* or *Chronicles of Astro Boy*) was serialized in a daily newspaper, *Sankei Shimbun,* from September 28, 1968, through February 28, 1969. In this 538-page epic, Tezuka took all the questions fans had asked (such as why the pacifistic Atom had such superweaponry built into him), and answered them in a dark and mature story. Atom was presented as a thoughtful, somber character dealing with problems of moral complexity, rather than as a spunky boy-robot facing simplistic confrontations of good versus evil.

The Atom Chronicles was Atom's final major manga tale. Tezuka brought him back in a handful of stories during the 1970s and 1980s to please popular demand, but he was clearly not really interested in them. Most portrayed Atom in notably out-of-character roles; some were outright self-parodies. Atom's final appearance, in 1986, was in funny-animal form as Atom Cat!

Meanwhile, TV's first anime hit in the 1960s had become old-fashioned animation by the 1970s. In the mid-'70s Tezuka received an unusual request from Japan's biggest animation company, Toei Doga. Toei asked him to create an authorized imitation of *Mighty Atom*—a new "sanctioned rip-off" as close to Atom as he was willing to make it.

Jetta Marsu (Jetter Mars or *Jet Mars)* ran for twenty-seven episodes— from February 3 to September 15, 1977. The setting was a similar future (A.D. 2015 instead of 2003) populated by humans with robot servants. If Mighty Atom was a ten- to twelve-year-old boy, Jet Mars looked closer to eight years old. The difference was that, where Atom was a virtuous Good Boy, Mars had no morals at all. He was built by Dr. Yamanokami (roughly a cross between Thomas Edison and Scrooge McDuck) as a "battle robot" for hire. This incensed kindly Dr. Kawashimo, who taught robots to be beneficent members of society.

Tezuka said that his idea was to portray Mars as closer to the blissful innocence of Disney's Pinocchio, who always went along with the most recent adult to talk to him. Mars would be a cheerful young robot bouncing back and forth between two arguing scientists, who would constantly jockey humorously to override the other's influence. Audiences would watch to see which scientist would "win" each week, whether Mars would altruistically help humanity or help to enrich the capitalistic Yamanokami. As it turned out, Toei wrote Dr. Yamanokami out of the series as quickly as possible. Mars moved in permanently with Dr. Kawashimo, and the two turned into bland imitations of Dr. Ochanomizu and Atom. The significance is that, even though *Jet Mars* was for young children, Tezuka had wanted to engage in philosophical debates about morality—unfettered egoism versus service to society—rather than a standard kiddie formula.

Three years later, Tezuka got his chance to retell *Mighty Atom*'s story his own way. The new, color *Mighty Atom* ran for fifty-two episodes from October 1, 1980, through December 23, 1981.

But Tezuka's own way followed his shift of interest from simplistic adventure to emotional inner conflict and moral struggles. His art style had also continued to evolve, and he felt that his new character designs looked more realistic. Possibly so, but the change was not necessarily for the better. The 1960s *Mighty Atom* had frankly looked like a mechanical replica of a ten- to twelve-year-old boy. Scenes in which he impersonated a real boy may have been unconvincing, but it increased the verisimitude of a super-strong robot for the action sequences. The 1980s Atom did look more like a real child, and a pudgy one at that. He now looked too soft and babyish for a dramatic hero. Dr. Ochanomizu (Dr. Elefun) and Higeoyagi (Mr. Pompus) were older men, but their 1960s versions showed them as feisty geezers who could plausibly accompany Atom on his adventures. Tezuka's 1980s presentation made them look too feeble and doddering to go into action.

The fatal change was the increased emphasis on tragedy and pathos. Tezuka had employed these to good effect in the 1960s TV cartoons. Viewers were hooked by the pilot episode's emotionalism of Dr. Tenma's grief over his son's death and his obsession with bringing him back to life through robotics, and of Atom's heartbreak when his "father" rejects him because he is not a real boy. Several episodes featured robot "innocent adversaries" forced into wrongdoing through no fault of their own, who were destroyed at the climax despite Atom's attempt to save them. But these intense scenes were sparingly used, so they had more impact upon viewers when they did occur.

In the color TV series, practically every episode seems heavy with overhanging doom. Dr. Tenma's real son is not just killed in an automobile accident, he lingers long enough for a three-hanky tearful hospital deathbed scene. Atom's increased realism has turned him into a little boy who is timid and insecure despite his super-strength. Instead of momentarily grieving at a tragic climax, he constantly agonizes over the victims that he may not be able to save—and far too many episodes do end with a sympathetic supporting character gasping a final farewell. Atom has become a super-wuss!

One major change had strong potential. The philosophical debate that was humorous in *Jet Mars* became dramatic in the 1980s *Mighty Atom* through the introduction of Atlas, Atom's "evil twin brother." In this new version of "The Birth of Atom," Dr. Tenma's blueprints for Atom are stolen by a European arms manufacturer, Count Walpur Guiss, who builds a duplicate super-robot not programmed with any morality. Guiss intends to rent Atlas to the highest military bidders as an invincible weapon. But the amoral robot sees no reason to serve Guiss, or any other weak human. After escaping from Guiss's castle, Atlas builds himself a new adult body suitable for a robot Greek god and decides to conquer humanity. Atom opposes him, in a series of nine episodes scattered throughout the fifty-two.

Unfortunately, Atlas is a wishy-washy adversary. He acts as though he does not really want to rule the world, but feels it is the logical goal for a being of his omnipotence. (And what else should an invincible robot do to pass the time? Play golf?) Atlas also seems confused by Atom's loyal defense of weak humans. Atlas's logical mind cannot comprehend Atom's emotionalism and moral values, but Atom's conviction is so intense that Atlas wonders what his own programming may lack. This indecision is intelligent and intriguing. It would have made an excellent single or two-part episode. But dragging it on throughout the series turns Atlas from a truly dramatic nemesis into a weakly hesitant foil whose menace dribbles away.

The flaws of the color series are nicely illustrated in the final episode, no. 52, "Atom's First Love." (This is a notable episode because Tezuka personally introduces it in a live-action sequence, in the tradition of Walt Disney's introductions to his TV series.) Dr. Ochanomizu discovers that plans for a super-robot have been stolen by a foreign country. Atom is sent to sneak into the country's military base and destroy the plans. On the outskirts of the base, he meets a cute girl, Nuka. She is also a robot. Atom's attempt to sneak into the base fails, but Nuka helps him to get in. They are captured by the

---

Astro Boy. The episode title translations are taken from the 1982–84 Australian broadcast but are listed in the original Japanese order, with the Australian broadcast order following in parentheses.

The Birth of Astro Boy (1)
Astro Versus Atlas (included with 1) [Astro Versus Atlas no. 1]
Robot Circus (2)
Save the Classmate (3)
Atlas Lives Again (10) [Astro Versus Atlas no. 2]
Robot Land (21)
Frankenstein (12)
The Red Cat (29)
The Crystal of the Desert (11) [Astro Versus Atlas no. 3]
The Robot President (31)
The White Planet (8)
Goliath's Head (47)
The Light Ray Robot (35)
Uran the Tomboy (13)
Robio and Robiette (44)
Astro Fights Aliens (7)
Save the Carolina 3 (5)
The Rainbow Comet (15) [Astro Versus Atlas no. 4]
The Death Balloon (49)
The Transformation Robot (9)
The Wreck of the Titan (30)
The Liar Robot (43)
The Girl From Alsoar (20)
The Greatest Robot in the World, Part 1 (50)
The Greatest Robot in the World, Part 2 (51)
The Robot Vikings (22) [Astro Versus Atlas no. 5]
The Time Machine (36)

The Robot Stuntman (34)
The Great Meltdown (23) [Astro Versus Atlas no. 6]
Uran's Twin (27)
Speeding Through the Storm (14)
The Return of Queen Cleopatra (46)
The Runaway Subway Train (16) [Astro Versus Atlas no. 7]
The Baby Elephant Pook (6)
The Secret of Bee City (42)
The Monster of Clarken (17)
Lily on Peligro Island (24)
The Anti-Proton Gun (41) [Astro Versus Atlas no. 8]
The Man-Made Solar Sphere (37)
Blackie Young (45)
The Genie From Outer Space (18)
The Robots Nobody Wanted (19)
Atlas Forever (48) [Astro Versus Atlas no. 9]
The Snow Leopard (25)
Uran's Quest (32)
Outer Spaceport R45 (28)
The Hijacked Airship (39)
The Human-Faced Rock (26)
Uran Falls in Love (38)
The World of Odin (33)
The Secret of the Mayas (40)
Astro's First Love (4)

scientist-commander, who reveals that Nuka is a disguised nuclear bomb. Dr. Lindolf launches Atom towards the Sun in an escape-proof rocket, but Nuka follows to rescue him. Lindolf activates her one-hour detonation device to punish her for treachery. Atom flies them both back to the base, where Nuka urges Lindolf and Atom to dismantle her to save themselves and the innocent humans around them.

Let's analyze this. Atom is a helpless pansy. His attempt to pass as a human boy is ludicrous. He fails to infiltrate the base and must be helped in by a conveniently friendly stranger. He is immediately captured, and must be rescued by the cute girl robot. She altruistically sacrifices her own life to save him (and others). Atom can do nothing but sigh mournfully and look as though he is about to burst into tears.

Tezuka may have beamed with pride at putting his personal touch on this and the other fifty-one episodes. But is it any wonder that the public preferred the more dynamic, never-give-up Atom of the '60s who did not look like a well-meaning but constant loser?

The fifty-two color episodes were dubbed into English for an Australian broadcast in 1982–84, which is now being released on video in Australia and Britain. This version's character names are a curious mixture of original Japanese names, names from the American 1963–64 version, and brand-new names. "Astro Boy," "Dr. Boynton," "Dr. Elefun," and "Inspector Gumshoe" are the old American names. "Uran" (Astro Girl) and "Hamegg" (Ringmaster Cacciatore) are the original Japanese names. "Daddy Walrus" (Higeoyagi/Mr. Pompus) is a new Australian name. To add to the confusion, there is also a separate 1980s Canadian dubbing with different names.

Pokémon: Ready for Its Next Success
Animation Magazine no. 92, July/August 2000.

Last November the gaming and TV mega-hit *Pokémon* scored another success in the motion picture field, when *Pokémon: The First Movie* set new records for a November theatrical release, earning over $50 million in its first five days. Now *Pokémon: The Movie 2000* is poised to duplicate the phenomenon with its July 21 premiere in theaters.

Pokémon (a Japanese juvenile slang abbreviation of *Pocket Monsters*, adopted in America as the official title) began in 1996 as a Nintendo children's video game. Game designer Satoshi Tajiri based the premise on his own childhood fascination for unusual insects. Its popularity quickly led to a comic book series and a weekly TV cartoon series in April 1997, both produced by Shogakukan Production Co. Ltd. *Pokémon's* launch date in America was September 1998, when both Nintendo's first *Pokémon* Game Boy video game and the TV cartoons premiered.

The animation began as a weekday syndicated TV series, but its ratings won it promotion to the Kids' WB! network less than six months later. The 1998 Japanese theatrical feature hit American theaters in November 1999, with results (including front-page news reports of battles over the fast-food kids' meal tie-in gaming cards) that stunned critics.

Pokémon's popularity with the seven-to-fourteen age group is based upon a combination of the eye-catching allure of numerous cute fantasy animals, and strong stories featuring a likeable cast centered around Ash Ketchum, a ten-year-old boy, and Pikachu, a pocket-sized "electric mouse." In the Pokémon world, all children compete to capture and tame one each of the exotic woodland and river creatures (originally 150, though each new video game and motion picture introduces at least one new Pokémon to the cast). Those who acquire a full set win the coveted title of Master Pokémon Trainer.

Ash set out at first to grab these Pokémon for fame and glory, but through his developing friendship with Pikachu he gradually came to recognize the animals as living creatures rather than mere possessions. *Pokémon* uses the mania to be "in" with the latest electronic games to steer children toward a deeper relationship with animals and nature, as well as an appreciation for the responsibility of caring for pets and the importance of ecological awareness.

This aspect is dramatized in *Pokémon: The Movie 2000.* The second theatrical feature follows the two-part format of the first. It opens with a twenty-two-minute humorous short, *Pikachu's Rescue Adventure,* starring everyone's favorite Pokémon at home in the forest during a storm, along with some of the rarer of the cute monsters, such as Hoothoot, Bellossom, Ladyba, Slowking and Elekid.

The hour-long main feature (the Japanese title is *Revelation Lugia*) is a dramatic adventure that introduces new Pokémon so powerful that they are closer to the gods of folk tales. Ash's questing around the world brings him to the Shamouti Islands, where he learns of four mighty Pokémon birds that control the elements of nature: Moltres (fire), Zapdos (lightning), Articuno (ice), and their leader, Lugia (water). The four live in harmony, maintaining nature's balance. But Lawrence (his Japanese name is Zildan), an arrogant and greedy Pokémon collector, captures them, which throws nature into chaos. Lugia chooses Ash as a representative of humanity to prove that humans do know the importance of ecological balance.

The movie pushes the *Pokémon* theatrical envelope with faster pacing, more dramatic battles and more CGI.

Pokémon: The Movie 2000 has been produced for American audiences by 4Kids Productions, the same creative team that makes the TV cartoons and that created last year's big screen release. Norman J. Grossfeld, the company president, is the film's producer, as well as co-adapter (with director Michael Haigney) of the original screenplay by Takeshi Shudo.

"I don't think kids see Ash as a superhero," Grossfeld says. "It's more like he's their surrogate in the world of Pokémon and that's what makes the stories so special . . . What we're hoping to show kids with this movie is what Ash learns—that one person can make a difference. You never know when you might be faced with a situation where you can do something good for someone and be a hero, even in a small way. It doesn't have to be huge and the whole world doesn't necessarily have to know about it. You just have to be willing, like Ash, to do the right thing."

The *Pokémon* movies have become a summer tradition in Japan since 1998. The third feature, *Pocket Monsters: Lord of the Unknown Tower,* was released in Japan July 9. And although each movie features a separate story, each is also tied to background elements in the ongoing weekly *Pokémon* TV cartoons.

The first *Pokémon* movie was released in America last November partly because the American TV series had reached the point by which background elements in the movie would be understood by the TV fans. This year the reverse is true. *Pokémon: The Movie 2000* will introduce new elements that will be followed up in the fall season of the TV series, *Pokémon GS.* The new elements in the movie and the TV series will also be expanded in the next generation of Nintendo's *Pokémon Gold and Silver* (hence GS) Game Boy video games.

The *Pokémon* TV series is still tops in the ratings (for the fourth quarter of 1999 and the first quarter of 2000, *Pokémon* ranked both No. 1 and 2 of the top ten Saturday morning programs for the children two-to-eleven group). With adventures and characters introduced in *Pokémon: The Movie 2000* and *Pokémon GS,* Warner Bros. plans to keep *Pokémon* on top.

Is Digimon Movie Destined for Success?
Animation Magazine no. 94, October 2000.

The popularity of Japanese "cute monster* cartoons" that began in America in summer 1998 with *Pokémon* is still riding high. There are three series on American TV featuring human children in a world of adorable fantasy animals that look designed for the plush-doll market: *Pokémon, Digimon,* and *Monster Rancher.*

Two *Pokémon* theatrical movies, distributed by Warner Bros., have hit America's big screens in 1999 and 2000. The first was a mega-success; the second, just out in July, seems to be establishing itself as second only to *Chicken Run* among America's theatrical animated releases of 2000. Now the *Digimon: Digital Monsters* TV series is about to make the transition to

---

*In Japanese, "monster" is a generic word for any imaginary creature. It does not have the pejorative implication of inherent menace or evil that the English word carries.

theaters. Twentieth Century Fox will distribute *Digimon: The Movie* to 1,700 theaters starting October 6.

Digimon: Digital Monsters premiered on the Fox Kids Network in August 1999, adapted for American TV from the weekly *Digimon Adventures* TV cartoons that started in Japan in March 1999. To parents, the principal story differences between *Pokémon* and *Digimon* are that *Pokémon* is set in a different world similar to Earth, in which all children try to catch and tame one each of 150 different species of cute pocket-sized forest monsters. The story centers on a few of these children and the particular creatures that become their special pets.

In *Digimon,* seven children at a summer camp on Earth are transported to a magical digital world which seems connected to the Internet. The idea of humans entering a fantastic electronic/Internet world is a science-fictional theme that goes back to the 1970s. Disney's *Tron* (1982) was one of the first such cinematic adventures.

In *Digimon,* children meet a group of intelligent digital animals (Digimon), and each child bonds with one that is attuned to his or her personality. An evil force of "Black Gears" is trying to take over the Digiworld by corrupting the Digimon. The children have been brought to the Digiworld to join with their Digimon companions; thus they've become "DigiDestined" to fight the evil that threatens our world as well.

Digimon characters are talking playmates rather than non-speaking pets. Each Digimon helps his or her human partner improve personality traits (become braver and more alert, concentrate harder when there is an important job to be done, etc.). Meanwhile, each child helps his or her Digimon partner transform from a cute little monster into a more robust and dynamic form in the face of danger. Naturally, there are collectible toys of both forms.

Digimon episodes flow together as a continuing serial—more so than the *Pokémon* episodes, which are self-contained yet feature a gradually advancing story line.

On TV *Pokémon* and *Digimon* have been running neck-and-neck in terms of popularity among their audiences. Newer *Digimon* episodes have put the series in the lead in that race. *Digimon* has become the Fox Kids Network's top-rated program on weekdays and Saturdays, as *Pokémon* has been for Kids' WB! During the last television sweeps period in May 2000, *Digimon* topped *Pokémon* by 63 percent in the two-to-eleven age group, and by 29 percent in the six-to-eleven group. Now we will see whether this TV popularity translates into theatrical popularity.

A subtle technical difference exists between the movies. The *Pokémon* movies were produced as complete feature-length adventures in Japan, and adapted for American audiences with English dubbing and minor editing. The *Digimon* movie does not exist as such in Japan. *Digimon* is produced by Toei Animation Co., Japan's largest animation studio; Toei also produces

Sailor Moon and *Dragon Ball Z*. For more than twenty years Toei has produced theatrical eighty- to ninety-minute "animation fair" compilation features, which consist of two to four new short adventures showcasing its most popular TV cartoons of the moment. This lets children see new adventures of their favorite TV cartoons in higher-quality theatrical animation.

The eighty-three-minute *Digimon: The Movie* was edited for U.S. release from three *Digimon* shorts taken from the spring and summer 1999 and 2000 Toei Animation Fairs. The first, a twenty-minute segment, is a prequel describing how the seven children first met and became friends. The second, a forty-minute featurette, links the events of the TV serial's first season (fifty-four episodes) and sets up the new plot and cast of the second season, *Digimon 02*. The third segment is a twenty-minute mini-adventure set during the second season, which began in Japan in April and in mid-August in the States. This has the advantage of encompassing the entire *Digimon* story line and main cast in the feature, but in a story that is somewhat more episodic than the usual movie adventure.

Subtle cultural differences can also be found between *Pokémon* and *Digimon*. *Pokémon*, which was launched in America in September 1998, may be the last Japanese cartoon import for which the American producers felt it necessary to Americanize the main characters' names. *Digimon, Monster Rancher*, and, most recently, *Cardcaptors* have retained original Japanese names.

Terri O'Malley, *Digimon*'s producer, says: "Bringing Japanese animation to American audiences is even easier this year than it was just last year. The public is aware today that programs like *Sailor Moon* and *Digimon* are from Japan, and that the cast really has Japanese names, and they don't care. They even expect to see Japanese signs in the background. The only time we have to change the writing now is when the audience is meant to read it, such as when there is a close-up on a handwritten note and the audience is expected to read the note.

"Since *Digimon* is for young children," O'Malley continues, "we have given some of the juvenile heroes American-sounding nicknames for easier audience identification. But they are based on their Japanese names. Yamato Ishida is "Matt." Koushiro Izumi's friends call him "Izzy." And Takeru Takaishi is "TK." We try to never change a name, unless the original foreign name turns out to coincidentally have unfortunate connotations in English or Spanish.

"In fact, in this feature," she adds, "the children from Japan meet a new boy in the Digiworld who comes from America. This emphasizes that *Digimon* is not about either a group of Japanese children or a group of American children. It is about children, period. Everything that happens to the kids in Japan is also happening to kids in America, and in the rest of the world. The Digiworld, the Internet, is international, just like childhood is universal."

Vampire Hunter D: The Next Anime Hit in America?
Animation World Magazine 5 no. 9, December 2000.

The question has arisen recently as to whether the American motion picture industry is ready for Japanese theatrical animation, which is not pre-sold through children's TV. For most of the 1990s (starting with *Akira* in December 1989), Japanese animated features for adolescent and adult audiences have toured America only on the fine-art theatrical circuit. They have played usually in only one theater at a time, for a half-week or a week before moving on to the next city. The only exception was Troma's 1993 small general release of the family film, *My Neighbor Totoro*. It was not successful enough to justify the costs of making dozens of 35 mm prints and taking out full-page newspaper advertising.

But a lot can change in a few years. Anime is better known to the general public than it was just five years ago. Animation in general has become more acceptable for adults, thanks to movies and TV programs like *Toy Story, Chicken Run, King of the Hill,* and *South Park.* Theatrical children's features based on the mega-popular Japanese TV cartoons *Pokémon* and *Digimon* have been notoriously profitable despite poor critical reviews. Is it time to experiment again with a theatrical release of a Japanese animated feature for general audiences rather than for young children?

Urban Vision Entertainment, an anime-specialty company, hopes so as it prepares to release *Vampire Hunter D,* a stylish fantasy thriller in the tradition of Britain's 1950s–'60s Hammer horror movies teaming Christopher Lee and Peter Cushing. The small Los Angeles-based company is working hard at lining up a wider theatrical release than the art-house circuit by the time the movie is finished in early 2001.

The Modest First Film
Vampire Hunter D has a respectable if somewhat confusing history, thanks to a 1985 anime movie of the same name. That was an adaptation of a 1983 horror-adventure novel by Hideyuki Kikuchi. Kikuchi has fashioned himself into one of Japan's leading horrormeisters during the past two decades, churning out paperback novels in the tradition of Western horror writers like Robert E. Howard, Fritz Leiber, Robert Bloch, H. P. Lovecraft and

This second *Vampire Hunter D* movie was titled *Vampire Hunter D: Bloodlust* at the last minute to distinguish it from the first movie. It was released only in its English-language version; the Japanese theatrical release was subtitled in Japanese. Unfortunately, its American theatrical release was just the traditional art-theater crawl; it premiered on September 23, 2001, in only six theaters throughout America. But it took in a $25,521 gross, which is excellent for only six art theaters. Its total gross during its theatrical run was $151,086. ■

Stephen King. Many Japanese live-action and animated horror movies of the 1980s and '90s have been based on Kikuchi's novels. The author is known for, every couple of months, hosting all-night seminars for horror fans at a bar near his Tokyo home.

The 1980s were a decade of transition for Japanese animation, and the first *Vampire Hunter D* was notable in several respects. It was one of Japan's earliest animated releases aimed blatantly at the older teen/adult market rather than for children or families. It was one of anime's first treatments of European horror mythology rather than boys'-adventure science-fiction or traditional Asian horror-fantasy. Although *Vampire Hunter D* did have a theatrical release (in December 1985 and early 1986), it was intended primarily for Japan's emerging home-video market, which was already demanding more dramatic action and adventure (i.e., more violence and gore) than was permissible in family-oriented animation. Animation allowed *Vampire Hunter D* to present frightening monsters and breathtaking fantastic action that would have looked embarrassingly laughable in a low-budget live-action film. *Vampire Hunter D* was a hit with horror-movie fans in Japan in the late 1980s. It was also popular with horror and anime fans as one of the earliest anime releases in America, on the fine-art theatrical circuit and home video in 1992 and on The Sci-Fi Channel in 1993.

But it was a limited-budget production. Its technical quality compared favorably with videos of TV animation and direct-to-video releases, but not with most animated theatrical movies. Ironically, one of the animated features that it suffered next to was another horror thriller based on a novel by Kikuchi, *Wicked City,* produced at the new Madhouse studio by director Yoshiaki Kawajiri, released in April 1987. Kawajiri's directorial debut had been *Lensman,* a *Star Wars*-imitation space opera based on an American 1930s SF novel, three years earlier. *Wicked City,* a Stephen King-type modern urban horror fantasy, was his second theatrical feature. It set Kawajiri's reputation as a major directorial *auteur* of sophisticated animated suspense. His productions for the next decade were dominated by adult thrillers set in a high-tech future or in a Japanese historical landscape haunted by mythological monsters. At this same time, Kikuchi's reputation as a horror writer was also growing, and his original *Vampire Hunter D* novel was followed by several sequels. Fan demand for another movie, "done right" (Kikuchi had complained about the cheapness of the first movie), started developing.

A New Ultra-Cool Version

Plans for a new *Vampire Hunter D* by Madhouse and Kawajiri had just started in 1997 when a new partner appeared. Mataichiro Yamamoto had been a Japanese animation producer since the early 1980s, working with both established major studios (he was a co-producer in 1983 for Tokyo Movie Shinsha's *Golgo 13,* one of the earliest animated theatrical features to combine traditional cel animation with computer graphics) and his own Filmlink International company (which also produces live-action movies). In July 1996, Yamamoto started Urban Vision Entertainment in America to become directly involved with the growing American demand for anime. One of Urban Vision's first video releases was a Madhouse production. Yamamoto also wanted to pick up the American rights to both *Vampire Hunter D* and Madhouse's *Wicked City* (previously released in America by Streamline Pictures).

During their negotiations, Madhouse mentioned that it was starting a new *Vampire Hunter D* movie that would be ready in three or four years. Yamamoto wanted to do more than reserve the American video license for it; he wanted to get involved in its production. Also, Urban Vision had started small as an anime video distributor only, but Yamamoto hoped that in a few more years—coincidentally, by the time the new *Vampire Hunter D* would be finished—Urban Vision would be ready to expand into American theatrical distribution.

The new *Vampire Hunter D* bears the same title as the 1985 feature, but it is based upon the third novel (of twelve, so far; none yet published in English) in Kikuchi's series, *D: Demon Deathchase* (1985). The setting is a Gothic medieval fantasy world of A.D. 12,090, long after nuclear and biochemical war destroyed civilization. Human survivors were forced to contend with mutant-spawned monsters that resembled the supernatural beasts of legends. At first the monsters gained the upper hand—blood-drinkers who established themselves as a new feudal aristocracy modeled upon *Dracula* and similar vampire literature, preying on human peasants and serfs. After thousands of years, the vampires are becoming feeble and decadent, and the humans are rising up against their domination. "D" is a stereotypical mysterious Lone Rider, a taciturn knight-errant/ronin who rides into a community embroiled in civil war and offers to help the humans fight their vampire lords, despite showing clear signs of being a human-vampire crossbreed himself.

In the new movie, "D" is summoned by a prominent family in one of the rising but still isolated human cities. Their daughter has been kidnapped by one of the most powerful remaining vampires, who has fled with her beyond the borders of their authority. They offer ten million dollars for her return, or proof of a clean death in case she has been converted into a vampire. But they are not relying on "D" alone; they have also called in a team of ruthless anti-monster bounty hunters. The movie becomes a running three-way chase across the countryside, through both human and monster towns. There are clear signs almost immediately that the daughter Charlotte has eloped voluntarily with the handsome, charismatic vampire.

The vampire and monster mercenaries in his hire try to kill both "D" and the team of bounty hunters. The five bounty hunters (a combination of Rambo-style commandos, ninja assassins, and a beautiful but cynical femme fatale) are out to kill the vampire, and some of them would not mind killing the girl and claiming the "clean death" rather than taking the trouble to capture her alive. They also set traps to kill "D" or at least take him out of the competition. "D" remains stony-faced, but he obviously wonders if he is really on the right side if the vampire and Charlotte are genuine lovers and are voluntarily going into exile to leave humans in peace. But is this a trick of the vampire, with Charlotte as an innocent dupe?

First Rate Execution

The movie has some clever dialogue, but it relies so heavily on its visual impact that it would not matter much if it were shown as a silent film. The suspenseful direction by Kawajiri (who also wrote the screenplay) is backed up by beautiful graphics. Most of the chase takes place by day, through bright forest settings filled with trees and flowers. The vampires' sumptuous palaces and court costumes are rococo marvels of filigree and lace and sparkling gold trim (no cobwebs or emaciated corpses here). The main character designs are by noted international fantasy artist Yoshitaka Amano, whose recent American projects have included the art for *1001 Nights,* an animated fine-art film commissioned by the Los Angeles Philharmonic Orchestra with original music by David Neuman, and the full-color illustrations for fantasy author Neil Gaiman's deluxe book *Sandman: The Dream Hunters.* Amano's art style was faithfully matched for the rest of the characters and costumes by animation director Yutaka Minowa. Although the character animation is not up to the highest Disney standards, Kawajiri's tight direction of facial expressions and body language conveys a convincing "illusion of life" despite a limited fluidity of motion.

While the animation of *Vampire Hunter D* was in production at Tokyo's Madhouse studio, Urban Vision arranged for the post-production work in California. The English sound track was recorded in Los Angeles in 1999 before the Japanese dialogue was completed. The sound effects and other post-production work were directed during 2000 by Kawajiri in Marin County at Marco Co., whose husband-and-wife owners, Marco and Terry D'Ambrosio, composed the score. The film's final print master was made at George Lucas' nearby Skywalker Ranch facility.

Urban Vision has also been working on publicity and distribution all this time. A two-and-a-half-minute theatrical trailer was finished in 1998 and has been shown often at American anime fan conventions; it is also downloadable on Urban Vision's Web site. Urban Vision has made a work-in-progress print available for international film exhibitions since mid-2000. It has played to enthusiastic audiences at the FANT-ASIA Asian Film Festival in Montreal, Canada in July; at Japanime: The Best of Japanese Animation, the major film event at the Sydney 2000 Olympics Arts Festival in Sydney, Australia in August; and at the New York Anime Film Festival in October. A sold-out Halloween screening at UCLA's Anime A-Go-Go film program in October-November was blurbed as, "Regency meets Transylvania in this visual knockout of a movie with exquisitely gothic atmospherics, creepy special effects, tense action, and von Helsing fashioned as a foppish, half-vampire, half-human outcast called 'D.'"

Now, plans are being finalized for a simultaneous theatrical release in Japan and America. A Japanese general theatrical release is assured, but tiny Urban Vision is still trying to arrange for an American release that will exceed the traditional anime art-theater crawl of one theater in a couple of cities at a time. Its goal is still modest for an American general release: five or more theaters per city in twenty cities at a time. If Urban Vision can achieve this, *Vampire Hunter D* may become the first anime feature to reach America's general science-fiction/horror fantasy theatrical audiences.

Thanks for information on Hideyuki Kikuchi and his *Vampire Hunter D* novels to the *Vampire Hunter D Archives* Web site (http://www.altvampyres.net/vhd/) run by Cathy Krusberg, an American fan who can be reached at ckberg@ix.netcom.com.

Blood: The Last Vampire—Anime's First Digital Feature
Animation World Magazine 6, no. 7, October 2001.

Theatrical anime has been trying to achieve theatrical distribution in America since 1989. Limited to film festivals and sporadic art theater tours during most of the 1990s, 2001 may be the year that theatrical anime has reached its goal—or at least qualified itself as an entry to be taken seriously at the starting line. 2001 has seen nationwide releases of anime features as diverse as *Akira, Blood: The Last Vampire, Final Fantasy: The Spirits Within, Jin-Roh, Pokémon 3, Spriggan,* and *Vampire Hunter D: Bloodlust,* with *Metropolis* and *Escaflowne: A Girl in Gaea* due in early 2002. Most of these still appear in art theaters rather than a general citywide release; but in more than just a single theater, with play dates of a couple of weeks rather than just a couple of days, and getting serious reviews in the local press.

Blood: The Last Vampire is one of the most unusual, innovative, and exciting of this roster. It is Japan's first fully digital-imaged animation combined with CGI, presenting richly detailed animated characters against backgrounds of photographic reality. The unusually short forty-eight-minute running time makes it arguably a featurette rather than a feature, but this has not kept reviewers from treating it as a regular movie. Reactions from its Los Angeles release:

"Director Hiroyuki Kitakubo (*Roujin Z*) has created a rare animated spook show that is genuinely chilling, not just gross or campy. . . . The realistically textured designs have been subtly heightened and distorted, in a hangover palette of grays and browns." David Chute, *LA Weekly*, August 24–30.

" . . . stylistically, it's a huge break from the past, incorporating digital effects (and a more realistic look) to a greater extent than any of its predecessors, and merging the 2-D characters in near-seamless fashion. . . . if you expect quantity (or closure) for your $8 ticket, you may feel shorted. The quality, however, is unlikely to be disputed. *Blood* is, if nothing else, a visual stunner . . ." Luke Y. Thompson, *New Times Los Angeles*, August 16–22.

That complaint about the lack of closure indicates what is possibly *Blood*'s most imaginative and daring gamble: a story that is deliberately, frustratingly confusing and incomplete. The setting is an American military base in Japan in 1966, just gearing up to support the American military action in Vietnam. The audience's point of view is with a civilian nurse, who suddenly finds herself swept up in a running firefight between vampiric, human-hunting monsters and a team of government agents (?) with a mysterious superhuman young girl (vampire?). At the conclusion the action moves on, leaving the nurse (and the audience) facing a massive government cover-up, wondering if they will ever learn the truth.

Production of *Blood* began around early 1999 at Tokyo's Production I.G studio. Founded in December 1987 by Mitsuhisa Ishikawa, the studio has produced animation for TV programs, direct to video releases, theatrical features and video games. Writer-director Mamoru Oshii, one of the major names in Japanese animation, has been associated with Production I.G since he directed the *Patlabor* OAV series and two theatrical features in 1988–89 and 1993. Oshii and Production I.G really became noticed by the public in 1995, with the release of the CGI-intensive, Oshii-directed theatrical feature *Ghost in the Shell*.

In 1998 Ishikawa asked Oshii if he could recruit some fresh talent for the studio. Oshii began a study group called "Oshii Jyuku" (Team Oshii), gathering promising young animation writers, artists and filmmakers into a series of informal tutorial sessions to discuss how to go about creating a professional animation project. After several weeks of covering the basics, Oshii asked the members to come up with their own project plans, which the whole group would analyze together. In the *Making of Blood: The Last Vampire* documentary, scriptwriter Kenji Kamiyama said, "Mr. Oshii's study group was intended to give us young directors the practical know-how to implement a project plan. It was difficult because I had to create a plan every week. . . . I used all of my free time between my day job but I always had to pull an all-nighter before the due date."

It was about a year before the first elements of *Blood* began to appear. Junichi Fujisaki submitted a project, which included a young woman in a schoolgirl's uniform angrily brandishing a sword. The group felt that

Fujisaki's story was weak, but they liked that image. Then Kenji Kamiyama proposed a plot titled "The Last Vampire." The group liked its basic concept, and felt that Fujisaki's strong female character, Saya, would be just right as its lead. At this point Ishikawa began to look for a new production for the studio, so Oshii proposed that he, Fujisaki, and Kamiyama develop this production plan into a serious proposal.

The "Blood Project" that Team Oshii came up with was more ambitious than just one movie. Oshii personally (with a film credit of "Cooperative Planning") constructed a thriller plot of a modern vampire story. Humanity is being secretly preyed upon by shapeshifting monsters called "chiropterans" (literally "bat people"). This is being kept from the public by a top-secret international agency of vampire hunters (or maybe a series of government agencies in each country) who must hunt down the chiropterans without the public becoming aware of them. Aiding the vampire hunters is a sullen young woman named Saya armed with an ancient samurai sword. Saya's true nature and personal history are never clarified, but she obviously has superhuman strength and is spoken of in awe by the government vampire hunters as "the last of the Originals" who has been personally fighting the chiropterans all around the world for over a hundred years.

Several Facets of *Blood*

The Blood Project was divided into three parts, each semi-independent and each revealing important details of the story. Oshii wrote a complete fantasy horror novel, *Blood: The Last Vampire—The Night of the Beasts,* set three years after the events in the movie. Despite Oshii's previous directorial work for the studio, Ishikawa asked Hiroyuki Kitakubo to direct the *Blood* movie while Fujisaki and Kamiyama finished its screenplay. Kitakubo had previously directed a different *Ghost in the Shell* for Production I.G—the animation for the Playstation video game as distinct from the movie—as well as the theatrical feature *Roujin Z* and the OAV *Black Magic M-66* for other studios. The third part was a Playstation 2 video game, *Blood: The Last Vampire—Tokyo Battle,* set in 2000 (then two years in the future). Animation for this game was designed and directed by Satoru Nakamura, another of the Team Oshii study group. There were further *Blood* spinoffs; a comic book adaptation of the movie and a novelization of the video game plot. But they were incidental to the basic story, which was told through the movie, Oshii's novel and the video game. They were all released in Japan between October and December 2000, with the movie released in mid-November.

In a written interview for this article, Mr. Kitakubo says: "I was asked by Mr. Ishikawa to think about creating the movie [once the Blood Project was agreed upon] so it took only a few months for the project to start. The master plan was to have as many different ways to exploit this project as possible. I was only personally involved in part of the plan, as I was only involved in creating the movie. All these different elements to the one big project were overseen by various people who had their assignment and had the freedom to express their own view of how *Blood* should be portrayed. It was one of the rules to this project; nobody would interfere with the other person's project."

One of Kitakubo's key decisions was to pick popular artist and SF movie designer Katsuya Terada as *Blood*'s character designer. Terada, who has drawn many cartoon characters for video games, was intrigued by the challenge of designing characters of an unusual degree of reality to be animated, including two Afro-Americans, a soldier and a Man-In-Black secret agent. Terada also drew the cover art and graphics for Oshii's *Blood* novel.

A New Boundary

Both Kitakubo and Ishikawa wanted the movie to push Production I.G to new limits in digital imaging technology. When asked if the unusually short running time was an artistic decision to reinforce the enigmatic stretching of the story between the three parts, Kitakubo said: "To be honest, the reason we made it forty-eight minutes long was because of our software and hardware limitations. Anything that was longer would have made the film of a lesser quality. We wanted to create a new style of animation appealing to a larger audience." The digital imaging developed by Production I.G did not break new ground; it is essentially the same procedures that Disney has been using for its features since *Pocahontas* and *Mulan*. But this was new ground for Japan, and it puts Production I.G at the forefront of the Japanese industry's advance from the old hand-drawn cel process to animation "in the computer." *The Making of Blood: The Last Vampire* thirty-five-minute documentary (included with the movie on the video and DVD releases) shows the studio's digital technicians and equipment in some detail.

The results have been appreciated in reviews like those cited at the beginning of this article. *Blood* is also racking up an impressive list of honors. In addition to four awards in Japan (from the Media Art Festival of the Agency of Cultural Affairs, the 55th Mainichi Film Competition, the Takasaki Film Festival and the Animation Kobe Festival), *Blood: The Last Vampire* was voted Best Feature Film at the 2001 World Animation Celebration in Hollywood in August. And it is one of four nominees for ASIFA-Hollywood's twenty-ninth annual Annie Awards in the category of Outstanding Achievement in an Animated Feature Film, where it is being measured against Disney's *The Emperor's New Groove,* Warner Bros.' *Osmosis Jones* and PDI/DreamWorks' *Shrek* for the award in November. Heady company for an anime feature!

What is the future for the Blood Project? In America fans of the movie are still awaiting news on whether the novels or the video game will be published in this country. In Japan there have been a couple more novels, but the project is essentially finished. Mr. Kitakubo concluded his interview with, "As far as I can say, this project has been completed and each one of us have gone on to new interests. We are not at this moment working on anything related to *Blood*. Production I.G owns the project in its entirety. Team Oshii still remains within the whole I.G. structure. There probably will be new projects born from Team Oshii in the future, but at this time nothing I can say that's concrete."

A Retro-future *Metropolis*
Animation World Magazine 6, no. 11, February 2002.

Every so often a landmark film appears which advances the state of the art of animated features. These usually project a modernistic or futuristic mood. It is unusual when one is equally successful as a tribute to the past. *Metropolis* (formally *Osamu Tezuka's Metropolis*, to distinguish it from the classic Fritz Lang 1927 feature) superbly straddles both the past and the future. It blends the soft, "cartoony" art style of the late 1930s American theatrical short cartoons (Disney, Fleischer, Harmon, and Ising) with the latest in computer graphics to tell a drama reminiscent of the SF adventures of the 1920s and '30s; Lang's *Metropolis* and other such mid-'30s serials as *The Phantom Empire* and *Undersea Kingdom* also did this.

The Re-Creation of *Metropolis*
Osamu Tezuka (1928–1989), Japan's "God of Comics" (Manga no Kamisama), is widely credited as the major creative influence on that nation's post-World War II comic book industry in the late 1940s and 1950s, and its animation industry in the late 1950s and 1960s. He was known at the time as "the Walt Disney of Japan" (a title which has since passed to Hayao Miyazaki). One of his earliest TV animation staff was Rintaro (Shigeyuki Hayashi). In one of Tezuka's last communications to American anime fans in the mid-1980s, he urged them to seek out the manga of Katsuhiro Otomo, a new writer-artist who was winning his first awards (*Domu, Akira*). *Osamu Tezuka's Metropolis*, directed by Rintaro from a screenplay by Otomo (as part of the "Metropolis Committee," the credited producers—five years in production at the Madhouse studio), is their tribute to Tezuka.

At the same time, it is their opportunity to have fun, just as Tezuka did when he drew his *Metropolis* cartoon novel in the late 1940s. Tezuka's first cartoons were published while he was still a student, just after World War II ended. They caught the public's attention because of Tezuka's flamboyant use of cinematic effects (close-ups, tracking shots, unusual camera angles) and dramas (e.g., Westerns, modern crime thrillers, etc. influenced by the movies imported into Japan by the Allied Occupation) while most other Japanese cartoonists were still drawing traditional Japanese themes. One of Tezuka's first influential works was a cartoon-art adaptation of *Crime and Punishment*. Tezuka always admitted that his *Metropolis* (155 pages, published on September 15, 1949) was much less serious. In fact, he had not yet seen Lang's movie when he produced his version, inspired by the reviews and plot synopses of it and a picture of its movie poster showing the robot woman. His was more a generic synthesis of old SF movies and adventure serials, with a Mad Scientist named Dr. Charles Laughton (after the actor who had played Dr. Moreau in the 1933 *Island of Lost Souls,* not the scientist Rotwang in Lang's *Metropolis*), a master criminal plotting to conquer the world with his army of robots (compare Tezuka's Duke Red with Eduardo Ciannelli in the 1940 *Mysterious Dr. Satan*), a tough Private Investigator, and a couple of adventurous young kids, one of whom is unwittingly the lost human-looking robot girl Michi (the equivalent of Maria in Lang's movie). When her robotic nature overcomes her innocence and she turns destructive, her climactic battle against the police atop a skyscraper is reminiscent of *King Kong.* Tezuka's rambling cartoon novel even contains obvious art references from the Disney-produced *Mickey Mouse* newspaper adventure strip of the '30s drawn by Floyd Gottfredson.

Looking at the 1949 *Metropolis* today, it is easy to see why Tezuka tended to dismiss most of his earliest work before the 1950s (although his robot girl Michi was clearly a prototype for his *Tetsuwan Atom/Astro Boy* created a few years later, indicating that Astro Boy owes as much to Lang's Maria as to Collodi's Pinocchio). Otomo and Rintaro have wisely completely revamped Tezuka's youthful light parody of 1930s SF movie themes into a tighter and more dramatic story, which is a much better tribute to Tezuka's whole career. It also works better as a tribute to Lang's original concept, since it restores the cinematic visual emphasis of a towering futuristic city that is mostly Art Deco in design (or 1890s to 1910s for the slums), and the plot emphasis of a class struggle between labor and a capitalistic elite (represented by their new robot working class). But they (and character designer Yasuhiro Nakura) have retained Tezuka's early art style from the 1949 manga rather than using his more familiar and sophisticated style from his later works such as *Astro Boy* and *Kimba the White Lion.*

Stunning ...

The first five minutes of the new *Metropolis* are worth the price of admission alone for the visual spectacle. It opens with a pseudo-1930s black-and-white newsreel of financial magnate Duke Red proclaiming the completion of his towering office building, the Ziggurat, which will confirm the status of Metropolis as the greatest nation in the world. The screen suddenly expands to a color CGI panorama of an inaugural celebration with thousands cheering in the streets, searchlights, fireworks, the sky aswarm with zeppelins crowded with sightseers. The camera swoops dizzyingly upward, downward, and outward from the immense skyscraper, including a brief look out from an elite glass-walled restaurant on an upper floor of the Ziggurat.

The scene continues long enough to introduce the main plot elements.

Duke Red is sharing the speakers' stand with Metropolis's President Boon. When reporters ask Duke Red if he is considering going into politics, he pledges his complete support to Boon's administration; but their glances and body language reveal that neither trusts the other. Conversation between a man and a boy in the crowd establish that they are strangers to Metropolis who have just arrived. Shunsaku Ban is an investigator from Japan with his young nephew Kenichi as his assistant. They are tracking a scientist guilty of illegal research in robotics. Shots are heard, and a group of men in similar clothing are seen shooting at a figure who turns out to be a robot disguised as a human. Ban and Kenichi overhear conversation that reveals that the men are in the uniform of the Marduks, a militant anti-robot political party that everyone knows amounts to a private army controlled by Duke Red, and that anti-robot prejudice has been growing stronger as more humans are becoming unemployed due to being replaced by them by the city's ruling capitalist elite.

The 1949 manga plot was mostly a straightforward confrontation between Ban and Duke Red, while the robot girl who believes that she is human searches for her parents. In the more complex movie plot, Duke Red has brought Dr. Laughton (no first name) to Metropolis to create a new-generation Artificial Intelligence to control the super-computer, which is secretly built into the Ziggurat. Duke Red insists that this A.I. be made in the form of a robot duplicate of his dead daughter, Tima (instead of Michi). Due to plot machinations, Tima is lost, activated without any instructions, and discovered by Kenichi, who believes that she is a traumatized human with amnesia. She does not merely have adventures as Michi did; Tima is also on a quest for identity. Is she a robot, or does her human-level Artificial Intelligence make her human in a moral sense? Many of the wonders of Metropolis are seen through the eyes of Tima.

A Clever Collection of Past and Future

The action in this 107-minute feature seldom slows down, but it is almost incidental to the vast city in which it takes place. This *Metropolis* with its newest and most imposing Ziggurat may derive from Fritz Lang's updating of the Tower of Babel, but it is easy to assume that the directors also studied such movies as *Blade Runner* and *The Fifth Element* to make sure that their ultimate future city would not be inferior to any others. Settings shift from the palatial offices of the elite to a gaudy entertainment district to squalid slums to ominous scientific laboratories (in different art styles; compare Dr. Laughton's lab, modeled upon those in 1930s Frankenstein movies, to the more obviously CGI mechanistic lab atop the Ziggurat at the climax) to huge underground sewers. The CGI is used masterfully to create the sensation of a teeming population. There are numerous scenes of crowded streets with dozens if not hundreds of characters seeming to move individually. But my favorite is a city square on a wintry morning after a failed anti-robot uprising. There is almost nobody in sight, just the empty square with the scuffed snow covered in what looks like thousands of footprints.

Many scenes and shots are designed to make individual characters appear insignificant in comparison to the city. This supports the continual struggle by several characters to refuse to let the city dominate them. An ongoing question is whether the robots should be considered as part of the city or as individuals. Tima is not the only one that seems self-aware. Pero, a junky robot contemptuously given by the Metropolis police to Ban as a local guide, looks as comical as the robots in the 1930s movie serials, but his intelligent dialogue and wise advice give him a tragic dignity.

One of the key elements in establishing the mood of the 1930s and '40s is the jazz music. The original score is by Toshiyuki Honda, one of Japan's leading jazz performers since the 1970s. Honda composed a 1920s Dixieland-style score for the movie, performed by a group named the "Metropolitan Rhythm Kings" that, according to the publicity, included director Rintaro on the bass clarinet. There are also a few vintage American numbers, most notably "St. James Infirmary" and "I Can't Stop Loving You," which are surprisingly effective.

Metropolis was released in Japan on May 26, 2001. It premiered in America at the Hollywood Egyptian Theater on August 17, and was supposed to be released by TriStar Pictures on November 9. But due to the post-September 11 sensibilities about movies showing the destruction of giant buildings, the release was postponed until January 25, 2002. It deserves to be a contender for the new Academy Awards category for Best Animated Feature.

A Winning *Spirit*
Anime Invasion no. 4, Fall 2002.

It's bigger than *Titanic*. It's buried *Star Wars*, *Spider-Man* and *Jurassic Park*. And none of that means anything in the United States.

The good news: *Spirited Away* is almost here. After watching it get award after award (including the Japanese Academy Awards' Best Picture Oscar) and beat record after record (at $240 million, it's Japan's No. 1 movie of all time and the highest-grossing non-American film in the world), America will finally get a chance to see *Spirited Away* for itself. The latest masterpiece by acclaimed director Hayao Miyazaki will hit U.S. theaters on September 20.

The bad news: *Princess Mononoke*, Miyazaki's 1997 masterpiece before *Spirited Away*, had the same awards and records in 1999 before Miramax released it in the United States. It was a flop, not even earning back the $3 million spent to bring it over (even though it's earned $140 million worldwide).

So what chance does *Sen to Chihiro no Kamikakushi* (as it's known in Japan) have?

Despite its worldwide success, can it even have half the business of an American animated film like *Monsters, Inc.?* One American is confident that it can: *Monsters, Inc.* producer John Lasseter.

Pixar Power

John Lasseter knows how to make animated movies for Americans. Besides producing *Monsters, Inc.,* he's the director of *Toy Story, Toy Story 2,* and *A Bug's Life,* all from Pixar Animation Studios, where he is executive vice president. Both Disney and Studio Ghibli (Miyazaki's animation studio, which made *Spirited Away*) asked Lasseter to serve as creative consultant for Disney's English-language version.

In a sense, however, he has been involved with *Spirited Away* almost from its start. "I visited Japan in March of 2000 for the release of *Toy Story 2* in Japan," recalls Lasseter.

"I took the opportunity to visit Studio Ghibli. They were just beginning production on *Spirited Away.* It looked fantastically exciting. Miyazaki storyboards himself, and as I was talking with him, I rummaged through his trash basket like any fan and asked if could keep some of the storyboard drawings that he had discarded. He laughed and said, 'No,' then took three of his good drawings, signed them and gave them to me."

Lasseter has been a personal friend of Hayao Miyazaki ever since the two met at the Disney studio in the early 1980s, when Lasseter was a beginning animator and Miyazaki had come from Tokyo to attend Disney's animation seminars for its new staff. Lasseter also credits Miyazaki's films as being a direct inspiration for Pixar's mixture of fantasy, humor, and adventure; Pixar's animators have been known to watch the Japanese laserdiscs of Miyazaki's films during the productions of its own features.

Shortly after its 2000 Japanese release, Ghibli president Toshio Suzuki came to Pixar with a subtitled film print of *Spirited Away.* "We showed it in the 235-seat screening room at Pixar," remembers Lasseter. "This was its first screening anywhere outside of Japan. Everyone was blown away. We were familiar with Miyazaki's previous films, and we felt that he had topped himself."

But despite Pixar's overwhelmingly favorable reactions, Disney still wasn't sure whether to bring it over, remembering *Princess Mononoke* before it. Full of weird gods, monsters, and magic, would *Spirited Away* be too Japanese for America?

Weird World

The story that had Disney so worried isn't overtly Japanese. What it is, is *weird.*

A young girl, Chihiro Ogino, and her parents get lost while driving through a forest on the way to their new house. They find an apparently abandoned fairy-like town which the parents assume is an out-of-business amusement park. Mr. and Mrs. Ogino are transformed into pigs for gluttonously eating the food there. When the town awakens at nightfall as a living hot springs resort spa for the spirit world, Chihiro must decide whether to escape and abandon her parents, or remain to try to restore them to humanity before they are slaughtered and eaten.

But when the spirits discover her, a mysterious boy named Haku tells Chihiro the only way to survive in this strange land is to get a job at a bathhouse run by the sinister witch Yu-Baba. There, Chihiro serves the many gods who come to the bathhouse to relax, while at the same time trying to figure out how to save her parents and save her name, which Yu-Baba has taken away, giving her the new name "Sen" (hence the Japanese title, "*The Spiriting Away of Sen and Chihiro*").

Lasseter feels that the film will resonate with all audiences, regardless of nationality. "Disney was concerned about American audiences not understanding some of the Japanese traditional cultural elements in the story," says Lasseter. "But I felt that it would be particularly accessible to Western audiences because it is seen from the point of view of a modern, materialistic young girl who is unfamiliar with her own cultural past." It was this argument that finally convinced Disney to commit to the film.

The Name Game
Who's Who and What's What in Miyazaki's Masterpiece?

You're soon going to see a movie where young Chihiro is pulled into a wacky fantasy world filled with crazy, far-out spirits. But in fact, those spirits aren't so crazy—they all have roots in Japanese folklore. For instance, the goblins you'll see (called "kami"; literally "gods," but gods as minor nature spirits) seem to have names. But these names are actually just descriptions in Japanese. Confused? Don't be, silly Americans. Here's a guide to help you identify the ghosts, goblins and gods within, though don't blame us if the names are different in the American release.

Yu-Baba: The witch who owns and runs the bath house of the gods. "Ba" or "Baba" is the Japanese familiar name for an old woman or grandmother. It's the same in Russian, too; the most famous old witch in Russian folklore is Baba Yaga; Old Granny Yaga. But "yu" is the Japanese for "hot water," so Yu-Baba is not so much a personal name as a description: the Old Lady Who Runs the Bathhouse.

Zeniba: Zeniba looks just like Yu-Baba, which makes sense since they're twins. But Zeniba is the good one; "Zeni" means good-will or well-meaning; "ba" means old woman. Yu-Baba's names leaves it vague as to whether she is good or evil, but Zeniba's name tells you immediately she is friendly.

Kamaoji: The spider-like gent who runs the resort's boiler room is Kamaoji.

American Style

Which is when John Lasseter's work really began. As the creative consultant, he has been involved in every step in the localization process. First off, this means overseeing the translation of Miyazaki's Japanese script to ensure that it remains as faithful to the original story as possible while sounding perfectly natural in English. "The number one thing to me was to protect Miyazaki's vision," Lasseter says. He worked closely with Disney's voice director, Kirk Wise, in selecting the voice cast, most of whom were already Disney veterans.

Daveigh Chase, the voice of Lilo in *Lilo and Stitch,* plays Chihiro, and Jason Marsden, Max Goof in Disney's *A Goofy Movie,* plays Haku. The other roles are filled by veteran voice actors and Pixar familiars like David Ogden Stiers and John Ratzenberger. The final verdict? Lasseter says that Ghibli has complimented the Disney dub as the best English dub that any Miyazaki film has ever had. (High praise, considering that Ghibli held creative control over the dubs of *My Neighbor Totoro, Kiki's Delivery Service,* and *Princess Mononoke.*)

As for changes to the plot or names, Ghibli fans can rest easy. "We did not change any character names," promises Lasseter. "When she meets someone whose name is really a description of their appearance or their

---

But "kama" is "boiler" or "furnace," and "oji" is "old man," so he's just Old Man Furnace.

Kasuga: The spirits dressed in the style of ancient lords who arrive at the bathhouse in a group tour. They drift through the streets like transparent ghosts. This is a double entendre; "kasuka" or "kasuga" means "dim" or "indistinct," and one of the most revered Shinto shrines in Japan is Kasuga Shrine in Nara, dating back to A.D. 768.

Ohgaeru: Ohgaeru are staff members at Yu-Baba's bathhouse; they are the frogs (all men) who clean the baths.

Okusare: When the spirit dripping with sludge slithers in to take a bath, he is addressed as Okusare-sama, which might be euphemistically translated as honorable Lord Stinky. When he is finally cleaned, he is revealed as Kawa-no-kami, literally God of the River.

Oshira-Sama: The colorless fat spirit with the pendulous cheeks whom Sen meets in the elevator is Oshira-sama, which can be translated as Lord Whitey. He is actually an anthropomorphic Japanese radish called a daikon, and obviously an agricultural spirit.

Kao-Noshi: Literally, "face no" or "negative," but most often translated as "No-face." This mysteriously vague name is a clue that the other spirits have no idea who he is, either.

job, we sped up the dialogue to add a translation," he explains. "So she might address Kamaoji as both 'Mr. Kamaoji' and 'Mr. Boiler Room Man' the first time she meets him, and then as just 'Kamaoji' as in the Japanese dialogue for the rest of the time."

Nor did they add any graphics, no matter what. "If Chihiro sees a building which has a sign in Japanese that American audiences can't read, we might add a, 'Hmm, a bathhouse,' type of talking-to-herself line to the dialogue," says Lasseter.

Spirit in the Sky

Thanks to Lasseter and Pixar, *Spirited Away* will be a Disney release. This means, unlike *Princess Mononoke* (released by Disney subsidiary Miramax), *Spirited Away* will be going to most major theaters. And although the story and world is very Eastern, Lasseter has no doubt it will find its American audience.

"Miyazaki told me how his grandchildren, girls about 10 years old, seemed very apathetic and shallow," explains Lasseter. "They were only concerned with the latest popular trends; they did not know or care anything about the past. Miyazaki felt he had to make a movie for modern children, to introduce them to the fascination of their cultural heritage, and to show them the importance of responsibility."

Hopefully, American audiences will feel the same way. And maybe a new tradition will begin.

Cowboy Bebop: The Movie . . . At Last
Animation World Magazine 7, no. 12, March 2003.

Anime fans do not need to be told how good *Cowboy Bebop: The Movie* is; they have been waiting impatiently for almost two years. In fact, fans have been suffering for the past year squinting at blurry bootleg video copies, or wincing at the pidgin-English subtitles on the imported Hong Kong DVD release. Now it is finally coming to American theaters with a superb English dubbing, co-distributed by Destination Films and Samuel Goldwyn Films. The initial release, on April 4, will be in seventeen major cities across the United States If the box office is favorable, this may be expanded.

Hot, Hot, Hot

Cowboy Bebop has been a controversial favorite since it was created by Japan's Sunrise animation studio as an adult TV series five years ago. TV theme popularity tends to come in waves, and late 1997–early 1998 in Japan looked like the time for "space adventure" shows. Two of the better examples that season were Sunrise's *Outlaw Star* (an interstellar *Treasure Island*) and Madhouse's *Trigun* (a space Western on the planet Gunsmoke).

Cowboy Bebop was not just an average TV anime series for Sunrise. It was one that the entire studio got really enthusiastic over and assigned its top talent to. (*Cowboy Bebop*'s creator-of-record is "Hajime Yatate," Sunrise's well-known house pseudonym for a team effort.) The leader of the creative team was director Shinichiro Watanabe, a fan favorite as the director of the futuristic military adventure series *Macross Plus* and *Mobile Suit Gundam 0083: Stardust Memory.* Watanabe wanted to design not just a space adventure series for adolescent boys but a program that would appeal to sophisticated adults. His main inspiration was the *Lupin III* anime series, which had been mega-popular from the late 1970s through the mid-'80s, about a debonair roguish international jewel thief and his "cool" gang in jet-set locales. They were sympathetic because they preyed upon truly despicable rich villains rather than the innocent.

Other leading members of Sunrise's creative team were scriptwriter Keiko Nobumoto, character designer Toshihiro Kawamoto, mechanical art designer Kimitoshi Yamane, and composer Yoko Kanno. Most of them had worked together before, in addition to having credits on other popular anime titles. Nobumoto had scripted *Macross Plus,* Kawamoto had designed the characters for *Gundam 0083,* and Kanno had written the music for *Macross Plus* (which needed an extremely strong score to support the plot about the rise of a popular singing idol who turns out to be a computer-generated Artificial Intelligence) and *The Vision of Escaflowne.* Yamane had not worked with Watanabe, but his credits included such other anime hits as *Bubblegum Crisis* and *The Vision of Escaflowne.*

The space-adventure update of *Lupin III* that Watanabe's team came up with was a "frontier" interplanetary culture of A.D. 2071. The Solar System has been colonized (forget the American publicity ad copy about humanity spreading "to the stars;" the action is all between Venus and Neptune), but it is a grungy society of mostly bubble-domed small communities on asteroids and the moons of the gas-giant planets, plus artificial space stations. Only Venus and Mars have any large cities. The cultural influences of this space society are as much Chinese as Western. There is a confusing conglomeration of independent governments, alliances, and spheres of influence. The only system-wide organizations seem to be a unified police force, the ISSP (Inter Solar System Police), which is widely considered to be corrupt and ineffective, and powerful crime families which combine the worst aspects of the Italian Mafia and the Chinese Triads.

Due to the general helplessness of individual police forces at dealing with anything more serious than local petty crime, most governments have fallen back on posting rewards for the capture of serious criminals. This has created a new occupation of bounty hunters, popularly called "cowboys," who roam the Solar System looking for criminals with big rewards. *Cowboy Bebop* is about one particular "odd couple" team of these cowboys aboard the *Bebop,* a decrepit used spaceship. The core duo, introduced in the first episode, are Spike Spiegel and Jet Black, two macho good buddies who (it turns out from their conversation) only met shortly before deciding to team up and do not really know much about each other's pasts. The next few episodes add the remaining three of the team: Faye Valentine, a *femme fatale* bounty hunter, who alternates between joining their hunts as a partner and competing with them as a rival; "Ed," a young adolescent brilliant computer hacker (technically a she, although Ed is so androgynous that it is easier to think of her as an "it"); and Ein, an apparently normal dog (Welsh Corgi) with cryptic hints of abnormal capabilities. (One of the running gags of the series is leading the audience into trying to catch Ein doing something super-canine.)

Bebop History

The most important of the many elements that made *Cowboy Bebop* so successful is its sophisticated and mature attitude. Watanabe made no secret that, in addition to *Lupin III,* it was largely his tribute to his favorite American movies and TV series, which were shown in Japan during the 1970s and '80s including *Butch Cassidy and the Sundance Kid* (the relationship between Spike and Jet), anything with Bruce Lee (Spike is a martial-arts fanatic), anything with a blues or jazz sound track, and lots of Blaxploitation movies (the series has a very racially diverse supporting cast). Individual movies from *Alien* to *Midnight Run* were pastiched and parodied. One main attraction was that the audience was always kept guessing over the nature of the next episode. Would it be a comedy, a detective caper, an action thriller, a somber mood piece which would reveal some more of one of the main cast's past, or something else unexpected? The hot music motif was emphasized in many of the episode titles (in English), such as "Asteroid Blues," "Honky Tonk Women," "Ballad of Fallen Angels," "Heavy Metal Queen," "Jamming With Edward," "Jupiter Jazz," and "Mushroom Samba."

The dialogue was kept "clean," but its level of sophistication was appropriate to adults in a criminal milieu. Drug dealing and homosexuality were key elements of some episodes. As a result, *Cowboy Bebop* achieved the unique record that only half of its twenty-six episodes were considered suitable for TV broadcast during its initial run on the TV Tokyo network as a Friday primetime 6:00 P.M. series (April 3 through June 26, 1998). The remaining thirteen episodes were initially available when the whole series was released on video. The entire series was finally shown on TV on the WOWOW satellite channel on Fridays at 1:00 A.M., October 23, 1998, through April 23, 1999. The TV series won awards in Japan including the Third Kobe Animation Festival's award in the Best TV Animation category, and the 2000 annual Japan National Science Fiction Convention's Uchusen SF Award for Best Media science-fiction.

Cowboy Bebop has been a similar fan favorite in America. It originally appeared as one of Bandai Entertainment's early anime home video releases, two episodes dubbed or subtitled on thirteen videos between September 1999 and October 2000. Anime fans who are often critical of the quality of English dubbing agreed that *Cowboy Bebop*'s was one of the best dubs yet. That was quickly superseded by a bilingual DVD release in six volumes between April and November 2000. The conventional wisdom among anime fans was that *Cowboy Bebop* was too mature to ever appear on American TV. When it did finally show up on The Cartoon Network's new "Adult Swim" block on September 2, 2001 (at 11:30 P.M. EST), the edits and omitted episodes served as new publicity for the uncut DVDs. A fancy *Cowboy Bebop: The Perfect Sessions* complete DVD boxed set was released in November 2001 for not quite $200. More recently, *Cowboy Bebop: Best Sessions* (November 2002) is a two-disc DVD of the six most popular episodes "reedited and remixed . . . under the direct supervision of series director Shinichiro Watanabe." All of this new marketing would not be possible if *Cowboy Bebop* did not continue to be extremely popular.

The Big Screen Release

And now the movie! The TV/DVD series was so popular in Japan that there was never any doubt that there would be a theatrical release. *Cowboy Bebop: Knockin' On Heaven's Door* is crafted by the same "dream team" of creators: "Yatate," Watanabe, Nobumoto, Kawamoto, Yamane, and Kanno. The theatrical budget permitted the story to be set in "Alba City, the capital of Mars," the major human city off Earth. This is the excuse to create a much larger and more detailed metropolitan cityscape than in any of the TV episodes, which blends aspects of New York City, Tokyo, and an ethnic Near-Eastern "Morocco Street" neighborhood. The 116-minute running time allows for the slow buildup of a tremendously suspenseful plot. Each of the main cast is given at least one scene in which to stand out to please their fans, but the main protagonist is Spike Spiegel. He has two lengthy action scenes in which he gets to demonstrate his martial-arts expertise, which has been only hinted at in the TV episodes.

The studio press kit for the American-retitled *Cowboy Bebop: The Movie* English-dubbed theatrical feature (featuring the same popular voice cast as the TV series) says that it made "its world premiere at the Big Apple Anime Fest 2002 (BAAF) in New York City [on Labor Day weekend]." But its original Japanese release was on September 1, 2001. (It was in Japan's top fifteen box office for five weeks. In July 2002 it won the SPJA Industry Award, presented at Anime Expo in Long Beach, Calif., in the 2001 Best Japanese Anime Theatrical Release category.) This is significant because, if it had been delayed for just a few weeks, it would have looked like a blatant and unimaginative imitation of the September 11, 2001 NYC terrorism combined with its follow-ups. *Cowboy Bebop: The Movie* features a deadly terrorist threat involving massive explosions and what appears to be the release of an unknown bioplague that kills thousands in a cityscape that is practically rotoscoped from NYC. The suspects include a mysterious Rachid in an Arabic district. At the same time that the largest reward in history is offered for the terrorists (which attracts our *Bebop* gang), the authorities (both government and some powerful corporate villains) react with authoritarian force against all possible suspects. There are ominous implications that any bounty hunters who do actually find the terrorists may not be rewarded but "disappeared" for Knowing Too Much. One wonders whether a reason for the delay in the movie's general release since its film festival premiere last August has been that it was still too close to the September 11 attacks.

So it is finally being released. But, despite *Cowboy Bebop's* popularity with the American fans, it is only getting an art-theater release: one theater each in seventeen cities (well, two in NYC). Will it do well enough to earn a wider release for itself, or for the next anime theatrical feature to be released in America? Let's hope . . .

The Animatrix: Anime Reloaded
Animation World Magazine 8, no, 3, June 2003.

In 1999, *The Matrix* immediately became one of the top films of the year. In May 2003, *The Matrix Reloaded* set new box-office records. Now has *The Animatrix* done the same for a direct-to-video/DVD release on its June 3, 2003 release?

From the moment of its release in 1999, the buzz about *The Matrix* acknowledged its inspirational debt to Japanese animation. Andy and Larry Wachowski, the film's young creators, were big fans of anime. This was no news to anime fans, who could clearly see the influence of its dark SF story concepts and its directorial moves throughout.

Just how much the Wachowski brothers were anime fans is now even more obvious with *The Animatrix,* an eighty-nine-minute movie released directly to DVD and video. The compilation feature consists of nine separate short animated films set in the live-action *Matrix* story-universe, tying the first two theatrical features together. The nine films are by seven different directors, five of whom are among the tops in the Japanese animation industry. The other two, both Americans, were already working with Japanese animators before joining *The Animatrix* project.

According to the "making of" information in the DVD's seventy-eight minutes of special-feature documentaries, *The Animatrix* began as early as 1997 when the two Wachowskis and producer Joel Silver made a press tour to Tokyo to set up the Japanese theatrical release of *The Matrix*. The Wachowskis took the opportunity to meet many of their favorite anime directors. After the 1999 release of *The Matrix* (a major hit in Japan), they asked whether these directors (most of whom had loved *The Matrix*) would like to help create an animated version of it, showcasing their individual artistic and directorial styles.

Joel Silver picked Michael Arias, an American computer special effects and digital technology expert working with the anime industry, as their representative in Tokyo. Arias was already associated with Studio 4° C, which became one of the project's two main production studios. The first step was deciding that *The Animatrix* should be a feature consisting of several separate short films rather than a TV series. A TV series would require more episodes of longer stories (averaging twenty-two minutes each). That would stretch the budget so the quality of each episode would be less, and it would be harder for the styles of different directors to stand out. Arias invited the anime directors. Some could not accept because of prior professional commitments, but a "dream team" was soon assembled.

Yoshiaki Kawajiri ("Program") was one of the founders of the Madhouse studio in the 1980s. His mature-themed anime features *Wicked City* (1987) and *Ninja Scroll* (1993) had already made him one of the most popular directors and character-design artists with American anime fans. Kawajiri's Madhouse became the second main production studio. He had ideas for two *Animatrix* stories that the Wachowskis liked, but he only had time to produce one of them himself. The second that Kawajiri outlined, "World Record," was given to his protégé Takeshi Koike to fully develop and visualize.

Koji Morimoto was one of the founders of Studio 4° C, which also became the workshop for Shinichiro Watanabe and Mahiro Maeda. Morimoto ("Beyond") was best known for his dark-humor SF sequence "Franken's Gears" in the 1987 anthology feature *Robot Carnival,* but he was also an animation supervisor on 1987's mega-popular *Akira.* Watanabe was co-director of the 1994 *Macross Plus,* but he really established his name by directing the prestigious *Cowboy Bebop* TV series and theatrical feature, one of the biggest anime hits in America. Maeda had recently directed the OAV series *Blue Submarine No. 6,* which set fans and professionals alike talking about his bold mixture of computer graphics and traditional animation.

It was at this time that *Final Fantasy: The Spirits Within,* being produced by a team of American and Japanese animators at the Square USA studio in Honolulu, was publicized. The Wachowskis wanted its CGI style of anime in *The Animatrix,* and its director Andy Jones was recruited for "The Final Flight of the Osiris." The final director, American animator Peter Chung (*Aeon Flux*) was already working on projects with Madhouse and with the

As *Watching Anime* was being edited, Quentin Tarantino's *Kill Bill: Vol. 2* was released (April 2004) to major critical and box office success ("$45.9 million in thirteen days and counting . . .," reported the Box Office Mojo Web site). The publicity included the announcement that Tarantino plans to add an anime feature "prequel" to the two-part live-action feature. Most news reports of this cite *The Animatrix* as a precedent. ■

South Korean studio DNA when he learned about *The Animatrix* from Kawajiri. Chung sold his own story idea, "Matriculated," to the Wachowskis. Chung produced it at DNA in Seoul.

The directors all worked by remote control through Arias, who sent their developments of the Wachowskis' story outlines (or their original stories) to the two brothers who were in Australia directing both *The Matrix Reloaded* and *The Matrix Revolutions,* and returned their comments to the directors. All agree that Andy and Larry supervised with an extremely light control, mainly making sure that each story remained consistent to their overall concept of the *Matrix* universe, since they wanted each short film to demonstrate its creator's own artistic personality, and the completed feature to display as many different anime styles as possible.

It has not hurt that a couple of these directors have become even more popular in America during the three years since work on *The Animatrix* began. Kawajiri's *Vampire Hunter D: Bloodlust* got rave reviews in the fan community, while Watanabe's *Cowboy Bebop* gained new fans through its Cartoon Network screenings and the 2003 release of the theatrical feature. Watanabe also became personalized through his self-caricature as "Nabeshin" in the zany TV series *Excel Saga,* a popular DVD release.

Warner Home Video does not release sales figures, so it will be difficult to tell whether *The Animatrix* sets any new records or not. But a theatrical preview on May 14 at the 1st Annual Los Angeles Anime Festival in Hollywood (its only theatrical screening in America) was the only feature to sell out before the two-week festival opened. Among the DVD stores that report their sales online, on the day after *The Animatrix*'s release, the Planet. DVD Web site listed it as No. 1 on its Top 10 sales chart, while allDVDprices.com listed it as No. 4 and dvdovernight.com placed it at No. 7 (and sold out). Whether or not *The Animatrix* sets any records, clearly it is already a hit—good enough that anime fans are encouraged to hope that other major SF movie franchises will commission their own anime projects. An anime *Spider-Man* or *X-Men?* An anime *X-Files* or *Jurassic Park?* An anime *Terminator?*

September 1963: *Astro Boy* Premieres in America
This Month in Anime History column in *Newtype USA* 2, no. 9, September 2003.

It was in September 1963 when *Astro Boy,* the first TV anime, premiered in America.

Oh, you already knew that?

Actually, September is the month that most "pre-anime" Japanese TV cartoons which made it to America went on the air as "just kids' cartoons."

This is because, in the broadcast entertainment industry, September is traditionally the month when summer reruns end and the Fall season introduces its new programs. This goes back to TV in the 1950s, if not to radio even earlier. It goes for syndicated programming (TV series sold to local channels on an individual basis) as well as for network programming (TV series sold to one of the major TV companies whose programs are broadcast nationwide).

None of the early anime TV series that were considered by American TV executives as suitable for remolding into American TV cartoons were "big" enough to make it onto the networks. Even *Astro Boy,* which was bought by the giant National Broadcasting Company, was never broadcast on the NBC channel. In the 1960s NBC had a subsidiary, NBC Enterprises, which managed NBC's entertainment ventures beyond its own TV and radio broadcasting. These ranged from finding or producing TV programs that were not good enough for NBC but were still marketable to local TV stations, to producing Broadway plays. (In 1970 the federal government ruled that this violated anti-trust laws. NBC was forced to give up everything beyond its own national broadcasting.) It was technically NBC Enterprises that licensed *Tetsuwan Atom* for TV broadcasting in America and hired independent producer Fred Ladd to Americanize it, and another NBC subsidiary, NBC Films, which sold it on a station-by-station basis throughout America, usually for a one-year license. (This explains why different histories of anime may conflict as to whether it was "NBC," "NBC Enterprises," or "NBC Films" that brought *Astro Boy* and *Kimba the White Lion* to America.) *Astro Boy,* and all syndicated TV programs, would have appeared in different cities at different times over a period of several years (however long the American distributor had licensed the American TV rights from the Japanese producer). But they all had to start somewhere, and for *Astro Boy,* its first American appearance was on September 7, 1963, on New York's WPIX channel on Saturdays at 6:00 P.M.

For *8th Man,* marketed by ABC Films, it was exactly two years later on

For over twenty years prior to my writing this column, articles about anime or about *Battle of the Planets*—including my own "Fifteen Years of Japanese Animation Fandom, 1977–1992" in *The Complete Anime Guide*—had reported its American broadcast premiere as October 1978. When I tried to find out a specific date rather than just "sometime in October," nobody knew. Even Sandy Frank Film Syndication, whose actual 1978 records had long since been packed away, had only the "October 1978" date in its publicity. But an actual examination of *TV Guide* no. 1329, the September 16–22, 1978, issue for several different cities, showed an illustrated half-page "the premiere of *Battle of the Planets* today" display advertisement on the Monday, September 18, afternoon programming page (but listing different times and different syndicated channels). I would like to acknowledge veteran *Battle of the Planets* fan James Long of San Diego, who had kept his copy of that *TV Guide,* for pointing this out. ■

September 7, 1965, also on NYC's WPIX. But September 7th was a Tuesday in 1965; *8th Man* was an afternoon kid's cartoon on Tuesdays at 4:00 P.M.

For *Kimba the White Lion,* it was September 11, 1966, on Los Angeles's KHJ on Sundays at 6:00 P.M. *Prince Planet* also premiered during September 1966, but it was marketed by long-gone American International Television and records are no longer available as to exactly which city and on what day during September 1966 *Prince Planet* first appeared.

NYC's WPIX channel was a major purchaser of first-run syndicated programming, and in September 1967 it premiered two anime series: *The Amazing 3* (from Modern Programs) on September 6 as a daily 3:00 P.M. cartoon, and *Speed Racer* (from Trans-Lux Productions) on September 28 as a weekly Thursday 6:00 P.M. cartoon.

After 1967, it looked for over a decade as though no more Japanese TV cartoons would ever be sold in America, due to their "increased violence." This changed a decade later, thanks to *Star Wars.* That movie was a major hit in 1977, and every TV station wanted a *Star Wars*-type TV cartoon. Sandy Frank Film Syndication performed major plastic surgery on *Gatchaman* to turn it into one, and *Battle of the Planets* premiered on Monday, September 18, 1978, in multiple cities as a Monday-Friday afternoon TV cartoon, at different times (3:30 P.M. on San Diego's KFMB, 4:30 P.M. on Los Angeles's WTTV, etc.) *BotP* made "space adventure" TV cartoons respectable, and it was quickly followed by *Star Blazers* on September 10, 1979, and *Voltron, Defender of the Universe!* on September 10, 1984, among others.

By the 1990s anime was appearing in the American video market and its Japanese origin was no longer unknown, but the TV industry still had to sell any anime intended for syndicated broadcasting as "children's TV cartoons" for the fall season's programming. New programs sold during the 1990s included *Sailor Moon,* which premiered in the United States on September 11, 1995 (although on August 28 in Canada); *Dragonball Z* on September 13, 1996; and *Pokémon* on September 8, 1998. (And, to stretch a point, *Monster Rancher* on August 30, 1999.)

So September continues to be a very important month for anime, at least concerning regular TV broadcasting outside of the cable channels with specialized anime blocks like The Cartoon Network's Toonami (or the brand-new Anime Network) which may premiere new TV anime in any month.

Millennium Actress: The Struggle to Bring Quality Animation to Theaters
Animation World Magazine 8, no. 6, September 2003.

Millennium Actress, one of the best animated features of the new millennium (and likely to remain so, no matter how many more are produced during the next 997 years) has finally come to American theaters—although in a release so limited that you will miss it if you blink.

Millennium Actress (*Sennen Joyu*) is the second critically acclaimed/ anime fan favorite theatrical animated feature created by artist/writer/ director Satoshi Kon and screenwriter Sadayuki Murai, produced by Tokyo's Madhouse studio (best known for *Wicked City, Ninja Scroll, Vampire Hunter D: Bloodlust,* and some of the sequences in *The Animatrix*). Their first was the 1997 *Perfect Blue,* a murder mystery that was likened to an animated Alfred Hitchcock thriller.

Millennium Actress has superficial similarities: Kon's distinctive art style, a mystery set within Japan's cinematic industry, and a surrealistic viewpoint from inside the heroine's mind. But where *Perfect Blue* emphasized a nightmarish paranoia to make both the heroine and the audience wonder whether she has become a psychotic killer, *Millennium Actress* is a more benign look into a retired actress's bittersweet memories. If *Perfect Blue* is comparable to Hitchcock, then *Millennium Actress* is similar to James Cameron's *Titanic,* as an elderly woman's flashback of romantic reminiscences, which are so vivid they draw her audience back into the past with her.

It starts with a SF scene very like *2001: A Space Odyssey,* but featuring a female astronaut. This turns out to be from a movie being watched by Genya Tachibana, a middle-aged independent documentary filmmaker. It was the final feature made by Chiyoko Fujiwara, Japan's greatest actress from the 1930s until the late 1960s when she abruptly vanished into seclusion. Now, thirty years later, Chiyoko's old studio has hired Genya to produce a documentary about her. Genya and his brash young cameraman Kyoji Ida track her down and persuade her to give them a personal interview.

As the frail but gracious Chiyoko relives her past, Genya and Kyoji become supporting characters in her memories. These present a behind-the-scenes look at both the Japanese movie industry of this period and the individual features in which she starred. Viewers "in the know" will recognize pastiches of Japan's greatest films, from *Throne of Blood* to *Godzilla,* although they work equally well as an enjoyable sampler of Japanese movie genres for viewers who do not know the specific films.

Regarding Chiyoko's personal story, it turns out that Genya had met her as a bashful teen assistant on the studio lot just before her final film. He still has a puppy-love crush on her, and although it is not necessary for his documentary, he wants to know the secret of what drove Chiyoko into hiding so long ago.

Filming *Millennium Actress* in detailed 2-D animation, rather than live-action, permits a more seamless transition through the scenes from the "real present" to the "real past" to the often jarring contrast of Chiyoko's different movie roles. (Animation also enables the monsters and sets in the SF movies to look more realistic than the actual '50s and '60s live-action movies ever did.) This becomes an intellectual puzzle as Genya and Kyoji gradually realize that Chiyoko's memories may be more romantically enhanced than what really happened, and they must consciously separate the truth from her idealized view of reality.

Satoshi Kon's *Millennium Actress* was released at about the same time as Hayao Miyazaki's *Spirited Away*. But while both garnered critical praise— the two tied for Japan's Agency of Cultural Affairs' 5th Media Arts Festival Grand Prize in December 2001—*Spirited Away* went on to box office success in Japan, while *Millennium Actress* went after international film festival fame. Its world premiere was at Montreal's Fantasia 2001 Asiatic fantasy film festival in July 2001, where Kon personally introduced it to a sold-out audience. (It won first place in the Best Animation Film category, as well as The Fantasia Ground-Breaker Award.) It next played at the Sitges 2001 festival in October, winning the Orient Express Award. Then came the Media Arts Festival in December, a screening in Japan but a limited one.

Millennium Actress's Japanese theatrical release did not come until September 14, 2002, in the midst of playing at other international festivals from Singapore to England to Australia to the United States (Kon appeared at its screening at the AFI Fest 2002 in Hollywood in November) to Japan again (it won the Best Entry Award in the Theatrical Movie category at the Tokyo International Anime Fair in March 2003). Kon seems to be following this route again with his newest feature: *Tokyo Godfathers* (also animated by Madhouse) has just had its world premiere at the Big Apple Anime Fest (BAAF 2003) in New York on August 29–31, where Kon was a guest of honor.

The publicity went out in August. "As part of the recent studio trend, DreamWorks SKG has formed a new specialty division, Go Fish Pictures, with *Millennium Actress,* the critically acclaimed anime title by Satoshi Kon, as its first release. *Millennium Actress* opens September 12, 2003, in Los Angeles, New York, Chicago, Boston, San Francisco and Toronto." But it only shows at only one theater in each of those six cities.

The announcement goes on to say that Go Fish Pictures' expected second release, in spring 2004, will be the anime feature *Innocence: Ghost in the Shell II*.

"Go Fish, considered by DreamWorks as a lab experiment, will look to indie filmmakers and small production companies for product. We are looking for anything that is compelling whether it is animation or live-action," DreamWorks president of distribution Jim Tharp told *VFXWorld*. While Tharp admits that anime has had a difficult time in the theatrical marketplace (with all of its kudos, *Spirited Away* was not a commercial success), Go Fish will experiment with *Millennium Actress* and *Ghost* to see if it can attain better box office results.

"It is very difficult, and we realize that you can't overpay for them," he added. You can't overspend, either, which is why the new specialty division will focus first on targeting the core anime fan base with *Millennium Actress* before reaching out more broadly if the movie performs in its limited theatrical run. And if it exceeds expectations, Tharp said the studio may even push back the DVD release, which is now scheduled for October 28 through DreamWorks Home Entertainment.

This press release has a resigned air compared with DreamWorks' high hopes for *Millennium Actress* less than a year ago. And why not? *Millennium Actress* had been winning international film awards for more than a year. *Spirited Away,* highly publicized in the United States by Disney since its limited theatrical distribution began in September 2002, was getting into the news around the country for its record-setting international (outside the United States) grosses, its rave reviews, and all the prestigious awards that it was garnering.

Spirited Away was up for the 2003 Academy Awards in the new Best Animated Feature Film category. Everyone in the animation industry was hoping that if it won, it would go on to popular success similar to the live-action *Crouching Tiger, Hidden Dragon.* And DreamWorks hoped that *Millennium Actress* could quickly follow it.

On March 23, 2003, *Spirited Away* won the coveted Oscar. On the March 28–30 weekend, Disney increased *Spirited Away*'s theatrical distribution from its previous maximum of 151 theaters nationwide to 711 theaters. It was wasted money. Despite all the acclaim, the public was not interested in seeing this foreign theatrical animated feature. *Spirited Away* had grossed $5,616,071 by the weekend of the Academy Awards presentation. As of September 4, *Spirited Away*'s grosses stood at $10,055,859, meaning that Disney's rerelease in more than 500 more theaters brought in less than $4,450,000 more. (Statistics from the Box Office Mojo Web site.)

This decisively killed any dreams that *Millennium Actress* could become a box office hit in America. If the American public could not be convinced that *Spirited Away* is worth seeing as a delightful family film, it appears impossible to win large audiences for an animated feature "about the Japanese movie industry" that is "not for children."

Considering these strikes against it, DreamWorks is to be congratulated for giving *Millennium Actress* a theatrical release at all. It is well worth seeing on the big screen, if you are lucky enough to live in one of the six cities showing it. If you are not, don't miss the DVD release. Critics from animation and major consumer publications and newspapers in the United States are enthusiastic, giving it high praise. Some are even calling it a contender for the animation theatrical Oscar.

Perfect Blue Revisited
Animation Magazine no. 129, October 2003.
(Originally published as a sidebar to cover-featured article by Michael Mallory on Satoshi Kon's *Millennium Actress*.)

Millennium Actress is not Satoshi Kon's first feature to draw reactions of, "Why is this animated instead of live-action?" Kon was first introduced to American audiences with the 1999 art-theater release of his 1997 Hitchcockesque thriller *Perfect Blue* (also animated by Madhouse).

Mima Kirigoe is the beloved lead singer in a hit teen pop-idol singing group. But teen pop singers have meteorically short careers, so when Mima gets a chance to try out as a TV-movie actress, she risks taking it. The change is brutally shocking. Some of her old fans vilify her for sabotaging her group by leaving it, while her new professional peers dismiss her as lacking real acting talent. The modest and insecure Mima is also seriously disturbed by her graphic role as a rape victim out for revenge.

Then reality starts apparently shifting into paranoia. A new Web site purportedly by Mima appears for her fans; she is not posting it, but it contains accurate personal details that nobody else knows about. She begins to feel she is being watched by a stalker. When the unreality reaches the level that Mima sees events which she knows are physically impossible, she must wonder whether she is going insane or whether some enemy is making her seem to be, either out of personal maliciousness or to set her up as the apparent perpetrator of psychotic violence against her new TV associates.

The use of animation rather than live-action enhances *Perfect Blue*'s surrealistic elements. It is harder to tell how much of "what the camera shows" is real and how much is Mima's imagination, or what someone is trying to convince Mima is her imagination—or whether the camera is showing both.

From the beginning Mima seems to have a more ethereal loveliness than the movie's other women. Does this mean that she really is an unusually beautiful girl, or does it artistically signify her naive innocence confronting the reality of the acting industry—or maybe a possible stalker's idealized view of her? Kon uses the psychological nuances of animation in a different way than he does in *Millennium Actress* (where the appearances of the two documentary filmmakers in Chiyoko's past signifies what a vivid actress and storyteller she is without implying that they think, or the audience should think, they have actually been transported into her past), but the effect is equally striking and imaginative.

January 1917: First Animation Produced in Japan Is Released

This Month in Anime History column in *Newtype USA* 3, no. 1, January 2004.

It wasn't much, a five-minute one-reeler titled *Imokawa Mukuzo Genkanban no Maki* (*Mukuzo Imokawa, the Doorkeeper*). The animator was Oten Shimokawa (1892–1973), a young cartoonist from Okinawa who began his career at Japan's pioneering humor magazine, *Tokyo Puck,* inspired by and named after Britain's world-famous humor magazine.

By the 1880s, the civil strife of the 1860s and '70s surrounding the Meiji Restoration (celebrated in anime dramas such as *Ruroni Kenshin* and *The Dagger of Kamui*) had ended with the victory of the reformers over the isolationists. Japanese society was firmly and enthusiastically committed to modernizing itself (the custom of high school and college student uniforms was adopted from the then-current Prussian educational system) and joining the rest of the world.

Early American, British, and French cinematographic films were shown in Japan during the 1890s and 1900s. Japanese artistic technophiles and business entrepreneurs quickly tried to create Japanese movies and start a movie industry. The Japanese movie industry dates its beginnings to 1896 or 1897. The first Western animation seen in Japan was during 1910. The short films of moving drawings by such American and French cartoonists as J. Randolph Bray, Winsor McCay, Emile Reynaud, Raul Barré, and Emile Cohl, among others, were an immediate challenge to Japan's young cartoonists already inspired by American and British newspaper comic strips and magazine gag cartoons. Shimokawa, a twenty-four-year-old editorial assistant at *Tokyo Puck* in 1916, first experimented with filming chalk drawings on a blackboard. When that did not work, he drew in ink directly onto the film.

Shimokawa's film was released during January 1917 (the exact date does not seem to be known) by the early film producer/distributor Nikkatsu (founded in 1912). Seitaro Kitayama (1889–?), an actual Nikkatsu employee (a graphic artist making subtitles and caption cards for their live-action films), was already working on his own animated film, *Sarukani Gassen* (*The Battle of the Monkey and the Crab,* also known as *The Crab's Revenge Against the Monkey*). Also five minutes, it was released on May 20, 1917. Japan's third animated film, *Hanahekonai Meitou no Maki* (*Hanahekonai's*

After twenty-five years I am still learning new details about Japanese animation. When I wrote this column for NTUSA in November 2003 I did not know when Seitaro Kitayama had died. I have since learned it was in 1945. There is still much to discover. ■

New Sword, a.k.a. *The Fine Sword*) by Jun-ichi Kouchi (1886–1970), another *Tokyo Puck* cartoonist, was the last released during 1917 (June 30). Kouchi's film got the best reviews.

Shimokawa made five more short animated films, but failing eyesight soon forced him to return to magazine and newspaper cartoons while he could still draw at all. Kouchi animated several Japanese folk tales into the 1920s and at least one animated political cartoon in 1924, *Ninki no Shouten ni Tateru Goto Shinpei* (*The Spotlight is on Shinpei Goto*, the former mayor of Tokyo who, as minister of home affairs, was responsible for rebuilding the city after the 1923 earthquake). Today Kouchi's main claim to fame may be that he was the sensei of Noburo Ofuji, a cut-paper silhouette animator who became Japan's first internationally known film-festival animator after the War (his 1952 *Kujira* got a rave review from Pablo Picasso). Kitayama made a second cartoon, *Taro no Banpei: Senkotei* (*Taro the Sentry: Submarine*), featuring the folk-tale hero Momotaro, the Peach Boy, as a modern little-boy sailor patrolling the harbor in his toy submarine. This film, released on August 4, 1918, was the first anime to become known outside of Japan. Kitayama then returned to making dialogue cards for silent movies until 1921, when he left Nikkatsu to start his own company, Kitayama Eiga Seisakujo (Kitayama Movie Factory). This was Japan's first actual animation studio. All previous films had been made (and were mostly still made until after World War II) by hobbyist animators working at home, although some were advanced money by distributors like Nikkatsu. However, Kitayama's company produced mostly educational and industrial films for the government such as *Kiatu to Mizuageponpu* (*Atmospheric Pressure and the Suction Pump*, 1921) and *Shokubutu Seiri: Seishoku no Maki* (*Plant Physiology: the Story of Reproduction*, 1922) rather than art or entertainment films. There was one notable exception: *Usagi to Kame* (*The Tortoise and the Hare*), released to the public in 1924.

The Great Kanto Earthquake and fire of September 1, 1923, which leveled Tokyo, destroyed all known prints of Japanese animation produced up to that time. All that is known of them today comes from newspaper reviews and movie-industry publicity descriptions. The oldest anime still in existence is the twelve-minute *Ubasute-yama* (*The Mountain Where Old Women Are Left to Die*), independently produced during 1924 by former Kitayama studio animator Sanae Yamamoto (1898–1981) but not released until 1925. In a way the pioneers of Japanese animation are considered to be Yamamoto, Ofuji, Yasuji Murata, Kenzo Masaoka, and others who produced the post-earthquake silent films from 1924 to the beginning of sound films; while Shimokawa, Kitayama, and Kouchi are the evolutionary forerunners who led to the pioneers.

So Japanese animation began in 1917. And of the three films released that year, the first was in January.

Index

Some frequently used words such as "anime" or names such as "Tezuka" appear on almost every page. To keep such headings from becoming cluttered with so many page citations as to become useless, this index is limited to significant citations only. Alphabetization is by the "word first" method, so that *All You Need Is Love* appears before Allers, Roger. Anime whose titles begin with numerals are listed twice in this index, at the beginning in numerical order and within the alphabetical entries according to spelling based on their pronunciation: e.g., the anime *8th Man* appears at the beginning of the listings as well as under the reasonably assumed pronunciation/spelling *Eighth Man*. Personal names are indexed under the last names of real persons, but fictitious characters are listed under either first or last names depending on how people are most likely to look for them. Thus Osamu Tezuka is under T, but Ataru Moroboshi is under A, while Prof. Packadermus J. Elefun is under E.

1001 Nights, 76, 112, 148, 344
20,000 Leagues Under the Sea, 187, 242
8th Man (a.k.a. *8 Man*), 54, 74, 193, 219, 223, 231, 248, 277, 314, 363–64

Academy Comics, 26, 34
Academy of Motion Picture Arts and Sciences, 139, 149, 210
A.D. Vision. *See* ADV Films
Adams, Roe R. III, 39, 130
ADV Films: adult anime market, 112, 114–15; anti-piracy, 120–21; at Anime Expo 2003, 82–83; Carl Macek at, 8, 78; founding of, 43, 63, 123; numbering (of series), 127; professional industry, 128–30, 133–34
Aguilar, Michael, 12, 37
Aim for the Top! See Top O Nerae!
Akira: British release, 131; cable TV, 124, 135; critical reviews, 21, 63, 69; Marvel comic book, 38; prestigious feature, 76, 79–80, 107, 125, 129, 281; production in Japan, 132, 349, 361; theatrical release in America, 40, 101, 123, 128, 138, 140–41, 345; video release, 41;
Akira Production Report, 40, 101
Akita Shoten, 11, 15, 73
Alakazam the Great: Ishinomori involvement in, 207; *Spaceketeers* TV anime, relation-

ship to, 251, 302; theatrical release in America, 22–24, 27, 52, 65, 73, 98, 135, 140; Tezuka involvement in, 146, 198; Toei release in Japan, 279, 294
Alexander, 138, 139
"All You Need Is Love," 30
All-Purpose Cultural Cat Girl. See Bannô Bunka Neko Musume
Allers, Roger, 163, 176
amateur films and videos: by American fans, 30, 32, 36–37, 41–42, 84; pre-1956 anime by amateur filmmakers, 278–79, 369–70
Amateur Press Association (APA), 25, 31, 34
Amazing 3, The, 23, 54, 222, 249, 364
Amazing Spider-Man, 56
Anacleto, Matthew, 37, 41
Animag: The Magazine of Japanese Animation, 37–38, 61, 68, 72, 103
Animag BBS, 38
Animage, 26, 58, 65, 71–73, 142–43, 209–11, 232, 269, 281
Animanga, 36
Animation Adventure, 29
Animation in Asia and the Pacific, 52–53
Animation Magazine, 72, 98, 100, 103, 122, 143, 161, 175, 275, 322, 336, 338, 368
Animation World Magazine, 9, 10, 72, 80–81, 104, 110, 135, 209, 213, 278, 325, 341, 345, 349, 356, 360, 364
Animatrix, The, 83, 360–62, 365
anime: adopted in Japan

from "animation," 270; as animated SF, 20; contrasted with Japanimation, 85–86, 277; as a cultural/economic genre in America, 41–43, 63–64, 70, 98, 128–35; educational value for teaching Japanese history, 282–85; influence on American filmmakers, 360–62; as a word meaning pornographic or poor-quality animation, 64, 108–11
Anime, The, 26, 73, 143
A.N.I.M.E., 35, 37, 41
Anime 18, 112, 114–17
Anime America '94, 177
Anime Archive column, 85, 285, 287
Anime Café, 70
Anime Central, 62
Anime East, 51
Anime Expo (AX), 51–52, 359; AX 1992, 42, 61, 81–82; AX 2000, 139; AX 2003, 80–85, 286
Anime Hasshin, 36
Anime Janai, 36
Anime North, 62
anime specialty companies and shops, 63, 70, 80–83, 99, 123, 125, 128
Anime U.K., 23, 181
Anime V, 73, 105–6, 143, 274–75
Anime Web Turnpike, 60, 122
Anime Weekend Atlanta, 62
AnimeCon '91, 41, 61, 81–82, 122
Animedia, 16, 73, 143
AnimEigo, 39–40, 43, 63, 102, 118, 123, 128,

130, 134
Animenominous!, 40, 72
Animerica, 43, 51, 68–69, 71–72, 124, 129, 131, 144, 179
Anime-Zine, 25, 35, 61, 72, 124
ANNIE awards, 174, 197
Anno, Hideaki, 41, 185
Anpanman, 136–37
Antarctic Press, 26, 34, 42–43, 72, 322
anti-piracy, 119–22
APA-Hashin, 36
Appleseed, 38
Area 88, 37, 260, 265–67
Argo Notes, 31
Arias, Michael, 361
Army Surplus Komikz Featuring Cutey Bunny, 30
Arrivederci Yamato, 32, 97, 224
Art of Japanese Animation II, The: 70 Years of Theatrical Films, 65, 269
ASIFA-Hollywood, 165, 174, 197, 198, 348
Astro Boy: 1959 Japanese live-action TV series, 200–1, 293; 1963 Japanese anime series, 53, 89, 92, 111, 147–49, 152, 198, 219, 221–22, 271, 280, 323; 1963 U.S. TV series, 22, 25, 44–46, 57, 74, 98, 103, 128–29, 135, 140, 152, 155, 193, 219, 247–48, 313–34, 316–20, 362–63; 1980 Japanese TV series, 231, 331–36; 1980s U.S. merchandising, 34, 37; 1989 U.S. video release, 26, 40, 99, 130, 170, 322; appearance in *Phoenix: Dawn*, 202; manga in

Japan, 149, 199, 241; spelling of, 220; statue of, by Robin Leyden, 201; Tezuka as creator/artist of, 19, 59, 173–74, 183, 234, 237, 264, 279, 332–33, 350
Ataru Moroboshi, 47, 258
Atkinson, Lisa, 140
Atlantic Anime Alliance, 42
Atlantis: The Lost Empire, 149, 185
atomic bombing, 25, 31, 247
Atwell, Brett, 121
awards: Academy Award (Oscar), 210, 212, 367; anime fan awards, 8, 51, 122; ASIFA ANNIE/Winsor McCay Award, 165, 197–99; Comic-Con's Inkpot Award, 67, 174; international awards won by anime, 148, 257, 275, 348–49, 352; Japanese SF, manga, and film awards, 204, 208, 349, 358; *Kimba* as 1960s award winner, 11; SPJA Industry Awards, 42, 50–52, 61, 85
AX (magazine), 73, 143

BAKA!-con, 62
Balticon, 29, 67
Bambi, 69, 140, 146, 152, 161, 166, 171–72, 179, 182, 234
Bannô Bunka Neko Musume, 49
Banzai Anime, 44, 70, 120, 123
Barefoot Gen, 25, 33–34, 247
Baron, Gustav, 120
Battle of the Planets,

25–26, 57, 66, 305; differences between *Battle of the Planets* and *Gatchaman*, 224, 250; U.S. release date, 53, 363–64
Battledroids, 33
Battlestar Galactica, 44, 58, 298, 302–3
BayCon, 35, 39, 41, 82
Beck, Jerry, 10, 12, 24–26, 28, 38, 63, 65, 77, 100, 130, 140–41
Bird Scramble!, 36
Blood: The Last Vampire, 141, 345–48
Blooper, Inspector Ignatz, 46
Books Nippan, 12, 28–32, 35–36, 70, 102, 265
Bramer, Doug, 36
Brave Raideen, 24, 43, 55, 66, 246, 293, 295–96
Braviak, Su, 127
Brilliant, Dr. Bob, 46, 248, 314, 316–17
Broken Down Film, 148, 164, 199
Brown, Ryan, 36
Brownlee, Guy, 36
Bruce, Roy and Cathy, 12, 37
Bruton, Heather, 36
Bubblegum Crisis, 38, 125, 129, 289, 357
Buchanan, Joey, 27
Burress, Charles, 145, 161, 176–78
Byers, Reggie, 36

Cal-Animage, 38
Canada, 53, 81, 121, 136, 138, 163, 254, 344, 364
Candy Candy, 19, 76, 201, 228
Canino, Ralph, Jr., 12, 27
CAPA-alpha, 74
Capcom, 31
Capital City Distribution, 42, 178, 181

Capricon, 29
Captain Harlock, 11, 26, 29–30, 32, 57, 96, 98, 201, 225, 241, 254, 256, 304, 313
Captain Harlock and The Queen of a Thousand Years, 254, 256, 313
Card Captor Sakura [a.k.a.] *Cardcaptors*, 84, 133, 135–36, 340
Carlton, Ardith, 12, 31–32, 34–35
Cartoon Network, The, 69–70, 109, 111, 134–35, 359, 362, 364
Cartoon/Fantasy Organization (C/FO), 7, 9, 11–12, 16, 19–20, 24–92, 32, 39, 57–60, 66–67, 75–77, 151, 197–201, 232, 298
Casshan: Robot Hunter, 288
Castle of Cagliostro, The, 7, 29, 77, 142, 188, 201, 209–11
Cat Girl Nuku Nuku, 49
Central Park Media, 41, 63, 99, 112–15, 119, 123, 127–28, 130, 330
Change-TAMAIDA!, 237–38
Chin, Oliver, 121, 131
Cholodenko, Dr. Alan, 145
Choppy and the Princess. See *Princess Knight*
Chronic Rift, The, 41
Chung, Peter, 12, 138, 361
Cinema Anime, 20
Cirillo, Joe, 116
Cirulnick, Brian, 31–32, 36, 42
Cleopatra, 76, 280, 335
Cliff Hanger, 31
collectibles, 81, 103–4, 124
comic books, 9, 11, 15, 26–27, 30–34, 40, 42–43, 56, 62, 67–68, 74–76, 93–94, 99, 101, 117, 124, 145–46, 149, 178, 181, 196, 207, 209, 220, 232–47, 259–68, 293, 297, 304, 306–8, 311–13, 322, 325, 332, 336, 347, 349
Comic Party, 9
Comic-Con (San Diego), 17, 176; 1978, 26, 201; 1980, 16, 18–19, 25, 28–29, 59, 67, 173–74, 202–3; 1982, 30; 1986, 265, 267; 1989, 39; 1996, 79, 120
Comico, 33–34, 303, 306, 308, 311–12
Comics Buyer's Guide, 10, 175
Comics Collector, 61, 71
Comics Journal, The, 10, 61, 124, 232
Complete Anime Guide, The, 22–23, 63, 69, 71, 183–84, 363
computer networks: anime fan sites, 37–38, 60, 67, 122, 144, 210, 345; box-office statistics on cinema-industry websites, 216, 361–62, 367; commercial and professional anime sites, 70, 134, 170, 344; *Digimon, Perfect Blue* Internet plot elements, 339–40, 368; *Nadia-Atlantis* controversy on the Internet, 185–89; "Save *Sailor Moon*" Internet campaign, 50
conventions, 22, 60, 80–82, 84, 99, 119, 122, 177. *See also specific conventions such as Anime Expo, Comic-Con, LosCon, etc.*
Corman, Roger, 62
Cosmo Police Justy, 244, 260, 267
cosplay, 29, 32, 62, 80, 84
Cowboy Bebop, 132, 134, 356–62
Crispin, Mark, 37
Critical Mass, 112, 114
Crystal Triangle, 38
Cutey Honey, 30, 44, 49–50, 142, 194
Cyborg 009, 97, 194, 201, 207–8, 223, 245, 288

Dairugger-XV, 33, 253
Dangaio, 40, 102
Danguard Ace, 96, 193, 251, 300–1
Davis, Julie, 129, 131, 133
Del Rey Books, 37, 40
Detroit News, The, 31
Devil Hunter Yohko, 26, 43, 48, 125
Devilman, 76, 194, 196, 220
DeWeese, John, 37
Diary of Anne Frank, The, 110, 230, 280
Dick Tracy, 54
Digimon: Digital Monsters, 338–39
Dippé, Mark, 140
Dirty Little Girls, 36
Dirty Pair, 34, 36, 39, 204, 259
Disney (company): attack on anime, 70–71, 108–9, 111; Disney World TV movie starring Tezuka, 163, 173, 199; formula followed by Toei, 52, 76, 279; influence on early anime, 269; influence on Tezuka, 140, 220, 234, 333, 349; in Japanese video market, 104, 106–7; in *Nadia-Atlantis* controversy, 187–89, 199; popularity of

animated features, 20, 56; in Simba-Kimba controversy, 144–85; U.S. release of Miyazaki features, 64, 101, 125, 140, 142, 209–12, 214–45, 353–56, 367

Disney, Roy E., 144, 161, 182

Disney, Walt: death of, 56, 155; introducing TV program, 335; meeting with Tezuka, 183

Dr. Slump, 89, 91, 96, 233, 242–43, 263

dojinshi. *See* fanzines

Dokonjo, 34

Dominion Tank Police, 26, 49

Doraemon, 111, 125, 136–37, 226, 237, 276

Dragon Ball/Dragon Ball Z, 11, 103, 107, 123–25, 132–33, 135–37, 276, 340

Drax, Simon, 73

DreamWorks SKG, 366

Duffy, Jo, 32, 41

Dunn, Ben, 12, 34, 36

Dynamic Productions, 195–96, 240, 264

Dynamo Joe, 32

Earth Defense Command (EDC), 30, 60–61, 68

Earthquake, Great Kanto, 284, 371

Ebert, Michael, 37

Eclipse International, 37–38, 260, 266

Educomics, 31

8th Man (a.k.a. *8 Man*), 54, 74, 193, 219, 223, 231, 248, 277, 314, 363–64

Eldred, Tim, 40–41

Electric Holt, 37

Elefun, Dr. Packadermus J., 46, 248, 332

Elfquest. See Pini, Wendy

Engel, Jim, 29

Epic Comics, 38

Escaflowne, 139, 345, 357

Eternity Comics, 34, 40, 43

Family Home Entertainment, 30, 128, 323

Fanfare, 10, 28, 72, 219–21

Fangoria, 10, 28, 68, 72, 293, 297

Fanta's Zine, 9, 27, 61, 75

Fantastic Films, 61

Fantastic Four, 56

fanzines, 9–10, 16, 23–24, 27, 31, 36–37, 47, 60, 68, 74–75, 99. *See also* specific fanzines such as *Anime-Zine* and *Bird Scramble!*

FASA Corp., 33

Fenelon, Robert, 12, 29, 31–32, 35, 41

Fernandez, Peter, 317–78, 323

Filmation, 54

Final Fantasy, 79, 83, 123, 139, 345, 361

First Comics, 32, 37, 260

Fist of the North Star, 131, 305

Flash Gordon, 54, 331

Foglio, Phil, 32

Fong, Dana, 37–38

Force Five, 10, 28–30, 251, 254, 297–300, 302–3

Frazier, Scott, 12, 36

Fujii, Satoru, 43

Fujio, Fujiko, 206, 226–27

Fushigi Yugi, 80, 134

Gafford, Carl, 12, 25, 66, 85

GAGA Communications, 38

Gaiking, 96, 251, 296–97, 300–301

Gainax, 39, 41, 51, 102, 125–26, 185, 189

Galaxy 2 Express (feature), 25, 30, 62, 95, 97, 225, 241–42, 250–51, 272, 281

Galaxy Express 999, 11, 16, 29, 44, 57, 92, 95, 224–25, 230, 237, 241–42, 272, 281, 298, 302

Galvez, Enrique, 44

Gamilon Embassy, The, 29, 67

Gatchaman, 16, 36, 57, 97, 121, 142, 223–24, 231, 250, 287–88, 305, 364

General Products-USA, 39

Getta Robo/Getta Robo-G, 56, 66, 96, 193, 223, 286, 296, 300

Giant Robo, 42, 280

giant robots, 27, 93, 103, 105, 220, 223, 246, 248, 251, 258, 271–72, 286, 293–301. *See also* specific giant robot series such as *Force Five* and *Mazinger Z*

Gigantor, 22, 46, 54, 223, 231, 240, 248–49, 263, 293, 313–22

Gilliam, Phil, 29

Gleicher, Marvin, 120, 128, 131, 134

Go Fish Pictures, 366

Go Lion, 33, 253, 286

Godzilla, 23, 67–69, 91, 103, 115, 130, 235, 242, 297, 365

Goldberg, Eric, 140

Golgo 13, 35, 74, 132, 240, 259, 265–66, 288, 342

Goodnough, Christopher, 126

Grandizer, 16, 96, 193, 196, 220, 251, 280,

298, 300
Graphic Story Bookshop, 11, 15, 23
Graphic Story World, 15, 23, 74
Grave of the Fireflies, 115, 125, 140, 281
Green, Howard, 144, 162, 176–77
Greenfield, Matt, 43, 130
Grenald, Seth, 37
group tours, 28–29, 34–36, 59, 205
Gulliver's Travels Beyond the Moon, 23, 53
Gunbuster, 40, 48, 102
Gundam, 29, 33, 40, 95, 97–98, 126, 132, 134, 219, 258, 272; *Gundam 0083*, 357; *Gundam W*, 276
Guyver, The, 131, 208

Haller, Michael, 298, 302
Hanna-Barbera, 44, 54, 110, 150, 219, 221, 261, 270, 279
Harmony Gold U.S.A., 7–8, 26, 33–35, 77, 100, 109, 255, 305–10, 312–23
Harrison, Steve, 31
Headley, Beverly, 35
Heidi, Girl of the Alps, 110, 211, 280
Hernandez, Lea, 39
Hernandez, Mark, 31
Heroic Legend of Arslan, The, 328–29, 331
Highly Animated, 32
Hill, Claude, 31
Himiko, Queen, 202, 284
Hiramatsu, Yuji, 12, 29
Hiroshima, 25, 31, 34, 247
Ho, Mario and Glen, 34
Hole in One, 237
Homma, Masumi, 41
Horibuchi, Seiji, 43, 264, 266

Horn, Susan, 29, 70
Horvath, JoLynn, 29, 32
Howell, Shon, 39
Hozumi, Teruko (Pico), 9
Hughes Aircraft, 10, 199

I Saw It, 31
IANUS Publications, 73
Igarashi, Yumiko, 19, 29, 67, 202, 228
Ikegami, Ryoichi, 37, 260
Ikuhara, Kunihiko, 141
Internet. *See* computer networks
Iron Man No. 28. See *Tetsujin 28-go*
Ishi[no]mori, Shotaro, 92, 194, 206–9, 223, 245, 269, 288
Ishikawa, Mitsuhisa, 141, 346

Jack and the Witch, 23, 53
JAILED (Japanese Animation Industry Legal Enforcement Division), 119–22
Japanese Animation Network (JAN), 37, 39
Japanese bubble economy, 286–87
Japanese Fantasy Film Faire, 25, 61, 68
Japanese Fantasy Film Journal, The, 23, 67–68
Japanese National Science Fiction Convention, 35
Japanimation, 10, 24–25, 42, 44, 63, 66, 85–86, 99, 104, 124, 177, 184, 198, 246–47, 253, 277; Japanimation '86 tour, 35
Jarrad, Jonathan, 41
Jasinski, Chet, 42
Jetter Mars, 333
Johnson, Michael, 70, 108, 111
Jones, Andy, 361

Jones, Mike, 33
Joy's Japanimation, 70, 86, 123, 126–27
Jumping, 148, 164, 199
Jungle Emperor (Tezuka's manga and Japanese anime version), 144, 147–56, 159, 161, 163–66, 169–76, 179–80, 183–85, 234, 239, 271; symphonic suite, 97

Kabuto, 42, 193, 223, 294
Kagami, Joji, 237
Kamui, 37, 80, 96, 98, 229, 260, 264, 266–67, 370
Kaposztas, James, 29, 30
Karahashi, Takayuki, 38
Kato, Kazuhiko. *See* Monkey Punch
Katsucon, 62
Katzenberg, Jeffrey, 161–62, 175
Kausler, Mark, 171
Kawajiri, Yoshiaki, 138, 342, 361
Kawamoto, Kihachiro, 273
Keller, Chris, 41
Kiki's Delivery Service, 70–71, 101, 125, 128, 140, 188, 206, 211, 215, 281, 356,
Kikuchi, Hideyuki, 138, 341, 345
Kimba the Lion Prince, 170, 184
Kimba the White Lion (U.S. version), 11, 22, 54, 57, 59, 98, 140, 144–85, 199, 219, 221, 226, 249, 313, 317, 363–64
Kime, Chad, 131, 133, 135
Kimono My House, 29, 39, 70
Kitakubo, Hiroyuki, 345, 347

Kitayama, Seitaro, 268–69, 278, 370
Kitty Films, 94, 126
Kitty Media, 112, 114–45, 117, 130
Kleckner, Shawne, 114, 120, 129, 132
Kodansha, 31, 33, 72, 125, 165, 172, 174, 195, 204, 208, 234, 239, 241, 246, 260, 273
Koike, Kazuo, 37, 260, 283
Kojima, Goseki, 37, 260
Kon, Satoshi, 365–66, 368
Kondo, Yoshifumi, 214, 276
Kouchi, Jun-ichi, 371
Kudo, Kazuya, 37, 260
Kuri, Yoji, 205, 273, 279
Kyle, Richard, 9, 11, 15, 23, 74

L.A. Hero, 42
Ladera Travel Agency, 34
Laputa: The Castle in the Sky, 39, 96, 125, 188, 275, 281
Lasseter, John, 211, 214, 216, 353, 355
Lazzo, Mike, 70, 109, 111
Ledford, John, 129–30, 133
Ledoux, Trish, 22–23, 43, 69, 131, 145, 176, 179, 183–84
Legend of the Forest, 148, 164, 199, 205–6
Lemon APA, 36
Lemon People, 238
Lensman, 33, 40, 77, 96, 101, 273, 342
Lent, John A., 52
Leyden, Robin, 11, 16–17, 19, 24, 172, 176–77, 200–3
Little Norse Prince, The, 23, 53, 294
Little Tokyo, 33–34, 74, 200

Locke the Superman, 94, 243–44
Lone Wolf and Cub, 260, 264, 283
Los Angeles, 9, 12, 16, 19–20, 22, 24, 28, 33–34, 44, 57, 59, 63, 66, 73, 89, 99, 155, 173, 303, 362, 364
Los Angeles Comic Book and Science Fiction Convention, 38, 40, 175
Los Angeles International Animation Celebration, 164, 205, 257
Los Angeles Science Fantasy Society (LASFS), 9, 19, 24, 73, 75
LosCon, 24, 37–38, 61, 66
Lum-chan, 34, 89, 243, 258
Lumivision, 41
Lunacon, 25, 31
Lupin III, 7, 18, 29, 31, 76–77, 84, 93, 97, 142, 188, 201, 209–11, 220, 228, 240–41, 258, 276, 357–58

M.D. Geist, 38, 124
Macek, Carl, 7–8, 10, 12, 304; Carl F. Macek Gallery, 30, 304–5; *Robotech*, 33–34, 69, 109, 304–13; Streamline Pictures, 38, 63, 100, 113, 130, 140
Mach Go Go Go. See *Speed Racer*
Macross, 33, 35, 77, 89, 93, 96, 130, 285–86; as a component of *Robotech*, 34, 254–55, 304–12; *Macross: Do You Remember Love?* 34; *Macross II*, 42; *Macross Plus*, 50, 125,

357, 361; *Macross 7*, 276
Madhouse, 125, 273, 342–44, 349, 356, 361, 365–66, 368
Madox-01, 38, 40, 103
Maeda, Mahiro, 81, 361
Maeda, Toshio, 113, 117
magazines, 16, 26, 32, 35, 43, 51, 53, 58, 60–61, 68, 72–73, 105, 123–24, 142–43, 261–63, 293
Magic Boy, 22–24, 52, 55, 65, 73, 279
Magness, Don, 31
Mai the Psychic Girl, 37, 260, 266
Man from U.N.C.L.E., The, 11, 74, 234
Manabe, Johji, 41
manga, 9, 15, 23, 25, 31–32, 39, 46, 51, 68, 74, 83, 99, 104, 117, 124, 142, 145–46, 149, 193–96, 199, 200, 203–4, 206–11, 220, 232–47, 259–68, 279, 288–89, 314, 332, 349–51; Tezuka as "God of Manga," 59, 163, 174, 198, 206, 349
Manga (magazine), 30
Manga Entertainment, 83, 112–14, 120–21, 123, 125, 128, 131–32, 134
Manga! Manga!: The World of Japanese Comics, 31, 72, 174, 195, 204, 234, 237, 260
Manga Max, 50–51, 68, 72, 119, 126, 128, 328, 331
Manga Newswatch Quarterly, 43
Mangazine, 34, 42, 72
Marc Davis Lecture on Animation, 139
"March is Manga

Month," 42
Marine Boy, 23, 54, 219, 249, 271, 317
Markalite, 103, 313
Marmel, Mitch, 37
Mars (comic book), 32
Marvel Comics, 9, 27, 32, 56, 66, 93, 101, 227, 288, 294, 296
Masaoka, Kenzo, 269, 371
masquerades. *See* cosplay
Matrix, The, 84, 132, 133, 140, 360, 362
Matsumoto, Leiji (Reiji), 11, 92, 206, 224, 237, 241, 256, 272, 281, 302
Mattel, 27, 56, 103, 193, 297–99, 301
Mazinger Z, 23, 55, 98, 193, 196, 223, 240, 255, 264, 271, 280, 286, 294–96, 300
McKinney, Jack, 37
McLaughlin, John, 41
Mecha Press, 41
Media Blasters, 112, 114–15, 120, 127–30, 133
Mediascene, 25, 68, 304
Megazone 23, 47, 125
Mekton: The Game of Japanese Robot Combat, 32, 68
Menichelli, Luke, 35, 40
Merlino, Mark, 11, 19, 24, 26, 28, 75
Metropolis (Osamu Tezuka's), 80, 141, 345, 349–52
MGM (Metro-Goldwyn-Mayer), 22–23, 56, 65, 106, 155
Mighty Atom. See Tetsuwan Atomu
Mighty Morphin' Power Rangers, 207–8, 277
Mikimoto, Haruhiko, 41
MileHiCon, 28
Millennium Actress, 364–68

Miller, Frank, 31, 259, 268
Minkoff, Rob, 161–62, 165, 175–76
Minmay, Lynn, 89, 93
Miyagawa, Hiroshi, 90, 97
Miyazaki, Hayao, 35, 118, 137, 170, 204, 206, 273, 275, 281, 349, 366; association with Disney, 64, 70–71, 106, 111, 125, 140, 142, 147, 164, 169, 183–85, 188–89, 209–16, 352–56; book about, 69
Mobile Suit Gundam. See Gundam
model kits, 26, 32, 41, 104, 241, 276, 307–8
Momotaro's Gods-Blessed Sea Warriors, 65, 204–5, 269, 278, 326, 328
Momotaro's Sea Eagles, 65, 326
Monkey Punch, 7, 12, 18, 29, 67, 173, 202–3, 228–29, 240, 258
Monster Rancher, 108, 133, 135, 338, 340, 364
Moon Kingdom, 50
Morimoto, Koji, 361
Mountain Where Old Women are Abandoned, The, 278, 370
Mukuzu Imokawa, the Doorkeeper, 65
Munson-Siter, Patricia, 36
Murata, Yasuji, 278, 371
Mushi Production, 147–48, 156, 170, 173, 175, 199, 221, 231, 270–71, 273, 280, 314, 316, 320
music, 37, 41, 43–44, 48, 53, 58, 81–84, 89–95, 97, 102, 104–5, 123, 131, 143, 150, 154–55, 202, 229, 232, 243–44,

262, 270, 322, 344, 352, 357–58
music videos, 41, 48, 84, 91, 105
My Anime, 26, 73, 143
My Neighbor Totoro, 123, 125, 140, 206, 275, 281, 341, 355

Nadia: The Secret of Blue Water, 126, 149, 185–89
Nagai, Go, 19, 29–30, 50, 67, 92, 193–97, 202, 206, 223, 227, 237–38, 240, 255, 264, 271, 280, 286, 294, 296, 300
Nakazawa, Keiji, 25, 31, 247
Napton, Robert, 36, 102
Nausicaä of the Valley of the Winds, 21, 96, 142, 209–11, 254, 257, 281
nausicaa.net, 188, 189
NBC (National Broadcasting Company), 46, 54, 70, 109, 150, 152–56, 161, 170, 172–73, 221, 226, 316–17, 319, 320, 363
New World Pictures, 30
New World Video, 35
New York Creation Convention, 32
Newtype, 73, 83, 143
Newtype USA, 10, 83, 85, 142, 144, 285, 287, 362, 369
Ninja High School, 36
Nippan Shuppan Hanbai. *See* Books Nippan
Nippon Columbia, 90–91, 93
Niver, Judith, 11, 24
Nobunaga, Oda, 283–84
Norakuro, 228, 239, 278
NOW Comics, 37
NTA (National Telefilm Associates), 156, 173, 320

NTSC. *See* video broadcast standards
Nuku Nuku, 49
numbering (of series), 126

O'Connor, Paul, 40
O'Donnell, John, 41, 113, 119–20, 130
Ofuji, Noburo, 269, 278, 371
Oh! My Goddess, 11, 49, 124, 138
Okada, Toshio, 41, 102
One Thousand and One Nights [a.k.a.] *1001 Nights*, 76, 112, 148, 344
Ono, Kosei, 146, 151, 206
Opyt, Danielle, 112, 121
Orguss, 42
Original Astro Boy, The, 37
Oshii, Mamoru, 281, 346
otaku, 64, 184
Otogi Cartoon Calendar, 219
Otomo, Katsuhiro, 38, 141, 206, 281, 349

Pacific Comics, 32
PAL. *See* video broadcast standards
Palmer, Tom, 32
Panda and the Magic Serpent, 22–24, 52, 65, 73, 278–79
Panda.com, 37
Paniccia, Mark, 43
Parents' Magazine, 11
Pascuzzi, Mike, 118, 129, 131, 133
Patten, Fred, 7–8, 16–17, 23–24, 26, 35, 37, 67–69, 73–80, 140, 151, 175, 177, 206, 232
Pearl, Stephen, 42
Pelletier, Claude, 38
Perfect Blue, 131, 134, 140, 365, 368

Philcon, 36
Phoenix 2772, 19, 29, 80, 96, 173, 241
Pini, Wendy, 12, 19, 27, 37
Pinto, Michael, 28, 31–32, 42
Pioneer Entertainment, 131–33
Pixar Animation Studios, 209, 216, 353
Pokémon [a.k.a.] Pocket Monsters, 64, 109, 123, 126, 131–33, 135–36, 336–41, 345, 364
Pollotta, Nick, 32
Pom Poko, 125, 212, 275, 281
Pondsmith, Mike, 32, 37, 68
Pony Toy-Go-Round, 30
popular culture, 45, 50, 62, 65, 75, 130, 163, 172, 206, 212, 234, 282
pornographic anime, 110–18
Prince Planet, 22, 54, 103, 231, 249, 364
Princess Knight, 23, 65
Princess Mononoke, 70, 108–9, 111, 125, 138, 140, 188–89, 210, 212, 215–16, 352–33, 355–56
Production I.G, 141, 346–49
Project A-Ko, 36, 38, 40, 61, 81, 122, 124–25
Project A-Kon, 40, 61, 81, 122
Protoculture Addicts, 38, 40–41, 61, 68, 73, 99, 108, 124, 139, 144, 180
Puss in Boots, 23, 53, 272, 294

Quagmire, Joshua, 30, 196

R. Talsorian Games, 32,

69, 73
Raideen. See *Brave Raideen*
Rankin-Bass, 231, 273
Ranma 1/2, 62, 123–24, 126
Ranney, Doug, 22–23, 69, 183–84
Raskin, Gene, 46
rec.arts.anime, 37, 60, 67, 122
Record of Lodoss War, 48, 62, 84, 123, 125
Redmon, Kara, 121, 132
Reed, Aaron, 36
Revell Inc., 307–8, 310
Rhino Entertainment Company, 43–44, 150
Rice, Doug, 12, 29, 32
Riddick, David K., 34
Rifas, Leonard, 31
Right Stuf (International), The, 26, 40, 63, 99, 112, 114, 120, 123, 128–30, 132, 149–50, 170, 282, 322
Rion 2990, 36
Roady, Jeff, 12, 35
Robotech, 7, 12, 26, 33–38, 40, 45, 50, 62, 69, 72, 76–77, 99–100, 102–3, 109, 122, 128–30, 202, 247, 253–55, 276, 285, 303–5, 307–13; *Robotech: The Macross Saga*, 34, 308, 312; *Robotech: The New Generation*, 34, 310, 312; *Robotech Masters*, 34, 254–55, 309, 311–12
Robotech Art 1, 35
Robotech BGM Collection, 37
Rodregez, Felix, 41
Roman Album series, 26, 31, 142, 210
Ronin, 31
Rose, The, 37
Rossi, Valerio, 113, 115

S and J Productions, 127
Sadamoto, Yoshiyuki, 41
Sailor Moon, 44, 50, 64,
  84, 103, 107, 109–10,
  118, 124, 126, 128,
  132, 135–37, 141,
  276–77, 340, 364
Saito, Takao, 11, 35, 74,
  234, 240, 259, 264–65
Sam the Olympic Eagle,
  235
San Diego Comic-Con.
  See Comic-Con
San Francisco Chronicle,
  144–45, 161–62, 164,
  176–78
Sasha, 25, 31
Satonaka, Machiko, 169,
  178–79
Savage, Lorraine, 12, 36
Schindler, Robin, 12, 35
Schodt, Frederik L., 31,
  40, 146, 172, 174, 183,
  185, 234, 260
Schubert, Ann, 12, 35,
  37, 41, 67, 122
Schweizer, Peter, 148
Sci-Fi Channel, The, 19,
  63, 69, 124, 135, 322,
  342
Seo, Mitsuyo, 65, 269–70,
  278, 326
Shameless School, 195
Shimamoto, Kazuhiko,
  206–7, 209
Shimokawa, Oten, 65,
  269, 278, 370
Shintani, Kaoru, 37, 260,
  265
Shirato, Sanpei, 37, 229,
  260, 266
Shirow, Masamune, 38,
  281, 287
Shoemaker, Greg, 12,
  23, 67
Shogakukan, 39, 43,
  68, 71, 126, 131, 260,
  266–68, 336
Shogun Warriors, 27, 56,
  66, 103, 193, 296–99

shojo, 112
Shuriken, 36
Silent Möbius, 48
Silver, Joel, 360, 361
Sirabella, John, 114, 116,
  118, 120, 129–30,
  133–34
Siskel and Ebert, 69
Sito, Tom, 171
Skull Man, The, 206–7,
  209
Smith, Toren V., 34–35,
  38–39
Society for the Promo-
  tion of Japanese
  Animation (SPJA), 42,
  51–52, 80, 84–85, 359
SoftCel Pictures, 112, 114
Sonoda, Kenichi, 41
Space Adventure Cobra,
  41, 242
Space Battleship [a.k.a.
  Cruiser] *Yamato*, 113,
  224, 253, 302
Space Fanzine Yamato,
  31, 60, 62
*Space Pirate Captain
  Harlock. See Captain
  Harlock*
Spaceketeers (*The Space
  Musketeers*), 251, 298,
  300, 302
Sparks, Jimmy, 46, 223,
  248, 314, 317–18
Speed Racer, 23, 44, 46,
  54, 70, 98, 109, 111,
  118, 128–29, 219, 250,
  271, 276, 318, 320,
  322–25, 364; Japanese
  versions, 228, 286,
  323–24; *The New Ad-
  ventures of . . .*, 323;
  theatrical features,
  323; U.S. merchandis-
  ing, 37, 323–25
Spirited Away, 83, 140,
  142, 209–16, 352–53,
  356, 366–67
Star Blazers, 27–32, 45,
  57, 59–62, 67, 113,

128–29, 202, 224, 232,
  250, 253, 272, 297–98,
  302–3, 364
Star Blazers fan club,
  28–29, 60
Star Trek, 16–17, 44, 58,
  69, 78, 98, 122, 136,
  232, 286, 298, 303
Star Wars, 32, 57–58, 66,
  75, 90, 224–25, 281,
  364
Starblaze Graphics/The
  Donning Company, 35
Starlog, 61, 72, 124, 247,
  253
StarQuest, 19
Starvengers, 96, 251, 296,
  300–301
Sternbach, Rick, 41
Streamline Pictures, 7–8,
  10, 12, 38–41, 43, 63,
  77, 79, 100, 112–13,
  123, 128–30, 140, 188,
  277, 305, 323, 343
Studio 4° C, 361
Studio Ghibli, 76, 106,
  125, 137, 142, 185,
  209–15, 275, 281, 353
Studio Gonzo, 82
Studio Pierrot, 82–83,
  126, 272
Studio Proteus, 38–39,
  41, 68
Stukey, Randall, 36
Sudlow, Paul, 36
"Survival in 3DK,"
  236–38
Suzuki, Toshio, 209–10,
  353
Sweet, Matthew, 41–42
syndicated TV, 57, 100,
  122, 173, 252–53, 303,
  307–8, 310–11, 319–
  20, 323, 337, 363–64

Takahashi, Rumiko, 34,
  36, 89, 91, 206, 243
Takahata, Isao, 137, 211–
  12, 214, 275, 280–81
Takai, Tatsuo, 46

Takemiya, Keiko, 244

Tatsugawa, Mike, 38, 42, 52, 65, 80

Tatsunoko Production, 77, 92, 230, 271–72, 276, 280, 305–6, 323

TCJ (Television Corporation of Japan), 231, 271, 280, 314–16, 318–19

Teenagers From Outer Space, 37, 62, 68

Tekkaman the Space Knight, 92, 97, 252–53

"Television Isn't Ready For This," 31

Terry, Jim, 9, 12, 27, 298–99, 302

Testicle Boy, 237

Tetsujin 28-go, 46, 240, 249, 263, 293, 314–19, 322

Tetsuwan Atomu, 16–17, 45–46, 53, 73, 89, 91, 97, 147, 149–50, 152, 155, 237, 248, 264, 270–71, 293, 314, 316, 331–34

Tezuka Awards, 51

Tezuka, Osamu, 17, 75, 92, 140, 145–46, 174–75, 194, 197–99, 203–7, 220, 222, 227, 230–31, 233–34, 239–41, 261, 264, 270, 279–80, 293; adult and art films, 111–12, 148, 273; ; in America, 30, 39, 40, 62, 98, 100–1, 131, 135–36, 138–39, 141–42, 183–84, 209–11, 250–51, 257, 305, 336–61, 364–68; *Astro Boy* creator, 46, 53, 147, 149, 237, 331–36; *Kimba* creator, 140, 144–84, 226, 239; meeting American fans, 7, 12, 17, 19, 25, 27, 29–30, 59,

67, 173–74, 199–203; *Metropolis* creator, 141, 349–51; theatrical releases; in Japan, 22, 23, 52–53, 65–66, 76, 112, 123, 125, 136–37, 146, 148, 170, 202, 208, 221, 224–25, 229, 231, 241, 244, 258, 268–69, 272–73, 275–76, 278–81, 294, 325–28, 369–70

This Is the Story, 35

Thomas, William III, 27

Thompson, Jeff, 40

Those Obnoxious Aliens. See *Urusei Yatsura*

Thunder Sub, 254, 256

Thunderbirds 2086, 251

Toei Animation, 27, 91–92, 106–7, 125–26, 137, 195–96, 203, 208, 211, 225, 230, 271–72, 276, 280, 286, 294, 296, 303, 305, 333, 339–40; first anime theatrical features, 52, 76, 146, 198, 270, 279; providing anime for U.S. test-marketing, 9, 25–26, 28, 59, 75, 201, 220–21

Toei Doga. See Toei Animation

Tokuma Publishing, 26, 142, 210, 273

Tokyo Movie Shinsha (TMS), 19, 29, 31, 59, 125, 132, 201, 209, 211, 229–30, 272, 276, 280, 322, 342

Tomb of Dracula, 93, 98, 313

Tomino, Yoshiyuki, 33, 40, 258, 272

Top Craft, 231, 273

Top O Nerae!, 48

Toriyama, Akira, 91, 242, 263, 264

transforming robot toys, 56

translation booklets, 34–35

TranZor Z, 255, 264

Trelaina, 31

TV programming, 24, 57, 124, 298, 305, 319, 325

20,000 Leagues Under the Sea, 187, 242

Twilight of the Cockroaches, 41, 101

U.S. Manga Corps, 41–44, 63, 113–35, 123, 131

U.S. Renditions, 36–37, 40, 42, 63, 101–2, 123, 128, 130

U.S.A. Yatsura, 36, 47

UFO Dai Apollon, 56, 193, 286

unauthorized merchandise, 33–34, 119–22, 156

United States, 53

Urban Vision, 118, 121, 128, 132, 133, 341, 343, 344, 345

Urotsukidoji: Legend of the Overfiend, 86, 113, 114, 116, 117, 123, 125

Urusei Yatsura, 34, 36–37, 41, 44, 47, 49, 89, 91, 94, 96, 98, 130, 205, 243, 258

USA Today, 69–70, 109, 111, 162, 177

Vampire Hunter D [and] *Vampire Hunter D: Bloodlust*, 96, 124–25, 132, 135, 138–39, 274, 341–35, 362, 365

VCR (video cassette recorder), 24, 53, 55, 67, 74–75, 129

Verne, Jules, 101, 187, 189

video: commercial anime videos, 35, 40–43,

45, 51, 63, 77, 80, 86, 101–9, 111–23, 126–35, 147, 149, 183–84, 188, 196, 274–75, 277, 281–82, 306, 311, 321–23, 325, 329–31, 342, 360, 362; *Kimba* on video, 150, 156, 161, 163, 165, 170–71, 176, 178, 180, 182; programs at clubs, 16, 24, 44–45, 58, 75

video broadcast standards, 21, 66

video game, 62, 79, 106, 123, 132, 133, 138, 143, 276, 338, 346, 348

video rooms (at conventions), 19–20, 24–26, 28–29, 31–33, 35, 38, 44–45, 59–60, 66–68, 80, 83, 99, 121, 165, 247, 322

Viz Communications, 37, 39, 68, 72, 121, 128, 131, 260, 266, 267

V-MAX, 41

Voltron, Defender of the Universe!, 33, 62, 252, 303, 364

Wachowski, Andy and Larry, 360–62

Wakefield, Derek, 30

Wakefield, Mary, 40

Wall, Rik, 121

Warriors of the Wind, 26, 35, 62, 254, 257

Washer, Wendell, 11, 24, 74

Watanabe, Shinichiro, 357, 359, 361

Web sites. *See* computer networks

West Cape Corporation, 32, 113

Westchester Films, 27, 31–32

Westercon, 11, 20, 26, 28, 59, 67, 322

Wheeler, Scott, 320, 322

Williams, Janice, 114

Williams, John, 58, 89–90

Windaria, 47–48

Winters, Colleen, 12, 29

Wise, Kirk, 187–88, 215, 355

women's anime/manga. *See* shojo

Wonderworld (magazine). See *Graphic Story World*

Wonderworld Books. *See* Graphic Story Bookshop

Woodhead, Robert, 39, 130

World Events Productions, 33, 252

World Science Fiction Convention, 26, 32, 33, 81, 201, 209, 308

World War II, 141, 197; distrust of government a legacy of, 285; *Gigantor* as weapon of, 314, 318; propaganda anime, 325, 326; Tezuka career and manga industry beginning at end of, 198, 233; *Yamato* as refighting WWII in space, 224, 250, 272, 281, 287

Yabushita, Taiji, 146, 270, 279

Yagyu, Jubei, 283

Yamamoto, Eiichi, 153

Yamamoto, Mataichiro, 132, 342

Yamamoto, Nobu, 132, 134

Yamamoto, Sanae (Zenjiro), 269, 278, 371

YamatoCon, 31, 32, 68

Yokoyama, Mitsuteru, 223, 226, 240, 263, 293, 313, 314

Yoshida, Tatsuo, 222, 223, 228, 323

Yotoden, 38, 283

You Say Yamato, 32

Young, Paul, 40

Yuzuki, Hikaru, 236

Zitomer, Jeff, 115, 116

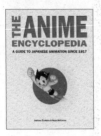